INTERNATIONAL
TRADE AND FINANCE

INTERNATIONAL TRADE AND FINANCE

Readings

THIRD EDITION

Robert E. Baldwin

J. David Richardson

University of Wisconsin

Little, Brown and Company

Boston   Toronto

Library of Congress Cataloging-in-Publication Data
Main entry under title:

International trade and finance.

   Includes bibliographical references and index.
   1. International economic relations — Addresses,
essays, lectures.   2. Commerce — Addresses, essays,
lectures.   3. International finance — Addresses, essays,
lectures.   I. Baldwin, Robert E.   II. Richardson, J.
David.
HF1411.I5182   1986   382.1   85-30035
ISBN 0-316-07927-8

Library of Congress Catalog Card No. 85-30035

ISBN 0-316-07927-8

9 8 7 6 5 4 3 2 1

HAL

Published simultaneously in Canada
by Little, Brown & Company (Canada) Limited

Printed in the United States of America

Preface

As interdependence in the world economy continues to increase, the distinction between domestic and international economic issues becomes less and less meaningful. No longer can the typical business, labor, or political leader devote minimum attention to international trade and financial policy issues. There is, for example, scarcely a part of the country where profits and employment in some local industry have not been adversely affected in recent years by the high international value of the dollar. With increased international financial flows and greater product competition from foreign suppliers, businesspersons, labor leaders, and elected officials now must become familiar with such issues as the adequacy of the current exchange-rate systems, managing the debt problems of developing countries, and offsetting "unfair" foreign trade.

This book of readings deals with the above topics and other key monetary, commercial and investment issues that we face in the late 1980s, and with important analytical developments that help illuminate these problems. A selected list of topics is examined in detail rather than providing brief coverage of every issue arising in international economics. Although this approach necessitates the omission of some topics and causes some overlapping among the papers, the advantages of permitting readers to examine the views of different authors in some depth was thought to outweigh these costs. Textbooks must necessarily be brief on many topics; the purpose of a book of readings should be to delve more deeply into matters of special importance.

We selected a particular analytical or policy issue by asking ourselves whether there was wide or growing interest in it among trade economists. We then looked for papers by authors especially knowledgeable on the subject which were written in a straightforward, interesting style that could be easily understood by students, even those taking their first course in international economics. In the more controversial policy fields, we also tried to include papers that represented divergent views. Although we have had varying success in meeting these standards for each topic, we believe that the readings supplement the material covered in trade textbooks in a way that can enrich and enliven courses in international economics.

We have written introductions to each part in order to place the various selections in better perspective as well as to sometimes supplement, synthesize, or critique different viewpoints. Some of the material covered in these introductions may need to be updated because of the rapid pace of developments in international economics, but we are confident that students will benefit considerably from reading them. We have further tried to help students by providing an index (unlike most books of readings) and by including the bibliographical references listed by the various authors.

The readings are divided into ten parts with all but two of the thirty-four selections new to this edition. Part I consists of two papers that analyze the competitiveness of U.S. producers in international markets and consider the question of whether the United States is deindustrializing. The readings in Part II examine evidence on the costs and benefits of protection and various policies for facilitating adjustment in import-injured industries. A selection that compares various political-economic explanations of protection is also included. Part III deals with recent analytical work that explores how interventionist trade policies may increase a country's welfare if international markets are imperfectly competitive. In addition, the nature of industrial policy in Japan and other countries is discussed and evaluated. Part IV traces shifts in U.S. trade policy over the past forty years and then considers some of the new issues for negotiation in the next GATT-sponsored multilateral negotiating round as well as proposals for strengthening the existing set of international trading rules. Trade policies in the developing countries are analyzed in Part V, particularly the effectiveness of export-promoting versus import-substitution policies. Part VI concerns multinational corporations (MNCs). The selections indicate both how many countries that at one time were only hosts to such corporations are themselves now forming MNCs and how the bargaining relationships between these firms and governments have been changing. The important question, "Are current exchange-rate systems working?" is explored in Part VII in macroeconomic and microeconomic terms. Besides evaluating the systems, the authors of the various papers suggest ways to improve the operation of these systems. Part VIII addresses the issue of whether fundamental changes are needed in the international monetary order and presents selections with a wide range of opinion on this matter. The causes of the recent international debt crisis are examined in Part IX together with the actions taken to deal with the crisis. On this issue there is also a wide range of opinion, represented in the readings, about how well the crisis was handled and whether it is likely to emerge again. Part X concludes the readings with selections that describe the structural and institutional changes in international financial markets that are at the root of current problems with exchange-rate systems and international debt.

Contents

I

Can America Compete? Is the United States Deindustrializing?

Introduction *1*

1 Changes in U.S. Industrial Structure: The Role of Global Forces, Secular Trends, and Transitory Cycles *3*
   Robert Z. Lawrence
2 Trade Deficits, Industrial Competitiveness, and the Japanese *19*
   Rachel McCulloch

II

Import Protection Versus Open Trade

Introduction *37*

3 Trade Policies in Developed Countries *39*
   Robert E. Baldwin
4 Costs and Benefits of Protection *48*
   Organization for Economic Cooperation and Development (OECD)
5 Import Quotas and the Automobile Industry: The Costs of Protectionism *62*
   Robert W. Crandall
6 Adjustment, Protection, and Employment *74*
   Charles Pearson and Gerry Salembier
7 Why Open Trade Is Better Trade *85*
   GATT Study Group

III

Responding to Trade-Distorting Policies of Other Countries

Introduction   *93*

8   Strategic Trade Policy: A Survey of Issues and Early Analysis   *95*
     Gene M. Grossman and J. David Richardson
9   Unfair Trade Practices: The Case for a Differential Response   *114*
     Judith L. Goldstein and Stephen D. Krasner
10   Industrial Policy and Trade Distortion: A Policy Perspective   *122*
     Richard N. Cooper

IV

Background and Issues in New Trade Negotiations

Introduction   *141*

11   The Changing Nature of U.S. Trade Policy Since
     World War II   *143*
     Robert E. Baldwin
12   Protectionist Threat to Trade and Investment in Services   *161*
     Jeffrey J. Schott
13   Trade Policy Aspects of International Direct Investment
     Policies   *180*
     Harvey E. Bale, Jr.
14   The Way Forward   *199*
     GATT Study Group

V

Trade Policies in Developing Countries

Introduction   *215*

15   The Effects of Trade Strategies on Growth   *216*
     Anne O. Krueger
16   A Cool Look at "Outward-looking" Strategies for
     Development   *222*
     Paul Streeten

VI
Multinational Enterprises

Introduction *233*

17 Multinational Reshuffle *236*
     Geoffrey S. Carroll
18 Multinationals Revisited *248*
     Paul Streeten

VII
Are Current Exchange-Rate Systems Working?

Introduction *255*

19 Whither the Exchange Rate System? *259*
     Morris Goldstein
20 The Many Disappointments of Flexible Exchange Rates *268*
     Robert M. Dunn, Jr.
21 Unexpected Real Consequences of Floating Exchange Rates *290*
     Rachel McCulloch
22 The Overvalued Dollar *305*
     Rudiger Dornbusch
23 What Can Central Banks Do About the Value of the Dollar? *313*
     Dallas S. Batten and Mack Ott
24 The EMS and UK Membership *324*
     Geoffrey Dennis and Joseph Nellis

VIII
Background and Issues in International Monetary Reform

Introduction *335*

25 Is There a Need for Reform? *337*
     Richard N. Cooper
26 Is There an Important Role for an International Reserve Asset Such
    as the SDR? *358*
     W. M. Corden

IX
International Debt Problems

Introduction *383*

27 International Debt: From Crisis to Recovery? *385*
     William R. Cline
28 The Case by Case Approach to Debt Problems *391*
     Azizali F. Mohammed
29 Dealing with Debt in the 1980s *398*
     Rudiger Dornbusch

X
Structural and Institutional Change in International Finance

Introduction *415*

30 The Changing Environment of Central Bank Policy *416*
     Alexandre Lamfalussy
31 The International Money Market: Perspective and Prognosis *422*
     Gunter Dufey and Ian H. Giddy
32 The One-World Capital Market *431*
     From *Euromoney Magazine*
33 The Rise of the Foreign Currency Futures Market *437*
     Norman S. Fieleke
34 New Markets in Foreign Currency Options *441*
     Brian Gendreau

Index *451*

INTERNATIONAL
TRADE AND FINANCE

I

Can America Compete? Is the United States Deindustrializing?

Is the United States deindustrializing and becoming a service economy? Is a major reason for the deindustrialization the increasing inability of American industries to compete in world manufacturing markets? The papers in Part I by Robert Z. Lawrence and Rachel McCulloch address these questions. If, as some have recently argued, the answer to the two questions is yes, important policy questions must be faced. Is it possible for the United States to continue to be a superpower with high and rising income levels if this country loses much of its industrial base because it is unable to compete effectively against other countries? If not, then is there not a need for major changes in government policies aimed at preventing continued decline in the manufacturing sector and at improving the competitive ability of U.S. industries in international markets?

By examining economic evidence from the 1970s and earlier, Lawrence argues that the United States is not deindustrializing, if what is meant by this term is an absolute decline in manufacturing employment or output. However, there has been a small decline in the share of total real output produced in the manufacturing sector between 1950 and 1980 (from 24.5 to 23.7 percent) and an appreciable drop in the employment share of this sector (from 35.9 to 22.4 percent) as productivity has grown rapidly. Still, recent U.S. growth in manufacturing compares favorably with that of other industrial countries. Between 1973 and 1980 the growth rate of U.S. manufacturing production was considerably above that of Germany, France, and the United Kingdom, although not as high as that of Japan. The comparison between the United States and other industrial countries in manufacturing employment is even more favorable for this period, since employment actually declined in Europe and Japan, whereas it increased in the United States.

Lawrence also finds that foreign trade was not an important deindustrializing force in the 1970s. Value added in the manufacturing sector increased by $2 billion between 1970 and 1980 due to the trade balance. Although for the entire decade there was a decline of 10,000 jobs attributable to foreign trade, trade increased job opportunities in manufacturing by nearly 400,000 from 1972 to 1980.

Lawrence then shows that the United States has been developing a comparative advantage in high technology and resource-intensive goods, while its comparative advantage in labor-intensive and capital-intensive products has been eroding. Foreign trade in the former categories of goods has been contributing to employment and output in the manufacturing sector, whereas trade in the latter two has tended to cause net job and output displacement.

McCulloch asks whether the massive trade deficits of 1984 and 1985 reflect a decline of U.S. industrial competitiveness and whether the many recent proposals aimed at improving industrial competitiveness by raising productivity, combatting unfair foreign trade practices, and promoting exports will in fact reduce the deficit. Her answer to both questions is negative. The deficit, she points out, is largely determined by macroeconomic conditions at home and abroad that have little to do with microeconomic policies aimed at improving the competitiveness of individual firms or industries.

Her point about macroeconomic conditions is based on the following equality that must hold between a country's aggregate investment and aggregate saving:

$$X - M + I = S - (T - G)$$

where $X - M$ is exports minus imports of goods or net U.S. investment abroad, I is private domestic investment, S is private saving, and $T - G$, taxes minus government expenditures, is public saving. As McCulloch says, the current trade deficits have their roots in the recent fall in saving brought about by the increase in federal government expenditures (G) relative to taxes (T). Since private saving has not increased, the effect of the increased government deficit must be to crowd out or decrease either domestic investment or net U.S. investment abroad. The rise in interest rates that has occurred as the government has bid for funds to finance the federal deficit has not only tended to discourage private domestic investment but has led to a return of U.S. funds previously invested abroad and an inflow of new foreign funds. Consequently, the trade balance has turned significantly negative as the demand for dollars and thus the value of the dollar has increased sharply. Policies that increase exports or reduce imports in a particular industry will increase employment in that industry but also will reduce employment elsewhere as the higher value of the dollar due to the larger net demand for dollars either discourages exports or increases imports in other industries.

As McCulloch points out, however, this does not mean that measures to improve competitiveness are worthless. By raising productivity in export industries such measures increase our real gains from trade as they increase the volume of imported goods that can be obtained from a given collection of domestic resources devoted to export production. But this is quite a different matter from improving the balance of trade. The trade balance is determined by macro-

economic policies and the current microeconomic policies recommended as the means of improving U.S. competitiveness are
doomed to failure if success is defined in terms of the U.S. trade
balance.

1

Changes in U.S. Industrial Structure: The Role of Global Forces, Secular Trends, and Transitory Cycles

Robert Z. Lawrence

INTRODUCTION

For the first time in postwar history, employment in U.S. manufacturing has fallen
for three consecutive years. The 10.4 percent decline in the number of workers in
U.S. manufacturing from 1979 to 1982 is the largest since the wartime economy
was demobilized between 1943 and 1946. The current slump is also unusual
because international trade has made an important contribution: normally the
volume of manufactured goods imports falls steeply in a recession — yet from
1980 to 1982, it rose by 8.3 percent; normally U.S. manufactured exports reflect
growth in export markets abroad — yet despite a 5.3 percent rise in these markets
from 1980 to 1982, the volume of U.S. manufactured exports dropped 17.5
percent.

　　　Are these developments the predictable consequences of three years of
demand restraint and a strong dollar, or do they result from deep-rooted structural
changes?

　　　There are widely held views that the recession has simply dramatized a
secular decline in the U.S. industrial base. One of these views blames U.S.

This paper draws upon research undertaken for a . . . book . . . published by the Brookings
Institution entitled *Can America Compete?* and upon a paper, "Is Trade Deindustrializing America? A Medium Term Perspective," *Brookings Papers on Economic Activity*,
1:1983. . . .

From *Industrial Change and Public Policy: A Symposium Sponsored by the Federal
Reserve Bank of Kansas City, Jackson Hole, Wyoming, August 24–26, 1983* (Kansas City,
Mo.: Federal Reserve Bank, 1983), pp. 29–71. Reprinted by permission. Some text, tables,
and footnotes omitted.

producers for the trend. Americans fail to produce quality goods because managers are myopic and care only about short-term profits, workers lack discipline and are shackled by work rules, and labor and management look on one another as adversaries. Others blame the U.S. government. On the one hand are those who fault it for excessive interference — for restrictive regulatory practices which have raised production costs, for faulty tax rules which have discouraged investment, savings, and innovation, and for trade protection, which has slowed adjustment to international competition. On the other hand are those who blame government neglect. The U.S. has failed to plan and coordinate its industrial evolution. It ought to have policies to promote industries with potential and to assist those in decline. Finally, there is also the more fatalistic view of the decline in U.S. manufacturing as the inevitable result of the rapid international diffusion of U.S. technology.

While some argue that particular U.S. deficiencies have become worse over time, others point to changes in the environment which have made U.S. structural flaws increasingly costly. As long as competition was primarily domestic, U.S. weaknesses were obscured. As global trade expanded, however, U.S. firms were forced to meet foreign competitors staffed with superior workforces and managers and backed by superior government policies.

Even before the recession and the recent decline in the U.S. manufactured goods trade balance, the erosion of the U.S. international competitiveness had become a national obsession. As an award-winning article in *Business Week* observed in 1980, "U.S. industry's loss of competitiveness has been nothing short of an economic disaster."

The perceived effect of international competition has now grown to the point that it is frequently cited as the major source of structural change in the U.S. economy and the primary reason for the declining share of manufacturing in U.S. employment. This shift of U.S. production away from manufacturing is viewed with some alarm, both because manufacturing activity is considered intrinsically desirable and because of the adjustment costs associated with the shift. In addition, some argue that this decline in comparative advantage does not result from an inevitable process of technological diffusion or from changes in factors of production, but rather from the industrial and trade policies adopted by other nations. Without similar policies, some contend that the United States will eventually become an economy specialized in farm products and services — "a nation of hamburger stands."

Yet, while the role of the deficiencies in U.S. policies and practices in retarding U.S. productivity growth over the past decade remains unresolved, the links between these deficiencies, U.S. trade performance and shifts in our economic structure have not been convincingly demonstrated. . . .

Given the radical changes in the world economy after 1973, the period from 1973 to 1980 is the most relevant sample for current policy discussions. The data for this period measure performance in the new international environment that is marked by stagnation, volatile exchange rates, and increasing government intervention in trade; and it is during this period, it is alleged, that foreign industrial policies have damaged the U.S. manufacturing base. The data for this period also allow a comparison of U.S. industrial performance with those of other major industrial countries in a period in which comparative performance is less heavily influenced by relative stages of development.

Observations for the 1973–80 period, however, may be unduly influenced by the different cyclical positions prevailing in the end point years. Because capacity utilization in manufacturing was similar in 1970 and 1980, U.S. data for the entire decade are used to provide a second, cyclically neutral, measure of structural changes.[1] Observations for 1970–80 are still influenced by changes in the real exchange rate of the dollar in these years. As measured by the International Monetary Fund, relative U.S. export prices for manufactured goods were 13.5 percent lower in 1980 than in 1970. In evaluating the results, therefore, it should be kept in mind that the U.S. trade performance during the 1970s depended in part upon this price-adjustment process.

In this paper I analyze the changing role of manufacturing in the U.S. economy and structural change within U.S. manufacturing. . . .

THE MYTH OF U.S. DEINDUSTRIALIZATION

The contention that declining U.S. international competitiveness has induced the deindustrialization of America is wrong on two counts. First, in the most relevant sense, the United States has not been undergoing a process of deindustrialization; and second, over the period 1973 to 1980, the net impact of international competition on the overall size of the U.S. manufacturing sector has been small and positive.

The term "deindustrialization" requires further elaboration for precise communication. First, what is industry? Does it, for example, include the construction and mining sectors or refer more narrowly, as we will interpret it here (partly for reasons of data availability), to the manufacturing sector alone? Second, does "deindustrialization" refer to a drop in the *output* of industry, or to the *inputs* (e.g., capital and/or labor) devoted to industry? And third, does "deindustrialization" refer to an *absolute* decline in the volume of output from (or inputs to) manufacturing, or simply a *relative* decline in the growth of manufacturing outputs or inputs as compared to outputs or inputs in the rest of the economy?

Since industrial policy is generally concerned with facilitating adjustment, absolute deindustrialization with respect to factors of production would probably be the definition appropriate to current policy concerns about the manufacturing sector as a whole. While a declining *share* of output or employment could change the relative power of industrial workers, or the character of a society, an absolute decline in industrial employment entails much greater adjustment difficulties. Absolute deindustrialization at rates in excess of normal voluntary quits by workers and depreciation of capital requires the reallocation of workers and capital to alternative sectors in the economy with all of the attendant costs

Changes in U.S. Industrial Structure

TABLE 1

Share and Size of U.S. Manufacturing Sector

| | TOTAL | | | | | | SHARES | | | |
	GNP (1)	IPMAN (2)	EMP (3)	EMP-MAN (4)	NCAP (5)	NCAP-MAN (6)	Real out-put	Em-ploy-ment	Cap-ital	Expen-diture*
1950	535	131	42.50	15.24	n.a.	n.a.	24.5	35.9	n.a.	29.2
1960	737	172	54.19	16.80	543.2	104.4	23.3	31.0	25.8	28.4
1965	939	237	60.77	18.06	662.9	158.1	25.5	29.7	23.8	28.6
1970	1086	261	70.88	19.37	860.1	202.2	24.0	27.3	23.5	25.4
1973	1255	325	76.79	20.15	971.1	215.3	25.9	26.2	22.2	24.5
1975	1232	290	76.94	18.32	1033.7	232.7	23.5	23.8	22.5	23.1
1979	1479	367	89.82	21.04	1184.6	275.1	24.8	23.4	23.2	23.3
1980	1474	351	90.56	20.3	1226.3	293.6	23.7	22.4	23.9	22.1
1981	1503	359	91.54	20.2	1268.5	311.8	23.7	22.1	24.6	21.9
1982	1477	338	89.62	18.9	n.a.	n.a.	22.9	21.1	n.a.	20.7

GNP	= GNP (in billions of 1972 dollars)
IPMAN	= Value added in manufacturing (in billions of 1972 dollars)
EMP	= Employees in nonagricultural payrolls (in millions)
EMPMAN	= Employees in nonagricultural payrolls, manufacturing (in millions)
NCAP	= Net fixed nonresidential business capital (in billions of 1972 dollars)
NCAPMAN	= Net fixed nonresidential business capital in manufacturing (in billions of 1972 dollars)
*	= Ratio of GNP to value-added in manufacturing in current dollars

Sources: National Income Accounts: Bureau of Economic Analysis; *Employment and Earnings,* Bureau of Labor Statistics (March 1972); *Statistical Abstract of the United States,* 1981, U.S. Department of Census, 1981, p. 562; and *Survey of Current Business,* October 1982.

associated with such dislocations. Relative deindustrialization, on the other hand, is far less costly to accomplish, for it may entail simply devoting less resources to manufacturing in the future.[2]

As indicated in Table 1, these distinctions are relevant for characterizing U.S. deindustrialization:

Measured by the size of its manufacturing labor force, capital stock and output growth, the U.S. has not experienced absolute deindustrialization over either 1950–73 or 1973–80. Employment in U.S. manufacturing increased from 15.2 million in 1950 to 16.8 million in 1960, 19.4 million in 1970, 20.1 million in 1973 and 20.3 million in 1980.[3] The capital stock in manufacturing grew at an annual rate of 3.3 percent from 1960 to 1973, and 4.5 percent between 1973 and 1980. And output in manufacturing increased at a 3.9 percent annual rate between 1960 and 1973, and a 1.1 percent annual rate from 1973 to 1980.

Judged by the output share of goods, the United States was virtually no more a service economy in 1980 than it was in 1960. In 1960, 1973, and 1980 the ratio of goods to GNP measured in 1972 dollars was 45.6, 45.6, and 45.3 percent, respectively. Similarly, the ratio of value added to manufacturing (in 1972 dollars) was actually somewhat higher in 1973 than it was in 1950. Nonetheless, from 1950 to 1973, the *shares* of expenditure, employment, capital stock, and R&D devoted to the manufacturing sector declined. Factors on both the demand and the supply side account for manufacturing's diminishing share. As incomes have risen, Americans have allocated increasing shares of their budgets to items in the service sector such as government services, education, medical care, finance, and real estate services. At the same time, productivity in manufacturing has increased more rapidly than elsewhere in the economy. Although the more rapid growth in manufacturing productivity has resulted in slower increases in manufacturing prices, the demand stimulated by the relative decline of manufacturing goods prices has not been sufficient to offset the fall in the share of resources devoted to value added in manufacturing. As a result, overall real industrial output has risen about as rapidly as GNP, but the share of employment and capital in manufactured goods has declined.[4]

From 1973 to 1982, there was a marked acceleration in the rate at which the share of manufacturing in output and employment has declined. But this should have been expected, given the slow overall growth in GNP and the fact that labor productivity growth (output per man-hour) fell less in manufacturing than in the rest of the economy. (See Table 2.) The demand for manufacturing output is particularly sensitive to fluctuations in income. The demand for goods, particularly durables, is inherently more sensitive to short-run income fluctuations than the demand for services because many such purchases can be easily postponed. In slack periods the demand for consumer durables and plant and equipment products slumps, while during booms consumers allocate much of the transitory increases in their incomes to the purchase of consumer durables and housing, while producers invest in plant and equipment. Thus the generally slow growth in U.S. GNP from 1973 to 1980 was reflected in disproportionately slow growth in the manufacturing sector.

The relationship between the growth of manufacturing and the overall growth of the economy can be summarized statistically by regressing industrial production on GNP. Such an equation confirms that industrial performance is a magnification of that of the overall economy. If GNP grows at 1.7 percent per year, there will be no increase in manufacturing production. However, for each percentage point increase (decrease) of GNP growth above 1.7 percent, manufacturing output will rise (fall) by 2.2 percentage points. As indicated below, when an equation such as this, fitted using data from 1960 to 1973, is used to forecast industrial production for the period 1973 to 1982 given actual GNP, it does so with remarkable accuracy. Thus, there is no puzzle in explaining aggregate manufacturing production: It is almost exactly what one should have expected given the performance of the total economy. . . .

TABLE 2

Bureau of Labor Statistics Estimates of Average Annual Rates of Growth in Output per Hour, the Contribution of Capital Services per Hour and Multifactor Productivity 1968 to 1980*

Private nonfarm business	(1) 1968 to 1973	(2) 1973 to 1980	(3) Slow- down (1)–(2)
Output per hour	2.5	0.5	−2.0
Minus: Contribution on capital services per hour†	0.8	0.5	−0.3
Equals: Multifactor productivity‡	1.7	0	−1.7
Manufacturing: Output per hour of all persons	2.9	1.3	−1.6
Minus: Contribution of capital services†	0.7	1.0	+0.3
Equals: Multifactor productivity‡	2.2	0.3	−1.9

*Average annual rates leased on compound rate formula.

†Change in capital per unit of labor weighted by capital share of total output.

‡Output per unit of combined labor and capital input.

Source: United States Bureau of Labor Statistics USDL-83-153

THE MYTH OF INFERIOR U.S. INTERNATIONAL COMPARATIVE PERFORMANCE

A comparison of the performance of U.S. manufacturing with that of other major industrial countries should be useful for separating the problems that are shared by other countries, and are therefore reflective of broader global forces, from those unique to the United States. A comparison might also assist in gauging comparative U.S. strengths and weaknesses. Proponents of a radical change in industrial policies contrast the ad hoc and laissez-faire policies of the United States with the systematic, interventionist practices abroad. While conceding that there are marked differences in the degree to which foreign practices have succeeded, they argue that the conscious policy of managing the decline of older industries and the rise of new industries has been superior to the U.S. approach, which has been marked by malign neglect. Similarly, the broader provision of social services in European economies, the more extensive rights to their jobs enjoyed by workers, and the greater restrictions on plant closings have all been held up as worthy of emulation. On the other hand, opponents of such policies argue that they will delay adjustment, for the government is most likely to be captured by forces seeking to preserve the status quo, and strictures on mobility are likely to retard adaptation.

It is particularly important that international comparisons be made on the basis of performance since 1973, for policies that enjoyed success in an environment of strong global growth and economic expansion might not be appropriate for the current era of stagnation.

The 1972–74 commodity boom and the inflation that accompanied it ushered in a new era. All developed countries have been plagued by low rates of investment, slow growth, and inflation. The problems associated with high inflation and energy shocks have destroyed the confidence of investors. They have learned from their experiences in 1973 (and again in 1979) that at any time a political disruption in the Middle East or a sudden increase in domestic inflation may force their governments to adopt policies that bring on a recession, leaving them with excess capacity. . . . The rate of investment has slumped, the growth of the heavy [manufacturing] industries has been cut, and consumption expenditures have risen as a share of GDP. Industries with long gestation periods for investment, such as steel and shipbuilding, have been particularly hard hit by the post-1973 slump. There is insufficient demand for the products of plants that were built on the basis of overoptimistic projections of market growth in the late 1960s.

By a wide variety of indicators, the relative performance of U.S. manufacturing since 1973 has improved. The declines in the growth of manufacturing production, productivity growth, employment, and investment in manufacturing were all smaller in the U.S. than in other industrial nations. In Table 3, I report rates of growth for GNP and manufacturing production in the major industrial economies. While U.S. growth was among the slowest prior to 1973, since that time, U.S. growth has been quite typical for a developed country.[5] From 1973 to 1980, the overall increase in U.S. GDP of 17.3 percent was about the same as that in the rest of the developed countries (up 19.1 percent in the OECD), and U.S. manufacturing production grew at about the same rate as that in the OECD as a

[TABLE 3]

Growth in Gross Domestic Product and Manufacturing Production in Major Industrial Economies (1960–1980, average annual rates of change)*

Country	GROSS DOMESTIC PRODUCT[†]		MANUFACTURING PRODUCTION[‡]	
	1960–1973	1973–1980	1960–1973	1973–1980
United States	4.0	2.3	5.4	1.8
Germany	4.5	2.3	5.2	1.1
France	5.6	2.8	5.0	1.3
Japan	9.2	3.8	12.5	2.9
United Kingdom	3.1	0.9	3.0	−2.2
OECD	5.0	2.5	6.0	1.7

*Rates are annually compounded.

†GDP data calculated at the 1975 price level.

‡Industrial production index for manufacturing, 1975 = 100.

Sources: *National Accounts, 1951–1980*, Vol. 1, OECD; *Main Economic Indicators — Historical Statistical, 1960–1979*, OECD; and *Indicators of Industrial Activity, 1982–IV*, OECD.

[TABLE 4]

Growth in Industrial Output — Selected Developed Economies

		United States	Japan	Germany	OECD Europe	OECD total
Textiles	63/73	2.7	5.7	1.5	1.7	2.6
	73/80	−0.3	−1.6	−1.7	−1.1	−0.7
Chemicals	63/73	7.9	13.7	9.0	8.8	8.9
	73/80	4.0	2.4	1.4	1.7	2.7
Basic metals	63/73	4.2	14.2	4.8	4.9	5.6
	73/80	−2.9	1.0	−0.7	−0.3	−0.9
Iron and steel	63/73	3.7	14.5	4.9	4.2	5.4
	73/80	−3.9	−0.7	−1.5	−1.4	−1.7
Nonferrous metals	63/73	5.3	13.2	5.8	4.7	6.2
	73/80	−1.6	31.5	1.8	0.9	−0.3
Metal products	63/73	5.4	14.9	4.7	3.7	6.1
	73/80	1.0	−0.1	0.8	0.1	0.5
Nonelec. machinery	63/73	7.0	14.3	3.5	3.4	6.8
	73/80	2.9	3.2	1.8	1.9	2.7
Elec. machinery	63/73	6.5	18.1	8.5	6.8	7.9
	73/80	2.8	8.2	1.9	1.8	3.5
Transp. equipment	63/73	4.6	18.0	5.9	4.6	6.3
	73/80	−0.1	3.5	1.4	1.1	1.2
Professional	63/73	7.4	8.7	4.5	n.a.	n.a.
scientific equipment	63/73	3.1	19.5	1.1	...	...

Source: OECD Industrial Production, various issues.

whole (13.0 vs. 12.8). Although trailing behind that of Japan, U.S. industrial production grew more rapidly than in Germany, France, or the United Kingdom.

It is in Europe rather than in the United States that employment is undergoing absolute deindustrialization. Compared with historical trends, industrial production in Japan was abnormally strong while industrial production in Europe was unusually weak. Regressions relating industrial production to GNP in European countries from 1960 to 1973 substantially overpredict the level of industrial production in 1980. In the case of Japan, they underpredict industrial production (by 12 percent in 1980).

In [Table 4], I report growth rates in industrial output for several industries:

With the exception of basic metals, U.S. output growth from 1973 to 1980 for food, textiles, apparel, chemicals, glass, and fabricated metals products was more rapid than that of either Germany or Japan. Although U.S. growth lagged behind Japan in the various engineering categories, it trailed German growth only in basic metals production and transportation equipment.

Employment

The employment record of the U.S. manufacturing sector may come as an even greater surprise to those concerned about U.S. deindustrialization: From 1973 to 1980, the United States increased its employment in manufacturing more rapidly than any other major industrial country including Japan. (See [Table 5].)

Moreover, since, as indicated in [Table 5], the average work week declined more rapidly abroad, the relatively larger growth in U.S. manufacturing employment is even more conspicuous. A comparison between U.S. and Japanese employment growth indicates that from 1973 to 1980, Japanese employment in sectors such as transportation, electrical machinery, iron and steel, nonelectrical machinery, chemicals, and nonferrous metals grew less rapidly or declined more than that in the United States. . . .

As the case of Japan makes clear, in the current global environment of relatively slow growth in demand, rapid increases in output do not necessarily increase employment. Indeed, compared with the United States, the faster increases in Japanese productivity have entailed the more rapid process of labor-force deindustrialization. In the case of Europe, employment opportunities in manufacturing have decreased because faster productivity growth has been combined with relatively slower growth in output. . . .

Research and Development

Since 1972, the United States has maintained its share in R&D spending among industrial countries, reversing the relative decline in U.S. spending that occurred in the late 1960s and early 1970s, when government-funded R&D was cut back while R&D spending in other major countries advanced rapidly. From 1972 to 1980, the growth in business-funded R&D in the United States has been similar to that of France, Germany, and Japan; and while government-funded R&D in the U.S. has not grown at the Japanese pace, it has exceeded the rise in support provided by the governments of France, Germany, and the United Kingdom.

According to estimates made by the OECD by a wide variety of indicators the U.S. continues to dominate other industrial countries in its commitment to R&D. In 1977, for example, spending on R&D in U.S. manufacturing was equal to about 6.5 percent of the domestic U.S. industrial output. By contrast, spending on manufacturing R&D in Japan, the United Kingdom, and Germany amounted to 3.7, 5, and 4.0 percent of the industrial output. Indeed, privately funded U.S. R&D alone was equal to 4.4 percent of manufacturing product. In absolute terms in 1979, measured at purchasing power parity levels, the U.S. spent about 1.5 times as much as Japan, Germany, France, and the United Kingdom combined and employed about 1.3 times as many scientists and engineers. By contrast, in 1979 manufacturing employment in these countries was 1.5 times that in the U.S. The OECD has also ranked industrial countries according to the

[TABLE 5]

Changes in Employment and Hours in Manufacturing for Seven Countries, 1960–80 (average annual changes, in percent)*

Year	United States	Canada	Japan	France	Germany	Italy	United Kingdom	Eight European countries†	Ten foreign countries‡
Aggregate hours:									
1960–80	0.9	1.0	0.8	-0.1	-1.3	-0.3	-1.7	-1.1	-0.5
1960–73	1.6	1.7	2.1	0.6	-0.2	-0.1	-1.2	-0.4	0.4
1973–80	0.7	-0.3	-0.7	-2.1	-2.6	-0.1	-2.9	-2.3	-1.7
Employment:									
1960–80	1.0	1.3	1.6	0.6	-0.4	1.2	-0.9	-0.1	0.4
1960–73	1.5	1.9	3.0	1.2	0.5	1.4	-0.5	0.5	1.1
1973–80	0.6	0.3	-0.8	-1.2	-1.8	0.1	-2.2	-1.5	-1.3
Average hours:									
1960–80	0.0	-0.3	-0.8	-0.7	-0.9	-1.5	-0.8	-1.9	-0.8
1960–73	0.1	-0.2	-0.9	-0.5	-0.8	-1.5	-0.7	-0.9	-0.8
1973–80	-0.1	-0.5	-0.1	-0.9	-0.9	-0.3	-0.8	-0.8	-0.5

*Rates of change computed from the least-squares trend of the logarithms of the index numbers.

†France, Germany, Italy, United Kingdom, Belgium, Denmark, the Netherlands, and Sweden.

‡The eight European countries plus Canada and Japan.

Source: Bureau of Labor Statistics, *Monthly Labor Review*, December 1981, p. 15.

percentage of manufacturing output spent on R&D in a variety of industry groups during the 1970s. The U.S. ranked first in manufacturing overall as well as in the electrical, aerospace, machinery, and transportation categories.

As this brief comparison suggests, if U.S. manufacturing performance since 1973 is considered to have been relatively poor, this should not be ascribed to a relative failure to commit resources either to capital formation or to R&D. While the use made by U.S. manufacturers may or may not have been inefficient, the U.S. capital stock and real R&D in manufacturing have grown as rapidly as those abroad.

Productivity

Measured both in terms of the ratio of total output to all inputs and in output per man-hour, U.S. productivity growth in manufacturing, as in the economy as a whole, has slowed down in the period since 1973. Over the same period, however, there has been an even larger slowdown in foreign productivity growth, both in manufacturing and in the whole economy. Careful studies have been unable to provide convincing explanations for these slowdowns, and I will not attempt an investigation of them here. It should, however, be noted that, despite some convergence in the period since 1973, the U.S. productivity growth rate in manufacturing remains the slowest of any major industrial country. . . .

Measured by output per man-hour, however, the United States continues to be the world's most productive manufacturing nation. According to Roy, for example, in 1980 output per employed worker-year in United States manufacturing was about 16 percent higher than in Japan, 21.7 percent higher than in Germany, and 31.3 percent higher than in France.[6] To be sure, the United States no longer leads in all industries. According to the 1981 White Paper on International Trade issued by the government of Japan, Japanese productivity levels in 1979 were above those of the United States in steel (108 percent above U.S. levels), general machinery (11 percent higher), electrical machinery (19 percent), transportation equipment (24 percent), and precision machinery and equipment (34 percent). . . .

Concluding Remarks

In this section I have pointed to the marked contrast in European economic performance before and after 1973, a contrast that is particularly evident in data on European industrial performance. European manufacturing production has declined by more than might have been expected, given GNP. Employment has fallen, and productivity growth slowed down. While Germany has been relatively successful in shifting out of slow-growing industries, it has been less successful in moving into new ones. In fact, just as Americans have responded to the slowdown in manufacturing by decrying the short-sighted nature of their decisionmakers, in Europe the concern stems from excessive rigidity.

European governments have assumed much greater responsibility than those in Japan or the United States for providing steady increases in standards of living, and a much greater degree of job tenure is provided in Europe than is common in the United States. In the 1950s and 1960s, these guarantees were relatively costless, for rapid demand growth facilitated job retention, and rising productivity growth made higher wages affordable. With the shocks and slow growth in the 1970s, however, governments were forced to make good on the guarantees. Partly because they were backstopped by generous social payments by schemes such as indexation, growth in European real wages exceeded the pace warranted by changes in productivity and the terms of trade. This squeezed profits, discouraged investment, and slowed growth. With slow growth and high wages, firms wished to reduce their work forces. Governments were forced both to support employment by job subsidies, trade protection, schemes for job-sharing, reductions in work hours and early retirement and to provide extensive unemployment benefits. While manufacturing employment declined, the services sectors in Europe were unable to provide employment for new labor force entrants and those displaced from manufacturing.

Whereas European unemployment rates have been considerably lower than those in the United States for most of the postwar period, by 1982 the average unemployment rates in the United States and the European community (EC9) were 9.7 and 9.5 percent, respectively. Although they stand at similar levels, structural unemployment seems much higher in Europe. According to the OECD, in the United States in 1982, about 16.6 percent of the unemployed had been unemployed for more than six months. By contrast, in Germany, France, and the United Kingdom, the long-term unemployed were 38.1, 55.8, and 45.7 of the unemployed. In 1979, males over the age of 45 constituted 36 percent of all unemployed German males, whereas in the United States, older males were 17 percent of all unemployed males. Similarly, older women were 29 percent of the unemployed in Germany, and 15 percent in the United States.

There is, therefore, overwhelming evidence that the structural problems facing European economies far exceed those in the United States. . . .

MYTHS ABOUT THE SIZE AND SOURCES OF STRUCTURAL CHANGE

While much of the discussion about U.S. deindustrialization has been couched in terms of the manufacturing sector as a whole, in fact it reflects a concern about a few specific industries. Several of these industries have a number of characteristics which are likely to make employment loss particularly conspicuous: Adjustment is particularly difficult and costly in sectors in which capital investments are long-lived, workers earn wage premiums that reflect nontransferable benefits (such as seniority, monopoly rents, and the impact of strong unions), and production occurs in large plants that are important for the economic health of the areas in which they are located.

The erosion of employment has occurred in industries in which it is likely to be most vocally resisted because the industries are likely to be politically powerful and the burdens of adjustment on the workers are likely to be especially great. It has been especially concentrated among unionized workers, in large plants, and in large industries.

In 1980, based on a disaggregation of industries of two-digit SIC codes, 58 percent of U.S. workers were in a two-digit industry which had experienced an overall decline in employment since 1973. In addition, four of the industries with slow employment growth (tobacco, autos, primary metals, and textiles) are among the five industries which have the largest average plant size.

Indeed, a comparison of the features of the industries which grew rapidly in the 1960s with those growing rapidly in the 1970s indicated two important differences. Industries with large plant size and with high concentration ratios were more likely to grow slowly in the 1970s than in the 1960s. Both these variables suggest a declining importance of economies of scale, the predictable result of slow over-all market expansion.

To get behind the structural shifts in manufacturing, the 52 industries of the input-output categories have been classified by production process.

In the trade literature it is customary to group goods into three categories: goods that require the relatively intensive use of natural resources ([termed] Ricardo goods), goods that require high proportions of research and development or employ scientists and engineers fairly intensively (product-cycle or high-technology goods), and goods that use relatively standardized production technologies (Hecksher-Ohlin goods). In this paper, for the process categories I adopt the Ricardo (resource-intensive) and product-cycle (high-technology) groupings and divide the Hecksher-Ohlin group according to relative capital-labor ratios into capital- and labor-intensive categories.

The data in [Table 6] highlight the change in the composition of U.S. output and employment in manufacturing. They indicate the long-run shift toward high-technology sectors in both output and employment. The employment shift proceeded at about the same pace between 1970 and 1980 as during the previous decade, although the shift measured by valued added accelerated somewhat. But from 1973 to 1980, the shift toward high technology accelerated according to both measures. In the thirteen years from 1960 to 1973, the share of high-technology products increased in total value added from 27 to 32 percent. In the next seven years, it rose from 32 to 38 percent. The acceleration in employment share in high-technology sectors is even more dramatic: After increasing from 27 percent in 1960 to 29 percent in 1973, it rose to 33 percent by 1980.

[Table 7] breaks down the striking divergence of the high-technology sector from the rest of manufacturing into the parts accounted for by domestic use and foreign trade. Between 1973 and 1980, output of high-technology products increased by 30.6 percent and employment rose by 15.7 percent; in industries characterized by other production processes, output grew sluggishly and employment declined. The compositional changes were related to growth resulting from both trade and domestic use. Although most of the employment growth in the high-technology sector can be ascribed to the rise in domestic use, growth in

[TABLE 6]

Shares of Value Added and Employment in U.S. Manufacturing, by Production Characteristics of Industries (selected years, 1960–80, by percent)

Item	1960	1970	1972	1973	1980
Value added*					
High-technology	.27	.31	.31	.32	.38
Capital-intensive	.32	.30	.31	.32	.27
Labor-intensive	.13	.13	.14	.13	.12
Resource-intensive	.28	.25	.24	.23	.23
Employment†					
High-technology	.27	.30	.28	.29	.33
Capital-intensive	.29	.30	.30	.30	.28
Labor-intensive	.21	.20	.21	.21	.19
Resource-intensive	.23	.21	.21	.20	.20

*Value added computed for each input-output (I-O) industry by multiplying gross output in 1972 dollars by the ratio of value added to output in the 1972 I-O table.

†Employment is derived from the Bureau of Labor Statistics series on employment and earnings. The series has been aggregated to the two-digit I-O industry and then to the process categories.

Sources:[DRI (Data Resources Inc.) tape and 1982 Employment and Training Report of the President, pp. 255–58.]

[TABLE 7]

Percentage Change in Value Added and Employment in U.S. Manufacturing Due to Foreign Trade and Domestic Use, by Production Characteristics of Industries (1970–80 and 1973–80)*

Item	1970–1980			1973–1980		
	Total	Domestic use	Foreign trade	Total	Domestic use	Foreign trade
Value added						
Total	33.1	32.3	0.8	9.6	7.8	1.9
High-technology	61.9	54.7	7.2	30.6	25.2	5.4
Capital-intensive	18.4	22.2	−3.8	−7.3	−6.7	−0.6
Labor-intensive	16.5	20.7	−4.1	−2.1	−0.2	−1.9
Resource-intensive	23.4	22.6	0.8	10.7	8.2	2.5
Employment						
Total	4.7	4.7	0.0	0.7	−0.7	1.3
High-technology	16.4	12.9	3.5	15.7	11.1	4.6
Capital-intensive	0.3	2.3	−1.9	−6.0	−5.9	−0.1
Labor-intensive	−1.8	1.8	−3.6	−8.2	−6.3	−2.0
Resource-intensive	0.5	−0.6	1.1	−1.5	−4.1	2.6

*See notes to [Table 6.]

Sources: Same as Table 1.

employment from foreign trade was greater in this sector than in any other. Foreign trade also raised employment in resource-intensive industries, where domestic demand was sluggish. Stagnant or falling domestic demand, combined with a reinforcing decline in net foreign demand, thwarted growth in both capital- and labor-intensive industries.

Despite smaller changes due to trade than those due to domestic use, public perceptions may be exaggerating the role of trade because the effects of trade and domestic use have been positively correlated. For reasons unrelated to international trade, the U.S. manufacturing sector has been undergoing major structural shifts in output and employment because of domestic demand and technology. The impact of trade has in some cases reinforced these domestic changes; in other cases, industries experiencing employment losses because of domestic use have had only minor offsets as a result of trade. This correspondence between trade and domestic use is apparent at the relatively disaggregated level of the 52 I-O industries. From 1973 to 1980, for example, there was a 0.49 correlation between the contributions to value added of domestic use and those of foreign trade. The correspondence between growth related to domestic use and growth related to trade can be seen clearly when the 52 industries are aggregated according to the nature of the production process. . . .

The Role of U.S. Trade

The growing importance of high-technology trade to the United States is illustrated by Chart 1, which contrasts the U.S. trade balances in R&D and non–R&D-intensive products.[7]

The literature disputes the precise sources of the U.S. advantage in high-technology manufactured goods. Does it result from the relative abundance of engineers and scientists, the relatively large amounts spent on R&D, or the market inducements to innovate a rich economy? The strong interactions among these factors inhibit quantification of the contribution of each. However, it is quite possible to provide a snapshot of the kinds of manufactured goods the United States succeeds in exporting and those in which import penetration has been the greatest.

U.S. export industries have made large investments in R&D and are at the technological frontier. The products are often novel, require specialized production methods, and benefit during their development from being close to the market in which they are sold. Staying ahead requires continual innovation to offset the inevitable standardization of the production process and the international diffusion of technology. Conversely, U.S. imports, especially those from developing countries, are by and large mature and standardized products that can be mass-produced using skills that can be quickly acquired. They may be manufactured products requiring unskilled labor (such as apparel and footwear) or products requiring capital relatively intensively (such as steel).

In summary, therefore, the impact of trade has not been to shrink the U.S. manufacturing sector, and the United States has not lost its comparative advantage in manufacturing as a whole. The United States has been developing a comparative

[CHART 1]

U.S. Trade Balance in R&D-Intensive and Non–R&D-Intensive Manufacturing, 1960–79

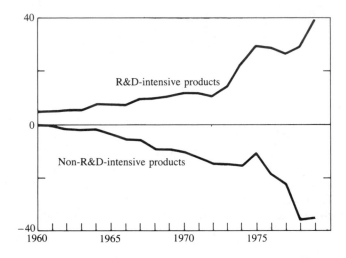

Source: National Science Foundation. *Science Indicators 1980* (U.S. Government Printing Office, 1961), p. 32

advantage in high-technology (and resource-intensive) products, while its comparative advantage in labor-intensive and capital-intensive products manufactured with standardized technologies has been eroding. There is, therefore, a correspondence between the U.S. industries experiencing slow economic growth because of sluggish domestic use and those experiencing declining comparative advantage.

Notes

1. Capacity utilization in U.S. manufacturing, measured by the index of the Federal Reserve Board, was 79.3 percent in 1970 and 79.1 percent in 1980.
2. Of course, as we will show later in this study, absolute declines of employment in individual industries may entail considerable adjustment difficulties, even when offset elsewhere by employment gains in other manufacturing industries.
3. By contrast, the nation has experienced an absolute decline in agricultural employment from 8.6 million in 1945 to 3.3 million in 1980.
4. There are two measures of manufactured output which provide somewhat different growth rates. The industrial production index of the Federal Reserve Board consistently suggests more rapid increases than the deflated value of manufactured goods output in the GNP accounts.
5. In fact, according to United Nations data, North American industrial production from 1973 to 1980 grew as rapidly as that in all market economies.

6. Overall U.S. GDP per man-year in the U.S. was 49 percent above that in Japan, 13.3 percent above that in Germany, and 7.7 percent above that in France. A. D. Roy, "Labor Productivity in 1980: An International Comparison," *National Institute Economic Review* No. 101, August 1982, p. 29.
7. The United States has maintained its share in world trade of high-technology products far better than in more routine goods. See Bela Balassa, "U.S. Export Performance: A Trade Share Analysis," Working Papers in Economics, 24, Johns Hopkins University, 1978.

2

Trade Deficits, Industrial Competitiveness, and the Japanese

Rachel McCulloch

Are U.S. industries in serious trouble? As nearly every month brings new record deficits in U.S. merchandise trade and the current account, the competitive position of U.S. industries has become the subject of increasing public concern. Several years of ever larger trade deficits have convinced many Americans that the nation does indeed face a basic "competitiveness problem." The causes of dismal U.S. trade performance, once confined to the realm of dry technical analysis, now serve as the centerpiece of television news features, after-dinner speeches, and even political platforms. Committees and commissions are formed almost daily to study the competitiveness problem, devise recommendations for its speedy solution, and promulgate the inevitable report. A hefty stack of these reports now awaits the interested reader, and still more reports continue to pour in as additional groups complete their collective labors and publish their findings.

The mammoth trade deficits, we are told repeatedly, reflect the decline of American industrial competitiveness. Our spending for new plant and equipment and for research and development is lagging woefully, with disastrous consequences for productivity growth. Many of our industrial products have lost the reputation for high quality that once commanded premium prices in world markets. Our labor-management relations are destructive, our business executives myopic, our educational system chaotic. Under a U.S. President ideologically committed to reduce government spending and balance the budget, the Federal deficit has grown to proportions even more mind-boggling than our trade deficits. And despite all this, the fate of our industries continues to be shaped by a

From *California Management Review*, vol. 27, no. 2, pp. 140–156. © 1985 by the Regents of the University of California. Reprinted by permission of the Regents.

crazy-quilt of ad hoc laws and administrative decisions, a structure so lacking in consistency that we actually do not know the extent to which we are using the power of government to promote the well-being of any particular industry.

THE COMPETITIVENESS CONSENSUS

While predictably divergent in tone and detail, the reports of the various groups are in some ways remarkably similar. Almost all point to a large and growing trade deficit, concur that "competitiveness" is the root problem, and recommend a variety of direct measures to solve it. Almost all assume implicitly that firm-by-firm and industry-by-industry gains can produce corresponding gains at the national level. Although some groups stress measures to improve the productivity of U.S. industries while others emphasize policies to combat unfair trade practices and promote U.S. exports, all highlight the competitive position of U.S. products in world markets.

 With so many distinguished voices crying in unison for steps to improve industrial competitiveness, it seems indiscreet and almost unpatriotic to ask whether this campaign is based on sound economic logic. Regrettably, the answer to this unasked and possibly unwelcome question is: "Probably not." While compelling in its appeal to common sense, the competitiveness consensus is based on an incomplete and flawed evaluation of the underlying problems and their causes.

 In this article, I argue that the U.S. trade deficit — the most frequently cited "symptom" of declining U.S. competitiveness — is largely determined by macroeconomic conditions at home and abroad. As a consequence, most of the policies currently advocated as means to restore U.S. competitiveness are likely to have little effect on this aggregate; only changes in macroeconomic conditions can eliminate the huge trade deficit. On the other hand, competitiveness policies *can* improve industry and firm performance. However, in most cases there will be domestic losers as well as gainers from such policies, and there is no reason to expect a net gain in total domestic employment.

 This does not imply that the current recommendations lack merit. On the contrary, the national campaign to restore industrial competitiveness has generated many worthwhile proposals, which, if implemented, will surely promote the economic well-being of the country. Nonetheless, the campaign is doomed to failure as long as "success" is defined in terms of the U.S. trade balance, and policy measures taken to achieve it are limited to those with a direct influence on industrial competitiveness. As I argue below, the real benefits attainable through these policies are increased gains from trade (not necessarily an improved trade balance) and higher-productivity jobs (not necessarily more jobs).

 Is this nitpicking? I think not. We need sound policies, but we also need a clear understanding of what these policies can be expected to do. "Failure" of sensible policies to achieve their presumed objectives may promote the adoption of other, less desirable measures to restore competitiveness. Only changes in macroeconomic policy can reverse the large trade deficit without creating significant new problems. The erroneous belief that direct competitiveness-oriented measures will do the job sets the nation up for disappointment and lays the groundwork for a new protectionist initiative predicated on the false assumption that all else has failed.

WHAT DO WE MEAN BY COMPETITIVENESS?

A curious feature of the many recent books, articles, and reports devoted to the decline of U.S. industrial competitiveness is that the authors rarely attempt to define what it is. In the reports of committees, the omission is perhaps not surprising — competitiveness means different things to different people. In fact, there seem to be at least four distinct meanings in current usage.

The first and most common meaning refers to aggregate trade performance — the merchandise trade balance or the balance in goods and services trade. By this definition, a country is losing competitiveness when its trade balance is declining. A second and related definition refers to the sectoral trade balances (multilateral or with a specific partner) in particular industries or product categories. Industrial competitiveness in this sense could be declining even if the overall merchandise trade balance were improving. For those concerned about the sectoral composition of exports and imports, an improving merchandise trade balance generated by, say, agricultural exports might be less desirable than an equal improvement brought about by reduced imports of autos and steel.

A third definition of competitiveness is in terms of market share, either for total trade or in specific sectors. In a growing world market, it is possible to have declining share-competitiveness at the same time that the sectoral trade balance is rising, if the U.S. fails to capture enough of the total growth in demand. This has been the recent situation for the U.S. aircraft industry.

As these definitions suggest, competitiveness may be defined in terms of the composition of output or employment. Are services growing relative to manufacturing? High-technology production relative to basic industries? Many concerns about competitiveness are actually concerns about changes in the composition of output relative to some unspecified ideal. One of the problems inherent in industrial targeting is that there is no evident consensus about the right composition of national output.

Finally, relative rates of productivity improvement, typically measured by output per hour of labor input, are sometimes used to assess competitiveness. It is almost universally assumed that greater productivity gains at the industry level translate automatically into increased employment and enhanced competitiveness as measured by trade performance, although neither result is logically implied.

With these definitions in mind, how does the U.S. economy stack up? In terms of all four, there is a strong suspicion that we are losing out in relation to at least one major competitor — Japan.

WHY ARE THE JAPANESE GAINING?

Central to the current preoccupation with declining U.S. competitiveness, and with the national failings that may explain it, is the inevitable comparison to our economic arch-rival, Japan. The bilateral deficit on merchandise trade with Japan is now almost a third of the total U.S. merchandise trade deficit, and the bilateral imbalance in U.S.–Japan trade in manufactured goods trade is even more striking. Worse yet, the Japanese seem to be gaining fastest in the markets for high-technology products, where U.S. firms previously enjoyed unchallenged dominance.

Many academic analysts and professional Japan-watchers (along with some observers in government and even the U.S. business community) view Japanese economic gains relative to the United States as the natural consequence of their superior play in a basically fair game: they do well what we do poorly. This view emphasizes economic "fundamentals" and looks primarily at the possible causes of lagging productivity growth in American industries. Policy prescriptions derived from it typically urge the United States to improve education at all levels; increase incentives for investment, research and development, and especially commercialization of new technologies; reevaluate Federal antitrust policies to take account of the global nature of industrial competition; and seek new, more cooperative modes of labor-management interaction.

These recommendations in effect suggest that the United States ought to adopt the methods and policies deemed responsible for Japanese economic successes, thereby allowing U.S. industries to benefit from similar advantages. Here the most difficult question to answer is what *particular* features of the Japanese society and economy are critical to those successes. The fallacy of *post hoc ergo propter hoc* is an obvious peril in generalizing from the Japanese experience. Too, some key Japanese institutions are unlikely to prove effective in the very different U.S. context. (Quality circles? How about a company song or a sushi bar?) Nonetheless, the American public has been inundated by articles and books on Japanese education, Japanese technological advancement, and particularly Japanese management practices. Most carry at least an implicit message that the United States has much to gain from emulating Japanese ways.

But not everyone shares the view that Japanese successes are mainly the natural reward for working smarter and harder. To some, the world looks markedly different. Many Americans in business, labor, and government (especially but by no means exclusively those whose objectives have been directly threatened by competition from Japan) readily acknowledge such factors as the Japanese work ethic, educational system, and high national savings rate. However, this group believes the *primary* advantage of the Japanese in competition with the United States arises from the different rules or norms guiding the actions of their governments. In their view, United States policy toward industrial competitiveness is constrained by an outmoded laissez-faire philosophy unsuited to actual world conditions. By contrast, the Japanese (and almost everyone else) feel free to augment or circumvent market forces whenever the national interest seems better served by doing so.

This second group is highly critical of certain Japanese practices, including targeting, nontariff trade barriers, and manipulation of the exchange rate. However, their fundamental dissatisfaction is reserved for the actions (or, often, inaction) of United States officials. Policy recommendations typically highlight the urgent need for a more aggressive U.S. stance in trade law and its administration. Top priority is also accorded to major new export-promotion efforts. Overall, this latter group places far less stress on the determinants of industrial *productivity* while emphasizing the role of government action in determining the ability of United States firms to compete successfully in world markets.

Although predicated on different assessments of the underlying problem, these two views of U.S. trade performance and of competition with the Japanese have important common elements. Both are fundamentally microeconomic in orientation and emphasize the competitive position of U.S. products in world markets. Furthermore, there is agreement that the U.S. trade imbalance, worldwide and especially with Japan, can and should be remedied through appropriate *direct* measures, whether this entails restructuring U.S. industry to improve American productivity, altering the context of competition between United States firms and their foreign rivals, or perhaps (especially for committees) some of each.

COMPETITIVENESS IS NEITHER THE PROBLEM NOR THE SOLUTION

A fundamental defect in the campaign to restore American trade competitiveness is that it sets up as an ultimate objective what is not even the primary means to achieve that objective. We should be concerned about international competitiveness, whether across the board or in particular industries, because of its further implications for overall national well-being. Yet competitiveness is rapidly being elevated to an end in itself rather than a likely concomitant of a rising standard of living.

This distinction is crucial because some proposed policies could indeed reduce the U.S. trade deficit or increase the market share worldwide of specific U.S. industries but would achieve their results *at the expense* of future gains in productive capacity, employment, and national well-being. Other proposals chart a desirable course of action in terms of the national interest, but would have at most minor consequences for aggregate trade performance. Moreover, even broad-based measures would create domestic losers as well as gainers.

Policies to promote effective education, capital formation, and research and development serve the national interest primarily by increasing overall productive capacity. However, this would be true even in an economy that had no trade and thus no possibility of a "competitiveness problem." On the other hand, such changes by themselves, even in the longer term, have no direct implications for aggregate trade performance, because they would tend to advance the performance of some industries at the expense of others.

Likewise, sensible trade policies help to promote the growth of exports and imports along lines that allow maximum national benefits from trade. They may also defend domestic producers from "unfair" foreign competition and provide temporary domestic insulation from the full consequences of rapidly changing conditions in world markets — a kind of safety net. Again, effects of these policies may well be significant at the industry level but there are no immediate implications for aggregate trade performance or employment.

Recent recommendations from groups concerned about U.S. industrial competitiveness include many sound and even necessary steps for the nation. At the same time, they are unlikely to "succeed" in the narrow sense of reducing the red ink in the trade numbers or raising total employment. To understand why, it is necessary to look at the relationship of the trade balance to the nation's overall balance of payments.

DETERMINANTS OF AGGREGATE TRADE PERFORMANCE

Put simply, *aggregate* trade performance is determined primarily by factors *other than* those highlighted in the competitiveness approach. The aggregate current account deficit (merchandise trade plus services, income from foreign investment, and unilateral transfers of resources such as foreign aid) must be equal to the aggregate capital account surplus (net inflow of investment funds from abroad). This does not mean that competitiveness policies would have no effect on trade. Rather, these policies would increase the trade balance of some industries and with some trading partners, but these gains would come largely at the expense of deterioration elsewhere in U.S. trade performance. Aggregate current account performance can be altered only if there are corresponding changes in the capital account.

Competitiveness analysts are basically looking for changes that can enhance the attractiveness of U.S. goods and services relative to their foreign counterparts. Applying to the capital account the same sort of logic used in analyzing trade performance, we need to ask how to make U.S. assets *less* attractive to investors. Somehow this approach is not as compelling, because we recognize that the strengths of the U.S. economy account for some of these inflows and that reduced inflows would aggravate one of the very problems pinpointed by the competitiveness analysts — the high cost of capital to U.S. firms. Another way to put this is that we have a large trade deficit mainly because we have a large capital-account surplus. To understand the deterioration in U.S. trade performance, we thus need to look at the reasons for the corresponding improvement in the capital account.

Roughly speaking, current trade deficits have their roots in the recent fall in total U.S. saving. National saving is equal to private saving plus government saving. The latter is the fiscal surplus or deficit. Thus, the large recent increase in the Federal budget deficit translates into lower total national saving unless offset by a corresponding increase in private domestic saving (or larger state and local budget surpluses). After the fact, total national investment (capital formation at home plus net acquisition of foreign assets) must be equal to total national saving. Reduced national saving must therefore be matched by reduced national investment. It is in this sense that a budget deficit financed by government borrowing can cause "crowding-out" of capital formation and lower productivity growth.

In an economy that had no capital transactions with the rest of the world, the total fall in national saving would have to be met by a corresponding fall in domestic capital formation — conventional crowding-out. This would be achieved through an increase in real, i.e., inflation-adjusted, interest rates that would deter marginal private-sector borrowers. These higher rates might also discourage some deficit-financed government activities at the local level. In principle, private-sector *lenders*, i.e., savers, might also increase their supply of funds to the market by raising the proportion of their incomes allocated to savings, but there is no empirical evidence of significant interest responsiveness on the part of U.S. savers.

In an open economy such as the United States, the process is complicated by international movements of financial capital. As national saving drops and the real interest rate rises in the United States, there is a tendency for part of the fall in saving to be met by reduced net U.S. investment abroad. This takes the form of a return flow of U.S. funds previously invested abroad and/or an inflow of new foreign funds. As funds shift toward the United States from other financial markets, the higher real interest rates resulting from decreased national saving in the United States are transmitted abroad. Some part of the crowding-out of private capital formation is thus shifted to other nations. Since the world remains, at least for now, a closed economy, the decline in total world saving must be met by an equal reduction in total world capital formation.

Thus, the turnaround in the U.S. capital account is the immediate consequence of a growing Federal deficit that has not been matched by increased private domestic saving or reduced demand for private domestic capital formation. The nation's capital-account position is determined by the resulting increase in the domestic interest rate and its effect on international flows of financial capital. The "improved" capital account means a corresponding dollar-for-dollar deterioration in the current account. The mechanism ensuring this result is the market-determined appreciation of the dollar.

DEFICITS AND THE DOLLAR

In the present exchange-rate system, the dollar's value in terms of other currencies is determined primarily by private supply and demand. The demand for dollars is the counterpart of foreign purchases of U.S. goods, services, and assets. As U.S. residents purchase fewer foreign assets and foreigners purchase more U.S. assets, the net demand for dollars increases, raising the value of the dollar relative to other currencies and especially relative to the currencies of countries with high national savings rates and low real interest rates, such as Japan.

Equilibrium in the foreign-exchange market is restored when the net demand for dollars to purchase U.S. goods and services has fallen enough to match the increased net demand for dollars to purchase U.S. assets. The inflow of funds to U.S. financial markets in effect crowds out U.S. net exports of goods and services, just as the outflow of funds to the U.S. crowds out capital formation in other countries.

What this implies is that the ingredients of industrial competitiveness cannot be regarded as *independent* determinants of trade performance. In particular, induced movements in exchange rates tend to offset the aggregate consequences of any improvement in industrial competitiveness. Unless national saving rises relative to the demand for funds for private investment, any increase in the competitiveness of an industry will be accommodated mainly through a *further appreciation* of the dollar — squeezing out marginal exports and squeezing in marginal imports across all industries.

One consequence of the inverse relationship between capital inflows and trade performance is that policies to discourage capital flows to the United States *would* produce a corresponding improvement in the current account. This improvement would arise through a decline in the value of the dollar. If national saving is not altered, however, reduced capital inflows entail shifting back to the United States some part of the crowding-out of capital formation that is currently occurring abroad. Putting this in slightly different terms, U.S. real interest rates would be higher and foreign interest rates lower. Substantially the same result would be produced by a shift in investor preferences away from U.S. assets. In either case, the price of better trade performance would be reduced demand and employment in interest-sensitive sectors such as housing and automobiles. Moreover, to the extent that higher real interest rates discouraged domestic capital formation or research and development, productivity growth in U.S. industries would be further stunted.

EXPORTS DO MEAN JOBS, BUT WHOSE?

At one level, the concern about industrial competitiveness is a concern about American jobs. Administration trade officials are much given to emphasizing the importance of exports in total domestic employment, while labor unions stand ready to remind us that imports mean fewer U.S. jobs. Our record trade deficits are interpreted as showing the net current impact of trade transactions on demand for domestically produced goods and services, and, therefore, on domestic employment. Accordingly, it is tempting to conclude that measures to expand exports or reduce imports represent effective means to increase U.S. employment, either across the board or in specific industries.

This logic is correct only in a very limited sense. Looking first at employment in a specific industry, it is reasonable to assume that total industry demand worldwide at a given time is largely fixed. Competitiveness policies at the industry level, whether oriented toward increasing exports or reducing imports, tend to increase U.S. jobs in that industry without any appreciable effect on total industry employment worldwide. Thus, any gain in U.S. jobs must come primarily at the expense of foreign jobs in the same industry. It is therefore quite true that if we succeed in exporting more or importing less in a given industry we are likely to expand employment in that industry, while at the same time reducing employment more or less proportionally elsewhere in the world. Measures to achieve this are called "beggar-your-neighbor" policies for obvious reasons. Curiously, most well-informed people are aware that import restrictions protect jobs at home at the expense of those abroad, but only a few appear to recognize that similar logic applies also to export-promotion efforts.

Whatever the desirability of pursuing policies that shift unemployment abroad, in practice our ability to manipulate trade flows for this purpose is likely to be quite limited. Other nations are equally concerned about employment growth in the aggregate and employment in particular sectors (e.g., high-technology industries). Most have been decidedly less successful than the United States in creating new jobs. If many countries try simultaneously to increase their world market shares in steel, autos, or semiconductors, it is obvious that not all can succeed. Moreover, their efforts are likely to reduce global productive efficiency and thereby shrink income and welfare worldwide. This is what happened in the early 1930s, when a number of countries, including the United States, erected high tariff barriers to protect domestic jobs. Now as then, broad U.S. actions to raise import barriers or expand export incentives can be expected to trigger prompt, widespread retaliation by U.S. trading partners.

However, even if a given U.S. industry succeeds in increasing its total employment, this does not imply a comparable increase in national employment. Rather, the improved trade performance of one U.S. industry will tend to *worsen* the trade performance of other sectors. The aggregate trade balance of the nation is determined by macroeconomic factors. When one industry's performance improves, increases in input costs, interest rates, and especially the international value of the dollar squeeze out marginal U.S. exports and squeeze in marginal U.S. imports. The net result is an offset that leaves the overall trade balance unchanged. Measures that raise a specific industry's employment through changes in the microeconomic determinants of its international competitiveness might thus be termed beggar-your-brother policies, since they tend to shift unemployment between sectors of the U.S. economy.

Again, it is important to emphasize that some competitiveness policies can provide real benefits, although not the ones typically used to justify their adoption. Offsetting macroeconomic changes at home and retaliation abroad undercut the possible employment gains to be achieved through measures whose main objective is to spur exports or deter imports, i.e., measures intended to alter the competitive context of U.S. producers. The fundamental reason is that industry gains from such policies must come at the expense of our trading partners and/or employment in other domestic sectors.

The situation is somewhat different for measures that increase economic efficiency. Because these measures raise the productive potential of the nation and of the world, they open the possibility of mutual gains for the United States and its trading partners. However, productivity improvements alone tend to change the pattern of employment and trade performance across industries rather than aggregate performance for the nation as a whole.

THE BILATERAL DEFICIT WITH JAPAN

The competitiveness approach views as separate and independent the various factors that influence U.S. trade performance. One consequence of this mode of analysis is the extraordinary degree to which resulting policy prescriptions focus on the bilateral relationship between the United States and Japan. The implicit assumption is that measures which reduce the bilateral deficit with Japan will achieve a corresponding reduction in the overall trade deficit, i.e., will not be offset by opposite movements in other bilateral balances.

In a well-functioning multilateral trading system, there is no reason to expect any two nations to have balanced trade, even in the long run. As a nation that imports virtually all its industrial raw materials and much of its food, Japan must run a global surplus in manufactured goods trade to maintain balance in overall merchandise trade. This surplus cannot be taken, as many observers are inclined to do, as evidence of insidious nontariff barriers to imports of manufactured products (Japan's average tariff rate is very low relative to other major nations). In fact, industry-by-industry analyses of Japanese trade patterns suggest that Japanese trade flows with other nations, including the United States, are about what one would expect on the basis of overall resource endowments.

The real significance of the large bilateral deficit in U.S. trade with Japan is that it gives U.S. officials considerable leverage in negotiating with their Japanese counterparts — the Japanese have much to lose from further restrictions on their access to the lucrative U.S. market. However, as suggested above, the result of exercising that leverage may be mainly to alter the relative success of different U.S. industries rather than to improve overall U.S. trade performance. Likewise, any reduction in the bilateral trade deficit with Japan will be largely offset by deterioration in other bilateral balances.

A somewhat more complex and intriguing issue is raised by recent vigorous efforts by the United States to promote liberalization of Japanese financial markets. These efforts have been justified in rather vague terms as having the desirable but admittedly long-term goal of increasing the use of the yen as a form of international money, a function currently dominated by the United States dollar. To the extent that the persistently high value of the dollar is due to this role, a substitution of yen for dollars might help to bring down the market-determined value of the dollar while raising that of the yen. This argument is a dubious one, however, since the dollar served as the main form of international money even when, in the late 1970s, it was as clearly undervalued in terms of relative purchasing power as it has been overvalued since 1981. Furthermore, the widespread international use of the German mark and the British pound seems not to have prevented overvaluation of the dollar relative to those currencies as well as the yen.

The implications for Japanese capital outflows and the value of the yen rest on the net effect on Japanese saving relative to domestic investment demand, or, roughly speaking, the real rate of interest available to asset holders. Major liberalization of credit markets in Japan affects firms as well as households, so that both investment and saving behavior are likely to be altered; the net effect is difficult to predict. However, the current yen-dollar exchange rate reflects not only private choices but also the fiscal policies of the United States and Japan. Just as U.S. fiscal policy has put upward pressure on the value of the dollar, Japanese fiscal policy depressed the value of the yen by maintaining a budget deficit for the nation that is low relative to national private saving. A substantial increase in Japanese government expenditures, whether for defense, infrastructure, or other categories where Japanese spending is currently quite modest relative to that of other affluent countries, would mean lower net national saving and upward pressure on domestic interest rates.

While the long-term effects of financial liberalization are of uncertain size and even direction, there are also important short-term consequences of the agreements reached by the negotiators. These concerns improved access for foreign firms to the Japanese market for financial services. Here the potential gains for a particular sector of American business are evident — and perhaps not very surprising, given negotiations led by a Secretary of the Treasury who has spent his professional life in the U.S. financial community. But the likely short-term effect on the yen-dollar rate, most now acknowledge, will be a further *weakening* of the value of the yen. This is because Japanese saving and domestic investment are more or less fixed in the short run, while the liberalization will make it easier for the existing pool of Japanese savings to move into foreign assets.

THE REAL GAINS FROM TRADE

I have argued that policies to improve industrial competitiveness cannot, by themselves, reduce the trade deficit or domestic unemployment. Direct measures to increase domestic employment by raising exports or reducing imports in any particular industry invite foreign retaliation. Changes that enhance industrial productivity will primarily improve the trade performance of some firms and industries at the expense of others. Through exchange-rate adjustment, competitiveness becomes what it has to be to produce a trade deficit or surplus that fits overall macroeconomic conditions. Measures that reduce capital flows to the United States can improve trade performance and increase employment in industries that export and import, but these gains will be offset by the domestic effects of higher real interest rates on domestic spending.

A more basic problem with the view that exports are desirable because they create jobs at home and imports are undesirable for corresponding reasons is that it totally misrepresents the real sources of gains from trade. Policies based on this view are thus unlikely to produce a pattern of mutually beneficial trade growth over time.

Fundamentally, mutual benefits from trade between two nations arise through the exchange of products or services embodying domestic resources for foreign products whose production at home would require a larger collection of resources. Thus, international trade can be seen as a kind of superior technology that allows us to derive more from our productive inputs than would be possible otherwise. Trade that reflects the nation's *relative* productivity in exports and imports is said to be based on comparative advantage. The gains from this kind of trade do not depend on precisely *why* foreigners are willing and able to deliver a particular product in exchange for our own. All that matters is that we exchange our product for one that would be more costly in terms of domestic resources. In particular, foreign subsidies, targeting, and unfair trade practices do not reduce the nation's current gains from trade. However, they may be an important concern for a different reason, to which I return later.

Trade based on comparative advantage is trade that allows *mutual* gains — gains that are not matched by losses abroad. In fact, mutual gains are the *only* kind of gains from trade that can serve as the basis for U.S. policies; these are the only kind of gains that are sustainable over the long run. Policies that attempt to create benefits for the United States mainly at the cost of other nations will evoke retaliatory action from our trading partners. Nations sufficiently minor relative to the world market can pursue almost indefinitely policies to enhance the position of domestic interests at the expense of foreign competitors; the same option is not available to the dominant country in the international system. This does not mean that the United States will or should continue to run a trade deficit as large as the present one. But, as I have already argued above, direct measures to influence U.S. competitiveness are in any case unlikely to have much bearing on the aggregate trade deficit.

In addition to gains based on comparative advantage, trade is also beneficial because it promotes the integration of national markets into a single world market. With more firms potentially serving a given market, there is increased competition among suppliers. Moreover, because industrial activities have some minimum efficient scale of operation, a larger market allows lower unit cost and greater variety of products and services. Perhaps most important among these gains from a larger potential market is the enhanced incentive for research and development. Like the gains based on comparative advantage, the gains from a larger market are mutual gains.

To ensure the greatest gains from trade, the long-run goal for the United States ought to be a balanced expansion of exports and imports, where the main expansion of exports reflects what the U.S. economy does best and the main expansion of imports reflects what the U.S. economy is least suited to produce. Unfortunately, our current trade policies tend to do the opposite, limiting imports precisely from those suppliers that are best in a particular industry, as we have done with Japanese automobiles and with textiles and apparel from the newly industrializing countries.

THE REAL GAINS FROM MEASURES TO IMPROVE COMPETITIVENESS

An appreciation of the real gains from trade allows us to understand why some of the policies recommended to promote competitiveness are valuable and important even though they do not constitute effective means of reducing the trade deficit. If we think of trade as a superior technology for transforming domestic capital, labor, and other inputs indirectly into the goods and services we obtain from abroad, an improvement in the efficiency of our export production has the effect of boosting the overall productivity of that indirect technology, i.e., increasing the amount of imported goods and services obtained from a given collection of domestic resources employed in production of exports.

In short, higher productivity in our export industries usually means greater gains from trade. Again, these are typically mutual gains, since some of the enhanced productivity in the export industries will be passed along to trading partners in the form of lower prices or improved quality of our products. Obviously, increased efficiency and better quality in goods produced at home for domestic use are also beneficial, allowing higher consumption or investment levels to be achieved from given productive inputs.

Like measures to improve productivity at the industry level, efforts to alter the competitive context can be valuable in securing greater gains from trade. If barriers restrict access to foreign markets or if domestic policies discourage exporting, the nation's gains from trade are necessarily reduced, even though, as already emphasized, the effect on aggregate trade performance as measured by the merchandise trade or current account balance is likely to be minor. The loss of potential benefits from trade will be especially great if foreign barriers discriminate against the industries in which the relative advantage of U.S. producers is largest.

Similarly, the case against protection of our own industries is that it reduces the nation's potential gains from trade. Protection inhibits purchases from abroad of those goods and services in which the U.S. advantage is least. This means a lower standard of living for U.S. consumers and higher costs for U.S. producers. Protection also reduces gains from trade abroad and thus curtails foreign demand for U.S. products. In addition, protection at home may spur retaliation against our own most competitive products. As a result, we can lose high-productivity jobs in order to protect ones in less productive sectors. Finally, protection segments markets, reducing the gains that come from market size.

CAN FREE TRADE BE THE WHOLE ANSWER?

Does this mean that the United States would be best served by a policy of free trade? Unfortunately, things are never quite that simple. There are costs of full exposure to world markets to be taken into account in setting the nation's trade policies. These costs, which must be set against the benefits already discussed, suggest that a unilateral move to free trade would not necessarily be in the nation's best interest, even if this revolutionary policy change were to become politically feasible.

To begin with, it is often suggested that we might, over the long term, derive national gains from fostering the growth of certain industries not currently competitive in world markets. This idea was once labelled the infant-industry argument; today we are more likely to hear about dynamic learning, forward linkages, or maintaining the industrial base. The central idea is that current domestic production may yield a significant future benefit which cannot be captured by the producing firms. This might be due to problems of technological appropriability or the inability of private capital markets to handle large, risky, long-range projects. In such an instance, intervention can be beneficial, but only if the eventual gain is large enough to offset, in present-value terms, the cost of the temporary protection required. Thus, it is not enough that the industry have a fully competitive status ahead, but also that the rewards to be reaped in the future more than offset the costs of protection along the way.

The actual cases (often Japanese) cited to demonstrate the validity of this line of reasoning usually begin and end with the fact that a previously protected industry eventually becomes internationally competitive. However, this evidence is seriously deficient, as it establishes neither that the industry would not have flourished in the absence of intervention nor that the eventual national benefits merited the earlier costs. These costs typically extend well beyond the affected industry, through competition among industries for capital, labor, and other inputs. For example, salaries of scientists and engineers are likely to rise when specific high-technology activities are targeted for fast-track development, with adverse consequences for competing high-technology sectors.

Problems of adjustment pose a different concern for policy. As world supply and demand conditions change, sometimes quite rapidly, open international markets entail the redeployment of domestic resources among productive activities and often geographical regions as well. Labor and/or capital may be unemployed or underemployed during this process. U.S. trade policies reflect a social and political consensus that the burden of such changes should not be borne entirely by those directly affected. Rather, where an industry's position is adversely affected by import competition, the law provides temporary relief from the full consequences of foreign competition. This temporary relief usually takes the form of tariffs or quotas on imported goods.

In principle, such policies provide breathing room for the affected industry, time in which to improve its competitive position or, in some cases, to phase out domestic production of goods where comparative advantage has shifted unambiguously abroad. In practice, however, neither adjustment to a status of full competitiveness nor phasing out of domestic production will necessarily occur during the limited period of import relief, so that the same industries return again and again for additional "temporary" relief. An obvious solution to this problem is to tie import relief to an adjustment plan, but this would make Federal officials the de facto administrators of a national industrial policy, responsible for deciding whether and how a given industry might be restored to international competitiveness.

In addition to temporary relief from changed conditions of "fair" trade, U.S. trade law also faces the task of dealing with the panoply of devices that give foreign firms an "unfair" advantage, i.e., one which arises primarily from the use of government powers for the specific purpose of creating an advantage over competitors abroad. Production, export, or credit subsidies are only the most obvious examples of what has become a pervasive phenomenon in world markets. As in the case of fair competition from abroad, the interests of domestic purchasers are pitted against those of producers. Here, however, the issue is more complex. It concerns the interface between our own economy, in which the market remains the primary force guiding resource allocation, and those of nations where direct government guidance of resource allocation is far more extensive.

United States reliance on the market reflects the notion that entrepreneurs should be rewarded for risk-taking, and we are (in most cases) comfortable with the idea that this involves losses as well as profits. But it is one thing to say that an entrepreneur who guesses wrong about tastes, technology, costs, or potential competition should be penalized by lower profits, and quite another to say that an entrepreneur should accept losses caused mainly by the actions of foreign *governments*. The long-term viability of our own market system may be reduced if U.S. firms are forced to compete on equal terms with foreign enterprises bankrolled by national treasuries.

The case for protection against unfair competition financed by foreign governments does not apply to another situation often lumped together under the same heading, i.e., foreign sales below full average cost. As long as this pricing is determined by foreign firms as part of their overall business strategy, it ought to be regarded as another variety of fair competition. Dumping as defined in U.S. statutes is a normal business practice of most firms with substantial fixed costs and fluctuating demand — including our own firms in cyclical industries. Requiring firms to refrain from such pricing, whether in the domestic market or in international trade, reduces allocative efficiency.

Finally, a reciprocal liberalization is preferable to a unilateral one on several grounds, including greater national gains and easier adjustment. Probably more important, reciprocal liberalization, whether on a multilateral or a bilateral basis, is likely to meet less political resistance at home, because it creates readily identifiable domestic winners as well as losers.

All of this suggests that government intervention may, under certain circumstances, improve national well-being. However, it by no means ensures that actual intervention will be beneficial or that trade policy is the best means to achieve particular national objectives. Import relief may indeed be desirable in some circumstances, but this relief necessarily comes at the price of foregone benefits from open international markets. Moreover, because such policies permit domestic firms to maintain higher prices for their products and services, they raise costs and thus reduce competitiveness in other sectors of the economy. And, since favored industries nearly always benefit from direct intervention on their behalf regardless of the effects on the nation as a whole, the one *sure* consequence of an activist trade policy is the diversion of managerial attention from the shop floor, research lab, or marketing department to the corridors of the nation's capital.

THE REAL GAINS FROM WORRYING ABOUT INDUSTRIAL COMPETITIVENESS

The competitiveness analysts tend to view as separate and independent the various factors that at a point in time influence a given industry's trade performance. Similarly, they almost always assume that measures to improve a particular industry's trade performance or improve a particular bilateral trade balance (e.g., with Japan) will have a corresponding effect on the aggregates. I have argued that this approach neglects the relationships among the individual factors shaping competitiveness at the industry level and the macroeconomic determinants of aggregate U.S. trade performance. As a consequence, direct policies to improve competitiveness, whether by improving productivity at the industry level or by changing the competitive context of U.S. trade, are likely to fail in their announced goal of reducing the U.S. trade deficit.

Nonetheless, many of the policies currently put forward as means to increase U.S. industrial competitiveness are clearly beneficial to the health of the U.S. economy. Thus, the real gain from the mobilization of national concern about competitiveness is the increased scrutiny devoted to the functioning of our economy and society. Carrying through in such areas as educational improvements, enhanced incentives for industrial research and development, tax reform, and better labor-management relations will surely benefit the nation in both the short and the long run, although the same would be true in an economy entirely closed to international transactions. We can indeed benefit from emulating some aspects of the Japanese economy, although the primary reason for the benefit is not that we increase our competitiveness but that we increase our productivity.

Likewise, policies to promote open international markets are surely in the nation's interest, not for their effects on our aggregate trade balance but on our aggregate gains from trade. We will see these gains reflected not in reduced unemployment but in improved quality of employment opportunities.

At the same time, it is vital for the nation to recognize that direct measures alone cannot restore the balance in our international accounts. If we want to reduce the trade deficit without creating serious problems elsewhere in the economy, we must look to appropriate macroeconomic solutions. There is a real danger in selling direct competitiveness-oriented measures as means to correct the trade deficit. The certain failure of this approach paves the way for a new and destructive wave of protectionism, justified by the egregious fallacy that nothing else can save American jobs.

II
Import Protection Versus Open Trade

As pressures to protect industries facing intense import competition mount in the 1980s, economists are attempting to ascertain more accurately both the benefits and costs of protection and the effectiveness of alternative means of assisting injured industries. They are also trying to understand better the various political and economic factors that determine why one industry receives protection while another that also appears to be highly sensitive to import competition does not.

The selection by Robert E. Baldwin surveys the main hypotheses dealing with this last issue and the evidence available empirically from testing these hypotheses. Political-economic explanations of the differential ability of industries to obtain import protection range from the pressure group and the voting machine models, which stress the importance of an industry's ability to organize into a lobbying group and its voting strength, to models postulating that government officials seek to minimize the adjustment costs to workers of import competition or simply continue to shield industries with historically high levels of protection. All the various models receive some empirical support. But since the same variable is often used to reflect different political or economic behavior, it is difficult from existing empirical tests to distinguish among the models in terms of their relative explanatory powers.

The papers by the OECD Secretariat and by Robert W. Crandall deal with the costs and benefits of protection. Citing evidence of a significant increase in the use of nontariff import barriers in recent years, the OECD survey examines the impact of these measures on trade flows and prices, employment, and structural adjustment in the industrial nations and on the exports of the developing countries. One of the main conclusions from the survey is that the domestic employment goals of the discriminatory nontariff barriers introduced in recent years have been undermined by shifts in production not only to noncontrolled countries but to regions within the protecting country other than those where the displaced workers live, by an upgrading of product quality within commodity groups subject to quantitative restrictions, and by substitution of capital for labor in the injured industries. The costs to consumers have still been substantial, however. Crandall estimates that total U.S. consumer costs of the voluntary export restraints in Japanese automobiles are $4.3 billion as a consequence of an average $400 increase in U.S. car prices and a $1,000 price rise in Japanese cars. The consumer cost per job saved was nearly $160,000.

In some industries, such as automobiles, the rents earned by domestic firms as a result of protection have been used to restructure the industries and make them more competitive internationally. However, in others with low entry barriers, such as clothing and footwear, these rents have not brought about adjustment but simply attracted new domestic establishments.

The reading by Charles Pearson and Gerry Salembier focuses on the concept of adjustment costs and compares protection and trade adjustment assistance programs as means of facilitating adjustment. Economists make a distinction between the social and private costs of adjusting to a change in the pattern of trade. The former refer to the value of output or income foregone by the economy when productive factors are temporarily unemployed, while the latter pertain to the costs, net of transfer payments, borne directly by these displaced resources. For a change in the pattern of trade to be desirable from an economic efficiency viewpoint, the benefits of the change, appropriately discounted, must exceed the temporary output loss brought about by the change. As the authors note, however, the political decision on whether a trading change will be allowed without any government intervention is more likely to be determined by the magnitude of the private costs associated with the trade shift. Pearson and Salembier's analysis of trade adjustment assistance suggests that such programs as technical assistance to firms and loans or loan guarantees to facilitate modernization of productive facilities as well as job retraining, job placement, and wage subsidies for workers may be more effective than protection in reducing the private costs associated with rapid changes in trading patterns, while still securing the benefits to the economy of open trade.

The last selection, written by a group of international leaders appointed by the Director-General of the General Agreement on Tariffs and Trade (GATT) to report on problems facing the international trading system, summarizes briefly the case for an open trade policy. Recognizing the difficulties to enterprises and workers of adapting to rapidly changing economic conditions, the authors argue that a policy of open trade is essential to economic growth. Protection not only stunts an economy's growth and produces a loss of real income but, by postponing adjustment, makes it more painful when it finally occurs. They also maintain that arguments such as that protection saves jobs in an economy or is needed to defend against low foreign wages do not hold up on close examination.

3

Trade Policies in Developed Countries

Robert E. Baldwin

THE POLITICAL ECONOMY OF PROTECTION

Since the early 1970s a growing body of literature has emerged that attempts to explain the differences across industries in both levels of protection and the extent of tariff reductions undertaken by governments in GATT-sponsored multilateral trade negotiations. . . . Although much has been written on the subject, there is still widespread disagreement as to which of the various competing hypotheses best explains the structure of protection within industrial democracies. Disagreement exists at three different levels of analysis. There is, first, a lack of consensus concerning the nature of the political decision-making process. Secondly, authors differ widely with respect to what they believe are the key political-economic characteristics that enable an industry to obtain greater protection or successfully to resist duty cuts. Lastly, there is a significant divergence in views over which economic variables are the best proxies for a particular political-economic characteristic. These three differences are explored in more detail below.

1.1. The Nature of the Political Decision-Making Process

Two extreme positions exist concerning the manner in which political decisions are reached. One treats government officials simply as intermediaries who balance the conflicting interests of various groups in society in order to maximize their likelihood of remaining in power. According to this view, the nature of political decisions depends upon the preferences of voters and various interest groups, with the state having little independent influence. A quite different position regards the state as being largely autonomous in the decision-making process. Although writers [who] explicitly [propound] this position recognize that there are societal constraints on autonomous actions by the state, [such as] elections, they stress the ability of the government to use its power to circumvent these constraints.

Most authors adopt an intermediate position between these two positions. However, those closer to the first view devote considerable time to explaining just how a particular individualistic or social objective associated with protection is actually translated into political action. Those who put more emphasis on the

From R. W. Jones and P. B. Kenen, eds., *Handbook of International Economics*, vol. 1 (Amsterdam: North Holland, 1984), pp. 572–582. Reprinted by permission of the publisher. Some footnotes and references omitted.

autonomy of the state tend, by contrast, to test for the empirical relevance of a particular social goal without dwelling upon the political process by which it is implemented.

Authors favoring the intermediation view of government differ among themselves with regard to the extent that they assume that the actors in society are motivated by short-run or long-run economic interests and by altruistic or ethical concerns toward others. Those emphasizing the importance of short-run individualistic economic interests focus upon the ability of individuals benefiting directly and immediately from protection to exert their power through voting and group pressures. However, by taking a longer-run view of self-interest or by introducing altruistic or ethical attitudes on the part of the various political actors in the economy, it is possible to account for the willingness of individuals not directly affected by the level of economic activity in a particular industry to grant protection for that industry. For example, supporting protection for an import-injured industry as a form of social insurance is political behavior consistent with the notion that individuals are motivated by long-run economic interest. And, of course, the willingness of individuals to support temporary protection for the industry, even though they know the cost of the industry's products will rise somewhat, is easily explained if the utility level of those individuals is related positively to the utility level of employees in the injured industry or simply if ethical considerations prompt this support. . . .

1.2. Alternative Models and Key Industry Characteristics

The differences among writers in the field become most evident, however, when they describe the political behavior-process that leads to protection for an industry and then select the economic characteristics of the industry that reflect this behavior. At least seven distinct (though not necessarily incompatible) models or hypotheses of political behavior can be discerned in the literature. There are several more that deal with protection for particular sectors such as national defense industries. All receive some empirical support. Unfortunately, however, there is no general agreement on just which models (or group of models) perform best.

The seven models and the key political-economic characteristic of an industry that each one stresses as being the main determinant of the industry's ability to secure protection are as follows.

1. The common-interest or pressure group model — the ability of an industry to organize as a political pressure group;
2. The adding-machine model — the voting strength of an industry;
3. The adjustment assistance model — the ability of workers to adjust to greater import competition;
4. The equity-concern model — the income and skill levels of workers;
5. The comparative-costs model — the international competitive strength of an industry;

6. The international-bargaining model — the bargaining ability and political importance of the countries from which competing imports are supplied;

7. The *status-quo* (or historical-influences) model — the historical level of an industry's protection.

The *interest-group model* is probably the best known of the different hypotheses directed at explaining the structure of a country's industrial protection. Writers who formulated this model stress that the actual political outcome in a democracy may not reflect the views of a majority of the country's citizens because of imperfect knowledge as well as costs of redistributing income and undertaking political action. For example, for a country facing fixed terms of trade, a policy of free trade is welfare-superior to a protectionist policy in the sense that it is possible in a world of costless income-redistribution to make everyone better off than they would be under protection. However, because of the existence of redistribution, knowledge-acquisition, and political-action costs, this free-trade policy may not be implemented in the political process. What may occur instead, according to the interest-group hypothesis, is that industries benefiting from protection organize into political pressure groups and succeed in obtaining protection against competitive imports.

Whether groups with a common economic interest do in fact organize depends upon the gains and costs expected by their members. As Mancur Olson (1965) points out, tariff protection for an industry is a collective benefit (the tariff protects all firms in the industry) and industry efforts to exert political influence are financed by voluntary contributions on the part of its members. Therefore, the free-rider problem hampers efforts to organize for political purposes. An individual firm has an incentive to withhold its contribution and enjoy the benefits of the protection secured by the rest of the industry. The outcome may be that the industry does not organize at all, even though it is in the interests of all its members to do so. Olson reasons that the voluntary formation of pressure groups is more likely if the group is small [or] the benefits are unevenly distributed, since individual members or at least a group of members has more at stake.[1] While some industries may be small enough in terms of the number of firms or sufficiently concentrated to organize, he maintains that consumers generally are unable to do so. Pincus (1975) further argues that an industry's lobbying efforts will be greater the more geographically concentrated it is, since this improves its ability to coordinate and monitor these activities.

In testing these different relationships, a seller-concentration ratio, e.g. the share of industry shipments accounted for by the [four largest] firms, and the number of establishments in an industry are usually used to capture Olson's hypotheses about group size and the distribution of benefits, whereas a geographic concentration ratio is utilized to reflect Pincus's argument. A positive correlation between the level of protection (or changes in the level of protection) and seller and geographic concentration ratios is expected and a negative one between the number of firms and the protective level. Since purchasers of goods for intermediate-input purposes are thought to be more effective opponents of protection than final consumers (for the preceding reasons stated by Olson and Pincus), a measure of the extent to which an industry's sales go to other industries rather than final consumers is often introduced to measure the resistance by others to protection. One also expects greater resistance to protectionist pressures in sectors with extensive exports and foreign direct investments because of the fear of foreign retaliation.

Olson (1982) has argued that the ability of a group to organize is influenced not only by the number and size-distribution of its firms but the extent to which its common interest has been threatened. A series of . . . shocks or crises may be necessary before a group organizes or, if already organized, increases its lobbying pressures. Thus, a variable such as the growth rate in employment or output can be introduced as part of the interest-group model with the expectation that duty levels will be higher and duty cuts lower the lower the growth rate in an industry.

Those who apply the common-interest group model to explain protection generally assume that capitalists and workers in an industry share the same view about the desirability of import protection. However, on the basis of the Stolper–Samuelson theorem (1941), one would predict a conflict between the views of these two groups. If a country is relatively capital-abundant and exporting capital-intensive goods (and thus importing labor-intensive goods), labor should, according to the theorem, favor protection because its real wage will rise whereas capitalists should favor an export subsidy on the capital-intensive goods.

Magee (1978) earlier tested the Stolper–Samuelson theorem by examining the congressional testimony of labor and capitalists when the Trade Act of 1974 (a tariff-liberalizing proposal) was under consideration. He found that in almost all instances labor and management in a particular industry shared the same view on liberalization versus import protection. As he points out, this result is consistent with a specific factors model. . . .

The *adding-machine model* was formulated as a separate hypothesis and so-named by Caves (1976). Like the pressure group approach, this model postulates that individual consumers do not actively oppose protection because of a lack of knowledge and the high costs of individual political activity relative to the benefits. Consequently, the pattern of protection is shaped by the interests of producers, who have more at stake in particular industries than consumers do. However, rather than focusing on the incentives that each industry has to organize and exert political pressure through campaign contributions and other forms of assistance to politicians, this model emphasizes the voting strength that an industry possesses. Since the government officials act to maximize the probability of their election, what matters in obtaining protection is the number of votes that an industry has. Caves also postulates that an industry's voting strength increases, the higher its labor-output coefficient and the more decentralized and geographically dispersed it is.

Both the interest-group and adding-machine models are based on a view of the political decision-making process that considers the state to be an intermediary responding to the short-run, individualistic economic interests of producers and consumers. The remaining five models to be considered rest upon a view of the political process that considers producers and consumers as either taking a long-run view of their self-interests or being concerned about the economic welfare of others or, alternatively, that regards the state as having some scope for autonomous actions.

The *adjustment assistance* model, first stated explicitly by Cheh (1974), hypothesizes that governments aim at minimizing short-run labor adjustment costs in deciding which industries should receive the smallest duty cuts in a multilateral trade negotiation or the largest increases when injured by increased imports. Variables used to measure the ability of workers in an industry to adjust to duty cuts include the labor-output coefficient, the percentage of unskilled workers, the percentage of workers over 45 years of age, the proportion of workers in rural areas, the height of the initial duty, and the growth-rate of industry shipments. A positive relationship is hypothesized between the first four of these variables and changes in an industry's import duties on the grounds that it takes longer for unskilled, older workers living in rural areas to find new jobs than it does for other workers. Low cuts are also expected in high-duty industries, since a given percentage cut in a high-duty item tends to reduce its import price relatively more (and thus put more adjustment pressure on domestic producers) than the same percentage cut in a low-duty item. On the other hand, since rapid industry growth facilitates adjustment to duty reductions, growth rates and the extent of duty cuts are likely to be negatively correlated.

The *equity-concern model* focuses primarily upon the governmental objective of ensuring that low-income workers are not hurt by economic change . . . . Authors who have stressed its importance in explaining levels of and change in protection . . . utilize such measures as average wages, the proportion of unskilled workers, and an industry's labor-output ratio in testing the model's validity.

Several investigators have pointed out that one would expect protective levels to be relatively high (and duty cuts comparatively low) in those industries in which a country is at a comparative-cost disadvantage. This *comparative-costs model* takes account of the obvious point that relatively low-cost domestic industries tend to be net exporters and therefore tend to oppose protective actions because of the fear of foreign retaliation. Consequently, even though an export-oriented industry may, for example, be highly concentrated or large in employment terms and thereby capable of exerting considerable protectionist pressure, it will not do so. To take account of this point in testing the interest group, adding-machine, and other models, it is therefore necessary to introduce a comparative-cost measure as a control variable. A concern by the government over excessive dependence on imports could also be the basis of high protective levels in sectors of comparative disadvantage. An industry's labor-output coefficient, average wage, and proportion of unskilled workers are often utilized as measures of comparative disadvantage in industrial countries.

The *international-bargaining model,* first proposed by Helleiner (1977), supplements the interest-group model in that it deals with the ability of one government to influence the trade policies of another government. One obvious consideration affecting a country's bargaining power is whether it is prepared to cut its own levels of protection when others reduce their trade barriers. Since the less developed countries (LDCs) have generally been unwilling to do so, Helleiner expects that duty levels in industrial countries will be higher (and duty-cuts less) on products of export interest to the LDCs than on items supplied by countries practicing reciprocity. He uses average wages and an economies-of-scale variable to indicate those manufactured products in which the LDCs have an export interest. . . .

The last model, the *status quo* or *historical influences model,* is attributable to Lavergne (1983). In his view, there are two reasons for current duty levels (and recent duty cuts) to be positively correlated with duty levels that existed several years ago. One is a desire by government officials to avoid large adjustment costs for an industry. The other is conservative respect for the *status quo* that is based either on a regard for existing property rights (even in the form of rents generated by protection) or on a cautious response to uncertainty concerning the effect of change. In his concept of the conservative social welfare function, Corden (1974, pp. 107–111) also stresses the public goal of not disturbing the economic *status quo* so much that some income groups incur significant income losses. To test the historical-influences hypothesis for the United States, Lavergne employs the tariff levels that prevailed under the 1930 Smoot–Hawley Act.

Table 1 summarizes the relationships expected in the various models between levels of and changes in protection and the key economic characteristics used to reflect the political behavior assumptions of the different hypotheses. The relationships usually found in empirical tests of the models are also listed in the table.

An alternative approach to analyzing the structure of protection in terms of the type of specific behavior hypotheses or control factors considered thus far has been suggested by Anderson (1978). Anderson views protection as being determined in a political market in which import-competing producers are the demanders and the government is the supplier. In his view the demand for assistance is affected by factors determining both the expected benefits of favorable action to import-competing producers and the expected lobbying costs, while the supply is determined by the benefits of assistance to the government, e.g. loss of financial support and votes. All of the variables mentioned in discussing the seven models described above (plus a few more) are listed as demand or supply variables by Anderson. Since he is more interested in predicting the structure of protection than in separating out the relative importance of demand versus supply forces, he lists several of the variables as both demand and supply determinants.

TABLE 1

Expected and Actual Relationships Between Key Industry Characteristics and Levels of and Changes in Protection

Industry characteristic	VARIOUS MODELS (expected relationships)							Actual empirical relationship
	Pressure group	Adding machine	Adjustment assistance	Equity concern	Comparative costs	International bargaining	Status quo	
1. Seller and geographic concentration ratios	positive	negative	—	—	—	—	—	pos. & neg.
2. Number of firms	negative	—	—	—	—	—	—	negative[a]
3. Growth rate	negative	—	negative	—	—	—	—	negative
4. Extent of foreign investment	negative	—	—	—	—	—	—	positive
5. Extent of sales to other industries	negative	—	—	—	—	—	—	negative
6. Number of workers	—	positive	—	positive	positive	—	—	positive[a]
7. Labor-output coefficient	—	positive	positive	positive	positive	—	—	positive[a]
8. Proportion of unskilled workers	—	—	positive	positive	positive	—	—	positive[a]
9. Age of workers	—	—	positive	—	—	—	—	positive
10. Proportion in rural areas	—	—	positive	—	—	—	—	positive[a]
11. Average wage	—	—	negative	negative	negative	—	—	negative[a]
12. Import penetration ratio	—	—	—	—	positive	—	—	positive[a]
13. Extent of imports from LDCs	—	—	—	—	—	positive	—	positive[a]
14. Historical level of protection	—	—	—	—	—	—	positive	positive[a]

[a]Indicates the relationship is usually statistically significant at the 10 percent level or less.

1.3. Empirical Tests: Results and Appraisal

An impressive number of empirical tests of the various models described in the preceding section already exist, and new studies are emerging at a rapid pace. . . .

One of the first issues to be settled in any empirical analysis is whether to measure protection in terms of nominal or effective rates. At a conceptual level effective rates are preferable, since these rather than nominal duties indicate the benefits from protection to the factors employed in an industry. However, industries may in fact focus mainly on nominal (output) rates because of a desire to avoid political conflicts with other industries. It is also necessary in some cases to utilize nominal rates because effective rate estimates are out-of-date or too aggregative to capture the desired level of detail. Fortunately, the entire issue is not very important as a practical matter, since there is generally a high degree of correlation between nominal and effective rates.

A more serious matter concerns the absence . . . of measures of protection that take account of other forms of industry assistance besides tariffs. If subsidies or quotas, for example, are substitutes for tariffs, regression results based only on tariffs can be misleading. In the United States industries with high tariffs are also highly protected by nontariff measures, so that the problem may not be serious in practice, but it is not known whether this relationship also exists in other industrial countries.

Problems of interpreting the results from the regression analyses also arise because of the high degree of correlation among some of the independent variables, e.g. average wages, the labor-output coefficients, and the proportion of unskilled workers. An additional problem is the likely existence of two-way causal relationships between some of the variables. For example, even if (potentially) high import-penetration levels lead to high levels of protection, there may be no statistically significant relationship across industries at a given point in time between duty levels and the actual ratio of imports to consumption because high duty levels reduce the ratio of imports to consumption.

As can be seen from the last column in Table 1, the various empirical tests indicate that industries receiving the greatest protection (and the lowest duty cuts during multilateral trade negotiations) are ones in which the workers tend to be unskilled, low-paid, older, and live in rural areas. These industries are also characterized by a large number of workers, a high labor-output coefficient, a small number of firms, slow growth, a high import penetration ratio, and historically high levels of protection. It is difficult at this stage of the empirical testing to determine the relative explanatory power of the different models, since the same independent variables are employed to test several of the hypotheses. To do so, it is necessary to find economic variables that delineate the various models more sharply and thereby reduce the overlap that now exists.

Consider, for example, the common-interest or pressure-group hypothesis. This model assumes that, if an industry organizes into a pressure group, it will secure higher levels of protection. However, the failure of the concentration variables to be significantly related to protection may be due either to the fact that industries with low concentration ratios also organize and secure protection or alternatively, that while only concentrated industries tend to organize into common-interest groups, these pressure groups are not effective in securing protection. It is this latter relationship, i.e., whether those industries that organize into pressure groups — a directly observable relationship — do in fact succeed in obtaining protection, that is of more interest than the characteristics of those industries that organize. Consequently, we need to relate direct measures of political pressures across industries to protectionist results in these sectors. Although there is no single ideal index of political pressure and difficult data collection problems exist in the field, regressing tariff levels or duty cuts on such indicators of active political pressure as the size of lobbying expenditures and political contributions by an industry, the extent to which members of an industry make their view known to government officials through letters or personal visits (this also provides evidence on the adding-machine model), the volume of testimony and public statements in favor of the industry's position, etc. would seem to be a better way of testing the model than relating tariff levels to such variables as concentration ratios and the number of firms.

There are also more direct measures available for testing most of the other models. As Bale (1977) has shown, the actual magnitude of adjustment costs (in terms of foregone income) associated with a given reduction in protection can be estimated for each industry. Similarly, instead of using partial and imperfect indicators of comparative costs such as average wages and the proportion of unskilled workers, it is possible to utilize estimates of revealed comparative costs based either directly on a country's trade performance or on differences in factor prices inferred from this performance. Furthermore, the willingness of other nations to offer trading concessions in return for concessions granted by others could be measured directly on a sector-by-sector basis by examining the "offers" of the various participants in a trade negotiation.

While collection of the data needed to come up with these kinds of direct measures of the behavior characterizing the various models is a formidable task, such an effort seems to be required if we are to make significant further progress in understanding the political-economic determinants of the structure of protection. Presently we are able to predict this structure reasonably well from various industry characteristics, but we do not understand what type of political and economic behavior these variables reflect. . . .

Note

1. Olson points out, however, that even if an industry does not meet these criteria it may succeed in organizing if it produces a private good, e.g. a journal that provides useful technical information to its members, and collects funds for lobbying by selling this good.

References

Anderson, K. (1978), "Politico-economic factors affecting structural change and adjustment" in C. Aislabie and C. Tisdell, eds., *Institute of Industrial Economics Conference
Series*, no. 5 (University of Newcastle, Australia).

Bale, M. D. (1977), "United States concessions in the Kennedy Round and short-run labor
adjustment costs: Further evidence," *Journal of International Economics, 2*, 145–148.

Caves, R. E. (1976), "Economic models of political choice: Canada's tariff structure,"
Canadian Journal of Economics, 9, 278–300.

Cheh, J. H. (1974), "United States concessions in the Kennedy Round and short-run labor
adjustment costs," *Journal of International Economics, 4*, 323–340.

Corden, W. M. (1974), *Trade policy and economic welfare* (Oxford University Press,
London).

Helleiner, G. K. (1977), "The political economy of Canada's tariff structure: An alternative
model," *Canadian Journal of Economics, 4*, 318–326.

Lavergne, R. P. (1983), *The political economy of U.S. tariffs: An empirical analysis*
(Academic Press, New York).

Magee, S. P. (1978), "Three simple tests of the Stolper–Samuelson theorem," in P.
Oppenheimer, ed., *Issues in international economics* (Oriel Press, London), 138–153.

Olson, M. (1982), *The rise and decline of nations: Economic growth, stagflation, and
social rigidities* (Yale University, New Haven).

Olson, M. (1965), *The logic of collective action: Public goods and the theory of groups*
(Harvard University, Cambridge).

Pincus, J. (1975), "Pressure groups and the pattern of tariffs," *Journal of Political
Economy, 83*, 757–778.

Stolper, W. and P. A. Samuelson (1941), "Protection and real wages," *Review of Economic
Studies, 9*, 58–73.

4
Costs and Benefits of Protection

Organization for Economic Cooperation and Development (OECD)

The main focus of [this] report is on import restrictions in OECD [Organi-
zation for Economic Cooperation and Development] countries affecting manufactures. [The membership of the OECD consists of the countries of Western
Europe, Canada, the United States, Japan, New Zealand, and Australia. Eds.] . . .
The study does not deal with agriculture, mining, energy, high-technology products or services. Nor does it address the problems of government support for new
promising activities and export promotion, including associated finance. . . .

Excerpted by permission from Organization for Economic Cooperation and Development,
"Costs and Benefits of Protectionism" (Paris: OECD, 1985), pp. 9–24. The project was
carried out by Wolfgang Michalski, Henry Ergas, and Barrie Stevens.

The membership of the OECD consists of the countries of western Europe, Canada, the
United States, Japan, New Zealand, and Australia. Eds.

THE EVOLUTION OF TRADE POLICY

World trade in manufactures encounters lower tariff obstacles today than at any time in the past. Subsequent to full implementation of the reductions agreed to in the Tokyo Round, average MFN [Most Favored Nation] tariffs on industrial imports for 17 major OECD countries will stand at around 4.5 percent. The results of the Tokyo Round also embody moves towards liberalisation of some major nontariff barriers. Access by developing countries to OECD markets has been significantly broadened by the Generalised System of Preferences, now entering its second decade, reflected in the steadily rising share of the developing countries in OECD imports of manufactures.

Despite a prolonged period of slow growth and high unemployment, the OECD countries' commitment to the multilateral trading system has ensured that the vast majority of manufactured trade goes free of hindrance and interference. However, a relatively small, but recently increasing number of sectors — accounting for more than a quarter of manufactured trade — is still subject to high nominal and effective tariffs, to severe nontariff barriers and to distorting subsidisation. Though the sectors traditionally most affected by such measures include textiles, clothing, footwear, steel, and shipbuilding, protection has more recently been extended to previously less- or unaffected sectors, such as automobiles, consumer electronics, and machine tools.

The nontransparency of many of the trade barriers recently put in place makes it difficult to assess their extent or coverage, and any such assessment must be treated cautiously. On one plausible estimate, the share of restricted products in total manufactured imports increased over the period 1980 to 1983 from 6 to 13 percent for the United States and from 11 percent to 15 percent for the EEC [European Economic Community]. In 1983, the product groups subject to restriction accounted for around 30 percent of total manufactured consumption in the countries covered, up from 20 percent in 1980. These results are drawn from a study that adopts a relatively narrow definition of NTBs [Nontariff Barriers]; the increases in nontariff protection are even more dramatic in some of the other research reviewed.

Within the protected sectors the scope of protection has both deepened and widened. Taking steel, automobiles, motorcycles, consumer electronic products, textiles, and footwear together, it has been estimated that the absolute number of NTBs quadrupled between 1968 and 1983. While less than 1 percent of OECD automobile trade (excluding trade within the EEC) was affected by discriminatory restrictions in 1973, this share had risen to nearly 50 percent a decade later. Other estimates suggest that the proportion of trade under nonliberal treatment rose in recent years from 31 to 73 percent in steel and from 53 to 61 percent in textiles and clothing.

Changes in the mix of policy instruments used to control imports have increased the extent of discrimination. There has been a marked shift away from

. . . safeguards, applied on a nondiscriminatory basis, towards bilateral instruments such as voluntary exports restraints and orderly market arrangements. From 1980 to 1983 the share of Japan's and the Asian NICs' [Newly Industrializing Countries'] exports affected by discriminatory restrictions rose from 15 to over 30 percent. At the same time, the range of supplying countries subject to such restrictions has also expanded.

The spread of discrimination undermines the free flow of goods between countries which — at least in theory — are not subject to restrictions. Thus measures adopted to prevent transshipment impose heavy documentation requirements on products from unrestricted sources. According to experts in trade procedures, the execution of the average transaction in international trade now requires 35 documents and 360 copies, partly as a result of trade restrictions. A study for Finland found that documentation costs amounted to 1.4 to 5.7 percent of the total value of 1982 imports — a heavy burden, when set against the profit margins typically involved in foreign trade.

Domestic subsidies, too, may be exercising an increasing impact on trade flows. Narrowly defined, the share of the OECD countries' GNP accounted for by financial transfers to enterprises has increased by over four-fifths since 1965, while the share of such transfers in the operating surplus of firms has more than doubled. Of course, not all subsidies are distorting; but it is important to note that the industries benefiting most from the increase in public assistance are by and large the same in the various OECD Member countries. Apart from high-technology activities, they include steel, shipbuilding, textiles and clothing, and more recently, automobiles.

The Impact on Trade Flows and Prices

It is frequently argued that the protectionist backlash has had a limited impact, since trade in manufactures, even in the product groups most subject to restrictions, continued to grow rapidly in the 1970s. Equally, the countries to whose exports most of the discriminatory measures apply, managed to increase their share of OECD imports. However, the trade performance of the more restricted product categories deteriorated markedly in the 1980s. It would seem that — after being largely ineffective in the earlier period (with the possible exception of the MFA) — protectionist measures were gradually reinforced and eventually began to bite. [The MFA, that is, the Multifiber Arrangement, is an international agreement regulating trade in textile and apparel products. Eds.]

In the 1970s, the impact of discriminatory restrictions on trade flows was limited by pervasive trade diversion, as imports from the more restricted sources were replaced by imports from other suppliers. Trade diversion has been greatest in industries where there is a multiplicity of potential sources of supply and where trade is highly responsive to price and quantity signals, for instance, clothing and footwear. In the EEC, diversion as a result of MFA restrictions has occurred from the most affected Asian exporters to sources with preferential access to the EEC market, notably those on the Mediterranean rim (and the very small ACP suppliers). [ACP stands for African, Caribbean, and Pacific countries that are associated with the European Economic Community and that were former African territories of France, Belgium, and Italy or are non-Asian Commonwealth countries. Eds.] Over the period 1976 to 1980 the volume of EEC imports of MFA products from the Asian NICs increased at an average of 2.2 percent annually, while the figure for the Mediterranean and ACP suppliers was 9.5 percent.

Nonetheless, trade diversion has also been important in less mobile activities such as steel and consumer electronics, mainly because of the growing diffusion of technological and industrial capabilities, improvements in worldwide marketing and distribution channels, and the great sensitivity of multinational enterprises to opportunities for shifting the localization of production. The 1977 Orderly Market Agreement for colour television receivers between the United States and Japan is a good illustration. Though at the time of the agreement Japan accounted for 90 percent of U.S. imports of complete receivers, its share two years later was down to 50 percent, while that of the Asian NICs has increased from 15 to 50 percent.

In addition to changing the geographical origin of imports, quantitative restrictions have affected the nature of the products traded. In particular, faced with a volume limit on their exports, the more restricted suppliers have been encouraged to move up-market within the controlled group, thus maximising the value of a fixed total volume of exports. According to one estimate the share of luxury cars in Japanese automobile exports to the United States increased by 13 percentage points as a result of voluntary export restraint. There is also considerable evidence of such shifts in product composition occurring in the other industries reviewed.

All these protection-induced changes in the country and product composition of trade have tended to undermine the specific objectives of import control. Governments have therefore come under continuous pressure from domestic producers to extend the number of countries subject to the restrictions, and to more precisely specify the product categories in which the restricted producers can operate. Thus, during MFA I, the United States had bilateral agreements with 19 countries but none of these agreements specified explicit limits on imports of so-called "sensitive items." During MFA II, specific limits were introduced into U.S. bilateral agreements with seven countries; and during MFA III, this number rose to 14. Equally, for the EEC, the number of countries covered by bilateral agreements increased from 33 in MFA I to 43 in MFA III, while the number of categories specified went from 23 to 48.

The progressive extension of discriminatory restrictions suppresses an increasing volume of trade. Econometric evidence suggests that the tightening of the MFA at its second renewal has reduced imports of textiles and clothing into the OECD by nearly 10 percent in volume terms. With the economic recovery and changes in exchange rates boosting demand, the restrictive impact of import controls has been compounded.

Throughout the period discriminatory quantitative restrictions have created upward pressures on prices in protected markets: first, because the most restricted sources tend to be those with the lowest costs; and second, because these restricted sources raise their export prices to capture the rents from the restrictions. Particularly in industries where demand is — at least in the short term — fairly inelastic, these increases in import prices provide an important "price umbrella" for domestic producers. As restrictions tightened and the scope for offsetting effects diminished, the upward pressure on prices may have strengthened over the period.

A study on the UK clothing industry suggests that the average increase in UK clothing retail prices due to the second MFA was already in the order of 20 percent and for lower-quality items such as jeans, 30 to 50 percent. Prices for children's wear — a highly labour intensive product — doubled. These changes can have a regressive impact on income distribution, because clothing accounts for a larger share of poorer households' consumption expenditure. One estimate finds that protecting the Canadian clothing industry costs lower-income households four times as much as it costs higher-income households.

Protection, notably by voluntary export restraint, also provides large transfers to foreign producers. It is estimated that protection has increased the profit margin on Japanese steel sales in the U.S. market by at least 10 percent. This is around $200 million a year — about equivalent to half of Japan's annual expenditure (the world's highest) on steel R&D. As regards textiles and clothing, UK restrictions under the MFA are estimated to transfer twice as much income to foreign exporters as to UK producers. A plausible overall assessment is that the annual transfer from OECD consumers to Asian NIC exporters of textile and clothing products is at least U.S. $2 billion. This is equivalent to around 4 percent of the total value of NIC exports to the OECD region.

The Impact on Employment

Employment in industries (and regions) facing structural difficulties has declined faster than in manufacturing as a whole. Over the past ten years manufacturing employment in the EEC fell by 11 percent, but in textiles and clothing the drop was about 40 percent (i.e., 1.7 million jobs) and in steel over 40 percent (equivalent to 330,000 jobs). As for the United States, total manufacturing employment fell 7 percent between 1978 and 1982. In the same period employment in textiles and clothing declined by 16 percent (almost 400,000 jobs) and in steel by 31 percent (a job loss of 150,000). Employment declines of this magnitude, particularly in a period of overall recession, impose high adjustment costs on the labour force.

Governments have therefore come under increasing pressure to attenuate the speed of the adjustment process and the rate of job losses. However, import restrictions appear to have only a limited positive impact on employment in the protected sectors. First, even in the sectors most exposed to international competition, trade flows are usually a fairly minor determinant of employment levels; second, because of trade diversion, discriminatory restrictions have a relatively limited impact on overall import volumes; third, the scope for substituting domestic output for imports may be limited.

Protection is most likely to be effective in maintaining employment in the few industries which have structurally low productivity, little scope for modernisation and hence compete mainly with developing countries, for example, the clothing industry. It was estimated in 1980 that Canadian restrictions on apparel imports protected 7.5 percent of the industry's jobs. Another study found that 1977 U.S. tariffs on apparel preserved nearly 90,000 jobs, equivalent to 10 percent of the industry's employment. Finally, a 50 percent increase in allowable MFA imports of apparel under Swedish VERs [Voluntary Export Restraints] would, it was concluded, reduce clothing employment by 6 percent, twice as large a job loss as a similar increase in textiles imports would entail.

In most other industries the proportion of domestic employment potentially protected by import restrictions is typically in the order of two or three percentage points, though in the very short term the effect may be larger. This is still a small sum relative to the changes induced by shifting macroeconomic circumstances. On one estimate, the U.S.-Japan automobile VER increased U.S. employment by no more than 22,000 over the period to 1982, while the recession was cutting required labour input by more than ten times this figure.

In the longer term, protection can accelerate capital-labour substitution, further reducing industry employment. Capital-labour ratios in the textile industry, for instance, have gone from being well below the manufacturing average in the 1950s to some 20 percent above average now. Together with relatively slow demand growth, capital deepening accounts for two-thirds or more of the industry's long-run employment decline in the advanced OECD countries, with changes in import penetration being a rather minor factor. A recent UK study estimates that given the slow growth of demand, productivity growth in the UK textile industry will reduce employment by nearly 40 percent over the period 1983–97. Abolishing the MFA would, over the same period, involve a fall in employment of only 7 percent, equivalent to 13,000 jobs. "Saving" each of these jobs costs UK consumers annually about twice as much as the yearly wage of a textile worker.

Productivity increases, partly as a result of accelerated offshore assembly, were also at work when employment in the U.S. colour television industry declined despite protection, passing from 29,000 in 1977 to 26,000 in 1979 and 21,000 in 1981. It is, however, estimated that job losses between 1979 and 1981 would have been 1000 to 1500 greater, had import restrictions not been in effect. Saving each of these jobs cost U.S. consumers over $60,000 a year (on the conservative assumption that the price of a $200 set increased by $5).

The employees who benefit from protection have in a number of cases not been those at whom protection was originally aimed. This is because of major shifts in the regional and occupational composition of employment within the protected country. Thus, in the U.S. textile industry, total employment was virtually constant from 1968 to 1977, but within this total the industry created some 60,000 white-collar jobs, which went to employees with considerably higher educational qualifications than the manual employees they were replacing. Over roughly the same period, and again with approximately constant total employment, the industry created some 50,000 jobs in the South, while suppressing 75,000 jobs in the North. Protection has done little for those workers who face the most difficult adjustment problems. Rather, whatever jobs have been created have gone to fairly mobile, better trained employees.

Finally, job-maintenance in the protected industry may be offset by adverse macroeconomic impacts. Protection sufficiently extensive to have a major impact on imports and employment in a wide range of industries is likely to lead to currency appreciations reducing total exports, thus curtailing employment in other sectors of the economy. Protection induced changes in price and wage behaviour can compromise the effectiveness of macroeconomic policy and necessitate a tighter demand management stance.

Restrictive trade policies are more likely to redistribute income and employment than to create new bases for growth. In most instances, import restrictions remove employment from one set of industries — those which are more export-oriented and more technology intensive — to industries which mainly compete with imports. The small number of lower-pay, lower-quality jobs being saved by protection are replacing other jobs which, over the longer term, would contribute more to overall productivity and higher real incomes.

The Impact on Structural Adjustment

By raising prices and increasing the domestic producers' share in the home market, import restrictions can increase the resources available for industrial adjustment. The improved cash flow of domestic firms makes it possible for them to carry out modernisation investments, underwrite the costs involved in adjusting capacity to demand, and/or diversify into more promising areas of activity. Moreover, protection can change the incentives for cooperation between foreign and domestic firms. At the same time, however, by reducing the pressures for adjustment to occur, and given the substantial costs adjustment entails, protection can perpetuate technical and economic inefficiency.

In fragmented, labour-intensive industries such as clothing and footwear, competition occurs primarily on a cost basis. There is limited scope for product differentiation and capital-labour substitution. As a result, protection does little to establish durable market segmentation or to reduce the cost differential between OECD producers and major developing country exporters. In the clothing industry, for example, advanced technology is being introduced into ancillary operations such as cutting and grading, but stitching operations, which account for 80 percent of value added, are — and in the medium term will remain — highly labour intensive. Cost differentials in this stage of production between developed and leading developing country exporters are in the order of 1 to 5 or 6; even by drawing on peripheral labour markets (such as home workers or the "underground" economy), OECD manufacturers cannot reduce wage costs by this amount.

The argument that protection facilitates a run-down in these activities is clearly contrary to the evidence. In effect, given low entry barriers, the rents created by protection in these activities simply attract new resources, not only labour and capital, but also entrepreneurship. In the United States, one-third of the clothing and textiles establishments existing at the end of 1982 had been created since 1976. In France over a fifth of new manufacturing firms are in the textiles and clothing industries. Protectionist measures have permitted adjustment only to the extent that they have allowed the international division of labour to operate through such indirect means as off-shore assembly and licit or illicit trade diversion.

In oligopolistic industries, competition depends chiefly on product differentiation, economies of scale, technology, marketing, and service. By changing industry behaviour, quantitative restrictions can provide a substantial flow of rents both to domestic and foreign producers. According to one analysis, the automobile VER increased the profitability of Japanese sales in the U.S. market by 12 percentage points. Notably when their market share is restricted, foreign firms can seek to further increase the rents they derive from the protected market by selling technology and other intangible assets to domestic producers. Indeed, cooperative agreements between restricted foreign suppliers, particularly Japanese, and domestic firms have proliferated in the oligopolistic industries receiving protection.

There are cases in which protection, coupled with adjustment programmes, has encouraged firms to utilise the resources made available for restructuring. Prominent examples are the car industry in the United States and certain parts of the steel industry in the European Community. Frequently, however, there are factors at work which impede adjustment from occurring. If price and quantity signals from the marketplace are distorted, import controls can make it difficult for firms to assess long-term relative costs and set investment plans accordingly. If there is widespread excess capacity, and modernisation investments would involve construction of large-scale plants, as is the case, for example, in the steel industry, the risk of reinvesting in the activity may outweigh the potential benefits. Firms may also face political or institutional constraints on their restructuring choices, for instance, if assistance has been granted to firms on condition that employment levels be maintained.

Over time, the response of foreign suppliers to protection can also substantially narrow the domestic firms' adjustment options. To the extent that foreign rivals generally respond to quantitative restrictions on imports by product upgrading and moving upmarket, domestic firms face increased foreign competition in those sections of the market which are least price-elastic. This is precisely where their long-run competitive edge could otherwise lie. Foreign firms can also offset the benefits of protection to domestic rivals by investing in the protected market. In the longer term, neither the domestic nor the foreign firms may derive much net advantage, but real economic costs are incurred in the process, bearing largely on the protecting country.

PROTECTION AND DEVELOPING COUNTRIES

Uncertainty about the future of trade regimes depresses investment and business confidence not only in many OECD economies, but also in developing countries. So far, OECD protection has had more impact on the composition than on the level of LDCs' [Less Developed Countries'] exports. However, the vulnerability of LDCs, and particularly those at an earlier stage of industrial development, to protectionist measures (or their threat) has remained very high. Moreover, as protectionist measures spread, narrowly economic feedback effects may be magnified throughout the multilateral trading system as income levels, financial solvency, and capacity to import are affected.

In the nine years up to 1982, LDC manufactured exports to the OECD area grew by less than 8 percent per annum, a substantially slower rate than in the period prior to the 1973 oil shock. There are strong indications that in the absence of, or at least with less protection, these exports would have been higher. In the 1982–84 recovery, they accelerated to well above 20 percent per annum, despite protection, and import penetration of manufactured goods on some major OECD markets has continued to increase strongly. Moreover, the five major NICs — the main target of protectionist measures — have largely benefited from this upsurge. It seems plausible, therefore, that, on the whole, variations in the growth of aggregate demand in the OECD countries have had more impact on the rates of LDC export growth than has OECD protection.

The spread of trade restrictions has changed the pattern of LDC exports. Developing countries, and particularly the more advanced NICs, have rapidly stepped up the diversification of their exports, moving into new regional markets and more skill intensive products. At the same time there has been a deliberate shift of certain production activities away from those countries particularly restrained by protection in industrial countries into less-restricted, low-labour-cost countries. Protection has compounded the impact of changing patterns of cost competitiveness in prompting and accelerating these developments.

Other developing countries have captured market shares left by the more restricted exporting countries, benefiting in some cases from the shift of production facilities out of NICs. Attempts to circumvent quotas under MFA and to benefit from GSP tariff quotas have been important factors in this regard. Nonetheless as restrictions tighten, many of the second and third generation of manufacturing exporters, rather than the more flexible NICs, may run into mounting difficulties. These difficulties may include resistance from established exporters anxious to preserve market shares, and a network of trade restrictions which take effect quickly as export volumes expand fast from a low base.

The manifest willingness of protecting countries to extend existing restrictions to new sources of supply plays an important role in this respect, discouraging investment in potential LDC exporters. A striking instance is provided by the U.S. colour television receiver Orderly Marketing Agreement. Initially aimed at Japan, the emergence of Korea and Taiwan as alternative sources of supply led to the agreement's extension to these two countries. Though a number of other sources — for instance Mexico, Singapore, and Thailand — were well placed to enter the U.S. market at that time, the deterrent effect of the initial extension was clearly sufficient to dissuade them.

Debt service ratios for developing countries fluctuated around 15–16 percent during the 1970s, but rose sharply to around 24 percent in 1982–83. The recession, the dollar appreciation, and the rise in interest rates which followed the second oil shock, played a larger part in this increase than did OECD protection. But had the developing countries been able to achieve in the 1980s even half the annual average growth rate in export earnings they recorded in the 1970s, their 1982 debt service ratio would have been more than 4 percentage points lower. Indeed, the rapid upsurge in LDC exports after 1982 has been a crucial factor in keeping indebtedness within manageable limits. This experience underlines the importance of both sustained growth in the OECD area and the LDCs' ability to secure access to world markets and expand export earnings for coping with high indebtedness.

Sharply increased debt service ratios and the limited inflow of real resources mean that in many developing countries there will be a higher premium on the efficient use of capital. But uncertainty about future trade regimes makes it increasingly difficult for developing country exporters to predict market outlets. Resources tend to be diverted to activities which are highly protected domestically and/or where product mixes and production schedules are highly flexible rather than going to those with the greatest development potential.

Any break in the complex chain of expanding LDC manufactured exports and imports, servicing external debt, and sustaining investment will work to the detriment of developing and developed countries alike. It has been estimated that a gradual increase in protection in the OECD region equivalent to a 15 percentage point rise in tariffs would cause a significant reduction by 1995 of GDP both in developing and developed countries. The middle income oil-importing LDCs would sustain a loss in GDP of 3.4 percent, but the industrial countries would equally suffer a 3.3 percent cut in their GDP as a result of the self-inflicted effects of their own protective measures.

Beyond the purely economic feedback effects of protectionism, broader considerations are also relevant here. In the first place, the industrial countries have to avoid that the heavily indebted LDCs — partly on account of the spread of protection — see no politically and socially acceptable way of restoring their economic health in the foreseeable future. Second, although protectionism in many LDCs has been part of the landscape for many decades, its advocates consider their position vindicated by the attitude of pressure groups in industrial countries. Protectionism thus feeds on itself in a circular and cumulative process, undermining the open multilateral trading system. North-South relations are not the only ones at stake; trade among industrial countries and intra-LDC trade could be just as much affected.

The Politics and Economics of Protectionism

Ultimately, trade policy is determined by politics, domestic and international. Whether protectionism spreads, imposing major harm on the world economy, depends on three factors: the costs and benefits of trade for domestic political actors; these actors' access to and control over the process of government; and the extent to which international commitments and obligations with regard to trade policy are viewed as binding by national governments.

The process of growing economic interdependence, though making an important contribution to overall macroeconomic performance, has created major adjustment pressures over the last decade. Shifts in the structure and dynamics of the OECD's trading relations, notably the emergence of new actors in the world economy, have increased the need for adjustment. But at least until the early 1980s, the flexibility of most OECD economies — and hence their capacity to adapt to change — diminished. The burdens this gives rise to have been aggravated by a context of slow growth and high unemployment.

In the mature oligopolies — automobiles, steel, consumer electrical equipment — intensified international competition has compressed profit margins, in a trend which the recent recovery has reversed, but unevenly. At the same time, there has been a strong association between greater import penetration and employment losses in industry, while the cost of losing one's job in these industries has increased. (According to one estimate, workers dismissed from the U.S. steel industry suffer an earnings loss equal, on average, to 10–15 percent of their lifetime earnings.) Moreover, import competition may have affected those who remained employed through its impact on wage setting.

While raising the "potential demand" for protection, the extent to which shifting trade patterns actually lead to protectionist measures will depend on the receptiveness of the political system to interest group pressures. Two salient changes can be identified: first, governments must deal with increasingly articulate, narrowly defined pressure groups unconcerned by the macroeconomic impact of their behaviour. This is partly because the growing scope of public involvement in the economy has itself encouraged more sectional interests to become politically organised, as the frequency and density of their contacts with governments rises.

Second, the range of policy instruments governments can use for responding to these pressures has diminished. Increasing economic interdependence constrains individual government's choices. Because of the inefficacy of macroeconomic policy in maintaining full employment and budgetary constraints on social welfare programmes, consensus maintenance has become more difficult. The attractiveness of import protection — which is off-budget, highly visible to the protected group, but much less visible to others in terms of its costs — has consequently increased.

These changes in the domestic policy system have been paralleled by the diminishing efficacy of multilateral instruments in regulating, if not preventing, protectionist measures. This is partly the result of changed economic circumstances — the observance of international rules and regulations being to some extent a "fair-weather" phenomenon. However, it is also due to more far-reaching, and less readily reversible, changes in the structure of international relations. These include the growing range and diversity of participants in international negotiations; the widening agenda and increasing technical complexity of the issues to be dealt with; and the emergence of a multipolar economic power system.

The medium-term prospects for the world trading system will depend on this interaction of economic and political, domestic and international, factors. While sustained recovery and greater flexibility in product and factor markets may reduce the costs of adjusting to change, it would be illusory to expect protectionist pressures to disappear. Moreover, the prospects for increasing the resilience of domestic political systems to interest-group pressures should not be overrated. Nonetheless, a decade of structural change in the OECD economies has produced new actors with a growing interest in an open trading regime — notably in the high-technology and service industries. Much rests on the capacity of the multilateral system — and especially of its OECD participants — to respond to the needs of these new actors and resolve newly emerging problems and major long-standing issues, rather than concentrate on defending the industries and activities of the past.

CONCLUSIONS: PROTECTION AS AN INSTRUMENT OF POLICY

Protectionist measures are usually intended to meet two broad objectives: to provide visible and immediate relief to industries experiencing severe difficulties, and notably to their workforce, while allowing ongoing adjustment to changed circumstances. These objectives correspond to an employment and social equity concern on the one hand, and to a general goal of promoting greater economic efficiency and industrial restructuring on the other. Relative to the complexity of these objectives, protection is a fairly simple and blunt instrument of policy.

By reducing imports, protection seeks to raise the market share of domestic producers and the price they receive for their goods. Greater output and profitability in the domestic industry is presumed to increase employment and promote modernisation. The highly indirect nature of this link between the instrument — import controls — and the variables of policy interest — jobs and investment — provides a first source of ineffectiveness. Trade diversion reduces the impact of discriminatory restrictions on import volumes; domestic producers may not be able to provide an attractive substitute for imports; if the pressure of competition or of excess capacity on the home market is sufficiently strong, an increase in domestic output may involve little increase in employment, producers' profits, or capacity to finance investment.

Even when protection does effectively transfer resources to the protected industry, the outcomes may still fall far short of policy goals. To begin with, the objectives of industry modernisation and job preservation are frequently incompatible, at least in the short run. More rapid modernisation usually involves shutting obsolete plants and reducing the industry's labour force. Conversely, preserving jobs may mean keeping these plants — often the industry's most labour-intensive ones — in operation, at an obvious cost to efficiency. Protection may help achieve one objective or the other; in none of the cases surveyed did it achieve both.

Moreover, the jobs saved or investments promoted may themselves not reflect the policy's original goals, notably with respect to income distribution. It has proved very difficult to ensure that whatever jobs are "saved" go to the less mobile and skilled workers located in problem regions. Equally, rather than promote investment and modernisation in the domestic industry, a large share of the rents from protection have accrued to their foreign competitors, notably in cases involving "voluntary" export restraints.

Ultimately, the bluntness of protection as a policy instrument means that its precise effects — the extent of the "benefits" and their distribution — are extremely difficult to predict when the policy is being designed, while the outcome frequently fails to meet the objectives in some important respect. This creates pressures for yet more assistance to the industry in question. Trade diversion leads to demands for extending the import controls to new sources and products; the persistence of high adjustment costs for workers in the industry makes the social cost of cheap imports seem excessive; while the fact that the industry is not increasing its competitiveness relative to rivals casts a return to normal trading conditions as premature.

The ineffectiveness of protection has a pervasive impact on its costs. The tangible costs to consumers — both individual households and, in the case of intermediate goods, user industries — have been extensively documented. . . . But to these must be added the indirect costs of protection, which are less tangible and more difficult to quantify. Even in economies operating far from full employment, it may be possible to ignore the macroeconomic impact of a single protectionist measure, but not the cumulative effect of the spread and persistence of such measures.

Poorer economic performance as a result of protection is aggravated by a deteriorating environment for policy making. Macroeconomic policy is more difficult to implement when a large part of the domestic economy expects to be shielded from the competitive discipline of product and labour markets. The "demonstration effect" of protection encourages more and more interest groups to become organised and active, diverting adjustment policy from promoting overall efficiency to arbitrating among competing sectoral claims. Protection itself becomes less effective in promoting adjustment when — as a result of the repeated renewal of protectionist measures — the firms being protected have no reason to expect that they will ever be exposed to the full challenge of international competition.

Similar processes operate at an international level. Protectionist measures implemented by one country may seem to legitimate similar measures adopted by other countries. Retaliation is more likely to occur in an environment where protection is pervasive than when protectionist measures are a clearly confined exception to the rules. As countries act to neutralise the impact on their own producers of policies adopted elsewhere, it becomes more difficult for each country to predict and control the outcome of policy choices.

Taken on their own, import controls have therefore not been a cost-effective instrument of adjustment policy. The disproportion between costs and benefits has been particularly great in cases involving highly discriminatory and complex restrictions imposed on a large number of potential suppliers — as, for example, in the MFA. Widespread discrimination and complexity results in cumbersome and costly administration, an extreme lack of transparency and uncertainty for all trading parties. Conversely, the costs of protection have been lower when the measures implemented were nondiscriminatory and transparent, with minimum distortion of the price system. The cases surveyed confirm that quantitative restrictions generally impose higher costs than tariffs, because the effective protection they accord increases as the domestic industry loses competitiveness, is particularly great in phases of cyclical recovery, and is inevitably less transparent.

Equally important in determining the costs of protection is the scope it leaves for the domestic industry's ongoing adjustment to changes in the international division of labour. In the clothing industry, for example, tariff provisions favourable to outward processing trade are a major factor explaining why the industry has adjusted better in some OECD countries than in others.

Some forms of protection are consequently less costly than others, but the "first-best" solution of returning to normal trading conditions should not simply be set aside. This does not mean providing no adjustment assistance whatsoever — in fact, certain assistance policies can clearly improve the functioning of market economies. But there are cases where the assistance being provided through protectionist measures is imposing costs far in excess of the conceivable benefits. Ultimately, choosing among these options depends on careful and ongoing assessment of the costs and benefits of policies — not only from a narrow budgetary point of view but in terms of the economy as a whole. A clear understanding of the costs protection imposes is essential to mobilising the groups it harms, particularly since these costs are frequently widely dispersed and indirect. . . .

5

Import Quotas and the Automobile Industry: The Costs of Protectionism

Robert W. Crandall

The American automobile industry had a very good year in 1983: New-car sales jumped up by nearly one million units, and, as has been well-publicized, after-tax profits soared to a record $6.2 billion. But the industry is not quite as robust as these statistics suggest. U.S. automobile companies have been playing with a home-field advantage — quotas on Japanese imports, negotiated in 1981 and now extended through 1985.

This article explores the effects of the quotas — on automobile prices and on the profits of domestic manufacturers. The essay begins, however, by tracing the recent history of the automobile industry; it is important, in assessing the impacts of the quotas, to understand why they were sought in the first place.

THE PAST AS PROLOGUE

Sales

Before the 1958 recession, the U.S. automobile industry appeared to be a stable, invincible oligopoly. From time to time, ardent trustbusters would suggest that the government should initiate antitrust proceedings against General Motors in order to increase competition in the industry. It seemed highly unlikely that foreign producers would ever be able to capture a substantial share of the U.S. market. Although Volkswagen enjoyed some success in the late 1950s, import sales then tapered off — dropping below five percent of total sales by 1962, as Table 1 indicates.

That decline proved to be short-lived; in the next eight years, the proportion of U.S. sales accounted for by imports tripled, settling at about 15 percent for the years 1970–74. Ford and General Motors responded to the stepped-up competition from small imported cars by launching their Pinto and Vega model lines, but neither of these proved particularly successful. When the second oil shock occurred in 1978–79, fuel-efficient foreign cars became more popular than ever; in 1980, 28 percent of the new cars registered were imports.

While the sales of imports have increased since 1965, growth in the demand for new cars has decreased. From 1965 through 1970, sales were essentially flat, deviating little from an annual rate of nine million cars; this

From *The Brookings Review*, Summer 1984. Copyright © 1984 by The Brookings Institution, Washington D.C. Reprinted by permission of the publisher. Some tables omitted.

TABLE 1

U.S. New Car Registrations 1960–1983 (millions)

Year	Domestic cars	Imports	Total	Import share
1960	6.1	0.5	6.6	7.6%
61	5.2	0.4	5.6	6.5
62	6.6	0.3	6.9	4.9
63	7.2	0.4	7.6	5.1
64	7.6	0.5	8.1	6.0
65	8.7	0.6	9.3	6.1
66	8.3	0.7	9.0	7.3
67	7.6	0.8	8.4	9.3
68	8.4	1.0	9.4	10.5
69	8.3	1.1	9.4	11.2
70	7.2	1.2	8.4	14.7
71	8.5	1.3	9.8	15.1
72	9.0	1.5	10.5	14.5
73	9.7	1.7	11.4	15.2
74	7.3	1.4	8.7	15.7
75	6.8	1.5	8.3	18.2
76	8.4	1.4	9.8	14.8
77	8.8	2.0	10.8	18.3
78	9.0	1.9	10.9	17.8
79	8.0	2.4	10.4	22.7
80	6.3	2.5	8.8	28.2
81	6.0	2.4	8.4	28.8
82	5.5	2.3	7.8	29.3
83	6.4	2.5	8.9	27.5

Source: Automotive News, Market Data Book Issue, April 27, 1983.

leveling-off came after more than a decade of substantial sales growth. Sales were at a higher plateau between 1971 and 1979, averaging about ten million cars per year, but most of this increase was absorbed by imports, particularly those from Japan. As a result, even during the relatively prosperous period of 1976–79, the demand for domestic cars was about the same as it had been in 1965–66. That demand then plummeted during the first four years of the 1980s, as U.S. manufacturers managed to sell only about six million new cars per annum — far below their totals in the recession-plagued years of 1970 and 1975.

     . . . The profit rates of U.S. automobile manufacturers fluctuated wildly during the 1970s, ranging between 6.1 percent and 18.7 percent on equity. Then, in 1980, the bottom fell out; the firms lost $4 billion on sales of 6.3 million cars. This was the worst year in the industry's history; its profit rate of −9.3 percent was 23.2 percent below the average for all manufacturing. When sales had declined sharply in 1970 and again in 1975, U.S. manufacturers had managed to earn positive rates of return. In 1961, with sales of only 5.2 million cars, the companies had earned 11 percent on equity. Clearly, the industry's difficulties in 1980 — and in the two years that followed — reflected more than just cyclical swings in the economy. What had gone wrong?

Regulation

One source of vexation has been the federal government, which has saddled the industry with a succession of new regulatory requirements. Safety regulation began in 1966, federal emissions controls in 1968, and fuel-economy regulation in 1978. The costs of safety and emissions regulation have been substantial; . . . they reached nearly $2000 per car by the early 1980s.

Prior to 1972, emissions control costs were negligible, and safety equipment costs were less than $200 per car. Both categories of costs then rose sharply, however. Automobile manufacturers struggled with the technology of emissions control while trying to convince the government that its timetable for control was much too stringent. For at least two years and perhaps longer, the companies used relatively inefficient fixes to constrain emissions. The results were poor performance, severely depressed fuel economy, and widespread customer dissatisfaction.

At about the same time, the Department of Transportation was imposing two major new safety regulations on the industry — requirements for seat belt interlocks and energy-absorbing bumpers. The interlock requirement was quickly repealed by Congress in response to bitter complaints from new-car buyers, but manufacturers had already spent time and money on the design and fabrication of interlock systems. The bumper requirement was surely a masterstroke of bad timing; it added substantially to the weight of cars — and detracted significantly from their fuel economy — just as the Arab oil embargo was driving gasoline prices up.

The second big regulatory surge came in 1980–81. The industry managed to stave off a new requirement for passive occupant restraints, but only at the last minute. Product planners had to be prepared to install passive seat belts or air bags in some models in 1982 before the Department of Transportation relieved them of this requirement in mid–1981. In addition, emissions standards were tightened substantially in 1980–81, necessitating major changes in ignition systems and control devices.

Unfortunately, these regulatory initiatives came right after the second oil shock and an attendant surge in the sale of Japanese imports. At the same time that U.S. manufacturers were struggling to redesign and downsize their cars as quickly as possible, they had to introduce new emissions-control technologies and to develop passive restraint systems. The Japanese car companies appear to have adjusted to the regulatory requirements more readily than their American rivals, perhaps because they did not need to downsize their product lines simultaneously.

The safety regulations and the pre–1980 emissions controls appear to have been effective, but the gains they produced have not been without their costs. For consumers, safety and emissions standards have increased the prices of new cars by at least $1000 and reduced both fuel economy and performance. As a result, they have reduced the demand for new cars. Had emissions controls been kept at 1979 levels and the energy-absorbing bumper left a matter of market choice, new car sales would have been higher and regulatory headaches fewer for an increasingly besieged Detroit.

More recently, the Corporate Average Fuel Economy (CAFE) standards, legislated by Congress in 1975 and implemented by the Department of Transportation, have placed U.S. companies in the difficult position of trying to meet the resurgent demand for larger cars while still making progress towards the 1985 goal of 27.5 miles per gallon for their fleets.

Product Quality

An unfortunate consequence of the turbulence of the 1970s was a sharp decline in the product quality of U.S. automobiles relative to that of Japanese imports. This decline was reflected not only in the "fit and finish" of cars — that is, the fit of body panels and the general quality of exterior finish — but also in the frequency of repairs. In 1970 . . . the repair records of U.S. cars were only marginally worse than the records of Japanese imports in the first few years of service. These differences may have narrowed or disappeared in later years of service. By 1976, however, Japanese cars had much better repair records than their American counterparts — and this gap has persisted and even widened in the years since then. It should be noted that the continuing declines in quality . . . are not confined to the new down-sized front-wheel drive models, but have occurred across the entire model lines of the U.S. companies.

Production Costs

The quality advantage of Japanese cars was no doubt one factor in the shift of American buyers toward imports; another factor was the loss of U.S. competitiveness in the production of smaller cars. Since 1980, there have been numerous attempts to quantify the differences between U.S. and Japanese production costs for subcompact cars. Estimates of the Japanese advantage range from $1300 to $2500 per car, a substantial fraction of the average delivered price of these models. Those who have studied this question agree that the main sources of the cost disparity are differences in wage rates, labor productivity, management practices, and inventory costs.

Part of the U.S. industry's problem derives from its own collective bargaining; it has granted large wage increases to its unionized workers rather than risk strikes or labor unrest. As indicated in [Table 2], the result has been hourly employment costs that are about 60 percent above the average for all U.S. manufacturing firms. In Japan, by contrast, automobile companies pay their workers only 25 percent more per hour than what the average Japanese industrial worker receives. Moreover, the differences between the hourly employment costs of U.S. and Japanese car manufacturers has been widening — from about $6 in

[TABLE 2]

Total Hourly Compensation in the Motor Vehicle Industry and
All Manufacturing — U.S. and Japan ($/hour)

| Year | U.S. | | JAPAN | |
	Motor vehicles	All manufacturing	Motor vehicles	All manufacturing
1975	9.44	6.35	3.56	3.05
1976	10.27	6.93	4.02	3.30
1977	11.45	7.59	4.82	4.03
1978	12.67	8.30	6.85	5.54
1979	13.68	9.07	6.90	5.49
1980	16.29	9.89	6.89	5.61
1981	17.28	10.95	7.65	6.18
1982	18.66	11.68	7.18	5.70
1983	19.02	12.31	7.91	6.24

Source: Bureau of Labor Statistics

the mid–1970s to about $11 now — even though productivity growth in the Japanese firms has been more rapid.

The surge in demand for Japanese imports was followed by a sharp upturn in the value of the dollar. From the beginning of 1980 through the third quarter of 1982, the dollar appreciated against the yen by more than 30 percent. Even today, the value of the dollar in terms of the yen is 20 percent higher than it was in January 1980. This depreciation of the yen has added considerably to the Japanese cost advantage over U.S. automobile producers.

PAYING FOR PROTECTION: THE IMPORT OF QUOTAS

In 1980, the U.S. industry began to appeal for temporary protection from Japanese imports. In July 1980, the International Trade Commission initiated an investigation under Section 201 of the Trade Act of 1974. This proceeding did not result in an ITC decision to recommend trade relief measures. In 1981, however, President Reagan announced that agreement had been reached with Japan on a voluntary export restraint (VER) that would limit Japanese automobile exports to the United States, beginning that April, to 1.68 million cars per year.

The Reagan decision did not arouse much opposition since it followed a year in which U.S. automobile manufacturers lost approximately $4 billion. Employment in the industry had fallen by more than 20 percent; approximately a third of that decline was due to a sharp rise in import sales. Moreover, the Chrysler Corporation had recently been saved from bankruptcy by federal loan guarantees, and Chrysler workers had taken substantial pay cuts.

The voluntary export restraint negotiated with Japan was renewed in 1983 for the 1984–85 period, but with a slightly higher limit of 1.85 million cars per year. By 1983, however, the industry had returned to at least the appearance of financial health, generating more than $6 billion in after-tax profits. The price of Japanese cars surged, U.S. manufacturers paid substantial bonuses to their executives, and commentators began to question the wisdom of continuing the restraint agreement with Japan.

The Rationale

The Reagan administration obtained temporary quotas on Japanese imports in order to buy the U.S. automobile industry and its workers time to adjust to the new rigors of world competition. It anticipated that during this adjustment period, car companies might undertake the substantial tooling required for the manufacture of new models, launch major investment programs designed to lower production costs in existing plants, establish new plant configurations, reduce inventory costs, and seek changes in union work rules and wage agreements. After a few years, the industry would be able to compete effectively once again — unless its cost disadvantages were rooted in fundamental economic forces beyond its control, such as exchange rates, raw material costs, or a shift of comparative advantage to lower-wage countries.

There was and is another possible outcome: Trade protection might simply provide an opportunity for increases in automobile prices, wages, and company profits. A reduction in the availability of imports inevitably increases the demand for U.S. automobiles, opening the door for price hikes. The resulting increases in profits could provide an enticing target for union negotiators in the next round of bargaining. With foreign competition temporarily (or permanently) reduced, workers have less incentive to moderate their wage demands or to allow fundamental changes in work rules.

Which of these outcomes seems more likely? Past experience with trade restrictions hardly suggests that they offer a guarantee of industrial renaissance. The steel industry has enjoyed some form of protection over most of the past 15 years, but it has not recovered. Trade protection for manufacturers of television receivers or shoes has hardly returned the United States to a dominant position in these industries. If past experience is any guide, one should not expect the Japanese VERs to be a miracle cure for the U.S. automobile industry.

The Industry's Adjustment

In fact, U.S. companies had begun to adjust to the new world of high gasoline prices and international competition some time before the VERs took effect. There is every reason to believe that the industry was well on its way to renewed competitiveness. Manufacturers had focused more on small cars since the two oil shocks, and by 1981 had reduced the average weight of a domestic car 30 percent from its 1972–73 high. Similarly, by 1980 the industry was selling 40 percent of its cars with four-cylinder engines, up sharply from 9 percent in

1972–73. Fuel economy was up by more than 25 percent over what it had been in 1972–73 for cars of the same weight and horsepower; actual fuel economy increased much more than that, as buyers shifted to smaller cars.

The investment expenditures of the automobile companies are further evidence of their pre–1981 adjustment efforts. Between 1975–76 and 1979–80 . . . real investment outlays increased by more than 88 percent. More focused census data show that investment in plant, equipment, and special tooling rose more than 87 percent over the same period. In short, the industry had invested enormous sums in new models before the establishment of quotas. Since 1981, real investment expenditures by the automobile industry have fallen by 30 percent. Buyers have begun once again to demand larger cars; eight-cylinder cars accounted for 31 percent of 1983 sales, up from 24 percent in 1981. New or modified models abound: Ford has introduced a new series of front-wheel drive cars and a modified version of its older rear-wheel drive Thunderbird; Chrysler has added a new sports car and a series of vans to its product line; and General Motors has downsized its larger cars. But the major changes were in place before the quotas were; by March, 1981, Ford's Escort, Chrysler's Aries-Reliant, and General Motors' X-, J-, and A-body cars were either on the market or nearly ready for introduction. It is difficult to trace any differences in product offerings to the quotas.

Nor has productivity soared as a result of the quotas. Between 1977 and 1982, productivity growth in the motor vehicle industry was 0.4 percent, as compared with 0.2 percent in the nonfarm business sector. From 1980 to 1982, the industry outperformed the rest of the nonfarm business economy, but, given the depth of the 1982 recession, it is difficult to draw any firm conclusions from these data. In 1982, the UAW agreed with Ford and GM to forego some wage increases in order to stem the flow of red ink from these companies' domestic financial statements. These agreements followed similar, but larger concessions granted to Chrysler in previous years. In addition, the industry has attempted to increase productivity by investing in labor-saving equipment and improving worker morale. At this juncture, there is insufficient evidence to judge the success of these attempts. Indeed, General Motors' decision to produce subcompacts jointly with Toyota in California appears to be an attempt to break out from the restrictive work rules with which it is saddled in other plants. . . .

Effects on Automobile Prices

There is no doubt but that by creating an artificial scarcity of Japanese imports, the voluntary restraints have increased the prices charged for these cars; the only question is by how much. A 1983 Wharton Econometrics study estimated that as a result of the quotas, the prices of Japanese imports jumped up an average of $920 to $960 per car in 1981–82 alone. With the surge in demand that took place in 1983, this price effect has surely increased substantially — which means that our assistance for the U.S. industry has benefited Japanese producers and their dealers by at least $2 billion per year in price enhancement. From the standpoint of American taxpayers, a tariff clearly would have been a better policy choice than the voluntary restraints.

The effect of the restraints on the prices of U.S. cars is more open to dispute. It is not easy to estimate this effect because the mix of automobiles is constantly changing. Indeed, some industry officials believe that any recent price increases above the cost of producing cars have been due to mix changes, not imports. But if the VERs reduce the potential supply of new Japanese cars in the United States (and they surely do), they must increase the demand for American automobiles. Historically, the average price of automobiles in the United States has varied directly with the strength of demand; therefore, one would expect the VERs to increase the prices of domestic cars.

Assume for a moment that the VERs have simply increased the U.S. industry's market share by 5 to 8 percent, without increasing prices; given the trend in import sales between 1978 and 1981, this range probably represents the maximum effect of the quotas on market shares. In 1983, a 5 to 8 percent shift would have meant the purchase of an additional 445,000 to 712,000 domestic cars, assuming no effect on total car sales. My current research suggests that the marginal profit on these cars, before taxes, would have been about $2000 per car — for a total of $0.89 to $1.42 billion, less than the gain realized by Japanese companies and their dealers. (Of course, if the VERs have increased domestic car prices, then the additional profits made by U.S. manufacturers would be substantially higher.)

I used several techniques to estimate the impact of the quotas on domestic car prices, and while I would not claim that the results of any one of the tests are definitive, the fact that the outcomes are so similar does suggest that the price effect of the quotas is in the range indicated.

One way to gauge that effect is to relate U.S. car prices to costs and demand over a substantial period of time and then to use the resulting equation to predict prices under the VERs in 1981–83. I developed a pricing model for the period 1961–80, incorporating labor costs, capital costs, regulatory requirements, the price of steel, the strength of demand, and dummy variables for years of price controls. As indicated in part 1 of [Table 3], the model tracks the annual average prices of new cars in this 20-year period with an average error of only about $56. However, the equation underestimates prices for 1983 by more than $800 per car and for 1981–83 by a yearly average of $430. Since the model was built using the Commerce Department's series on actual transactions prices, it reflects discounts from list prices. It does not, however, standardize for changes in the mix between small and large cars or in the mix of options. These changes occurred in the 1960s and 1970s, and the equation tracked prices very well for those two decades. The only major difference between the 1970s and, say, 1983 is the presence of an import restraint; it seems reasonable to infer that the VER must account for a substantial share of the excess of actual prices over predictions.

A second method for analyzing shifts in automobile prices is the use of a

[TABLE 3]

Three Estimates of the Effect of Quotas upon U.S. Car Prices

1. Average price of new domestic cars sold = f(labor cost, capital cost, regulatory cost, price of steel, 1972–74 price controls, vehicle sales)
Period of estimation: 1961–1980. Standard error: $56.

Excess of actual prices over predicted prices:

1981	$237
1982	$236
1983	$829

2. Hedonic model: Price of a new domestic car = f(weight, ride, handling, acceleration, size class, gasoline cost, dummy variables for various years); Period of estimation: 1970–83 models (172 cars).

Increase in estimated value during quota years for small cars:

Year	Total ($/car)	Additional regulatory costs ($/car)	Net value ($/car)
1981–83	826	454	372

3. Annual increase in consumer price index:

Period	(1) Total CPI	(2) New-car CPI	(2)/(1) Ratio
1960–70	2.7%	0.3%	0.11
1970–80	7.5	5.1	0.68
March 1981–Dec. 1983	4.9	4.5	0.92
March 1981–Dec. 1983 (at 1970s' ratio)	4.9	3.3	0.68

Difference in behavior of new-car CPI relative to total CPI in March 1981–December 1983 compared with difference in 1970s:

$$4.5\% - 3.3\% = 1.2\% \text{ per year.}$$

Effect on new domestic car prices of 1.2% greater increase per year:

Actual 1983 average price	Predicted 1983 average price	Difference
$10,484	$10,116	$368

so-called hedonic model that reflects the qualitative attributes of each car. I gathered data on 176 domestic models tested by *Consumer Reports* from 1970 through 1983; complete data were available for 172 of these cars. The following factors were included in the model: weight, acceleration, the estimated quality of ride, the estimated handling capability, the cost per mile of gasoline consumed, and the size-class of the car (subcompact, compact, intermediate, full size, or luxury). When specific dummy variables are used for each year, the model estimates that the real list price of small cars increased by 12 percent, or $826 per car, in the 1981–83 period. These increases in the real price of cars, holding the qualitative attributes constant, include the effects of tighter emissions control standards set by the government in 1980–81. These standards added $454 (1982$) to the cost of small new cars, which must be deducted from the estimated increase in the real, quality-adjusted price. Thus, as shown in part 2 of [Table 3], the hedonic model estimates that the quotas increased list prices by an average of about $370 per car in 1981–83. This calculation does not reflect changes in dealer discounts and rebates; inasmuch as rebates have narrowed substantially since March, 1981, the estimate is undoubtedly biased downward.

Finally, one can assess the impact of the VERs by examining the behavior of the Consumer Price Index for new cars since March, 1981. Historically, the CPI for cars has risen less rapidly than the total CPI. Part of the reason for this differential is that the Bureau of Labor Statistics deducts estimated improvements in quality — including regulatory costs — from price increases for automobiles. The total adjustment for quality improvements in 1981–83 was nearly $850, of which about $700 reflects regulatory costs. Since most other components of the CPI are not similarly adjusted, the new-car CPI should rise less rapidly than the total index, *ceteris paribus*.

The new-car component of the CPI increased by only 0.3 percent per year in the 1960s, while the CPI as a whole rose by 2.7 percent per year. In the 1970s, the corresponding figures were 5.1 percent and 7.5 percent. But since the inception of import quotas, the difference has narrowed remarkably. From March, 1981, through December, 1983, the new-car component of the CPI increased by 4.5 percent per year and the overall CPI by 4.9 percent. Had the 0.68 ratio of the 1970s persisted, we would have expected the new-car component to advance only 3.3 percent per year during this period — 1.2 percent less than actually observed. If the prices of domestic cars had risen at this lower annual rate, then, as part 3 of [Table 3] indicates, they would have been an average of $368 less than they were.

Equally striking is the behavior of the new-car CPI in the period just after the import quotas were introduced. From April through December 1981, the new-car CPI increased at a 10.3 percent annual rate, after rising at a 4.1 percent rate for the preceding 15 months. This surge occurred during a continuing decline in demand.

The various calculations just discussed are likely, for four reasons, to underestimate the impact of the quotas. First, they do not take into account the sizable interest rate subsidies that were offered in 1981. Second, the continued appreciation of the dollar and the improvement in the relative quality of Japanese automobiles would have placed relatively more downward pressure on U.S. car prices in 1981–83 than in previous periods. If there had been no quotas, we surely would have expected U.S. car prices to reflect increasing import competition. Third, wage rates paid by U.S. automobile producers grew somewhat less rapidly than average U.S. wages in 1980–83, after having increased more rapidly in 1975–80. Absent the quotas, these lower wage costs would have been reflected in new-car prices. Finally, with gasoline prices falling since 1982, federal fuel economy standards have undoubtedly led U.S. companies to restrain the prices of smaller cars.

Profits

As a check on these estimates, one might look at the before-tax profits of the companies. If prices increased abnormally relative to costs, profits should have risen relative to their historical relationship with volume. To test for this outcome, I used the Commerce Department's estimate of domestic profits (before taxes) in the motor vehicle industry, adjusted for changes in inventory valuation. [Table 4] shows the very strong recovery in pretax profits since 1980. Despite much lower sales volumes, the real profit per domestic vehicle produced has rebounded to 1978–79 levels. In fact, on the sale of fewer vehicles than were sold in 1975, real profits per vehicle in 1983 were more than double what they had been in that earlier year. When before-tax profits, deflated by the CPI, are fitted to total vehicle sales (including trucks and buses), the import share, a dummy variable for the 1973–74 price controls, and a dummy variable for the 1981–83 period, the results show that profits have risen by 50 percent over 1960–80 levels for the same levels of vehicle production. This translates into $280 per vehicle, including large cars, trucks, and buses. Since import restraints have not raised truck and bus prices and have had less of an impact on the prices of large cars than on those of small cars, the effect per small car must have been substantially greater than $280. These increases in profits may have been due in part to productivity gains, but a substantial share of the explanation must be the price effects of import restraints.

Employment

It is difficult to see how the VERs could have shifted more than 8 percentage points of the market from Japanese imports to U.S. cars by 1983. If the higher prices caused by the quotas had no effect on automobile sales in 1983, a market share shift of this magnitude might have saved, at most, 46,200 production jobs in the automobile industry. (A swing of 8 percentage points to U.S. automobiles would have produced an 11 percent increase in domestic sales. Assuming that the elasticity of production workers with respect to output is 0.7, this translates into a 7.7 percent increase in employment on a 1983 average base of 600,000.)

If, as was almost certainly the case, higher prices reduced total automobile sales, the effect on employment was smaller. Quotas appear to have raised

TABLE 4

Profits Before Taxes,* 1970–83

Year	Before-tax profits (billions of $)	Before-tax profits (billions of 1972 $)	Before-tax profits per vehicle** (1972 $)
1970	1.2	1.3	160
1971	5.0	5.2	490
1972	5.9	5.9	520
1973	5.7	5.3	423
1974	0.1	0.0	472
1975	1.9	1.5	165
1976	7.2	5.3	461
1977	9.4	6.5	513
1978	8.9	5.7	443
1979	4.7	2.7	235
1980	-3.8	-1.9	-239
1981	-0.6	-0.3	-37
1982	0.9	0.2	27
1983	7.7	3.2	353

*With inventory valuation adjustment.

**Vehicles include all cars, trucks, and buses.

Sources: Bureau of Economic Analysis, Department of Commerce, *Survey of Current Business,* annual issues; Motor Vehicle Manufacturers Association, *Motor Vehicle Facts and Figures,* annual issues.

prices by an average of about 5 percent, which, assuming a unitary elastic demand, translates into a 5 percent reduction in sales. Absent this reduction, total sales would have been 9.4 million units instead of about 8.9 million. If U.S. producers had obtained a 65.5 percent share of this larger total, their domestic sales would have been 6.0 million units instead of 6.4 million — and the number of production jobs in the industry would have declined by 26,200. What that cost has been depends upon the extent of relative-price effects, welfare losses in production, and welfare losses in consumption caused by constrained consumer choice. Concentrating only on the price effects, if the average price of U.S. cars has risen $400 and the average price of Japanese imports has gone up $1000, the cost to consumers in 1983 was $4.3 billion plus additional losses in consumer welfare due to the VERs' constraint on the choice of cars. The cost per job saved, therefore, was nearly $160,000 per year. Employment creation at this cost is surely not worth the candle.

It is possible that the number of jobs saved was substantially less than 26,200 and that the per-job cost estimate just presented is overly conservative. Falling gasoline prices and the increasing demand for larger cars should have offset some of the rising pressure on small-car sales caused by a depreciation of the yen against the dollar in 1981–83. An 8 percentage point shift in market share translates into an import share of 35.5 percent in 1983 without the quotas. This would have required Japanese imports of 40 percent more than the quota level in 1983. While it is conceivable that Japanese imports would have risen by this much, it seems unlikely; such an increase would have required a very high price elasticity of demand for these cars, little reduction in U.S. auto prices to meet the competition, or both. Without the quotas, it is likely that U.S. automobile prices would have been lower, thus restraining the shift to the Japanese models.

CONCLUSION

Given the scant evidence that these quotas are advancing the competitiveness of the U.S. automobile industry, their desirability turns on whether Americans wish to pay large premiums on their cars in order to increase the employment of auto workers at wages far above the manufacturing average. Indeed, because they have produced high profits in the industry, the VERs may actually lead to a widening of this wage differential in the 1984 contract negotiations. If that happens, the political necessity for quotas will increase, and future presidents will have difficulty arguing that the domestic automobile industry should once again face the rigors of international competition.

6

Adjustment, Protection, and Employment

Charles Pearson and Gerry Salembier

There is nothing unique about international trade as a source of adjustment costs, particularly labour adjustment costs. Technological change, shifts in the pattern of demand, relocation of industry within a country, and other factors can all lead to worker displacement and social adjustment costs. . . . The main differences appear to be a greater willingness to resist trade-induced change through protection measures, and separate government programs in some countries (United States, Germany, Canada, Australia, Netherlands) to deal with real and potential trade-related job losses. . . .

From *Trade, Employment, and Adjustment,* Essays in International Economics (Montreal, Canada: The Institute for Research on Public Policy, 1983), pp. 12–31. Reprinted by permission of the publisher. Some footnotes omitted and text rearranged.

ADJUSTMENT COSTS

What exactly are the economic costs of adjusting to changes in comparative advantage, and how should they be measured? Traditional international trade theory is not especially helpful. The usual textbook presentation assumes full employment, perfect mobility of resources (labour and capital) among domestic industries, and equilibrium exchange rates. In this fashion, adjustment itself becomes automatic, instantaneous, and costless. The only cost identified in the traditional comparative static trade analysis is the loss of economic efficiency and social welfare involved in *not* adjusting to shifts in comparative advantage. In other words, the cost of long-term misallocation of resources is dealt with, but the transitional cost involved in the process of re-allocating resources is ignored.

The traditional presentation does recognize that not everyone gains from freer trade. Specifically, owners of scarce productive factors — labour in a capital-abundant country — find their price in factor markets is bid down, and they may be made worse off. In that sense, some domestic groups may suffer economic losses from a freeing of trade. . . . On the basis of narrow self-interest, it is rational for these groups to seek protection even at the expense of the general welfare. From this, one can build a theory explaining protectionist pressure. . . .

As a practical matter, however, resource adjustment is not automatic and instantaneous. Workers released from declining industries are not immediately re-employed elsewhere in the economy. Plant equipment and skills are not easily transferred to other types of production. Thus, not only are there long-term costs to the economy involved in not adjusting, but the process of adjustment itself also involves real costs to workers, owners of capital, and to the economy as a whole. Theories of protectionist pressure should also account for these costs.

The sources of transitional adjustment costs are imperfect mobility of resources, the most extreme case being human and/or physical capital that is specific to one industry or firm. It is necessary at this point to distinguish between social and private adjustment costs. By social adjustment costs we mean the costs borne by society as a whole during the adjustment period. By private adjustment costs we mean the net cost, after adjusting for transfer payments, borne directly by the displaced resources during the adjustment period.

Social adjustment costs are due to the loss of output to the economy when resources are made temporarily unemployed due to a change in the pattern of trade. They can be defined as either the value of output or income forgone when resources are made temporarily unemployed and are typically measured by wages forgone while workers are unemployed. The underlying premise is that wages reflect the value of labour's output, and thus lost wages measure the value of lost output. This may be an acceptable measure, but it is not perfect. It would be preferable to adjust for the value of additional leisure (if any) while unemployed. Also, when the trade-displaced worker finds alternative employment, he may "bump" the unemployment to others in the job market. Measures of social adjustment costs should include the direct and indirect unemployment effects. Finally, the wage rate prior to the lay-offs may overstate the social cost, as the correct measure is the value of unemployed labour in the next best alternative occupation.

Should lower wages in subsequent employment be part of social costs? It would appear not, as the subsequent wage reduction reflects the write-down of the value of human capital that was specific to the initial job, but which, due to trade change, has now lost some of its economic value. As noted below, however, lower wages in subsequent employment are part of workers' total private costs.

A similar argument applies to losses suffered by the owners of plant and equipment. Trade change can reduce the market value of the capital — indeed, make it without value and idle if it cannot be transferred to other industries. But this is a private cost and does not represent a social cost. Physical capital that is made obsolete or uneconomic to operate because of trade change has lost its economic value. The fact that it is idle does not constitute a social cost. Nevertheless, some capital (e.g., trucks) can be used in many activities. There may be a period of temporary unemployment for this capital, and the value of its services lost during unemployment does represent a social cost.

Adjustment costs can be viewed from another perspective. One might argue that workers could, if they wish, bid down their wages to meet import competition and maintain their employment. If they do not, then unemployment can be regarded as voluntary, and presumably workers rationally expect the costs of unemployment to be less than the (discounted) difference between the two income streams — accepting temporary unemployment with subsequent re-employment versus maintaining their initial employment at depressed wages. In this event, the concept of social adjustment cost loses considerable force. But the existence of transfer payments (unemployment payments) affects workers' decisions and it is not clear that social adjustment costs disappear entirely. Also, workers may anticipate receiving trade protection and this influences their wage demands.

It is more fruitful to recognize that labour markets are not perfect — for example, medium-term labour contracts for worker groups may preclude individual wage negotiations and downward wage adjustment. In this case, the focus is properly shifted to viewing the social cost of adjusting to trade as a reflection of distortions in the labour market.

Another bothersome problem in the concept of social adjustment cost is the length of unemployment, which is presumably influenced by the wage at which the unemployed trade-displaced worker is willing to work. The troubling conclusion is that measured social adjustment costs are determined in part by workers' willingness to accept other employment at some (lower) wage. The higher a worker's wage demand, the higher are the social adjustment costs (indeed, it may have been high wages that caused import competition and decline in domestic production in the first place). This may also be further affected if unemployment benefit programs are based on, or take into account, the previous wages paid. Thus, for a social cost-benefit analysis of a prospective trade change, we are left in the uncomfortable position of comparing the gains from the trade change with the adjustment costs to society that are in part determined by worker-wage demands.

A final issue is whether the real resources expended by displaced workers in retraining themselves and in job search costs (travel, relocation expenses, etc.), and the real resource costs incurred by society in trade adjustment assistance programs for retraining and relocation, are part of social adjustment costs. The answer appears to be 'no,' as presumably retraining increases skill levels, and job search expenditures result in a better match between worker skills and job requirements. Assuming workers are rational and the market for training is working reasonably well, the benefits to society of training (and of job search activities) are at least equal to resource costs involved in the training and relocation activities. Retraining and job search costs need not, therefore, be considered additional social costs arising directly from the trade change. If they are to be so considered, however, the separate benefit (e.g., increased skills) must also be included in the social benefit-cost calculus.

Overall, from an efficiency viewpoint, social adjustment costs give rise to two principal policy considerations. First, do the benefits from trade, properly discounted, outweigh the temporary adjustment costs? That is, are the costs to society of maintaining these resources in their initial production greater or less than the benefits of maintaining their output? Secondly, are there government measures that would reduce the period of unemployment and hence minimize adjustment costs?

Private adjustment costs to trade change are conceptually distinct from social adjustment costs. For trade-displaced workers, private adjustment costs include the after-tax wage loss while unemployed, net of any transfer payments (unemployment benefits and trade adjustment assistance payments) and net of the value of additional leisure, the loss of valuable seniority and pension rights and indirect benefits such as health insurance, and the loss of the value of job-specific human capital. The latter can be measured as a stock loss, or as the present discounted value of the reduction in wages when re-employed. It is also possible to consider the psychic costs of becoming unemployed and having one's specialized skills become worthless as additional private costs. (The social welfare function could, in theory, include these as social costs as well.) If lay-offs are concentrated in smaller communities, there is a possibility that home prices are depressed, an additional private cost. There can be "second round" private costs, especially in smaller communities, as local income, spending, and tax revenues decline. Shopkeepers and local taxpayers are frequent examples of those who bear indirect private costs. Voluntary and involuntary transfers among groups in society form a large part of the calculation of private adjustment costs, but are not part of social adjustment costs.

Owners of capital also suffer private adjustment costs as asset prices are written down to reflect new competitive pressure. This cost, however, may not fall on the current owner of the plant and equipment if the trade change was anticipated, and market values therefore adjusted downward, at the time of last sale of the assets in question. The owner of the capital at the time of increased imports may have bought the assets at the reduced price, and there would be no justification for providing him with compensation. Indeed, correct anticipation of trade change can reduce private costs to both labour and capital. As a practical matter, such anticipation is often impossible for owners of long-lived fixed assets. Furthermore, ownership and management are often intertwined in smaller firms, and "sunk" capital inhibits shifting into other types of production. As a result, workers and management combine to resist adjustment and request protection or subsidies.

Private adjustment costs are important for two reasons. First, for reasons of equity or social justice, society may feel an obligation to compensate firms and workers for losses due to a trade change that is in the general interest. This obligation may be more strongly felt when the trade change is the direct result of a deliberate government action such as a tariff reduction. Such was the case under the 1962 U.S. trade legislation and the 1968 establishment of the Canadian GAAP [General Adjustment Assistance Program] program, both of which tied adjustment assistance to increased imports resulting from earlier tariff liberalization. At present, the link between earlier tariff reduction and increased imports need not be demonstrated in either country; increased imports, for whatever reason, can trigger adjustment assistance. In any event, compensation for equity purposes must consider private adjustment costs, and not social adjustment costs.

Secondly, to understand resistance to adjustment and the sources of protectionist pressure, one must look to private and not social adjustment costs. To the extent that an adjustment assistance program is designed to reduce protectionist pressure and "buy" a more liberal trade policy, it must compensate for private adjustment costs. However, even an adjustment assistance program that fully compensates trade-displaced labour and capital, and compensates communities, would not entirely dispel protectionist pressure. It is important to realize that resources that *remain* employed despite import competition will prefer protection to adjustment assistance. . . . Profits and wages would be higher with protection for those workers and capital owners who are able to compete. The constituency for protection is larger than those who might become unemployed or whose firms might close down, and for that reason it is not realistic to expect a trade adjustment assistance program to dissipate protectionist pressure fully.

To conclude our discussion of adjustment costs, it should be stressed that the benefits of adjusting to changes in comparative advantage and changes in international competitiveness should not be ignored. The prospect of greater economic efficiency and the accompanying longer-term benefits form the desirability as well as the impetus for adjustment. However, the act of adjustment is not costless. It is for these reasons — the benefits from adjustment, the cost of adjustment, and the distribution of costs and benefits — that adjustment is a public policy issue. . . .

TRADE ADJUSTMENT ASSISTANCE VERSUS PROTECTION

It is tempting to contrast trade adjustment assistance (TAA) and trade protection by claiming that TAA programs are designed to facilitate adjustment, whereas protection measures such as tariffs and quotas impede the adjustment of resources. There is considerable merit to this view when TAA programs are designed exclusively to improve efficiency in the allocation of resources, and when protection is of a permanent nature. In that case the rationale for adjustment assistance is adjustment, and the rationale for protection is to maintain resources in their current (uncompetitive) activity. But when actual adjustment assistance programs are compared to temporary trade protection, the contrast loses some of its sharpness. To some extent the U.S. TAA program and many Canadian adjustment assistance measures share objectives similar to those of temporary protection. They tend to emphasize assistance as much as adjustment, and both adjustment assistance and temporary protection can fail to achieve these objectives for somewhat similar reasons. It is necessary to identify these objectives, and the reasons why they are often not achieved, to reconcile divergent views of adjustment assistance and trade protection as a response to import competition.

In principle, both protection that is perceived by the beneficiaries to be temporary and TAA programs can facilitate adjustment by inducing resources to become more competitive in their current activities, or by moving resources to more productive activity. In that sense they may share a common efficiency objective. Temporary protection can, in principle, accomplish this by offering the distressed industry a breathing spell, which enables it to make productive investment and rationalize its operations, emerging with an improved competitive position in the same product lines. But why is the additional investment and rationalization not undertaken privately if the industry ultimately becomes competitive?

One answer may be that there are defects in the private capital market or in private entrepreneurship that inhibit the private sector on its own from making the necessary investments to again become competitive. Another related answer might be that the discount rate applied to future income streams by private investors may be greater than the social discount rate implicit in efficiency objectives. For example, the risk of expensively trained workers moving to competing firms within an industry raises the private discount rate applied to the benefits of a training program but does not affect the social discount rate. In such cases, the government is justified in correcting the private market distortion by offering temporary protection (or better yet, direct subsidies). Another answer, however, is that the industry may feel that it is cheaper and more secure to obtain protection from the government. Seeking protectionism can be as lucrative as responding to market forces, and, if given the option, rational people can be expected to pursue protection. This is particularly common where the private sector is traditionally fairly risk averse and accustomed to government intervention, as in Canada. However, it does not justify policy measures to protect the industry.

Temporary protection, especially with phased declining levels, can also, in principle, allow for the orderly movement of resources out of the industry by attrition, thus contributing to the efficiency objective of minimizing social adjustment costs (minimizing involuntary labour unemployment). We immediately see, however, the first of a series of dilemmas. Temporary protection can slow the outflow of resources or even encourage resources to flow into the industry, which conflicts with the objective of phasing down the industry through attrition. Unless the government can correctly identify which industries will ultimately become competitive and which will not, trade protection gives confusing signals and often fails to promote efficient allocation of resources. More specifically, temporary protection designed to slow the decline of an industry and moderate labour adjustment costs may be excessive and impede the outflow of resources. Import legislation generally fails to differentiate between protective measures that encourage industry adjustment, either through inducing enhancements in competitiveness or prompting resource outflows, and those that inhibit adjustment.

The second dilemma is that trade measures give blanket protection to all firms in an industry, some of which are apt to be viable and others not. By providing higher profits to the stronger domestic firms, weaker firms may be driven out of business even more rapidly, with unemployment concentrated at the firm level. This appears to have been the case in the U.S. stainless steel flatware industry. Many years of high protection coincided with sharp contraction of the number of domestic firms, and increasing domestic concentration by the two dominant domestic producers (Pearson, 1979). True, the smaller firms may have been eliminated with or without trade protection, but the point is that involuntary unemployment occurred at the firm level, even as overall employment was being maintained through protection.

Thirdly, increased protection that encourages investment may displace additional workers, as capital is substituted for labour. In that event the objective of minimizing labour adjustment costs is subverted even if the protection is successful in restoring the competitive position of the industry. Finally, temporary protection in practice may turn out to be long term, as has been the case with the textiles and clothing and shipbuilding industries in many countries. Clearly this obstructs rather than facilitates adjustment. In summary, although temporary protection can be defended on the grounds of increasing efficiency and minimizing labour adjustment costs, there are some serious difficulties in attaining these objectives.

Adjustment assistance programs are also defended on efficiency grounds, either making resources more efficient in their current activities or minimizing adjustment costs by helping resources move to other sectors. In that respect, the programs can have an objective that is similar to, not different from, protection. In both Canada and the United States, the main vehicle for making resources more efficient in their current activities are the provisions that assist firms — technical assistance, grants, loans and loan guarantees for working capital and expansion and modernization of productive facilities, and other forms of assistance. The main vehicle for reducing labour adjustment costs is worker services — training, job placement, and reimbursement for job search and relocation expenses. Canadian programs provide, in addition, portable wage subsidies, temporary employment opportunities, and early retirement benefits for displaced older workers.

But these programs, like protection, may frustrate rather than further the objectives of efficiency and minimum labour adjustment costs. Assistance to firms can increase the flow of resources to the distressed industry, blocking adjustment through attrition. And assistance to firms can lead to labour displacing investment, increasing unemployment in the industry and increasing labour adjustment costs. Finally . . . assistance payments to workers can reduce the private costs of unemployment, prolong periods of unemployment, and increase rather than decrease social adjustment costs.

Both temporary trade protection and adjustment assistance have been defended on equity grounds. Liberal trade policies are in the general interest and bring economic gains to society. For reasons of fairness, however, many would argue that there should be some mechanism whereby the relatively small group that loses from trade should not bear the full burden, but should be compensated or offered relief for their injury.

Not only do adjustment assistance programs and temporary protection share to some extent an equity justification, but, in both instances, the equity motive can be in conflict with the efficiency motive. The conflict is clear with trade measures, which in practice often lock resources into uncompetitive and inefficient industries. And, as mentioned above, adjustment assistance can, under some circumstances, impede rather than facilitate adjustment.

The two policy alternatives are not identical in assisting capital and labour, however. One important difference is that trade protection assists *all* resources in the industry, whether or not they would have become unemployed due to imports. Both strong and weak firms receive protection. Workers who would have remained employed may also benefit from higher wages than they otherwise might receive. In contrast, adjustment assistance mainly assists specific firms, communities, and/or workers affected by increased imports. In that respect, the latter policy can target assistance more finely.

Another difference is that adjustment assistance can be purposefully directed towards workers, rather than firms, whereas both firms and workers benefit from protection. Such an emphasis on assisting workers makes sense if owners of capital are able to diversify their portfolio and protect against trade-related capital loss. Workers with a substantial investment in job-specific human capital skills cannot easily diversify and insure against loss. In such cases, the equity case for assisting workers is stronger than the equity case for assisting capital owners, and the ability to direct policy towards the former group becomes important.

Adjustment assistance programs and temporary protection share a third objective. Trade policy is made in a political context in which the interests and strength of various groups are reconciled. Both temporary protection and adjustment assistance can be seen as devices for "buying" a more liberal trade policy than otherwise would be feasible. They permit more liberal trade and contribute to economic efficiency in a larger sense. To be successful, however, they must be an acceptable "payment" to important interest groups as insurance against possible subsequent injury.

The problem with such "purchases" in the Canadian political environment is that certain groups, such as the textile producers, may be in a position to co-opt the influence of other political forces in order to raise their "price." The long-standing Canadian political imperative of reducing regional economic disparities undoubtedly plays a role in the making of textile sector trade policy. The geographic concentration of the industry in economically sensitive regions in Ontario and Quebec adds considerable strength to the voices of producer interests. Hence, sizeable trade adjustment assistance programs like the $250 million Canadian Industrial Renewal Board of 1981 may be a relatively expensive trade-off for the degree of trade liberalization achieved.

The evidence for the United States suggests somewhat greater success in this regard. Liberalizing the escape clause procedures and the TAA program helped sell the 1974 trade legislation that established the U.S. negotiating mandate for the Tokyo Round. Since the special deals were made prior to the negotiations, the 1979 trade legislation implementing the Tokyo Round met no serious problems in Congress. Similarly, the International Trade Commission (ITC), in considering 42 escape clause cases between 1975 and 1979, rejected 16, and the President rejected a further 18, bringing the number of cases receiving increased trade protection down to 8. Surely the existence of the TAA programs helped the ITC and the President to resist protectionist pressure in a large number of specific situations.

Discussion of the political context of trade policy brings up the issue of the "appropriate" role of government in the economy. The use of commercial policy instruments such as tariffs and global quotas is accepted in all countries, and, while regulated, is allowed under the GATT as being within the ambit of government activity. Financial assistance or direct government financial participation may have significantly greater potential for controversy, depending on the country. For example, direct government intervention to support a major import-competing company facing financial difficulty might be politically accepted, or indeed expected, in, say, France or Canada. The same government action in the United States could easily become the focus for extended public debate. Were it a question of imposing a tariff surtax or a quota, reactions in these countries would likely be much less divergent. The perceptions of the role of government in the economy are an important influence on both the "price" that may have to be paid and the range and viability of trade policy options.

Another factor to be considered in evaluating the political effectiveness of trade adjustment assistance programs is their small "take-up," or actual usage. Neither Canadian nor U.S. programs were initially very heavily utilized following the tariff reductions of the Kennedy Round. Nevertheless, this should not be taken as an indication that they have not acted to mitigate protectionist pressures. The important aspect of these programs as far as the acceptability of trade liberalization is concerned is not the amounts paid out but rather the amounts available. Provided the announced allocation of resources to the program is a credibly large amount, they can function as a psychological safety net to firms and workers anticipating (incorrectly) injury due to import competition. Whether or not benefits, grants, or loan insurance are in the event accepted may be immaterial to their political effectiveness. On the other hand, . . . when the U.S. program was heavily utilized in 1980 and 1981, it led to a backlash, and far more restrictive legislation.

PROTECTION AND EMPLOYMENT

There are several points of an analytical nature that are deserving of emphasis in the discussion of trade adjustment assistance versus protection. Industry-specific trade measures such as tariffs and quotas are far less effective at maintaining employment than is commonly supposed. Jobs preserved in one industry by trade barriers are at the expense of jobs lost elsewhere in the economy. Moreover, while trade measures can affect the structure of employment among industries, they are less effective at preserving jobs in the protected industry than might first appear for a number of reasons.

First, it is generally not possible to expand domestic output and employment in an industry on a one-for-one basis with the reduction in imports, but only by some fraction of the reduced imports. The reason is that tariffs and quotas drive up price and reduce overall consumption of the product. Thus imports will decline by a greater amount than domestic production will increase. The more responsive domestic demand is to price increase, and the less responsive is domestic supply, the smaller will be the increase in domestic output and employment.[1]

Secondly, as mentioned above, trade protection can encourage capital deepening, or the substitution of capital for labour as the protected industry attempts to rationalize and become more productive. This is exactly the investment strategy pursued by the Canadian textile and clothing industry, the beneficiary of the country's highest level of protection (Textile and Clothing Board, 1980). A study of the U.S. textile industry also shows considerable labour-saving investment and innovation taking place behind protective trade barriers. . . . Cable (1977) makes the same point with respect to the U.K. apparel industry. This again illustrates the potential conflict between the policy objectives of enhancing productivity and maintaining employment.

Finally, if the protected domestic industry is monopolized, the response to higher prices caused by tariffs and quotas may be to continue to restrict output and capture monopoly profits. Quantitative restrictions on imports with a domestic monopoly can, at least for a large economy like the United States, actually lead to a further reduction in domestic output and employment.

Even when employment is increased in the protected industry, it is likely that an equivalent number of jobs are lost elsewhere in the economy, although they may be difficult to identify. One channel is through inter-industry linkages. Trade barriers operate to insulate domestic producers from foreign competition, enabling them to raise their prices. Any industry that uses the output of a protected industry as an input faces higher production costs as a result and is made less competitive internationally. This leads to the possibility of lay-offs in that industry (and possibly to the demand by that industry for protection).

Another channel is through induced currency changes. In a floating exchange-rate system, trade barriers that reduce imports in one sector tend to appreciate the home currency over what it would otherwise have been. This, in turn, reduces the international competitiveness of the full range of export- and import-competing sectors with consequent loss of jobs. Similarly, if the reduction in expenditure on imports decreases foreign incomes, there may be some loss of exports for the home economy. These negative effects are indirect and difficult to associate with specific jobs lost.

The inclusion of these indirect effects on employment is not an argument against protection in all cases. If temporary protection does lead to adjustment, it may be warranted. But the protection remedy can easily be abused, and the impact on employment is not limited to the protected industry. Jobs created artificially through protection in one sector affect jobs elsewhere in the economy, and these employment consequences are indirect and difficult to identify separately. Trade protection can reshuffle jobs among industries, but it is not effective at creating general employment. . . .

Notes

1. Two extremes will yield no increase in domestic employment following a tariff assuming perfect substitutes — zero domestic supply elasticity and zero foreign supply elasticity.

References

Cable, Vincent. 1977. "British Protectionism and LDC Imports." *Overseas Development Institute Review 2*, 29–48.

Canada. 1980. Textile and Clothing Board. *Textile and Clothing Inquiry*, Vol. 1. Ottawa: Ministry of Supply and Services, Canada.

Pearson, Charles. 1979. "Protection by Tariff Quota: Case Study of Stainless Steel Flatware." *Journal of World Trade Law 13* (July–August), 311–21.

7

Why Open Trade Is Better Trade

GATT Study Group

Ever since ancient times, people have found that they can increase their incomes by developing specialized skills and trading the fruits of their labour in the market-place. A farmer may know how to sew and a tailor may know how to raise chickens — but each can produce more by concentrating on doing what each can do most efficiently.

The same applies to countries. Trade allows countries to concentrate on what they can do best. No two countries are exactly alike in natural resources, climate or work force. Those differences give each country a "comparative advantage" over the others in some products. Trade translates the individual advantages of many countries into maximum productivity for all. This is the classic theory of international trade. It is still valid today.

In reality, the world is more complicated and cluttered than an economist's abstract model.

In the real world, enterprises and their workers cannot move instantly and painlessly into whatever industries are favoured by comparative advantage. Workers need time (and sometimes help) to change jobs. And, when investment and employment are depressed severely for several years, further job losses, from whatever cause, will not be tolerated.

In the real world, most prices in international trade are partly determined by the exchange rates of the currencies involved — and exchange rates can reflect factors other than the relative prices in the exporting and importing countries. For example, when the value of the U.S. dollar is bid-up by investors seeking higher interest rates or security in a turbulent world, U.S. exports become more expensive (and more difficult to sell) around the world — regardless of comparative advantage.

In the real world, no matter what the economic factors, some goods are central to a country's national security. Such goods will not be offered in open trade. Nor will a nation always seek the price advantage offered by open trade if the result may be to weaken an industry vital to security.

Finally, in the real world, developing countries may find that the only way to launch "infant industries" quickly is to shelter them temporarily from foreign competition.

Faced with these political and economic realities, governments in both

From General Agreement on Tariffs and Trade Study Group, *Trade Policies for a Better World* (Geneva: GATT, 1985), pp. 23–31. Reprinted by permission. Table omitted.

the developed countries and the developing world have frequently imposed protectionist restrictions on trade — understandably. Pure economic theory conflicted with other national objectives. But more often, these valid arguments for temporary restrictions are seized on as excuses for the wholesale protection of special-interest industries. Most protectionist measures wrap themselves in the language of job preservation or national security or infant industries but, more often than not, only as a cover for special pleading.

Restrictions on trade may be obvious and overt, like high tariffs on imports, or disguised, like voluntary export restraints. They may result from policies with a mixture of initial aims, like subsidies, procurement policies and investment restrictions. But they all damage the trading system. If we are serious about promoting open trade, we must confront these disguised restrictions as well as the more obvious ones.

Restrictions on trade often represent an immediate, easy choice for political leaders faced with hard problems. Most governments admit that open trade promotes efficient use of their country's resources, but they often have other concerns — like protecting jobs in the short run or meeting the next instalment on the foreign debt. The restriction allows the policymaker to have an answer to today's immediate crisis. "Yes," he says, "the quota will stop the foreign product from entering the country, and protect our jobs." Few people ask, or think about, whether they will be better off tomorrow.

Protectionism is an attempt to avoid the consequences of economic change. Such a course is economic folly. Change, in the form of continuous adjustment in patterns of production and employment — adjustment to new technological opportunities, to changes in consumer demands, and to shifts in international competitiveness — is essential to economic growth. Trade continuously guides workers and capital into the most productive uses, because it acts as a carrier of new technologies and other forms of innovation between countries (thereby stimulating both savings and investment).

Attempts to avert change through trade restrictions thus end up stunting an economy's growth, and produce a loss of real income. This sacrifice will increase the longer an economy is "protected" against its need to adjust to reality. The longer an adjustment is postponed, the more painful it will be when it finally occurs. For these reasons, when protectionist measures are proposed, they should be made explicit and open — so that their hidden costs can be weighed against their supposed short-term benefits. Otherwise, an economy may suffer serious and cumulative damage.

THE ILLUSION OF PROTECTIONISM: VISIBLE BENEFITS, INVISIBLE COSTS

The advocates of protectionism start with built-in advantages.

Most government policymakers and business leaders undoubtedly recognize — in principle — that whenever some people gain from a protectionist measure, others will lose. But the "benefits" of protection are easily visible; the real costs of protection are more difficult to see.

One reason is that the "benefits" of protection are concentrated, while the costs are spread invisibly among many people, scattered across the country. Those who stand to gain from a particular trade restriction — the workers and owners of a specific industry — are obviously more visible and vocal than the general body of consumers, workers, taxpayers, and shareholders in export industries, all of whom stand to lose.

Consumers lose from protection by paying higher prices for a poorer choice of goods, taxpayers lose by paying higher taxes to finance subsidies, workers lose because of lost opportunities for new jobs, and shareholders lose because their companies suffer from shrinking markets for export products.

But these losers seldom even know that they are being made to bear the costs. No one, at present, sees a full balance sheet for protectionist measures. So it is easy to find strong and vociferous advocates for protection, and rare to find equally vigorous opposition.

Even the structure of most governments encourages those who want protectionist help. Ministers of commerce, industry, or agriculture are always available to listen to the pleas of a particular industry. But few countries have a minister to whom consumers can address demands for greater freedom of choice, or one to whom taxpayers can complain about the hidden costs imposed on them by subsidies.

The powerful force of nationalism is frequently used by those who will benefit from protection to bolster their political case; governments and makers of public opinion often encourage this kind of thinking. The appeals are familiar: "Buy American," "Buy British," and, in India, "Swadeshi is Swaraj," or "Self-determination means buying domestic products." There are even appeals to regional solidarity ("Europeans buy European cars") and local loyalty ("Made here in Virginia"). It is easy to make protectionism appear patriotic — even though it actually weakens a nation over the long run.

Further, the costs and benefits of protection are generally felt at different times: the gains come early, while most of the losses are postponed. When a trade restriction is imposed, the apparent benefit to the protected industry is soon clear in the form of jobs saved or profits increased. But those benefits seldom last, and over time they weaken the prospects for employment and profits elsewhere in the economy. Unfortunately, the short-term, concentrated "benefit" is apparent; the longer-term and diffused costs in lower growth are not.

Developing countries face similar difficulty with infant industries. Vague hopes, wishful thinking, and a failure to appreciate that everything has a cost (if only in the sense of alternative opportunities sacrificed) lead to much unfruitful and expensive protection. The same mistakes are common in industrialized countries providing support to infant high-technology industries.

In most public discussion of protection, the right questions are seldom asked. What will the total costs be if trade restrictions are imposed? Is protection the most efficient way to help the industry in trouble? Will paying higher consumer prices protect jobs for more than just the short run? What will be the effects on inflation? On long-term economic growth?

It would represent a real advance, both nationally and internationally, if techniques could be developed to improve the evaluation of demands for support through protection: not just in the choice between one claim and another, but in deciding, for instance, what kind of support should be given, how much of it, and for how long. . . .

The final invisible cost of protectionism is political. Open and expanding trade tends to ease friction between countries and help international cooperation in other fields. It provides an economic incentive to maintain good relations. Attempts to restrict, regulate, and manage trade, on the other hand, inevitably make international relations more difficult. Supplanting the multilateral trading rules with discretionary actions, establishing exclusive trade agreements which discriminate against outsiders, and engaging in tit-for-tat trade conflicts increases the friction among nations.

We are concerned about the recent deterioration in goodwill among trading nations. It is important to good international relations that trade be conducted in ways that all participants see as fair and mutually rewarding.

DO THE ARGUMENTS FOR PROTECTION HOLD UP?

Doesn't Protection Save Jobs?

The belief that imports create unemployment is widespread.

With unemployment in the industrialized world at its highest levels since World War II, the fear of losing more jobs to foreign competition is strong. In almost all developing countries, unemployment is endemic, and jobs in the modern sector of the economy are few and jealously guarded against competition from imports.

But the belief that protectionism can preserve jobs is mistaken. The need for more open trade is not a question of balancing an abstract notion of economic efficiency against the real prospects of unemployment with all its waste and misery. Trade helps create jobs.

Protectionist pressures are strongest, and public sympathy for them greatest, when there is imminent danger that factories will close and jobs will be lost. No society can be indifferent to large-scale and concentrated unemployment — democratic societies least of all. In the short run, to be sure, protection can help keep employment in particularly favoured industries higher than it would otherwise be. But that does not mean that protectionist measures in favour of one or several industries can increase the total number of jobs in the economy; quite the contrary.

There are several reasons for this.

First, even in the "protected" industries themselves, the number of jobs is likely to shrink. In industries where labour-saving machinery is available, protectionist measures award companies windfall profits which can be invested in automation — thus accelerating the substitution of machines for people. This has been a common experience in the textile industry of developed countries, where special protection failed to stop employment in the industry from falling by one-third during the years 1973–1982.

This kind of investment diverts capital away from its most efficient use, including creating new enterprises that could be viable without protection.

Experience in the steel industry has been similar. And because steel is such an important component in the manufacture of many other products, protecting the steel industry has also led to a loss of competitiveness — and jobs — in steel-using industries such as automobiles.

Second, any jobs which are "saved" from the competition of imports are preserved only at the expense of jobs lost in the same country's export sector. Quite simply, if your country buys less of a foreigner's products, he will have less money to spend on your products.

Third, protection damages export industries in less obvious ways. When given to individual industries it tends to push up the costs of the others — by raising prices, particularly for labour, and by directing capital away from them. And in a world of flexible exchange rates, import restrictions tend to push up the price of a country's currency, further hurting exports.

Fourth, protection prevents the creation of the further new jobs that spending by higher-paid export workers would bring into existence in industries and services not related to trade.

It is true that the import-competing sector is generally made up of labour-intensive, low-wage industries. Workers in these industries who lose their jobs because of import competition cannot count on easily finding jobs in the export sector. But the answer to this dilemma is not trade restriction; it is energetic policies to help workers adjust. The way to maximize job opportunities is to help workers take advantage of change. In the short run, that means retraining; in the long run, and even more important, it means a commitment to make high quality education available to all. The workers of tomorrow's advanced industries will have to be perpetual students, technologically adept and intellectually flexible, if they are to take full advantage of the changes which will drive economic growth.

Doesn't Cheap Foreign Labour Justify Protectionism?

Advocates of protectionism often portray "cheap" labour or "low wages" as a kind of infection against which domestic wage levels must be defended. To argue this way is to deny the poor almost the only competitive advantage they possess, and to prevent them from expanding their capacity to buy goods from others. Besides, the facility to import products from countries where labour is more abundant releases labour in the importing countries for more productive purposes.

— and What About Slave or Prison Labour?

Of course, there is no disagreement that countries do not have to accept the products of slave or prison labour. A specific GATT rule allows countries to prohibit imports of such products.

Don't Farmers Need Protection?

Protection for agriculture is defended with an assortment of age-old arguments, including the need to maintain essential elements in the national economy, and to preserve the small farmers' way of life. Yet as an element in the economy, and as a way of life, in many richer countries agriculture is essentially now just another kind of industry, and often a rather prosperous one. We accept that the pace of adjustment may have to be slower in agriculture than in industry, and we recognize that the emotional basis for protecting it remains strong. But we do not believe that agriculture deserves to be a sacred cow of policy. And at the very least, the general public ought to be permitted a clear view of the costs of protecting agriculture.

What About National Security?

When it comes to defence industries, definitions can be surprisingly broad. Farmers claim national security as grounds for protection. Sweden's footwear producers argue that the Swedish army cannot be assured of boots unless a viable domestic industry is kept alive. Similar claims are put forward worldwide in favour of failing steel and textiles companies, uncompetitive manufacturers of aircraft and machinery, and a host of other producers who dislike competition. Such arguments cannot be completely dismissed; in an unstable world some goods that truly relate to national security will and should be protected. But even if some of these claims are valid, they should always be examined carefully. They are the thin end of a protectionist wedge, capable of imposing heavy burdens on the economy and of causing great damage to trade.

Can't Protectionism Help Stabilize Exchange Rates?

Claims for protection are being put forward today because of the fluctuation of currencies in the post-Bretton Woods régime of floating exchange rates. The rise in the value of the U.S. dollar has demonstrated how strong inflows of external capital can drive up the exchange rate of a currency, sucking in imports, discouraging exports, and harming otherwise competitive industries.

This clearly goes far to explain the present upsurge in calls for protection of U.S. industries against imports. Trade policy, however, can provide no effective answer to these difficulties. In fact, any reduction in imports that protection may cause will make the existing imbalance between supply and demand for a currency still greater, pushing its exchange value even higher.

The real causes of the problem lie elsewhere. Recent experience strongly suggests that abnormal fluctuations in exchange rates are mainly the result of the sensitivity of international flows of capital to differences in interest rates, expectations about future rates of inflation or the desire to find a safe haven for funds. When domestic interest rates are high, pushing up the exchange rate, they are generally the result of large fiscal deficits and unanticipated restraints on the money supply. If exchange rates appear overvalued from the viewpoint of importers and exporters, tighter fiscal policies and a more predictable monetary policy are needed. Trade policy has no remedy to offer.

Can't Protectionism Protect Us from the Difficulties of Change?

An odd twist to the protectionist argument, briefly popular in some advanced industrialized countries, suggests that so much economic progress has been achieved that people now want stability more than anything else. A few advocates of protectionism actually assert that some loss of efficiency or even growth can be accepted because high living standards are now a reality, and because people prefer to maintain their current jobs and surroundings rather than be exposed to further change. Such prophecies about the saturation of wants have often been made and equally often been proved wrong: they were proved wrong again during the past decade of recession.

Another version of this "stability" argument for protection suggests that an open trade policy requires such frequent and far-reaching adjustments that most democratic countries find them politically impossible to undertake.

From the point of view of trade policy, the "stability" arguments ignore both the two-sided nature of trade (if you deny markets, you also lose them) and the fact that the greatest pressure for change comes from domestic advances in technology.

In a world that is changing as rapidly as ours, no society can stand still. Trends in technological, social, and economic change cannot be held back by restrictions on trade. The countries with the fastest-growing economies today are generally those which have performed best in trade — and those have been the countries most ready to adjust to market opportunities and changed conditions. The impressively rapid growth of a number of developing countries in Asia is the best example.

The choice is not between changing or standing still; it is between embracing change or postponing it. A country which attempts to avoid the effects of change simply ensures that the strains will be more disruptive when they eventually occur. A country whose policies encourage open trade and rapid adjustment can take advantage of the continuing transformation of the world economy to maximize economic growth.

The concrete challenge before government policy-makers is to reverse the tide of protectionism and make more open trade possible, through both national and international actions. . . .

III

Responding to Trade-Distorting Policies of Other Countries

The protectionism analyzed in Part II is based on national and sectoral economic and social concerns about permitting the unconstrained operation of the free-market forces of changing comparative advantage. However, a new set of reasons for the government to intervene in international markets for goods and services has become much more important in recent years, namely, to counter both the monopolistic actions of foreign traders and the trade-distorting measures of foreign governments.

The reading by Gene M. Grossman and J. David Richardson surveys the literature that has recently developed on this subject. As they point out, when international markets are organized competitively, there are few grounds for trade policy intervention to raise a country's real income. But such is not the case in imperfectly competitive environments where there are excess profits. For example, if a country purchases all of the quantity of a good it consumes from a foreign monopolist, it can capture part of the monopolist's supernormal profits by imposing a tariff on the imports of the good.

A more important case is the situation where a single home firm and single foreign firm compete in a third-country export market. An equilibrium will be reached when each firm has no profit incentive to change the quantity it exports, given the quantity of exports of the other firm. While a different quantity of the home firm's exports would yield the firm a higher profit, the foreign firm does not believe the home firm would continue to export that different quantity once the foreign firm responded in a manner which was optimal from its viewpoint. Thus, the foreign firm would not in fact accede to exporting the quantities that would enable the home firm to obtain higher profits. If, however, the government of the home country precommits itself to provide a certain export subsidy to the home firm regardless of what either firm does, the foreign firm may change its view about how the home firm would respond and believe that the home firm's most profitable response with the government export subsidy will in fact be a quantity that yields the home firm and country a higher income level than in the absence of the government subsidy. The equilibrium then will shift to this new distribution of export quantities by the two firms.

Not only is strategic interplay among firms likely in imperfect markets but strategic trade policy actions among governments are quite possible. One familiar example that Grossman and Richardson discuss is a sequence of tariff retaliations between two governments. As they point out, at the equilibrium level of tariffs, where it is not in the interest of either government to change its tariff, one country may be better off than under free trade or both countries could be worse off. In the latter case, each government would agree to free trade only if some forum such as the GATT exists that would ensure that the other would not cheat by starting a trade war again.

The authors note that the analysis of strategic trade policy environments is relatively new, with many unresolved theoretical issues and a lack of good knowledge about how important this type of behavior is or will become in the real world.

The paper by Judith L. Goldstein and Stephen D. Krasner illustrates the type of strategic behavior that many individuals in the trade policy community are advocating. Specifically, they argue that the United States should adopt a tit-for-tat strategy when other countries defect from accepted GATT rules and norms. Under the tit-for-tat strategy the United States would follow GATT rules until other countries failed to do so and then adopt the same practices as the countries who break the international rules of "good" behavior. If these countries again began to follow these rules, the United States would then also do so. The authors maintain that the United States can best ensure international compliance with GATT rules and thus the maintenance of a liberal trading regime by responding in kind to foreign practices. In their view there are, however, some government trade-related policies on which there is no international agreement as to what is good behavior and consequently which are not likely to be abandoned by foreign governments if a tit-for-tat strategy is followed. In these circumstances, they argue, this country should either accept these deviations from our concept of fairness or adopt similar policies ourselves.

A comprehensive industrial policy such as the Japanese have followed is often advocated as a response to foreign trade-distorting policies. Richard N. Cooper explains the nature of Japanese industrial policy since the end of World War II and also details U.S. government policies affecting our trade. He then appraises various possible policy directions the United States might pursue, given the widespread use of industrial policies by other countries. The United States, for example, could try to get other governments to eliminate their subsidies, attempt to harmonize the extent of subsidizing policies among countries, or seek international agreement that extensive consultation must precede any major change in government industrial policies and that such changes be introduced gradually. Retaliation may be appropriate in cases where the action has a reasonable chance of inducing a behavior change beneficial to this country, but Cooper believes that general retaliatory rules are not likely to be helpful. Above all, he urges, the United States should choose measures that are best suited for *this* country rather than simply adopt measures that seem to have worked well abroad.

8

Strategic Trade Policy: A Survey of Issues and Early Analysis

Gene M. Grossman and J. David Richardson

[1] INTRODUCTION

A well-defined literature has developed recently on the conduct of trade policy in strategic environments. This paper surveys the research reported there and discusses its implications. Strategic environments are those in which a relatively small number of economic agents make interdependent decisions. Strategic environments contrast with the more familiar perfectly competitive environment in which a large number of agents make independent decisions because each agent considers itself too small to influence market outcomes. Until recently, most research on trade policy dealt with the perfectly competitive environment. Governments were deemed to act in the belief that their policies affect market equilibrium, but without regard for the effects of their actions on the behavior of other governments. When agents take the actions of their rivals to be immutable, strategic behavior plays no role.

It is increasingly important to analyze trade policy in the context of strategic environments, because circumstances do not fit the orthodox paradigm. Firms have grown multinationally over the past few decades. The development of

From G. M. Grossman and J. D. Richardson, *Strategic Trade Policy: A Survey of Issues and Early Analysis,* Special Papers in International Economics No. 15, April 1985, pp. 1–2, 7–8. Copyright © 1985. Reprinted by permission of the International Finance Section of Princeton University; and from G. M. Grossman and J. D. Richardson, *Strategic Trade Policy: A Survey of Issues and Early Analysis,* National Bureau of Economic Research Progress Report (Cambridge, Mass.: NBER, 1984), pp. 10–35. Some footnotes and references omitted.

the European Community, of co-production and joint ventures, and of ambitious national development plans has encouraged firms to assume a global identity. In some national markets, a few firms compete for a "prize" that is essentially control of the whole nation's industry. In such oligopolistic environments, firms clearly recognize the effect that their actions have on the behavior of other firms, and each firm must conjecture about its rivals' reactions to its decisions. These same features cause governments to play strategic "games" among themselves. Their choices regarding trade policy influence global market decisions and may induce either retaliation or cooperation by rival governments.

Strategic economic conflict over markets and policy can involve threats and promises, bluffs and commitments. These are familiar features of games and war, and make for rich and complex analyses. None of them has any place in competitive environments. Their object is always to influence the outcome of a conflict in one's own favor. This may imply that the outcome will become more unfavorable for one's opponents — but not necessarily. In some cases, if participants are competing for shares of a pie of roughly fixed size, trade policy is bound to be contentious. In other cases, strategic behavior may dictate cooperation that can lead to mutual benefit. In all cases, however, the standard tenets of the orthodox theory of trade policy may fail to apply. Or, if they apply, it may be for new reasons.

Strategic trade policy is topical in the United States because of the perception that governments abroad are taking unfair advantage of the U.S. commitment to open trade and of their countries' relatively small size. This perception underlies support for a new and aggressive "reciprocity" requirement in U.S. trade policy. It is also topical because strategic moves by foreign firms, often with the support of their governments, seem to some observers to be placing U.S. firms under unprecedented pressures. These pressures lie behind many of the recent demands for a U.S. industrial policy. Strategic trade policy is controversial, too. Critics of recent initiatives and proposals wonder whether strategies designed to deter foreign governments will end in mutually destructive trade wars, and whether industrial targeting may merely stimulate unproductive rent-seeking by special-interest groups. They wonder further whether the conduct of trade policy along strategic lines will require a case-by-case approach that the U.S. government may be ill-equipped to carry out.

This paper aims to survey only "early" analysis of these matters, because that is all there is. The strategic approach to trade policy is a new, or — perhaps more accurately — reborn, area.[1] Much more research must be undertaken. Some of it will no doubt develop thoughtful counterarguments to those favoring strategic trade policy. Much of it should be empirical and historical. . . .

[2] TRADE POLICY IN IMPERFECTLY COMPETITIVE MARKET ENVIRONMENTS

When the behavior of foreign nations, firms, and individuals is sufficiently competitive, there are only weak arguments for trade-policy intervention. In the absence of market distortions, market-determined trade wastes fewest resources;

in the presence of market distortions, correctives other than trade policy waste fewest resources. But that may not be the case in imperfectly competitive settings, where trade policy can alter the entire economic environment in which firms make their strategic decisions.

The economics of trade policy in an imperfectly competitive environment is scarcely developed by comparison with its exhaustive development in a competitive environment. Such policy is almost certainly more complex than competitive policy. One reason is that the characterization "imperfectly competitive" can take on many different meanings. The specific trade-policy implications may depend on whether static or dynamic scale economies are important, on whether competition in research and development (R&D) plays a major role in industry development, on the ways in which advertising and promotional activities affect the type of competition, on whether competing firms regard quality or product characteristics as strategic variables, and so on. The literature has only just begun to explore the trade-policy implications of these many forms of competition.

Supernormal Profits

A common feature of imperfectly competitive environments is the existence of supernormal profits (sometimes described as "pure" or "economic" profits, or, pejoratively, as "excess" profits). These are profits larger than the minimal amounts necessary to provide an incentive for entrepreneurial activity. The source of supernormal profits is often market power, which may be identified with the existence of significant barriers to entry or may arise in an R&D-intensive environment from the application of patent-protection laws.[2] Supernormal profits may be ongoing or transitory and in either case have important implications for trade policy.

In a series of papers, Brander and Spencer (Brander and Spencer, 1984a, 1984b, and Spencer and Brander, 1983) have pioneered a line of research that investigates the conditions under which "our" country can use trade policy to capture (or preserve) a larger share of these supernormal profits. They consider an oligopolistic global industry with a fixed number of firms and assume that, at least temporarily, barriers to entry prevent economic profits from being driven to zero. Other things being the same, we would prefer that "our" producers had a larger share of the total industry profit pool than "theirs." That preference seems compelling whether such a pool is ongoing or transitory (because new entrants could eventually compete it away). And it seems compelling whether we are consciously aggressive (out to maximize our share of the spoils from oligopoly, much as we might maximize our share of the gains from trade by setting an optimal tariff) or conservatively and honorably defensive (out to prevent our oligopolistic trading partners from maximizing *their* share at our expense).

The basic Brander-Spencer point is very simple. If oligopolistic profit is inevitable, then trade patterns that give "us" greater access to it are economically superior to other trade patterns, given everything else. Policy would seem at first blush to have no place here, and especially not trade policy. "Our" private oligopolists would seem to have exactly the same goals as outlined above and to be perfectly capable of taking care of themselves if they are given the market freedom to do what comes naturally to oligopolists. The Brander-Spencer contribution is to show that this intuition is misleading in some cases. Depending on the nature of the strategic competition among firms, policy may have a role. Depending on the degree of segmentation among national markets, even trade policy may be appropriate.

In the simplest setting they consider, Brander and Spencer examine a duopoly consisting of one home firm and one foreign firm, with competition taking place only in a third-country market. If domestic consumption is zero, the only effect the third market has on national economic welfare is as a source of "producer surplus" — the difference between export revenue and the opportunity cost of resources devoted to production. When factor prices accurately reflect opportunity cost in the home and foreign economies, producer surplus is nothing other than the profit of the exporting firm.

When the two firms compete in the absence of policy intervention, each firm can be deemed to calculate a range for quantity sold by its foreign competitor. For each conceivable foreign quantity sold, the home firm can calculate its optimal response on the assumption that foreign sales remain constant. We can depict this behavior graphically. . . . The home firm's "best response" function is RR in Figure 1. It slopes downward because the more the foreign firm offers for sale in the third-country market, the lower will be the market price for any quantity sold by the home firm, and therefore the less the home firm will wish to offer. Similarly, R*R* illustrates the best response of the foreign firm to any home firm quantity, when the foreign firm takes home sales as given. The intersection E is a market equilibrium in the sense that each firm's strategy (its export quantity choice) is optimal given what the other firm has chosen to do.

Now the home firm would in fact earn higher profits at a point like P than it does at E. At P, it has a larger market share, whereas the total market quantity (and therefore market price) is roughly the same as it is in the actual equilibrium. So the home firm might threaten to produce an amount Q_1 "no matter what," in which case the optimal foreign response would appear to be Q_1^*. However such a threat is not "credible." The foreign firm knows that the home firm would not actually want to carry out its threat, if it, the foreign firm, were to go ahead with its plans to offer Q_0^*.

Policy Precommitments

In an equilibrium without policy, information that every oligopolist has about others deprives each of any credible new threat. The information is that each oligopolist has chosen optimally in light of the underlying environment. This information removes any incentive for further alteration in oligopolistic instruments. Price, quantity, quality, investment, R and D, and so on are already at their optimal values when there is genuine equilibrium.[3]

Credible policy, however, may be able to change the underlying environ-

FIGURE 1

Equilibrium and Optimal Response Curves in a Two-Firm Market, Given Competitor Sales

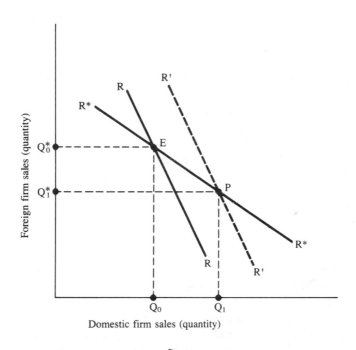

ment and shift the equilibrium. Suppose that the home government acts first, and announces a subsidy for exports. Suppose further that the policy declaration is taken to be credible, in the sense that foreign competitors take the subsidies into account as "precommitments" — inhospitable aspects of the competitive environment. In this case, the curve RR is no longer the optimal response function for the home firm under an export subsidy policy. Instead, the home firm should want to supply more at every level of foreign output than it would without the subsidy. The export subsidy would thus shift the home firm's response function to R'R', and the new oligopolistic equilibrium would be indeed at P, with a permanently higher share of the industry's pool of supernormal profits accruing to the home firm.

The key question in this example is what the government can do for its firm that the firm cannot do for itself. Intuition suggests that firms themselves can undertake such strategic "first strikes" or precommitments. . . . But in equilibrium all such actions that are in the firm's interest have already been taken, and threats of further thrusts by some firms are dismissed by other firms as mere bluffs.

The government, by contrast, may have the potential to threaten and credibly precommit even after the firms attain oligopolistic equilibrium, shifting the equilibrium to obtain a nationally desirable distribution of profits. Therein lies the key asymmetry between governments and firms in Brander's and Spencer's conception.

There are of course conditioning factors. Dubious or inscrutable policies have no influence — influence stems from both credibility and public transparency. Recurrent policy may also lose strategic effectiveness. It may become so regularized that it too can be described by a stable behavioral relation.[4] Then firms may be able to predict policy accurately, treat government as another "player" in the competitive game,[5] and dismiss any discretionary policy divergence from regular rules-based patterns as incredible.

Brander and Spencer generate an *example* of how trade policy *can* improve national welfare. Eaton and Grossman (1983) extend this analysis to consider a wider range of potential behavior by oligopolistic market participants. Their aim is to determine whether there is any presumption toward trade intervention, and what its optimal form might be. They first study alternative specifications of the firms' decision-making process. One such specification, used above, is that each firm chooses its optimal export quantity on the assumption that the opponent firm would not respond by further altering its own quantity choice. In other words, each firm conjectures a zero response from its opponent to its own optimal choice. More general behaviors allow nonzero conjectures about opponent behaviors. Each nonzero conjecture generates a different "best-response function," and consequently different equilibria. The Brander-Spencer analysis deals with the special case where conjectured responses are zero.

Eaton and Grossman first show how Brander's and Spencer's conclusion holds for a broad set of alternative conjectures. An export subsidy will raise national economic welfare whenever the home firm conjectures a more aggressive foreign response to its action than the foreign firm actually undertakes.[6] [They] then show that the opposite is true when the home firm holds conjectures that underestimate the true aggressiveness of its rival's response. In that case an export *tax* is optimal.[7] Finally, if the conjectures that the home firm entertains are "consistent" in the sense that its belief about the foreign firm's response to its own initiatives is exactly how the foreign firm responds (when, for example, a subsidy policy causes the home firm to alter its decisions), then free trade is an optimal policy.

Eaton's and Grossman's work demonstrates that there is no guarantee that any specific trade policy, such as an export subsidy, will shift supernormal profits toward one's "own" competitors in oligopolistic markets. In fact, when expected responses by rival competitors are not systematically biased toward optimism or pessimism, then export subsidies (or any other given policy) shift profits away from the nation about as often and as much as they draw them in. Thus the case for active trade policy in an imperfectly competitive environment rests crucially on the behavior of oligopolistic firms. One might even say it rests "uneasily" since the behavior in question has to do with intrinsically subjective conjectures. It is worth recalling from the earlier discussion that the case also rests on firms' perception that government is not a wholly predictable market participant itself, and that when it acts, its actions are credible. . . .

Extensions: More Than Two Firms, Consumption Effects, Several Oligopolies

Other extensions of the Brander-Spencer analysis provide additional insights into the potential rules for trade policy in imperfectly competitive trading environments. Dixit (1984) . . . [studies] oligopolies with more than two firms. [He] shows in the framework that underlies Figure 1 (the so-called "Cournot model") that the efficacy of an export subsidy continues to apply so long as the number of home firms is not "too large." . . . There are two potential motives for export policy in these regimes. The profit-shifting motive for policy intervention remains present when there are more domestic firms than one, as long as firms conjecture an aggressive rival response. Against this is the more familiar "externality" motive for an export *tax*, which says that home firms do not take into account the effect of their actions on the profits of other home firms, and therefore produce too much relative to what would be called for by a coordinated or collusive production plan. Since the government aims at increasing total national welfare, and hence the *sum* of profits from exports to third-country markets, it will wish to move the equilibrium toward the collusive outcome. This can be done with an export tax. The larger is the number of domestic firms the greater will be the "externality effect," and the larger the tax necessary to offset it. Thus, the profit-shifting motive for a subsidy . . . will be outweighed by the externality motive for a tax when the number of firms is large. . . .

Two additional motives for intervention are present when domestic consumption takes place. First, the government may be able to shift some of the profits earned by foreign oligopolists at the expense of home consumers into the domestic treasury in the form of tariff revenue. Second, the existence of supernormal industry profits implies a wedge between consumer valuation and the resource cost of producing an extra unit. The value of home consumption exceeds the value of the resources that would be needed to produce it. Eaton and Grossman (1983) discuss trade policy as a second-best substitute for antitrust policy in this case, but show that optimal intervention for this purpose can involve either taxing or subsidizing trade.

All of the work discussed thus far rests on a convenient but restrictive conception of general equilibrium. Attention is focused on one imperfectly competitive industry, and it is assumed that expansion in this industry can be achieved by drawing resources from perfectly competitive industries elsewhere in the economy. This approach begs the central question of industrial targeting — namely, *which* sector(s) merits government support among the many that might satisfy the Brander-Spencer criteria. Dixit and Grossman (1984) have recently studied this question in a less restrictive general-equilibrium structure. They conceive of an economy with one large competitive sector and many small oligopolistic industries comprising an imperfectly competitive "high-technology sector."

Dixit and Grossman assume that all the industries in the high technology sector draw on a common scarce resource that they call "scientists." To highlight their argument they assume initially that scientific effort is in fixed supply in the short run, and that this factor is required in fixed proportion to output in each of the oligopolistic industries. They assume the "Cournot behavior" of Figure 1 to generate a profit-shifting motive for subsidies. But they note that in this structure a subsidy to one industry will cause the salary of scientists to rise, as more are needed for expansion there, and that this change in factor prices acts as an implicit *tax* on all the other domestic oligopolists. In a symmetric situation where each industry is a duopoly with one domestic and one foreign firm, and where all domestic firms are similar with respect to demand and cost conditions, the optimal policy is free trade. The profit-shifting gains from targeting any one industry are dissipated by the profit-shifting losses of other industries in the high technology sector. When industries are not symmetric, then government could sensibly seek to target those industries in which the amount of profit-shifting (that is, the induced change in the foreign firm's behavior per unit of scientific labor expended) is highest. There is also somewhat more scope for successful industry promotion when the supply of scientists can respond to its rate of return, or when other factors can be substituted for scientists in the production of high-technology goods. Nevertheless, Dixit and Grossman conclude that the potential benefits from strategic trade policy are exaggerated when the analyst considers only a single imperfectly competitive industry against a backdrop of an otherwise perfectly competitive economy.

Other Distortions and Economies of Scale with Imperfect Competition

Imperfectly competitive environments thus far have been identified principally by the existence of supernormal profits. Such supernormal profits are often associated with positions of "natural monopoly" or market power due to economies of scale. When markets are also imperfect — perhaps even "missing," due to informational deficiencies and/or aversion to risk — then policy may have at least a potential for ameliorating these other market distortions.

Krugman (1982) has described the effects of trade policy in competitive environments made imperfect by static and dynamic scale economies. Whether or not trade policy is a sensible policy in such environments was not addressed by Krugman. Some discussion of the issue is possible below, however, by considering further imperfections in competitive markets for insurance and finance.

Krugman considers several alternative sources of scale economies. Cost curves may decline as output increases. Cost curves may be flat but nevertheless shift down when larger outputs justify larger productive R&D spending. Or cost curves may be flat, yet shift down when larger historical output imparts improved productivity through learning-by-doing. Krugman's conclusions are the same irrespective of the source of scale economies. His chief conclusion is that protection of domestic markets and promotion of export markets can reduce per unit costs, thereby saving resources. Cost and resource savings improve the international competitive position of "our" producers in *all* markets, not only those protected or promoted. The potential national-welfare gains from improved competitiveness are the same as in the discussion above — a larger share of global oligopolistic profit. But the mechanism for achieving these gains is different. In Krugman's work trade policy is directly a demand-side policy, but ultimately a supply-side policy. The size of markets facing our producers directly influences the productivity of their resources and effort.

Stable equilibria in each national market would imply ongoing oligopolistic equilibrium there. Yet Krugman's equilibria need not be stable. When they are not, a small policy change can be predatory. One firm may succeed in driving others out of the market, thus establishing a monopoly.

The existence of scale economies and learning-by-doing provides only a potential for policy in all these circumstances, not a case for it. The scale economies described by Krugman are internal to the firm, so its incentive to exploit them corresponds perfectly with the government's objective to have it do so. When information is reasonably complete, and when insurance and financial capital markets work reasonably well, then markets will have no scope for policy. The financial market will correctly identify the firm with the most productive prospects in each market and underwrite its ventures to the exclusion of its competitors. The insurance market will underwrite any risk. The most competitive firm will become a "natural monopolist" in the designated market. Markets will have made sure that all scale economies are captured, leaving none for trade policy to seize.[8]

However, when private information is imperfect, or when risks are very large, or when certain externalities are present, then policy potential may be restored. This observation is trivially true, of course, whether scale economies are present or not. Scale economies can increase the practical relevance of these causes of market failure, however, by creating multiple market equilibria. . . . Some of the many equilibria are preferable to others from the perspective of national economic welfare. But the economy may be stuck at an inferior equilibrium if lenders and insurers are unable or unwilling to accept the risk involved in underwriting a dramatic change in resource allocation, even when the expected reward is quite high. Good information about the immediate neighborhood of a (stable) equilibrium helps keep the economy there; poorer information about more distant neighborhoods and equilibria is heavily discounted by risk aversion and institutional limits to the size of down-side loss that any firm can accept. Of course once again these observations establish only a potential case for policy. And it is a potential that rests on the assumption of superior government information and risk management. When markets do badly, governments may do worse.

Policy Alternatives

Voluntary export restraints. The foregoing discussion has taken taxes and subsidies to be the instruments of trade intervention. Krishna (1983), building on prior analyses of trade policy under monopoly . . ., has shown how taxes and quantitative restrictions are not equivalent when markets are imperfectly competitive. In a model like Brander's and Spencer's with domestic consumption, Krishna demonstrates that voluntary export restraints (VERs) act as "facilitating" devices for greater implicit collusion between the duopoly firms (at the expense of consumers in the importing country). The way in which they do so is best understood in the light of our earlier discussion. Each firm would like to cut back its sales toward the monopoly level, if its rival were also willing to respond accordingly. The firms would certainly restrict output if they could behave collusively, and move to a cooperative equilibrium. But in the absence of coordinated action any promise by one to refrain from aggressive marketing behavior is not credible. A VER can make this promise credible. The exporting firm is bound by policy not to expand its export sales beyond the agreed-upon limit. Then the firm in the importing country can raise its price, knowing that its rival will not be able to expand market share. The result is that VERs can raise the profit levels of *both* firms in a duopoly at the expense of consumers in the importing country. Tariffs do not generally have this property.

Domestic policies. Trade policies are of course not the only tools available for governments to alter equilibrium in imperfectly competitive environments. Other instruments might be superior to trade intervention, whether the aim is to compensate for market failures implicit in imperfect competition or to shift profits when this objective is achievable.

The argument for trade policy is strongest when national markets are not well integrated. Then trade policy, and especially discriminatory trade policy, allows governments to treat each market competition separately, and devise intervention that is appropriate for the state of the oligopolistic competition there. On the other hand, when transport costs are low and arbitrage opportunities are easily exploited, it may be best to conceive of the oligopolistic competition between "our" firms and "theirs" as one integrated conflict. Trade policy may remain an attractive instrument since the objective of national welfare implies concern for home but not foreign consumers. Yet a nondiscriminatory trade policy that ignores source and destination is more likely to be indicated in this case.

Spencer and Brander (1983) have noted that other policies besides trade policy may have a natural place in industrial stages that precede international competition for sales. Policy may aid in a first-stage thrust to install capacity, promote products, or reduce production costs through R and D.[9] Strategic development of first-stage precommitments can then alter the nature of the output-stage competition. A national government may wish to shift the "best response functions" in the first stage to yield an outcome at a later stage that is more favorable to home participants. This objective, which is similar in its justification to that for policy precommitments at the output stage, suggests a potential motive for such policies as investment tax credits, R and D subsidies, and research joint ventures.[10]

Antitrust policies. Dixit (1984) and Ordover-Willig (1983) have noted the close interdependence between trade and antitrust policy when market environments are imperfectly competitive. When domestic firms earn supernormal profits at the expense of foreign consumers, antitrust policy aimed at preserving competition at home generates a by-product welfare cost due to foregone market power in international markets. Dixit and Ordover-Willig find that allowing a merger of two home firms in an oligopolistic industry confers a welfare gain that outweighs consumer losses provided that the share of imports in home consumption is small. If the home and foreign markets can be separated with respect to antitrust policy, as, for example, might be accomplished by establishment of "export trading companies" or cartels, then the welfare effect of allowing domestic firms to exploit their monopoly power abroad is unambiguously positive. Of course, such policy is clearly predatory, and begins to resemble monopoly tariffs, which forces the issue of foreign retaliation that we examine below.

Summary: Distortions and Precommitments Under Imperfect Competition

To summarize, the arguments for policy intervention discussed in this section are of two sorts. The more familiar type emerges from consideration of the market distortions that are frequently encountered in imperfectly competitive environments. Trade policy analysts are familiar and in principle accepting of this second-best motive for policy intervention, which has its direct analog in the perfectly competitive environment.

What is novel here is the argument for policy intervention as "preemption" or "precommitment," an argument that suggests that government become a facilitator in the global competition for supernormal profits. This section has demonstrated that such policy may or may not be justified, depending upon the credibility of governments and the expectational behavior of firms.

There are many reasons for care in applying these conclusions. For example, a key requirement for all the strategic trade policies discussed above is that "our" firms and projects be distinguishable from "theirs." Many real firms are transnationally owned, and many real projects are joint ventures by firms with different nationalities. Trade policies that redistribute profits toward some favored project or toward some favored firm will fail to aid "us" significantly unless our residents have disproportionate stakes and shares in the favored projects and firm. Global integration of capital markets seems to be moving the world closer to an extreme in which profit-earners worldwide hold comparable portfolios of investments. In this extreme, national trade policies would be completely ineffective for capturing or preserving supernormal profits for "us."

Another observation is that all the strategic trade policies discussed above redistribute income from foreign firms, and from consumers worldwide, to large national corporations. Even if this redistribution yields an increase in overall national welfare it might nonetheless be opposed on income distributional grounds. The oft-noted tension between efficiency and equity objectives of trade policy becomes all the more dramatic when the beneficiaries of policy are those firms already earning supernormal profits.

One might argue on the contrary that global supernormal profits should be taken as a given. Nations compete over their international distribution. The larger the share that "our" policy can claim for "us," the larger is "our" national purchasing power and economic welfare. The division of the gains among "us" can be settled separately. Furthermore, given the imperfectly competitive global market structure, no nation need lose absolutely from "us" claiming a larger share of its rents. Other nations lose only the opportunity to enjoy a larger windfall share for themselves. And the defensive version of the counter-argument is even less objectionable. We would not sensibly choose as a nation to encourage foreign oligopolists, possibly with the assistance of their governments, to collect supernormal profits at our expense.

These arguments notwithstanding, trade policy can itself be used to influence the market structure, as measured by how many firms participate in an imperfectly competitive industry and which of them will be domestic firms. For example, protection of a domestic market may provide the incentive for a domestic firm to undertake entry. Export subsidies can have the same effect.[11] Furthermore, a country with an incumbent in an industry might close off its home market to foreign firms in order to *deter* entry that would threaten its own oligopolists. Or the same government might threaten retaliation if a foreign government attempted to promote entry by subsidies.

Dixit and Kyle (1984) have studied the use of trade policy as a means for entry promotion and entry deterrence. They find in a simple framework that a country gains from protectionist entry-promotion whenever entry would occur with such a policy but not without it. Such protection for entry promotion is, however, generally harmful to world economic welfare, and countermeasures by other governments that discourage these policies are beneficial. In contrast, subsidies as instruments of entry promotion may be desirable from a world perspective, and countermeasures against them, when successful, are harmful to world welfare.

Many practical and conceptual objections temper the conclusions outlined in Section [2]. One might question the information requirements for implementing sensible preemptive policy. As always, there is also the risk that self-serving, rent-seeking, special interest groups will use these conclusions for exploitative purposes. More conceptual reasons for caution are discussed in Section [4].

[3] RESPONSE AND COUNTER-RESPONSE IN A STRATEGIC TRADE-POLICY ENVIRONMENT

Trade policy analysts frequently assume that trade policy abroad, like technology and consumer preferences, is a predetermined given. "Our" optimal policy is calculated taking "their" policy as an "exogenous" parameter. It is not surprising, therefore, that most early studies of trade policy under imperfect competition have maintained this familiar assumption.

Yet recognition of strategic interplay among firms of different nationalities leads naturally to consideration of strategic interplay among governments. Even in a perfectly competitive market environment, policy can potentially be used by "us" to improve "*their*" calculation of optimal policy. That is, we may be able to choose some active policy, or menu of active policies (contingent on foreign response), that would shift "optimal" policy abroad to an outcome more desirable to us than the outcome under policy independence. In an imperfectly competitive market environment, the potential may be even stronger. Being "first" with policy precommitments may reduce the payoff to reactive foreign policies of the same sort, and may also deter firms abroad from similar attempts at market pre-emption.

The classic analysis of strategic trade policy as a reactive "game" between governments is Harry Johnson's ([1954]) study of the optimum (monopoly) tariff in the presence of retaliation. We summarize it here since recent analysis has built upon it. Johnson analyzes retaliatory tariff conflict in a perfectly competitive market environment that can be depicted in a diagram similar to Figure 1. In Figure 2, TT represents the "best response" of the home government to alternative tariff rates that the foreign government might set. If the tariff abroad is zero (and is not expected to change), then the optimal home response is to set the familiar optimal tariff (OT). This tariff best exploits the home nation's market power in world markets (power that competitive firms cannot capture). If, instead, the tariff abroad is at some positive level, then it is optimal for the home government to choose a lower tariff, since the foreign tariff diminishes demand for U.S. goods, and fewer national monopoly rents can be extracted. In general, the higher is the (given) tariff abroad, the smaller is the home country's optimal tariff. T*T* shows a similar "best response" of the foreign government to alternative home country tariffs. It too is downward sloping, by analogous reasoning. At point E each government has chosen a trade policy that is optimal given what the other has chosen. If each believed that the other's policy were immutable then neither would have any incentive to change. In fact each would find the conjectured stubbornness of its opponent confirmed. E would be an equilibrium.

One problem with the equilibrium E is that it is quite possible for each country to be worse off there than at 0, where each country would forswear the use of trade policy entirely.[12] This unfortunate property of a noncooperative conflict is known as the "prisoners' dilemma." Each government would agree to an alternative outcome (free trade) if only there were a way that the other could make

FIGURE 2

Equilibrium and Optimal Response Curves for Two Governments, Given the Tariff Rate Abroad

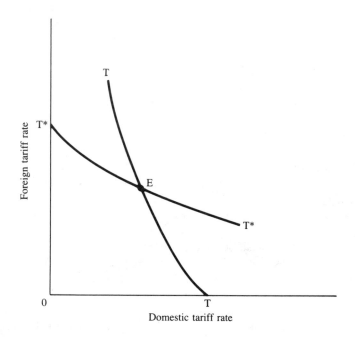

credible a promise not to cheat. This is a role that a forum for cooperation (such as the GATT) might play.

Mayer (1981) has studied the incentives for negotiated tariff settlements — cooperative equilibria — in just such a tariff game. He argues that reasonable conditions for a negotiated tariff settlement are: (i) that neither nation should be worse off at the cooperative equilibrium than at the noncooperative equilibrium E; and (ii) that no combination of changes in tariffs should exist after the settlement that could raise the welfare of both nations. Mayer shows that free trade by both countries satisfies the conditions he sets forth for "reasonableness." However, so too do many other policy combinations, all of which have the property that one government engages in export subsidization under the settlement. The exact outcome that results from negotiating will depend upon the bargaining abilities of the respective negotiators and the relative strength of the bargaining positions they bring to the negotiating table. The latter, in turn, hinges on which country stands to be harmed more if the talks break off, in which case the noncooperative equilibrium at E would be restored.

One problem with the cooperative equilibrium is that after a negotiated settlement is reached, the incentive remains for each government to "cheat." This certainly has its counterpart in reality. Governments may seek alternative policies that accomplish their original goals (exploitation of national monopoly power in this case). For example, domestic taxes or quantitative trade restrictions may be implemented by each government independently to restore an equilibrium similar to E. For each policy tool that is ruled out by cooperative negotiation, another may spring up in its place.

This dilemma has led Jensen and Thursby (1983, Thursby and Jensen (1983)) to ask whether government behavior in the Johnson analysis is plausible (and uniquely so) in the short and long run. The authors explore the issue of "conjectures" (consistent, optimistic, and pessimistic) that is discussed . . . in Section [2]. In the short run, a government might expect reactions from its counterpart abroad other than the "zero-response conjectures" assumed in the Johnson analysis. Thursby and Jensen consider a range of possible parameters for conjectured response, and find that so long as marginal propensities to import are sufficiently small, increased conjectured retaliation results in lower equilibrium tariffs.

In a longer-run analysis governments may recognize that setting trade policy is a "repeated game," involving *sequences* of equilibria like those discussed above. They might adopt more sophisticated strategies such as "follow free trade unless and until the foreign government deviates, then respond in kind for one, two or many periods." Strategies might involve threats and promises of other kinds (of course only those that are credible will be given weight).

The analysis of dynamic, repeated games is still in its infancy. Applications to trade policy are few. Jensen and Thursby (1983), for example, have considered the outcome of a repeated tariff-setting "game" in which each government follows a "trigger" strategy. A trigger strategy is one where a cooperative option (in this case free trade) is played either for the first k years (where the government chooses k optimally) or until the opponent acts noncooperatively, whichever comes first. Jensen and Thursby find that if each government correctly evaluates the incentives facing its rival, then the outcome will be for each to choose its noncooperative strategy (that is, implement its optimal tariff) in *every* play of the sequence. Essentially the process unravels from the end. Each government has a clear incentive to act noncooperatively in the final period. Then in the second-to-last period each will conjecture a noncooperative outcome in the final period. Thus, there is no reason to take a cooperative initiative in the second-to-last period, since it can have no effect on future outcomes. So the second-to-last period is just like the last, and so on, leading to noncooperation in all periods.

The results are somewhat more sanguine if each government is imperfectly informed about the motives of the other. In particular, if each government believes there is some probability that its rival simply will be "a nice guy," or that the rival would be willing to try out a cooperative stance until and unless it was exploited, then free trade can prevail for some part of the repeated game. It is interesting that if each government merely believes that its opponent may act cooperatively (contrary to its strategic incentives), then the outcome is a situation in which these beliefs are in fact validated.

Future research might consider practical questions and dynamic strategies. How can a government make credible its threats of retaliation? Equally important, how can credibility be vested in promises not to engage in "beggar-one's-neighbor" policies? International institutions that, in effect, change the rules of the game may help in this regard. For example, a negotiated trade policy settlement might rest on firmer ground if violations could be litigated in an international court for trade disputes.

All the discussion in this section has been of optimal tariff policy in a perfectly competitive market environment. The same principles apply to nontariff trade policies and in the imperfectly competitive environments discussed in Section [2]. Brander and Spencer (1984b), for example, have shown that if each government can set a "preemptive" export subsidy to shift the equilibrium in a duopoly in favor of its own firm's profits, then both will in fact do so. Each government chooses an optimal subsidy that is the best response to the subsidy chosen by the other. But each country ends up worse off in the resulting equilibrium than if both had agreed not to intervene at all. The general point is that many trade policies beggar one's neighbor. What is gained by one country is lost by another, and even the initial gain may be dissipated by retaliation. In such settings the most sensible challenge for trade practitioners may be to devise mechanisms for cooperation that are credible, enforceable, and verifiable, rather than to plot new and strategically effective thrusts.

[4] UNRESOLVED ISSUES AND RESEARCH EXTENSIONS

Research into trade policy and industrial organization in strategic environments is in an early stage. Some directions for subsequent stages are outlined below.

1. In frameworks with only two governments, there are two broad classes of equilibria: cooperative and noncooperative. When additional governments are introduced, there are many classes of intermediate equilibria. These spring from formation of cooperative coalitions among some but not all participants. Many practical policy questions seem to rest on which of these intermediate, mixed cooperative/noncooperative equilibria are "better" than others (higher economic welfare, more stable, less susceptible to cheating, and so on). Among such practical questions are the following: Are U.S. trade negotiations best aimed at bilateral, regional, or multilateral cooperation? Is the United States injured by preferential expansion of the European Community? Are developing countries really better off as a group seeking noncooperative equilibria with developed trading partners? Research of both an abstract and practical kind seems useful in considering multicountry "policy games."

2. Cooperative equilibria had a more prominent place in Section [3's] discussion of strategic policy competition among governments than in Section [2's] discussion of strategic market competition among firms. Yet illustrations of corporate cooperation abound: joint ventures, global sourcing, licensing of tech-

nology, and international corporate mergers and conglomeration. Research seems to be needed on preconditions for cooperative equilibria among firms. What aspects might trade policy choose to sanction, perhaps even encourage? What aspects might be better labelled as cartel-like collusion, and regulated by policy? Section [2] summarizes work on how policy might shift noncooperative market equilibria. Research seems needed on how policy might shift cooperative equilibria of various types.

3. The concept of "equilibrium" needs refinement in additional research on the imperfectly competitive environments described in Section [2]. Supernormal profits were assumed implicitly to persist there. This may be appropriate for some truly natural monopolies. Yet in many industries, supernormal profits will eventually be competed away by entry, so that the long-run environment is monopolistically competitive even if the short run is oligopolistic. "Pre-emptive" trade policy may then have different short-run and long-run effects, including potentially permanent impacts on competitive market structure, and transitional effects on incentives to expand, merge, and collude. Furthermore, industrial stages may be even more complex, with concomitant complexity for trade policy. Early stages of conflict among firms may be highly competitive — for example, competition in R and D, competition in experimental testing of new products and processes. Expected profits may be zero in early stages, with current profits subnormal rather than supernormal. As industries mature, supernormal profits may develop as the payoffs to successful participants at the earlier stages. Late-stage profits may provide the incentive necessary for firms to undertake further research and product development. Then as maturation continues, "late" new entrants may arrive (using perhaps the standardized technology that was established in the competitive first stage), and supernormal profits may shrink again toward zero.

4. Trade policy interacts with R and D policy to determine the dynamic evolution of technology-intensive industries. The promise of a protected home market (via import barriers or closed government procurement practices) may be necessary to induce firms to undertake research projects involving large risks and substantial "up-front" outlays. Conversely, a subsidy to R and D or a more stringent patent-enforcement policy may enhance competition in the later production and trade stage. Future research might spell out policy interdependence more exactly. There are also important questions concerning trade in technology itself. Should a domestic enterprise be permitted to license new technology to foreign firms, who then use it to compete vigorously with other domestic firms? Would a government licensing board be able to improve the terms on which a country buys and sells technology, for example, by restricting or eliminating competition between its own firms in bidding for or offering what is essentially a public good? How does policy regarding trade in technology affect the incentive firms have to innovate?

5. Conjectured responses of rivals fundamentally influenced the conclusions of much of the work summarized. Consistency (accuracy) of conjectures

was one important influence, credibility of threats and promises, explicit or implicit, another. Both consistency and credibility are judged by whether conjectured responses match equilibrium responses. Those that do not are labelled inaccurate or incredible responses. These observations beg two important questions. One is how "equilibrium" is defined, for example, with or without supernormal profits (see point 4 above); in quantity measure, price measure, or something else. A second question is how "equilibrium" is recognized by participants, and whether or not there is some learning process that has its own technology and strategic dynamics. More research is needed on these questions.

6. The concept of "scale economies" also needs refinement. Trade policy implications may be different for any of several different conceptions. Helpman (1983) distinguishes economies of scale that are internal to firms only, internal to nations but not to firms, and internal to global industries but not to firms or nations. Spillovers can also cross industry lines, either within or between countries. The precise form of the scale economies conceptually could be derived from more basic microeconomic structures, but this has not yet been done. Helpman (1983) and Markusen (1984) further distinguish economies of scale from those of "scope" — aspects of the production process that allow a single organizational entity to provide several product lines at lower cost than could a set of independent producers. Such economies of scope gave rise to multiproduct firms, and when different products are produced most cheaply in different locations, multinational multiproduct firms. The trade policy implications of globalization based on economies of scope have yet to be explored.

7. Firm versus government conflict and strategy has been neglected in this survey. Section [2] focussed instead on firm versus firm conflict in the presence of government policy, Section [3] on government versus government conflict. Research seems needed on the way strategic trade policy, specifically performance requirements (export targets, local content rules), influences large, self-conscious multinational firms. A crucial part of such research would involve examining the way that small numbers of self-conscious multinationals strategize against governments, perhaps playing some off against others for tax advantages and other forms of preferential treatment.

The potential research extensions outlined in this and previous sections are numerous. Timely undertaking of at least some of them seems essential as the structure of international trade and policy becomes more "strategic" — more concentrated among small numbers of interdependent multinational firms and blocs of governments. Over the longer term, a worthy research target might be knowledge of the costs and benefits of trade policy in strategic environments that is as thorough as it now is for perfectly competitive environments.

Notes

1. Its roots extend back into U.S. economic history and into familiar arguments for protection aimed at development based on infant industries, backward linkages, etc.
2. Supernormal profits also accrue to firms (or individuals) that adjust most rapidly to

structural change, even in competitive environments (to be exact, between the equilibria of a structurally shocked competitive environment). Furthermore, quick capture of supernormal profits is analytically the same motivation as quick escape from subnormal profits. On the obvious importance of defining equilibrium and "extra-equilibrium phenomena" in these matters, see note [3] and Section [4] below.

3. The point being made and the power of policy in this section depend crucially on the definition of equilibrium, and on firms' ability to recognize it. In Section 4, we discuss the need for further refinement of the concept of equilibrium.
4. This is sometimes called a policy reaction function.
5. Increasingly, governments own some or all of a firm's equity. In such cases they are closer to being just another player.
6. The zero conjecture or "Cournot equilibrium" does indeed imply a conjecture that is more aggressive than actually occurs, because each firm believes its rival's output to be given, whereas each firm in fact cuts its output as its rival increases its own.
7. Such is usually the case in so-called "Bertrand equilibrium," where each firm sets a price for its output under the belief that its rival has set a price which is given and unresponsive to the first firm's choice.
8. The possibility for strategic trade policy of the Brander-Spencer sort might remain, however, under these circumstances. Credible government policies might alter the international competitive environment in the assessment of both firms and the capital market, and therefore alter also the equilibrium configuration of natural monopolies and oligopolies. Each government will have preferences over configurations aimed at optimizing with respect to its opportunity to claim a share of supernormal profits.
9. That would seem to be what commentators have in mind when they describe the ability of policy to influence "dynamic" comparative advantage.
10. Note, however, that just as in the case of market-share competition, the form of the optimal policy response (which may be no response at all) will depend upon firms' conjectures of their rivals' reactions in the first-stage game.
11. A possible instance of the use of trade policy for this purpose in an imperfectly competitive market environment is the case of the European consortium to manufacture the Airbus. It can be argued that protection of the Airbus' home market and subsidies from the partner governments w[as] necessary to allow the consortium to recover a sufficient fraction of the huge sunk costs of development, in order to make entry into the competition against Boeing profitable.
12. At least one country must be worse off at E than at O, since in perfectly competitive environments free trade maximizes world purchasing power (welfare).

References

Brander, James A. and Barbara J. Spencer (1984a), "Tariff Protection and Imperfect Competition," in H. Kierzkowski (ed.), *Monopolistic Competition in International Trade,* Oxford: Oxford University Press.

Brander, James A. and Barbara J. Spencer (1984b), "Export Subsidies and International Market Share Rivalry," Working Paper no. 1404, Cambridge, Mass., National Bureau of Economic Research.

Branson, William H. and Alvin Klevorick (1984), "Report on the NBER Meetings on Analysis of Trade Problems, August 19, 1983 and December 2, 1983," processed, March.

Dixit, Avinash K. (1984), "International Trade Policy for Oligopolistic Industries," *Economic Journal* (supplement), pp. 1–16.

Dixit, Avinash K. and Albert S. Kyle (1984), "On the Use of Trade Restrictions for Entry Promotion and Deterrence," Discussion Papers in Economics No. 56, Woodrow Wilson School of Public and International Affairs, Princeton University.

Dixit, Avinash K. and Gene M. Grossman (1984), "Targeted Export Promotion with Several Oligopolistic Industries," Discussion Papers in Economics No. 71, Woodrow Wilson School of Public and International Affairs, Princeton University, February.

Eaton, Jonathan and Gene M. Grossman (1983), "Optimal Trade and Industrial Policy Under Oligopoly," Working Paper No. 1236, National Bureau of Economic Research.

Jensen, Richard and Marie Thursby (1983), "Free Trade: Two Noncooperative Equilibrium Approaches," Ohio State University, processed.

Johnson, Harry G. (1954), "Optimum Tariffs and Retaliation," *Review of Economic Studies, 21,* 142–153.

Krishna, Kala (1983), "Trade Restrictions as Facilitating Practices," Discussion Papers in Economics No. 55, Woodrow Wilson School of Public and International Affairs, Princeton University.

Krugman, Paul (1982), "Import Protection as Export Promotion," forthcoming in H. Kierzkowski (ed.), *Monopolistic Competition in International Trade,* Oxford: Oxford University Press.

Mayer, Wolfgang (1981), "Theoretical Considerations on Negotiated Tariff Settlements," *Oxford Economic Papers, 33* (February), pp. 135–153.

Ordover, Janusz A. and Robert D. Willig (1983), "Perspectives on Mergers and World Competition," processed, March 16.

Spencer, Barbara J. and James A. Brander (1983), "International R&D Rivalry and Industrial Strategy," *Review of Economic Studies, 50* (October), 707–722.

Thursby, Marie and Richard Jensen (1983), "A Conjectural Variation Approach to Strategic Tariff Equilibria," *Journal of International Economics, 14* (February), 145–162.

9

Unfair Trade Practices: The Case for a Differential Response

Judith L. Goldstein and Stephen D. Krasner

Trade-distorting practices by other states did not seriously affect U.S. commercial interests until the mid-1960's. However, growing overall and sectoral trade deficits, as well as rapid changes in trading patterns, have made such practices a more salient political issue. The modal and preferred American policy response has been to rely on U.S.-supported liberal institutions, notably the General Agreement on Tariffs and Trade (GATT), to provide a framework for multilateral negotiations designed to eliminate such practices. Although GATT negotiations have sharply reduced tariffs, certain nontariff barriers (*NTBs*) continue to have a deleterious impact on American corporations and more general national economic interests.

To further long-term objectives related to both American economic prosperity and an open global system, two strategies should be adopted. First, the United States should pursue a tit for tat strategy with states that violate explicit

From *American Economic Review Papers and Proceedings* 74 (May 1984), pp. 282–287. Copyright © 1984 by the American Economic Association. Reprinted by permission of the publisher and authors. Some references omitted.

GATT rules. Conciliation and unimplemented threats, the mainstay of existing policy, will not work. Rather, the United States should retaliate against such violations. Second, for nonconventional *NTB*s, that is, practices not understood to be nor easily capable of becoming incorporated into the GATT, the United States should abandon its policy of attempting to conclude new agreements that would broaden the scope of international rules. The United States has had and will continue to have limited success with such a policy. As an alternative, the United States should develop a more efficacious set of domestic industrial policies, even recognizing that given American institutions and values, this will not be an easy task.

In short, we make the following argument. American interests lie with the continuation of a liberal trading regime. The United States can best insure international cooperation by responding in kind to foreign practices. If states are willing to cooperate, so should the United States; if states defect from accepted GATT rules and norms, the United States should retaliate. If the practice is halted, American sanctions should be stopped. Alternatively, when U.S. economic interests are threatened by nonconventional *NTB*s or export-promoting practices, the United States should accept such behavior as inherent in the trading system and consider adopting similar practices of its own. The principled rejection of industrial policy must be replaced by a pragmatic assessment of options given American institutional and material resources.

I

In conception, the postwar trade regime was to regulate all trade distortions. Liberal rules, norms, and procedures were to be adopted by states and patrolled by international organizations. Problems with this image, however, were evident from the start. The International Trade Organization was never created. In GATT's formative period, 1947–58, two deviations from liberal design appeared. First, a series of national protectionist practices were sanctioned through a "grandfathering" provision. These included the U.S. escape clause provision and the 1921 Anti-Dumping Act. Second, although regime norms were accepted as the prototype, strict adherence to rules and procedures was not immediately expected.

Between 1958 and the close of the Kennedy Round, deviations from liberal norms were tacitly sanctioned in several critical areas. GATT coordinated and monitored the reduction of tariff barriers, but some *NTB*s such as the EEC's Common Agricultural Policy (CAP) were considered to be beyond the regime's legitimate control. Although seen as violating the spirit of GATT, such practices were not challenged. For U.S. policymakers, bolstering growth in noncommunist economies took precedence over strict adherence to liberal norms.

By the early 1970's, however, America's concern about discrimination rose. The overall balance of payments situation deteriorated and sectoral problems multiplied. While many of these changes reflected macroeconomic factors, including the effort to maintain ambitious social and military activities in the late

1960's, others were related directly or indirectly to state activities in other countries. New issues, such as the impact of foreign subsidies on the American position in third markets, became more sensitive.

The GATT has been ineffective in dealing with a wide range of problems, especially those not directly related to explicit tariff barriers. Its dispute settlement mechanism is weak and infrequently utilized. . . . Many forms of state intervention which impact on international market performance are not directly dealt with in the General Agreement. The GATT secretariat does not even have a mandate to maintain a comprehensive inventory of nontariff barriers. (Under Article X, GATT members are obligated to publish their trade regulations but not in any systematic comparable manner. . . .) Thus, as trade tensions increased in the 1970's the fundamental weaknesses of this organization, originally viewed only as a temporary bridge to the International Trade Organization, became apparent. The U.S. response to these problems was to press for the inclusion of nontariff barriers into the GATT framework in the Tokyo Round of multilateral trade negotiations *(MTN)*.

II

With regard to the relevance of present international rules there are three kinds of practices that influence international transactions: tariff barriers, conventional nontariff barriers, and nonconventional nontariff barriers. Tariff barriers have been the primary concern of the postwar trading regime. Several rounds of multilateral trade negotiations have resulted in dramatic reductions.

Conventional nontariff barriers are those that are accepted as being subject to the rules of the international regime for trade. Some, such as quotas, are explicitly dealt with in GATT. Others, such as some voluntary export restraint agreements, have come under the panoply of GATT during the postwar period. The defining characteristic of these conventional *NTB*s is that policymakers recognize them as being on the agenda of the international regime for trade. Some consensus exists as to what constitutes fair and unfair practices.

Nonconventional *NTB*s, however, present a more difficult problem. Nonconventional *NTB*s are practices that have not been accepted as part of the agenda for the trading regime. Basic standards of fairness are subject to debate. The issues involve not how a particular activity should be classified, but the classification scheme itself. The right of one state to challenge the legitimacy of an explicit export subsidy or a quota is not questioned, but the right of a state to demand changes in the banking or distribution systems of a trading partner is much more suspect.

The various *NTB* codes negotiated during the Tokyo Round represent the most significant effort thus far to expand the scope of the GATT to make nonconventional *NTB*s into conventional *NTB*s. While it is too early to reach a definitive conclusion about the success of these agreements, initial experiences are not hopeful. For example, the long and caustic debate between the United States and Japan over purchases of telecommunications equipment associated with the new code on government procurement has had very limited results. Not only has Japan's Nippon Telephone and Telegraph had considerable difficulty opening itself to American producers, the U.S. government was involved in American Telephone and Telegraph's rejection of a low cost bid from a Japanese company for fibre-optic equipment, a decision justified in terms of national security. . . . Moreover, the new codes themselves, whose provisions are limited to the signatories, represent a departure from the fully multilateral principles of the General Agreement. Further, the grievance settlement procedures of the codes have done little to revive the authority of GATT. For example, the first two cases filed under the new subsidies code, initiated by Australia and Brazil, claimed that the EEC's sugar export subsidy program was in violation of GATT Article XVI. Although the EEC subsidy was clearly at odds with GATT standards, no sanction was imposed. . . . And, in practice, had GATT ruled against the EEC, moral suasion would have been the only instrument at its disposal. Thus, while norm-based arguments have led to some changes in the EEC subsidy program, these modifications have not satisfied complainants.

Given the weakness of dispute settlement mechanisms, the United States should adopt a policy of appropriate unilateral trade retaliation as defined by GATT rules rather than multilateral diplomacy in cases involving conventional unfair trade practices. The international system for trade can be regarded as a prisoner's dilemma. The best outcome for an individual player is for that player to cheat (by, for instance, imposing an optimal tariff) while the other player cooperates. However, if both players cheat they will be worse off than if they both had cooperated. The ironic logic of single play prisoner's dilemma, which drives both parties to defeat, is well known. However, cooperation is much more likely under conditions of iterative prisoners' dilemma, but only if both parties are quick to punish and quick to forgive. Experimental findings suggest that the winning strategy for iterative prisoners' dilemma is tit for tat. . . . tit for tat is a strategy in which the player cooperates on the first move and then does whatever the other player did on the preceding move.

The United States is in an ideal position to play tit for tat because of its large domestic market, provided that both parties are clear about the values in the matrix and the classification of behavior as cooperation (fair) and defection (unfair). With regard to conventional *NTB*s, which are covered by existing international agreements, these conditions are likely to be met. Retaliation by the United States is likely to alter the behavior of trading partners, if those partners understand American demands and regard them as legitimate. However, if the United States fails to defect itself, it can expect continued defection from its trading partners.

Use of a tit for tat strategy may be exemplified by a number of recent American actions. In the case of Chinese textiles, retaliation after Chinese refusal to sign new accords led to a return to the bargaining table. Although the short-term Chinese response was further retaliation, a similar American response on the second move convinced the Chinese to cooperate. Similarly, the American response to the Canadian sale of subsidized subway cars to the United States led to a rescinding of the controversial financing program. In two other cases, future actions favorable to the United States may be predicted. Retaliation for EEC export subsidies led to the 1983 flour, butter, and cheese sales to Egypt. By using its own subsidization program, America supplanted a traditional French market and created incentives for negotiations. In a like manner, the U.S. refusal to compensate the Common Market for American import tariffs on specialty steel is likely to lead to European quotas.

Tit for tat is not aimed at starting a trade war. It is a program that should elicit cooperation and "freer" trade. It is a strategy that could be implemented given existing American institutions, although this would require that American policymakers change their basic attitudes toward retaliation. For the last thirty years, the executive-centered decision-making structure for trade has viewed legal rules and procedures within the United States that protect American producers from foreign unfair practices as a threat to free trade. Laws, such as antidumping and countervailing duty which were enacted before America's liberal period, have been seen as particularly troubling compared with safeguards passed after 1934, because these statutes do not give the executive any discretionary authority. . . . As opposed to escape clause procedures where the president can negate a ruling by the International Trade Commission (ITC), unfair trade practices carry mandatory duties. In the past, the executive response to this situation has ranged from attempts at persuading industries to retract petitions, to *ad hoc* devices such as "trigger-prices," to the extensive use of the waiver provisions for countervailing duty cases provided under the 1974 Trade Agreement Act. In general, the executive's strategy has been to undercut American actions for fear of stepping onto the "slippery slope" which leads to spiralling retaliation and the end of an open trading system.

This strategy has been misconceived. The defense of liberalism by the most liberal solution to trade distortions has not worked in practice . . . for it does not work in theory. The United States should meet protectionism in kind. We *cannot* defend liberalism unilaterally; without pressure, our trading partners *will not* act in accordance with GATT norms. Thus, the removal of both dumping and countervailing duty responsibility from the Treasury to the Commerce Department is a progressive step toward further international liberalization. Commerce is less reluctant to use existing legal provisions against unfair foreign trade practices.

III

The third group of barriers to trade cannot be treated as the other two. This group is composed of practices that have not come under even minimal regime control. They have been so excluded because they are difficult to quantify and compare; they are often viewed as part of the individual state's sovereign rights. Development of Anglo-American state-society relations made both the United States and

Great Britain the logical progenitors of a liberal international regime. Both polities have historically deemphasized the need for a positive state role in economic affairs. The late industrializers and nations which needed to restructure their economies after World War II had no proclivity to accept the model of a *laissez-faire* state. State intervention into a range of economic activities was accepted.

Most American central decision makers have had difficulty comprehending cross-national variations in state-society relations. Other states were expected to follow the American model: liberal with regard to both international exchange and domestic social groups. This is not a tenable position for guiding policy. Neither international negotiations nor unilateral retaliation will easily convince other states to change basic institutional characteristics of their political economies. It is futile and possibly counterproductive to attempt to negotiate the removal of nonconventional *NTB*s. Even with the expenditure of substantial resources, the United States can expect at best only symbolic changes. The Common Agricultural Policy (CAP) of the EEC and the Japanese industrial policy illustrate these propositions.

The EEC's agricultural policy covers 90 percent of Europe's farm production. It guarantees producers a uniform international price, usually above the world market price. To make products internationally competitive, the EEC must use export subsidies. In the early 1960's, the United States had little problem with the CAP; European integration was considered to be in America's interest and the CAP was an unfortunate but necessary part. By the 1970's, however, U.S. acquiescence to the CAP faded. Not only did the subsidies program undercut American agricultural exports to Europe, but it also weakened the U.S. position in third markets.

The U.S. strategy has been to show that EEC policies violate GATT norms. Although unquestionably the case, negotiation and enactment of a subsidy code during the MTN has had little impact on EEC policy. In effect, the United States is attempting to make the EEC subsidy program a replica of its own, that is, one based on domestic but not international state intervention. This task is problematic. Negotiations on subsidies are difficult to conclude, especially with respect to adjudication procedures. Once institutionalized they invite complainants to use GATT's procedures. However, since GATT is incapable of handling such cases, the codes can be counterproductive to their liberal intent. Weak institutional mechanisms further undermine GATT's credibility. And, of central importance, applying pressure to the EEC to change the CAP may threaten general political goals by exacerbating tension between the United States and Europe.

Japanese industrial policy offers an even clearer example of practices that were not envisioned by American policymakers in either the drafting of the GATT or of domestic legislation. Industrial policy refers to state sanctions targeted to specific sectors or industries. Industrial policy can take four different forms: protection, adjustment, relief, and enhancement. . . . While protection, adjustment, and relief either fall under existing international rules or are generally consistent with liberal norms, enhancement or nurturing presents overwhelming problems for international regulation or unilateral American initiatives.

The relationship between the state and the private sector in Japan is radically different from the tacit Smithian model upon which American rules have been predicated. The presumption in Japan "is that the state is there to do whatever is appropriate and necessary to promote industrial growth and prosperity.". . . Nurturing has involved specific government support such as low interest funds for targeted industries, direct subsidies, special amortization provisions for capital investments, and exclusion of critical capital equipment from import duties. Although it would be difficult, some of these practices might be directly challenged by the United States. However, there is a wider array of actions that fall under the concept of administrative guidance that reflect even more vividly the unique characteristics of Japan's political economy. The ability of Japan's central economic bureaucracies, the Ministry of International Trade and Industry (MITI) and the Ministry of Finance, to exercise administrative guidance comes not so much from the direct allocation of resources, but rather from "respect for the bureaucracy, the ministries' claim that they speak for the national interest, and various informal pressures that the ministries can bring to bear" (Chalmers Johnson, 1982, p. 266). The MITI has acted as a clearing house for information involving the development of national research strategies for critical industries. It has organized Diet caucuses to support specific high technology sectors in exchange for relatively modest political contributions to the Liberal Democratic Party. Major public financial institutions are heavily influenced by MITI preferences. The *keiretsu,* or conglomerates composed of several industrial firms, a trading company, and a bank, which dominate Japan's industrial structure, were constituted by MITI in the 1950's to concentrate capital for key development projects. . . .

Neither international arrangements in the GATT or elsewhere, nor American trade policy, can provide an adequate response to Japanese initiatives. Japan is not going to abandon an industrial strategy that has provided such spectacular results in the postwar period. Rather, American pressures could provoke retaliatory or defensive pressures that would threaten market-oriented international behavior. First, Japan would regard such pressures as infringements on existing sovereign prerogatives. One need only contemplate the reaction if U.S. allies demanded that support of defense industries be abandoned because it has provided American firms with commercial advantages. Second, it would be extremely complex to quantitatively specify an appropriate American response. In reflecting on the decision of the Reagan Administration to reject the Houdaille relief petition, the most thoroughly documented case ever presented by an American corporation, Lionel Olmer, the Under Secretary of Commerce, stated that the petition "did make a fairly persuasive case that the Japanese machine tool industry got off to a very successful start on the basis of government assistance of some order of magnitude. The difficulty was to try to allocate that amount of government assistance to a specific product" (JEI *Report,* November 11, 1983, p. 4). In sum,

Japanese industrial policy, even more so than the CAP, is not amenable to regulation through international agreement or unilateral international pressure.

The United States should accept deviation from a Keynesian, much less a Smithian, model of state society relations as an inherent characteristic of the international system. Various national policies will cause trade to depart from the pattern that would have developed under purely liberal conditions. Such nonconventional *NTBs* or trade promoting measures are unlikely to change. American interest will not be realized by either expanding the scope of GATT and using tit for tat or dispute settlement procedures on these *NTBs*. Rather, the United States, too, may need to rely on "less-than-liberal" solutions to American trade problems. In the coming decades, industrial policy should become one of the state's policy tools. Adjustment to foreign competition, often reflecting the activity of government bureaucracies or publicly owned firms, will require a more active role for the American state. In sum, the United States should learn from the manner in which other nations have under-cut American economic supremacy.

IV

In the coming decade, American producers will be increasingly challenged at home and abroad by foreign products. In response, the U.S. should pursue two strategies. When American goods are being supplanted due to foreign use of tariff and nontariff barriers in violation of accepted international norms, the United States should retaliate in kind. A tit for tat strategy is optimal. It is the best guarantor of other nations abiding by the "rules of the game." However, a tit for tat strategy will not succeed when the trade distortion is not clearly in violation of accepted rules and norms. America's policy in the past in such situations has been to attempt to widen the scope of the liberal regime. However, the United States does not have the power to bring about agreements that would make nonconventional *NTBs* into conventional *NTBs*. Moreover, such an effort could be counterproductive. Rather, the United States should accept certain deviations from the Keynesian/Smithian model, and when necessary use nonliberal means to bolster the competitive position of United States industries in the international market.

References

Japanese Economic Institute, *Report No. 43A*, November 11, 1983.
Johnson, Chalmers, *MITI and the Japanese Miracle*, Stanford: Stanford University Press, 1982.

10

Industrial Policy and Trade Distortion: A Policy Perspective

Richard N. Cooper

U.S. industry these days feels under siege from foreign competitors, and points to rising shares of imports in their home market and falling shares of U.S. exports in world markets. Attention has been drawn to a host of foreign practices that apparently help to explain the increased competition from foreigners, ranging from specific export promotional tactics and specific import prohibitions to broadly drawn industrial policies and industrial targeting that allegedly provide impetus to foreign exports and simultaneously discourage imports from the U.S. and elsewhere. These practices in one variant or another have been discovered to be widespread, being used not only by other industrial countries, but by less developed countries as well, particularly the newly industrialized countries such as Korea and Brazil. But Japan is held up as the main culprit, not so much because its practices are more extensive than those in other countries, but because they are somewhat mysterious and lost behind Japanese reticence and linguistic ambiguity, and above all because Japan has emerged as the most successful competitor in a number of industries in which Americans have hitherto considered themselves unrivalled. It is foreign success rather than the practices themselves — which in many cases have existed for many years and in some cases have actually diminished in importance — which has given rise to such widespread concern, and has led to calls for U.S. action ranging from retaliation to emulation.

This essay addresses these American concerns about what have come to be called "unfair trade practices" from the perspective of public policy. What response should the U.S. government make to these foreign practices and their alleged impact on the foreign trade — and even the industrial viability — of the United States?

With respect to the future viability of American industry, the view has been expressed that the theory of comparative advantage which provides the intellectual underpinnings for a liberal trade policy is fundamentally misleading, since it takes comparative advantage as given, whereas in fact it is determined by government policy. In particular, it is claimed that the country that gets the head start in a period of rapid technical change is likely to develop a "comparative advantage" in the product in question. Government actions that lead to early development thus determine comparative advantage.

From Richard N. Cooper, "Industrial Policy and Trade Distortion: A Policy Perspective," paper presented at the International Competition Conference, Ft. Lauderdale, March 7–9, 1985. Reprinted by permission of the author. Some text, tables, and references omitted.

The paper will take up the objectives and instruments of industrial policy in several other countries, focussing on Japan. It will then enquire into governmental influences on the American economy and its structure of trade, which on close inspection turn out to be more pervasive than most Americans think, and with some unexpected twists. The paper then addresses the "making" of comparative advantage by government policy, and finally turns to various alternative approaches to U.S. policy for dealing with the pervasive influence of governments on the composition of output and trade, both in a cooperative framework and by acting on its own. . . .

INDUSTRIAL POLICY IN JAPAN AND ELSEWHERE

"Industrial policy" has no well-defined boundaries, and at its broadest we can take it to mean any government policies that affect the structure of output, or, slightly more narrowly, any government policies whose intended purpose is to affect the structure of output. But perhaps the best way to characterize industrial policy of the type that concerns many Americans now is to discuss briefly but concretely the policies of the country that is seen to be most threatening, i.e., Japan.

This task is somewhat more difficult than it might seem, since Japanese policies have changed substantially over the past 25 years, and some of the measures most frequently cited, in fact, belong largely to the past. So Japanese industrial policy will be described here in the three phases frequently cited by Japanese analysts: end of postwar price control (1952) to the early 1960s, aimed at establishing the base for a modern industrial economy; 1960–1972, following elimination of foreign exchange controls, aimed at excelling in exports; and 1972 to the present, aimed at shifting the structure of the Japanese economy from capital-intensive to knowledge-intensive activities. The dividing lines between these periods are of course somewhat artificial, and some continuity of both policies and problems can be found during the past 40 years, but over the period, substantial changes in both policy orientation and instruments of policy occurred.

The Fifties

In the early 1950s, the Japanese desired to build a modern industrial society, drawing insofar as possible on the strengths they already had, which included a skilled workforce in steel-making, shipbuilding, and optics (for binoculars) built up during the Second World War. Strong government guidance in modernization had been part of Japanese history during the previous eighty years, and it was turned to again. Crucial industries were identified, forecasts of demand were made, and the industries were encouraged to invest accordingly. A rationalization program was begun for steel in 1951. Special industry promotion laws were passed for synthetic fibers (1953), petrochemicals (1955), machinery (1956), synthetic rubber (1957), electronics (1957), and aircraft (1958). Assembly of automobiles was made a priority in Japan in 1952. The Occupation-imposed Anti-Monopoly Act was amended in 1953 to permit the formation of "recession" and "rationalization" cartels with government approval in order to prevent cut-throat price competition and to induce orderly reduction in capacity during periods of slack demand (such as immediately following the Korean War, when the revisions were passed). The Export and Import Trading Act was also passed in 1953, permitting cartels to fix prices and to limit imports. By 1971 there were 195 legally recognized cartels under the Export-Import Trading Act, 13 under the Anti-Monopoly Act, and 23 under separate legislation pertaining to the machinery, electronics, and fertilizer industries, a decline in number by about 20 percent from the mid-1960s.

It was during this period too that the Fiscal Investment and Loan Program (FILP) was created, whereby postal savings accounts (historically an important depository of household savings) and public pension reserve funds were channeled into a series of trust funds (about 40 today) for the promotion of public policy. These trust funds include the Japan Development Bank (JDB) and the Export-Import Bank of Japan.

Investment by the favored industries was encouraged by special tax incentives and by loans from JDB. Japanese industry drew 13 percent of its external financing from JDB in 1952–55 and another 15 percent from other FILP programs (these figures had declined to 4 and 10 percent, respectively, by 1971–75). Four key selected industries — electric power, shipping, coal, and steel — got 24 percent of their external financing from JDB and another 13 percent from other FILP programs in 1952–55. So this government finance was a key instrument of policy; moreover, a JDB loan often provided a signal for lending (at commercial terms) by the quantitatively more important private banks, on the grounds that the favored firms were likely to involve lower risk than other business loans.

Finally, foreign exchange control existed throughout this first period, and import licenses were used to further the industrial policy. For instance, foreign cars were more durable and commodious than domestic cars, and as the taxi industry revived and thrived, its demand rose for foreign cars (including used cars from American forces resident in Japan). Purchase of such cars was limited under foreign exchange regulations in 1951, imports were liberalized in 1952 but sharply tightened again in early 1954, and a "buy domestic" campaign was started with the taxicab companies. Japanese production with improved quality required foreign technology. MITI [the Ministry of Trade and Industry] in 1952 promulgated guidelines for auto assembly licensing agreements which, *inter alia,* stipulated that after a specified period of time 11 key auto parts had to be produced in Japan. Foreign exchange regulations were used to limit imports in many other industries as well, and to shape the development of each favored industry.

The Sixties

Although Japan recognized the importance of exports from as early as 1949, when export promotion was adopted as MITI's main goal, the 1950s can be characterized principally as a period of import substitution, as Japan began to produce more sophisticated products that permitted a reduction in imports of those products. In 1960 there was a major trade and foreign exchange liberalization, associated with pressure from the United States and Europe to move toward currency convertibility and to accept fully the obligations of the General Agreement on Tariffs and Trade (GATT), which Japan had joined in 1955, preparatory to Japan's admission to the Organization of Economic Cooperation and Development (OECD), the club of industrialized countries, in 1964. This move eliminated exchange controls and general use of overt import restrictions as a major instrument of industrial policy, although some approved cartels continued to limit imports, presumably with MITI knowledge. The relative importance of the JDB also declined sharply, as the private banks became both stronger and more assertive.

A consequence of the liberalization of foreign exchange regulations and of the growing strength of sources of domestic credit in Japan is that MITI had to rely more on moral suasion, less on directives. It did not always work. An effort to pass a new law supporting selected industries unexpectedly failed due to domestic opposition in the early 1960s, and in 1965–66 the Sumitomo steel company flouted MITI's administrative guidance to cut back steel production. The growth of independent banks inhibited the development of "national champions" in Japan, since each bank wanted to have within its "family" of firms a representative from each major industry. The degree of competitiveness among major Japanese banks and firms, and the difficulty it sometimes poses for government, was already encountered in 1955 when a MITI plan to create a single small, inexpensive People's car (along the lines of Volkswagen) to open the mass market was leaked to the press (Japan's press is more competitive and more aggressive than that in the United States) and created a storm of protest from the actual and would-be auto makers. The plan was abandoned, and vigorous competition developed among Japan's auto makers.

A general policy can continue in the face of even major exceptions and derogations. But it is also likely that such exceptions remind the officials, if they need reminding, that there are distinct limits to their authority, and they therefore influence what MITI calls for, and what industry calls on MITI to call for if the industry is not unanimous. It is not true, as foreigners are sometimes led to believe, that Japanese business leaders are unwilling to take risks on their own and to stand out from the crowd.

By the 1960s steel and shipbuilding were commercial successes, and relative emphasis shifted to encouragement of the machine tool industry, which, like steel, and on the basis of close observation of the American economy, was seen to be a prerequisite for a modern industrial economy. It continued to get tax breaks, modest subsidies, and favored procurement.

The Seventies

In the early 1970s there was a marked shift in Japanese policy in a number of respects. The Japanese public had become restless about growing pollution, about the inadequate welfare system, and even about the fact that they had to pay much higher prices for some Japanese products than Japan's overseas customers did (television sets, especially, became a local *cause célèbre*). Moreover, MITI and other officials became concerned about the rapid growth of Japan's imports of oil, even before the oil shock of late 1973. In response to general public pressure, Japan adopted in 1972 a much more generous social security system and introduced stiff pollution standards. In response to the dollar crisis of 1971–72, Japan took a number of steps to liberalize imports, to liberalize direct investment inflows, and to monitor exports with a view to restraining too rapid growth. Japan also eliminated its "buy only Japanese" policy with respect to government procurement, and loans under FILP were made subject to Diet approval, something that had not been required before 1972, and which greatly reduced their flexibility as an instrument of industrial policy.

Looking to the future, MITI emphasized the growing importance of "knowledge-intensive" industries and encouraged Japanese industry to move in that direction. The Agency for Industrial Science and Technology (AIST) was created within MITI to finance research projects in ceramics, computers, seabed mining, and flexible computer-aided manufacturing systems. The criteria for AIST support are that the item in question is not yet on the commercial market and that the research effort would be too large or too risky for private firms to undertake alone. An early success was a desalination process that was later commercialized by private firms and sold in the Middle East. MITI in 1983 had a total R and D budget of about $250 million, which was divided between MITI's own 15 laboratories and support for R and D by private firms, compared with about $10 billion in total spent annually by Japanese firms on research and development.

The most heavily publicized cases of government R and D support concern the VLSI (very large-scale integrated circuit) project started in 1976, on which some $120 million in conditional loans (repayable only if there was commercial success) was made by the government between 1976 and 1979; and government support of a so-called fifth generation computer in the early 1980s. But there are other sources of support of high technology industries than research grants and conditional loans. Since 1978 the National Aeronautics and Space Development Agency has given preference in its procurement to satellites with high local content, which now exceeds 60 percent. However, Japan's semiconductor market "can be said today [1984] to be completely open to American-owned companies."

Japan does not only help the products of the future. Since 1978 it has had a program to "restructure" Japanese industries that are depressed, for whatever reason. Firms accounting for two-thirds of a depressed industry's output can petition the government for a restructuring plan, which involves an agreed reduction in capacity, with loan guarantees and tax benefits accruing to firms that scrap capacity under the plan. In mid-1984 there were 22 officially designated industries, of which five (paper, ethylene, compound fertilizer, polyolefins, and PVC resin) had formed legal cartels to restrict output and price competition. . . . This represents a substantial decline in the use of cartels from 20 years earlier. In addition, FILP support for Japanese industry is very much less (proportionately) than it used to be, and the government loan rate differential below market rates dropped from around 3 percent in the early 1960s to about one percent in the early 1980s. . . . In general, Japanese government involvement in determining industrial structure is far less than it once was — in part because the two instruments of foreign exchange licensing and credit control are now unavailable for disciplining large firms. But it continues to provide hortatory guidance in MITI's "Visions" and other government pronouncements, and to back these up with direct or indirect funding on a modest scale, and with directed government procurement.

Europe

Other countries have industrial policies which are similar to those in Japan and generally more extensive. For example, Britain, France, and Italy all have had organizations analogous to JDB, that channel publicly raised funds to private enterprises. All provide tax breaks to encourage investment in general and favored investment (by industry and by region) in particular. All have extensive state-owned industrial enterprises, something that is rare in Japan, that receive periodic infusions of new "equity" capital, which is difficult to distinguish from subsidies when the firms are running operating losses. All have given extensive support to their steel and textile industries, to consolidate operations and to scrap obsolete capital. Britain, France, and Germany have also provided government support to cushion declining demand in their shipbuilding industries. In the high technology area, all have provided extensive government funding and preferred government procurement in aerospace, computers, and telecommunications. . . . For instance, national Post, Telephone, and Telegraph (PTT) organizations in these countries rarely procure foreign-made equipment; the same is true of national power companies with respect to heavy electrical generating equipment.

Newly industrializing countries also have adopted strong industrial policies, apart from the traditional technique of restricting imports that compete with the production of favored industries. Korea has, at least in one area, adopted a novel incentive: Koreans who work on contract engineering and construction projects in the Middle East have been exempt from the draft and given priority in public housing when they return home. . . .

OBSERVATIONS ON INDUSTRIAL POLICIES

The purpose of this sketchy survey is to illustrate how widespread are the uses of "industrial policies" and how diverse are the instruments of support that governments may use. They raise the question of how can such extensive interference with market forces be reconciled with a liberal trading system predicated on the mutual gains that flow from reliance on comparative advantage to determine each country's structure of output and trade, with certain acknowledged exceptions having mainly to do with national security.

In particular, the discovery that foreign governments intervene extensively in national economic development even at the sectoral level, and that these interventions may impinge on the market for American products both at home and abroad, has recently led to a number of stated or implied recommendations for U.S. policy. . . . The U.S. government, it is suggested, should:

1. insist that other countries give up the practices which allegedly represent "unfair competition" for American firms;
2. adopt measures similar to foreign actions that are deemed to have been successful, e.g., create a revived Reconstruction Finance Corporation modelled on the Japan Development Bank;
3. raise import barriers to goods enjoying "unfair competition," sometimes only after (1) has failed, or as a threat to encourage foreign compliance with (1); and
4. match the foreign competitive measures in third-country markets (e.g. through generous Exim Bank financing) and/or restrict unrelated imports into the United States from countries engaging in unfair competition in third markets.

Before we turn to policy issues for the United States, however, several remarks should be made about the overall economic impact of these industrial policies.

First, most of them are not new and have been around for a long time, so whatever real stimulus they provide should have been adjusted to by adaptation elsewhere in the economic system. France, Italy, and Japan, among major countries, began extensive industrial policies in the early 1950s. Britain launched on this course in earnest in the mid-1960s. Indeed, if anything, the impact of industrial policies has been declining in Japan in recent years, and the Thatcher government in Britain has attempted to reduce that country's sectoral policies in the early 1980s.

Second, in many cases a costly *quid pro quo* is exacted for government support of a firm or industry, especially in terms of loss of freedom or flexibility over decisions regarding employment, plant closings, new investment, and diversification. This loss of freedom and flexibility is directly or indirectly cost-increasing. Such factors are typically not allowed in the reckoning as "negative" unfair competition, a partial offset to the aids that are received.

Third, it is often forgotten that the United States, while not having an industrial policy as such, nonetheless has many measures which directly or indirectly assist American business. These are sufficiently extensive and variegated to warrant extensive treatment in a moment.

Fourth, it should not be forgotten that measures which discriminate in favor of certain firms or industries by that very fact discriminate *against* other firms or industries. In economics there are only rarely opportunities for a "free lunch," and someone has to pay for the special aids that are granted to others. This is an important analytical point and will be discussed further below.

The United States government has had and continues to have extensive sectoral involvement in the U.S. economy. For example, in the nineteenth century it gave land grants to the railroads and more recently it has constructed a vast highway system to open up areas of the country and provide cheap inland transport. It provides cheap, under-priced water to irrigate Arizonan and Californian farms, producing the citrus which growers complain about being unable to sell "fairly" to the Japanese and Europeans. It has extensive research and development programs by the Department of Defense and by the National Aeronautics and Space Administration which generate commercially valuable spin-offs such as jet engines, helicopters, and the Boeing 747. . . . It is true that Europeans and Japanese exaggerate the quantitative importance of the commercial impact of defense R and D, but most American analysis of foreign government policies is also qualitative, leaving the impression of greater quantitative importance than is generally warranted. Extensive charitable deductions under the U.S. tax system permit the United States to provide higher education to a much larger percentage of the labor force than the Europeans could afford with their tax-supported systems and in "unfair competition" with the private universities of Japan.

It is perhaps useful to address more systematically government subsidies and other policies that influence American exports, since the U.S. government engages in a host of actions that influence the competitiveness of American exports, ranging from direct actions to encourage exports through activities to stimulate production and general support for business activity to actions which, by discouraging certain industries, lead indirectly to encouragement of others. The following list proceeds from the most direct form of export encouragement to less direct forms (this list is adapted from Cooper in Warnecke).

1. Economic and military assistance to less developed countries, tied to the procurement of American goods. In this case the U.S. government, in effect, buys the American goods and gives them away or lends them on very easy terms. Foreign aid represents an extreme form of export subsidization, but it is accepted as contributing to economic development or national security, and the importing countries in this case would be unlikely to hold the United States accountable for unfair import competition or to impose countervailing duties. But third countries may lose export orders because of foreign aid shipments tied to U.S. procurement. The subsidization of American exports would cease if foreign aid grants and loans were freely useable for the purchase of goods and services anywhere, as is the case with loans from The World Bank. U.S. foreign assistance and military credit sales amounted to about $15.5 billion dollars in 1982, or about 4½ percent of total U.S. exports of goods and services.

2. Under U.S. tax laws until 1984, corporations that derived at least 95 percent of their gross receipts from exports could qualify as domestic international sales corporations (DISCs) and could defer payment of corporate profits tax until dividends were remitted to the parent corporation. This provision, which cost in excess of $1 billion in annual revenue foregone in the mid-1970s, amounted to an

interest-free loan from the government for expenditures involved in the promotion of exports. The subsidy element — about $60 million a year — was thought to be much less than the foregone revenues, since the taxes would have eventually to be paid. In fact, in the 1984 Tax Act, which eliminated the DISC and permitted in its place the Foreign Trade Corporation, many of the unpaid taxes were waived, so the interest-free loan turned out ex post [facto] to be a direct subsidy.

3. The U.S. government subsidizes both the construction and operation of merchant vessels under U.S. registry. Construction subsidies do not increase exports since such subsidies are available only to purchases by U.S. flag companies, but of course operating subsidies to shipping make it easier for Americans to export shipping services. Both programs are of long standing, and in the mid-1970s the operating subsidy amounted to around $200 million a year. Ship construction and shipping services generally involve heavy government involvement throughout the world.

4. The Export-Import Bank provides medium-term credit for American exports. For a number of years the interest rates were below market rates, so a direct subsidy was involved. More recently, the Bank has tried to keep its lending rates above its borrowing rates by enough to cover its operating costs, except when necessary to meet foreign competition. The subsidy to American exports is thus now the more subtle (and smaller) one which arises from the use of U.S. government credit in borrowing in the capital market plus the absence of a requirement to pay dividends on the Bank's capital.

5. Until 1973 the Commodity Credit Corporation (CCC) gave substantial subsidies to U.S. exports of many agricultural products, the counterpart of a system of high domestic price supports combined with the view that in the absence of agricultural policy the United States would be a substantial exporter of agricultural products, especially grains, cotton, tobacco, etc. The high price supports stimulated output, so the program also involved limitations on acreage. This system was reinstituted on a lesser scale in the early 1980s. It is difficult to say whether agricultural exports would be larger or smaller than they would have been in the absence of the government support program, since the support prices and the acreage controls could be expected to have opposite effects on farm production.

6. Investment in plant and equipment in the United States enjoys a 10 to 25 percent investment tax credit. The credit in effect lowers the cost of domestic investment by that amount, and thus stimulates the productive capacity of the economy. The credit operates for all investment, however, so it is not obvious whether on balance exports or imports are stimulated more by the tax credit. The first-round effects of increased production and income could go either way. The major long-run effect of the investment tax credit is to make American industry somewhat more capital-intensive than it would be without the credit, both in each industry taken separately and in its overall industrial structure. In addition, since 1981 there have been extremely generous write-off provisions for the depreciation of new investment. These provisions have a similar effect [to] the investment tax credit.

Depletion allowances for oil and other minerals have the effect of stimulating domestic production of such products and thus serve to reduce imports or to increase exports of these products. Until 1975 this tax privilege was available to American-owned mineral investment anywhere in the world, but now it is limited to production in the United States.

7. There are many areas of direct government expenditure for activities that support business enterprise. Examples are federal spending, net of user charges, for airports and air traffic control, for dredging rivers and harbors, and for providing postal service. Government funds by the billions have been devoted to development of water resources, which provide both cheap hydroelectric power in the areas covered by them, and cheap water for irrigation in the southwestern part of the country, resulting in a great stimulation of agricultural output there. In addition, the Rural Electrification Administration has subsidized the electrification of the rural parts of the American economy for nearly fifty years at low interest rates, thus making farming somewhat less costly than it would otherwise be.

8. Price controls on domestically produced natural gas cheapen energy for Americans with access to the price-controlled gas and hence provide "subsidies" (but not revenue-reducing ones) for American exports as well as for domestic sales of products that require gas to be used in their production. In 1985 some, but not all, gas price controls were removed, so this "subsidy" will diminish in importance over time. For nearly a decade before 1981, U.S. oil prices were also held below world market prices, with similar effect.

9. Government expenditures on research and development help to cover the initial cost of new economic activities, which often later lead to exports. The classic example is agricultural research, which has been financed by government for over a century and has led to vast improvements in the productivity of American agriculture and to improvements in the quality of agricultural products. Sometimes too, large export sales are a distant by-product of military research and development expenditures, as was the case with the jet engine. Currently the government is spending substantial sums on research and development in the energy sector, both on nuclear power and on such possibilities as liquefaction of coal. To the extent that the latter proves to be economically feasible, it may augment future exports of American coal.

10. Extensive government purchases sometimes lead to the development of products which are highly competitive in world markets, by helping private firms to spread their own research and development costs as well as other overhead expenditures over a larger number of sales. The list of products here in principle is a long one, but the point is quantitatively important in relatively few industries, such as military equipment, avionics, some kinds of telecommunications equipment, and ground tracking stations for satellites.

11. The most pervasive influence, and quantitatively probably the most important stimulus to exports of particular goods, but also the least obvious, is the host of government regulations on U.S. production which have been introduced to improve the working environment or the natural environment. Such items as

effluent controls, safety regulations, minimum wage legislation, and restrictions on child labor can have a profound effect on the competitiveness of particular industries, and hence on the relative competitiveness of other industries less directly affected. Since most observers would not mention such government actions in a list of export "subsidies" — and indeed they do not normally give rise to a loss of government revenue, except where the government occasionally incurs some of the costs, for example, of anti-pollution actions — it is worthwhile to trace through the influence on exports of one of these regulations, the minimum wage. The key assumptions in this analysis are that, over time, balance is maintained in international payments, for example by movements in the exchange rate of the dollar, and that the government takes whatever steps are necessary to assure full employment of the labor force. So we are looking here for the *sectoral* effects, the relative stimulation or retardation of production in particular sectors of the economy which arise from the regulation in question.

The minimum wage, if it is set high enough to exceed the wages that would otherwise be paid in some industries, reduces the international competitiveness of those industries by raising their costs. The industry will find it is more difficult to compete with products from abroad. Imports will rise, and restoration of equilibrium in the balance-of-payments will require some depreciation of the dollar relative to what it would otherwise be. The depreciation, in turn, will *increase* the competitiveness of all sectors where wages are not influenced by the minimum wage. Put more concretely, it is likely in the United States that the minimum wage discourages the production of apparel (displaced to some extent by imports) and encourages the production and export of machinery. Thus, in an indirect fashion, via adjustment of the exchange rate, the export of machinery is "subsidized" (but, again, not in a fashion that reduces revenue to the government). A similar argument holds, *mutatis mutandis,* for other government regulations. For example, meeting required safety standards will raise costs more in some industries than in others, and via adjustments in the exchange rate will increase the competitiveness of industries or firms whose costs for safety have increased least. (See Kalt for a finding that environmental regulations have had a discernible effect on the composition of U.S. trade.)

So the influence of government actions on international competitiveness is pervasive, but it may also be so indirect as to be difficult to trace in detail with any confidence. It may nonetheless be substantial, even when it flows from actions aimed at objectives quite different from a desire to stimulate exports. . . .

We can now return to a point raised at the outset: Can comparative advantage be made? Of course it can. In a tradition going back at least to Frank Taussig, it has been recognized that comparative advantage is determined not only by a country's natural endowments, but also by its social and political and educational systems. It is determined by the quality as well as the quantity of its labor force, by the motivation of its workers, and their willingness to work diligently. Insofar as government provides for inland transport, education, efficient banking and other financial transactions, these too can influence comparative advantage, as can the long list of items discussed above for the United States, especially the regulatory environment. It would be absurd to pretend otherwise and to treat each geographic area as a *tabula rasa* with natural endowments but with no social or political system.

That is perhaps not what is meant when people talk about "making" comparative advantage rather than "finding" it. Rather, they may have in mind permanent cost advantages that are generated by a head start or by extensive production of a particular product. If important and durable economies arise from "learning by doing," then "doing" can give an advantage, however it is brought about. . . . However, two points should be kept in mind before rushing headlong to do many things in the interests of reaping the learning-by-doing cost advantages that they may engender. First, undertaking production which is not at once profitable in order to reap the advantages of learning by doing represents an investment, and to undertake any investment on the supposition of future positive rates of return is not sufficient. It will be a good investment only if the yield on the investment is at least as high as that on alternative investments. If, on analysis, that seems to be the case, then as with any new investment opportunity many parties may simultaneously want to undertake it, and that would not necessarily be a bad thing.

Second, "decisive" cost advantages for a given product or product group achieved by learning by doing turn out to be remarkably transient in many instances, given the large number of products which have had their commercial introduction in the United States, but the production of which has subsequently been relocated abroad. Evidently there are cost factors which eventually over-whelm the cost advantages achieved even by a relatively long head start in production and the learning-by-doing gains that are thus achieved. There remains the possibility, however, that other countries do not recognize these two points, and that they therefore undertake government support for activities which turn out to be bad investments, but which in the meantime create competition for otherwise successful American firms. What, if anything, should be done about it?

POSSIBLE POLICY DIRECTIONS

The problems posed above have been around for a long time. What we now call industrial policy goes back, in the strictly commercial arena, at least to the time of the early eighteenth century, when France tried (successfully) to create a high quality porcelain industry in competition with the Saxon industry in Dresden. The effort in textiles is even older, as when in the early seventeenth century, England attempted (unsuccessfully) to start a finished textile industry in competition with the Flemish cities, by prohibiting the export of wool.

Existing Arrangements

The General Agreement on Tariffs and Trade (GATT) of 1947 dealt with the problem of subsidies and international trade by suggesting (in Article 16) that export subsidies on manufactured goods — note the exclusion of primary products — should generally be eschewed, and permits Contracting Parties to impose countervailing duties when such subsidies cause material injury. (In addition, Article 19 provides a general escape clause from GATT commitments, permitting countries to reimpose tariffs, but only on a nondiscriminatory basis, whenever a domestic industry is subject to substantial injury by imports.) A GATT working party attempted to define more precisely in 1960 exactly what export subsidies were. In the mid-1970s the United States introduced its "traffic light" proposal, distinguishing between subsidies that were prohibited (red), subsidies that were clearly permitted (green), and subsidies which were potentially trouble-some and which were subject to consultation and possible countervailing action when they cause injury to some other Contracting Party to the GATT (yellow). This proposal was not adopted in the form in which it was presented, but it provided a framework for the Code on Subsidies and Countervailing Duties that was adopted in 1979 as part of the Tokyo Round of multilateral trade negotiations.

The 1979 Code prohibits export subsidies except on certain primary products and except by developing countries. Code signatories undertake not to use such subsidies (Article 9) and their use creates a (rebuttable) presumption of adverse effects, and are thus subject to countervailing duties without an injury test, but subject to international approval. The Code also provides, in its Annex, an illustrative list of export subsidies, which goes a long way toward defining them. The Code acknowledges the widespread use of, and permits, many other subsidies, but signatories recognize that these can hurt the trade interests of other countries and they therefore "seek to avoid causing such effects through the use of subsidies." In evaluating the use of subsidies in pursuit of domestic economic objectives, signatory countries are to "weigh . . . possible adverse effects on trade" (Article 11). If other countries are injured by such subsidies, they can countervail the subsidies in question (see the appendix for the relevant Code articles and the illustrative list of export subsidies).

This general language leaves a very large area for interpretation, not to mention the cracks and overlaps in the illustrative list of prohibited subsidies. U.S. practice is gravitating toward an interpretation that requires a domestic subsidy to provide a "special favor" to a firm or industry before it is countervailable under U.S. law. That is to say, the United States tries to rule out as countervailable subsidies such broad legislative favors as accelerated depreciation, investment tax credits, research and development tax credits, and so on. Thus a domestic subsidy is countervailable if it causes material injury to an American industry through stimulated exports and if the subsidy is selective rather than general in its impact on the foreign firm or industry.

On the whole, the approach embodied in the GATT Code and in evolving U.S. practice seems very sensible. Export subsidies are prohibited, and other subsidies are permitted but are countervailable if they are selective and if there is injury to another party. But several practical problems remain. First, on this track we must await sharper definition of the distinction between selective and general subsidies on a case-by-case basis. Second, during the period in which this sharper definition is taking place, the possibility exists for harrassing imports by bringing test cases, and creating uncertainties whenever there is a preliminary finding of subsidy, through "suspension of liquidation," under which an importer is put on notice that he may have to pay a higher duty at some subsequent date, but does not know what the duty will be. Third, there is no assurance that other countries will move in the same direction as the United States in their interpretation of the distinction between selective and general subsidies. The United States tends to be the most active country in developing the case law, perhaps because other countries have less formal mechanisms for restricting imports if they choose to.

In their detailed study of treatment of subsidies to international trade, Hufbauer and Erb (1984) suggest that the list of prohibited export subsidies needs to be tightened and that the distinction between general and specific subsidies needs to be substantially clarified. But they basically accept the existing framework. Their most novel suggestion is in the area of remedies to subsidies, where they propose the countervailing *subsidy*, to be financed by an (internationally approved) import duty on goods coming from the country providing the offending subsidy. The advantage of a countervailing subsidy as opposed to a countervailing duty is that it permits the injured country to continue to sell in third markets and even in the home market of the subsidizing country. Its obvious disadvantage is that it would affect fourth-country competitors, who now would have to compete with two subsidizing countries, and that might engender a race toward subsidies. It would perhaps ultimately lead to a "disarmament" negotiation to remove the subsidies, as happened during the late 1970s and early 1980s with respect to official export credits, thereby reducing the distortions to international trade. But once subsidies are introduced, eliminating them is a prolonged, difficult, and often not wholly successful process as the effort to get consensus on official export credit restraint also illustrates.

Three Alternative Criteria

A major difficulty with public debate in this area is that it mixes three quite different criteria in assessing subsidies: distortions to resource allocation, fairness or equity, and injury. It is reasonable to conjecture that if there were no injury the issues of fairness and distortion would not arise in the practical world of policy, although academic economists would be concerned with the misallocative effects of distorting subsidies. However, when injury does arise, the three different criteria tend to be co-mingled, yet each points to a rather different solution.

Subsidies, domestic or export, induce distortions in the allocation of resources and hence should be eliminated or offset in the interest of economic efficiency, except in those cases where the subsidy is itself designed appropriately to offset some other distortion, e.g., an externality of some kind. This is the principle that underlies the prohibition on export subsidies, and the permissible imposition of a countervailing duty. As pointed out above, however, the countervailing duty cannot undo the distortion with respect to competition in third markets. A plan to eliminate all of the distortions introduced by government action would be a counsel of perfection given the extensive government intervention in modern economies, enumerated above. It would even be difficult against all selective subsidies, which would invariably be justified on grounds of correcting a distortion in capital or labor markets, or as exploiting an externality, or on national security grounds, or in extreme cases as necessary to insure domestic peace and political harmony. Governments are likely to abandon their extensive array of domestic subsidies only when they come to deem the costs, defined broadly, to be greater than the rewards.

Emphasis on equity or fairness leads to a second approach to policy, which would be to harmonize domestic measures among countries. If an activity has positive externalities or national security value, that attribute is presumably not limited to a particular country. Most countries are concerned about having substantial local production of the staple food, perhaps of steel, perhaps of small arms, and increasingly of electronics on grounds of national security. Nations can negotiate broad ground rules on what is and is not acceptable. That would offer one concrete meaning to the otherwise obscure phrase, providing "a level playing field." The rules would be permissive rather than obligatory, but they would also be limiting, in that countries could not subsidize beyond what was agreed. The United States did try in the Tokyo Round to negotiate a more detailed elaboration of acceptable but possibly troublesome subsidies, but the result was the less specific Code described above. However, the United States could try again to get greater international agreement on domestic subsidies that are permissible and those that are sufficiently potentially troublesome that they should be avoided. Inevitably such a negotiation would have to be on a conditional MFN basis, as the subsidies Code was, since the interests of over ninety GATT members are too diverse to permit any meaningful harmonization among all of them. By general consensus, developing countries are held to a lesser standard than are the fully industrialized countries, although the extent to which the standard should be relaxed is still a matter of considerable and continuing dispute.

Negotiation on harmonization of subsidies would be a cooperative approach. If other countries decline to cooperate willingly, the United States could approach the matter unilaterally. One way to do this is through the notion of "reciprocity," as embodied in Senator Danforth's telecommunications bill. This bill is motivated by the fact that Japanese and major European markets in telecommunications equipment are effectively closed to American (and other foreign) sellers, since most of this procurement is undertaken by government-owned (PTT) monopolies. Danforth's bill would require other countries to open their individual markets to imports of U.S. telecommunications equipment within three years under the threat of a sharp increase in U.S. tariffs on telecommunications products coming from them, from roughly 8 percent today to about 35 percent. The underlying principle is that the terms of access should be the same in each product field, telecommunications in this case, and that the United States should persuade others to adopt U.S. practices — which, with the recent breakup of AT&T, means relatively open procurement by private telecommunications companies in the

United States. In the absence of foreign adoption of U.S. practice, the United States will greatly reduce their access to the U.S. market.

There are two problems with this as a general approach. First, it does not address the question of exports of third countries. (That is perhaps not a major problem in telecommunications; indeed, the United States continued to hold 38 percent of the world market in telecommunications products in 1982, compared with only 11 percent for Japan despite its alleged export prowess.) Second, success flowing from the threat embodied in the Danforth bill is likely to vary from country to country. Japan has a large stake in the U.S. market. France, whose practices are if anything even more exclusive than Japan's, does not. Japan might comply in its negotiations with the United States, Britain and Germany might comply partially, and France might not comply at all. The result at the end of three years would be that the United States would have to have different levels of restriction on products from each of these countries and value-added criteria to prevent geographic arbitrage among them. The issue is even more complicated when one allows for the difference between national ownership and location of production, through foreign subsidiaries. Thus new distortions would be introduced into international trade, the discrimination implied would represent a sharp break with the most-favored-nation principle embodied in the GATT, and the consequence would be much closer surveillance over imports, with correspondingly greater opportunities for threats and harrassment. These developments would not be in the overall U.S. interest.

A second unilateral approach toward a "level playing field," or more accurately toward reducing the protectionist mischief that can be done under that label, would be to introduce a uniform tariff of, say, 10 percent on all U.S. imports of manufactures, against a presumed entitlement of zero, combined with a stipulation that any industry wanting protection above that level would bear an exceptional burden of proof to show that it was substantially injured by a substantial foreign subsidy, one that was well above ten percent, except in the case of prohibited subsidies. By imposing a levy on all imports of manufactures, the uncertainty that foreign exporters now face with respect to U.S. administrative law in the area of subsidies and countervailing duties could be greatly reduced. The disadvantage of this kind of measure, of course, is that it imposes a burden on all consumers of imports, and also directly and indirectly reduces the competitiveness of U.S. exports, mitigated only in part by giving drawbacks of the duty on their imported inputs. Also, over time it might be difficult to sustain the principle that the 10 percent duty covered most foreign subsidies, against an asserted entitlement of no duty.

The third major approach shifts the emphasis to injury, and away from the subsidies as such except for the clearly prohibited subsidies. It recognizes that government influence is pervasive and of long standing, and that in many ways such influence has been absorbed into the existing prices and economic structure. It focuses instead on large changes in government policy and the injury that such changes may cause. This approach would call for prior notification of all major changes in government policy, and gradualism in the implementation of these changes. When gradualism is not followed, it would permit degressive (that is, gradually phased out) relief to the injured party, with a view to encouraging ultimate adjustment to the new situation. Procedures would be necessary for discussing new policies and for considering measures that would achieve the same objective with smaller external impact. They would cover any major change in policy with external repercussions on particular industries and would have the objective of modifying the proposed action so as to reduce the imposition of costs on other countries. A gradual introduction of the new measures, like the multi-year staging of tariff reductions, is one way to reduce the costs of adjustment. The principles involved here cover subsidization of domestic production that competes with imports as well as subsidization of exports.

Instead of calling for harmonization of policies, an exacting requirement in a world of independent nation states, this approach calls for extensive prior consultation on any industrial policy changes that are likely to cause injury, with a view to avoiding those changes but also with a view toward mitigating any injury that does occur.

Variants of the harmonization approach and the approach emphasizing injury are not incompatible with one another. It would be possible to emphasize injury as the main strategy, while still negotiating with other countries to reduce the discrepancies among their industrial policies. But extreme harmonization would not be necessary.

Advice to the United States

In framing U.S. policy, it is necessary to consider what is in the best interest of the United States, given its capabilities and limitations. The United States cannot favor particular industries secretly; that is not consistent with the way American government operates. Should it do so openly? My answer would be that open support for particular industries should be given only if a strong public policy case can be made for such support on its merits: either on grounds of national security, or if there are strong and demonstrable externalities which are engendered by such support. This approach, while sounding blandly obvious, in fact has strong implications with respect to some of the proposals that have been made. For example, the Labor Industry Coalition for International Trade has complained of closed markets in other industrial countries for electric power generating equipment, in contrast to imports by the United States that on occasion have reached 20 percent of U.S. purchases. This, they contend, is unfair. . . . But under the present regime the United States is not losing any of the economies of scale that it might otherwise obtain. In fact the U.S. share of world exports actually rose between 1965 and 1980, from 5 to 10 percent. In addition, Americans presumably get lower cost power by permitting import competition. Power is an important input into industry. It is possible, for instance, that part of the difficulties of aluminum refiners in Japan is due to preferred Japanese procurement of domestic electric generating equipment. While it would certainly be desirable to be able to sell U.S.

equipment in France and Japan, it is not obviously in the U.S. interest to stop purchases from those countries even if they decline to open their markets to U.S. equipment, and indeed the existing regime may, on balance, even favor U.S. industry as a whole. We simply do not know about the general equilibrium effects.

Furthermore, U.S. actions should not be motivated by arguments that rest on the fallacy of composition, that is, that the action would generate employment or improve the overall trade balance. Except in the short run, employment and the overall trade balance are determined by the macroeconomic conditions of each economy, not by particular trade policies.

In short, the United States should look at other countries (1) for practices which are illegal under GATT and its codes and (2) for policy measures that may have useful application in the United States. But in the end the United States should adopt measures that are best for the United States in the institutional setting of the United States, not just because they seem to have worked well abroad. Many actions by foreign governments have been costly and largely unsuccessful; those that have been successful would not necessarily or generally be successful in the American context. The United States could adopt many of the practices of Europe or Japan; but it would be unwise to do so. In particular, Americans should have to make a specially strong case for discriminatory treatment in favor of any particular industry. It is much easier for foreign countries to "pick winners" because they observe successful new industries in the United States. How would the U.S. government pick the industries of the future? To what experience could Americans turn? Instead, the United States relies on private rewards to thousands of firms and individuals, each making a guess as to which activities will be winners in the future. Most will be wrong. Some will be right.

But what kind of position does this leave the United States in with respect to bargaining with other countries on their practices? Might it not be desirable for the United States to introduce Danforth-style reciprocity or in other ways to threaten to close U.S. markets with a view to getting foreign countries to open theirs? Here we must recognize limitations of the United States. The American government cannot bargain subtly in the economic arena, and it has always found it difficult to back away from a publicly stated and argued position introduced for bargaining reasons, but not fully acknowledged as such. Many Americans will believe the arguments that have been advanced. In short, a pluralistic, open society cannot bluff. It simply cannot carry it off. Foreigners will be skeptical of any nonserious threat, and once domestic political support has been built for the threat, the threat becomes serious but it ceases to be a bluff. For this reason the United States should threaten actions only when it is clearly willing to undertake them. And in general it should be willing to undertake them only if they are in its best interests, not simply as a bargaining tactic.

It is true that the ambiguity surrounding decision-making within the United States, and particularly the relationship between the President and the Congress when it comes to trade matters, is sometimes helpful in bargaining with foreigners, since foreigners can never be certain that Congress will not take the upper hand and move in a way which puts them at a disadvantage. This uncertainty is a reality of American politics, and it can sometimes be used successfully in the bargaining context. But it is rather different from the bluff of a poker player.

If other countries continue to be recalcitrant in pursuing practices that the United States considers unacceptable, should the United States retaliate as a demonstration that it is willing to take action hurtful to the other country, even if it is also hurtful to the United States? As suggested above, the general answer to this question is negative. However, it cannot absolutely be ruled out, if the action has a reasonable prospect of inducing a change in [the other country's] behavior that is beneficial to the United States. But this prospect is so heavily conditioned on the exact manner, timing, and context of the threatened retaliatory action that general rules are not likely to be helpful. It is a case where "playing it by ear" is preferable to playing by score or, to mix metaphors, by recipe. That is where the art of diplomacy comes into the economic arena.

References

Hufbauer, Gary Clyde and Joanna Erb, *Subsidies in International Trade,* Washington: Institute for International Economics, 1984.

Kalt, Joseph P., "The Impact of Domestic Regulatory Policies on International Competitiveness," mimeo, March 1985.

Warnecke, Steven J., ed., *International Trade and Industrial Policies,* London: Macmillan, 1978.

IV

Background and Issues in New Trade Negotiations

For over forty years the United States has been the major international supporter of a liberal international trading regime and the driving force behind the seven trade-liberalizing multilateral negotiations that have taken place under the auspices of the General Agreement on Tariffs and Trade (GATT) over this period. Since 1982 the United States has again been calling for a new round of multilateral trade negotiations, and this is quite likely to take place during the last half of the 1980s.

The first reading in this section by Robert E. Baldwin discusses the rise of the United States as a hegemonic power devoted to an open trading regime largely for foreign policy reasons and explains how U.S. trade policy objectives have gradually become more domestically oriented as the dominance of the United States among market economies has gradually declined. The selection also traces the shifts in the positions and power of various domestic economic groups and political institutions during this period.

There are still some issues left over from the Tokyo Round of multilateral negotiations (1974–1979) that many think should be dealt with in any new negotiations. These include the formulation of a new safeguards code covering injury to domestic firms and industries due to increased imports, the introduction of rules that curtail the subsidization of agricultural exports, and the improvement of the GATT's dispute settlement mechanisms. However, the readings by Jeffrey J. Schott and Harvey E. Bale, Jr. focus on two important new issues for the upcoming negotiations: barriers to international trade in services and trade-related investment policies that distort world trade.

U.S. negotiators in the Tokyo Round actually had the authority to negotiate on various barriers that impede the flow of services across international borders, but the difficulties of reaching agreement on the various codes covering trade in goods precluded much negotiating activity in this area. Schott presents data on the growing importance of services trade in international commerce and indicates the type of measures that restrict trade in financial, telecommunications, and transport and travel services. He also explains the reactions of the European Community, Japan, and the developing countries to the American initiative to undertake negotiations in this field.

Bale points out that many countries not only limit foreign investment but require foreign firms permitted to invest to undertake certain performance requirements such as purchasing a fixed percentage of intermediate inputs locally, exporting a minimum proportion of the final value of output as a way of contributing to the foreign exchange earnings of the country, employing a certain proportion of local personnel as administrators, and transferring a certain amount of the firm's technology to nationals in the host country. While such measures can obviously distort the pattern of world trade, it will be difficult to reach multilateral agreements that specify the extent to which such practices should or should not be permitted. Bale argues that a bilateral negotiating route may be more effective for the United States.

The last selection in this part presents the proposals for a new round of trade negotiations by a group of international leaders appointed by the Director-General of the GATT. Not surprisingly, the authors argue that the traditional liberal approach of the GATT must be strengthened by abandoning discriminatory trade restrictions like voluntary export restraints and eliminating exceptions to the import adjustment rules such as the Multifiber Arrangement, which has restricted the development of trade in textiles and apparel since 1973. They also articulate the growing conviction that there is a need for better international coordination of macroeconomic policies and greater consistency between trade and financial policies.

11

The Changing Nature of U.S. Trade Policy Since World War II

Robert E. Baldwin

[1] INTRODUCTION

Future economic historians will undoubtedly stress trade liberalization as the most distinctive feature of U.S. commercial policy over the past fifty years. As [Table 1] indicates, through a series of thirty bilateral agreements and eight multilateral negotiations, tariffs have been steadily cut to only about 20 percent of their 1930 average level.[1] The increased use in recent years of nontariff protective measures modifies this liberalization picture somewhat, but the trend in protection over the period has clearly been downward.

Although tariff reduction has been the dominant theme of U.S. trade policy since the early 1930s, important changes have taken place in the nature and extent of U.S. support for this trade liberalization. A consideration of these developments is helpful not only to better understand American international economic policy over the period but also to predict possible significant shifts in future U.S. trade policy. To further these objectives, this paper focuses on five closely related trends in or features of U.S. trade policy since the end of World War II. They are: (1) the shift from the use of trade policy in the immediate postwar period as a means of promoting broad international political and national security goals of the United States to its greater use in recent years as a means of advancing national economic objectives and responding to domestic political pressures based on particular economic interests; (2) the continuing efforts by Congress over the period to modify the trade powers of the president to make U.S. international commercial policy more responsive to its wishes; (3) the changes in the positions of the Republican and Democratic parties concerning the desirability of trade liberalization versus increased protectionism; (4) the shifts in the attitudes of business, labor, and the farm sector toward the liberalization-versus-protectionism issue; and (5) the increased use of nontariff measures to regulate international trade at the same time that tariffs were being significantly reduced.

Underlying the different shifts in postwar U.S. trade policy outlined

From R. E. Baldwin and A. O. Krueger (eds.), *The Structure and Evolution of Recent U.S. Trade Policy* (Chicago: University of Chicago Press, 1984), pp. 5–27. © 1984 by the National Bureau of Economic Research. Reprinted by permission of The University of Chicago Press. Some footnotes and references omitted.

TABLE 1

Duty Reductions Since 1934 Under the U.S. Trade Agreements Program

GATT conference	Proportion of dutiable imports subjected to reductions	Average cut in reduced tariffs	Average cut in all duties	Remaining duties as a proportion of 1930 tariffs[a]
1. Pre-GATT, 1934–47	63.9%	44.0%	33.2%	66.8%
2. First Round, Geneva, 1947	53.6	35.0	21.1	52.7
3. Second Round, Annecy, 1949	5.6	35.1	1.9	51.7
4. Third Round, Torquay, 1950–51	11.7	26.0	3.0	50.1
5. Fourth Round, Geneva, 1955–56	16.0	15.6	3.5	48.9
6. Dillon Round, Geneva, 1961–62	20.0	12.0	2.4	47.7
7. Kennedy Round, Geneva, 1964–67	79.2	45.5	36.0	30.5
8. Tokyo Round, 1974–79	n.a.	n.a.	29.6	21.2

[a]These percentages do not take account of the effects of either structural changes in trade or inflation on the average tariff level.

Source: Real Phillipe Lavergne, The Political Economy of U.S. Tariffs, Ph.D. thesis, University of Toronto, 1981.

above are three more basic economic and political influences that help explain why these changes occurred and the manner in which they affected the U.S. commitment toward a liberal trade policy. They are, first — and most important — the emergence and subsequent decline of the United States as a hegemonic power; second, the persistent pressure exerted over the entire period by a politically significant group of domestic industries (whose composition changed somewhat over time) against trade liberalization and in favor of increased import protection for themselves; and, third, the efforts by Congress to reduce the greatly increased powers granted the president during the economic emergency of the 1930s and the military emergency of World War II.

[2] U.S. LEADERSHIP IN ESTABLISHING A LIBERAL INTERNATIONAL TRADING REGIME

Well before the end of World War II, the foreign policy leaders of the Democratic party had concluded that the lack of an open world economy during the 1930s was a major contributory cause of the war and that the United States must, therefore, take the lead after the end of hostilities in establishing an open international trading system to make "the economic foundations of peace . . . as secure as the political foundations."[2] Thus, even before the war had ended, the Roosevelt administration had not only drafted a proposal for a multilateral trade organization but had also requested substantial, new, tariff-reducing powers from Congress.

[2.1] The Basis of Democratic Support for a Liberal International Regime

A desire on the part of political leaders for a new international regime is quite different from actually bringing about such a change, especially when — as in this case — there is a lack of strong direct pressures for the change from either the country's electorate or other governments. One factor that helped the Democratic leadership gain the support of members of their own party for the adoption of a liberal international economic order was the compatibility of such a regime with the trade policy position that the party had long supported. Since the late nineteenth century, the Democrats had associated high tariffs with monopoly profits for the rich and low tariffs with low prices for goods consumed by the average citizen. Furthermore, they maintained that low U.S. tariffs encouraged low foreign tariffs and thus indirectly stimulated increases in U.S. exports, especially agricultural goods. This latter argument was crucial in obtaining passage of the Trade Agreements Act of 1934. The gradual recovery during the 1930s in employment and exports as the trade agreements program was implemented served to reinforce this ideological commitment of Democrats to liberal trade policies. Consequently, the greater emphasis in the postwar period by the party leadership on the foreign policy merits of a liberal trade policy, in addition to its domestic benefits, represented an extension of the party's recent position that was not difficult for most Democrats to accept. It was also consistent with the stance adopted by the Wilson administration at the end of World War I. Thus, over 80 percent of the Democrats voting in the House of Representatives supported the party's position on extending the trade agreements program during the 1940s and 1950s.

The fact that implementing an open international trading system did not involve any significant new increase in the powers of the president also was important in gaining domestic support for the regime change. As a consequence of what almost all regarded as the excessive use of logrolling during the enactment of the Smoot–Hawley Tariff of 1930, coupled with the sense of crisis created by the depression that followed shortly thereafter, the Congress in 1934 gave the president the authority to lower U.S. tariffs by up to 50 percent in negotiations with other countries in return for reciprocal cuts in their import duties. Consequently, the 1945 request for another 50 percent duty-cutting power to enable the United States to take a leadership role in international trade liberalization did not entail any basic changes in existing presidential powers.

The most important reason, however, for the success of the Democratic leadership in first gaining and then maintaining support for the U.S. leadership role in creating a liberal international economic regime was the hegemonic trade and payments position that the United States assumed in the immediate postwar period. The United States emerged from World War II with its economic base greatly expanded, while the economic structures of both its enemies and industrial allies were in ruins. Except for Great Britain's position at the outset of the Industrial Revolution, economic dominance of this extent is unique in the history of the industrial nations. Even as late as 1952, the U.S. share of total exports of the ten most important industrial countries was 35 percent whereas it had been only 26 and 28 percent in 1938 and 1928, respectively. . . . The 1952 U.S. export share of manufactures was also 35 percent in contrast to only 21 percent in both 1938 and 1928. Furthermore, there was an export surplus in every major industrial group (e.g., machinery, vehicles, chemicals, textiles, and miscellaneous manufactures) except metals. These abnormally favorable export opportunities, together with the vigorous postwar domestic economic recovery, served both to mask protectionist pressures from industries whose underlying comparative cost position was deteriorating and to build support for liberal trade policies on the part of those sectors whose international competitive position was strong.

The ability of government leaders to obtain domestic support for trade liberalization was further enhanced by the emergence of the cold war in the late 1940s. The public generally accepted the government view that the communist countries represented a serious economic and political threat to the United States, its allies, and the rest of the market-oriented economic world. The argument that the United States should mount a vigorous program to offset the communist threat by providing not only military aid to friendly nations but also assistance in the form of economic grants and lower U.S. tariffs, therefore, also received public support.

There was still considerable opposition to trade liberalization in the immediate postwar period, however. As in the 1930s, a long list of industries testified during the 1940s and 1950s against giving the president the power to cut duties on imports competing with domestically produced goods. The products covered included textiles and apparel, coal, petroleum, watches, bicycles, pottery and tiles, toys, cutlery, ball bearings, glass, cheese, lead and zinc, copper, leather, and umbrellas. The decision in this period not to apply a liberal trade policy to agriculture significantly weakened the sectoral opposition to liberalization and established a precedent that has been used several times since to offset protectionist opposition.

Pressures to halt further tariff cutting were also strengthened by the opposition of many Republicans to liberalization on doctrinaire grounds. The Republican advocacy for protectionism on the grounds that this policy promoted domestic economic development and high living standards had an even longer tradition than the Democratic position in favor of liberalization.

From the outset of the trade agreements program, the Roosevelt administration assured Congress that no duty cuts would be made that seriously injured any domestic industry. However, in 1945 the administration recognized the possibility that such injury might occur by agreeing to include in all future trade agreements an escape clause permitting the modification or withdrawal of tariff reductions if increased imports resulting from such a concession caused or threatened to cause serious injury to an industry. Furthermore, under prodding from Republican members of Congress, President Truman in 1947 issued an executive order establishing formal procedures for escape clause actions whereby the International Trade Commission (ITC) would advise the president whether such a modification was warranted.

The strength of the early opposition to across-the-board liberalization is further illustrated by the history of the peril point provision that directed the president to submit to the ITC a list of all articles being considered for tariff negotiations and required the commission to determine the limits to which each duty could be reduced without causing or threatening serious injury to import-competing domestic industries. This provision was introduced in the 1948 extension of the trade agreements program when both houses of Congress were controlled by the Republicans. It was repealed in 1949 when the Democrats regained control of the Congress but was then reintroduced in the 1951 extension act, even though the Democrats possessed a majority in both the House and the Senate. The escape clause was also made an explicit part of the law at that time.

These developments indicate that the U.S. trade policy commitment at the beginning of the postwar period was to a policy of liberal trade rather than to a policy of free trade. It was recognized at the outset that protection of particular industries would be permitted if these sectors would otherwise be seriously injured by increased imports. Furthermore, as indicated by the provisions of the charter for an International Trade Organization (ITO) and the General Agreement on Tariffs and Trade (GATT), the commercial policy section of the ITO, pertaining to such practices as dumping and export subsidization, the United States as well as the other major trading nations condemned so-called unfair trade.

The failure of the U.S. Congress to ratify the ITO or even to approve the GATT as an executive agreement is another indication of the early concerns of domestic political interests for import-sensitive U.S. industries. Among other concerns, Congress was fearful that establishing a strong international organization to deal with trade matters would lead to the destruction of many U.S. industries as a result of increased imports. Numerous members of Congress and some of the groups they represented were also concerned about the increase in presidential power that the approval of such an organization might involve. They believed that the division of political powers among the legislative, executive, and judicial branches of government had shifted excessively in favor of the executive branch as a result of the unusual problems created by the depression and World War II and were, consequently, reluctant to extend new authority to the president, especially in an area specifically reserved for Congress under the Constitution.

[2.2] *Gaining International Support for a Liberal Regime*

As previously noted, the implementation of the change from an inward-looking to an open international trading regime required the support of other countries as well as of the U.S. electorate. The hegemonic model is the major explanation put forth by political scientists to account for this support. The reasoning behind this model is as follows.

An open international trading (and payments) system has elements of a public good. For example, adopting a mercantilistic viewpoint, if one country reduces its tariffs under the most-favored-nation principle, other countries benefit from the improved export opportunities this action creates even if they do not make reciprocal duty cuts themselves. Consequently, any individual country has an incentive not to reduce its duties and to hope that it will benefit from the cuts made by other nations. This "free rider" problem may well result in the failure to secure a balanced, multilateral set of duty reductions even though they would benefit all participants. As Olson (1965) and other writers on collective goods have pointed out, it is less likely that the public good will be underproduced from a social viewpoint if one member of the concerned group is very large compared to the others. The dominant member is so large that the costs to it of free rides by other members tend to be small compared to its gains. Furthermore, the large member may be able to use its power to force smaller members to practice reciprocity. Thus, proponents of the hegemonic theory of regime change point to both the dominant trading position of Great Britain in the nineteenth century and the United States in the immediate post–World War II period to account for the creation of open world trading regimes in these periods.

More specifically, in the immediate postwar period the United States was willing and able to bear most of the costs of establishing a liberal international economic order. The other major industrial countries were plagued by balance-of-payments problems, and they rationed their meager supplies of dollars to maximize their reconstruction efforts. Consequently, the tariff concessions they made in the early multilateral negotiations were not very meaningful in terms of increasing U.S. exports. U.S. negotiators were fully aware of this point, and they also offered greater tariff concessions than they received, even on the basis of the usual measures of reciprocity. . . . In effect, the United States redistributed to other countries part of the economic surplus reaped from its usually favorable export opportunities to enable those countries to support the establishment of an open trading regime.

While the hegemonic model has considerable appeal, it should be noted that just as U.S. domestic support for an open trading system was qualified in several ways (e.g., no industry should be seriously injured by duty cuts), so too was the support of other countries. For example, the British insisted upon a provision in the GATT permitting the use of quantitative restrictions to safeguard a country's balance-of-payments position. Furthermore, they were successful in preventing the complete elimination of imperial preferences and in excluding customs unions and free-trade areas from the nondiscriminatory provisions of the GATT. Other illustrations of the limited support of GATT signatories for free trade are the provisions permitting preferential government purchasing policies, allowing (at the insistence of the United States) quantitative restrictions on primary products, and imposing almost no restraints on domestic subsidies.

[3] SHIFTS IN DOMESTIC SUPPORT FOR LIBERALIZATION

The shifts in traditional party positions on trade policy that became evident in 1951, when the Democrats voted in favor of the peril point provision and the escape clause, and when a surprisingly large proportion of Senate Republicans supported the administration's earlier efforts to establish a liberal world trading system, continued over the next thirty years. They were the consequence of basic reassessments of attitudes toward liberalization versus import protection by the various economic groups making up the two major political parties. Congress also continued to restrict the president's ability to refuse to provide protection to industries judged by the ITC to be seriously injured by increased imports. At the same time, however, Congress granted significant new duty-cutting powers to the president.

[3.1] Political Parties and Income Groups

When the Republicans gained both the presidency and control of Congress in 1952, some Republicans expected a return to traditional protectionist policies. However, President Eisenhower and his main advisors within the administration and in Congress believed — like earlier Democratic administrations — that trade liberalization was an important foreign policy instrument for strengthening the "free world" against communism. As became apparent with the issuance of the report of a commission established in 1953 by the president to study foreign trade (the Randall Report), Republican business leaders — especially those in large corporations — also had concluded that a liberal trading order was desirable from their own economic viewpoint. Thus, after a standoff period in 1953 and 1954 during which protectionist-oriented Republicans in the House blocked any further tariff cutting, the liberalization trend was renewed in 1955 when, with the help of a Democratic Congress, President Eisenhower succeeded in obtaining a further 15 percent duty-cutting authority. In 1958 he was granted an additional 20 percent tariff-reducing authority.

Just as more and more Republicans came to accept the desirability of a liberal trade policy as a general principle, more and more Democrats began to press for exceptions to this principle. In the late 1940s, the industries requesting import protection tended to be relatively small and not very influential politically. However, by the mid-1950s the politically powerful cotton textile, coal, and domestic petroleum industries, whose employees tended to vote Democratic, were asking for protection. In 1955, the Eisenhower administration, as part of its efforts to obtain the support of the Democrats for its liberalization efforts, pressured the Japanese into voluntarily restricting their exports of cotton textiles to the United States. This did not fully satisfy the textile interests, however, and in 1962

President Kennedy agreed to negotiate an international agreement permitting quantitative import restrictions on cotton textiles as part of his efforts to gain the support of Southern Democrats from textile areas for the Trade Expansion Act of 1962.

The coal and oil industries succeeded in obtaining a national security clause in the 1955 trade act that permitted quantitative import restrictions if imports of a product threatened "to impair" the national security. Voluntary oil quotas were introduced on these grounds in 1958 and made mandatory in 1959.

The most significant change in the nature of the support for protectionism occurred in the late 1960s when the AFL-CIO abandoned its long-held belief in the desirability of a liberal trade policy and supported a general quota bill. Basically, the shift in labor's position was related to the rapid rise in import penetration ratios (and thus to the increase in competitive pressures) that occurred in many manufacturing sectors in the late 1960s. These included wool and man-made textiles and apparel, footwear, automobiles, steel, and electrical consumer goods, such as television sets, radios, and phonographs. . . . Workers also believed that large numbers of domestic jobs were being lost because of extensive direct investment abroad by U.S. manufacturing firms.

Still another reason for organized labor's change in view was its disappointment with the manner in which the Trade Adjustment Assistance (TAA) program under the Trade Expansion Act of 1962 had operated. The AFL-CIO had supported passage of this act in considerable part because its leaders believed that the extended unemployment benefits and retraining provisions of the TAA program would greatly ease not only any adverse employment effects of the Kennedy Round tariff cuts but also the job displacement effects of ongoing shifts in the structure of comparative advantage in the world economy. However, not a single decision providing adjustment assistance to workers was made under the program until November 1969. Congressional modifications in the administration's original proposal on adjustment assistance that were not fully appreciated by labor or the Democratic leadership produced this unfortunate effect. As a result of the program's disappointing performance, the AFL-CIO leadership became more and more disenchanted with a liberal trade policy, and in 1970 the organization testified in favor of protectionist legislation.

As would be expected, this change in organized labor's position was reflected in the trade policy votes of Democratic members of Congress. In 1970 Wilbur Mills, the chairman of the Ways and Means Committee and long a strong supporter of liberal trade policies, yielded to the pressures of many of the members of his committee and sponsored a bill establishing import quotas for textiles and footwear and requiring the president to accept affirmative import relief decisions of the ITC if certain conditions relating to the extent of import increases were fulfilled. In the House of Representatives, 137 Democrats voted in favor of the bill in contrast to only 82 against it. Republicans, on the other hand, opposed the bill 82 to 78. Further protectionist features, such as quotas on fresh, chilled, or frozen meats, were added in the Senate Finance Committee, but when the various trade provisions reached the Senate floor as an add-on to a social security benefits bill, the threat of a filibuster by a small group of Democratic senators who strongly supported liberal trade policies forced recommittal of the trade features of the bill to the Finance Committee where they died.

The shift in the positions of the two parties was again demonstrated in the voting pattern on the Trade Act of 1974, which provided an additional 60 percent duty-cutting authority to the president. In the final House vote, 121 Democrats voted against the bill whereas 112 supported it. Republicans favored the bill 160 to 19. Part of the increased Republican support can be attributed to the significant surplus of agricultural exports that began to emerge in the early 1970s. The agricultural sector has become one of the most internationally competitive parts of the American economy, and most farmers, who tend to support Republicans as members of Congress, now press for trade liberalization as a means of reducing foreign trade barriers against their own export products. At the same time, however, because the international competitive position of certain large-scale industries, such as steel and automobiles, began to deteriorate (and continued to do so in the late 1970s and early 1980s), some Republican members of Congress who rely heavily upon the support of big business began to adopt a more selective approach to liberalization.

It is doubtful, however, if the Trade Act of 1974 would have been approved had not the president made certain concessions both to organized labor and to particular industries subject to considerable import pressure. The criteria for obtaining adjustment assistance were made much easier to meet labor's objections, and the multilateral arrangement on textiles was extended to cover textile and apparel products manufactured from man-made material and wool as well as cotton. In addition, the voluntary export restraints agreed upon in 1968 by Japanese and European steel producers were extended in the early 1970s. The shift to a flexible exchange rate system in 1971 was also an important factor enabling the president to obtain new powers to reduce trade barriers.

Although the pattern of congressional voting on trade policy measures in the early 1970s shows that Republicans favored and Democrats opposed liberalization, it is probably not correct to conclude that this represents a permanent shift in party positions. The fact that there was a Republican president at the time considerably influenced the nature of the voting by Republican and Democratic members of Congress. A more accurate description of what has happened is that liberalization versus protectionism is no longer a significant party position. The vote of an individual member of Congress on trade policy is now more influenced by economic conditions in his district or state and by the pressures on him by the president (if they are both in the same party) than by his party affiliation. . . .

[3.2] Congressional Restraints on the President

From the outset of the trade agreements program, many members of Congress felt that the president was too willing to reduce tariffs in import-sensitive sectors and — along with the ITC — too reluctant to raise them for import-injured industries. Furthermore, they believed that the executive branch was not sufficiently "tough" in administering U.S. laws dealing with the fairness of international trading practices. Consequently, Congress frequently took the occasion of the program's renewal to introduce provisions designed to force the president and the ITC to comply more closely with these congressional views. Much of the pressure for these provisions came from import-sensitive domestic industries and labor groups. However, part of the readiness on the part of members of Congress to limit presidential authority on trade policy matters seemed to stem from a belief that Congress had given the president too much of its constitutional responsibility "to regulate commerce with foreign nations" and to levy import duties.

Restricting the power of the president by introducing the peril point provision and a formal escape clause provision in 1951 has already been mentioned. The peril point provision was eliminated in the Trade Expansion Act of 1962, but the ITC was still charged with making a judgment "as to the probable economic effect of modifications of duties." More important, at congressional insistence, the chairmanship of the inter-agency committee established to recommend tariff cuts to the president was shifted from the State Department (long regarded by Congress as being insufficiently sensitive to the import-injury problems of U.S. industry) to a new agency, the Office of the United States Trade Representative (USTR), which reports directly to the president. The requirement of the 1974 law that an elaborate private advisory system be established has somewhat further restricted the degree of independence that the president has in selecting items on which cuts are to be made and in determining the depth of those cuts. The creation and subsequent strengthening of congressional delegations to trade meetings and negotiations under the 1962 and 1974 laws have had the same effect. Since 1954 the president has also been specifically directed not to decrease duties on any article if he finds that doing so would threaten to impair the national security. Furthermore, in granting the president the authority in 1974 to permit duty-free imports from developing countries, Congress specifically excluded certain articles, such as watches and footwear, from preferential tariff treatment.

Congress first put pressure on the president to accept affirmative recommendations of the ITC on escape clause cases when this provision was introduced into law in 1951 by requiring the president to submit an explanatory report to Congress if these recommendations were rejected. Since this seemed to have little effect on the president, Congress included a provision in the 1958 renewal act that enabled the president's disapproval of any affirmative ITC finding to be overridden by means of a two-thirds vote of both the House and Senate. This was eased in 1962 to a majority of the authorized membership of both houses and then in 1974 to only a majority of members present and voting.[3]

Congress has also included numerous provisions in the trade laws passed since the end of World War II aimed at increasing the proportion of affirmative import-relief decisions on the part of the ITC. The most obvious way to accomplish this has been to change the criteria for granting increases in protection when an industry is threatened with or is actually being seriously injured by increased imports. For example, the Trade Agreements Extension Act of 1955 narrowed the definition of an industry and required an affirmative decision as long as increased imports contributed "substantially" toward causing serious injury. The 1962 trade act sharply reversed this move toward easier injury criteria as Congress apparently mistakenly believed that the new Trade Adjustment Assistance program would ease the pressures for import protection, but in 1974 the language was again changed to resemble closely what it had been in the 1955 law. Moreover, the requirement that the increased imports be related to a previously granted tariff concession was eliminated.

Less obvious ways that Congress used in trying to make the ITC more responsive to its views were utilizing its confirmation powers to try to ensure that commission members were sympathetic to its views and changing certain adminis- trative arrangements relating to the agency. Beginning in the late 1960s, the chairman of the Senate Finance Committee, Senator Russell Long, and his committee colleagues began to argue forcefully that "it is to the Congress, not the Executive, that the Tariff Commission is expected to be responsive,"[4] and they began to be very critical of nominees whose professional background was largely in the executive branch of the federal government. In the period between 1953 and 1967, five of the thirteen commissioners appointed had extensive employment experience in the executive branch and another two in the commission itself. However, between 1968 and 1980, none of the twelve newly appointed com- missioners had either of these backgrounds. Instead, seven of the approved nominees had significant congressional experience, either as a member of Con- gress (one person) or as congressional staffers. In a further effort to weaken the influence of the president over the commission, Congress in 1974 removed all controls of the executive branch over the commission's budget and eliminated the power of the president to appoint the chairperson of the commission. This latter change was modified in 1977, but the president still cannot appoint either of his two most recent appointees as chairperson.

Similar steps were taken by Congress to try to ensure a stricter enforce- ment of U.S. trade laws relating to unfair foreign practices. For example, many members of Congress long felt that the Treasury Department was too lax in administering U.S. antidumping and countervailing duty legislation. One step designed to change this was to transfer in 1954 the determination of injury (but not the determination of dumping) from the Treasury Department to the ITC. Further- more, under pressure from Congress, the president in 1980 transferred the author- ity to determine both dumping and subsidization from the Treasury to the Com- merce Department — an agency that Congress believed would more closely carry out its intent in these areas. The 1974 change in the manner of administering U.S. legislation pertaining to unfair import practices (sec. 337 of the Tariff Act of 1930) is another illustration of the decline in presidential authority over trade matters. Prior to 1974 the ITC conducted the investigations into alleged violations of this law and then transmitted its findings to the president. If the President was satisfied that unfair import methods had been established, he could ban the importation of the relevant products. However, in 1974 Congress gave the ITC the authority to ban imports of the affected products or to issue a cease-and-desist order to the person practicing the violation. The only power remaining with the president under this law is his ability to set aside the actions of the ITC within sixty days "for policy reasons."

Perhaps the most significant reduction in the president's authority over trade policy concerns his ability to negotiate agreements with other countries covering nontariff measures. When Congress directed the president to seek such agreements under the Trade Act of 1974, it stipulated — unlike it has done with tariffs — that any agreements must be approved by a majority vote in both the House and Senate. This provision was extended in the Trade Agreements Act of 1979 and both gives Congress much greater control over the nature of any agreement and increases its control over the pattern of tariff cuts undertaken by the president in a multilateral trade negotiation, since the tariff and nontariff concessions made by the participants are closely linked.

[4] THE INCREASING IMPORTANCE OF NONTARIFF TRADE-DISTORTING MEASURES

As the reduction in tariffs by the industrial countries continued during the 1950s and 1960s, greater attention began to be given to nontariff trade-distorting measures, not only because they became more obvious as tariff rates declined, but also because there seemed to be a trend toward their greater use. During the 1960s, the extension in the use of quantitative restrictions from primary product sectors, such as agriculture and petroleum, to manufacturing activities, such as cotton textiles and steel; the greater utilization of various export-rebate and import-deposit schemes to improve a country's balance-of-payments position; and the introduction of many new domestic subsidies aimed at stimulating growth in depressed areas, easing structural adjustments, and promoting high-technology industries, all served to direct attention to the fact that the benefits of tariff liberalization could be offset by nontariff trade barriers (NTBs).

As the above illustrations indicate, the increased use of NTBs, particularly beginning in the 1960s, stemmed both from the efforts of particular sectors to secure protection or special export assistance through these measures and from the concerns of governments with balance-of-payments problems and with various social and economic policy objectives. In the case of the United States, for example, the sharp increase in the lending and guaranteeing authorizations of the Export-Import Bank in the late 1960s and early 1970s and the approval of the Domestic International Sales Corporation (DISC) in 1971 represented efforts to increase the country's exports within the constraints of the then fixed exchange rate system. While the United States also followed other industrial nations during the 1960s in greatly expanding domestic programs directed at improving social and economic conditions for disadvantaged income groups and depressed sectors, most American programs had little direct or indirect effect on the pattern of trade. Such did not appear to be the case in a number of other industrial countries, however. Substantial financial assistance by other governments to specific industries and particular economic activities appeared to public and private officials in the United States to represent a serious threat to U.S. trade competitiveness and to the liberal international order in general. Consequently, widespread support began to develop for a new GATT-sponsored effort to provide more detailed NTB codes that would reduce the injurious effects on others of such measures as a country's domestic subsidies or its rules pertaining to product standards.

U.S. officials did possess the authority to undertake negotiations on NTBs during the Kennedy Round of trade negotiations, and a GATT committee was established to deal with this subject. Agreement on an antidumping code was reached, as well as on eliminating a number of particular nontariff measures, such as the American selling price (ASP) system of customs valuation and European discriminatory road-use taxes. However, reaching agreement on tariff issues proved to be so difficult and time-consuming that negotiations in the nontariff field were not very extensive. Moreover, Congress felt that the president had exceeded his authority by trying to implement the new antidumping code as an executive agreement rather than submitting it to Congress for approval and therefore passed a law directing the ITC to ignore the new code when making its injury determinations. Congress also rejected the proposal to eliminate ASP.

In the markup sessions on the Trade Act of 1974, key members of the Senate were adamant about the necessity of submitting international agreements reached on nontariff matters to Congress for final approval, and, as noted earlier, such a requirement was included in the act. However, once this matter was settled, Congress fully supported the efforts of the president to negotiate new NTB codes in the Tokyo Round, and the set of codes eventually agreed on was approved without difficulty by the Congress.

At the same time, efforts were undertaken to negotiate new agreements that would mitigate the adverse effects of foreign NTBs. U.S. producers were pressuring government officials for stricter enforcement of existing U.S. "fair trade" legislation, such as the antidumping and countervailing laws, and were seeking import protection under these laws to a greater extent than in the past. Furthermore, domestic producers were demanding the greater use of quantitative restrictions (as compared with import duties) as the means of protecting their industries against injurious import increases.

One factor accounting for the greater number of less-than-fair-value cases has been the difficulty of obtaining protection through the traditional provisions pertaining to injury caused by import competition. Despite the 1974 easing of the criteria for determining whether import relief should be granted, only forty-seven cases were decided by the ITC between 1975 and 1982, and in all but twenty-four of these a negative decision was reached. Furthermore, the president rejected import protection in all but ten of the twenty-four cases. The likelihood that the routine acceptance of affirmative ITC decisions would be interpreted by foreign governments as an abandonment of the postwar international economic leadership role on the part of the United States appears to have made the president reluctant to accept more than a relatively small proportion of these decisions. Even the Congress has been hesitant on similar grounds to weaken the import-relief criteria much beyond what they were in the 1950s.

Providing protection to offset alleged unfair trade practices is much less likely to be interpreted as representing a basic shift in policy, either by other governments or domestic interests supporting a liberal trading order. Thus, within reasonable bounds a president can support efforts to achieve "fair trade" through measures that protect domestic producers while still being regarded as a proponent of liberal trade policies.

Not only has a better understanding of this point led domestic industries to utilize U.S. fair trade legislation more extensively in seeking import protection, but legislative and administrative changes relating to these laws have facilitated this shift. Congress, though diluting the president's power to reduce trade barriers and to set aside ITC decisions, has at the same time given him new authority to limit imports on fairness grounds. For example, the 1922 and 1930 tariff acts granted the president the authority to impose new or additional duties on imports or even to exclude imports from countries that impose unreasonable regulations on U.S. products or discriminate against U.S. commerce. The 1962 Trade Act further directs the president to take all appropriate and feasible steps to eliminate "unjustifiable" foreign import restrictions (including the imposition of duties and other import restrictions) and to suspend or withdraw previously granted concessions where other countries maintain trade restrictions that "substantially burden" U.S. commerce, engage in discriminating acts, or maintain unreasonable import restrictions. The Trade Act of 1974 restates these provisions and in section 301 also gives the president the authority to take similar actions in response to "subsidies (or other incentives having the effect of subsidies) on its [a foreign country's] exports . . . to the United States or to other foreign markets which have the effect of substantially reducing sales of the competitive United States product or products in the United States or in foreign markets" and "unjustifiable or unreasonable restrictions on access to supplies of food, raw materials, or manufactured or semimanufactured products which burden or restrict United States commerce." However, Congress could veto any actions taken by the president. In amending this provision, the 1979 Trade Act stressed the president's responsibility for enforcing U.S. rights under any trade agreement and simplified the list of foreign practices against which he is directed to take action. Interestingly, this act also eliminated the authority of Congress to nullify presidential actions taken under this provision by a majority vote of both houses within ninety days.

The extension of the definition of dumping in the Trade Act of 1974 to cover not only sales abroad at lower prices than charged at home but to include sales of substantial quantities at below cost over an extended period (even if domestic and foreign prices are the same) is another legislative change that encouraged the use of fair trade legislation to gain protection. Under this provision, the steel industry filed dumping charges in 1977 covering nearly $1 billion of steel imports from Japan, all the major European producers, and India. However, as Finger, Hall, and Nelson (1982) point out, cases of this magnitude in key sectors attract so much political opposition (both domestic and foreign) that they cannot be disposed of at a technical, bureaucratic level and consequently spill over into the political route for gaining import protection. In this instance, the domestic industry was successful in convincing President Carter that its claims were justified, and the so-called Trigger Price Mechanism for steel evolved as an alternative to pursuing the antidumping charges to the final stage.

A similar political solution was reached in 1982 when the steel industry filed charges that European steel producers were receiving extensive subsidies and therefore should be subject to countervailing duties. The possibility of countervailing duties had such significant economic and political implications that the governments of the parties involved did not wish the matter to be settled on technical grounds and sought a solution at the political level. Eventually the Europeans agreed to quantitative export limits on a wide range of steel products to the United States.

Other important sectors that have been protected in recent years by nontariff barriers are the footwear, television, and auto industries. Voluntary export restraints were negotiated by the president in the first two sectors after affirmative injury findings by the ITC. However, the ITC rejected the auto industry's petition for import relief. Nevertheless, the industry was successful in persuading the administration of the need for import controls, and the Japanese eventually agreed to restrict their sales of cars to the United States.

The increased use of nontariff trade-distorting measures obviously has weakened the liberal international trading regime, not simply because they represent a move toward protectionism, but because many of them have been applied in a discriminatory manner and are negotiated outside of the GATT framework. Some of the political decisions reached at the presidential level have also occurred without the opportunity for all interested parties to be heard, as would be the case if a technical route such as an import-injury petition before the ITC were being followed, or even if a political route at the congressional level were being pursued.

[5] DECLINING U.S. HEGEMONY AND THE LIBERAL INTERNATIONAL ECONOMIC ORDER

The hegemonic model of regime change predicts openness in world trading arrangements when a hegemonic state is in its ascendancy and a shift toward a closed system as this nation declines in power and is not replaced by another dominant state. Although this theory is consistent with the early part of the postwar period, there is general agreement . . . that the model does not perform very well as an explanation of regime change for more recent years.

Most writers . . . date the decline in America as beginning in the 1960s. The decline in relative economic power is evident, for example, from the fact that the U.S. share of merchandise exports of the fifteen largest industrial countries fell from 25.2 percent in 1960 to 20.5 percent in 1970, and then to 18.3 percent in 1979. The percentages for exports of manufactures for the same years are 22.8, 18.4, and 15.5. The U.S. share of the GNP of these countries was 57.1 percent in 1960, 50.2 percent in 1970, and only 38.1 percent in 1979. It became quite clear during the long and difficult Kennedy Round negotiations concerning the appropriate tariff-cutting rule to adopt that other industrial countries, especially the European Community, were no longer prepared to continue to accept the U.S. leadership role in a routine manner. As the reduction in cold war tensions during the 1970s reduced the perceived need for U.S. military protection against the Soviet Union, the decline in American economic and political influence became even more evident.

Despite a shift in power from a situation where one country dominated the economic scene to one where there are now three major economic blocs (the United States, the European Community, and Japan), most observers agree that the trade and payments regime continues to be essentially an open and liberal one. As [Table 1] shows, the tariff cuts made in the 1960s and 1970s were actually much deeper than those made in the 1940s and 1950s. Furthermore, the new nontariff codes negotiated during the Tokyo Round, though often very general in their wording, do represent a significant accomplishment in providing the basis for preventing nontariff measures from undermining the liberalization benefits from the postwar tariff cuts. While the GATT ministerial meeting in November 1982 again demonstrated the inability of the United States to dominate international deliberations on trade policy issues, it did reconfirm the continued commitment of the major industrial nations to a liberal international economic order. The increased use of nontariff trade-distorting measures described in the last section represents derogation from this order, but the trading regime still remains essentially an open one.

A consideration of either the economic theory of market behavior or the production of collective goods suggests that the failure of the hegemonic model to predict the continuation of an open system should not be surprising. A single firm that dominates a particular market is likely to stabilize the price of the product at a monopolistic level while still tolerating some price cutting by the smaller firms making up the rest of the industry. However, oligopolistic market theory suggests that the same result is likely if two or three large firms dominate an industry. Similarly, as Olson (1965) pointed out, the free-rider problem associated with collective action by an industry can be overcome if a small number of firms (as well as just one firm) produce a significant share of the industry's output. Thus, the continued support for a stable, open trading order as the distribution of power changed from an almost monopolistic situation to an oligopolistic one is quite consistent with market behavior theory.

The shift from a hegemonic position to one in which the country shares its previous economic and political power with a small number of other nations is, however, likely to alter the country's international behavior somewhat, just as the change in the status of a firm from a monopolist to an oligopolist is likely to change the firm's market behavior. In the U.S. case, the nature of the change has been to initiate trade negotiations mainly to achieve economic benefits for the country rather than to further general U.S. foreign policy and national security goals. This shift in emphasis first became apparent in the Dillon and Kennedy Rounds of negotiations when government leaders stressed to the public the economic gains that would be achieved by lowering the European Community's tariff level and thereby reducing the trade diversion resulting from the formation of this customs union. The usual arguments about the need to strengthen the free world as a means of meeting the threat of communist expansion were also presented, but with less vigor than in the past.

Support for a multilateral trade negotiation based on the view that it was in the economic interests of the United States to participate in such a negotiation was even more evident in the Tokyo Round. In early 1973 President Nixon sent a generally worded bill to Congress that provided the president with the authority to modify tariffs as he thought appropriate and to conclude agreements with other nations on nontariff issues. Congress took the opportunity of a proposed negotiation to reshape the bill so that it dealt with many of its concerns about the nature of the international trading system. In doing so, it soon became apparent that business, labor, and agricultural interests were very fearful that the increasing use of nontariff measures by other countries would significantly curtail U.S. export opportunities and lead to injurious increases in imports. Congress reacted in part by strengthening U.S. fair trade legislation, but its main response was to give the president detailed directions about negotiating new international codes aimed at reduced nontariff trade-distorting measures. In other words, both the Congress and the president agreed that strengthening the liberal international economic order was in the economic interests of the United States, quite aside from its political and national security implications.

As might be expected, the less altruistic behavior on the part of the United States in its international economic relations has resulted in an increased number of trade disputes between the United States and other countries. Many who support a liberal trading order are concerned that these disputes will become so numerous and difficult to solve that the system will collapse with each of the major trading powers pursuing inward-looking trade policies. This is, of course, a possibility. However, most of the trading frictions do not arise because of disagreements on the principles involved in the commitment to an open trading system but on matters of interpretation within these principles. For example, as pointed out earlier, the key parties in the system have always agreed that it was proper to shield an industry from injurious increases in imports. Consequently, when the United States protects the auto and steel industries from import competition or the Europeans subsidize industries from import competition or the Europeans subsidize industries as a means of retaining their domestic market shares, this is not regarded by most countries as a departure from the basic liberal trading rules. Disagreements sometimes arise, however, over whether a country is going beyond the intent of the rules and engaging in what in effect are beggar-thy-neighbor policies. The settlement of major disputes at a high political level and the continuing efforts to improve the GATT dispute-settlement mechanism are a recognition by the major trading nations of the damage to the system that could occur from such disagreements.

Krasner (1976) argues in his amendment to the hegemonic model that the abandonment of the commitment to a liberal trading order on the part of the United States (or the other major trading nations) is likely to occur only when some major external crisis forces policy leaders to pursue a dramatic new policy initiative that they believe to be in their country's interests. However, it may be that the existing power-sharing arrangement between the United States, the European Community, and Japan reduces the likelihood of this outcome compared to the case of a declining hegemony in the midst of many smaller states. In this latter situation, the dominant power is tempted in a crisis to take advantage of its monopoly power over the terms of trade. But when power is shared, the recognition both that a country's market power is quite limited and that retaliation is likely to be swift and significant tends to discourage such adventurism. Of greater concern than the possibility of a dramatic abandonment of the liberal international economic order is the likelihood of a continuing gradual erosion in the openness of international trade because of the inability of the major industrial powers to agree on international measures that take into account the economic interrelationships between trade policies and policies in the exchange rate, monetary, fiscal, and social areas.

Notes

1. If the effects of structural shifts in trade and of inflation on specific duties are included along with the negotiated tariff cuts, the average tariff on dutiable imports drops from a 1931 level of 53 percent to about 5 percent after completion of the Tokyo Round cuts.
2. Statement by President Roosevelt to Congress on 26 March 1945.
3. [In June 1983 the Supreme Court declared the congressional veto to be unconstitutional.]
4. Hearings before the Senate Committee on Finance, 23 June 1971. In these hearings, Senator Long explained the actions of the committee during the late 1960s on various presidential nominees to the commission.

References

Finger, J. M., H. K. Hall, and D. R. Nelson. 1982. The political economy of administered protection. *American Economic Review 72*, 452–66.

Krasner, S. D. 1976. State power and the structure of international trade. *World Politics* 28:317–47.

Olson, M. 1965. *The logic of collective action*. Cambridge, Mass.: Harvard University Press.

12

Protectionist Threat to Trade and Investment in Services

Jeffrey J. Schott

William E. Brock, the United States Trade Representative in President Reagan's Cabinet, has called barriers to international trade in services "perhaps the most important of the emerging trade issues" for the 1980s.[1] Because of the increasing importance of services in overall world trade, the growing incidence of restrictions on international transactions in the services sector and the absence of rules to ensure that trade in services — like that in goods — is conducted on a fair and equitable basis, the United States has pressed for the liberalisation of trade in services in the framework of the General Agreement on Tariffs and Trade (GATT).

When trade ministers gathered in Geneva in November 1982 to consider the deteriorating condition of the international trading system, and to agree on a new GATT work programme, they declined to approve an American proposal, supported by Japan and the European Community, for a working party of GATT signatory countries to be formed to study problems affecting international trade in services. Instead, the ministerial declaration invited signatory countries to conduct national studies on the subject and share the results through international organisations, including the GATT, for consideration at the GATT session in 1984 to decide whether multilateral action would be appropriate and desirable. The GATT Secretariat was charged with acting as a clearing house for collecting, collating and distributing information. But the refusal of the signatory countries to establish a working party has been interpreted by the Director-General of the GATT to mean that the GATT Secretariat should not engage in analysis of issues in the services sector of the world economy.

The limited results of the GATT ministerial meeting confirmed that most countries remain sceptical of the need to develop new rules to cover trade in services. The reasons are not hard to fathom. Countries are still having trouble implementing the results of the Tokyo Round of multilateral trade negotiations conducted in 1973–79 and are loath to embark on new trade talks. In this regard, the rash of trade disputes between the United States and the European Community has distracted attention away from new areas such as services and has disrupted cooperative efforts to liberalise trade and strengthen the international trading system.

More specifically, there is a general lack of familiarity with the produc-

From *The World Economy* 6, no. 2 (June 1983), pp. 194–214. Reprinted by permission of Basil Blackwell Limited. Some footnotes omitted.

tion and trade of service industries on the part of government officials. Many of these industries, especially those involved in the provision of financial services, are looking to the government for the first time for support in the resolution of their problems affecting international trade. Their problems do not involve the traditional kinds of trade restrictions (tariffs or import quotas), but they are manifested in more subtle administrative ways, as through restrictions on the right of establishment, discriminatory taxation or capital requirements, as well as controls on the transmission of data. They are uncharted waters for the GATT and, not surprisingly, many trade officials are a bit at sea in incorporating the services dossier into their portfolios.

The United States is partly to blame for the confusion and caution exhibited by foreign trade officials. Due to the zeal of the American effort to draw international attention to trade problems in the services sector, there have been exaggerated fears of the complexity of the issues affecting trade in services and their importance to the trading interests of the United States.

On closer examination, however, the problem of dealing with trade in services is not as great as it seems. Two common misperceptions can readily be dispelled. The United States is not the predominant exporter of services. Nor is it alone in having a considerable interest in the liberalisation of trade in services. The European Community and Japan also have a lot to gain from new intergovernmental negotiations.

While this should provide some comfort to the harried trade negotiator, it should not diminish the urgency of dealing with trade problems in the services sector. Work needs to be begun in earnest to explore what can and should be done to strengthen the international trading system through the adoption of new disciplines on trade in services. We cannot afford to put the issue on the back burner. There is a clear threat that if they are not attended to now, restrictions on trade in services are likely to proliferate and contribute to the increasing protectionism that is undermining the GATT system.

SERVICES AND INTERNATIONAL TRADE

What is meant by international trade in services? And how much trade in services is actually being conducted? Those are the questions addressed in this section for the purpose of defining the parameters of the international debate on the subject.

It is hard to imagine how trade could be conducted without service industries. Trade must be financed, cargo insured and goods transported, distributed and marketed. Such services, however, can also be "traded," that is, provided to a resident of a foreign country without a link to goods. Banks and insurance companies transact huge volumes of business every day, managing financial resources and providing insurance coverage, without reference to physical products. Planes, ships and railways transport people as well as merchandise. These activities are part of a growing segment of world trade which is quaintly described as "invisible" trade.

There are many other types of services which are traded internationally, ranging from travel, tourism and motion pictures to expertise provided by lawyers, accountants and other professionals.

In addition, there is a service which provides a conduit for the trade of other goods and services, namely data flows. This is a relatively new field. But it is one that is rapidly changing the nature of a wide range of international economic activities. High-speed telecommunications have shrunk the world to a size that is more accessible and understandable to a vast number of people. As such, it has dramatically narrowed one of the most important impediments to international trade and investment, the "knowledge gap," which in the past made it much more costly to engage in overseas business.

One need only consider that such diverse activities as banking, insurance, travel, construction and engineering, shipping, legal and accounting work as well as telecommunications are all part of the services sector to appreciate the scope of the conceptual problem of integrating trade in services into the rubric of principles and rules of the international trading system. Indeed, the complex and heterogeneous nature of service industries makes it difficult, or so it would appear at present, to develop a coherent and comprehensive set of principles and rules applying to trade in services and is one of the main reasons why many governments are reluctant to address the subject.

While it is clear what service industries produce, it is not so clear how to measure their output, for individual governments and international organisations use different accounting methods to determine the value of traded services in national accounts. This makes international comparison and analysis of data rather difficult. Moreover, the data on trade in services are not very good, for analytical and other purposes, and what exist [are] patently incomplete. One is thus left up in the air over the actual scope and magnitude of international flows of services. There are two main reasons for this problem:

a. Because services by nature have no physical presence, they are difficult to value and, for various reasons (for example, tax avoidance), they are often under-reported.
b. Services are often subsumed in a contract for goods and the value of the services provided is counted as part of the cost of the goods.

The data available on world trade in services, however, permit some rudimentary international comparisons. Although the statistics undoubtedly underestimate the value of trade in services, they do provide at least a reasonable estimate of the relative *magnitude* of trade in services in relation to overall trade in goods and services. For the purposes of this article, which is to examine whether there is a need for *normative* rules to govern trade in services and for negotiations to be planned, this is not a great handicap. By contrast to negotiations on tariffs, precise data on trade flows are not especially relevant when deliberating on rules to regulate government conduct, as was the case with the Tokyo Round discussions on nontariff measures. As such, it is probably sufficient to have a "feel" for the magnitude of trade in services, sufficient to evaluate the trading interests of various countries.

According to statistics compiled by the Committee on Invisible Exports in the United Kingdom, world trade in services grew at an annual rate of almost 20 percent during the 1970s and it almost kept pace with the rapid rate of growth of trade in goods (see Table 1). During this period, trade in services accounted for only a little more than one fifth of world trade in goods and services. The United States was the world leader, accounting for about 20 percent of this total in 1980; France and the United Kingdom were a distant second at just over 9 percent.

The magnitude of world trade in services and its rapid growth have been widely given as a major reason why there is a need for a stable institutional environment, for a framework of principles and rules, to foster further development of the services sector. The numbers alone are impressive, over half a *trillion* dollars of exports in 1980, but not necessarily all of this trade would be covered in prospective negotiations on trade in services. About a third of global receipts from services are derived from investments. Transport and travel take another 40–45 percent and the category of "other services" (which encompasses the bulk of the trade in the services noted above) accounts for a little less than a quarter of total trade in services.

Practically none of the investment income *per se* could come under the purview of the GATT's trade rules. These flows are generated from foreign direct and portfolio investment; in many cases, they are influenced more by tax and monetary regimes than by trade rules. While some receipts from "pure" transactions of financial services — that is, fees and commissions — are subsumed in this category, the bulk of the total is composed of interest and dividends earned from foreign assets.

If investment income is subtracted from the aggregate of receipts from trade in services, however, there is still a large volume of trade that falls outside the purview of the GATT which could benefit from the development of new rules. And, interestingly enough, once investment income is factored out of the equation, the United States no longer holds a dominant position among the world's international purveyors of services. As is shown in Table 2, the United States, the United Kingdom, France and West Germany all account for a little under 10 percent of global receipts from services when investment income is excluded. In this light, negotiations on services may not seem so indigestible to trade officials, who have been worried about biting off more than they could chew.

CURRENT RESTRICTIONS ON TRADE IN SERVICES

International transactions in the services sector face a variety of restrictions in different markets. Some take the same form as those applied to goods, be it through "traditional" measures such as tariffs and import licences and quotas or through more opaque means of protection such as subsidies and discriminatory government-procurement policies. Other restrictions hamper trade in services by

TABLE 1

World Trade in Goods and Services, 1970–80
(billion dollars)

	1970	1971	1972	1973	1974	1975	1976	1977	1978	1979	1980	Annual average growth 1970–80
A. Total goods and services	375.4	421.5	498.4	686.8	988.2	1,023.5	1,154.2	1,320.7	1,551.3	1,965.6	2,398.5	20.9
B. Merchandise exports	282.6	315.3	375.0	522.7	773.6	798.2	909.4	1,035.2	1,201.6	1,517.5	1,855.7	21.4
C. Services[a] of which:	92.8	106.2	123.4	164.1	214.6	225.3	244.8	285.5	349.7	448.1	542.8	19.6
D. Transport[b]	25.9	29.2	32.4	41.3	56.5	59.5	62.3	71.8	83.5	106.1	129.4	17.9
E. Travel	20.7	21.6	25.8	33.1	35.6	42.3	44.9	55.8	70.1	86.4	99.0	17.2
F. Investment	26.6	30.4	34.6	53.6	78.8	69.5	73.6	83.1	98.5	143.3	189.5	23.3
G. Other services	19.6	25.0	30.6	36.1	43.8	54.0	63.9	74.8	97.5	107.2	124.8	20.5
C/A (%)	24.7	25.2	24.8	23.9	21.7	22.0	21.2	21.6	22.5	22.8	22.6	
F/C (%)	28.7	28.6	28.0	32.6	36.7	30.8	30.0	29.1	28.1	33.0	34.9	
(C – F)/A (%)	17.5	18.0	17.8	16.1	13.7	15.2	14.8	15.3	16.2	15.5	14.7	

[a]Excludes transfers and miscellaneous government receipts.
[b]Includes passenger fees.
Sources: World Invisible Trade, Committee on Invisible Exports, London, various issues; and *Direction of Trade*, International Monetary Fund, Washington, 1977 and 1981 yearbooks.

TABLE 2

Exports of Services[a] by Country, 1980
(billions of SDRs[b])

	Value minus investment income	% of total
United States	26.6	9.8
United Kingdom	25.6	9.4
France	25.2	9.3
West Germany	24.8	9.1
Italy	17.2	6.3
Japan	14.5	5.3
Netherlands	13.5	5.0
Rest of the world	124.1	45.7
Total	271.5	100.0

[a]Excludes miscellaneous government receipts.
[b]1 Special Drawing Right = $1.3015.

Source: World Invisible Trade. Committee on Invisible Exports, London, June 1982, Table 5a.

limiting investment opportunities in a foreign country. Barriers can be absolute, barring outright foreign participation in a market, or only partial, limiting the scope of activities of foreign firms or placing discriminatory requirements on their operations in order to help domestic firms to compete.

Many of these barriers were instituted to meet broad objectives of national economic policy and, as such, they serve purposes other than trade protectionism, which may be just a side effect. Monetary policy, foreign-exchange controls and development subsidies often tend to discourage participation by foreign service industries in a market. Yet at the same time they often serve very important functions such as the regulation of the banking system and the development of a local capital market.

One must therefore take a close look at what restrictions exist and why they were imposed and remain in force. The fact that certain measures restrict trade in services may not mean, in and of itself, that it is desirable to reduce or eliminate them, for they may serve legitimate nontrade purposes.

Financial Services

Financial services pose a special problem for inter-governmental negotiations because most countries regulate their banking and insurance industries to ensure prudential business practices and to guarantee performance. Each country has its own regulatory regime which lays down guidelines for foreign participation in the market. In some cases, as in the United States, regulatory review is de-centralised, with "provincial" bodies often settling conflicting policies with regard to the granting of licences.

What is at issue is not the regulation of these industries but whether certain statutory or administrative practices discriminate against companies solely on the basis of their residency or ownership — and thus deny or limit business opportunities in those markets to foreigners.

International insurance operations involve coverage of the principal risks involved in world trade — including bonding, performance and transport insurance — as well as coverage of investment projects that are too large to be handled solely by domestic companies. In addition, companies engage in reinsurance transactions to transfer risk insurance to another company or a pool of companies, to meet regulatory requirements or to take advantage of more favourable tax and regulatory policies in foreign markets. Many transactions — for example, those covering transport, bonding and liability insurance — can be carried out in principle without a foreign company's presence in the market in question. Others are facilitated by the presence of an agent or representative resident in the market.

Restrictions on insurance transactions by foreign firms generally take the form of controls on investment, capital and foreign exchange and discriminatory trade and tax policies:

(a) Investment-policy concerns often translate into restrictions on the right of establishment of a foreign company in a market. Companies may be barred outright from doing business in a country or may be forced to limit their participation in the market to a certain class or line of insurance. Such policies are often effected through restrictive licensing requirements which may, for example, limit participation only to locally licensed firms and, at the same time, set a required share of domestic ownership or control as a prerequisite for such a licence.[2]

(b) In order to inhibit foreign activity in a market further, some countries may also impose various discriminatory exchange controls, as well as capital and labour requirements, which place foreign firms at a competitive disadvantage *vis-à-vis* local firms. Foreign-owned firms may face more stringent restrictions on access to foreign exchange or on remittances of capital. Regulations on the activity of foreign-owned firms often set higher capital requirements than on domestic firms (for solvency margins, say), imposing a higher capital cost and thus reducing profits of foreign-owned operations.

(c) Finally, certain government practices erect barriers to trade in insurance that are quite similar to barriers affecting trade in goods. Licensing and discriminatory tax provisions both clearly violate the tenet of "national treatment," which is one of the keystones of the GATT system; some tax measures also confer an implicit subsidy on the operations of domestic firms. Moreover, countries often restrict transactions by governmental entities to domestic firms, barring foreign-owned firms in many cases from a large and lucrative market for public-sector contracts.

Reinsurance poses a special area of problems. Reinsurance is simply the trade of insurance policies among companies. It is a way of spreading risk over a larger capital base than was available to the original insurer or of forming in effect a syndicate to insure large overseas projects or liability risks. In this sense reinsurance is a commercial transaction.

Companies may also, however, transfer risks to other firms, or their foreign affiliates, for financial reasons not purely related to the insurance function. This is an important reason why the value of international reinsurance transactions has grown so rapidly over the past decade.[3]

All governments actively regulate banking operations in their economies both for prudential reasons and to implement monetary and economic policies. Regulations are designed to ensure the soundness of banking operations; measures such as reserve requirements, credit restraints and capital controls are often employed to implement various domestic monetary policies and to safeguard against balance-of-payments problems. In developing countries, government regulations are often designed to protect the domestic "infant industry" against foreign competition, in order to help stimulate and develop the local capital market. While these are all legitimate objectives, in many cases government regulation is implemented in a way that discriminates against foreign banks and lessens competition and thus fosters inefficiency in the domestic economy.

Like insurance companies, banks face a wide array of restrictions on their international operations, ranging from outright barriers to entry to limitations on the type or scope of activities in which they may engage in foreign markets. Many of these are effected through discriminatory regulations that in essence undercut the profitability and competitiveness of foreign banks in the market in question through the imposition of requirements that (i) raise the capital cost of operations of foreign banks in the market (through, for example, higher reserve requirements, tighter credit and lending ceilings and barriers to access to rediscount facilities) and (ii) prohibit certain kinds of banking activities (by refusing to allow the solicitation of certain types of deposits and by limiting the number of branch banks, if branches and subsidiaries are permitted at all). These restrictions are particularly prevalent in the developing countries, especially among the rapidly developing and highly open trading countries of South-east Asia.

Certain problems faced by banks stem less from discriminatory measures imposed by foreign governments than from capital controls and other monetary policies which are applied in a uniform way. Because of their position in the market, their greater reliance on international capital markets for their resources, or for a variety of other reasons tied to the particular global operations of the bank, foreign [banks may sometimes find themselves] in a disadvantageous competitive position *vis-à-vis* domestic banks in a market.

Telecommunications and Data Flows

The rapid development of new technologies for the transmission and utilisation of data has led to the creation of a widespread range of new products and services and has made it easier and cheaper for many more people and industries to take advantage of data banks and advanced communications services. One needs only go to any street corner to see how banks are pushing a new line of services made possible by advances in electronic transfers of funds and using automated 24-hour teller machines to facilitate the processing of banking services. The new technologies have also created a new set of trade problems, those relating to the right of access to data banks and, also, to telecommunication inter-connect markets in foreign countries. As with financial services, most of the trade problems arise out of restrictive government regulations.

Telecommunications and information services are subject to a significant degree of government regulation through the control (usually by public telecommunication monopolies) of the main channels for the provision of these services — leased lines, inter-connect systems and satellites. The regulations limit the right of access to data banks, information systems and communication networks — in many cases exclusively to domestic companies. When permitted, foreign participation in the market is usually controlled through restrictive licensing policies and high taxes. There are a number of reasons for such controls.

First, as in insurance and banking, governments have a legitimate role to play in the protection of the *users* of telecommunication services — in this case the concern is with the privacy or confidentiality of the information stored in data banks. This in part concerns the safeguarding of individual privacy, the maintenance of cultural sovereignty from foreign influences and the protection of national-security interests. The last is based on a concern about the dependence on, and the security of, data stored overseas — in particular, whether one can guarantee access to such data in the event of an emergency.

Second, on the other side of the coin, the national-security rationale is also used to justify protection for public monopolies from foreign competition on the grounds that the control of access to, and the transmission of, vital information is essential for national-security reasons. As such, many governments bar or restrict foreign participation in the domestic telecommunication industries through licensing and tax policies (high transmission tariffs). Many developing countries have charged that such actions effectively block the transfer of new technology to developing countries and that the national-security rationale is used to mask the desire to protect domestic industries from foreign competition.

Third, restrictions are also sometimes imposed on the use of computer facilities in the domestic market in order to encourage the use and development of local systems and the activities of local producers or assemblers. This is particularly prevalent in developing countries, where governments often require firms to use domestic sourcing for their data processing. Brazil, in particular, set up a special secretariat for "informatics" in 1979 to control information flows into and out of the country. Basically the Brazilians do not want to be left out in the cold in the "information revolution" and have thus restricted access to foreign data banks and imposed import restrictions on computer hardware in order to spur the growth of the domestic "informatics" industry.

Because of the rapid pace of change in information and data-processing technologies, there is more concern about the possible future imposition of restrictions than about existing measures. As such, the key concern for policy makers should be how to prevent a further backsliding into protectionism.

Transport and Travel

Another area where rapid changes in technology have revolutionised the provision of services is in the transport and travel industries. The development of containerised cargoes has transformed the transport industry, allowing the use of lighter and more fuel-efficient vessels and facilitating the loading, off-loading and storage of cargo. Such changes have also, however, undercut the market position and competitiveness of certain shipping lines and bulk-cargo carriers and have led to increased calls for protection.

This is not very surprising. Governments have regulated the transport industry for years in order to provide incentives for the development and maintenance of national flag carriers. Because transport services require large capital investments, there is a need to have a fairly good estimate of the future revenue from the service before a decision can be made to sink funds into new ships or aircraft. Governments have attempted to afford a kind of guarantee of profitability for their transport industries through domestic regulations and the negotiation of international agreements which restrict price competition and fix market shares for national flag carriers.

Protection of national interests in the maritime trade is provided *inter alia* through the following.

(a) Cabotage. One of the most common practices is the restriction of marine transport between ports in the same country through various cabotage rules. Transport is often reserved exclusively to national flag carriers; the main exception to this is the transport of crude oil and products, where shipments are controlled by the major multinational oil enterprises and delivered on international bottoms. The oil trade, however, is the exception that proves the rule. Typical of such measures is the Jones Act, of 1920, which restricts inter-coastal trade in the United States to American bottoms.

(b) Subsidies. Governments often support their domestic maritime industry both through direct operating subsidies to maintain and operate the domestic fleet and through construction subsidies to support the domestic shipbuilding industry. The subsidies often take the form of low-interest loans and tax preferences for the domestic industry. Both types of measures are justified on national-security grounds, the rationale being that a country needs to have a fleet that can be pressed into military service in the event of war. This point was amply demonstrated during the recent war over the Falkland Islands when the British Government consigned a number of merchant ships to its naval task force.

(c) Cargo preference. Governments can discriminate against foreign flag carriers in a variety of ways, namely through blatant quotas which reserve all or a certain percentage of cargo to be carried on domestic bottoms, by granting preferential rates or imposing discriminatory taxes on the operations of certain carriers and, as noted above, by providing subsidies. Such practices can have a pronounced effect on the competitiveness of the goods offered in international commerce, especially those bulk commodities where the transport cost is a large part of the total price.

The international provision of transport services is also heavily regulated by such bodies as the International Maritime Consultant Organisation, which deals with the health and safety standards for ocean-going vessels, and the United Nations Conference on Trade and Development (UNCTAD), under whose auspices the notorious Code of Conduct for Liner Conferences was negotiated in the mid-1970s. The UNCTAD Liner Code deals with the sticky issue of cargo sharing and attempts to lock in a fixed share of global revenues from shipping for flag carriers from developing countries. As such, it impedes competition in transport rates in an effort to bolster revenues and secure a larger market share for countries that are not members of the Organisation for Economic Cooperation and Development (OECD). The trade preferences impose a significant cost on internationally traded goods and provide a ready conduit for countries to subsidise their exports through the transport industry. Nevertheless, the UNCTAD Liner Code is now likely to enter into force in 1983, in spite of the nonadherence of the United States.

Air transport is also heavily regulated on both the national and the international level, although the recent trend towards de-regulation in the American market is having some impact in Western Europe as well. National governments restrict landing rights and operations of foreign carriers for both national-security and safety reasons. Such restrictions, however, often hamper the foreign carriers from establishing a profitable route structure or limit their ability to provide on-ground services. International routes and fares are complicated further by the regulations of various organisations, in particular the International Air Transport Association (IATA).

In the travel industry, transactions covered include the usual expenses — lodging, meals, internal transport, entertainment, *et cetera* — and ship, rail and airfares collected from foreign residents. Some of these activities are already covered by agreements negotiated under the auspices of various international organisations; others by their nature (for example, lodging, meals) are not amenable to international rules. The only real restrictions that arise in this area are monetary-control measures designed to stem capital outflows (usually by setting limits on how much money a resident can take out of the country). Such controls are reactions to more general economic problems and are not a proper topic for a discussion on trade.

Other Services

There are [a] number of other kinds of services that are traded internationally and face restrictions which are similar to those hindering the provision of the major services discussed above. Subsidies, restrictive government-procurement policies, quotas and other administrative measures affect trade in, for example, (i) construction, engineering and consultancy services, (ii) professional services such as those performed by lawyers and accountants, and (iii) motion pictures and other forms of entertainment.

The provision of construction, engineering and consultancy services has become a major trade issue over the past few years because of the number of "big-ticket" industrial development projects that have been undertaken in developing countries, especially in the Middle East. In these cases the problems derive not from protection of domestic industries in the "importing" country but rather from subsidised competition from other bidders for the lucrative contracts. Importing governments do, however, resort to a kind of arm twisting to get a better deal out of the competing bidders, sometimes through administrative red tape (such as delayed or cancelled visas) and demands for outright graft. This situation has led American companies to lobby hard in Washington for changes in American laws (particularly sections 911–13 of the tax code and the Foreign Corrupt Practices Act of 1979) to allow them to compete more effectively against foreign suppliers of goods and services for such projects.

The ability to perform professional services abroad is also sometimes hampered by restrictions or administrative difficulties in gaining accreditation to practice in a foreign country and/or membership of foreign professional associations. In addition, visas are often denied to foreign professionals, in order to force companies to retain local experts.

Restrictions on the import of motion pictures and other forms of entertainment are imposed for reasons of cultural sovereignty (to prevent foreign cultures from "polluting" domestic society) and to protect the market for local industry and performers. Protection for motion pictures, in particular, has in effect been sanctioned for years by both the GATT and the OECD. Article IV of the GATT explicitly permits screen quotas as long as the portion of time that is not reserved for films of national origin is not allocated among foreign suppliers. While the OECD Code of Liberalisation of Current Invisible Operations requires the elimination of restrictions on the "exportation, importation, distribution and use of printed films and other recordings," many countries have lodged reservations to this particular provision, which has effectively gutted its discipline.

AMERICAN PERSPECTIVE ON TRADE IN SERVICES

The above section has set out an impressive array of barriers that interfere with the free flow of services among countries. The restrictions break down into two categories: (i) those implemented by familiar nontariff trade measures such as import quotas, subsidies and discriminatory procurement, licensing and technical-standards practices; and (ii) those implemented by capital controls and discriminatory tax policies. There are, of course, areas of overlap between the two and, indeed, many industries, particularly those dealing in financial services, suffer from both trade and capital restraints. But they all have one common purpose, namely, to make it more difficult for foreign firms to compete in the market in question, the former by affecting the ability to perform the service (that is, the access to the market) and the latter by undercutting the profitability of firms engaged in the service trade. Either way, the restrictions hit the bottom line of companies providing services and thus tend to reduce the trade advantage of foreign firms in the market.

The question is how to deal with these problems in the context of the international trading system. The United States has proposed that all the restrictions on trade in services should be examined in the GATT to determine whether new trade rules should be developed to address the significant problems that arise in this trade. Some of the restrictions can probably be resolved through the development of new international trade rules; others probably stand beyond the pale of the GATT because of overriding considerations of monetary and macroeconomic policies.

There is a real danger that unless rules on services are somehow incorporated into the framework of the international trading system, barriers are likely to grow and contribute to the increasing protectionism that is eroding the GATT system. The extent of the trade problems in the services sector and their significant impact on trade in goods points up the urgency of such an effort. This section describes what the United States has proposed in this regard and why.

Because the United States has done the missionary work in drawing worldwide attention to the issue of trade in services, there is understandable concern among other countries about the motives behind the American initiative in the GATT. Although the United States has not yet clarified its specific objectives and priorities, it has outlined in general terms a proposed work programme for the GATT in the area of trade in services.[4]

In essence, American trade officials envisage the negotiation in the GATT of an umbrella agreement that would set out a code of conduct that governments would follow in formulating their policies towards trade in services. But unlike the codes negotiated during the Tokyo Round deliberations, which work because they in effect interpret existing GATT provisions, the prospective services "code" would have to go beyond the scope of the Tokyo Round codes and include, in addition, new well-defined and binding obligations which are at present lacking in the GATT. The agreement would contain *inter alia* an affirmation of the principles of national treatment and the right of establishment and possibly other hortatory provisions that seek to accord to trade in services the same protections against formal restrictions and administrative barriers that now exist for trade in goods. Such an agreement would be similar in many respects to the GATT Standards Code that arose out of the Tokyo Round negotiations. In addition, the agreement would provide a platform for further negotiation of additional rules for particular service industries, if desired.

It is not hard to explain why the United States has taken the lead in pressing for multilateral negotiations on trade problems in the services sector. Clearly the United States has a major stake in the continued viability of the GATT system and the growth of world trade. There is concern that if a significant segment of world trade is not subject to international discipline, the GATT trading system may be further weakened.

But why now? The United States Administration has had a Congressional mandate since the Trade Act of 1974 to negotiate on trade in services. Yet little was done during the Tokyo Round deliberations to address any of the trade problems in services. In fact, negotiators had all they could handle during the Tokyo Round negotiations just trying to extend GATT discipline over nontariff measures affecting trade in goods, that is to say, breaking new ground on services was clearly premature. Perhaps more important, however, in explaining the new interest in services on the part of the United States has been the growing interdependence of national services markets. Many service firms now have an international perspective that was lacking only a few years ago. Moreover, in part because of technological advances, there is now a new mix in the types of services provided internationally, which has spurred greater interest and provoked more concern about restrictions on trade in services.

FOREIGN REACTIONS TO THE AMERICAN INITIATIVE

Because of the extensive attention given to issues in trade in services by American officials, it appeared that the United States was planning for a massive new round of trade negotiations in the mid-1980s. Ambassador Brock dispatched his deputies around the world to drum up support for new GATT talks. These representatives had mixed results; while they succeeded in elevating trade problems in the services sector to the agenda of bilateral and multilateral trade discussions, they also created exaggerated expectations of what needed to be done and thus led some foreign trade officials, who were struggling to implement the Tokyo Round agreements, to shy away from the American initiative.

The above analysis shows that such fears are unfounded. Given the limited scope of the proposed talks, many countries may find, on a second look, that negotiations on services in the framework of the GATT may not be all that bad. The following provides a thumbnail sketch of the interests of the main participants in the prospective GATT talks on services.

European Perspective

With the exception of the United Kingdom, the European Community's response to the American initiative on services has been decidedly restrained. Although many government officials see the logic of extending rules on trade in goods to trade in services, especially where the services facilitate trade in goods, they do not see a current need to place this subject high on the agenda of multilateral trade negotiations. Moreover, given their unfamiliarity with the subject, they are wary of what is involved in trade in services (particularly the investment-related ones), what the United States wants and what's in it for them.

This does not mean, however, that the European Community is not in principle interested in trade rules on services. The Community has been engaged since its inception in a slow and tortuous process of liberalising trade in services between the member countries. The Treaty of Rome, which established the European Economic Community in 1957, set out in Article 59 a framework for the liberalisation of trade in services.

In particular, the Treaty of Rome provided for the progressive elimination of restrictions on the right of establishment (Article 52) of nationals of a member country anywhere in the Community and included (in Article 62) a "standstill" provision, in which member countries were committed not to introduce "any new restrictions on the freedom to provide services," unless "otherwise provided in the Treaty."

That liberalisation was to be accomplished within the twelve-year transition period for the entry into force of the Treaty of Rome in line with the terms of internal directives which would be promulgated by the European Community's Council of Ministers. For certain services, however, progress on liberalisation or harmonisation of member countries' practices was tied to a parallel movement on rules on capital flows. This is particularly important for the banking, insurance and transport industries. The requirements that (i) rules for key industries should depend on progress in other areas and (ii) the development of common procedures to *implement* the agreement to liberalise trade in services should depend on agreement on internal directives, which has been very difficult to attain, have opened up major loopholes which, in practice, have stymied progress on the liberalisation of trade in services.

There is now pressure, particularly from the United Kingdom, for the European Community to do more. The British are especially interested in the liberalisation of trade in financial services, in which they enjoy a substantial comparative advantage. A private-sector report by the Committee on Liberalisation of Trade in Services in the United Kingdom called for "the GATT Secretariat to undertake studies aimed at defining more accurately the nature and extent of problems relating to trade in services," noting the "net advantage to the British economy that could be expected" from liberalisation.

Outside the European Community, Sweden has become increasingly interested in trade in services, for she seeks to expand the international operations of her service industries, particularly in banking and transport. The Swiss, who have negotiated bilaterally with the Community on trade in insurance, are also active.

Japanese Perspective

Japan has gone further than any other country in supporting the American initiative in the GATT on trade in services. Zenko Suzuki, as Prime Minister of Japan, noted at the Versailles Economic Summit meeting in June 1982 that his

country "will cooperate in a positive way" in work in the GATT on the liberalisation of services, investment and high-technology trade. The Japanese clearly want
to be seen as good international citizens and hope this forthcoming position on
services will offset some of the bad press they have been getting abroad because of
their trade surpluses with the United States and the European Community.

Over the years, the Japanese have run a large deficit on trade in services,
primarily due to payments for transport and travel which in 1981 accounted for
about $6.4 billion of red ink of their $12.3 billion deficit in services. Except for
shipping, Japan has less of a stake in exports of services than the United States or
the European Community. Total exports of services amounted to $31.5 billion in
1980, but if investment income and government military receipts are deducted, the
total slims down to $18.9 billion, or about 5 percent of all exports. Of this figure,
almost two-thirds is generated by transport receipts.

The Japanese recognise, however, the important role that services play in
world trade and, too, the need to maintain open markets if that trade is to develop.
In this regard, trade in services is one area where the Japanese have been responsive to demands for them to open their domestic market to foreign competition.
Steps were recently taken to reduce restrictions to foreign activity in the Japanese
banking and securities industries. This was ostensibly done to appease those
calling for Japan to import more. The reforms, however, also possibly presage a
big surge in international activity by Japanese firms in this area. Clearly there is
ample room for growth in Japanese exports of services.

Developing-Country Perspective

Trade in services is important to the developing countries, but the
possibility of multilateral negotiations to develop rules to govern that trade is not,
apparently, very welcome. Developing countries are wary of new trade talks on
services for three main reasons:

> First, developing countries are concerned that talks on services would
> deflect attention, and diplomatic resources, from more pressing trade
> problems for them, such as rules for "safeguard" action and the
> restrictions on trade in textile and agricultural products maintained by
> developed countries.
> Second, they are worried that new trade rules would freeze them into a
> position of inferiority as service users, not service providers. As such,
> they want to restrict trade in order to allow time for their domestic
> services industries to develop, typical of such concern being the
> Brazilian "informatics" policy mentioned earlier.
> Third, in this regard, developing countries see trade restrictions as a lever
> to force developed countries to transfer advanced technology to their
> economies.

It should be noted, however, that not all developing countries are opposed
to the liberalisation of trade in services. Some, such as Singapore, would like to see

reforms in international shipping rules to allow them to benefit from their comparative advantage in this area. In addition, the GATT does not normally require developing countries to assume all the obligations to liberalise trade that are demanded of developed countries. It is likely that any rules that would be negotiated for trade in services would leave ample room for the development of indigenous service industries in developing countries, protected from foreign competition by "infant-industry" trade barriers.

Perhaps the key reason why developing countries shy away from negotiations on trade in services is that many of the restrictions they maintain are integrally linked to their policies for economic development. In particular, restrictions on capital flows, which are a key problem in financial services, are often critical in meeting domestic monetary stabilisation and balance-of-payments objectives. Their impact on trade in services is of second-order importance to policy makers in developing countries in comparison with their value as more general tools of economic policy. If they are to include the developing countries, future talks on trade in services will have to recognise the inter-relationship of trade, investment and monetary policies in the developing countries and the limitations it places on their ability to liberalise trade, although these considerations also carry weight in many developed countries.

PROSPECTS FOR INTERNATIONAL NEGOTIATIONS

The final sorting-out process in this examination of trade in services involves what should be done internationally and where. A lot of work has already been done by several international organisations — particularly in the area of transport services. IATA has regulated the skies for years and UNCTAD hopes to rule the seas in the future through its Code on Liner Conferences. Future negotiations on trade in services have little to gain from a rehash of debates which took place in UNCTAD or IATA on maritime rules and civil aviation, respectively.

The main work currently under way is a series of sectoral studies within the OECD of key service industries. Various OECD committees are conducting reviews of trade in such services as insurance, banking, shipping and construction-engineering and consultancy services. In addition, a working party on information, computer and communications policy has begun to examine issues related to international information flows. The Trade Committee of the OECD is trying to coordinate the results of these studies and develop a comprehensive inventory of problems affecting trade in services. Based on this work, it will then try to draw some general conclusions on the need for and objectives of a possible negotiation on trade in services. These efforts are being hampered, however, by the lack of current and complete data as well as the apparent inability of different parts of the OECD to work with each other.

In spite of constant prodding by the United States, most OECD member countries have not been enthusiastic in support of efforts in the OECD related to the liberalisation of trade in services. Work has been allowed to proceed, but only grudgingly. The language of the 1982 OECD ministerial *communiqué* attests to this tepid attitude: "Ministers . . . decided to encourage the competent committees to progress as soon as possible in their analytical and fact-finding work." This is hardly a rousing call to action.

Moreover, the agreements that have been reached in the OECD — in particular, the Code of Liberalisation of Capital Movements and the Code of Liberalisation of Current Invisible Operations — have been noted more for their reservations and derogations than for their obligations to liberalise transactions in the services sector. The discipline of these OECD codes has been quite weak, although attempts are being made to shore up the invisibles code in the area of insurance. In a similar way, a 1976 OECD declaration that sets out an obligation to provide national treatment to foreign companies already established in the country suffers from two major weaknesses: first, it does not deal with barriers to entry and, second, it is not legally binding on OECD countries.

This last point underscores one of the basic problems with OECD agreements: for the most part, they consist of hortatory provisions of what countries should do rather than commitments by countries of what they will do. The OECD is a valuable *consultative* forum for the developed countries. But it is not an effective negotiating body.

The other key problem with the OECD is its limited membership. Without the participation of developing countries, it is hard to put together a clear picture of the global service-trade problems and what can be done about them. Many of the restrictions in the inventory compiled by the Office of the United States Trade Representative, in the Executive Office of the President, are imposed by developing countries; rules on the liberalisation of these measures will either have to take into account the particular reasons why they are maintained or provide for special exemptions from the general discipline for developing countries. In this regard, one argument that is often raised for advancing work in services in the OECD before entering into negotiations in the framework of the GATT is to coordinate the position of developed countries on this very question of special rules for developing countries. Such an "us-against-them" approach has not been successful in the past and is unlikely to be helpful in talks on trade in services in the future. One need only look at the OECD experience on the government-procurement code and OECD preparations for UNCTAD meetings to judge the value of "coordinated" OECD positions in international trade negotiations.

By contrast, the GATT is a better forum for talks on trade in services, for it is the only international body that seriously negotiates binding agreements. It is the only place where both developed and developing countries feel they can do business with each other.

Signatory countries to the GATT should not shy away from this task. Although the ministerial meeting last year failed to open the door for a GATT study, work should proceed in individual countries to analyse their interest in services in order to define more succinctly what issues need to be addressed in the international context. This is particularly important for the United States: a clear exposition of specific American objectives and a range of specific possible concessions is urgently needed to stimulate the international debate.

In addition, Western leaders would do well to address services not as a separate item on inter-governmental agendas but in the context of protectionism and the future of the international trading system. There has been a serious erosion of confidence in the GATT system, one that must be arrested if international trade is to increase and support a more general recovery. Reinforcing the GATT through new rules on trade in services would be a significant step forward.

Notes

1. Testimony of William E. Brock before the Subcommittee on Trade of the United States Senate Finance Committee, 14 May 1982.
2. See Brian Hindley, *Economic Analysis and Insurance Policy in the Third World,* Thames Essay No. 32 (London: Trade Policy Research Centre, 1982).
3. A study by the United States Department of Commerce concludes that much of the growth in transactions in international reinsurance by American firms derives from their desire to shift profits to foreign affiliates residing in countries with a more favourable tax and regulatory regime. Almost 50 percent of the increase in premium payments by American firms in the period 1970–80 went to foreign companies in the Caribbean (mainly Bermuda). The study notes that the loss ratio on risks reinsured by firms in Bermuda was significantly lower than in other areas, indicating that the transactions were probably made for financial rather than for commercial reasons. See Anthony J. Dilullo, "Service Transactions in the US International Accounts, 1970–80," *Survey of Current Business,* United States Department of Commerce, Washington, November 1981, pp. 29–46.
4. See Brock, "A Simple Plan for Negotiating on Trade in Services," *The World Economy,* November 1982.

13

Trade Policy Aspects of International Direct Investment Policies

Harvey E. Bale, Jr.

INTRODUCTION

For a decade now, the primary objective of U.S. trade policy officials has been to increase international discipline over governments' use of nontariff barriers and distortions to merchandise trade. In the GATT, advances were made in the Tokyo Round regarding subsidies, government procurement, and technical product standards policies. Since the end of that round of multilateral trade negotiations in 1979, the United States has made efforts to extend progress made in these areas and consideration has been given to other forms of nontariff barriers.

At least a decade ago, it was recognized that the manipulation of international direct investment flows by governments ranked high on the list of serious nontariff barriers. . . . Both business and labor organizations have urged trade policy officials to address two types of issues: (1) investment performance requirements that distort the pattern of U.S. and international trade and protect foreign industries from import competition, while exposing U.S. industry and labor to "unfair" competition; and (2) restrictions on the establishment of direct investment that impede access to foreign markets for U.S. exporters. . . .

U.S. government officials have become increasingly concerned about the trade ramifications of certain investment policies being implemented by some of our major trade partners. In its July 1981 White Paper summarizing the administration's trade policy objectives, the government expressed its intention to address foreign investment policies that "obstruct international trade just as seriously as do tariff and nontariff barriers," particularly export performance and local content requirements and associated investment incentives (Brock, 1981). . . .

This paper discusses several topics concerning the interrelationship between international trade and foreign direct investment policies noted above. The underlying theme is that these issues must be effectively addressed, both to preserve the trade liberalization goals (and results) of the GATT and to enhance global production efficiency.

From R. E. Baldwin (ed.), *Recent Issues and Initiatives in U.S. Trade Policy* National Bureau of Economic Research Conference Report (Cambridge, Mass.: NBER, 1984), pp. 67–100. Reprinted by permission. Some text, tables, and references omitted.

TRADE AND INVESTMENT: A MULTILATERAL CONTRAST

While the interrelationships between trade and investment issues have become increasingly recognized, until now they have not been addressed together in the same manner. With respect to both objectives and issues that need to be addressed, investment policy has commanded far less international consensus than has trade policy.

The General Agreement on Tariffs and Trade (GATT) represents a major international achievement in liberalizing international trade transactions. By joining the GATT, a majority of the world's developed and developing countries have agreed to "substantial reductions of tariffs and other barriers to trade" (GATT, 1969). Of course, the process of trade liberalization has not been entirely free of setbacks. Pressures have been present in the past, and have greatly increased recently, for protectionist trade actions and subsidized exports to stimulate industrial employment, provide artificial support for high technology industries, and help reduce balance of payments and domestic fiscal deficits. Despite these pressures, however, the maintenance of an international political commitment to trade liberalization under the GATT has been reaffirmed on several occasions. . . .

The institution of the GATT and the commitments made under it . . . provide a fundamental basis for further multilateral trade liberalization. In contrast, no such comparable multilateral commitment to the liberalization of foreign direct investment (FDI) exists. This is the case despite almost continuous U.S. efforts in this regard over the past several decades, and a consensus among economists that freer flows of FDI would substantially enhance efficiency in the use of the world's resources and provide important benefits to both home and host countries.

Shortly after the Second World War, when the Havana Charter for the International Trade Organization (ITO) was being negotiated, the United States proposed that the ITO cover direct investment as well as trade flows. The U.S. proposal was designed to promote FDI liberalization by including in the Charter binding provisions that would encourage international investment through guarantees of national treatment for foreign direct investment among ITO member states. As in the case of the binding trade provisions in the ITO's successor organization — the GATT — there would also be a right to compensation or retaliation by a member state against those members of the ITO that violated the investment "bindings" of the Charter. Unfortunately, the U.S. proposals were so diluted with allowances for "escape actions" and permissible derogations from national treatment that U.S. domestic support for the Charter was substantially diminished. In the end, for various reasons, including the absence of acceptable investment provisions, the United States Congress refused to give its approval to the ITO. . . .

The espoused United States international investment policy has been to seek to strengthen "multilateral discipline and restraint over government actions which affect investment" (National Advisory Council, 1977). In relation to developed countries, this policy has met with limited success. In 1961, the United States negotiated with countries of the Organization for Economic Cooperation and Development (OECD) a Code of Liberalization of Capital Movements which seeks to provide a framework for the progressive abolition of investment restrictions. In 1976, the OECD countries agreed upon a Declaration on International Investment and Multinational Enterprises. It provides that OECD countries should accord foreign direct investments, once they are admitted by the host country, "treatment . . . no less favorable than that accorded . . . domestic enterprises" (OECD, 1976, 1982[a]). . . . While these Codes seem to cover most U.S. objectives in the field of international direct investment, they still have major shortcomings. First, they apply only to the developed countries (and not all of them — Canada is not a signatory to the 1961 Capital Movements Code). Second, countries adhering to the codes are not necessarily bound by their provisions, and major reservations to the coverage of the Codes are permitted (OECD, 1982[b]). Canada, for example, which adheres to the 1976 Declaration, introduced measures in 1981 and 1982 that discriminate against *existing* foreign enterprises in Canada's energy sector; furthermore, Australia's membership in the 1961 Code carries "reservations" that justify its policy of restricting a broad range of foreign direct investment (OECD, 1982[a]). Finally, *all* of the OECD countries maintain restrictions against foreign investment in certain "sensitive" sectors, typically those related to national defense and petroleum and such service sectors as banking, insurance, and shipping (OECD, 1982[b]).

Negotiations among the developed and developing countries on the subject of FDI flows have been much less productive. There have been "North-South" deliberations in the United Nations; however, these have tended to focus on issues and "problems" posed by activities of "transnational corporations" and how to deal with them. There has been an accompanying tendency to downplay the issues of government policies toward FDI flows. . . .

In sum, we have not achieved broad commitments and enforcement in the domain of direct investment comparable to those achieved in the trade field via the GATT. In the GATT, countries make best efforts to maintain their trade commitments, in part because of the knowledge that retaliation is invited when those agreements are abrogated, or even when permissible escape clause actions are taken. In the investment area, a global investment agreement is lacking, while the agreements among the developed countries are partial and lack enforcement mechanisms.

There are, of course, understandable reasons for the lack of a GATT-like discipline in the field of investment. They are the same as those that led to a failure of the United States to obtain strong free trade provisions for investment flows in the Havana Charter in 1947, and resulted again in the failure to address investment performance requirements at the GATT Ministerial meeting in November 1982. FDI issues are normally considered politically sensitive, particularly by governments of host countries. They are typically considered in the context of national industrial competition, taxation, financial and social policies; furthermore, host countries' consideration of the economic benefits of inward FDI is frequently overridden by nationalistic and domestic political considerations — for example, the degree of foreign ownership and control over domestic economic resources. . . .

The absence of an international consensus on the liberalization of international direct investment policies are of significant concern to policymakers in the United States and some other capital exporting countries, because of the adverse effects these policies can have on international trade and investment flows. The danger to the GATT trading system is that certain national policies and practices toward foreign investment — particularly performance requirements, incentives, and screening — could increasingly constitute important barriers and distortions to international trade in goods and services.

The following sections survey major U.S. concerns and discuss various policy responses and initiatives to deal with them.

PERFORMANCE REQUIREMENTS

Foreign investors are expected to operate according to the legal system in host countries; however, frequently their host country obligations take the form of performance requirements extending beyond those generally imposed on host countries' own firms. Performance requirements most commonly encountered are:

a. *local content requirements,* which mandate that foreign investors purchase locally produced goods and services as a fixed percentage of the final product's value, or to establish certain manufacturing operations locally; these requirements can have the same effect as import quotas or tariffs on intermediate goods or raw materials . . . ;

b. *export requirements,* which obligate the investor to export: (1) a minimum proportion of the value of final output; (2) a certain absolute quantity of goods; (3) a quantity sufficient to balance import purchases by the firm; or (4) an amount that covers expenditures of foreign exchange; these requirements have the same impact on trade as do export subsidies: that is, exports of the MNC [multinational corporation] will be higher as a result of the requirements . . . ;

c. *technology transfer requirements,* which necessitate the licensing of technology to nationals of the host country;

d. *local equity participation requirements,* which impose a minimum equity position to be held by host country nationals in the operation (even up to a majority equity position);

e. *employment, size, location, and financing requirements,* which may specify use of local labor and management, minimum or maximum size, location (for example, in regions that are considered depressed), and limits on access to local financing. . . .

Performance requirements normally arise as part of the process of screening of foreign investments by host country governments. They may occur under the mandate of statutes or regulations, but they are also often negotiated between the foreign investors and the host government's screening agency — typically, the government's investment-authorizing agency or ministry of finance acting in consultation with other interested government departments. Frequently, performance requirements are linked to the granting of investment incentives (for example, tax holidays, remissions of duties on imported inputs, infrastructure development). They represent a tax levied on the benefits or rents received by foreign investors through incentives or entry into the host country market. In effect, this "tax" is used to support certain domestic economic activities.

All of the above categories of performance requirements can affect the flows of world trade and investment; but those which tend to have the most direct effect on trade are the local content and export performance requirements.

In the absence of direct incentives, the existence of performance requirements which significantly affect firms' behavior implies either the presence of a significant degree of protection from imports, relative local cost advantages, or a sizeable local market. The countries mentioned below as being those that utilize performance requirements most extensively — Canada, Australia, Mexico, Brazil, and India — have relatively large and protected domestic markets. Mexico and Brazil also offer substantial financial incentives. . . .

. . . There are several surveys and samples of the occurrence of performance requirements based upon the experience of MNCs. The most complete survey available has been done by the Commerce Department in 1977 as part of a benchmark survey of U.S. investment abroad (U.S. Department of Commerce, 1981). This survey found that 14 percent of all U.S. affiliates overseas were subject to export, local content, employment, or equity participation requirements as a condition for entering their host countries. The ratios are 6 percent and 29 percent in developed and developing countries, respectively. This survey, however, probably substantially underestimates the application of performance requirements by host countries to recent investments, particularly local content and export requirements, which were found for only 6 percent of all the affiliates surveyed worldwide (14 percent in developing countries). This is because the Commerce survey does not reflect the apparent upsurge in the use of trade-related and other forms of performance requirements in recent years. Of course, it could not measure those implemented since 1977, when protectionist pressures arising out of the recent global recession and foreign debt crisis have increased the tendency to impose local content and export requirements. For example, the 1977 survey found that less than 5 percent of U.S. affiliates in Canada were subject to performance requirements. However, most observers of Canadian investment policies would probably agree that the Canadian government has negotiated local content, export, and other requirements in connection with the *large majority* of foreign direct investment projects over the last several years.

For a few countries, the survey may also overstate the current use of

TABLE 1

Selected Countries with Significant Occurrences of Investment Performance Requirements

Country	Local content and exportation	Equity participation	Technology transfer	Employment, size, location & finance	U.S. direct investment position 1981 (US$ — millions)
Argentina	X	X			$ 2,735
Australia	X	X			8,779
Brazil	X	X	X		8,253
Canada	X	X	X	X	46,957
Colombia	X	X			1,178
Egypt	X	X		X	1,082
France	X		X	X	9,102
India	X	X	X		431
Indonesia	X	X			1,861
Japan		X	X	X	6,807
Malaysia	X	X	X	X	849
Mexico	X	X	X		6,962
Morocco	X	X			42
Nigeria		X			218
Saudi Arabia		X		X	580
South Korea	X	X			778
Spain	X	X			2,887
Taiwan	X				574
Turkey	X		X		210
Venezuela	X	X			2,175
					$ 100,275

Sources: LICIT, 1981; Robinson, 1983; U.S. Department of Commerce, 1981; Conference Board, 1983; USTR, 1983.

investment performance practices. This is probably the case for Japan which has liberalized its investment policies gradually since the late 1960s. (The 1977 survey indicates that Japan imposed requirements on 9 percent of U.S. affiliates operating in that country.)

Based upon the Commerce survey, but also upon more recent samples of companies and other sources of information (for example, from U.S. embassies), Table 1 presents a list of major host countries that have demonstrated a significant use of performance requirements over the past decade. The frequency of occurrence of developing countries on this list is consistent with the relatively high incidence of performance requirements in the LDCs found in the earlier Commerce survey. This list tends to indicate that the two most frequently employed performance requirements are local content requirements and requirements for local equity participation.

Regarding the extent of the use of trade-related performance requirements (TRPRs), an inventory of investment restrictions maintained by the U.S. Trade Representative monitors the policies of 76 countries. Of the 76 countries covered, 52 of them (13 developed and 39 developing countries) are making use of at least one TRPR instrument. U.S. FDI stock in countries with TRPRs amounted to more than $150 billion in 1981, or 68 percent of all U.S. FDI (USTR, 1983[a]). Another study by the Conference Board (1983) produced from a survey of more than 100 U.S., Canadian, and European companies with substantial foreign investments, found that local content requirements are commonly imposed by host governments of advanced developing countries (for example, Brazil, Mexico, and India). The study also found that for about half of these companies, local content requirements have an adverse effect on their local operations by significantly raising the cost of doing business and impairing management's ability to control operations.

Table 2 indicates that the industries most frequently targeted for TRPRs by foreign governments are the mining, electrical machinery, and transportation equipment sectors. . . . In the mining sector, resource-endowed countries have often attempted to encourage raw material processing in order to capture more of the value-added downstream by imposing domestic processing and manufacturing requirements as a condition for entry. . . . The world automobile industry is characterized by a high degree of protection and by the use of TRPRs. . . .

The Mexican automobile program illustrates the operation of local content and export requirements. Mexico's automotive industry objectives have been to: create employment-maximizing local content; substitute local products for imports; generate foreign exchange; strengthen majority-Mexican-owned companies in the production of automobile parts; and attain international levels of productivity. Following a series of auto decrees dating from 1962 through 1977 and development of its National Industrial Development Plan, the Mexican government has developed the following set of regulations for its automotive industry. Investment is to be encouraged by offering various incentives in the form of tax and import duty rebates, investment grants, relaxed safety and environmental regulations on the industry, no restrictions on profit remittances, special tax credits for new investments in certain depressed areas and for purchases of Mexican-made machinery, and preferential energy prices. Linked to these incentives are certain performance requirements. Company imports and other payments abroad must be fully offset by exports, and one-half of the obligation to export must be performed through the export of products made by Mexican-owned firms. The export requirements are raised to 110 percent of payments abroad if local content requirements are not met. For cars, the minimum local content is 50 percent of the exfactory value, with a recommended level of 75 percent. For trucks, the minimum and recommended levels are 65 and 85 percent, respectively. If the recommended

TABLE 2

Performance Requirements by Industry

Industry	Percent of U.S. affiliates subject to performance requirements	Percentage distribution of U.S. direct investment abroad — 1981
Total	14 %	100
Mining	27	3.3
Petroleum	16	22.9
Manufacturing	19	40.7
Food products	21	40.2
Chemicals & Allied products	19	8.8
Prim. & Fab. metals	18	2.9
Machinery (excl. electr.)	14	7.4
Electrical machinery	21	3.3
Transportation equipment	27	5.2
Other	17	9.1
Trade	9	12.4
Finance, insurance, real estate	8	15.4
Other*	10	5.3

*Agriculture, Forestry, Fishing, Construction, Transportation, Communications, Public Utilities, Services.

Source: Calculations based on a special tabulation of data, gathered through the BE-10 Benchmark Survey of U.S. Direct Investment Abroad — 1977, provided by the International Investment Division of the U.S. Department of Commerce, Bureau of Economic Analysis.

levels are not met by 1983, companies will have to increase exports above current levels (Ventana, 1981).

Fundamentally, the Mexican automotive industry policy is designed to: (1) attract new investment, both foreign and domestic, into its automotive parts industry through financial incentives; (2) provide high levels of protection for both parts and automobile production as part of its import substitution drive; and (3) encourage the development of scale economies through exports. Over the last several years, all of the major U.S. auto producers have located either assembly or engine or other parts plants in Mexico with substantial production capacity. These engine and parts plants will export most of their output, mainly to the United States.

Thus, the effect of the Mexican program is to shift some parts production from the United States to Mexico where the industry will be heavily protected and subsidized. It is expected that, as a result of the combination of incentives and performance requirements, U.S. automobile industry exports to Mexico will diminish and imports increase substantially. Whether the Mexican industry will become competitive internationally is questionable so long as the combination of incentives and TRPRs is considered an essential part of Mexico's policies in this sector.

Brazil also has a program in the automobile sector that combines investment incentives with local content and export requirements. However, Brazil imposes TRPRs only on firms that seek and obtain financial subsidies.

A likely result of the Mexican and Brazilian automobile programs is that U.S. production and exports to these countries will decline while imports increase. . . . A recent estimate of the effect of these programs is that nearly one percent of employment in the U.S. auto industry will be lost as a result of the Mexican and Brazilian incentives and performance requirements practices. . . .

. . . The incidence of TRPRs is relatively low among the developed countries — with notable exceptions in Canada, Australia, and Spain, and less frequent occurrences in the United Kingdom and France. Canada's investment policies and their effect on U.S.-Canada trade have received the greatest amount of attention.

In 1974, Canada established the Foreign Investment Review Agency (FIRA) for the purpose of screening foreign investments on the basis of "significant benefits" to Canada. In FIRA's guidelines, primary consideration is given an investment's local-sourcing, export and employment implications for Canada (FIRA, n.d.). The FIRA has actively sought and negotiated "undertakings" which commit firms, *inter alia,* to local sourcing and exports. Once the "undertakings" are made to the FIRA, they are enforceable by the Canadian government in Canada's courts.

The details of a number of cases where TRPRs have been associated with investments in Canada have been made public by the Canadian government. In one recent case, the Apple Computer Company was required to expand its production and value-added in Canada, to develop Canadian sources for Canadian-made power supply units and semiconductors, and to establish a task force to identify Canadian sources of supply for Apple worldwide operations. . . . In another recent case, the U.S. publishing firm, Gannett Co., made a number of trade-related commitments to obtain approval for an acquisition of a Canadian advertising company. (Initially, Gannett's application for approval of the acquisition had been rejected by Canadian authorities.) These commitments obligate Gannett to purchase the bulk of its newsprint requirements for *USA Today* from Canadian suppliers for three years. In addition, Gannett will work with the government to identify other Canadian goods and services to supply Gannett's input needs; and, further, Gannett is to study the possibility of a "major investment" in a newsprint mill in Canada (*Wall Street Journal,* 1981).

These two cases merely illustrate the general Canadian policy in recent years of negotiating TRPRs with MNCs that have sought to enter into Canada's market. Canadian policy with respect to trade-related "undertakings" has been applied as broadly as that of any other country and generally more so. The rationale for this policy is to shift more Canadian resources toward processing of natural resources, general manufacturing, and production of high technology goods and services. In this respect, Canada's performance requirements are consistent with its tariff structure, which is intended to provide greater protection for Canadian service and finished manufactured products. . . .

As with Mexico's performance requirements policies, it is far from certain that Canada's performance requirements and other policies will succeed in improving Canada's competitiveness in manufacturing. Yet, the potential future impact of Canada's policies for U.S. trade interests is substantial since Canada is the largest single country for both U.S. trade and direct investment.

THE "RIGHT NOT TO INVEST"

The previous section described the use of trade-distorting performance requirements placed on foreign investors as a condition for entry into production and sales within the host country's market. Such requirements constitute "content protection" to foster the local production of raw and intermediate goods. . . . But the insulation of host country production can, of course, be extended to the final good. Rather than placing local content conditions only on foreign investments as the price for a local presence, the host country may require *exporters* to establish all or most production of the final good locally in order to sell in its market.

It has been generally accepted that import barriers can generate significant flows of FDI. . . . Frequently, one of the major purposes of erecting tariffs is to attract foreign capital into the protected market. Nevertheless, in cases of low to moderate duties or quota restrictions that are generous, foreign suppliers can either invest locally or supply the protected market from their own country depending upon the marginal advantages of each alternative. If, however, foreign suppliers of a final product face prohibitive tariffs or an embargo on imports, or sales in the local market are conditioned on a value-based local content percentage that approaches 100 percent, then direct investment becomes necessary for local sales.

Some countries are insisting that foreign suppliers establish production capacity in the local market as a condition for *sales* there. Brazil and Mexico head the list of such countries. . . . Of course, this forced investment practice may be implemented with performance requirements designed to benefit domestic raw and intermediate goods producers. Thus, a foreign investor may be required to establish local production in order to sell his product; he may also be required to agree to performance requirements to source most of his inputs locally.

Thus, these two types of investment-related trade policies may be combined in their use by some countries. Brazil's auto industry combines both approaches, by prohibiting the importation of passenger cars (which ordinarily makes its nominal high tariffs from a trade perspective superfluous) and Spain maintains a very high protectionist tariff on finished cars. Furthermore, foreign investors are subject to substantial local content and export requirements in order to further encourage the development of the local automobile parts industries. . . .

The United States, at both the federal and local levels of jurisdiction, has so far avoided the use of trade-distorting performance requirements to domestic and foreign investment in this country. U.S. measures that most closely resemble foreign local content measures are federal and state Buy-America government procurement laws. Pressures to widen the scope of such laws, which favor goods with at least 51 percent U.S. content, have been great in recent years; however, recent U.S. administrations have supported the GATT government procurement code, negotiated in the Tokyo Round, which represents a start at liberalizing such U.S. and foreign procurement policies.

BARRIERS TO U.S. DIRECT INVESTMENT ABROAD

The U.S. government has been committed in the postwar period to an "open" investment policy, meaning that the U.S. government should not interfere with inward or outward direct investment flows. Moreover, U.S. officials have taken the position that such a policy should be adopted internationally. As mentioned above, this view was the basis for U.S. efforts to include investment provisions in the Havana Charter, and for the U.S. position in the OECD agreements mentioned earlier.

The major premise for this U.S. policy position is the proposition that, like free trade, liberalizing barriers to investment flows will tend to increase the economic welfare of both home and host countries. An important issue is the effect of outward FDI flows on a host country's trade, production, and employment. Labor unions and some academics assert that U.S. investment overseas displaces U.S. exports and reduces domestic employment and labor's share of national income. . . . Others find no systematic relationship between outward FDI and trade and employment, while another recent result of research shows a significant positive effect. . . . Certainly, business leaders and consultants strongly argue that U.S. direct investment abroad has a positive impact on U.S. exports and that overseas U.S. investment is vital to U.S. export competitiveness. . . . The 1977 Commerce Department benchmark survey of U.S. direct investment abroad indicates that 40 percent of U.S. manufactured exports are directed to U.S. affiliates abroad, and that there is a substantial surplus in manufacturers' trade between U.S. affiliates and parents.

The arguments put forth for positive linkage are: (1) that the establishment of U.S. manufacturing affiliates abroad provides new local marketing networks for exports from the home to the host country . . .; and (2) that typically, overseas affiliates purchase a significant level of their capital equipment and material inputs from the home country, although this effect may tend to diminish as the foreign affiliates mature. . . .

Host country local content requirements, of course, tend to reduce or eliminate trade benefits to the home country of outward FDI flows. This is a partial rationale for performance requirements that has been given for the use of local content and export requirements in Canada. . . . Without acceding to local content requirements in Canada, foreign firms have faced the almost certain prospect in recent years that their application for an investment will be denied.

Also, when potential host countries erect barriers to foreign investment, capital-exporting countries' potential merchandise and service exports may suffer. Japanese policies toward inward foreign direct investment have been very restrictive until recently. Further, continued problems associated with making acquisitions of existing Japanese companies appear to have been a significant element contributing to the poor U.S. export performance in the Japanese market. Meanwhile, large direct investments by Japanese automotive and consumer products companies in the United States have contributed positively to Japan's successful penetration of U.S. markets in these sectors. . . .

In 1980, Japan liberalized its basic investment legislation to require only the prior notification of inward direct investments. In principle, Japan grants the freedom to proceed with the investment after a short period of time. However, an investment proposal may be suspended or modified if it threatens Japanese industry competitive with the proposed investment (OECD, 1982[b]). In any case, U.S. flows of direct investment to Japan have not increased substantially over the last decade. . . .

Only six of the 22 OECD countries do not have some form of authorization or screening procedure for inward FDI flows, including the United States, Germany, Italy, and the United Kingdom. Among the major OECD countries with screening mechanisms, Australia, Canada, and France have tended to be quite selective concerning the type of investments admitted. Further, these countries have tended to attach both trade- and nontrade-related requirements to approved investments. . . . Further, as noted earlier, *all* OECD countries have *sectoral* restrictions or barriers to inward FDI, with most of these obstacles occurring in the fields of banking, insurance, mining, petroleum, aviation, and shipping (OECD, 1982[b]).

The developing countries exercise a considerably greater degree of screening and barriers to admitting FDI. . . . Among the LDCs, Latin American countries tend to be the most restrictive toward inward FDI and have substantial numbers of "market reservation" schemes in manufacturing and service industries that permit only locally owned firms to operate.

For example, the Andean Common Market (ANCOM) countries require that foreign investments be either initially or ultimately majority-owned and controlled by local nationals. . . . In Mexico, foreign investments made after 1973 may generally have a maximum of only 49 percent foreign ownership, with certain sectors, such as petrochemical and auto parts production, restricted even further. . . . Brazil has tried to greatly restrict FDI in certain high technology sectors, including petrochemicals, telecommunications equipment, and computers and semiconductors; and Brazil's "informatics" policy is designed to embargo imports and restrict production to locally owned enterprises, on the basis of a national security agreement, within the sectors of minicomputers, integrated circuits, and process-control instrumentation. . . .

Developing countries outside of Latin America which restrict access to sizeable markets through investment screening and restrictions — and, again, often tying performance requirements to those investors who do get admitted — include: South Korea, Malaysia, India, Indonesia, the Philippines, and Saudi Arabia. South Korea has recently announced, however, a major liberalization of its screening policies accompanied by a reduction in investment incentives. . . .

IMPLICATIONS FOR THE INTERNATIONAL TRADING SYSTEM

The policies and practices discussed above fall into the domains of both international investment and international trade policy. On the one hand, investment screening and performance requirements block and distort international trade flows. On the other hand, investment incentives and prohibitive barriers to trade distort the flow of international investment. Frequently, as in the case of Mexico, a combination of restrictive investment and trade practices is present: general screening and ownership limitations placed on foreign investment; selective investment incentives; local content and export requirements; and high tariffs and very limited quotas on imports of selected finished products (for example, automobiles, computers).

As noted earlier, international direct investment issues do not command the same degree of international consensus in principle as that accorded the issues of international trade. In the international trade area, there is general agreement that the system works best if governments are restrained; however, only a small minority of countries — approximately a half-dozen developed countries plus only a few developing countries — hold the same view with respect to flows of international direct investment. The predominant international view toward foreign direct investment flows is today as interventionist as it was at the time of the negotiation of the Havana Charter.

Current global debt and liquidity problems, however, are forcing many LDCs to reexamine the utility of screening and the imposition of equity participation restrictions for foreign investment. Direct investment provides LDCs with longer-term financing than that provided by commercial banks without adding to their immediate debt burden. Mexico's political leadership has suggested that their country is now willing to relax its requirement for minority foreign equity on a selective basis. South Korea, as noted above, has announced a forthcoming major investment liberalization program. Thus, there is a trend in international investment policies abroad toward the relaxation of barriers in the developing countries toward inward foreign investment. A U.S. bilateral investment treaty program (see below), designed to protect and provide better treatment for U.S. direct investment abroad, has generated considerable interest among the developing countries; this is the case even in Latin America, where a traditional anti-MNC attitude has prevailed and where governments have espoused the Calvo Doctrine, which argues against the international arbitration of investment disputes (a key position of developed countries).

Among the developed countries, Canada has shifted its position somewhat in its foreign investment review practices and is currently approving nearly all foreign investment proposals. This development has occurred following large-scale capital outflows in 1980 and 1981, which were generated by Canada's new policy to "Canadianize" the energy sector and the Trudeau government's adoption of a distinctly more hostile attitude toward foreign investment. . . .

Thus, there are strong pressures on our trade partners to improve the access to their markets for foreign investment. However, the same pressures of international debt and trade imbalances that are pushing countries in this direction also seem to be contributing nothing to the relaxation of trade-related performance requirements. Instead, the problem seems to be worsening. At the same time Mexican officials are announcing administrative actions to attract more flows of foreign investment, they are considering expanding the scope of local content and export requirements in the automobile sector. Mexico is also beginning to implement a similar program of performance requirements in the computer sector. Also, Mexico intends to liberalize access only for those who are prepared to export to the United States and who will agree on severe local content terms.

Similarly the new Canadian policy of welcoming foreign investment has not yet been accompanied by any significant shift in the "undertakings" policy of seeking local content, export commitments, R and D spending, and so forth. There are, nevertheless, signs that Canadian officials increasingly view these requirements as investment disincentives and are considering possible changes in approach. On the other hand, the government of the United Kingdom has been negotiating with a large Japanese automobile company for a major automotive plant investment in Wales, and these negotiations have been held up, in part, by the demands of the U.K. government for local sourcing commitments. . . .

Thus, while prospects are brighter today for the liberalization of screening barriers to investment overseas, they are probably worse for the relaxation of trade-related and other performance requirement practices. Of course, where such performance requirements are too onerous from a foreign investor's perspective, they could be relaxed. Rather than relax the performance requirements, however, countries may increase investment incentives instead.

U.S. companies, under pressures from competitors here and abroad, have tended to "make their deals" with foreign governments. . . . Those companies that accept performance requirements in order to gain entry to foreign markets become captive and therefore can become defensive about these practices. Not surprisingly, therefore, the U.S. business community is split somewhat on the question of performance requirements. Most major business organizations, such as the Business Roundtable and the National Foreign Trade Council, take a strong position against these requirements, both foreign and domestic. Some trade associations which represent companies captive to performance requirements, such as the automobile manufacturers, take a very cautious attitude toward them and, indeed, have defended them. . . .

Labor unions, most notably the UAW, have taken an "if-you-can't-beat-'em-join-'em" approach and are supporting legislation that would . . . implement local content requirements for the U.S. auto industry. However, labor groups still oppose the use of export requirements by foreign governments, as they can have a negative effect on employment in this country.

Those potentially injured by performance requirements are not those involved in the arrangements — namely, the foreign government and the foreign investor. Instead it is U.S. suppliers of machinery and parts for the foreign investment who are kept out of foreign markets by foreign local content regulations, and U.S. workers who may be displaced by foreign export requirements. Of course, in the longer run, both the country imposing performance requirements and the foreign investor may also lose. The host country will often find that it is necessary to continue costly protection and incentives programs indefinitely in order to maintain the profitability of the investment. The foreign investor may find that the performance requirements may become more burdensome, or that his protection from domestic or foreign competitors may be relaxed. This is, at least, the view of U.S. government officials, who believe that it is in everyone's interest to halt the spread of investment restrictions that distort trade and investment flows, and ultimately to roll back those in force now.

THE U.S. POLICY RESPONSE

The United States can address investment-related trade issues using multilateral or bilateral negotiating approaches. It can also take unilateral action. An approach which combines actions under all three categories will probably best advance U.S. objectives.

Multilaterally, the United States has led efforts to have the GATT, OECD, and World Bank work on investment practices that distort trade and investment flows.

In the GATT, two actions were taken . . . to address the problem of trade-related performance requirements. In early 1982, the United States initiated an action against Canada's use of local content and export requirements in the administration of the Foreign Investment Review Act. Specifically, the United States charged that under the FIRA, Canada sought and obtained commitments that violated Canada's GATT obligations: (1) to accord to imported products treatment "no less favorable than that accorded to like products of national origin in respect of all laws, negotiations and requirements affecting their internal sale . . . purchase . . . or use" under Article III; and (2) to act in accordance "solely" with "commercial considerations" in the application of "governmental measures affecting imports or exports by private traders" under Article XVII (GATT, *op. cit.*).

. . . Essentially the U.S. argument [was] that Canada's local content requirements are in violation of Articles III and XVII and that its export requirements violate Article XVII.

. . . A panel of three GATT experts found that Canada's local content requirements under the FIRA are contrary to its GATT obligations. With regard to violation of GATT's rules in Canada's use of export requirements the panel did not find that the GATT covers such practices. . . . U.S. officials were gratified that the panel found, at the least, that local content requirements imposed on foreign direct investment violate GATT's rules, as this case represents a precedent in dealing with investment performance requirements. It should also be noted that local content practices are currently more frequently employed than are export requirements (USTR, 1983[a]).

In addition to using the GATT dispute settlement process to address performance requirements for the first time, the United States proposed at the GATT Ministerial meeting in November 1982 that the Ministers direct the GATT to establish a work program to examine the use of performance requirements by member countries and its ramifications for the GATT and world trade. Opposition from many LDCs, however, blocked a GATT consensus on this proposal and the United States dropped it at the meeting. The U.S. government, of course, still reserves the right to raise this issue and its original proposal at any time in the forum of the GATT. . . . Nevertheless, the strong opposition from the LDC bloc to merely an examination of the issue indicates the difficulty of dealing with this issue in any multilateral forum.

In the OECD, a Working Group on Investment Policies under the Committee on Investment and Multinational Enterprises (CIME) has been addressing trade-related performance requirements as part of a broader exercise covering investment incentives and disincentives (OECD, 1983). The work is also being taken up in the Trade Committee of the OECD. Hopefully, a consensus can be achieved among the industrialized countries that they should avoid local content and export requirements. . . .

Bilaterally, consultations between the United States and its major trade partners have been used to communicate U.S. concerns about the long-term implications of performance requirements and barriers to investment flows. Most of these consultations have been with our major Western Hemisphere trade partners — Canada, Mexico, and Brazil. In the case of Mexico, bilateral contacts are the only way of addressing trade problems since that country is not a member of the GATT. The United States and Mexico have a Joint Commission on Commerce and Trade under which sectoral "study groups" have been established for automobiles and computers. In these groups both sides have an opportunity to discuss each country's objectives and policies.

Since late 1981 the U.S. government has also initiated an effort to negotiate bilateral investment treaties (BITs) with developing countries on the basis of a standardized prototype draft document. The U.S. draft contains provisions for national and MFN treatment of U.S. investments, avoidance of performance requirements, unconstrained repatriation of profits and other remittances of investors, prompt and adequate compensation in the event of direct investment expropriation, and mechanisms for the international arbitration of investment disputes (USTR, 1983[b]). The government has had consultations with approximately 30 countries and has active BIT negotiations now under way with approximately 10 countries. However, the advanced LDCs have yet to be drawn into negotiations. Most of the negotiations have involved middle-income LDCs such as Egypt, Morocco, Panama, and Costa Rica. Developed countries are not targets of U.S. negotiations because of the availability of the OECD framework, and the existence of Friendship, Commerce, and Navigation (FCN) treaties with most of our industrial trade partners (with the notable exceptions of Canada and a few major LDCs, for example, Korea and Taiwan). These FCN agreements contain provisions on national treatment, expropriation, and repatriation similar to those of the model BIT.

Unilaterally, the U.S. government has several options available. It can (and did in the case of Canada) initiate cases in the GATT to obtain decisions on the compatibility of individual country practices with the GATT's rules.

Domestically, private parties can initiate countervailing-duty proceedings against imports from countries which have offered financial investment incentives (that is, subsidies) tied to export requirements. . . . If the incentives are sufficiently significant, countervailing duties could be imposed with or without the determination of injury to the domestic party, depending on whether the country involved has signed the Tokyo Round subsidies code.

In addition, under Section 301 of the Trade Agreements Act of 1979, petitions can be made to seek presidential actions to deal with "unjustifiable, unreasonable discriminatory measures that burden or restrict" U.S. commerce. . . . The USTR may also self-initiate a 301 investigation. If a country is found to be using such measures, U.S. law permits the President to take action by imposing import restrictions against that country. It is likely that with the growth of trade-related performance requirements, Section 301 will find greater use in addressing such practices.

In the area of government assistance to U.S. investment abroad, the Overseas Private Investment Corporation (OPIC) sells long-term investment insurance and guarantees packages for U.S. direct investments in developing countries. In 1981, OPIC's legislative authorization mandated that it not provide insurance or guarantees when performance requirements that would result in a substantial negative effect on U.S. trade were attached to the investment project. A recent application for investment insurance covering a project in Brazil was denied on this basis.

Various other proposals have been made to deal with performance requirements and other restrictions on U.S. investment abroad. For example, it has been proposed that the United States use the leverage contained in its Generalized System of Preferences (GSP) program to obtain trade and investment concessions from those advanced LDCs which enjoy benefits of zero tariff preferences under GSP and employ performance requirements. . . .

CONCLUSIONS

The linkage between investment policies and trade flows is being drawn ever tighter by countries wishing to manipulate foreign direct investment to gain maximum trade advantage through screening and the imposition of performance requirements. At the same time, more countries may attempt to "force" direct investment by introducing new and prohibitive trade restrictions, such as Mexico's tight import restrictions on automobiles and the congressional auto local content bill. In the current economic environment characterized by . . . substantial LDC debts and structural adjustment problems in both industrial and developing countries, at least in the near term, we can expect to see beggar-thy-neighbor trade policies coupled with policies reflecting an increasing competition for capital. Thus, we would expect that investment restrictions will ease "at the border," while more restrictive conditions will be placed on the economic activities of admitted MNCs. With respect to performance requirements, we can expect to see a relaxation in the future of equity participation limitations, while local content and export requirements are tightened. . . .

U.S. policies might concentrate particularly on trying to prevent the establishment of new performance requirements, particularly by developed and advanced developing countries. . . . Efforts could also be made to roll back current practices. However, a rollback will be extremely difficult. The GATT can be used to address trade-related performance requirements, but progress will be slow. Multilateral approaches for dealing with trade and investment issues have, for a number of reasons, not been very successful recently. At the Ministerial meeting in November 1982, U.S. proposals for new work on performance requirements and other issues (including high technology and North–South negotiations) were rejected. And work in the OECD on investment issues, including performance requirements, is also going slowly.

The United States might also continue to reaffirm its belief in the effectiveness of the multilateral institutions by making proposals to deal with trade and investment issues in the GATT, OECD, World Bank, and elsewhere. However, the multilateral consensus in favor of trade liberalization has been weakened in recent years. . . . Thus, bilateral approaches with individual countries, or countries of a particular region, to address trade and investment problems may be relatively more effective now. The United States has initiated a bilateral investment treaty program and is pursuing bilateral trade and investment approaches with Japan and the Caribbean countries. . . .

However, it is unlikely that either multilateral or bilateral approaches will be sufficient to cope with circumstances in which foreign countries prefer restrictive and distorting trade and investment policies. Unilateral measures may be necessary to assist the development of longer-term multilateral or bilateral solutions by putting pressure on countries to negotiate. We can expect increasing pressures from the private sector and the Congress to examine methods by which U.S. trade and investment programs can be used in better coordination with U.S. trade and investment objectives abroad.

References

Brock, W. E. 1981. Statement on U.S. trade policy. Office of the U.S. Trade Representative, Executive Office of the President, Washington. July 8.

Conference Board. 1983. *Operating foreign subsidiaries*. New York.

General Agreement on Tariffs and Trade. 1969. *Basic instruments and selected documents* IV. Geneva.

Labor-Industry Coalition for International Trade (LICIT). 1981. *Performance requirements*. Washington.

National Advisory Council in International Monetary and Financial Policies. 1977. *International finance: annual report to the President and to the Congress*. Washington: Government Printing Office.

Organization for Economic Cooperation and Development. 1983. *Investment incentives and the international investment process*. Paris.

Organization for Economic Cooperation and Development. 1982[a]. *Code of liberalization of capital movements*. Paris.

Organization for Economic Cooperation and Development. 1982[b]. *Controls and impediments affecting inward direct investment in OECD member countries*. Paris.

Organization for Economic Cooperation and Development. 1976. *Declarations by the governments of OECD member countries and decisions of the OECD Council*. Paris.

Robinson, R. 1983. *Performance requirements for foreign business*. New York: Praeger.

United States. Department of Commerce. 1981. *The use of investment incentives and performance requirements by foreign governments*. Washington: Government Printing Office.

United States. Department of Commerce. Bureau of Economic Analysis, International Investment Division. 1981. *U.S. Direct Investment Abroad, 1977*. Washington: Government Printing Office.

United States. Executive Office of the President. Office of the U.S. Trade Representative (USTR). 1983[a]. Inventory of investment barriers. Mimeographed.

United States. Executive Office of the President. Office of the U.S. Trade Representative (USTR). 1983[b]. *Prototype bilateral investment treaty*, January. Washington.

Wall Street Journal. 1981. Gannett makes commitments in return for buying Canada firms. November 2.

14

The Way Forward

GATT Study Group

Before us lies a choice. One road leads to protectionism, distortion of competitive conditions, attempts to avoid change, and economic decline. The other road offers more open trade, observance of mutually accepted trading rules, readiness for change, and the promise of widespread economic growth.

Putting the world trading system on the right path requires concerted action. . . . We make fifteen specific recommendations for action. But the first requirement is that we recognize our shared and long-term interests.

THE COMMON INTEREST

The major participants in world trade must recognize that they share a common interest in the system's survival, far outweighing any differences among them.

This applies to relations between the United States, the European Community and Japan, and their disputes over bilateral trade balances, trade restrictions and agriculture. It applies equally to relations between the developed and developing participants in the trading system: they too often think and act at cross purposes, as if there were an inherent conflict between their long-term economic interests.

The multilateral trading system, if it is allowed to function properly, will benefit every country which participates in it. Viewing problems in a simplistic North-South context has seriously impaired international cooperation in many fields. In the area of trade, it is essential to get across the message — if the experience of the past few years needs any further underlining — that gains cannot be made "at the expense" of the other countries which are our suppliers and our customers.

A spirit of faction and mistrust already endangers international cooperation in many areas. It is particularly harmful in the field of trade.

The trade rules are being undermined by a combination of neglect at the highest levels of government and many separate actions taken at all levels of government. While the developed countries' forays outside the multilateral rules have played the leading role in this process, the demands of developing countries for special treatment have also damaged the system by encouraging the tendency to treat them as being outside it.

From General Agreement on Tariffs and Trade Study Group, *Trade Policies for a Better World* (Geneva: GATT, 1985), pp. 33–50. Reprinted by permission.

Both developed and developing countries have a contribution to make in reversing this process. We believe the initial move should come from the developed countries because, being the largest traders, they bear the largest responsibility for the functioning of the trading system. A convincing first step by the developed countries to unwind some of the restrictive measures introduced over the recent past (especially those which particularly affect developing countries) could help to produce a climate of confidence and encourage the developing countries to move towards trade liberalization.

CHANGE AND ADJUSTMENT

Economic growth of any kind requires change. Readiness to embrace change and adjust to its effects are indispensable to growth. But when particular firms, sustained by past protection, cannot compete against imports, an approach of gradual adjustment may be justified on economic grounds, as well as for human and political reasons. The costs of abrupt adjustment for these industries would be felt immediately, while some of the benefits — and in particular, the new job opportunities elsewhere — would probably appear more slowly.

Obviously, each country will choose adjustment policies which reflect its own economic philosophy. Nevertheless, in our view there is room in every economy for measures that go beyond creating a general policy environment favourable to adjustment. Such measures could aim at easing the transfer of workers out of declining industries, helping with their retraining and providing more opportunities for education. Indeed, readiness to meet new challenges depends not only on labour market policies such as retraining, which enhance the mobility of today's workers, but also on the general quality of education. Education is the foundation of a society able to compete in a growing, changing world economy.

Better adjustment policies should also be encouraged at the international level. That will require, above all, that the trading system and its rules function well. In an era of rapid change in the conditions of competition, the trading system must be responsive to problems, and efficient in mediating disputes.

PROPOSALS FOR ACTION

Recommendations for trade policy must, in our view, take as their starting point some basic principles: the need for trade to be based on fair competition (i.e., on genuine comparative advantage); the need to bring trade policy into the open; recognition that non-discrimination is the core of the multilateral trading system; the need for clear and accepted multilateral rules to govern trade policies; and recognition that trade policy is only one part of overall economic policy. With these considerations in mind, we put forward the following fifteen recommendations for specific, immediate action to meet the present crisis in the multilateral trading system:

1. *In each country, the making of trade policy should be brought into the open. The costs and benefits of trade policy actions, existing and prospective, should be analyzed through a "protection balance sheet." Private and public companies should be required to reveal in their financial statements the amount of any subsidies received. Public support for open trade policies should be fostered.*

A major reason why things have gone wrong with the trading system is that trade policy actions have often escaped scrutiny and discussion at the national level. Clearer analysis and greater openness in the making of trade policy are badly needed, along with greater public knowledge of how the multilateral trading system works.

Any proposal for protective action should be systematically analyzed. This could be done by what might be called a "protection balance sheet." Such statements, similar in aim to the "environmental impact" statements now required for construction projects in some countries, would allow periodic appraisal of existing measures and informed judgement on proposed new measures. They would set out the benefits and costs to the national economy of protectionist measures, as compared with withholding protection and/or with providing adjustment assistance. The idea has limitations in that the least quantifiable elements in the "balance sheet" will often matter most. But it would greatly improve the quality of public discussion by demonstrating the trade-offs in any protectionist measure, and would also help to create a constituency in favour of open trade policies. . . .

We recommend that the GATT Secretariat pursue efforts to develop the "protection balance sheet," possibly in the form of a technical handbook available to policymakers and the public. In the interests both of the general public and of company shareholders, we recommend that each country introduce a statutory requirement that annual financial statements of private and public firms give details of any subsidies (including tax subsidies) received from governments. Governments themselves should also provide clear and full information on subsidies granted and on preferential treatment provided in their own procurement of goods and services.

Most governments come to trade policy decisions behind closed doors, particularly on such questions as whether protection should be granted to a specific industry. A very few governments, by contrast, have quite elaborate formal procedures whereby proposals for protective action have to be reviewed by independent bodies, with full opportunities provided for public debate. The International Trade Commission in the United States and the Industries Assistance Commission in Australia, while not authorized to look into all of these matters, are useful as "magnifying glasses" which highlight the domestic distribution of the costs and benefits of protection. Organizations like these should be developed in all countries, so that all interested parties, and particularly consumers, can express their views on trade policy actions before the decisions are made. The expense and difficulty of putting these views should be kept to a minimum.

It is often argued that secrecy allows greater discretion to government authorities and permits them to block proposals for protection which, if publicized, could gain politically irresistible support. The more public approach, according to this view, fosters such support, and often involves traders in expense and uncertainty in defending in public hearings the maintenance of open markets. There is some force in these arguments. But we are convinced that the dangers of secrecy and administrative discretion are greater than those of more open procedures. The danger that a trade ministry will be too easily persuaded in private discussions to support a client domestic industry, without considering the interests of downstream users, the final consumer, or the economy as a whole, appears greater than when public procedures are followed. The open approach, exposing conflicting interests and helping to resolve them, also shields politicians better against protectionist pressures.

An essential first step in developing support for better trade policies is public awareness. We recommend that, in each country, governments make a conscious and continuing effort to expand public knowledge of the costs and hazards of protectionism, the benefits of open trading policies, and the functioning of the multilateral trading system. Channels for such an effort could include universities and schools, strengthened national consumer groups, and advisory groups made up of influential and active representatives of the main stakeholders in international trade — business, finance, labour and consumers. Such advisory groups could help not only to develop attention and commitment to liberal trading policies, but also to keep governments continuously aware of the national interest in such policies.

> 2. *Agricultural trade should be based on clearer and fairer rules, with no special treatment for particular countries or commodities. Efficient agricultural producers should be given the maximum opportunity to compete.*

Today, the most efficient agricultural producers — a number of developing countries among them — have good reason to feel cheated of their rights under the international trading system. A trading system which limits the liberalization process to certain sectors, and which accordingly does not accommodate the trade interests of all its participants, cannot fully perform its creative role in promoting growth and adjustment in an interdependent world economy.

If the anarchy that threatens agricultural trade is to be averted, countries' ability to restrict imports, or to resort to export subsidization in pursuing domestic goals, must be subject to more effective international discipline. A trading system that permits less efficient producers both to prohibit imports and to use export subsidies to compete with, and displace, more efficient producers on world markets, is fundamentally inequitable.

Quotas and other restrictions affecting access to markets for agricultural products, including restrictions maintained under past waivers and other exceptions from the GATT provisions, should be subject to strengthened rules. Measures such as variable levies and minimum import price arrangements that are not specifically covered by the GATT should also be brought under effective discipline. The underlying philosophy should be one of progressively greater scope for the interplay of market forces in agricultural trade.

Present GATT rules and disciplines governing the use of export subsidies in agricultural trade have failed to prevent major distortions in world markets. This situation is unlikely to be corrected unless efforts are made to limit not only the damage done by export subsidies but also their use. In the long run, the objective should be to eliminate export subsidization altogether.

> 3. *A timetable and procedures should be established to bring into conformity with GATT rules voluntary export restraints, orderly marketing agreements, discriminatory import restrictions, and other trade policy measures of both developed and developing countries which are inconsistent with the obligations of contracting parties under the GATT.*

The General Agreement contains several provisions which allow its signatory countries to grant protection in case of need. For example, selective protective action can be taken against injurious dumped or subsidized imports. Countries in severe balance-of-payments difficulties are allowed to apply import restrictions. "Safeguard" action can be taken against imports in cases where a domestic industry experiences temporary difficulty in adjusting to fair competition.

All of these "escape clauses" contain internal disciplines to prevent abuse. The "safeguard" rules (Article XIX of the GATT) are particularly strict, calling for nondiscriminatory application of whatever restrictions are imposed, and for compensation to contracting parties whose GATT rights are thus impaired.

A new development in the trading system in recent years has been the multiplication of trade restrictions "outside" the GATT, such as "voluntary export restraints" and "orderly marketing agreements." Most of these arrangements contravene specific provisions of the General Agreement.

The accumulation of such discriminatory restrictions, which are often applied precisely because they escape the discipline of the GATT rules, is destroying the authority of those same rules. These restrictions represent a market-sharing approach that could lead to the worldwide cartelization of entire industries. Moreover, countries which benefit from voluntary export restraints have often refused to consider their removal unless real trade concessions are made to them first by the exporting country. A programme should be initiated within GATT for the abolition of all existing illegal measures, including industry-to-industry restrictions inspired or tolerated by governments. Such a programme might take the form of:

- identification of all such restrictions;
- their conversion into clear, measurable and nondiscriminatory terms; and
- their elimination over an agreed, credible time scale.

4. *Trade in textiles and clothing should be fully subject to the ordinary rules of the GATT.* This means that all nontariff restrictions in this area, as in others, should be nondiscriminatory and time-limited, in accordance with the safeguard rules we propose in our Recommendation 9.

No clearer example exists of the mistakes made in deviating from the essential principles of a multilateral trading system than the Multifibre Arrangement which since 1973 has restricted the development of trade in textiles and clothing. Sectoral and discriminatory in nature, directed against developing countries as a whole, and inimical to the operation of comparative advantage even among developing countries, it should be brought to an end.

The present "MFA III" expires in July 1986. This presents an opportunity to set in place procedures to bring trade in textiles and clothing back within the normal GATT rules over a clearly-defined time period. Such a transition would have to be gradual. Even when completed, industries in trouble would of course still be able to make use of the safeguard protection available to them under the GATT rules.

Adjustment policies aimed at improving the ability of companies and workers to deal with change would undoubtedly be necessary to ease and speed up the process of transition. The more far-sighted and generous the adjustment policies are, the more rapid the transition can be.

5. *Rules on subsidies need to be revised, clarified and made more effective. When subsidies are permitted, they should be granted only after full and detailed scrutiny.*

Subsidies have become the main source of unfair competition and are at the root of the most serious and intractable trade disputes that have been brought before the GATT. Like other forms of protection, subsidies distort the economy by favouring one activity over the others. They represent a transfer to particular groups at the expense of the public at large. We recognize that such transfers may be used to achieve legitimate policy goals, but believe that they should only be made through procedures which ensure that all the costs of the subsidy, direct and indirect, are known to the public, and that those who bear these costs are heard.

GATT is not, to the extent it should be, a forum where subsidy actions affecting trade can be discussed and differences over them resolved. The present GATT rules on subsidies are far from clear. Moreover, because some of them are incorporated in a separate code negotiated in the Tokyo Round of the 1970s, the same rules do not apply to all GATT members.

Under the present rules, export subsidies on manufactured products are banned, except for developing countries. Export subsidies for primary products are restricted only by the condition that they should not lead to acquisition of "more than an equitable share of world export trade." We believe this concept is economically misconceived, since it implicitly endorses market-sharing. It is also too vague and subjective to permit clear judgement on whether a subsidy is acceptable or not — as was shown by the result of a U.S. complaint to GATT about European exports of subsidized flour. Although domestic subsidies are permitted, they are subject to retaliation if they damage the trade interests of other countries.

A better test of legitimacy than that of "equitable shares" is needed for subsidies on primary products; it is not evident to us why such subsidies should be legitimate at all, when those on manufacturers are banned. In the case of domestic subsidies, their full effects often emerge only some time after they are granted. If these effects are limited to the country where the subsidy is given, they are solely the affair of its citizens, but if international trade is affected, other countries may be legitimately concerned. In either case, more open procedures for considering subsidies can only be helpful.

Actions against subsidies must also be brought within clear rules; some measures now being taken against subsidies and dumping are illegal and therefore themselves unfair, as are domestic procedures which permit harassment of importers. The rules for defining injury should be clarified, and the type of offsetting procedures and actions permissible more strictly defined. Every effort should be made to bring all GATT members within the scope of the improved subsidy rules.

A country will often retaliate when it feels damaged by another country's subsidy practices; the result is a further deterioration in trade. A clearer GATT definition is needed of what is a subsidy. Tax subsidies? Agricultural price supports? Unless there can be agreement on definition, talk of "subsidy" is useless. Moreover, GATT should be the place where it can be determined what is acceptable under whatever rules are adopted. GATT's complaint procedures for subsidy cases should be broadened and strengthened. Only then will the system be able to determine what is fair and what is not.

> 6. *The GATT "codes" governing nontariff distortions of trade should be improved and vigorously applied to make trade more open and fair.*

The half-dozen agreements or "codes" on nontariff distortions of trade that were negotiated in the Tokyo Round of the 1970s represent an important step forward. Some of their provisions — and notably those of the subsidy code, to which Recommendation 5 refers — have proven inadequate and should be corrected. Most of the codes, however, have clearly established their value, clarifying the international trade rules, opening up new opportunities, and making trade fairer. Examples are the codes on customs valuation, import licensing and technical standards. We believe these codes should be vigorously and effectively applied, and that more countries should be encouraged to sign them.

> 7. *The Rules permitting customs unions and free-trade areas have been distorted and abused. To prevent further erosion of the multilateral trading system, they need to be clarified and tightened up.*

When two or more countries are prepared to establish free trade between or among themselves, creating a single market for all products, the GATT rules (in Article XXIV) permit them to do so. The European Community and the European Free Trade Association essentially meet the conditions of these rules. However, many other agreements presented under the rules, including some agreements between the European Community and its associates, fall far short of the requirements. The exceptions and ambiguities which have thus been permitted have seriously weakened the trade rules, and make it very difficult to resolve disputes to which Article XXIV is relevant. They have set a dangerous precedent for further special deals, fragmentation of the trading system, and damage to the trade interests of nonparticipants.

This situation has been ignored for too long. Possibilities of rectifying at least some past errors should be explored; above all, further mistakes and abuses should be prevented. We believe that the GATT rules on customs unions and free-trade areas should be examined, redefined so as to avoid ambiguity, and more strictly applied, so that this legal cover is available only to countries that genuinely use it to establish full free trade among themselves. Care should be taken that a tightened-up Article XXIV is not subsequently undermined by the grant of waivers to allow discriminatory arrangements by other means.

> 8. *At the international level, trade policy and the functioning of the trading system should be made more open. Countries should be subject to regular oversight or surveillance of their policies and actions, about which the GATT Secretariat should collect and publish information.*

We believe that governments should be required regularly to explain and defend their overall trade policies. As means to this end, one possibility would be periodic examinations, annually for the major trading countries, and less frequently for others. For each such examination, a panel representing three to five governments would be established to review a GATT Secretariat report on the trade policies of the country in question, subject its representatives to questioning, and make recommendations. This procedure would be somewhat similar to the examination of national economic policies in the OECD. Another possibility could be an independent Trade Policy Committee, serviced by the GATT Secretariat, that would publish periodic reports on policy developments. One or the other is needed to increase the accountability of governments for their trade practices.

In addition, the GATT Secretariat should be empowered to initiate studies of national trade policies; to collect, maintain, and publish comprehensive information on trade policy measures and actions; to call for further information and clarification regarding these measures and actions; and to invite discussion of them. By thus acting as watchdog (though not judge) on behalf of the trading system as a whole, the Secretariat would help to prevent departures from the rules and to strengthen the ability of all countries — and especially the smaller and developing countries — to defend their trade interests.

To help developing and smaller countries to play a fuller part in the GATT, the GATT Secretariat should be given the mandate and resources to provide additional training and advice to government officials dealing with trade policy.

> 9. *When emergency "safeguard" protection for particular industries is needed, it should be provided only in accordance with the rules: it should not discriminate between different suppliers, should be time-limited, should be linked to adjustment assistance, and should be subject to continuing surveillance.*

As already noted, the GATT rules include escape clauses which allow temporary protection to be given against imports of particular products if an industry can demonstrate that it is being injured by a sudden surge in imports. The main rule concerned with such "safeguard" action is Article XIX, which since 1973 has been the subject of continuing (and so far quite unsuccessful) negotiation. This failure to agree on one of the central elements of the trading system has itself contributed to weakening the GATT. The crucial issue in these negotiations has been whether safeguard restrictions may be imposed on a selective basis — that is, against the country or countries held to be causing the damage — or whether they should apply to all suppliers, in accordance with the principle of nondiscrimination.

The advocates of selectivity argue that to restrict imports from all sources when only one or two may be causing injury is unnecessarily disruptive. Application of Article XIX, however, is not a punishment for an offending exporter but an admission that the protected industry is not competitive. Since a nondiscriminatory safeguard action affects all suppliers, actual and potential, they have a strong common interest in early removal of the restriction. This concentrates the pressure for adjustment where it ought to be — on the protecting country and the protected industry. To apply a restriction to all one's trading partners is also, obviously, a more serious and difficult matter than to coerce a given supplier to enter into a "voluntary export restraint." The rule of nondiscrimination thus discourages governments from invoking the safeguard provisions unless the industry concerned really needs help.

We are in no doubt that the safeguard rules of GATT must outlaw discrimination. Time and again the negotiation of voluntary export restraints with one supplier (the most "disruptive" and therefore by definition the most competitive) has been followed by a proliferation of bilateral deals with *all* efficient suppliers who are not in a position to refuse, leading to virtual cartelization of world markets. The most obvious case in point is the Multifibre Arrangement, but cartelization of the steel sector is also far advanced. It is therefore untrue that "selective" action helps to limit the extent of disruption of trade. Moreover, the process of discrimination against the most efficient suppliers contravenes the principle of comparative advantage and maximizes the cost to the world economy of the protection granted to the inefficient.

We therefore recommend that safeguard action should be nondiscriminatory, that it should preferably take the form of tariffs rather than quantitative restrictions, and that it should be progressively phased out over a predetermined period. In order to ensure that it is time-limited, the action should be linked with adjustment assistance including help, where necessary, to ease the transfer of workers. The phasing-out process for the safeguard measures should be subject to review in the GATT, perhaps in a standing "adjustment committee" created specially for this purpose. The adjustment committee could coordinate closely with the surveillance body suggested in Recommendation 8, in order to oversee the safeguard actions. This would ensure that countries were living up to the phase-out commitments: if they were not, exporting countries could have grounds for additional compensation.

> 10. *Developing countries receive special treatment in the GATT rules. But such special treatment is of limited value. Far greater emphasis should be placed on permitting and encouraging developing countries to take advantage of their competitive strengths and on integrating them more fully into the trading system, with all the appropriate rights and responsibilities that this entails.* Additional help should be given to the least-developed countries of Africa and elsewhere in developing their trade. Removal of obstacles to their agricultural exports should be a primary target.

Most preferential tariff schemes in favour of developing countries are of very limited value. Developing countries have allowed themselves to be distracted by the idea of preferences, seeing them as a means of offsetting handicaps created by trade restrictions and distortions in developed country markets. They have done so at the cost of overlooking their fundamental interest in a nondiscriminatory trading system. Developed countries have used preferences as an easy substitute for action in more essential areas. Preferences may have value as a form of encouragement to infant industries, but developing countries should not depend on them indefinitely. The more advanced developing countries should also be expected to contribute market opportunities.

There is still room for further most-favoured-nation reductions in developed-country tariffs. In particular these tariffs now discourage developing countries from exporting semi-finished and finished products. The worldwide tendency toward "tariff escalation," whereby import duties are higher on semi-finished products than on raw materials, and higher still on finished products, gives high protection for processing activities (often of the order of 100 percent or more of the value added). This greatly handicaps many developing countries, as well as more advanced countries largely dependent on their natural resources, by discouraging resource-based industries such as metal refining and fabricating, and plywood and furniture manufacture.

The debt problems of developing countries provide an important reason for removing trade barriers against their exports and, even more, for making the trading system more stable and predictable. In no circumstances, however, should these problems be used as an excuse for introducing new discrimination into the international trading system.

Problems of human and material infrastructure, rather than of trade, dominate the economic situation of most African and other least-developed countries. However, trade policy, and especially production and export subsidies in other countries, should at least be prevented from hampering exports of primary commodities and other products from the least-developed countries. Preferences find their strongest justification when given to the least-developed countries. In general, it should be remembered that even if actions taken now have little immediate effect on exports of the least-developed countries, they will help to open up longer-term market opportunities, and thus to attract and induce export-oriented investment. Generally speaking, greater and assured access to export markets will encourage all developing countries to be more ready to accept foreign investment.

We see little basis for negotiations organized on "North-South" lines. The major problems of the trading system today are global; to put them into North-South terms is to oversimplify them. Moreover, the trade patterns and concerns of developing countries are just as varied as those of developed countries. Multi-lateral negotiations on market access, and on the improvement of particular trading rules, are likely to involve coalitions of interest that will vary according to the products and issues under discussion, and will only occasionally be clearly North-South in character. Individual developing countries will also have specific trade interests to pursue in negotiations. Since their own economies would benefit if they reduced their trade barriers, they would be well advised to turn such reductions to further advantage by obtaining, in exchange, improvements in access for their exports to the developed-country markets, and indeed to the markets of other developing countries.

> 11. *Governments should be ready to examine ways and means of expanding trade in services, and to explore whether multilateral rules can appropriately be devised for this sector.*

For all countries, the service sector represents an important and growing part of the modern economy, a large-scale source of employment and, in many cases, a focus of new ideas and technology. The development of trade in goods depends on adequate supporting services. Some governments believe the time has come to develop rules to encourage international trade in services; others are apprehensive about where such an initiative might lead.

We believe governments should look into the policy issues raised. We recommend this partly because of the obvious importance of the service sector, and partly because we fear that, if multilateral rules are not developed for services, discriminatory bilateral or regional rules will be developed instead.

But we are also convinced that there will be no progress on services without substantial progress on trade in goods. There is no future for an effort to involve GATT in services while neglecting its central and essential responsibilities. An attempt to extend a rule-based approach to new areas of economic relations while permitting the rules for trade in goods to continue to decay would lack credibility.

> 12. *In support of improved and strengthened rules, GATT's dispute settlement procedures should be reinforced by building up a permanent roster of nongovernmental experts to examine disputes, and by improving the implementation of panel recommendations. Third parties should use their rights to complain when bilateral agreements break the rules.*

The procedures for dispute settlement that have evolved in the GATT rely on panels of three or five independent experts which make findings and recommendations for adoption by the GATT Council. This procedure, which blends elements of third-party adjudication and negotiation, has served the world trade order well.

While problems have appeared in the dispute settlement process, not all can be attributed to weaknesses in the procedures. Sometimes panels have had to base their findings on rules that have been purposely left unclear for lack of agreement or that have been superseded by tacit or informal understandings. In such cases, solutions must be sought primarily in the creation, enforcement or renegotiation of the rules — in concrete terms, in the specific changes we are recommending in many of our other proposals.

A number of improvements, however, could be made in the dispute settlement procedures. Panels should be set up, and should complete their work, more speedily than in some past instances. Panels should always clearly indicate the rationale for their findings so as to give the GATT Council a firm basis for decision. The panels should be composed of experts fully familiar with the increasingly complex GATT legal system.

The best way to achieve these three goals is to build up a small permanent roster of nongovernmental experts in GATT matters to examine disputes. Such a roster would make it easier to select panelists. Moreover, frequent participation in panels by the same experts would lead them to accumulate expertise and experience that would help ensure the development of harmonious case law.

Under the existing GATT dispute settlement procedures, complaints may be brought against actions that impede the objectives of the General Agreement even if the action does not cause direct trade injury to the complaining contracting party. We regret that practically no use has been made of this possibility. If a bilateral arrangement impairs the objectives of the General Agreement, the parties to that arrangement can hardly be expected to bring a complaint in the GATT. In such cases, other contracting parties that are concerned about the broader consequences of the arrangement should initiate proceedings. We fear that, in the absence of third-party complaints, the restriction of trade through export restraint agreements and other cartel-like schemes will continue to escape the control of GATT.

In general, the functioning of the dispute settlement procedures would be improved if the Director-General of GATT were specifically entitled to initiate mediation and conciliation at an early stage in disputes.

We further suggest that greater and more systematic attention be given to the implementation of panel reports. Fixing dates for carrying out their recommendations, and regular Council reviews of how this is being carried out, would be steps in the right direction.

> 13. *We support the launching of a new round of GATT negotiations, provided they are directed toward the primary goal of strengthening the multilateral trading system and further opening world markets.*

The major "rounds" of trade negotiations held periodically in GATT, such as the Kennedy Round of the 1960s, or the Tokyo Round of the 1970s, serve an important purpose. They focus attention, permit issues to be grouped for negotiation so that all participants can hope to gain from the resulting package, mobilize political and technical support that is difficult to muster for more limited objectives, and help in forming a general view of what needs to be done. They also help political leaders to resist special-interest demands for protectionist measures.

The present accumulation of important trade policy issues in need of resolution is such that we believe a new negotiating round is now needed, and should be launched as soon as possible.

> 14. *To ensure continuous high-level attention to problems in international trade policy, and to encourage prompt negotiation of solutions of them, a permanent Ministerial-level body should be established in GATT.* Sessions of the GATT Contracting Parties should also be held at Ministerial level every second or third year.

Comprehensive GATT negotiating rounds are not always the best instrument for multilateral trade negotiations. The Tokyo Round took six years to complete. Many trade policy issues, including some of far-reaching importance, require more urgent attention and resolution than is possible in the framework of intermittent negotiating rounds. GATT's role as a forum for *continuous* negotiation should be developed.

We support high-level discussion of trade policy issues in the context of major economic meetings such as the Western "Summits," the IMF Interim and Bank-Fund Development Committees, and the OECD Ministerial Council. We urge the IMF Interim Committee to meet at regular intervals with both trade and finance ministers in attendance. Such meetings would allow trade policy to be looked at in the context of economic policies as a whole. Actual negotiation on trade issues, however, should take place in GATT itself.

For this purpose, and also with the more general aim of broadening understanding of problems and trends in the trading system, we see a clear need to create greater contact in GATT between governments, at a senior level.

We recommend establishment of a standing GATT Ministerial-level body of limited membership, but representative, through a constituency system, of all member countries. Such a body should enable the Ministers who set the course of their countries' trade and economic policies to come together frequently to share views and information, to help each other to resist protectionist pressures at home, and to carry forward international cooperation in support of the multilateral trading system. . . .

> 15. *The health and even the maintenance of the trading system, and the stability of the financial system, are linked to a satisfactory resolution of the world debt problem, adequate flows of development finance, better international coordination of macroeconomic policies, and greater consistency between trade and financial policies.*

Our recommendations on trade policy will achieve the results we seek only if sensible monetary and financial policies are also applied. . . . Monetary and financial developments bear on prospects for trade. We wish to comment on three specific aspects of these developments: debt, development aid, and policy coordination.

While the indebted countries need expanded trade, that will not be enough to enable them to pay the interest and principal they owe, much less to get the new funds they need to resume economic growth. As long as countries must limit imports, and pay much of their export earnings to banks, it is unlikely that they will be able to maintain vigorous economic growth or political stability over the long term. We are convinced that a systematic rescheduling of these countries' debt is needed, both in their own interests and in that of the world economy as a whole.

Flows of official development finance from the developed world to the poorer countries have stagnated in recent years. Trade alone cannot, for the majority of developing countries, provide them with a supply of capital adequate to their needs. For the poorest countries, particularly in sub-Saharan Africa, greatly increased aid flows on concessional terms are urgently needed. The World Bank and its sister institution, the International Development Association, the assistance programmes of the United Nations and its agencies, and the regional development banks, face growing and justified calls on their resources. All these multilateral sources of aid, as well as bilateral flows of assistance, should receive substantial and continuing reinforcement so that developing countries are able to grow and prosper, and thereby also contribute to economic expansion in the world.

Increased financial interdependence requires greater coordination of macroeconomic policies internationally, in order to prevent exchange rate instability and to encourage sustainable economic growth. The international consequences of changes in macroeconomic policy must be incorporated into national policy decisions, and should also be the subject of more effective international consultations. Greater consultation and coordination on fiscal policy would be beneficial, and may also be necessary for achieving sustained growth.

In general, trade and financial policies need to be made mutually consistent and reinforcing. This is not always the case now. When exports of the heavily indebted developing countries are limited by trade restrictions, their ability to service their debts is impaired; trade policy here works against financial policy. Similarly, illiquidity is driving countries to seek bilateral trade agreements, countertrade, and other special action damaging to the multilateral trading system. Restraints on capital spending, imposed as part of short-term adjustment programmes, impair the ability of the economy to adjust to longer-term structural changes. At the national level, cross-connections and inconsistencies like these call for much better coordination of policies between those responsible for trade and finance. At the international level, the International Monetary Fund, the World Bank and the GATT should work together more closely.

A FINAL CONCLUSION

We realize that many, or even most, of the recommendations we make will require negotiations, and that to be successful a negotiation must represent a balance of interests on the part of all the major participants. The difficulties of the trading system are manifold and cannot be solved overnight. But when sufficient consensus can be developed to launch a new round of negotiations — and the sooner the better — we hope that developed and developing countries alike will be bold and will take a fresh look at their common problems. . . .

V

Trade Policies in Developing Countries

Appropriate policies for developing countries to follow are still a matter of considerable controversy. One group of economists, typified by Anne O. Krueger, believes that export-promoting policies in contrast to import-substituting policies are the key to rapid economic growth in these countries. Others, like Paul Streeten, are more skeptical about the alleged benefits of outward-looking strategies for development. Part V presents the views of these two development experts.

Besides claiming that the logic of import substitution eventually leads to incentive-stifling complex quantitative controls over imports and domestic activities, an overvalued home currency that discourages exports, and a rising balance of payments deficit, Krueger argues that empirical studies of the policies pursued by developing countries support the view that export-promoting measures increase growth faster than import-substituting policies. In a study of ten developing countries, she finds that a one percent increase in exports led to a 0.1 percent increase in the rate of growth of gross domestic product.

Streeten agrees with much of the case for export orientation but argues that proponents of this approach go too far both in condemning import substitution and attributing to export policies effects that may be due to other policies. He argues that what matters for the success of an industrial policy is the quality of management, scale, technology, types of training and education, etc., and that it is as easy to envisage export-promoting policies being deficient in these matters as import-substituting policies.

As for the two countries often cited as confirming the merits of export-promoting policies — Taiwan and South Korea, Streeten claims that Taiwan is atypical because of the massive foreign aid the country received and its proximity to Japan, and that South Korea's growth cannot be attributed simply to export policies since it also practiced extensive import substitution and intervention by the government in the manufacturing and financial sectors. Export-promoting policies, he concludes, have been oversold, and in view of the possibly slower growth rates and increasing protectionism in the industrial countries for the rest of the 1980s, a more selective outward-looking strategy may be more appropriate for the developing countries than general trade liberalization.

15

The Effects of Trade Strategies on Growth

Anne O. Krueger

The determinants of a country's rate of economic growth are numerous, and there is no universally accepted method of quantifying the contribution of any particular factor to the growth rate. One of the problems of attempting to associate alternative trade strategies with growth rates is that the trade strategy itself is but one influence on the effectiveness with which other factors of production are employed.

Nonetheless, past research suggests a strong association between trade strategies and growth rates. Although countries could be expected to exhibit a varying mix of import substitution and export promotion, a number of factors tend to reinforce initial biases in trade regimes. Thus, each policy, over time, tends to be self-reinforcing.

ALTERNATIVE TRADE STRATEGIES

Consider first the salient characteristics of import substitution. In principle one could encourage domestic production of an import-competing good with subsidies; however, in practice, encouragement to domestic production is usually given by imposing either tariffs or quantitative restrictions (in the extreme case, import prohibitions) on imports of the commodity. The very act of protecting the domestic industry tends to discourage exports in several ways. First, exporters using the often more expensive protected commodity in their production process are placed at a disadvantage. Second, because the resources employed in the protected industry would otherwise have been employed elsewhere, protection of import-competing sectors automatically discriminates against all other sectors, including potential exporting ones. Third, establishment of a new domestic in-

From *Finance and Development* 20 (June 1983), pp. 6–8.

dustry usually requires imported capital goods, and in early stages of the industry's development the value of these imports is likely to exceed the international value added of import-substituting production. This tends to put pressure on the foreign exchange markets and while this could be offset by currency realignment, under import substitution regimes, there is resistance to doing so (partly in order to facilitate the import of needed capital goods). Usually additional quantitive restrictions are employed to reduce the size of the balance of payments deficit, further increasing the bias toward import substitution.

None of these tendencies constitutes an inexorable and inevitable outcome of import substitution regimes. In principle, a country could decide to protect, say, the metal products sector while simultaneously encouraging the export of petrochemicals. However, in practice such an outcome is seldom observed.

For a variety of reasons (including the important fact that the authorities necessarily have greater ability to affect decisions by domestic producers when the economy is relatively less open), measures to promote import substitution tend to consist of a mixture of pricing measures and of direct quantitative controls over various aspects of economic activity. Thus the hallmarks of an import substitution regime generally include: high levels of protection to a number of industries, with a very wide range of rates of effective protection (that is, protection against the value-added components of imports . . . [1]); fairly detailed and complex quantitative controls and bureaucratic regulations, both over imports directly and often over a number of areas of domestic economic activity (sometimes through the import regime); and an over-valued exchange rate with associated disincentives for exporting.

In contrast, under an export promotion strategy, since tariffs cannot induce production for the international market, a production (or an export) subsidy or a realistic exchange rate is required. Subsidies are costly to government budgets, and since they are clearly visible, excessively high subsidies tend to be politically unpalatable. Therefore, there is a tendency to maintain a realistic exchange rate as an alternative. That in itself encourages exports (and reduces the balance of payments motive for tariff protection), but simultaneously, exporting industries must be permitted to purchase their needed intermediate goods and raw materials at world prices if they are to be competitive. This puts pressure on the authorities to reduce barriers to imports, which in turn may encourage other producers to enter the export market. Thus a genuine export promotion policy must be accompanied by a fairly open and liberalized trade regime.

Export promotion has to rely upon pricing incentives rather than quantitative controls. But there are constraints on the degree to which incentives can be differentiated among exporting activities, as a substitute for a realistic exchange rate. The major incentives for export promotion other than a realistic exchange rate are export subsidies (usually expressed as a rate of local currency paid beyond the official exchange rate per unit of foreign currency sales); favorable treatment for exporters on their tax liabilities; and availability of credit at below-market rates of interest. The important point is that these incentives are provided to anyone who exports. They can provide a uniform degree of bias among exporting activities.

FINDINGS

The following analysis of the effects of alternative trade strategies on growth rates is based in part on the results of earlier research. . . . The relationship between the growth of exports and the growth of gross domestic product (GDP) was examined for a group of ten developing countries. An increase in the rate of growth of export earnings of one percentage point annually was associated with an increase in the rate of growth of GDP of about 0.1 percentage point. Even if this does not imply causation, the results indicate a strong relationship between export growth and the overall growth rate.

Although there appears to be a significant positive relationship between rates of growth of GDP and of exports, it is by no means a perfect one. [As Table 1 indicates,] Brazil's export earnings actually declined between 1955 and 1960, while real GDP grew at an average annual rate of almost 7 percent. A similar situation occurred in the Republic of Korea during 1953–60. On the other hand, Chile's relatively high rate of growth of export earnings in the 1960s was accompanied by a positive, though not equally rapid, growth of real GDP. In the case of Colombia the rate of growth of exports reversed from a negative 0.8 percent to a positive 17 percent annually, while real GDP increased by about two percentage points annually. To be sure, that represented a doubling in the rate of growth of per capita income, but it was far less striking than the change in the Brazilian or Korean growth rates following their reversals of trade policy and of trends in export growth.

The degree of bias of the trade regime toward import substitution changed for some of the countries studied during the period covered (see [Table 1]). Shifting to an export promotion policy generally resulted in much-improved performance in the country's export earnings. The switch from import substitution to export promotion strategies in Brazil, Colombia, and Korea led to significant increases in export growth rates. Pakistan's improved growth of export earnings represented a move toward a less unbalanced incentive structure in the 1960s, even though the bias toward import substitution was still substantial. The large positive rate of growth of export earnings for Indonesia also followed an abrupt departure from the extreme restrictiveness of trade policy in the period before 1965 toward a more "moderate" import substitution bias.

The important question is why the choice of a trade regime — import substitution or export promotion — contributed to differences in growth performance.

TABLE 1

Trade Strategy, Export Growth, and GDP Growth in Ten Countries

Country	Period	Trade strategy	Average annual rate of growth	
			Export earnings	Real GDP
Brazil	1955–60	IS	−2.3	6.9
	1960–65	IS	4.6	4.2
	1965–70	EP	28.2	7.6
	1970–76	EP	24.3	10.6
Chile	1960–70	IS	9.7	4.2
Colombia	1955–60	IS	−0.8	4.6
	1960–65	IS	−1.9	1.9
	1970–76	EP	16.9	6.5
Indonesia	1965–73	MIS	18.9	6.8
Ivory Coast	1960–72	EP	11.2	7.8
Korea	1953–60	IS	−6.1	5.2
	1960–70	EP	40.2	8.5
	1970–76	EP	43.9	10.3
Pakistan	1953–60	IS	−1.5	3.5[1]
	1960–70	IS	6.2	6.8
Thailand	1960–70	MIS	5.5	8.2
	1970–76	MIS	26.6	6.5
Tunisia	1960–70	IS	6.8	4.6
	1970–76	MIS	23.4	9.4
Uruguay	1955–70	IS	1.6	0.7

Note: EP = export promotion; IS = import substitution; MIS = moderate import substitution.

[1]Growth rate is for 1950 to 1960.

Sources: Trade strategy: based upon evidence in country studies (Krueger et al., Trade and Employment in Developing Countries, Volume 1: Individual Studies, University of Chicago Press for the National Bureau of Economic Research, Chicago, 1981). Export growth rates: computed from data in May 1977, IMF, International Financial Statistics. GDP growth rates: World Bank, World Development Report 1978 and World Tables 1976; United Nations, Yearbook of National Accounts Statistics, vol. 2, for 1971 and 1969.

IMPORT SUBSTITUTION

In most countries, after an import substitution strategy was adopted, the growth rate of export earnings (and earnings of foreign exchange from other sources) diminished. In part this was the conscious outcome of an import substitution plan, which aimed to diminish dependence on trade. However, while the growth of foreign exchange declined, the growth in demand for imports of goods and services frequently accelerated instead of decelerating. The resulting foreign exchange shortage caused severe difficulties in many countries and became a binding constraint upon the growth rate.

Virtually every import substitution industry required imports of raw materials, intermediate goods, and machinery and equipment. Policymakers were especially reluctant to deny permission for imports of these goods, since a reduction in capital goods imports would reduce the GDP growth rate and a reduction of intermediate goods and raw material imports would adversely affect output and employment. "Dependence" upon imports for final consumption goods was replaced by "dependence" upon imports for growth not only via the availability of capital goods but also for employment and output, because the newly established factories could not produce without imported intermediate goods and raw materials. Ironically, the import substitution strategy has frequently resulted in an economy even more dependent upon trade than had been the case under the earlier pattern of primary commodity specialization, while simultaneously discouraging the growth of foreign exchange earnings.

In many import substitution countries, increased dependence upon imports and laggard foreign exchange earnings were reflected in periodic balance of payments crises. Brazil, Chile, Colombia (before 1968), Tunisia, and Uruguay all had such episodes in the period studied. These crises, in turn, were associated with intervals during which import licensing was particularly stringent, if not prohibitive, generally resulting in slow growth, if not an outright reduction in output. Very often these periods of severe import restrictions ended with a devaluation and a stabilization program designed to make exporting more attractive, at least temporarily.

The exhaustion of the "easy" import substitution opportunities, even in large countries with sizable domestic markets, such as Brazil, also helped slow down growth. The domestic market was not large enough to support the development of other industries at economic sales of production after import substitution had taken place in industries such as textiles and shoes, where imports have been sizable and outputs fairly standard. Once easy import substitution was over, the incremental capital/output ratio in the industrial sector rose sharply, and the "leading growth sector" experienced a decline in its growth rate.

The tendency for import substitution strategies to be administered by a detailed and complex mix of policy instruments also contributed to the tapering off of growth rates. Imports were allocated by category of commodity, by type of domestic user, by source of foreign exchange, and by type of use — capital good, intermediate good, or raw material. The proliferation of the control network and its complexity has been a common feature of import substitution regimes and is certainly a characteristic that has had harmful consequences.

CONCLUSIONS

Perhaps the most important lesson that has been learned from the experience of the successful countries is that the approach to industrialization and the development of new industries under an import substitution policy tends to be less and less successful the longer it continues. Export-oriented strategies have generally generated higher growth rates than have import substitution. Export promotion, by its nature, avoids some of the costs of the import substitution strategy.

One factor contributing to the high cost of import substitution activities is the very small size of domestic plants. To the extent that there are significant indivisibilities or scale economies in industrial operation, the economic costs of failing to expand plants and industries to sizes adequate to serve more than the domestic market are significantly greater than the gains from trade implied by the static comparative advantage model. The lower the transport costs between a country and its major trading partners, the greater will be the advantages of building optimal-sized plants rather than introduce more, smaller new industries catering to the domestic market. The larger the minimum efficient size of plant, the greater are the economic costs of catering only to the home market.

Korea's experience provides quantitative evidence on this point. It was estimated that about 18 percent or one sixth of the growth in industrial output between 1966 and 1968 was the result of manufacturing industries achieving economies of scale or overcoming problems associated with small size.

There have also been occasional suggestions that capital-intensive industries tend to have larger minimum efficient sizes and higher costs of operating below those sizes than do labor-intensive industries. If that is the case, and if an import substitution strategy also tends to encourage the development of more capital-intensive industries than does an export promotion strategy, the gains achieved under an export promotion strategy are further enhanced.

Domestic markets of most developing countries are generally too small to support efficient-sized plants. This makes the traditional criticism that protecting infant industries imposes costs on consumers even more forceful. The development of new industries in most cases probably entails an expansion beyond the boundaries of domestic markets.

For all the countries studied that shifted toward export promotion, a striking feature of their success was the very rapid growth of manufactured exports, often of new products. A firm starting to manufacture a new product is very likely to sell to the domestic market first simply because of transport cost differences; experience demonstrates, however, that this is not always the case. In fact, one major way of starting new industries and new product lines in the exporting countries is for firms in developed countries to subcontract with foreign suppliers to fabricate particular parts and components. The foreign buyer may provide technical specifications, technical assistance, or even capital, and may enter into a joint management or ownership arrangement to produce the subcontracted product. In some cases the entire output may be sold abroad initially, with foreign orders filled first and the domestic market satisfied later. Such instances, though uncommon, nevertheless point to the important fact that new industries are developed and expand under an export promotion strategy, and industrialization is by no means synonymous with import substitution.

An efficient industrialization strategy is thus one in which incentives, when granted, induce activity at minimum efficient size. Incentives should therefore be based upon production, not the destination of output. The evidence is strong that growth performance is better under export promotion than under import substitution. The reasons are readily apparent. What is not known is the relative importance of each contributing factor and the interaction among them. It is probable that each of the phenomena discussed above has contributed to growth, perhaps in different degrees in different countries depending upon such factors as size of domestic market, per capita income level, and proximity to major industrial countries.

Note

1. The effective rate of protection measures the increase in value added made possible by a tariff as compared to the situation under free trade. For example, let us take a table that, in the absence of tariffs, sells for $100 (whether imported or domestically made) and that in its domestic manufacture utilizes imported wood worth $60. The domestic value added is therefore $40. If a tariff of 10 percent is levied on tables, raising their imported price to $110 (but wood imports remain duty free), then although the nominal tariff on tables will be 10 percent, the effective rate will be 25 percent — that is, $10 as a proportion of the $40 worth of domestic value added.

16

A Cool Look at "Outward-looking" Strategies for Development

Paul Streeten

Whereas world trade had grown by almost 8 percent a year in the 1960s, it slowed down to 5.5 percent in the 1970s. In spite of this, the nonfuel exports of the developing countries grew at 6 percent annually in the 1970s, compared with only 5 percent in the 1960s. These averages conceal the different experiences of some low-income countries, which have experienced poor trade performance, and some highly successful middle-income countries.

GROWTH OF MANUFACTURED EXPORTS IN THE 1970s

Manufactured exports of developing countries grew more rapidly in the 1970s than in the 1960s in spite of slower growth and rising protectionist tendencies. Successful performance is a function of volume increases and avoiding reductions in

From *The World Economy* 5, no. 2 (September 1982), pp. 159–169. Reprinted by permission of Basil Blackwell Limited. Footnotes omitted.

relative prices. The volume of manufactured exports of the low-income oil importers rose by 90 percent in the 1970s, but more than two thirds of this was lost by declining relative prices. The middle-income oil importers, on the other hand, raised the volume of their manufactured exports by almost 300 percent and lost less than one third of this through a decline in relative prices.

The success in expanding manufactured exports was fairly concentrated. In 1978 only ten countries, with 45 percent of the developing-world population, supplied more than 75 percent of its manufactured exports; and three countries, with less than 3 percent of the population, supplied more than 40 percent of the total.

Manufactured exports of the developing countries to the industrialised countries grew as rapidly as they did in the 1960s, although their share in the markets of the industrialised countries is still quite small. It has grown from 1.7 percent in 1970 to 2.9 percent in 1978.

Intra-Third World trade (excluding fuel) grew in the 1970s. The rising share of South-South trade, however, was almost entirely confined to the middle-income countries. Not only the oil exporters but also the growing newly industrialising countries presented expanding markets, but they were hardly captured by the low-income countries.

EXPORT ORIENTATION VERSUS IMPORT SUBSTITUTION

The ingredients of success were an initial growth in agricultural productivity and a switch from import-substitution to export-oriented policies for development. A successful export drive, in turn, depends on easy access to duty-free imported inputs (for example, export-processing zones), on adequate price and profit incentives for exports and on an existing industrial base.

The ingredients of the package that help the transition from a high-protection, import-substitution policy to an export-oriented policy are now well known. They include (i) devaluation, (ii) removal of discrimination against exports (so that incentives are comparable with those for production in the domestic market) and (iii) a reduction in quantitative restrictions and tariffs on imports. It is also important to avoid subsequent inflation which would erode the international competitiveness gained for exports. Anti-inflation measures are therefore part of the package. The transition period is a difficult one and adequate finance for the temporarily deteriorating trade balance is necessary.

The reasons for failure in the transition may be inadequate effective devaluation or inadequate removal of the bias against exports, resurgence of inflation or lack of political commitment. It is not easy to generate the long-term expectations in exporters for them to embark on production and design for foreign markets and marketing organisations. A contributing reason is that in many countries the governments themselves have set up inefficient industries and then they rig the price system, through import controls, in order to reduce losses. In such situations, it is not production that responds to given price incentives; it is the price system which has been made to fit given production decisions.

"Outward-looking" economies are more dependent on foreign trade and therefore suffer greater losses in relation to their gross national product (GNP) when external shocks, such as oil-price increases, occur. But their larger trade gives them a cushion which makes them less dependent on foreign finance and makes it less necessary to impose lengthy domestic deflation. Whether one should draw from this the conclusion that the best strategy for the 1980s for all developing countries is to adopt an "outward-looking" course is another question, to be discussed below.

In the last ten to fifteen years, disenchantment with import-substitution policies for industrialisation in developing countries has certainly led to a reappraisal of this strategy and to a new approach, emphasising export promotion and export-led growth — more generally, an "outward-looking" strategy. The old strategy was itself the result partly of the international trade pessimism of the 1950s and partly of the strong vested interests that import-substitution policies create.

The reasoning underlying the change in strategy, over-simplified, runs like this. Protectionist measures raise costs and reduce international competitiveness in manufacturing industry. In addition they differentiate between producers in the wrong way. Manufactured consumer goods generally receive the highest protection. The use of imported capital goods and other imported inputs into domestic manufacturing is often encouraged, whereas agriculture and exports are discouraged. In extreme cases the excessive encouragement of imported inputs leads to the phenomenon of negative value added (valued at the appropriate shadow prices).

The tariff structure, while encouraging all import-substituting manufacturing firms, whether large or small, domestic or foreign, is particularly advantageous to foreign (and domestic) companies that rely heavily on imported capital goods and intermediate products from their parent and sister companies. A substantial private profit earned by these companies is therefore consistent with a quite modest social benefit. If dividends are remitted abroad, the social gain may become negligible or turn into a loss. Many of the complaints against foreign investment must therefore be laid at the door of misguided protectionist policies.

The argument for the reorientation of trade policies is not only that protection, over-valued exchange rates accompanied by import restrictions and the resulting encouragement given to excessive import substitution have penalised exports but also that price elasticities for *manufactured* exports from developing countries are high and that *some* of these countries could have earned more foreign exchange by increasing *primary* exports.

Moreover, excessive import substitution thrives on a self-fulfilling prophecy. Import substitution is embarked on because of elasticity pessimism and the policy promptly leads to poor export performance, apparently justifying the initial pessimism. Alternative policies, labelled "outward-looking," could achieve, it is argued, greater efficiency, higher employment and a fairer income distribution.

A second and distinct thread in the argument of those advocating "outward-looking" strategies is that administrative centralised controls make for inefficiency and inequality and that prices should be used much more as an instrument of policy making and planning. The philosophy might be summed up as pro-free(r) trade, although not necessarily *laissez-faire*.

CRITICAL ASSESSMENT OF THE CASE FOR EXPORT ORIENTATION

While much of the case for export orientation and against a policy bias towards import substitution is by now generally accepted and has considerable validity, there is a danger that the new approach attributes to import-substitution policies for industrialisation faults which result not from the misallocation of resources between alternatives or inefficiencies arising from such misallocation but from inefficient use of the resources allocated to the given objective of import substitution. Conversely, the approach emphasising "outward-looking" policies may attribute to Taiwanesque price and export policies virtues that may be due to other causes. More particularly, there is a danger that the measures which receive most emphasis are those about which formal economic theory has most to say (movements along the production function), to the neglect of forces that are not amenable to formal modelling (moves towards the production frontier).

Self-Contradictory and Inadequate Arguments

Inefficient use of resources can have many causes, quite apart from those directly or indirectly linked to industrialisation behind high protection. It is just as possible to have inefficient export policies as it is to have inefficient import substitution. Indeed, the eagerness to prove the deficiencies of protection and the virtues of Taiwan's freer trade and price policies leads the advocates of "outward-looking" strategies to argue on mutually exclusive lines. Excessive protection is said to lead to high profits, excessive profit remittances, excessively high urban wages and excessive migration from the countryside to the towns. At the same time, inefficient use of resources, under-utilisation of capacity and waste are also generally ascribed to excessive protection. To the extent that high profits are earned, costs must be low and to the extent that inefficiency raises costs, profits must be reduced.

It would be useful to compare the potential gains to be derived from a reallocation of resources from import-substituting manufacturing industry to agriculture and exports with those that could be reaped from the more efficient use of resources in *both* sectors. It has been said that export-oriented industries cannot be as inefficient as import-substituting industries because world prices limit the extent to which social and private gains diverge and value added cannot be negative in exports. But this is a fallacy. Inefficient policies with respect to exports can take the form of excessive subsidies to inputs into export industries so that negative value added can occur just as readily there as in inefficient import-substituting industries. Malaysia, India and Brazil may have suffered from this in the past.

The degree of under-utilisation of industrial capacity due to poor management may be the same as, or even greater than, that due to small domestic markets made profitable only by excessive protection. More generally, the dichotomy between "outward-looking" and "inward-looking" strategies may focus attention on a less important set of decisions in industrial policy and may divert attention from the more crucial decisions relating to the quality of management, scale, technology, product-mix, product design, types of education, recruitment and training, administration *et cetera*. It is quite easy to envisage an export-oriented policy which suffers from defects very similar to those criticised by the critics of import substitution. The ultimate test of the respective merits of the "outward-looking" and "inward-looking" strategies is not their ability to allocate resources between sectors, but their power to mobilise domestic resources and skills and to create and activate incentives, attitudes and institutions for development.

It is sometimes argued that the pressures for efficiency are greater in an open economy with substantially reduced protection and "realistic" exchange rates. The *general* competitive pressures are of course stronger in such an economy, although it must be remembered that the cold winds of competition can wither, as well as strengthen, tender plants. But while import substituters face *more* competition and therefore may become *more* efficient when the exchange rate is lowered, exporters have an easier time and, by the same argument, should become *less* efficient. There is a curious (tacit) asymmetry in the arguments of the advocates of export-led growth that high profits weaken the competitive vigour of the import substituter, but they strengthen the competitive performance of the exporter.

The arguments for freer trade are normally based on (i) the doctrine of comparative advantage, (ii) economies of scale and (iii) increased competition. But the advocates of trade liberalisation are not always aware of the logic of their arguments. The three arguments are not additive, let alone mutually reinforcing. Whatever the independent merit of each, they are mutually inconsistent.

For example, comparative advantage and increased competition are difficult to reconcile. Take two countries, India and Japan. Assume that both produce machines and textiles, but that Japan has a comparative advantage in machines and India in textiles. Assume that efficient (that is, low-cost) and inefficient (that is, high-cost) firms are permitted to co-exist in each industry and each country, but cannot survive lower-cost competition from abroad. Assume that there are increasing unit costs in all four industries. When tariffs are removed, according to the theory of comparative advantage, Japan's machine industry and India's textile industry should expand, while Japan's textile industry and India's machine industry should contract. But in the expanding industries, inefficient firms will expand with the efficient ones; while in the contracting industries, efficient firms will shrink with the inefficient ones. Only if we assume that in India all machine firms are inefficient and all textile firms efficient would the comparative advantage and the competition argument reinforce each other. Otherwise, comparative advantage partly frustrates the beneficial effects of competition and competition prevents the full benefits from international specialisation.

It is true that if the dispersion between efficient and inefficient firms in each industry remains the same, there will be a move towards a better allocation of resources because of the move towards international prices, which represent opportunity costs. Moreover, there may be a tendency for the inefficient firms in the contracting sector to contract more than the efficient ones and for the efficient firms to expand more than the inefficient ones in the expanding sector. This would aid efficiency. But, equally, there may be a tendency for the efficient firms to contract more than the inefficient ones in the contracting sector, say because of firmer cartel agreements, and for the efficient firms to expand less than the inefficient ones in the expanding sector, because the efficient firms may want to take out their profits in the form of a quieter life.

Similarly, the arguments from competition are difficult to reconcile with those from greater economies of scale. If competition is measured by the number of firms in an industry and if the exploitation of economies of scale results in greater concentration, one excludes the other. It is true (i) that economies of scale may take the form of greater (horizontal and vertical) specialisation between firms no larger in size, so that the average size need not increase, (ii) that in spite of higher concentration a sufficient number may survive to safeguard competition, (iii) that greater national concentration may be accompanied by greater international competition and (iv) that competition is measured as much by potential rivals and the threat of innovation as by the number of actual rivals. But these points do not render the argument more consistent. The new specialised firms may not be competitive, and potential competition cannot be a powerful force where [a] large and expensive plant presents a barrier to entry.

There are often fallacies in the arguments presented about the effects of competition on efficiency and employment. A frequent argument is that (i) efficient firms and industries will expand considerably as a result of trade liberalisation while (ii) inefficient firms and industries will have to contract somewhat. But it could equally be argued that (i) efficient industries and firms will face less competition because their rivals abroad contract and (ii) inefficient industries and firms will contract considerably in the face of competition from abroad. In the first argument greater efficiency and expansion (both "good things" from the point of view of employment), and in the second argument reduced efficiency and contraction (both "bad things"), are combined.

Fallacy of Composition

The argument that there are high price elasticities of demand for manufactured exports depends, at least partly, on the policies which it condemns. The export success stories of the countries set up as paragons depend on the heavy import substitution and the resulting export failures of the other countries. Pakistan's success in the 1960s in increasing exports of jute textiles depended on

India's failure. Even though the share of developing countries in world exports of manufactures is still small (they account for 10 percent of the imports and less than 3 percent of the consumption of manufactured goods in industrialised countries), the demand elasticities for the most successful *products* are much smaller than for the exports of these products by a particular *country*. And although it is true that in the long run (i) the higher income generated by a larger international division of labour, (ii) greater economies of scale and (iii) international specialisation will generate additional demand for extra exports and that in the short run the foreign exchange earned by the developing exporters will be spent on the products of the importers, in the short and medium run the experiences of Taiwan and South Korea cannot be generalised. It is easy to show that if all developing countries were to register the same export performance relative to their labour force or to their gross domestic product (GDP) as Taiwan and Korea, import barriers would rise in the importing countries and the terms of trade would deteriorate. But if substantial price reductions of manufactured exports or substantial marketing costs were required in order to sell a larger volume in new and untested markets, this would undermine the basis on which the calculations for comparative efficiency between import substitution and exports were made. It would be ironical if we were to witness a wholesale conversion to export orientation in a decade when growth has slowed down and protectionism in developed countries is on the rise.

The dispute between those who say that exports of developing countries have been held back by demand and those who put the blame on supply limitations is to some extent a sham dispute. Both constraints are potentially present, even though only one is dominant at any particular time. It is fairly plain that if all trade barriers were removed overnight and developed countries were to resume high growth rates, the developing countries would not be able to meet that demand: supply would be quite inelastic and would conform to the constraint. But, equally, if all developing countries were to be as successful as Taiwan and South Korea in increasing exports, trade barriers would quickly be erected or terms of trade would deteriorate and the demand constraint would become operative.

Similar reasoning applies to the exports of primary products by the large traditional suppliers. The success of small East African competitors in encroaching on India's share of tea exports does not imply that India could have entered a price war without suffering large losses. So, once again, the lessons of the few cannot be generalised. A crucial proposition in the export-optimism argument is: "Other things being equal, it is easier to increase exports of a particular commodity if one has a small share in the world market for it than if one has a large one." But in the same circumstances it is also easier to be driven out of a market. At some point either the large rivals or other small rivals may completely knock out the budding exports. For precisely the same reason that exports may grow rapidly they may decline rapidly. If we take the phrase "other things being equal" seriously and apply it to supply elasticities, only differences in the size of suppliers are relevant. These will give a power advantage to the large and established suppliers if they wish to use their power.

Taiwan and South Korea as Models

"I like Taiwan" could be the campaign button of the outward lookers. Yet Taiwan is a special case. She enjoyed massive aid. Japan has a prominent position as a market and constitutes a nearby growth pole. Both immigrant and indigenous entrepreneurs are present. She receives favourable trade treatment and benefited from the boom caused by the Vietnam war. She had an effective land reform. Nobody, as far as I know, has sorted out the contribution of these various factors in Taiwan's success of achieving very rapid growth with equity, although their identification serves as a Rorschach test of the author's ideology. In particular, it would be interesting to compare in detail the effects of land reform with those of trade and price policies. It could, of course, be that the success depended on the interaction and mutual reinforcement of various factors, whereas the impact of any one in isolation could have been ineffective or counterproductive. For example, price policies reflecting scarcities in the face of an unequal land distribution would have reinforced inequality.

South Korea is another country with a spectacular performance in growth with equity, at least until recently. The success is often attributed to export-led growth through market forces. But the facts do not bear out the attribution. Korea has not only promoted exports but also massively substituted for imports. A whole range of products that were imported in 1960 were produced domestically in 1971. Moreover, Korea adopted import restrictions to achieve this objective. The promotion of export industries relied on many measures other than prices. The Government has a strong control of the banking sector and encouraged saving, as well as contributing by large government saving. The direction and composition of investment was controlled by differential interest rates that varied between 8 and 33 percent. Korea has a large public sector that absorbed nearly a third of total investment and 15 percent of manufacturing output. Since the ratio of capital to output is larger in state enterprises, the Government owns an even larger share of industrial capital. Moreover the share of employment in export industries of total employment is relatively small: 5 percent of total employment and 18.9 percent in manufacturing. Other factors apart from export promotion and policies other than the free play of market forces must therefore be responsible for Korea's success. . . .

Benefit of Developed Countries' Agricultural Protection

The advocates of trade liberalisation and "outward-looking" policies normally also plead for reduced agricultural protection in rich countries in order to enable poor countries to earn more from their agricultural exports. But nobody has seen that this policy may hurt the industrialising developing countries. It is, of course, well known that developing importers of agricultural products may have to pay higher prices for these imports. But I have a different argument in mind. The accelerated shift into manufacturing industry, subject to increasing returns, in the advanced countries — which would result from reduced agricultural protection (assuming that agricultural protection has been effective in raising agricultural production above what it would be in its absence, which can be doubted) — would make the manufactured exports from the developing countries less competitive and their industrialisation more difficult. Against this view one could argue that, although *incentives* to industrialise are reduced, *means* to industrialise (namely, export earnings from agriculture) are increased; that there is still scope for specialisation within the industrial sector; and that the favourable repercussions of accelerated growth resulting from abandoning protection more than outweigh the unfavourable effects of greater competitiveness. But these arguments do not dispel some doubts about the consequences of abandoning agricultural protection.

It is possible to doubt the three assumptions on which the case rests: (i) that agricultural resources in the advanced countries would flow into "industry," (ii) that "industry" is subject to increasing returns to scale and (iii) that "industry" is directly competitive with "industry" in developing countries. But as long as the argument is conducted in terms of "industry" versus "agriculture," the abolition of agricultural protection in the rich countries is bound to perpetuate the comparative advantage of the poor countries in (increasing-cost) "agriculture" and to delay the shift into (decreasing-cost) "industry." There is a contradiction in accusing the rich countries of condemning the poor countries to remain hewers of wood and drawers of water and at the same time blaming them for not buying enough "wood and water."

CONCLUSIONS

Not all options are exhausted by the contrast between "inward-looking" and "outward-looking" strategies. Some countries may choose a more selective strategy of looking outwards than general trade liberalisation and an indiscriminate welcome to foreign capital, multinational enterprises and foreign educational influences. A selective orientation towards other developing countries has been labelled "collective self-reliance." There are not only political and cultural arguments for such an orientation but also economic ones. The existing strong North-South orientation is partly the colonial heritage and the legacy of the network of communications, credit, transport *et cetera*. This has been reinforced since independence by aid-tying and investment by multinational enterprises. Once the alternative infrastructure has been erected, incentives for greater South-South trade will emerge. Moreover, in view of the probably lower growth rates of the countries of the Organisation for Economic Cooperation and Development (OECD), and the possibility of the erection of protective barriers, the encouragement of intra-Third World trade is a sensible way to insure against future losses. Even if buying in the North may be cheaper, lack of foreign exchange may make it impossible. A more poverty-oriented strategy for development will show that poor countries are more likely to produce for one another what they consume and to consume what they themselves produce. The strong North-South orientation of the past is partly built on the consumption patterns of a small Southern élite and the dual development this has implied.

The conclusions are as follows: First, it is over-simplified and misleading to claim that exports are the key to growth and that exports are achieved through the Invisible Hand. Second, both exports and import substitutes can be produced efficiently or inefficiently and this is a more important factor than reallocation from one to the other. Third, many arguments for trade liberalisation are mutually inconsistent. Fourth, the abolition of agricultural protection in advanced countries may have certain drawbacks for the developing countries. Fifth, the term "outward-looking" is too general and vague to present a good guide to policy.

VI

Multinational Enterprises

The "multinationalization of multinational enterprise" is one of the most significant trends of the 1970s and 1980s. Nations that were long-time hosts to multinational corporations (MNCs) have begun to parent MNCs themselves. Some of these new MNCs even come from developing countries. Many have made inroads into the United States itself, until recently the dominant MNC parent.

This trend is the most important theme in Carroll's paper, and has its place in Streeten's. Its importance is due in turn to another trend, only implicit in the papers: MNCs of all nationalities account for a steadily growing share of world exports and imports. Strictly national firms have become correspondingly less significant as exporters and importers. Almost all the growth of European, Japanese, and other MNCs has added to multinationals' weight in world trade. U.S. MNCs have grown, too. Very few have failed or stagnated or sold out or gone home. Other researchers demonstrate explicitly how MNCs have dramatically increased their shares of recent world trade — even U.S. MNCs — at the expense of national producers.

Thus the international competitive position of U.S. MNCs is reasonably strong, even though the competitive position of the United States as a geographical region may not be. Likewise Carroll can almost boast about the competitiveness of European MNCs, even though terms such as "Eurosclerosis" are applied to the dubious competitiveness of the largest European countries.

More and more of the world's trade seems linked to *corporate* factor endowments, skills, and technology rather than their *national* counterparts, on which so much of traditional trade theory focuses. Not that national endowments, skills, and technology are irrelevant. They obviously complement corporate endowments, skills, and technology that can be moved fairly easily across boundaries in the long run, contrary to the traditional assumption of factor immobility.

Some of the endowments, skills, and technology owned by every MNC are unique, protected by patents, experience, secrecy, specialized personnel, and scale economies due to sheer size. Thus MNCs are never perfect competitors. Trade patterns among them may differ widely from what perfectly competitive reasoning predicts. Economic rents may exist in the form of supernormal profits and create sharp conflicts over how to divide them between mobile MNCs and immobile governments and worker groups (Streeten). Gaming, bargaining, and organizational behavior may be crucial to explain international patterns of both trade and investment, as suggested by Grossman and Richardson's summary from Part III above.

Streeten perceives a shift in bargaining power in the conflict between governments and MNCs. One outcome, as he sees it, has been that U.S. multinationals have become more accommodating to host-country pressures, for example, by reducing their insistence on wholly owned affiliates. Streeten's vision is of increasing prominence for smaller, flexible multinationals, whose "special advantage would consist not in the monopolistic package of capital, technology, and marketing, but in special skills." These smaller multinationals would "use more capital-saving techniques . . . and design products more adapted to the consumption and production needs of the poor — hoes, simple power tillers, and bicycles, rather than air conditioners, expensive cars, and equipment for luxury apartments. . . ." This vision has been shattered by international debt problems, discussed below, and was always somewhat wishful thinking. Small may be beautiful, but it's not very likely: almost all the dramatic cross-penetration of U.S. markets by European and Japanese multinationals in the 1970s (see Carroll) has been by familiar oligopolistic giants.

This cross-penetration of multinationals poses some interesting puzzles. One is why it happened in the sequence it did, with burgeoning growth of U.S. investment in Europe during the 1960s, and burgeoning growth of European and Japanese investment in the U.S. during the 1970s and 1980s. Commentators sometimes point to the change in relative currency values as the most important reason. The dollar was overvalued in the 1960s; its depreciation corrected that overvaluation in the 1970s. Yet as McCulloch shows in her paper in Part VII, European and Japanese investment in the United States remained very strong in the 1980s even as the dollar soared toward overvaluation again. She discusses several more subtle explanations for trends in cross-penetration.

A second puzzle raised by cross-penetration is what direct investment does to the industrial market structure. The potential loss associated with worldwide oligopoly as multinational corporations displace or acquire smaller national firms and collude among themselves affects the whole world. But the matter is more complex than it appears, for certain direct investments may reduce monopolistic market power. Direct investment in a host country where one manufacturer previously had a monopoly position will reduce market concentration in that country; direct investment by smaller multinational oligopolists may reduce the world market power wielded by the largest multinational oligopolists.

Moreover, economic opinion is divided on whether market concentration and oligopoly is uniformly "bad." More market concentration may imply more research and development, with consequent innovation and faster growth. If so, the static losses from oligopoly and market power are the price paid for dynamic gains, which may outweigh those losses in terms of social welfare. Similarly, the corporation may consider market power a part of the return that makes innovation profitable. Streeten's argument that developing countries, because they are small, could be painlessly exempted from paying for such supernormal returns seems flawed. It fails to explain what would induce any sensible firm to accept a lower return on one part of its investments, even a very small part (investments in developing countries). Even small developing countries can kill the goose that lays the golden eggs, or more accurately, cause her to move her nest to more hospitable habitats.

Both papers in Part VI were written before international debt problems (Part IX) accelerated in 1982. Policy measures forced on the Latin American debtor countries, the Philippines, Indonesia, and Korea have clouded the outlook for MNCs there. Stricter performance requirements, desperate adjustments of regulations, virtual abolition of repatriation of earnings, and the inability of MNC affiliates to countenance new infusions of funds from their parents have all brought direct investment in problem debtors to a standstill. Some commentators have urged problem debtors to open their economies liberally so that direct investment by MNCs can replace the lending from international banks that has atrophied. There is no sign that more than token moves in this direction will be made, for reasons that are scattered liberally through Streeten's paper. And if liberalizing initiatives were taken toward MNCs, there is little chance that the MNCs would take them seriously. Debtor governments have no way of credibly guaranteeing that liberalization would remain after MNCs had sunk new roots into their economies. (This problem of credible precommitments is discussed in the Grossman–Richardson paper in Part III.) The consequence for MNCs of international debt problems may thus be a reconcentration of direct investment in Europe, Japan, and in the United States, and in those few newly industrializing countries (Part V) that remain untainted by debt.

17

Multinational Reshuffle

Geoffrey S. Carroll

In 1958 the original six members of the EC had a combined gross national product one quarter the size of the United States' GNP. In 1981, however, with a population of close to 270 million (as compared with 230 million in the United States), the 10 EC member countries have an aggregate gross domestic product of close to $3 trillion, or roughly equal to that of the United States. The consolidation of the 10 national economies has created the world's largest trading entity, and, together, the United States and the Community now account for approximately 50 percent of all world trade and more than 40 percent of the world's total output.

It became clear early on, however, that the remarkable levels of growth and the economic successes attained in the EC would not be achieved without cost to the United States. Over the past 25 years the costs have most visibly materialized in the form of trade disputes — numerous disagreements in the agricultural area, including the infamous trans-Atlantic "chicken wars," and in the steel industry — and in more recent years over the conduct of U.S. monetary policy. . . .

. . . The purpose of this article is . . . to show statistically the tremendous growth of the European [and Japanese] business and financial communities over the past 25 years — a fact not well known and an accomplishment which was aided in no small way by the existence of the Common Market.

The tables show the extent to which . . . industrial corporations and commercial banks have grown in size and scope vis-à-vis their principal competitors in the Organization for Economic Cooperation and Development. Each of the eight tables represents a large international industry, and each individual table compares the 10 to 15 largest firms in the world in that industry in 1959 to an equal number in 1981. Gross sales were chosen as the standard of comparison for corporations because this figure is less misleading than either of the other two possible standards of measure — net profits or gross assets. The commercial banks, however, were ranked according to their total assets. Although the gross sales figure is an inadequate measure of efficiency, it is a reasonably accurate barometer of market presence and control.

Though Europeans have found it difficult to discard the self-image of the economically weak, inefficient, and divided underdogs — particularly since Europe is currently suffering through . . . [several] consecutive years of . . . record rates of unemployment — the data suggests that this appearance is somewhat deceptive. Indeed, since the formation of the European Community, European-

From *Europe* Magazine, no. 231 (May–June 1982), pp. 12–15. Reprinted by permission. Some text omitted.

based industrial companies and commercial banks have sharply increased their shares of world markets, often at the expense of their U.S. competitors. European businessmen are by nature considerably more outward looking than their American counterpart. For every American company or manager who has knowledge of the outside world (and there are obviously many), there are thousands more whose mental horizons stop at the seaboard. Europe, whose history is deep in cross-frontier dealing, has not been able to afford that luxury.

Early in the 1960s it became clear that the United States did not have a monopoly on innovation, enterprise, efficiency, or quality control. First, many of the European firms successfully challenged U.S. multinational companies (MNCs) operating in their individual home countries. Then, in once U.S.-dominated third-country markets — ranging from Latin America to Africa to Asia — American MNCs found themselves competing with European firms which were increasingly as well-financed and well-equipped as themselves. By as early as 1971, the expansion rate of foreign manufacturing operations of large European and Japanese enterprises exceeded the rate of large U.S. enterprises. Not only was the growth rate of European MNCs' sales greater than that of U.S. multinationals, more foreign production outposts were being added to their systems than were being added to the network of U.S. multinationals. In fact, in these third-country markets the host governments welcomed other foreign-based corporations as alternatives to U.S. companies, for they brought not only similar products and processes, but also different national flags — flags that did not connote superpower.

And now, finally, in the most recent competitive development, many European [and Japanese] enterprises are making inroads into the U.S. market, initially through exports and then by taking over American companies or constructing new plants and distribution facilities in the United States. Although European [and Japanese] investment in the United States is still small compared to U.S. investment in Europe, it is growing rapidly.

[A] *Fortune* magazine listing of the largest industrial companies in the world (August 10, 1981) showed that of the top one hundred, 45 were from the United States, 42 from Western Europe, and 8 from Japan. Any way one measures it, there is no question that the United States is still the preeminent economic power in the world and is likely to remain so, but that preeminence is slipping. While the United States is still responsible for the large 21 percent of world GNP in 1981, this share has dropped from 45 percent in the 1950s.

Though there was only space available to display eight industry tables in this chapter, the original study included the examination of seven additional industries: food and beverage products, industrial and farm equipment, paper and wood products, industrial and farm equipment, cosmetics, rubber products, tobacco, and textiles and apparel. The tables show that the United States continues to maintain a predominate global position in the aerospace, paper and wood products, and food and beverage industries.

What the tables do not show is that Boeing saw its share of the non-Communist world market for commercial aircraft drop to 51 percent . . . [in 1981],

AEROSPACE

$ MILLIONS		1959	Ranking	1981	$ MILLIONS	
Net income	Sales	Company and country		Company and country	Sales	Net income
31.0	1,811.8	General Dynamics (US)	1	United Technologies (US)	12,323.9	393.4
12.4	1,612.1	Boeing (US)	2	Boeing (US)	9,426.2	600.5
8.7	1,301.6	Lockheed (US)	3	Rockwell International (US)	6,906.5	280.2
28.6	1,080.9	United Aircraft (US)	4	McDonnell Douglas (US)	6,066.3	144.6
30.7	1,044.9	North American Aviation (US)	5	Lockheed (US)	5,395.7	27.6
(−33.8)	883.8	Douglas Aircraft (US)	6	General Dynamics (US)	4,742.7	195.0
15.5	728.0	Hawker Siddeley (UK)	7	British Aerospace (UK)	3,309.4	266.3
10.0	435.9	McDonnell Aircraft (US)	8	Aerospatiale (Fr.)	3,120.7	28.1
8.5	435.5	Vickers (UK)	9	Rolls-Royce (UK)	2,926.4	(−62.8)
14.3	329.2	Curtiss-Wright (US)	10	Martin-Marietta (US)	2,619.3	188.1

AUTOMOTIVE (Autos & Trucks)

	1959				1981	
		$ MILLIONS				$ MILLIONS
Company and country	Net income	Sales	Ranking	Company and country	Sales	Net income
General Motors (US)	873.1	11,223.1	1	General Motors (US)	57,728.5	(−762.5)
Ford Motor (US)	451.4	5,356.9	2	Ford Motor (US)	37,085.5	(−1,543.3)
Chrysler (US)	−5.4	2,642.9	3	Fiat (Italy)	25,155.0	N.A.
American Motors (US)	60.3	869.9	4	Renault (France)	18,979.3	3,450.9
Volkswagen (Germany)	66.7	843.8	5	Volkswagen (Germany)	18,339.0	170.9
British Motor (UK)	21.2	742.0	6	Daimler-Benz (Germany)	17,108.1	605.1
Fiat (Italy)	23.1	700.8	7	Peugeot (France)	16,846.4	(−348.9)
Daimler-Benz (Germany)	5.9	588.3	8	Toyota (Japan)	14,233.8	616.0
Renault (France)	7.1	577.8	9	Nissan (Japan)	13,853.5	461.6
Simca (France)	0.5	418.7	10	Mitsubishi (Japan)	10,997.6	100.7

CHEMICALS

$ MILLIONS Net income	Sales	1959 Company and country	Ranking	1981 Company and country	$ MILLIONS Sales	Net income
418.7	2,114.3	E.I. Du Pont (US)	1	Hoechst (Germany)	16,480.6	251.6
171.6	1,531.3	Union Carbide (US)	2	Bayer (Germany)	15,880.6	356.3
110.1	1,423.8	ICI (UK)	3	BASF (Germany)	15,277.3	197.6
50.0	719.6	Allied Chemical (US)	4	E.I. Du Pont (US)*	13,652.0	716.0
37.4	708.0	Olin Mathieson (US)	5	ICI (UK)	13,290.0	(−46.5)
62.9	705.4	Dow Chemical (US)	6	Dow Chemical (US)	10,626.0	805.0
48.9	615.3	Monsanto (US)	7	Union Carbide (US)	9,994.0	890.0
25.1	585.5	Bayer (Germany)	8	Veba Oel (Germany)	9,645.7	35.9
52.3	583.6	American Cyanamid (US)	9	Montedison (Italy)	9,103.8	(−524.2)
23.7	540.0	BASF (Germany)	10	DSM (Netherlands)	7,514.2	12.5
20.5	529.0	Hoechst (Germany)	11	Rhône-Poulenc (France)	7,155.0	(−461.3)
19.3	471.5	Montecatini (Italy)	12	Ciba-Geigy (Switzerland)	7,113.3	182.1

*These figures do not reflect Du Pont's recent acquisition of Conoco, which moves Du Pont to the number one position.

COMMERCIAL BANKING

1960		Ranking	1981	
Company and Country	Assets ($ millions)		Company and Country	Assets ($ millions)
Bank America Corp. (US)	11,942.0	1	Citicorp (US)	114,920.0
Chase Manhattan (US)	9,260.4	2	Bank America Corp. (US)	111,617.3
Citibank (US)	8,688.4	3	Banque Nationale de Paris (France)	107,449.6
Barclays (UK)	7,457.1	4	Caisse Nationale de Crédit Agricole (France)	105,906.4
Manufacturers Hanover (US)	6,126.1	5	Crédit Lyonnais (France)	98,147.4
Chemical Bank (US)	4,539.0	6	Société Générale (France)	90,164.9
Royal Bank of Canada (Canada)	4,432.0	7	Barclays Bank (UK)	88,624.7
Morgan Guaranty (US)	4,423.9	8	Dai-Ichi Kangyo Bank (Japan)	88,519.8
Midlands of London (UK)	4,377.7	9	Deutsche Bank (Germany)	88,468.4
Lloyds (UK)	4,374.3	10	National Westminster Bank (UK)	82,585.3
Canadian Imperial Bank (Canada)	4,345.5	11	Mitsubishi Bank (Japan)	76,433.2
Bank of Montreal (Canada)	3,595.1	12	Chase Manhattan (US)	76,189.6
Security First National of L.A. (US)	3,593.7	13	Fuji Bank (Japan)	75,396.9
Bankers Trust (US)	3,430.3	14	Sumitomo Bank (Japan)	73,459.5
Continental Illinois (US)	3,312.1	15	Sanwa Bank (Japan)	70,268.9

METAL PRODUCTS

	1959 ($ MILLIONS)			1981	($ MILLIONS)	
Net income	Sales	Company and country	Ranking	Company and country	Sales	Net income
40.0	1,146.5	Continental Can (US)	1	Saint-Gobain-Pont-a-Mousson (France)	10,303.9	215.3
40.9	1,107.4	American Can (US)	2	Gulf & Western (US)	5,782.8	255.3
16.6	700.0	Mannesmann (Germany)	3	Continental Group (US)	5,119.5	224.8
36.1	618.3	Guest, Kenn & Nettlefolds (UK)	4	Degussa (Germany)	4,857.7	37.7
18.1	560.0	Tube Investments (UK)	5	American Can (US)	4,812.2	85.7
21.4	517.4	Am. Radiator & Std. Sanitary (US)	6	Guest, Keen & Nettlefolds (UK)	4,471.3	(209.1)
44.8	489.3	Reynolds Metals (US)	7	Reynolds Metals (US)	3,653.2	180.3
85.2	457.8	International Nickel (Canada)	8	Textron (US)	3,637.5	86.1
23.0	448.7	Aluminum (Canada)	9	Cockerill (Belgium)	3,462.8	(269.6)
6.2	384.8	Salzgitter A. G. (Germany)	10	McDermott (US)	3,282.5	88.4
15.9	332.0	Babcock & Wilcox (US)	11	SKF (Sweden)	2,958.7	105.7
6.9	325.9	Combustion Engineering (US)	12	Klochner-Werke (Germany)	2,781.2	(5.5)
19.6	322.3	Container Corp. American (US)	13	Vallourer (France)	2,758.2	15.0
6.5	310.2	Crane (US)	14	Tube Investments (UK)	2,693.4	(43.5)

ELECTRONICS-APPLIANCES

$ MILLIONS		1959	Ranking	1981	$ MILLIONS	
Net income	Sales	Company and country		Company and country	Sales	Net income
280.2	4,349.5	General Electric (US)	1	General Electric (US)	24,959.0	1,514.0
102.2	2,314.9	Western Electric (US)	2	I.T.T. (US)	18,529.7	894.3
85.9	1,910.7	Westinghouse (US)	3	Philips (Netherlands)	18,402.8	165.2
40.1	1,388.4	RCA (US)	4	Siemens (Germany)	17,950.3	332.4
92.3	1,100.5	Philips (Netherlands)	5	Hitachi (Japan)	12,871.3	503.4
72.3	1,081.0	GTE (US)	6	Matsushita (Japan)	12,684.4	541.9
23.1	866.2	Siemens (Germany)	7	Western Electric (US)	12,032.1	693.2
29.0	765.6	I.T.T. (US)	8	Générale d'Electricité (France)	10,847.1	96.4
27.4	683.8	Bendix (US)	9	Thomson-Brandt (France)	8,657.5	72.9
13.1	583.6	Associated Electric. Industries (UK)	10	Westinghouse (US)	8,514.3	402.9
15.2	579.5	Hitachi (Japan)	11	Toshiba (Japan)	8,146.4	198.1
8.9	512.6	AEG-Telefunken (Germany)	12	RCA (US)	8,011.3	315.3
21.3	496.1	Singer (US)	13	AEG-Telefunken (Germany)	6,755.9	(-163.8)
13.5	494.3	Raytheon (US)	14	Robert Bosch (Germany)	6,505.9	(-163.8)

METAL MANUFACTURING

1959			Ranking	1981		
$ MILLIONS					$ MILLIONS	
Net income	Sales	Company and country		Company and country	Sales	Net income
254.6	3,643.0	U.S. Steel (US)	1	Thyssen (Germany)	15,235.9	61.6
117.2	2,055.7	Bethlehem Steel (US)	2	Nippon Steel (Japan)	13,104.9	496.2
53.9	1,076.8	Republic Steel (US)	3	U.S. Steel (US)	12,492.1	504.5
77.1	1,022.4	Armco Steel (US)	4	Pechiney Ugine (France)	9,029.7	143.9
55.6	858.5	Aluminum Co. America (US)	5	Canadian Pacific (Canada)	8,539.5	498.7
NA	829.5	Fried. Krupp (Germany)	6	LTV (US)	8,009.9	127.9
29.5	765.7	Jones & Laughlin (US)	7	Krupp (Germany)	7,668.5	33.5
54.9	736.9	National Steel (US)	8	ESTEL (Netherlands)	7,046.1	(−245.8)
48.4	705.1	Inland Steel (US)	9	British Steel (UK)	6,772.7	(−3,891.3)
30.8	668.5	American Metal Climax (US)	10	Bethlehem Steel (US)	6,743.0	121.0
59.2	632.7	Anaconda (US)	11	Nippon Kokan (Japan)	5,930.5	114.2
10.4	609.1	Gelsenkirchener A.G. (Germany)	12	Armco (US)	5,678.0	265.3
30.9	608.1	Youngstown Sheet & Tube (US)	13	Sumitomo Metal (Japan)	5,558.9	117.1

PHARMACEUTICALS

1959 $ MILLIONS			1981	1981 $ MILLIONS	
Net income	Sales	Company and country	Ranking	Company and country	Sales	Net income
25.1	585.5	Bayer (Germany)	1	Hoechst (Germany)	16,480.6	251.6
NA	529.0	Hoechst (Germany)	2	Bayer (Germany)	15,880.6	356.3
46.7	420.8	American Home Products (US)	3	Johnson & Johnson (US)	4,837.4	400.7
15.4	297.7	Johnson & Johnson (US)	4	American Home Products (US)	3,798.5	445.9
24.9	253.7	Pfizer (US)	5	Roche/Sapar (Switzerland)	3,496.2	138.3
6.2	234.6	Ciba-Geigy (Switzerland)	6	Warner-Lambert (US)	3,479.2	192.7
29.9	216.9	Merck (US)	7	Bristol-Myers (US)	3,158.3	270.6
20.9	209.2	Sterling Drug (US)	8	Pfizer (US)	3,029.3	254.8
30.9	191.5	Parke Davis (US)	9	Sandoz (Switzerland)	2,925.5	120.6
23.4	187.0	Eli Lilly (US)	10	Merck (US)	2,734.0	415.4
16.4	182.8	Warner-Lambert (US)	11	Eli Lilly (US)	2,558.6	341.9
23.2	156.9	Upjohn (US)	12	Beecham Group (UK)	2,243.2	175.8

Source for all tables is *Fortune Magazine* (July, August 1960; May 4, August 10, 1981). Industry classification is also abstracted from *Fortune Magazine*. Figures are for 1980.

down from 67 percent in 1980, while that of Europe's Airbus Industrie jumped from 20 percent to 42 percent. With regard to the paper and wood products industry, while several European companies are annually making small inroads into this traditionally U.S.-dominated industry, the U.S. leadership seems relatively secure as 9 of the top 12 companies in the world are still American. Nor is the strong U.S. position in the world food and beverage products industry likely to deteriorate any time soon — of the top 25 firms in the world, 16 are American, each with annual sales in excess of $3.5 billion.

Of the 15 industries examined, there are several which have remained jointly dominated by European and American firms. Among these are rubber products, tobacco, cosmetics, and industrial and farm equipment. The international rubber industry is dominated by the American companies Goodyear Tire & Rubber, B. F. Goodrich, Uniroyal and General Tire and Rubber — with total sales of more than $16 billion in 1980 — and by the two European giants, Michelin and Dunlop-Perelli, with 1980 sales in excess of $15 billion. The dominant participants in the global tobacco industry are R. J. Reynolds, Philip Morris, and American Brands on the U.S. side — with joint sales [in 1981] of close to $20 billion — and British American Tobacco, Rothman's International, and Tabacalera on the European side, registering sales of more than $16 billion. With regard to industrial and farm equipment, no single continent was dominant 25 years ago and that holds true today as well. Whereas in 1959 the largest companies were evenly divided between the United States and Europe, in 1981, of the top 25 companies, 10 were European and 9 were American.

The larger number of industries examined in this study, however, show a declining U.S. share of the world market and a corresponding rise in the European [and Japanese] presence. Industries included in this group are automobiles, chemicals, commercial banking, electronics and appliances, metal manufacturing, metal products, and pharmaceuticals. Though the United States still possesses the two largest automobile companies in the world, the next 22 of 23 companies on the list are either European or Japanese. Though these tables do not show it, the second ten positions on the automotive list are occupied by such familiar names as British Leyland, Honda Motor, Volvo, Toyo Kogyo, BMW, Saab, Isuzu, Alfa Romeo, Yamaha Motor, and Suzuki Motor. An analysis of the second tier of companies is valuable in that it more often than not accurately shows where the next wave of competition is coming from.

In the chemical industry, whereas in 1959 seven of the top 10 firms were American, in 1981 seven of the top 10 companies are European and the three largest are German. This is a particularly remarkable accomplishment in light of the fact that the American chemical industry has been heavily subsidized, indirectly, through the regulation of natural gas and petroleum prices.

Of all the economic and financial changes which have occurred in the past 25 years, none is greater than the turnaround in the commercial banking sector. Whereas in 1960 the English speaking world (the United States, the United Kingdom, and Canada) overwhelmingly dominated the industry with all of the top

15 banks coming from these countries, in 1981 continental European banks and Japanese banks have essentially reversed the situation. Though the tables do not show it, 35 of the top 40 banks in the world in 1980 were based outside the United States, with five of the top seven and 22 of the top 40 being European.

In the electronics and appliances industry, European companies such as Philips, Siemens, and Générale d'Electricité have developed into formidable competitors of the likes of General Electric and ITT. A close examination of the companies currently ranked 15–25 in this field shows quite clearly that the greatest competitive pressures in the years to come will be provided by the Japanese firms.

The metal manufacturing industry is yet another area whose 25-year history has been characterized by significant growth on the part of European and Japanese companies. Whereas in 1959 11 of the first 13 companies were American, in 1981 20 of the top 25 companies are now foreign based, of which 12 are European and 5 are Japanese. The metal products industry was jointly dominated by the Americans and Europeans back in 1959, and it is still dominated by them today, but the European corporate presence is stronger.

In the pharmaceutical industry, several European firms have done extremely well and sales of each are now more than three times greater than [those of] their closest U.S. competitor. However, this does not mean that the Europeans dominate this industry internationally; they do not. Of the top 20 pharmaceutical companies in the world, 14 are U.S.-based and only 5 are European.

The U.S. economy is still the largest on the earth, but as the tables show, it has declined in terms of sheer power and influence, and it very well may continue to decline relative to the economies of some of its old and new competitors. It is highly unlikely, however, that European corporations will continue to grow over the next quarter-century as rapidly as they have over the last 25 years. The economic accomplishments of the EC — and Japan as well — are part of a natural cycle of growth that was to be expected as these areas recovered from the devastation of WWII.

It would be wrong for Americans, in both the public and private policy fields, to interpret what has happened as a defeat or some kind of national humiliation which both the Europeans and Japanese have enjoyed inflicting upon the Americans. To take this approach would be to misunderstand the process of change and thus run the risk of mishandling the necessary adaptation. It's not been a case of America bad, Europe good, but of both being profoundly different — internally and in relation to each other — from their condition and positions only 30 years ago. An independent version of Western affluence has been created, a version which is inevitably both a tribute to and a constructive criticism of the American original from which so much of Europe's creation of wealth has sprung.

18

Multinationals Revisited

Paul Streeten

The multinational is no longer so multifashionable. It is true that much is still being written about it, and this reviewer of some recent books and articles on the subject [see references at the end of the article] succumbs to the Swiftian thought that he who can make one word grow where there were two before is a true benefactor of mankind. Yet, in spite of the continuing controversy, some of the steam has gone out of the debate. There is no longer the sharp separation between those who think that what is good for General Motors is good for humanity and those who see in the multinational corporations the devil incorporated.

The reasons for this lowering of the temperature are to be found in five recent trends that suggest that the role of multinational corporations in development has to be reassessed.

First, there has been a shift in bargaining power between multinationals and their host countries, greater restrictions on the inflow of packaged technology, a change in emphasis from production to research and development and marketing, among other factors, that have increased the uncertainties of direct foreign investment. As a result, there is some evidence that it has become the policy of multinational companies to shift from equity investment, ownership of capital, and managerial control of overseas facilities to the sale of technology, management services, and marketing as a means to earn returns on corporate assets, at least in those countries that have policies against inflows of packaged technology (Baranson, 1978).

Second, many more nations are now competing with U.S. multinationals in setting up foreign activities, which means that the controversy is no longer dominated by nationalistic considerations. Japanese and European firms figure prominently among the new multinationals. The number of U.S. companies among the world's top 12 multinationals declined in all of the 13 major industry groups except aerospace between 1959 and 1976, whereas continental European companies increased their representatives among the top 12 multinationals in 9 of the 13 industries, and the Japanese scored gains in 8 (Franko, 1978). The reasons for this are to be found in the decline of U.S. predominance in technology transfer; in the fact that foreign production follows exports, and exports from these countries steadily rose; in the steady growth of European and Japanese capacity to innovate; and in the greater adaptability — both politically and economically — of these companies to the needs of host countries. For example, Michelin's radial tires, Bosch's fuel injection equipment, and French, German, and Japanese

From *Finance and Development* 16 (June 1979), pp. 39–42.

locomotives, aircraft, and automobiles are more energy saving than their American counterparts.

Third, developing countries themselves are now establishing multinationals. In addition to companies from the Organization of Petroleum Exporting Countries (OPEC), and firms established in tax-haven countries, the leading countries where multinationals are being established are Argentina, Brazil, Colombia, Hong Kong, India, the Republic of Korea, Peru, the Philippines, Singapore, and Taiwan. According to . . . Wells (1977), in Indonesia "Asian LDC investors together account for more investment than either Japanese, North American, or European investors, omitting mining and petroleum." It may well be that these firms use more appropriate technology and are better adapted and more adaptable to local conditions. Wells notes that there is a strong preference in the developing countries for multinational corporations from similar countries. Korean companies put up buildings in Kuwait, pave roads in Ecuador, and have applied to Portugal for permission to set up an electronics plant; Taiwanese companies build steel mills in Nigeria; and Filipino companies restore shrines in Indonesia. Hindustan Machine Tools (India) is helping Algeria to develop a machine tool industry; Tata (India) is beating Mercedes trucks in Malaysia; and Stelux, a Hong Kong–based company with interests in manufacturing, banking and real estate, bought into the Bulova Watch Company in the United States. C. P. Wong of Stelux improved the performance of the U.S. company. There are other instances of Third World multinationals that have aimed at acquiring shares in firms in developing countries (Heenan and Keegan, 1979).

The data on the extent of developing countries' foreign investment are inadequate and the evidence is anecdotal. A partial listing of major Third World multinationals in *Fortune* (August 14, 1978) contains 33 corporations with estimated sales in 1977 ranging from $500 million to over $22,000 million, totaling $80,000 million.

If there is a challenge, it is no longer uniquely American; and if multinationals are instruments of neocolonialism, the instrument has been adopted by some ex-colonies, and at least one colony (Hong Kong), and is used against others. (Excluding mining and petroleum, Hong Kong is, for example, the second largest investor in Indonesia.) Neither developed nor developing countries are any longer predominantly recipients of multinationals from a single home country.

Fourth, not only do host countries deal with a greater variety of foreign companies, comparing their political and economic attractions, weighing them against their costs, and playing them off against one another, but also the large multinationals are being replaced by smaller and more flexible firms. And increasingly alternative organizations to the traditional form of multinational enterprise are becoming available: banks, retailers, consulting firms, and trading companies are acting as instruments of technology transfer.

Fifth, some multinationals from developed countries have accommodated themselves more to the needs of the developing countries, although IBM and Coca-Cola left India rather than permit joint ownership. Centrally planned economies increasingly welcome the multinationals, which in turn like investing there, partly because "you cannot be nationalized."

Several distinguished authors, former U.S. Under Secretary of State George Ball, Professor Raymond Vernon, and Harry Johnson among them, had predicted that sovereignty would be at bay and some of these authors even suggested that the nation state, confronted with large and ever more powerful multinationals, would wither away.

> Competition among nation-states for the economic favours of the corporation and the xenophobic character of the nation state itself will prevent the formation of a conspiracy or cartel of nation-states to exploit the economic potentialities of the international business in the service of national power. Therefore, the long-run trend will be toward the dwindling of the power of the national state relative to the corporation.

Such was Harry Johnson's (1975) vision of the future. The nation state has shown considerable resilience in the face of multinationals; its demise, as with reports of Mark Twain's death, have been somewhat exaggerated. The Colombians succeeded in extracting substantial sums from their multinationals. The Indians dealt successfully with firms that introduced inappropriate technologies and products. The Andean Group and OPEC showed that solidarity among groups of developing countries in dealing with multinationals is possible and can pay.

STILL IMPORTANT FORCE

This is not to say that multinationals are no longer an important force. It has been estimated that the foreign production of multinationals accounts for as much as 20 percent of world output, and that intrafirm trade of these companies (defined narrowly as trade between firms linked through majority ownership) constitutes 25 percent of international trade in manufacturing. There has been an increase in the proportion of U.S. technology receipts, which are intrafirm. The share of total U.S. imports accounted for by intrafirm transactions of multinationals based in the United States rose from 25 percent in 1966 to 32 percent in 1975. The share of these transactions from developing countries showed a rise from 30 percent in 1966 to 35 percent in 1975; however, this rise can be accounted for by the rise in the price of petroleum imports, which constitute the largest category of imports from developing countries. The share of U.S. intrafirm trade in manufactures from developing countries declined from 16 percent in 1966 to 10 percent in 1976. But control can take many forms other than majority ownership in subsidiaries. And multinationals are adept in assuming these other forms (UNCTAD, 1978).

An essential feature of the multinational enterprise is a special advantage over the local rival, who knows the local conditions and the local language better than the foreigner. This advantage must be sufficiently large to permit rents to be collected that exceed the extra costs of geographical and cultural distance. It may consist in a natural monopoly, in size, in risk-spreading, in good will, or in proprietary knowledge acquired through research and development expenditure. It may be bestowed upon a firm by what Veblen called "business methods," like advertising, or by "production methods," like superior knowledge or larger scale.

It was recognized quite early that it is wrong for multinationals to benefit from a natural monopoly in which know-how is widespread, such as that enjoyed by public utilities. As a result, these enterprises were nationalized early. Host countries also learned to appropriate for themselves a larger share of the monopoly rents in minerals. In manufacturing, monopoly profits for multinationals were generated partly as a result of high levels of protection, on which the companies often insisted, and excessive subsidies and tax concessions, and partly as a result of trade names, market-sharing agreements, and other monopolistic practices.

Expenditure on the creation of this advantage does not vary with the unit operating costs in a particular country, which may be quite low compared with the prices charged. The large fixed costs that arise from research and development, exploration, scale, or advertising make the allocation of these costs between operations in different countries arbitrary within wide limits. But while one school of thought has used this to justify companies charging prices substantially in excess of the incremental costs of operating in a particular country, as a way of recouping what are regarded as necessary overhead expenditures, another school has emphasized the element of monopoly profit in these pricing policies. The existence of such profits or rents (which may be concealed, for example, through transfer pricing of imported inputs, management or license fees, interest rates on intrafirm loans, and royalties) implies that the "marginal productivity of investment curve," which relates returns to amounts invested, has vertical branches, within the limits of which the division of gains between the host country and firm is a matter for bargaining. Higher shares going to host countries would not be accompanied by reduced investment or lower operating efficiency, as the conventional theory has maintained.

This theory states that any policy that raises costs to the multinational is bound to lead to reduced capital or technology inflow. Policymakers have to "trade off" their desire for raising taxes, imposing conditions about local participation or training, or limiting remittances abroad against the advantages of more foreign capital and know-how. Though their relationship to the foreign enterprise may be a love-hate relationship, at the margin they have to make up their minds whether they love or hate the investment of the foreign company.

But the correct analysis must start from the monopolistic advantage of the firm and the monopoly rent that it yields. There will, therefore, be a range between a high "rate of return" to the company that will make the operation just acceptable to the host country and a low rate that will make it just worthwhile for the company. The maximum point of this range is determined by the host country's ability to acquire the advantage in an alternative way, or to do without it; the minimum point being set by the operating costs to the company of conducting the activity in the country.

It might be objected that if governments were to beat down returns to such low levels that they barely covered their local operating costs and did not permit firms to recoup a contribution to their overhead expenditures (such as those on research and development), they would kill the goose that lays the golden eggs. Pharmaceutical companies, for example, would have to go out of business if they were allowed to charge only the direct costs of producing drugs, for the sources of their research funds would dry up.

But this is not a valid objection as far as developing countries are concerned. The argument may hold for advanced, industrial countries. In deciding upon its research expenditure, the company usually has the large markets of the advanced countries in mind. Anything it gets from the small, relatively poor markets of the developing countries over and above operating expenses is frequently a bonus. To forgo that bonus would not reduce its research expenditure. The potential bargaining strength of the developing countries (where they have the ability, solidarity, and knowledge) lies precisely in their small size: an instance of the importance of being unimportant.

TOWARD A POLICY

Any developing country has to ask itself four questions in evolving a policy toward multinationals — a positive answer to each giving rise to the next question. (1) Are foreign enterprises wanted at all? Some countries, though their number is declining, may reject outright the idea of foreigners making profits in their country. (2) Is the particular product or product range wanted? Many products of multinationals are overspecified, overprocessed, overpackaged, over-sophisticated, developed for high-income, high-saving markets, produced by capital-intensive techniques and, while catering for the masses in richer countries, can cater for only a small upper crust in poorer countries. (3) Should the product be imported or produced at home? Home production could be for the domestic market or for export. (4) Is direct foreign investment the best way to assemble the package of management, capital, and know-how? The host country has a variety of choices. It can borrow the capital, hire managers, and acquire a license; use domestic inputs for some components of the "package"; or use consultancy services, management contracts, importing houses, or banks. If it is decided that direct foreign investment in the form of a multinational subsidiary is the best way of assembling the package, the terms of the negotiation will have to be settled, so that the host country strikes the best bargain consistent with efficient operation of the multinational. This is an area in which international organizations, like the World Bank, could give technical assistance to host countries. (Bilateral technical assistance would be suspected of taking the side of the companies.)

The correct approach is therefore a combination of cost-benefit analysis and a bargaining framework. In one sense, though not a very significant one, the two approaches amount to the same thing. It is always possible, formally, to regard forgoing the second-best bargain to any given bargain as an element in the "opportunity cost" (the cost of forgoing the alternative) of the bargain in question.

If, then, all bargains are ranked in order of preference, only the best bargain will show an excess of benefit over cost. But this is a purely formal way of getting round the difficulty of distinguishing between cost-benefit and bargaining issues. It would be more illuminating to say that cost-benefit analysis is useful in ranking the bargains, so that the host country knows what it should go for and what it will sacrifice with any concession, whereas the bargaining framework is necessary to strike the best bargain within the numerous items for negotiation. Here a number of issues may arise; do elements in the bargain in one country affect bargains in other countries? Can concession on one front be traded for counterconcessions on another? Are there clear areas of common interests that can be delineated from areas of conflicting interests? More fundamentally: can the government negotiators take a truly independent position that reflects the interests of their country, or do they not represent partial group interests within their own countries, that are aligned with the interests of the foreign company?

Bergsten, Horst, and Moran in their book *American Multinationals and American Interests* distinguish between four conventional schools of thought. The imperialist and mercantilist school argues that there is a joint effort by U.S. multinationals and the U.S. government to dominate the world both politically and economically. The sovereignty-at-bay thesis (Raymond Vernon, 1971) holds that multinational firms have become dominant over all nation states, both host and home, with largely beneficial effects on all concerned. The global reach school (Barnet and Müller, 1974), while agreeing that the firms have become dominant, concludes that the effects can be detrimental for both home and host countries. There is also the view espoused by labor unions in the United States that multinationals hurt the United States and benefit foreign countries. Bergsten, Horst, and Moran find that none of these (somewhat oversimplified) models really fits and propose a policy to get the best out of these firms. They find that the main distortions to be corrected arise from competitive government policies, by both host and home governments (with respect to tax policies, for example), and from the structure and behavior of the companies. The type of rules and procedures that we have evolved in the area of trade and money need also to be negotiated in the area of foreign investment and multinational behavior.

Can multinationals make a contribution to meeting basic human needs? Since it follows from the above argument, about the special advantage, that the multinationals from the developed countries are likely to produce and market rather sophisticated products on which oligopoly rents can be earned for some time, they are not likely to make a contribution to the simple producer and consumer goods that a basic needs approach calls for. (They may, however, contribute to intermediate goods, capital goods, and exports.) Such products would be readily imitated by local competitors and the rents soon eroded. There can be a conflict between the basic goods the poor need and the advertised consumer goods of the multinationals.

The chairman of a multinational food company writes in the *Columbia Business Journal* on the subject of marketing in developing countries:

How often we see in developing countries that the poorer the economic outlook the more important the small luxury of a flavored soft drink or smoke . . . to the dismay of many would-be benefactors the poorer the malnourished are, the more likely they are to spend a disproportionate amount of whatever they have on some luxury rather than on what they need. . . . Observe, study, learn. We try to do it at [our company]. It seems to pay off for us. Perhaps it will for you too.

It is probable that the new multinationals from the developing countries will be more adapted to local needs. The costs to the host country are likely to be lower and the technology and product design more appropriate to local conditions. They often are of smaller scale, use more capital saving techniques, create more jobs, are better adapted to the supply and social conditions in the host country, are more responsive to requests for exporting, local participation, joint ventures, or local training, and design products more adapted to the consumption and production needs of the poor — hoes, simple power tillers, and bicycles, rather than air conditioners, expensive cars, and equipment for luxury apartments. Their special advantage would consist not in the monopolistic package of capital, technology, and marketing, but in special skills. Their costs of overcoming geographical and cultural distance are often less than those of multinationals from industrial countries. Their relative bargaining power is weaker. The visible hand of these multinationals is less visible than that of U.S. companies. Because of these characteristics, their ability to survive in a world in which developing countries become increasingly interdependent among themselves is increased.

References

Jack Baranson, *Technology and the Multinationals* (Lexington, Lexington Books, 1978).

R. J. Barnet and R. Müller, *Global Reach: The Power of the Multinational Corporations* (New York, Simon and Schuster, 1974).

C. Fred Bergsten, Thomas Horst, and Theodore M. Moran, *American Multinationals and American Interests* (Washington, Brookings Institution, 1978).

Lawrence G. Franko, "Multinationals: The End of U.S. Dominance," *Harvard Business Review* (Nov.–Dec. 1978).

David A. Heenan and Warren J. Keegan, "The Rise of Third World Multinationals," *Harvard Business Review* (Jan.–Feb. 1979).

Harry G. Johnson, *Technology and Economic Interdependence* (London, MacMillan Press, 1975).

UNCTAD Seminar Programme, *Intra-firm Transactions and Their Impact on Trade and Development*, May 1978. Report Series No. 2, UNCTAD/OSG/174.

Raymond Vernon, *Sovereignty at Bay: The Multinational Spread of U.S. Enterprises* (New York, Basic Books, 1971).

Louis T. Wells, Jr., "The Internationalization of Firms from Developing Countries" in *Multinationals from Small Countries,* Tamir Agmon and Charles P. Kindleberger, editors (Cambridge, MIT Press, 1977).

VII

Are Current Exchange-Rate Systems Working?

Are current exchange-rate systems working? The most general answer provided by the assessments of Goldstein, Dunn, and McCulloch is: "not as well as proponents had hoped, yet not as poorly as detractors had feared." Each goes on to illustrate surprising successes and surprising shortcomings of the "generalized floating" that Goldstein claims to cover two-thirds to four-fifths of all world trade (despite widespread exchange-rate pegging in Europe and developing countries). Dunn's assessment of floating is largely macroeconomic; McCulloch's is microeconomic; Goldstein's is both.

There are several villains behind the shortcomings of floating exchange rates. Everyone's favorite is the lack of macroeconomic policy coordination among governments. In a financially integrated world economy, this allows irresponsible policy by one nation to spill over into others through capital movements and exchange-rate effects, illustrated most persuasively by Dornbusch. Yet this villain would be powerless to do any harm if international movements of financial capital were small. Then it is well known that floating exchange rates would insulate one nation from another's irresponsibility. So the second villain in the tale, the accomplice on whom the first depends, is financial capital mobility. It is chiefly responsible for destroying the traditional confidence that policy would be more independent under floating exchange rates than under pegged.

Two features of capital mobility are especially relevant. (1) International trade in financial assets has mushroomed in the past ten to fifteen years, growing faster even than trade in goods (see Chart 1 and Table 1 in the Batten-Ott paper). (2) This in turn has made it far easier for economic agents to make forward-looking financial decisions, sometimes speculative, sometimes precautionary, but always based on expectations of future events — real, financial, and governmental. These forward-looking decisions can swamp government attempts to intervene directly in foreign exchange markets, whether sterilized or unsterilized, as Batten and Ott show. They will also influence exchange rates markedly, and in turn the *current* economic variables that depend on exchange rates. Many of the current effects of forward-looking decisions are undesired, as discussed below.

One interesting observation is that these same villains are alleged (by Goldstein, and by Cooper in Part VIII) to have destroyed the Bretton Woods system and to undermine any system of pegged rates, such as the European Monetary System (Dennis–Nellis). If these villains thus destroy *all* exchange-rate systems, then the venerable question of whether "fixed or floating is best" is really secondary to two less familiar, more fundamental questions, each corresponding to one of the villains. The first is whether it is ever in the national interest to allow another sovereign state some say in one's own economic policies. In other words, is policy independence (one of the hopes of generalized floating) necessarily good? Might not cooperative constraint be good sometimes, even on narrowly nationalistic grounds? The second question is whether it is ever in the national interest to regulate international capital movements. In so doing one would also be regulating the expectations-based transactions that integrated world capital markets facilitate.

Different nations, of course, may answer these fundamental questions in different ways at different times. Dennis and Nellis illustrate this nicely in their discussion of whether the European Monetary System (a currency area) ought optimally to include Britain in its exchange-rate-pegging arrangements. They lean toward a yes in answer. Yet they weigh the arguments carefully, giving important weight to policy constraint/independence and to expectational movements in the pound's value motivated by North Sea oil production.

Two distinctions that recur in almost all the papers are important and relatively new to discussions of floating exchange rates. One is the distinction between nominal and "real" exchange rates. The second is the distinction between tradeables prices and nontradeables prices. Old thinking about floating focused on nominal exchange rates; "real" exchange rates could be ignored. (Real exchange rates are defined as index numbers of nominal rates adjusted for intercountry differences in inflation.) They could be ignored in the old thinking because they were assumed to hover around one (or 100 in index-number terms). Another way of phrasing that assumption is that nominal exchange rates hovered around their purchasing-power-parity (PPP) norms. Experience has forced new thinking about floating exchange rates to reject this assumption. Nominal exchange rates have wandered for long periods far from any PPP norms. Pronounced and protracted real appreciation of a currency has severely pressured a country's producers of tradeable products (exportables and import substitutes); sustained real depreciation has rewarded them. Both situations are described in the new thinking as "misalignment" of exchange rates. (The old thinking, by contrast, focused only on exchange-rate "volatility" and didn't worry much about it because of opportunities for hedging against short-run exchange risk.) The potential problems with misalignment are recessionary pressure from sustained real appreciation, inflationary pressure from sustained real depreciation, and resource misallocation from either.

The potential for exchange-rate misalignment to cause resource misallocation comes from the second fundamental distinction in new thinking. Prices of tradeable products track exchange rates much more closely than prices of nontradeables. Thus exchange-rate misalignments can lead to misalignments of relative prices *within* a country. These in turn can shift resources and alter the income distribution in ways that are often not wanted and not sustained in the long run.

This discussion helps explain the attraction of a zone of exchange-rate stability, such as the European Monetary System, described in the Dennis–Nellis paper (see their Note 1 and Table 2). It also helps explain Goldstein's proposal to stabilize *real* exchange rates. Doing so might also weaken the protectionist pressures that McCulloch describes as stemming from misalignment.

What this proposal approximates in a world with mobile financial capital and with reasonably accurate forecasting of expected inflation, is eliminating any "real" interest rate differential among countries. When the nominal interest parity condition, the Fisherian interest parity condition, and mean forecast accuracy all hold, the time trend in real exchange rates is approximately equal to the international difference in real interest rates:[1]

$$\dot{e} - \dot{p}_\mathrm{d} + \dot{p}_\mathrm{f} \approx r_\mathrm{d} - r_\mathrm{f}$$

where

$\dot{e}$ represents the time rate of change of any exchange rate (domestic currency price of foreign currency);

$\dot{p}_\mathrm{d}$, $\dot{p}_\mathrm{f}$ represent average domestic and foreign inflation rates for goods;

$\dot{e} - \dot{p}_\mathrm{d} + \dot{p}_\mathrm{f} = $ a measure of the average time rate of change of real exchange rates;

r_d, r_f represent measures of domestic and foreign "real" interest rates.

To stabilize real exchange rates by setting the left-hand side equal to zero would be, therefore, tantamount to eliminating international differences in real interest rates. It is notable that from the left side of the "equation" such policy looks like trade policy, but from the right side it looks like financial policy. With mobile capital, the two are closely linked. That is an important characteristic of today's international economy, stressed especially by McCulloch.

The "equation" also reveals one critical problem with policies that would aim to stabilize real exchange rates: they might introduce their own misallocation. Real exchange rates are after all, relative prices, too. They often *ought* to change, for the same reason as other relative prices change. Policies to stabilize them could impede movements of real capital that should desirably flow toward regions where real returns (interest rates) have risen and away from regions where they have fallen. Dunn sees and discusses this problem very clearly.

Others reflect it implicitly, for example, Goldstein and Dornbusch, in their uneasiness with defining "fundamental" values for the current account, capital account, and real exchange rate.

The main purpose of all the papers in Part VII is diagnosis — description of the health of current exchange-rate arrangements. Prescription, in the sense of international monetary reform, plays an important but subsidiary role. (It has the dominant role in Part VIII.) Among prescriptive suggestions in Goldstein's and Dunn's papers are crawling pegs, "target zones," "presumptive indicators," and regulation of international capital movements. Some of these are actually used in the European Monetary System, as Dennis and Nellis describe. All except the last are proposals for rules to govern monetary, fiscal, and exchange-market intervention policies. They would presumably aim at international harmonization of policies, and at maintaining "fundamental" real exchange rates. The questions being begged in these goals, however, are revealing. How do nations establish a consensus set of policies around which to harmonize? And how does one define and measure "fundamental" (optimal) real exchange rates? In Part VIII, Cooper attempts to answer both of these questions, but only for the year 2010 (he hopes). Corden does, too — provocatively: "not to worry," he says in essence, "the current interplay of governments and markets answers both questions well enough; 'reform' is not convincingly needed."

Note

1. If i_d and i_f represent measures of domestic and foreign nominal interest rates, and if forecasts are reasonably accurate, then the nominal interest parity condition is that $\dot{e} \approx i_d - i_f$, and the Fisherian interest parity conditions are that $i_d \approx r_d + \dot{p}_d$ and $i_f = r_f + \dot{p}_f$. Substituting the last two into the first and rearranging terms yields the "equation" in the text.

19

Whither the Exchange Rate System?

Morris Goldstein

The last few years have witnessed a resurgence of calls for a reexamination, or perhaps even a reform, of the international monetary system. In this context the lessons arising from the experience with the present system of managed floating, and the likely advantages and drawbacks of some options for its evolution over the medium term, are of considerable interest. This article summarizes the findings of a recent comprehensive appraisal of the exchange rate system.

Two restrictions limit the scope of the discussion. First, it does not discuss international liquidity. However, many of the important issues in the evolution of the exchange rate system can still be profitably discussed in the context of current reserve and liquidity arrangements. Second, the emphasis is on the larger industrial countries. This reflects the facts that these countries account for a large share of total international trade and capital flows; that much of world trade is denominated in their currencies; that most developing countries and many smaller industrial countries have adopted some form of limited flexibility in their exchange arrangements; that their exchange rate options are limited by "structural" factors; and, finally, that it is the variability of the currencies of major industrial countries that has prompted calls for a reexamination of the system. More stability in the exchange rates of the major currencies would go a long way toward providing greater stability for other currencies.

THE PRESENT SYSTEM

The current exchange rate system has four prominent characteristics. First, there is a wide diversity of exchange arrangements among countries. Peggers far outnumber floaters, but most of world trade and finance is conducted among countries whose exchange rates float against each other. In mid-1983, 93 countries, almost all of them developing, were pegging their currencies; 17 countries had opted for what the Fund calls "limited flexibility vis-à-vis a single currency or cooperative arrangements," including the 8 European countries that operate within the cooperative exchange arrangements of the European Monetary System; and 35 countries had adopted "more flexible" exchange arrangements, including "independent floating" by 4 of the largest industrial countries. During the period of flexible rates since 1973, there has been a trend away from pegged exchange arrangements, and, within these, from single currency to composite pegs (with former U.S. dollar peggers accounting for the bulk of the latter shift).

From *Finance and Development* 21 (June 1984), pp. 2–6.

Despite the large number of countries that peg their currencies, in trade-weighted terms, the current system is better classified as floating because most of the largest traders maintain more flexible forms of exchange arrangements. In fact, in trade-weighted terms, about two thirds to four fifths of world trade is conducted at floating rates.

The second feature of the system is that exchange rates continue to be viewed as a matter of international concern. A stable system of exchange rates is now seen, however, as dependent more on stable macroeconomic policies at the national level than on the form of the exchange rate regime itself. Present codes recognize explicitly that a system of stable exchange rates can be jeopardized as much by insufficient as by excessive exchange rate flexibility. Also, the Fund's obligations for surveillance over countries' exchange rate policies are now much greater than before.

Exchange rate variability is the third characteristic. This has been substantial — and for both nominal and real exchange rates, bilateral and effective exchange rates, and short- and longer-term time horizons. Exchange rate variability has been significantly greater than under the adjustable par value system and greater than variability in national price levels, but less than the variability of other "asset" prices.

By almost any measure, exchange rate variability has been much greater during the floating rate period (1973–82) than during the last decade of the adjustable par value system (1963–72). Further, the floating rate period has not shown a sustained tendency for exchange rate variability to decline over time. On most measures, it peaked in 1973, was on a declining trend for the next four to five years, and then rose sharply again during the late 1970s and early 1980s. The variability of nominal exchange rates under floating has also been substantially greater than implied by intercountry inflation differentials, yielding sizable changes in real exchange rates as well. The failure of purchasing power parity to hold has been particularly marked over the short to medium term. Going in the other direction, nominal exchange rate variability under floating has been much smaller than variability of some other asset prices (e.g., stock market prices, and changes in interest rates and commodity prices), suggesting that the floating rate period has been sufficiently turbulent to make all asset prices, not just exchange rates, fluctuate substantially.

Finally, although it is difficult to measure, it is clear that official intervention in exchange markets persists and the evidence is that the demand for reserves does not appear to have been appreciably diminished under floating rates. Most countries continue to regard exchange rates, at least in part, as a policy target. Intervention has not been aimed solely at countering disorder, or even at leaning against the wind, but has also included, inter alia, resisting rate movements that bear no relation to the fundamentals and resisting depreciation out of concern for its inflationary consequences or appreciation in order to maintain competitiveness.

CRITERIA FOR EVALUATION

With these broad characteristics of the present exchange rate system in mind, four criteria seem most appropriate in evaluating that system. First, does the system help or hinder macroeconomic policy in pursuit of fundamental domestic economic objectives (price stability, sustainable growth, high employment)? Second, how effective is the system in promoting external payments adjustment? Third, how does the system affect the volume and efficiency of world trade and capital flows (and thereby resource allocation in the international economy at large)? And fourth, how robust or adaptable is the system to significant changes in the global economic environment?

The *first criterion* reflects the view that the exchange rate system is basically a facilitating mechanism for more fundamental domestic economic objectives, like price stability, high employment, and sustainable economic growth. That is why, in sharp contrast to some earlier analyses of exchange rate systems, the degree of exchange rate variability, for example, is not put forward here as a normative criterion. In other words, exchange rate variability is only important to the extent that it impinges upon, or facilitates, achievement of the ultimate targets of economic policy.

The *second criterion* introduces considerations of external balance to supplement the internal balance objectives subsumed under the first. Connoting a desirable exchange rate system as one that promotes external payments adjustment implies that the system should set in train an (internationally acceptable) adjustment mechanism, either automatic or discretionary, that eliminates balance of payments disequilibria over a reasonable time period. To make such a criterion operational, it is, of course, necessary to have some definition or concept of balance of payments equilibrium. For the purposes of this article, it is sufficient to think of it as a condition under which the current account position can be financed by normal capital flows without recourse to undue restrictions on trade, special incentives to inflows or outflows of capital, or wholesale unemployment.

The *third criterion* derives from the proposition, given explicit endorsement in the purposes of the Fund, that global welfare is generally increased by an expansion of world trade and investment. This is another area where one wants the exchange rate system to act as a facilitating mechanism for some more basic economic objective. The criterion refers to the "efficiency" of trade and investment because in the real world, where international traders sometimes react to temporary relative price signals that bear little relation to longer-term changes in comparative advantage, not all increases in the volume of trade will be beneficial.

The rationale for including the *fourth criterion* is that, as with political constitutions, there are nontrivial costs associated with changing international monetary arrangements, especially under crisis conditions. Other things being equal, it is better to have an exchange rate system that is relatively robust or adaptable to changes in the global economic environment. Such an exchange rate system, for example, may have to work well under conditions of high international mobility of capital, or rapid or abrupt changes in comparative advantage, and accommodate changes in other environmental factors ranging from the degree of real wage flexibility to the preferences for a particular reserve currency or even the assumed behavior of one particular type of economic agent (be it the reserve center country or market speculators).

LESSONS OF FLOATING

If these criteria are applied to the past decade of experience with managed floating, what is the outcome? The study finds the overall performance of the exchange rate system "remarkably good given the harsh global environment but with plenty of room left for improvement." At the risk of oversimplifying the complexity of some issues and of ignoring others, the experience with floating rates also suggests the following lessons.

First, the capacity of the exchange rate system per se to do good or harm should not be overestimated. Neither the expectations of the proponents of floating rates nor those of its critics have been confirmed by experience. Floating rates have not provided complete or even good insulation against all types of external disturbances; they have not provided rapid and automatic equilibration of external payments imbalances; they have not eliminated or even significantly reduced the demand for international reserves; and they have not encouraged enough stabilizing speculation to keep real exchange rate movements within narrow bands corresponding to permanent changes in the terms of trade. On the other hand, they have not led to a collapse in international trade and investment; they have not destroyed the discipline to fight inflation; they have not trapped high-inflation and low-inflation countries in vicious and virtuous circles for long time periods, regardless of the authorities' policy efforts; they have not reduced the size of price elasticities in international trade nor produced perverse long-term effects on current account imbalances; and they have not led to large increases in structural unemployment due to workers shifting back and forth among industries in response to very short-term currency fluctuations. The first lesson has been that the exchange rate system matters, but not as much as was previously thought.

Second, by contrast, the importance of discipline and coordinated macroeconomic policies for the successful operation of floating rates should not be underestimated. Floating rates have allowed more autonomy than fixed rates did in the use or control of policy instruments, but in a world where goods and assets are traded freely and are close substitutes across countries, this increased autonomy will not translate into more effective policies if domestic monetary and fiscal policies are unstable, unbalanced, and uncoordinated with those of other countries. Such policies will eventually destabilize the exchange rate because current rates are heavily dependent on expected exchange rates; the latter are closely tied to expected future macroeconomic policies; and these, in turn, are strongly influenced by past policy behavior. Exchange rate policy can no more be divorced from basic macroeconomic policies under floating than it could be under fixed rates.

The existence of a wide diversity of exchange arrangements does not imply a nonsystem or a lack of logical foundation — this is the third lesson. The optimal degree of exchange rate flexibility differs across countries in large part because of differences in their economic structures. Both theory and empirical evidence indicate that exchange rate changes in the smaller, more open, more highly indexed economies have a proportionally larger impact on domestic prices and give them a less lasting relative price advantage than changes in the larger, less open, and less indexed economies. It is therefore not surprising that the former seek to avoid frequent or substantial movements in exchange rates, while the latter favor increased exchange rate flexibility. As a result, uniform judgments about whether exchange rates fluctuated too much over the past decade are not likely to be valid across countries, and for reasons that go beyond intercountry differences in philosophy about the efficiency of markets. Going one step further, these same cross-country viewpoints about optimal exchange rate flexibility strengthen the case for better coordination of policies. For in the absence of such consultation and coordination, it is unlikely that "common" views about the proper distribution of the adjustment burden between exchange rates and other policy instruments will emerge on their own.

Fourth, in appraising the present exchange rate system, it is crucial to distinguish the effects of floating rates from other developments occurring during the period of floating. Floating rates do not seem to have been responsible for high inflation and high unemployment rates nor for the slow growth in productivity experienced by industrial countries over the past ten years. Nor do they seem to have been the key factor behind the slowdown in the growth of world trade. No exchange rate regime would have emerged unscathed from the combination of shocks, portfolio shifts, and structural and institutional changes of the past ten years. For the same reasons, even if major changes in the exchange rate system could be brought about, such changes would not, by themselves, be likely to reduce unemployment significantly, eliminate pressures for protection, lead to a resurgence in investment or productivity, or make economies immune from future disturbances. The exchange rate system is an important facilitating mechanism for economic interdependence, but it is not a panacea for the world's current economic troubles.

Fifth, the present system has demonstrated some considerable strengths. Foremost is that exchange rate changes have made a positive contribution to securing effective external payments adjustment over the medium to long run. For example, despite some powerful external disturbances, the average size of payments imbalances of the larger industrial countries has been smaller and their duration shorter during the last decade than they were over the final ten years of the adjustable peg system. Asymmetries in adjustment between surplus and deficit countries, and between the most important reserve center and nonreserve currency countries, have been reduced. Similarly, given slowly adjusting national price levels, nominal exchange rate changes have made it possible for real rates to adjust to, inter alia, permanent changes in the terms of trade, significant natural resource discoveries, and continuing differences in trend rates of growth of labor productivity. Finally, although effective policy coordination among the major industrial countries has been the exception rather than the rule, and there have been serious lapses of discipline in national policymaking, the present system has at least maintained in the foreign exchange market a mechanism of conflict resolution that has involved neither suspension of currency convertibility nor large-scale restrictions on trade and capital flows.

Sixth, a good average performance in the harsh operating environment of the past decade does not mean that the present system has not had serious problems. The most critical one has been that real exchange rate movements (i.e., nominal exchange rate changes adjusted for inflation differences across countries) have sometimes gone far beyond those suggested by best estimates of "fundamentals" and have sometimes stayed out of line for periods of up to two to three years. Such maladjustments have created problems in two major areas.

First, they have handicapped efficient resource allocation. Large real exchange rate changes (for example, of 30 percent or more) over the medium term affect patterns of production, employment, investment, and consumption both within and across countries. Further, when these unsustainable exchange rate and payments positions do unwind, as they eventually must, there are likely to be adjustment costs because resources (especially labor) released from the over-expanded sectors do not quickly find employment elsewhere, particularly in the context of sluggish overall economic activity. Thus, even though such resource misallocation and adjustment costs were probably not the primary determinant of the recent inflation, growth, and unemployment performance, they made a difficult situation even more troublesome.

The second major difficulty has been in the policy reaction to disequilibrium exchange rates. Although the foreign exchange market does provide a decentralized solution to policy inconsistencies across countries, it has become increasingly evident that countries may resort to other more socially destructive administrative mechanisms to adjust to what they regard as a persistently "inequitable" rate. These mechanisms — most of which involve subsidies (overt or hidden), taxes, or quantitative restrictions on exports or imports — not only erode the gains from trade but also make cooperation more difficult in other areas of mutual concern. Again, even though exchange rate distortions have probably not been the prime cause of such restrictive measures, they have certainly not helped. This difficulty also highlights why it is so essential to take sufficient preventive measures in the future to keep an adjustment mechanism as imprecise as the exchange rate from having to shoulder too much of the adjustment burden.

OPTIONS FOR THE FUTURE

The discussion of the options for change assumes that the rest of the 1980s may be somewhat more hospitable than the 1973–82 period. That is, the exchange rate system will probably still have to contend with, among other things, real and monetary disturbances, high international mobility of capital, and so on, but the average rate of inflation, as well as its dispersion across countries, could well be lower, and there may continue to be a reservoir of goodwill that can be tapped for efforts aimed at greater coordination of policies.

A reasonable intermediate objective of any changes to the present exchange rate system would be to maintain enough flexibility in real exchange rates to aid external adjustment but at the same time create conditions under which they do not stray so far, so often, and for so long as they have from levels consistent with fundamentals. (As long as exchange rate behavior is specified in terms of real exchange rates, this objective can, in principle, be satisfied by fixed rates, flexible rates, or any combination in between.) The first part of this objective might be considered as the present system's principal strength and the latter, its principal weakness.

The first option is to return to *par values*. In this context, is it reasonable to envisage the return of conditions under which fixed exchange rates among the major currencies could be restored?

A negative answer rests on the following grounds: (1) the major countries would be unwilling to completely subordinate monetary policy to the dictates of a fixed exchange rate; (2) structural differences among countries are large enough to preclude the emergence of a common rate of inflation; (3) real exchange rate adjustments would be needed to reflect changes in comparative advantage; (4) prices and wages are too inflexible (particularly downward) to obtain the requisite real exchange rate movements without changes in nominal exchange rates; and (5) the absence of a willing or readily acceptable candidate for the central currency in the system.

The case for a positive answer is essentially that: (1) there is already in prospect a significant convergence of inflation rates for the four largest countries in 1984–85; (2) the discipline necessary to coordinate policies among the others will be given much impetus by the establishment of fixed rates; (3) the policy autonomy under alternative systems is largely illusory anyway; and (4) even a partial success (infrequently adjustable rates) would have a strong positive effect on domestic stability and the resumption of world trade growth.

Exchange rate formulas constitute a second option. If nominal exchange rates need to be adjusted to reflect fundamental changes, is there any rule or formula that could help determine the right structure of rates? How useful are "presumptive indicators" for signaling the need for adjustment?

The principal argument against the use of formulas or rules for determining appropriate changes in nominal exchange rates is that the factors that call for changes or that are symptoms of a maladjustment are too varied, too unpredictable, and too unstable over time to be captured *ex ante* in any formula or rule. While such a formula approach may have represented a reasonable second-best solution to the nominal exchange rigidities of the Bretton Woods era, it is not so in today's world, where exchange rates are, if anything, too flexible. The main counterargument is that exchange rate formulas represent a reasonable middle ground between the excessive rigidity of rates that are administratively set and those that are market-determined.

Presumptive or "objective" indicators for adjustment are, of course, in principle less restrictive because they usually do not specify which combination of adjustment measures the country should adopt. In brief, the case for them is that the regular examination of a set of multiple indicators could help to detect problems at an early stage and induce a more timely and more symmetrical pattern of adjustment than would occur in their absence (or at least trigger discussions of policy among countries that make coordinated surveillance workable). As with exchange rate rules, opposition to them is often based on the arguments that there is no simple indicator that will consistently transmit reliable adjustment signals and that even if there were one, practical problems over its precise definition, measurement, and monitoring would severely limit its applicability. (The only exchange rate arrangement that has actually implemented a presumptive indicator is the European Monetary System. In that system, once a country's actual exchange rate crosses a "threshold of divergence" from the ECU central rate, there is a presumption that the authorities will undertake corrective measures.)

A third option is *adjustable par values* with narrow margins. But would these be viable for the major currencies given the current high capital mobility?

Although this issue is similar in many respects to the first (on the restoration of fixed exchange rates), it is dealt with separately because capital mobility is widely cited as the key contributory factor to the breakdown of the Bretton Woods system. Indeed, the case against a return to adjustable par values with narrow margins is that none of the factors that made the Bretton Woods system so vulnerable to "hot money" flows would be less problematic today or tomorrow. Large and suddenly changing interest rate differentials would still arise because of the failure to harmonize monetary and fiscal policies across countries, there would be rumors of imminent parity changes due to a whole host of circumstances, and the resources of central banks would be insufficient to cope with the larger resources of private speculators. Some would say par values would be even more vulnerable today because liberalization measures and technological advances have combined to render capital much more mobile than during the 1950s and 1960s. Hence, if such an adjustable peg scheme could work at all, it would need both wider margins and some mechanism to ensure prompt adjustment of par values.

The opposing view is not so much that these problems are less serious today but that their intractability is exaggerated. Specifically, such a system can function even with relatively narrow margins if there are sufficient political commitment, generous support for riding out balance of payments difficulties, active exchange market intervention, a presumptive indicator for adjustment, and the acceptance of the need for occasional, and sometimes large, realignments of central rates.

A fourth option is to reduce excessive exchange rate variability by new taxes or *restrictions of international capital flows.*

This familiar issue has gained new support through the debate on how to cope with overshooting (or excessive fluctuation) of floating rates. The case against restricting the international capital market includes the following arguments: (1) there is no strong presumption that the costs in terms of resource misallocation from impeding the international flows of capital would be less serious than those arising from restricting the flow of goods; (2) there is no reliable method of separating in advance productive from nonproductive capital flows; (3) any tax on capital flows would make it more difficult for a country to finance a current account imbalance because it would have to raise interest rates enough not only to create a favorable interest rate differential but also to offset the cost of the tax; (4) even aggressive control programs, such as those of the early 1970s, often failed to stem private capital flows, and the subsequent development of offshore banking markets makes their efficacy today less likely; and (5) unless uniform restrictions or taxes could be negotiated and accepted by all parties, there would be a constant danger of escalation and retaliation, with damaging spillovers for other international transactions. The case for such impediments to capital flows does not ignore these costs; instead, it brings out the point that they will be smaller than the macroeconomic costs associated with larger exchange rate fluctuations under free mobility of capital.

Greater stability of floating exchange rates should be sought primarily in more *stable domestic macroeconomic policies* and in better coordination of these and of other policies across countries.

As emphasized earlier, it is now widely accepted that floating exchange rates would be less volatile if medium- and long-term private sector expectations about exchange rates were firmer. The case for stressing the implementation of stable, credible, and balanced policies is simply that, quite apart from their favorable impact on domestic economic objectives, these policies are the single most important ingredient in stabilizing exchange rate expectations. For if market participants cannot gauge the medium-term course of basic policies, and if they cannot be confident that the basic economic objectives can be reconciled across countries without either dramatic shifts in policy mixes and/or in exchange rates, they will have little basis from which to form a view about future exchange rates. In such circumstances, speculative "bubbles" and "bandwagon" effects become more prevalent because there are no natural bounds for the expectations of speculators.

Conversely, where countries have a history of stable policy behavior and where, therefore, forecasts of policy intentions have credibility, neither minor shocks nor short-term deviations of policies from targets are likely to be translated into large exchange rate movements because longer-term expectations about rates will not be much affected. (The relative stability of the floating Canadian dollar over 1950–61 is often cited as an example of such a stabilizing anchor at work.) Because better conduct is widely recognized as improving the functioning of any exchange rate regime, there is, of course, no case against better macroeconomic policies. But there are doubts and questions about if and how such improved policy conduct can be brought about within the present system.

A final major option is to establish *official "forecasts"* or "target zones" for exchange rates, to help both to reduce their variability and to increase the incentives for external adjustment.

The case for official forecasts or target zones rests on two arguments. First, in their absence, it is too difficult for market participants to form a view about future exchange rates. Even where policies are relatively stable, there are just too many factors that affect an exchange rate to make a firm judgment about its value six or eighteen months ahead. Second, because the authorities would be under some pressure either to keep actual rates within the target or forecast zone, or to explain departures from it, it is claimed that the speed of external adjustment would be increased. It is argued that without such official forecasts, authorities have insufficient incentives for adjustment, since they can always equate the "right" rate with the market rate.

The case against official forecasts of exchange rates is: (1) that given stable underlying macroeconomic policies, there is no need for an additional anchor for exchange rate expectations; (2) that negotiation of forecast rates or zones, and changes in them, would be subject to all the centralized management delays of the Bretton Woods era, thereby robbing the scheme of its flexibility; (3) that the best guide for domestic monetary policy is still that of achieving price stability; in contrast, the exchange rate can often give false signals; and (4) that forecast rates or zones would only have credibility if they were backed by broad coordination of macroeconomic policies — and if such coordination could be achieved, no change in the present system would be necessary.

20

The Many Disappointments of Flexible Exchange Rates

Robert M. Dunn, Jr.

The experience of the last ten years has made most academic supporters of flexible exchange rates sadder but wiser. During the early 1970s, the prevailing academic view was that flexible exchange rates would solve the increasingly obvious problems of the Bretton Woods system and thereby create a far less difficult

From R. M. Dunn, Jr., *The Many Disappointments of Flexible Exchange Rates*, Essay No. 154, December 1983. Copyright © 1983. Reprinted by permission of the International Finance Section of Princeton University. Some text and references omitted or altered.

environment for the management of domestic monetary and fiscal policies. A broadly accepted body of theory had been developed during the 1950s and 1960s that drew clear and strong contrasts between the workings of fixed- and flexible-exchange-rate regimes and produced a widespread preference among academic economists for the flexible-rate alternative.

When floating exchange rates were adopted by the major industrial countries in 1973, many academic economists expected that international finance was about to become a much less active area. Since the problems and conflicts of the fixed-exchange-rate regime were to be solved and since balance-of-payments problems were no longer possible, macroeconomic policy could return to a purely domestic focus. A few colleagues even suggested that those of us who worked in the area of international finance might find it advisable to develop new specialties in which to teach and do research.

Flexible exchange rates have not performed as expected. Nobody has been banished to labor economics, and international finance is at least as active as it was in the last days of Bretton Woods. Abundant theoretical and policy problems create continuing opportunities for teaching, research, and other remunerative activities. It is occasionally said that doctors bury their mistakes; economists often seem to prosper from theirs.

The current system of flexible exchange rates has not functioned in a manner that even approximates the predictions of previously accepted theory, and large and frequent exchange-rate changes have produced a range of unforeseen and generally disruptive side effects throughout the economies of the industrialized countries. The purpose of this essay is to review this disappointing experience. After a brief return to the body of theory that existed in the early 1970s to see what was expected of a system of flexible exchange rates and to note some of the assumptions behind those expectations, the predictions are compared with the events of the 1973–82 period. Recent theoretical and empirical work is then reviewed that suggests why the actual experience contrasts so strikingly with earlier expectations. The final issue is whether there are more attractive alternatives to the current international monetary system.

THE EARLIER PROMISES OF FLEXIBLE EXCHANGE RATES

Proponents of flexible exchange rates have almost always assumed that long-run trends in exchange markets would be dominated by relative rates of inflation, that is, that exchange rates would follow purchasing power parity. Friedman's (1968, pp. 419–420) classic defense of floating rates made this argument strongly, suggesting that it was far easier to allow exchange rates to adjust to differing rates of inflation than to compel price levels to adjust to a fixed parity. Other monetarists provided later support for this argument by suggesting that relative rates of growth of national money supplies would determine both relative rates of inflation and the exchange rate. Temporary factors such as shifting interest rates might cause temporary deviations from purchasing power parity, but both monetarists and other supporters of flexible rates expected constant real exchange rates beyond the short run. Friedman . . . argued that short-term factors should not significantly disturb exchange markets, because speculators would force the market toward its long-run equilibrium, thereby reducing deviations from purchasing power parity.

Supporters of flexible exchange rates like Friedman . . . argued that such a system would isolate the domestic economy from foreign business cycles. The well-known foreign-trade multiplier linkage through which such cycles are transmitted from one economy to another assumes a fixed exchange rate, and it was argued that a flexible rate would absorb the effects of sudden changes in foreign demand for exports in a way that would leave domestic aggregate demand largely unaffected. Under fixed rates, for example, a U.S. recession would cause a reduction in the demand for Canadian exports and a recession in Canada, but if the Canadian dollar were floating, it would have quite different impacts. With the exchange rate adjusting to maintain balance-of-payments equilibrium, a recession-induced decline in the U.S. demand for Canadian goods would produce a depreciation of the Canadian dollar sufficient to fully adjust the balance of payments, and most of the adjustment would occur in the trade account. The Canadian balance of payments would be totally unaffected by a U.S. recession, and the Canadian trade account would be affected only slightly.[1] The Canadian economy would become independent of the United States and would consequently be protected from the effects of misguided U.S. macroeconomic politics and the business cycles they cause.

Independence from the Keynesian process of business-cycle transmission was extended to independence in determining monetary policy. . . . [Many] argued that fixed exchange rates meant that national monetary policy could not be significantly different from policies prevailing abroad and that attempts to maintain an independent monetary position would be frustrated by the effects of the balance of payments on the domestic money supply. A fixed parity between U.S. and Canadian dollars made Canada the Thirteenth Federal Reserve District, an unkind but accurate phrase that was occasionally heard during the 1962–70 period when Canada had such a fixed rate. Flexible exchange rates, however, promised to emancipate central banks. A totally independent monetary policy could be maintained without undesirable impacts of balance-of-payments shifts on the domestic money supply. The exchange-rate changes caused by shifts in domestic monetary policy would actually augment the desired impacts of the policy on aggregate demand. An expansionary monetary policy in Canada, for example, would cause an outflow of capital, a depreciation of the Canadian dollar, and a resulting improvement in the Canadian trade account that would expand domestic aggregate demand. There would be a parallel decline in aggregate demand in Canada's trading partners such as the United States, but this was typically seen as a minor problem. Skeptics . . . suggested that flexible exchange rates would produce considerably less than complete macroeconomic independence, but supporters of floating exchange rates convinced most students of economics that the abandonment of fixed parities really would mean that central banks could pursue whatever domestically targeted policies they desired.

It is hardly surprising that young economists working for central banks tended to support floating exchange rates. What could be more enjoyable than working for an organization whose policies had suddenly become far freer and almost awesomely powerful in their effects on the economy? No longer would central banks have to tie their policies to those being determined abroad, only to see any attempts at independence washed out by the effects of the balance of payments on the domestic money supply. From being subservient to foreign monetary policy and the balance of payments, central bankers would become both free and powerful. It was occasionally noted by doubters that this wonderful prospect assumed that a central bank or government was prepared to accept whatever exchange-rate changes resulted from domestic or foreign shifts in monetary policy. Defenders of a floating-rate regime replied that the exchange rate was just another price; if it rose or fell occasionally, that would be no worse than similar changes in the price of copper or wheat. After all, how could an economist object to price flexibility, and why should the price of foreign exchange be different from any other price?

With the apparent elimination of the Keynesian business-cycle linkage and the increased independence and power of domestic monetary policy, flexible exchange rates promised a world of macroeconomic autarky. Inflate or deflate, manage your economy wisely or foolishly, the exchange rate would adjust to protect and even strengthen your policies. After decades of economic interdependence, in which economies were constantly affected or even dominated by foreign developments and were strictly limited in their policy options by balance-of-payments considerations, the prospect of national freedom for macroeconomic policy was inviting to those inclined toward a nationalistic view of economic policy.

In addition to gains for macroeconomic policy, flexible exchange rates also promised to eliminate mercantilism as an argument for tariffs and other protectionist devices, thus producing an era of free or at least more liberal trade. . . . [Many commentators] noted that a tariff merely causes an appreciation of the local currency that taxes export and unprotected import-competing industries without improving the trade account or increasing aggregate demand. The expectation that protectionism will improve the balance of payments and generate an increase in aggregate demand obviously makes no sense if the exchange rate adjusts to maintain payments equilibrium and most of the payments adjustment to the exchange rate occurs in the current account. . . . A tariff cannot be expected to generate an improvement in the balance of payments or in the level of aggregate demand. . . . It will instead impose a tax on unprotected traded-goods industries in a world of floating exchange rates. It was widely expected, or at least hoped, that the elimination of this ancient argument for tariffs would lead to a far more liberal trading environment.

SOME ASSUMPTIONS BEHIND THE EARLIER PROMISES

It is worth noting briefly the underlying assumptions behind the predicted macroeconomic effects of floating exchange rates.

Purchasing Power Parity

As was suggested earlier, Friedman and other supporters of flexible rates expected exchange rates to follow purchasing power parity. Yet, the circumstances under which real exchange rates can be expected to remain constant are decidedly unlikely. Purchasing power parity would prevail, for example, if the only source of significant shocks to the balance of payments were differing rates of inflation, or if the elasticities of demand for exports and imports were so high that shocks from other sources could be adjusted through very small exchange-rate changes.

The first possibility can be seen through a simple example. In a trade-only world with flexible wages and prices that starts from balance-of-payments and exchange-rate equilibrium, a 10 percent inflation in one small country will be just offset by a 10 percent depreciation in that country's currency. The new exchange rate will return all relative prices to their previous pattern and restore the earlier equilibrium. If the only source of shocks to the exchange rate is an event such as a 10 percent increase in prices caused by a 10 percent increase in the nominal money supply, a flexible exchange rate can be expected to follow purchasing power parity. But if the balance of payments and the exchange rate are affected by factors other than changes in relative price levels, another unlikely circumstance is necessary to produce a constant real exchange rate.

This second possibility is that short-term elasticities of demand for traded goods are so high that very small changes in the exchange rate would be sufficient to adjust to payments shocks from a variety of sources and no significant change in real exchange rates would occur. A large shift in the capital account, for example, would be absorbed or adjusted with only a slight change in the exchange rate, leaving the pre-existing purchasing-power-parity situation largely undisturbed. In the far more likely event that the relevant elasticities are lower, the same shift in capital flow would require a sizable exchange-rate change and purchasing power parity could not be expected to hold during the adjustment process.

Purchasing power parity might be saved in the case of low short-run and high long-run demand elasticities if Friedman's rational speculators always conclude that the long-run exchange-rate path will follow relative price levels and that recent rates of inflation are a good predictor of the future. . . . If these speculators move large sums of money on the basis of this expectation, relatively constant real exchange rates might be expected despite low short-run demand elasticities and a variety of shocks to the exchange market. The obvious problem is the requirement that speculators conclude that recent rates of inflation are a sound basis on which to predict future price changes and therefore the likely future exchange rates. This would be an extremely naive way to form expectations. Modern portfolio models of exchange-rate determination . . . sometimes produce sharp movements away from purchasing power parity despite the presence of speculators with rational expectations.

Finally, complete flexibility of domestic wages and prices would maintain purchasing power parity, because any shock to the exchange rate would first produce a change in the price of tradables and then rapid and parallel changes in wages and all other prices in the economy. A 10 percent depreciation from whatever source will raise the price of tradables by 10 percent, which will put upward pressure on wages and then on all other prices until the general price level has risen by 10 percent, thereby maintaining the real exchange rate. This scenario assumes that the central bank is willing to support such a result with an appropriate increase in the nominal money supply. Otherwise, tighter monetary conditions resulting from a decline in the real money supply will move the exchange rate and prices back toward their original level. Complete wage and price flexibility should mean, however, that purchasing power parity holds throughout the process.

Complete flexibility of wages and the prices of nontradables does not seem to be characteristic of the economies of the United States and other industrialized countries, however, particularly when the pressure on wages and prices is downward. Explanations are numerous, including the traditional kinked oligopoly demand curve, purported customer preferences for stable prices, and the direct costs of making and publicizing frequent price changes. Wage rigidity can result from union contracts that have less than full indexing. Downward rigidity in wages may also occur in nonunion sectors of the economy, because employers fear that wage cuts will both encourage the best workers (who may have options) to leave, and sharply reduce morale among remaining workers in the firm. Each of these two effects could reduce labor productivity to such an extent that lower wages would not produce lower unit labor costs.

Wage indexing is far more common in Europe than in the United States and is often designed to offset price-level changes completely. On this side of the Atlantic, fewer contracts are indexed and they typically provide for wage increases that do not fully cover price-level increases. . . . As a result, wages and perhaps nontradables prices are likely to be somewhat more rigid here than in Europe.

In all these situations, the law of one price is implicitly assumed for tradable goods. In particular, it is always assumed to hold for a single traded good where product differentiation does not exist. In general, however, broad price indices for tradables need not follow purchasing power parity even if the law of one price is valid. Product differentiation may make similar products in different countries less than perfect substitutes (e.g., prices of Volkswagens in Germany and Fiats in Italy may not follow purchasing power parity), or the same products may carry different weights in the price indices for two countries. The law of one price can be expected to operate only for single homogeneous traded goods, and even then it requires that markets be sufficiently competitive to produce prompt and effective arbitrage whenever the exchange rate moves.

If markets for homogeneous tradables are not sufficiently competitive to bring about such prompt adjustment of relative prices after an exchange-rate movement, the payments-adjustment process becomes far more complicated. The assumption that the law of one price obtains for single homogeneous tradables is crucial for any expectation that a flexible exchange rate will closely follow purchasing power parity for more broadly defined price levels. The law of one price for tradables is far from sufficient for the continuous maintenance of purchasing power parity, but it would appear to be necessary.

Adjustment of Current and Capital Accounts

Some large and simplifying assumptions also lie behind the suggestion that flexible exchange rates will greatly weaken the mechanism through which business cycles are transmitted between countries, strengthen an independent national monetary policy, and generally produce a world in which macroeconomic policies can be managed solely on the basis of domestic economic priorities.

In much of the work by proponents of flexible exchange rates, the current account was viewed as a simple function of relative price levels and of domestic and foreign levels of national income. The possibility was usually not considered that the current account and hence the exchange rate might be significantly affected by events such as OPEC pricing decisions or instabilities in other individual commodity markets. If such events were dealt with, it was assumed that they were inherently temporary and that rational speculators would keep the exchange rate at or close to its long-run equilibrium.

The view of capital flows implicit in [this early] work . . . on macroeconomic independence and monetary policy under floating exchange rates was based on a flow-adjustment model. Capital was assumed to flow continuously in response to a constant interest-rate differential. This assumption made it possible to conclude that a tight monetary policy would attract continuing capital inflows that would maintain an appreciated currency and a weaker trade account as long as a high interest rate remained in effect. It was widely recognized that a stock-adjustment model was a far more realistic approach to the capital account, but this approach was very difficult to incorporate in the policy-assignment models that were popular in the late 1960s and late 1970s. If domestic aggregate demand is a function of the interest-rate level and the capital account is a function of the change in interest rates, it is hard to reach firm conclusions on the use of monetary policy to deal with domestic business cycles through its effects on the capital account and the exchange rate. . . .

The early 1970s view of the capital account also said little about changing inflation and interest-rate expectations or about their potential impact on a floating exchange rate. Expectations were typically ignored or assumed to be neutral. It was not widely forseen that large changes in inflationary expectations, some of which were later reversed, could have disruptive impacts on exchange markets and rates.

From the perspective of 1983, it is clear that the preceding pages represent an excessively optimistic view of the prospects for a flexible-exchange-rate regime. Nevertheless, this discussion does approximate the conventional academic view of the late 1960s and early 1970s. At least, it roughly describes what my students were taught twelve years ago. What follows might be viewed as an attempt to atone for past sins.

EXPECTATIONS *vs.* EVENTS: 1973–82

Constant Real Exchange Rates

Purchasing power parity was a short-lived hope. Movements in real exchange rates have been large and have often been quickly reversed. The trade-weighted U.S. dollar depreciated in real terms by about 10 percent in 1976–78 and then appreciated by over 20 percent in 1981–82. Sterling depreciated in real terms by about 15 percent in 1975–76 before appreciating by over 60 percent in 1977–80. The Swiss franc rose in real terms by over 30 percent in 1977–78 and then fell by about 25 percent in the next two years. The yen followed a similar pattern, rising in real terms by over 30 percent in 1975–78 before falling by about 25 percent in 1978–79. . . . Since real exchange rates are measured after allowance for domestic and foreign rates of inflation, none of them would have changed significantly if purchasing power parity had held.

Data developed by Korteweg (1980, p. 18) indicate that the average change in the real exchange rate for sixteen industrialized countries between March 1973 and the end of 1979 was 6.8 percent. Sterling and the Swiss franc appreciated in real terms by 18.7 percent and 16.2 percent, respectively, over that period, while the Canadian dollar experienced a real depreciation of 7.2 percent. Expectations that exchange rates would follow relative price levels, thereby keeping real exchange rates largely unchanged, have certainly not been supported by the 1973–82 experience. . . .

If these real-exchange-rate changes were a long-run or permanent response to changing patterns of technological competitiveness or other factors that required fundamental payments adjustment, they might reasonably be viewed as necessary or even desirable. This has often not been the case, however; large changes in real exchange rates have often been a response to temporary factors and have often been reversed subsequently. For example, sterling appreciated sharply in 1979–80 when the arrival of a new Conservative administration led many market participants to expect a prompt deceleration of U.K. inflation. Since nominal interest rates remained very high, expected real yields increased sharply, making British assets very attractive. Increasing North Sea oil production, combined with increases in oil prices, added to the upward pressure on sterling. When inflation failed to decline promptly and oil prices stopped rising, sterling depreciated sharply. The dollar declined sharply in 1977–78 because of a weaker current account and widespread doubts about the macroeconomic policies of the incoming administration. It then appreciated sharply in 1981–82, when extraordinarily high nominal yields combined with an expectation of decelerating inflation to create very high expected real yields on dollar assets. These and other changes in real exchange rates have not been based on a need for adjustment to permanent shifts in payments patterns but have instead resulted from temporary factors, some of which were partially speculative.

Gains and Losses from Changing Real Exchange Rates

Large changes in real exchange rates have produced a range of disruptive and undesirable side effects within the economies of countries maintaining flexible exchange rates. One such effect was that sizable capital gains and losses were incurred on long-term debt that would not have been incurred if real exchange rates had been stable. If, for example, a Canadian firm or hydroelectric authority borrows U.S. dollars to finance a domestic investment, a constant real exchange rate means that any losses from exchange-rate changes are approximately offset by capital gains on real assets. A rise in Canadian prices of 10 percent relative to U.S. prices should be reflected in a 10 percent depreciation of the Canadian dollar and a 10 percent increase in the domestic-currency value of the real assets owned by the borrower, assuming that the price of these particular assets follows the general price level. If this assumption holds, the additional Canadian dollar cost of paying off the loan is covered by the capital gain on real assets. Fairly constant real exchange rates make long-term foreign borrowing relatively safe, despite the lack of forward markets with relevant maturities, because capital gains on domestic real assets should roughly offset losses on the exchange rate. If interest rates are 2 percentage points lower in New York than in Toronto, inflation is probably expected to average 2 points less in the United States than in Canada, and the Canadian dollar is expected to depreciate by 2 percent per year. As long as the real exchange rate is roughly constant, Canadian borrowers can compare implicit real costs of borrowing in the two countries with some confidence that they are facing correct relative prices.

When real exchange rates change sharply, however, this apparently safe system collapses and foreign borrowers can face huge losses. The Canadian dollar depreciated by about 15 percent between 1976 and 1979, despite the fact that Canadian prices rose by only one percent relative to U.S. prices over the period. This 14 percent real depreciation of the Canadian dollar imposed massive capital losses on Canadian firms and government agencies that had borrowed long-term funds in the United States. A few, such as Quebec Hydro, had partial hedges in the form of long-term contracts to sell electricity in the United States at fixed U.S. dollar rates. Most borrowers, however, lacked such hedges and have absorbed heavy losses.

Large changes in real exchange rates were often very expensive also for those who made forward price commitments on the assumption that real exchange rates would be relatively stable. Rolls Royce, for example, apparently expected high rates of inflation in the United Kingdom to be offset by a depreciation of sterling. It concluded that contracts to sell jet engines in the United States at fixed dollar prices need not be hedged, because it would be protected from prospective British inflation by dollar contracts to sell engines in the future. This conclusion was wrong, and a real appreciation of sterling produced losses that reportedly almost closed the firm.

A more long-lived side effect of changes in real exchange rates can occur in the form of shifts in the distribution of income within a country. If the Canadian dollar depreciates in real terms, prices of tradables rise in Canada relative to prices of nontradables. Firms producing tradables become more profitable than firms producing nontradables. To the extent that the tradables sector is regionally concentrated, localized booms or recessions can result. If, for reasons discussed earlier, wage rates are relatively fixed in the short run or if wages tend to follow the prices of nontradables, a real depreciation reduces real wage rates and shifts income from labor in general to capital invested in the tradables sector. But if exchange rates follow relative price levels, so that real exchange rates are roughly constant, none of these distributional effects will occur. That has obviously not been the case during the last few years.

The experience since 1973 has made it clear that a flexible exchange rate can be a source of constantly shifting implicit taxes and subsidies. A real depreciation subsidizes producers of tradables by taxing consumers of tradables who produce nontradables. If wages are sticky, such a depreciation also taxes labor. A real appreciation, such as that experienced in the United Kingdom in 1979–80, produces the opposite results. The real exchange rate is probably the most important price in an open economy, and any arrangement that allows frequent and large changes in that price will be disruptive. These disruptions may be seen as an unreasonable burden.

Monetary-Policy Independence and Changing Real Exchange Rates

The widespread recognition that large changes in real exchange rates have some decidedly undesirable side effects has meant that monetary policy has become far less independent of international considerations than had been expected. The earlier belief that flexible exchange rates would free monetary policy from international constraints assumed that central banks and governments were prepared to accept whatever exchange rates resulted from domestic or foreign monetary-policy shifts. That assumption no longer holds. Domestic monetary policy again faces an international-payments constraint: it must approximate the monetary policy being pursued abroad in order to avoid large exchange-rate movements.

This problem can be seen in the dilemma faced by many European central banks during 1981 and 1982. The Europeans made it clear that they did not believe their economies required the degree of monetary tightness maintained in the United States. Yet they felt compelled by their exchange-rate goals to maintain interest-rate yields approaching those in New York. If the European central banks had instead pursued a monetary policy based purely on domestic considerations, the resulting interest-rate differentials would have produced large capital outflows and sharp depreciations of the European currencies. Considerable downward movement of these currencies did occur in 1981–82, and undesirably high interest rates were necessary in Europe to avoid further depreciations, with all the disruptive effects described earlier. European governments and central banks were reduced to asking the United States to ease its monetary policy so that they could ease theirs. Canada found itself in a similar situation during this period as it maintained undesirably high interest rates to forestall an unacceptable depreciation of the Canadian dollar.

So much for the theory that flexible exchange rates make monetary policy independent and allow it to be targeted solely at desired levels of domestic aggregate demand. In the years of fixed exchange rates, the Europeans and Canadians had to follow U.S. monetary policy to avoid excessive swings in their payments balances; under flexible exchange rates, they have had to follow U.S. monetary policy to avoid excessive swings in their real exchange rates. There is not a great difference in the independence of national monetary policy under the two regimes.

The unwillingness of governments and central banks to allow excessive exchange-rate changes has also meant that the international transmission of business cycles remains in effect. When the United States entered a serious recession in 1981, Canada could have protected itself by allowing the decline in the U.S. demand for Canadian goods and for Canadian dollars to pay for those goods to produce a depreciation sufficient to maintain the Canadian current account. Relatively low short-run demand elasticities meant, however, that the depreciation required would have been large and disruptive. As a result, monetary policy was used to avoid such a sharp depreciation, and Canada appears to have imported the U.S. recession through a deterioration of its current account, almost as though the country were on a fixed exchange rate.

The macroeconomic independence that seemed to be promised by floating exchange rates has not amounted to much. Monetary policies are still determined in part by international payments considerations, and business cycles are still transmitted from large countries to smaller ones through the trade balance. Macroeconomic interdependence has survived and even prospered under floating exchange rates.

Another hoped-for result of flexible exchange rates, the end of mercantilism and a resulting movement toward free trade, has also failed to materialize. Despite a flexible-exchange-rate system that eliminates the mercantilist effects of tariffs, there has been a movement toward more protectionism in recent years. . . . Under flexible exchange rates, protection of one industry must come at the expense of all other domestic producers of traded goods. This linkage has apparently escaped those carrying on the political debate over protectionist measures. . . .

The hope that flexible exchange rates would encourage a more open environment for international trade has been disappointed.

OFFICIAL INTERVENTION AND THE MANAGEMENT OF EXCHANGE RATES

Expectations about the performance of flexible exchange rates were typically based on the assumption of a "clean" float or, at worst, of only modest official intervention undertaken for stabilization purposes. The situation since 1973 has been at some variance with this assumption. "Dirty," or managed, floats have been the rule rather than the exception, and intervention activities appear to have been biased toward undervaluing currencies against the dollar up to 1981–82. Central banks claimed that their activity in exchange markets was designed solely to stabilize exchange rates, but somehow reserves almost always rose. Unbiased stabilization should produce no trend in reserves, but the . . . [facts indicate] large and fairly persistent accumulations of reserves from 1973 through 1980 for a number of countries maintaining floating rates. This trend suggests that currencies may have been held down to encourage exports and discourage imports. . . . Intervention leaned toward undervaluing the currencies of . . . countries during this period. During some of these years, such as 1978, the dollar was falling against [other] currencies and accumulations of dollars would be expected. During other years, such as 1975, the dollar strengthened considerably, but [other] countries continued to accumulate reserves. Exchange-market intervention that keeps a currency below its market value might be viewed as a replacement for tariffs as a way to pursue the mercantilist goal of a trade surplus and increased domestic economic activity. A recent study of exchange-rate management concluded that the Japanese were particularly active in attempting to hold their currency below equilibrium levels from 1974 to 1977 (Argy, 1982, p. 73).

If excessive aggregate demand and inflation are the problem, exchange-market intervention might be used in an attempt to produce an appreciation of the local currency in order to repress the prices of tradables and the level of aggregate demand. This approach is suggested by the sizable losses of foreign-exchange reserves . . . for 1981 and 1982 [experienced by] a number of major OECD countries. Their central banks apparently concluded that it would be too inflationary to allow their currencies to follow market dictates while the United States was maintaining very high interest rates, and so used exchange-market intervention in an attempt to support their currencies [and hold down inflation].

Instead of being the means through which the balance of payments is kept in equilibrium, the exchange rate is apparently sometimes viewed as a policy tool in a domestic stabilization program. When inadequate aggregate demand is dealt with through large purchases of foreign exchange and a depreciated currency and inflation is attacked with sales of foreign exchange and an appreciation, problems may be created in the economies of the country's trading partners. They absorb the reverse effects on aggregate demand and prices, but the domestic problems of the intervening country are eased. This is hardly the view of flexible exchange rates that was presented by supporters in the 1960s and early 1970s. The IMF's fairly recent system of exchange-market surveillance is designed to discourage or prohibit the use of "managed" floating exchange rates for such domestic macroeconomic purposes, and it is important that this surveillance succeed. . . .

TWO UNSUPPORTED ARGUMENTS AGAINST FLEXIBLE EXCHANGE RATES

Many opponents of flexible exchange rates argued that the additional risks and transactions costs that would result from such a system would strongly discourage international trade and other international business activities. Firms were expected to respond to these presumed risks and costs by avoiding international business and instead stressing domestic activities. Studies of this problem have produced no evidence to support this fear. Trade grew rapidly throughout the 1970s, and econometric models showed no impact on its volume from the 1973 change in the exchange-rate regime. . . .

It has occasionally been suggested that flexible exchange rates had the additional disadvantage of containing an inherent inflationary bias. Supporters of the "ratchet effect" have argued that depreciations increase the prices of traded goods and are obviously inflationary, but that appreciations do not produce parallel declines. If a currency depreciates and later recovers its original level, a net inflationary result remains. Thus a system of flexible exchange rates makes all the participating economies more prone to inflation. Studies of this process by Goldstein (1977) . . . make it very clear that that there is no "rachet effect": exchange-rate movements do not produce a one-direction movement of prices, and so flexible exchange rates do not create an inflationary bias.

REASONS FOR THE FAILURE OF FLEXIBLE EXCHANGE RATES TO MATCH EXPECTATIONS

Why has the performance of flexible exchange rates confounded the predictions of earlier economic theory? It appears that no single flaw in the previous arguments is responsible, but rather a number of important factors.

Sources of Exchange-Market Shocks and the Law of One Price

First, purchasing power parity did not prevail, because shocks to the exchange markets came from a variety of sources besides differing rates of inflation, and elasticities of demand for traded goods were low enough to require sizable exchange-rate movements to produce adjustment. Proponents of purchasing power parity obviously did not allow for factors such as OPEC pricing decisions or the massive shifts in capital flows that resulted from changes in OPEC investment patterns and in inflationary expectations in the 1970s and early 1980s. . . . Low short-run demand elasticities meant that adjustment had to come primarily from speculative capital flows and official intervention at first, and only later from the trade account. Even over longer periods, demand elasticities were low enough to require sizable changes in real exchange rates in order to produce trade-account adjustment. In addition, wages and the prices of nontradables have not been perfectly flexible, particularly in a downward direction, so that exchange-rate changes that caused the prices of tradables to adjust did not produce a parallel adjustment in wage rates and in the prices of nontradables.

As was noted earlier . . . almost all . . . models of the behavior of a flexible-exchange-rate regime, assumed the law of one price. . . . Unfortunately, even markets for homogeneous traded goods are often not perfectly competitive, and there is considerable evidence that arbitrage pressures have not always been sufficient to maintain equivalent prices. . . . If prices of tradables remain unchanged for some period after the exchange rate moves, the adjustment of the trade account becomes more complicated and many models of how a flexible-exchange-rate system ought to behave are open to doubt. . . . Markets for many traded goods are decidedly oligopolistic, creating a preference for short-run price stability and permitting pricing behavior that violates the law of one price. When markets are oligopolistic, it is possible for both the domestic and the foreign prices of a homogeneous tradable to remain unchanged after the exchange rate moves within some limited range (Dunn, 1970).

Monetarism and Overshooting

Other factors besides fear of exchange-rate volatility kept monetary policy from achieving the independence and power that supporters of floating exchange rates had predicted. Monetarists argue that although a central bank can control the nominal money supply under floating exchange rates, it cannot control the real money supply beyond the short run. . . .

Thus, with wage and price flexibility, an independent monetary policy cannot alter output or employment beyond the short run, because the resulting exchange-rate changes will cause adjustments in the general price level that will return the real money supply to its previous level. A 10 percent increase in the nominal money supply will produce a 10 percent depreciation of the currency, which will cause a 10 percent increase in the prices of traded goods. The prices of nontradables will later adjust and the general price level will rise by 10 percent, which will return the real money supply to its original level. The monetary-policy shift has increased the domestic price level, including the price of foreign exchange, by 10 percent, but it has accomplished nothing else. . . . Prices of nontradables may take considerable time to adjust, but the ultimate result is clear: national monetary policy cannot be truly independent in a world of floating exchange rates, because exchange rates and the price level will adjust to keep the real money supply from changing significantly.

The fact that some goods prices may respond more slowly than do financial-asset markets to shifts in monetary policy produces a primary argument for overshooting and one explanation for the recent volatility of exchange rates. Dornbusch (1976) produced his original explanation of overshooting in a model with a domestic product that is an imperfect substitute for imports. Expansionary monetary policy causes the local currency to depreciate and the prices of imports to rise, but the price of the domestic product responds more slowly. As a result, the general price level rises by less than the percentage of the depreciation, and the real money supply [rises]. . . .

. . . The increase in the real money supply . . . causes a decline in the interest rate, creating a differential between foreign and domestic yields. If this differential equals the rate at which market participants expect the local currency to appreciate, as [suggested by the interest parity condition, then the domestic currency must almost instantly overdepreciate (overshoot) to create the expectation of subsequent gradual appreciation as the domestic price adjusts]. When the price of the domestic product has finally responded fully to the earlier monetary expansion and depreciation, the real money supply will fall [back to its original level,] allowing the local currency to appreciate to its final exchange rate. A 10 percent increase in the nominal money supply eventually produces a 10 percent depreciation, a 10 percent increase in the price level, and an unchanged real money supply, but the route to the final result is far from smooth [and involves depreciation that exceeds 10 percent temporarily].

Dornbusch (1980, pp. 205–210) later added the distinction between tradables and nontradables as a reason for a sticky price level. Tradables prices may respond quickly to the exchange rate, owing to arbitrage pressures, but prices of nontradables will lag considerably. To the extent that nontradables are a major part of the price structure, the overall price level will lag the exchange rate, creating the same argument for overshooting and the same process for getting to the final equilibrium. Whether the argument is put in terms of a sticky price for an imperfect substitute for imports or of a distinction between tradables and nontradables, the basic point is the same: if the price level does not respond quickly to changes in monetary policy and to the resulting movement of the exchange rate, overshooting results. The slow adjustment of the price level means that the real money supply does not respond promptly to the exchange rate, and the ensuing disequilibrium in the market for money means that larger short-run [than long-run] changes in exchange rates will result from monetary-policy shifts. Eventually, the exchange rate will return to the level suggested by the standard monetarist analysis, but in the meantime the exchange market will be volatile and potentially disruptive.

Overshooting of the type attributed to the slow response of prices to changes in monetary policy can also result from a simple stock/flow adjustment model of capital flows when expected real yields change. If, for example, a change in expectations causes portfolio managers to desire a 10 percent increase in the proportion of their funds that are invested in assets denominated in U.S. dollars, there will be a large flow of funds into U.S. dollars while the pre-existing stock of capital is redistributed. When this process is completed and actual portfolios match desired ones, the continuing flow of funds into assets denominated in U.S. dollars will depend on new savings that increase the size of portfolios. An extra 10 percent of new savings will flow into assets denominated in U.S. dollars, but this movement of capital will be far smaller than the shift during the original stock-adjustment phase.

The exchange rate must move by enough to cause some combination of current-account adjustment and speculative capital flows to accommodate a large but brief flow of capital followed by a much smaller but continuing flow. The exchange-rate change necessary to clear the exchange market during the stock-adjustment phase will be much larger than that needed during the continuing-flow phase. Thus a shift in portfolio preferences might be expected to produce exchange-rate overshooting. . . . The extent of the overshooting will be constrained by the market's expectation of a partial reversal of the original exchange rate and by speculative reactions to that expectation. As a result, this form of overshooting is self-limiting.

Alternative Explanations for Exchange-Rate Volatility

Recent writers have suggested a number of reasons other than overshooting for the unexpected volatility of exchange rates. One of these is the currency-substitution argument. Large firms and financial institutions hold money in several currencies. If money does not pay interest, a sizable change in relative inflationary expectations will cause a similar shift in the relative demands for the currencies, and hence in exchange rates. . . .

This argument rests on the assumption that money does not pay interest, so that changes in inflationary expectations cannot be offset by adjustments in nominal interest rates on money that will leave currency holdings and current exchange rates relatively undisturbed. Yet the importance of non-interest-bearing money has declined rapidly in recent years. Firms of the size that could be expected to be heavily involved in currency substitution are now very unlikely to hold any significant amount of money in non-interest-bearing forms. For such firms, the newer forms of money that are found in M-2 or in even more extended definitions of money have become dominant.

Money is now perceived as merely the liquid end of a range of interest-bearing assets held by firms, and shifts in holdings of money among currencies can be viewed as part of a traditional asset-diversification process. If nominal interest rates paid on money balances respond promptly to changes in inflationary expectations in order to maintain unchanged real yields, desired currency holdings and the exchange rate should not be greatly affected. . . .

Note that it is not necessary for the actual inflation rate in Britain to change, but merely for some event to lead a significant number of exchange-market participants to expect such a change. In recent years, exchange markets seem to have become very sensitive to new information (or misinformation) that implies future changes in relative rates of inflation. Let us suppose that "news" in the form of an election result, an announcement of changes in policy or senior personnel at the central bank, or an apparent change in the rate of growth of a currently fashionable definition of money suggests to exchange-market participants that a country's inflation rate is likely to accelerate. If this event is not accompanied by an offsetting increase in the interest rate on that country's currency, funds will flow out of the currency in large volume and sharp depreciation will result. The expectations of exchange-market participants may have been incorrect, and the actual rate of inflation may not increase. Perhaps the new information was wrong or was misinterpreted by the market. Even if expectations are soundly based, the exchange rate will move well before there is any change in domestic inflation rates, because goods prices are likely to be sticky and to lag changes in policies. . . .

The appreciation of sterling in 1979–80 and of the dollar in 1981–82 can be interpreted in this light. In both cases, the arrival of new conservative administrations and a monetarist approach to central banking apparently led market participants to expect inflation to decelerate. Nevertheless, nominal interest rates did not decline but instead remained very high. As a result, real interest rates appeared to have increased, making each of the currencies a more attractive way to hold money. Funds flowed in and appreciations occurred that were sufficient to produce large changes in real exchange rates. . . . When the expectation of a prompt deceleration of inflation in Britain was disappointed, sterling depreciated sharply. Inflation actually did decline rather rapidly in the United States, and the exchange rate was maintained through the summer of 1983 [and on into 1985].

Changes in desired currency holdings that cause large exchange-rate movements are not necessarily limited to private firms and financial institutions. If central banks holding foreign-exchange reserves in a number of currencies are sensitive to shifting expectations of relative rates of inflation, their behavior may be similar to that of private financial institutions. Although central banks are not typically thought of as trying to maximize returns on foreign-exchange reserves, some of them may reasonably be expected to move some of their reserves into currencies whose expected real yields are particularly high. Informed exchange-market participants have suggested informally that the 1978 decline of the dollar was encouraged in part by the aggressive movement by the central banks of a number of the larger developing countries and a few small industrialized countries out of dollars and into currencies that were appreciating. . . .

Kareken and Wallace (1978) have suggested that relatively constant real exchange rates are possible in a world of highly integrated capital markets and constantly changing expectations only if capital flows are prohibited. They argue that private capital flows are virtually certain to produce large and disruptive change in real exchange rates when portfolio managers view different currencies as close substitutes and consequently change the mix of the national monies they hold in response to frequent and sometimes temporary changes in expectations. It seems a bit extreme to argue that the only way to avoid constant changes in real exchange rates is to prohibit capital flows. Nevertheless, the increased sensitivity of currency holders to changing expectations clearly means that national monetary and fiscal policies must be managed with great prudence in order to avoid disruptive exchange-rate volatility. Macroeconomic policies will have to produce far more stable expectations than have prevailed in the industrialized countries if asset diversification is no longer to be a major source of frequent changes in real exchange rates.

What is left of the argument that flexible exchange rates make fiscal and monetary policies far more independent and allow them to be devoted to purely domestic goals? The apparent answer is, not much. Under fixed exchange rates, macroeconomic policies had to be oriented toward avoiding large and chronic balance-of-payments problems, with particularly severe constraints on monetary policy if capital markets were integrated. Flexible exchange rates now require that macro policies be oriented toward avoiding exchange-market volatility, with particularly severe constraints on monetary policy if capital markets are integrated. The independence for national macroeconomic policies promised by flexible exchange rates turned out to be greatly exaggerated. . . . The difference between alternative exchange-rate regimes turned out to be much smaller than had been expected. Like many other economic-policy panaceas, flexible exchange rates have failed to meet expectations.

ARE THERE BETTER ALTERNATIVES?

It is far easier to conclude that flexible exchange rates have not worked well than to suggest a replacement that is likely to be more successful.

Capital Controls and Dual Exchange Rates

Prohibitions or limitations on capital flows have been widely discussed as a possible route to a less volatile exchange market, but this approach has major disadvantages. To the extent that such controls prevent the movement of capital from where it has a low marginal product to where its productivity is higher, large losses of efficiency occur. If international capital flows are no longer possible, countries can invest only what is saved locally, producing an inefficient allocation of the world's capital stock.

An equally important objection is that capital controls are very difficult to enforce, and the difficulties increase the longer the controls are in effect. Ingenious investors can devise ways to move capital through almost any control system, false invoicing being the best known route. The primary impact of capital controls often seems to be loss of respect for the law, as many developing countries have discovered to their sorrow.

A recent study of the German experience with capital controls indicates that limitations imposed on one form of capital flows merely produced off-setting increases in other payments items (Argy, 1982, pp. 77–78). . . . Controls are likely to be effective only if they restrict almost every item in the balance of payments, and such all-encompassing controls are unlikely to be acceptable or to succeed in a market economy.

Dual exchange rates are sometimes suggested as an alternative to either fixed or fully flexible exchange rates, but this approach is subject to the same problems as capital controls. The most frequently discussed form of dual rates would fix a parity for the current account and allow the exchange rate to float for capital transactions. The goal is to protect the current account and domestic markets for traded goods from shocks resulting from shifting capital flows. . . .

The problem of evasion or cheating would arise whenever the two exchange rates differed significantly. The combination of avarice and ingenuity, upon which economic theory rests, virtually guarantees that market participants will find ways to shift transactions toward the more favorable exchange rate. Transfer pricing is an obvious option; if a currency is worth more for current- than for capital-account transactions, importers will be encouraged to overstate foreign purchases in order to move capital out of the country at the more favorable rate.

When Belgium had such a dual rate and its currency was worth more for current than for capital transactions, it was widely rumored that one year the trade data showed that Belgians had imported more eggs from the Netherlands than every Dutch hen had laid that year. The story may be apocryphal, but its basic point is valid: dual exchange rates encourage cheating, graft, and a general disrespect for the law. Dual exchange rates and capital controls might be viewed as the financial equivalent of prohibition. By outlawing a purely private activity to which many people are strongly attached, the government does not eliminate the activity, it merely encourages a large number of people to become lawbreakers.

An Exchange-Market Tax

Tobin (1982) has suggested a tax on all exchange-market transactions as a means of discouraging destabilizing short-term capital flows without providing an incentive to shift capital transactions to the current account through false invoicing. The major disadvantage of this approach is that if the tax was high enough to cause a sharp reduction in speculative capital movements, it would also be high enough to repress trade and other international transactions, and the resulting efficiency losses could be large. Economists have argued against tariffs for too long to approve a method of reducing exchange-market volatility that is merely a tariff on all international transactions. If the tax was not high enough to discourage trade and other transactions, it would probably not be high enough to reduce the volume of speculative capital flows by very much. Such a tax would be promising only in the unlikely event that there was reason to expect it to have a far greater impact on short-term capital flows than on other international transactions.

The problem of cheating or "tax avoidance" arises here also. If the tax was on purchases and sales of foreign exchange, as Tobin's article implies, barter would become attractive. The tax could be avoided by exchanging goods for other goods or for financial assets, and one could expect the rapid development of brokerage operations to facilitate such exchanges. Barter would fail to develop only if the tax was very low, and if it was very low it would not really discourage speculative capital flows. If the tax was on all international transactions rather than on purchases and sales of foreign exchange, the enforcement problems would become even larger. It would be very difficult even to identify all the transactions, and false invoicing would become an obvious way to reduce tax liabilities.

The Crawling Exchange Rate

The crawling peg has often been suggested as a route to exchange-rate flexibility without the volatility of freely floating rates. If a crawling peg was managed on the basis of purchasing power parity, changes in relative price levels would be reflected promptly in the exchange rate, but current-account shocks caused by factors other than differing rates of inflation and shifts in the capital account would not affect the exchange rate, and hence could not create undesirable disruptions elsewhere in the economy.

Unfortunately, this approach brings back most of the well-known disadvantages of fixed parities. Since sterilization of anything beyond modest payments disequilibria would probably be impossible for most countries, control over the nominal money supply would again be lost or at least greatly compromised. Balance-of-payments considerations would again become vital in determining macroeconomic policies, even when they conflicted with domestic goals. The only improvement over rigid exchange rates would be the prevention of disequilibria due to differing rates of inflation by a rapid adjustment of the exchange rate to offset such differences. But this leaves many other sources of trade-account shifts, including long-term changes in a country's terms of trade or in its competitiveness in world markets as a result of changes in technology or perceived product quality. These would not be offset through parity adjustments.

Under a purchasing-power [-parity] crawl, long-term shifts in the capital account could not be transferred into flows of real capital through the exchange rate. If, for example, a country became a more productive and consequently a more attractive location for investment, the resulting capital inflows would not produce [a real] appreciation that would cause a current-account deficit and an excess of domestic investment over saving. Because the exchange rate was being adjusted to offset relative rates of inflation, even if the country allowed the balance-of-payments surplus that resulted from the capital inflows to produce an increase in the domestic money supply, the resulting inflation would not bring about a current-account deficit and a movement of real capital into the country. Instead, the currency would be devalued to offset the inflation and maintain the current account. A purchasing-power-parity crawl does not offer any apparent mechanism through which shifts in financial capital flows can be transferred into movements of real capital in the current account. Even if a country becomes a more productive location for capital and therefore attracts larger financial capital inflows, it will not be able to increase its level of domestic investment relative to saving. As a result, the world's stock of capital cannot be efficiently allocated, creating the potential for sizable losses of output.

Presumptive Rules for Exchange-Rate Changes

It would appear that the problems of a crawling rate could be solved by the adoption of an exchange rate that is allowed to crawl in the short run to offset differing rates of inflation but can also be adjusted by larger amounts in response to major payments shifts. Presumptive rules for major parity changes, based on trends in the current plus long-term capital accounts or some other indicator of fundamental payments shifts, could be used to avoid competitive devaluations or other manipulative exchange-rate changes. Such presumptive rules would allow parity adjustments in response to terms-of-trade changes or basic shifts in the capital account but would not produce an exchange rate that moved constantly in response to volatile short-term capital flows.

Although this approach has obvious attractions, it also has at least two disadvantages. First, the industrialized countries that now maintain flexible exchange rates might not be able to agree on a set of presumptive rules and then accept their enforcement. There is a strong possibility that conflicts would arise between domestic economic or political goals and the exchange-rate changes called for by the presumptive rules, and it might not be possible to compel countries to change their parities in these situations. Such a system might not survive the first occasion on which a major industrialized country tried to encourage recovery from a deep recession when the presumptive rules called for a sizable appreciation of its currency.

The other difficulty involves speculators. If the relevant governments and officials of the IMF understand the presumptive rules, the private sector can also be expected to understand and use them to make fairly accurate predictions of future exchange-rate changes. If, for example, four quarters of large payments deficits are the presumptive basis for devaluation, every country that has had three (or perhaps only two) quarters of poor payments results can expect huge capital outflows. In such a situation, speculators will face a one-sided bet. There is a high probability that the currency will be devalued and virtually no probability that it will be revalued: speculators either make large profits or roughly break even. Because an exchange-rate regime that provided such possibilities would impose large financial losses on central banks that had to support currencies just before major parity changes, it could not be maintained. The ideal solution is unfortunately impossible — a set of presumptive rules that governments can follow but that speculators cannot understand and use to predict parity changes.

A Return to Fixed Parities

Recent suggestions for a return to rigidly fixed exchange rates, perhaps with an international gold standard, are even less attractive. The likelihood of success for such a system of fixed parities is suggested by the recent travails of the European Monetary System. If a group of decidedly similar countries committed to monetary integration and to a degree of policy coordination cannot make fixed exchange rates succeed and must instead change parities every few months, what are the chances for the successful maintenance of fixed parities among a much larger number of highly diverse countries that lack the European commitment to monetary integration? Any attempt to introduce a fixed-exchange-rate regime in the current economic and financial environment would almost certainly be doomed to rapid failure. Since there is no institutional mechanism to impose and maintain a "world monetary policy," fixed parities should be avoided.

Suggestions that the gold standard would provide such a mechanism introduce the interesting possibility that this monetary policy would be affected by the weather in the U.S.S.R. and the level of political stability in South Africa. If poor harvests force Moscow to sell large amounts of gold to pay for grain imports, world monetary policy will become more expansionary; if civil unrest in South Africa closes the mines for an extended period, tight money will follow. The numerous other arguments against a return to the gold standard are too well known to bear repeating. Recent arguments for a return to gold often seem to be based primarily on romantic yearnings for the imagined virtues and certainties of the past.

THE LIKELY CONCLUSION: RETAINING THE CURRENT SYSTEM

The answer may not be the best approach but merely the least bad: muddle through with the current regime of managed floats. . . .

The future of the current system of floating exchange rates may also depend in part on the nature of official intervention. As was noted earlier, intervention appears at times to have been aimed at manipulating exchange rates. . . . Intervention appears to have been more effective when it was coordinated between or among countries. Coordination was useful because it helped to convince market participants that the countries involved were working in the same direction and that their efforts were therefore to be taken more seriously. But even coordinated intervention had only short-term impact unless it was accompanied by supporting changes in macroeconomic policies. . . .

The annex to the Williamsburg Summit Communiqué [1983] indicated a general goal of "greater convergence in economic performance" among the seven major OECD countries. It further suggested that exchange-rate policy would be based on greater macroeconomic "policy convergence." . . . If economic-summit communiqués typically represented the policies that participating governments actually adopted, there would be reason for optimism about the prospects for less volatile exchange rates. Unfortunately, the recent history of such communiqués is not encouraging.

It is now clear that the earlier hope that floating exchange rates would make national macroeconomic policies largely independent . . . cannot be realized. Complete macroeconomic independence turns out to be a mirage under any exchange-rate regime. Only economic isolationism would produce such independence, and the economic performance of Albania suggests that few countries are likely to adopt that approach. For countries that do not find autarky attractive, macroeconomic policies must be designed with international payments constraints clearly in mind. The adoption of floating exchange rates may ease those constraints, but only modestly. Ten years of experience with floating exchange rates really have made us sadder but wiser.

Note

1. The conclusion that there is a net impact on the Canadian trade account is based on the assumption that part of the short-run payments adjustment to the exchange rate occurs in the capital account in the form of stabilizing short-term capital flows. This is particularly likely if the U.S. recession and the resulting depreciation of the Canadian dollar are viewed as being temporary.

References

Argy, Victor, *Exchange-Rate Management in Theory and Practice,* Princeton Studies in International Finance No. 50, Princeton, N.J., Princeton University, International Finance Section, October 1982.

Dornbusch, Rudiger, "Expectations and Exchange Rate Dynamics," *Journal of Political Economy, 84* (December 1976), 1161–1176.

Dornbusch, Rudiger, *Open Market Macroeconomics,* New York, Basic Books, 1980.

Dunn, Robert M., Jr., "Flexible Exchange Rates and Oligopoly Pricing: A Study of Canadian Markets," *Journal of Political Economy, 78* (January/February 1970), 140–151.

Friedman, Milton, "The Case for Flexible Exchange Rates," in Richard Caves and Harry Johnson, eds., *American Economic Association Readings in International Economics,* Homewood, Ill., Irwin, 1968, pp. 413–440.

Goldstein, Morris, "Downward Price Inflexibility, Ratchet Effects, and the Inflationary Impact of Import Price Changes," *IMF Staff Papers, 24* (November 1977), pp. 569–612.

Karekin, John, and Neil Wallace, "International Monetary Reform: The Feasible Alternatives," *Federal Reserve Bank of Minneapolis Quarterly Review* (Summer 1978), pp. 2–7.

Korteweg, Pieter, *Exchange-Rate Policy, Monetary Policy, and Real Exchange-Rate Variability,* Essays in International Finance No. 140, Princeton, N.J., Princeton University, International Finance Section, December 1980.

Tobin, James, "A Proposal for International Monetary Reform," in *Essays in Economics: Theory and Policy,* Cambridge, Mass., MIT Press, 1982, pp. 488–494.

21

Unexpected Real Consequences of Floating Exchange Rates

Rachel McCulloch

After a decade of floating exchange rates, international monetary reform is again in the air, and it is thus timely to ask how well (or badly) the current system is functioning. But compared to what? Because the current monetary arrangements came into effect following years of vigorous debate on the merits of exchange-rate flexibility, some observers appear to forget that these arrangements were not in reality "designed" or even "adopted" by the International Monetary Fund. Rather, the present regime was initiated by the collapse of the Bretton Woods system, following prolonged and heroic salvage efforts. As late as 1972, a report on

From R. McCulloch, *Unexpected Real Consequences of Floating Exchange Rates,* Essay No. 153, August 1983. Copyright © 1983. Reprinted by permission of the International Finance Section of Princeton University. Some text, footnotes, and references omitted.

international monetary reform by the Executive Directors of the IMF failed even to mention flexible exchange rates as a viable long-term option . . ., while an earlier report explicitly concerned with the role of exchange rates in the adjustment process had devoted only one of seventy-eight pages to floating rates. . . . The markedly after-the-fact Second Amendment of the IMF Articles of Agreement to legalize the status quo merely reflected recognition of member governments' inability to agree on an alternative — any system imposing even minimal restraints on national policies — rather than an affirmation of the benefits of floating.

The central and still unresolved issue in the fruitless debate over international financial arrangements was the desire to preserve national autonomy in the face of growing economic and political interdependence. Since the present time seems no more propitious than the early 1970s for the willing sacrifice of national sovereignty by IMF members, any argument for system reform must be solidly grounded in the accumulated experience with floating, not by reference to the dogmas of the Bretton Woods era. This essay is an eclectic assessment of that experience, with particular reference to the ways in which events have confounded both advocates and critics of floating. Although there is some discussion of the consequences of the floating-rate regime for worldwide macroeconomic performance, the main focus is on microeconomic issues — specifically, the role of floating rates in facilitating or retarding the growth of world trade and investment.

INTERNATIONAL MONEY AND THE GOALS OF BRETTON WOODS

National money, in its time-honored functions as medium of (indirect) exchange, unit of account, standard of deferred payment, and store of value, is supposed to facilitate the efficient allocation of resources in production and consumption. Although the precise nature and magnitude of the efficiency gains have never been spelled out fully in economic analyses, monetary history gives clear evidence of significant real resource costs and unanticipated redistributions of wealth when money fails to perform its traditional functions. At the same time, control of a nation's money supply also constitutes a potent tool of macroeconomic management and an alternative to taxation as a means of financing government expenditure. Thus, conflicting objectives confront those who conduct monetary policy, and there are both microeconomic and macroeconomic bases on which to judge their performance.

Analogously, the international monetary system is supposed to facilitate an efficient allocation of resources worldwide, presumably through trade guided by comparative advantage, but it also has important consequences for global macroeconomic conditions. This twofold function was explicitly recognized in the Articles of Agreement of the International Monetary Fund approved at Bretton Woods in 1944, which listed among the purposes of the Fund:

> To facilitate the expansion and balanced growth of international trade, and to contribute thereby to the promotion and maintenance of high levels of employ-

ment and real income and to the development of the productive resources of all members as primary objectives of economic policy (Articles of Agreement, Article I(ii)).

As inadequacies in the Bretton Woods system became apparent during the 1960s, criticisms and proposals for reform likewise fell into two distinct categories.

Macroeconomic Performance

The Bretton Woods system was held to impart a deflationary bias to the world economy on account of the asymmetrical positions of surplus and deficit countries — at least in the rules, if not in the actual behavior, of member nations. At a time when the prospects for "fine tuning" of national macroeconomic performance seemed bright, the obligations of member nations under the Bretton Woods rules appeared to limit the ability of elected governments to deliver the combination of inflation and unemployment desired by their constituents. Although theory suggested that control of two instruments — monetary policy and fiscal policy — should allow enlightened policymakers to achieve both "internal balance" and "external balance," thoughtful analysts stressed that other objectives, notably adequate long-run growth, could be jeopardized by this textbook solution.

Because the Bretton Woods rules appeared to constrain national governments, advocates of reform and especially of increased exchange-rate flexibility appealed to the need for greater macroeconomic independence. . . .

Subsequent events suggest that advocates of increased flexibility failed to distinguish adequately between institutional and economic constraints on the actions of national policymakers. The collapse of the Bretton Woods system clearly increased the national sovereignty of IMF members with regard to the conduct of macroeconomic policy but had at most a minor effect on the ability of member nations to achieve desired outcomes. Countries acquired the technical capacity to pursue autonomous monetary policies because they were no longer required to peg their exchange rates, but they were severely constrained in exercising this autonomy on account of the undesirable effects of large exchange-rate movements on their domestic economies. Furthermore, the system of flexible exchange rates could not suppress structural interdependence; the system proved to offer ample channels for the continued international transmission of macroeconomic disturbances. . . .

The standard [macroeconomic] arguments sometimes acknowledged the inflationary potential of exchange-rate changes themselves, . . . but only after 1973 did attention shift to this line of causation. . . . Although the inflationary pressures attending any devaluation or depreciation had long been emphasized by experts on less-developed countries, analyses for the industrialized nations tended to ignore the possibility, perhaps because of their Keynesian underpinnings. . . . [However,] the post-1973 inflationary experience was too dramatic to be ignored. Much subsequent debate has therefore centered on whether flexibility provides an independent source of inflationary pressure via a "ratchet" mechanism that pushes up domestic prices when a currency's value declines but fails to push them down at times of currency appreciation. Despite its intuitive appeal, however, empirical evidence for the ratchet effect appears to be weak. . . . One important competing explanation for the failure to anticipate fully the inflationary impact of devaluation or depreciation was the tendency to underestimate the true openness of industrial economies, or, more precisely, the strength of the linkage between international prices of traded goods and domestic prices of nontraded goods. . . .

Living with Exchange Risk

Pre-1973 microeconomic arguments for floating exchange rates stressed their role in encouraging unrestricted multilateral trade. . . . While rigidly fixed exchange rates like those of the classical gold standard were conceded to provide many of the benefits of a single world money, the Bretton Woods system of adjustable pegs had major shortcomings. Balance-of-payments disequilibria were frequently met by direct controls on trade and capital flows rather than the domestic macroeconomic policy responses prescribed by the "gold-standard rules of the game." Advocates of exchange-rate flexibility argued that it would produce appropriate exchange-rate movements, ensure prompt balance-of-payments adjustment, and thus obviate the need for direct controls that distort global resource allocation. But although proponents of flexible rates were virtually unanimous on this point, some critics foresaw incentives for protectionism. . . .

Of course, even pegged rates could and did change. Therefore, the appropriate comparison was not between floating and fixed rates but between rates changing by small amounts on a day-to-day basis and those changing by substantial percentages at longer intervals and usually only after macroeconomic policy debacles, welfare-reducing direct controls, and repeated foreign-exchange-market crises. Some critics warned, however, that the day-to-day movements of floating rates would not be small. Skeptics envisioned low price elasticities, long lags, exchange-rate overshooting, and destabilizing speculation that would result in wide fluctuations in market-determined rates — a specter of the 1930s that (along with competitive devaluation) the IMF Articles of Agreement specifically pledged to exorcise. Large fluctuations in rates, it was said, would increase the uncertainty facing international traders and investors. Although forward markets and a variety of other, more complicated mechanisms could provide transactors with insurance against rate changes, some warned that the additional cost would push world trade back toward barter. . . .

Subsequent events have provided ample reason for extreme modesty on the part of prognosticators in both camps. Market-determined exchange rates have exhibited instability beyond the fondest nightmares of fixed-rates fanatics, yet trade and investment flows seem relatively unaffected by these changes. . . . The volume of world trade continued to grow more rapidly than production throughout the 1970s, consistent with the hypothesis that the major determinant of changes in the level of trade is underlying GNP growth. Examining the effects of exchange-rate uncertainty on the multilateral and bilateral trade flows of the United States,

Germany, and several other industrial countries for the period 1965–75, Hooper and Kohlhagen (1978, p. 505) "found absolutely no significant effect on the volume of trade (at the 0.95 level) despite considerable effort and experimentation.". . . They did find a significant impact on prices, suggesting that the absence of any impact on volume might reflect relatively inelastic short-run supplies of exports or, alternatively, substantial hedging by importers and exporters.

These apparently contradictory phenomena may also be reconciled by the observation that the only alternatives to risky international transactions are risky domestic transactions. Of the many large risks of all types that any commercial endeavor now entails, exchange-rate uncertainty may be relatively minor compared with the benefits of foreign trade and investment. The risk is appreciable but the profitability even more so. As foreign-exchange risk is highly diversifiable, international operations provide an important means of diluting risks associated with domestic transactions rather than an independent addition to risk.

MARKET-DETERMINED EXCHANGE RATES

The central message of recent experience is that the foreign-exchange market is an asset market and that the economic laws governing exchange rates are fundamentally similar to those governing other asset prices — with stock and bond markets providing obvious domestic analogies. In fact, while exchange rates have indeed been volatile, their volatility has been less than that of stock prices. . . . Furthermore, even a determination of excessive volatility has no obvious policy implications.

Related to these findings is the discovery that the celebrated "law of one price" is not strictly enforced by real-world markets and that purchasing power parity, which perhaps ought not to have held in any case, has evidently collapsed. . . . As a consequence, the once-prevalent notion that an exchange rate behaves like the ratio of two national price indices must be scrapped and the role of exchange-rate movements in equilibrating international transactions reevaluated.

Controls on Trade and Capital Flows

A market-determined exchange rate necessarily equates day-to-day supply and demand for a nation's currency, whether or not supplemented by official reserve transactions. Thus, the need for direct controls motivated by overall balance-of-payments considerations is indeed eliminated by floating rates. The result has been, as predicted, an important reduction in the use of capital controls for balance-of-payments purposes. But asset preferences can and do produce significant prolonged divergences between the market price of a currency and its apparent "real" worth as determined by purchasing power parity. There is therefore no reason to expect a floating-rate system to eliminate incentives for direct controls motivated by current-account considerations.

While current-account balances have exhibited surprising (though lagged) responsiveness to rate movements, the reverse effect of current-account imbalances on exchange-rate movements is evidently much weaker. Indeed, floating rates react only to the extent that current-account imbalances constitute one type of "news" affecting asset preferences. Accordingly, macroeconomic incentives for protection, to increase domestic aggregate demand as well as to achieve sector-specific goals, are largely unaffected by floating rates.

The actual post-1973 experience has been characterized by the persistence and even extension of sectoral protection in the major industrialized countries, mainly for industries that are losing their competitiveness in relation to counterparts in Japan and especially the newly industrializing countries. Although there has been no apparent trend toward the increased use of protection (or competitive devaluation) as a means of macroeconomic stimulus, an assumed net gain in aggregate employment is customarily used — as in the Bretton Woods era — to bolster the case for proposed sectoral interventions, especially when large industries such as apparel and automobiles are involved. The Cambridge Economic Policy Group has promulgated a macroeconomic case for across-the-board protection of British industry, but with no noticeable effect thus far on the policies of the Thatcher government. Japan is sometimes accused of engaging in policies to prevent appreciation of the yen, especially through restrictions on inward foreign investment. But the main evidence presented in support of this hypothesis is unbalanced bilateral trade with the United States, a condition that also accompanied an allegedly overvalued yen in previous years.

Further aspects of the relationship between protection and exchange-rate movements are considered in subsequent sections.

Implications for Foreign Direct Investment

The "overvalued" dollar of the 1960s was singled out as an important reason, even *the* important reason, for the large volume of U.S. direct investment abroad, particularly in Europe. Through acquisitions of existing national enterprises and the construction of new plant and equipment, U.S.-based multinationals achieved a major presence in the protected markets of the newly created European Economic Community — investments all the more attractive at prevailing exchange rates. This role of disequilibrium exchange rates in foreign-investment decisions was initially confirmed by events of the 1970s. As the dollar plummeted in relative value through two devaluations and subsequent market depreciation, foreign direct investment in the United States grew with unprecedented rapidity — enough to make the United States the world's leading *host* country (in absolute but not relative terms) by the end of the decade. Yet the strengthening of the dollar since 1978 has not stemmed the flow of new foreign direct investment, and exchange-rate volatility has had no noticeable impact on its volume.

Why have foreign investors been undeterred by exchange-rate turbulence? There are several plausible lines of explanation, not mutually exclusive, that invoke the *relative* advantages of multinational firms over national enterprises. . . .

As already noted, one anticipated benefit of floating that has actually materialized is a marked reduction in the use of direct capital controls. This trend facilitates new or expanded investments, while at the same time increasing their attractiveness by improving prospects for the unimpeded repatriation of profits and royalties. Moreover, direct investment decisions are based on long-term plans, for periods during which even a pegged rate might well be expected to change. Over the life of an investment, the effects of volatility on profits largely cancel out, whereas cumulative movements in exchange rates, whether pegged or floating, mainly compensate for differential rates of domestic inflation or productivity growth across countries. A floating-rate system might even stimulate investment by easing such compensating exchange-rate adjustments and thereby reducing the likelihood of new direct controls on capital or trade flows during the investment period.

Foreign direct investment is also influenced by many considerations apart from exchange risk or the lack of it. If, as past studies suggest, protection is an important motive for direct investment, the recent protectionist swing in the United States — both actual and threatened — may have elicited investments intended to protect large expenditures already incurred in the development of the lucrative U.S. market. Recent Japanese investments in the United States may fall into this category. Furthermore, the accumulation of wealth by OPEC surplus nations has increased demands for assets of all kinds, and the post-1973 "internationalization" of the supply of saving probably favors U.S. assets because of the relative size and stability of the American economy. However, official statistics are uninformative on this point, since many OPEC investments are held anonymously through third-country intermediaries.

Finally, as suggested above and exactly contrary to pre-1973 conventional wisdom, floating may provide an important independent incentive for foreign direct investment. Input-price uncertainty is a recognized motive for vertical integration; a regime of floating rates accordingly provides incentives for vertical multinational integration. Together with centralized management, vertical integration allows a substantial reduction in the variability of profits due to exchange-rate movements between input-source countries and the downstream user. This explanation fits the Canadian floating-rate period, which was marked by continued expansion of U.S. direct investments in Canadian extractive industries. Likewise, the reduction of input-price uncertainty may be a second motive (in addition to increased actual and threatened protection) for recent Japanese investments in the United States. Horizontal global expansion may similarly be favored by floating rates. For production operations in which minimum efficient scale is relatively low or scale economies unimportant, global diversification of production facilities allows firms some opportunity to optimize with respect to medium-term movements in real exchange rates as well as enhanced leverage in dealings with national labor unions.

The vertical and horizontal expansions motivated by exchange-rate variability help to explain the rapid growth of intra-industry and intra-firm trade during the 1970s. They have opposite implications, however, for the responsiveness of trade flows to movements in exchange rates. While vertical integration allows a firm to ignore changes in the rate, horizontal integration offers opportunities to profit from them through adjustments in trade flows.

EXCHANGE RATES, RELATIVE PRICES, AND COMPETITIVENESS

A major surprise of the 1970s was the discovery that the United States is not a closed economy. The old and erroneous characterization . . . rested in part on a confusion of *traded* with *tradable* goods; for a large country like the United States, openness is consistent with low ratios of exports and imports to total domestic shipments. Closely linked was the failure to anticipate the importance of exchange-rate changes for domestic prices. Early and crude estimates of the inflationary impact of dollar devaluation assumed that the prices of imported goods would be the only ones affected.

Elasticities and the Law of One Price

Analysts had been misled in part by the traditional elasticities approach to exchange-rate changes. The elasticities approach entailed a basically Keynesian view of price movements. Domestic-currency prices (or supply curves) for exports and import substitutes were assumed to be independent of the exchange rate. A related assumption, crucial but always implicit, was that domestic and foreign goods are not highly substitutable, so that domestic producers of tradables face appreciably downward-sloping demand curves for their outputs even in the long run. Given these assumptions, the primary effect of a devaluation would be to alter the relative prices of domestic goods and their foreign counterparts, shifting domestic and foreign demands toward domestic goods. A devaluing nation with some excess capacity could therefore expect a durable improvement in the international price competitiveness of its export and import-competing industries and a resulting durable improvement in its trade balance. The same logic was carried over to open-economy versions of Keynesian macroeconomic models, in which the exchange rate served as a policy instrument for switching aggregate expenditure between foreign and domestic markets.

The unexpectedly large impact of exchange-rate changes on domestic prices in the United States, along with the many cases in which devaluation failed to produce a durable improvement in the trade balance, led analysts to discard the elasticities approach and its underlying assumptions. With considerable fanfare, the era of the monetary approach was ushered in. Central to the elasticities approach is the implicit assumption that the law of one price is not applicable; domestic-currency prices of domestically produced tradables can move independently of the domestic-currency prices of their foreign counterparts. Exponents of the monetary approach chose an opposite but equally extreme assumption, making the law of one price the centerpiece of their models. Domestically produced exports and import-competing goods were now taken to be perfect substitutes for their foreign counterparts; accordingly, their domestic-currency prices were necessarily identical at all times.

Under these new assumptions, a devaluation must increase the prices of domestically produced tradables to restore equality with the prices of their foreign substitutes. For a small country, the domestic prices of all tradables would rise by exactly the amount of the devaluation. Accordingly, an exchange-rate change affects primarily the prices of tradables relative to those of nontradables, rather than the prices of domestic goods relative to those of foreign goods. While the higher relative prices of tradables implies an increase in their domestic supply, domestic demand is shifted *away* from all tradables toward nontradables, eventually raising the prices of the latter and restoring the initial allocation of resources in domestic production. A key implication of such models is that devaluation cannot improve the internal price competitiveness of domestic suppliers.

But again events confounded theories, and again the problem centered on the law of one price — unduly disregarded in the elasticities approach but exalted beyond empirical justification by advocates of the monetary approach. As producers of almost any tradable good will be happy to affirm, exchange-rate movements *are* important for the overall international competitiveness of domestic industries; for some nonnegligible period, exchange-rate movements can and do alter the prices of domestic goods relative to those of foreign goods.

While the law of one price (for any one "good") assumes a high degree of substitutability in consumption or production between domestic tradables and their foreign counterparts, as well as markets that are highly competitive, empirical investigation reveals that these conditions do not hold for most tradable goods, at least over . . . relatively short periods. . . . Rather, for reasons having to do with product differentiation, trade barriers, delivery lags, distribution, and servicing, tradables are heterogeneous in their adherence to the law of one price, or, more precisely, in their adherence to its preconditions. "Substantial changes in exchange rates typically have substantial and persistent effects on the relative common currency prices of closely matched manufactures produced in different countries" (Isard, 1977, p. 948).

Recognizing that tradable goods are heterogeneous brings the analysis almost full circle to a framework in which elasticities again play a key role. An important implication is that the price effects of devaluation are not typically uniform across industries producing tradable goods.

Sectoral Consequences of Changes in Exchange Rates

Sector-specific consequences within the aggregate of "tradables" [are due to] . . . "structural" characteristics such as supply elasticities and wage rigidities or wage indexation. . . .

Where substitutability and therefore cross-price elasticities are high and markets competitive, there will be strong forces equating the domestic-currency prices of foreign-produced goods with those of domestically produced versions. A devaluation will therefore cause domestic prices to rise — by the full amount of a devaluation in the case of a small country that has no appreciable effect on international prices. Domestic supply, employment, and profits will rise; domestic consumption will fall.

For an industry in which domestic and foreign versions are highly imperfect substitutes, devaluation has much weaker short-run consequences for the domestic price. The increased domestic-currency price of the imperfect foreign substitute results in an outward shift in the domestic industry's downward-sloping demand curve. The effects on equilibrium price thus depend crucially on conditions of domestic supply. Domestic output, employment, and profits will rise; domestic and foreign consumption of the industry's output will rise on account of the favorable movement in its relative price. Moreover, with goods or services that are highly differentiated, each *producer* faces a distinctly downward-sloping demand curve, so that markets may be characterized by price discrimination. In such markets, [shifts in demand curves due to] an exchange-rate change may actually have a "perverse" effect on output and price, although not on profits.

Exchange-rate changes also affect industry supply curves through their consequences for the domestic-currency prices of tradable inputs. As noted above, the size of price changes depends critically upon the extent to which foreign and domestic versions are highly substitutable; the speed with which these price changes are reflected in higher production costs depends on the extent to which suppliers are bound by long-term commitments. One measure of the total impact of devaluation on a given industry through both output and input markets is the *net* effect on industry value added. As in the analysis of the "effective protection" that a nation's tariff schedule provides to a particular industry, i.e., the percentage by which industry value added per unit of output can exceed its free-trade level, a calculation can in principle be made of the *net* effect of "exchange-rate protection" on an industry's value added. A devaluation will raise domestic-currency value added by exactly the percentage of the devaluation only for an industry in which domestic and foreign goods are highly substitutable on both the output and input sides *and* effects on world prices of the industry's output sales and input purchases are negligible. Otherwise, either a smaller or larger increment is possible.

A last dimension of the sectoral consequences of devaluation concerns the division of increased industry value added between industry-specific and mobile factors. If the supply of mobile factors ("labor") is available at a fixed nominal reward, as in the case of a binding minimum wage, industry profits will increase by the full increment in value added. But because devaluation raises the cost of living and also tends to increase the demand for variable factors of production, there may be some upward adjustment in wages, whether determined by a competitive market, union contract negotiation, or legislation of a real minimum wage. On the other hand, devaluation — as opposed to depreciation of a floating rate — is often accompanied by an "incomes policy" intended to hold down wage adjustments, thus reducing the real wage and raising the proportion of increased industry value added accruing as profits.

Adjustments to Real Shocks

Although real shocks were hardly new in the 1970s, their interaction with a floating-rate system provided beleaguered policy analysts with considerable food for thought. As predicted, floating rates prevented the recurring exchange-market crises that no doubt would otherwise have accompanied the OPEC price shocks and ill-advised policy responses to them. And, although floating rates themselves did little to ease the adjustment of less-developed oil importers, most of which still peg their rates in any case, a largely private recycling process solved the immediate problem of inadequate balance-of-payments financing. Indeed, even critics of floating rates are usually quick to acknowledge that no alternative system could have survived the stormy 1970s. On the other hand, the actual adjustment process was quite different from that anticipated by most analysts, principally because of the unexpected ways in which OPEC surplus nations spent their vastly increased earnings.

According to the standard pre-1973 debate, flexible rates were supposed to insulate a country from external shocks, while fixed rates would allow the burden of internal shocks to be shared with trading partners. As already noted, the increased macroeconomic independence offered by flexible rates proved to be largely illusory. Moreover, the standard fixed vs. flexible arguments, based on conclusions from one-sector macroeconomic models, necessarily ignored the sector-specific impact of many shocks and thus obscured the sector-specific aspects of the resulting adjustment process. In response to this latter discovery, enterprising theorists have recently come forward with models of such hitherto uncelebrated maladies as "Dutch disease.". . .

As in the analysis of exchange-rate changes, the crucial missing insight was that "the" tradables sector is in fact a set of heterogeneous industries. Furthermore, each has at any time a collection of industry-specific factors that can be shifted elsewhere only at considerable cost. Therefore, in a floating-rate system, the good fortune of one tradable-goods industry, whether technological progress, a mineral discovery, or a favorable price movement in the world market, can become bad news for other tradable-goods industries through two mechanisms: exchange-rate appreciation and the bidding up of rewards to factors mobile between sectors. The result is "Dutch disease" or "de-industrialization" or the problem of "lagging sectors," i.e., ones in which output falls and the rewards to industry-specific factors decline. Moreover, "the decline in the relative size of non-booming sectors is a necessary component of the economy's adjustment toward a higher level of income" (Neary, 1982, p. 20). Thus, a conflict arises between efficient resource allocation and certain other national objectives, such as developing and maintaining an industrial sector of a certain size or maintaining the incomes of sector-specific factors.

All this assumes, of course, that the exchange rate moves in the direction suggested by the effect on the current-account balance, an effect that may be weak in practice. Furthermore, a national government wishing to avoid the consequences of appreciation can intervene in the foreign-exchange market, directly or indirectly, thus protecting other tradables sectors from injury. Corden (1981) has suggested that this is a primary motive for "exchange-rate protection." . . . Thus, the problem of adjustment can at least be postponed — for better or worse. . . .

. . . [Yet] the outcomes may be quite similar in the long run. The reason is that a macroeconomic policy cannot eradicate the "supercompetitiveness" of one tradable-goods sector over the rest. Through internal mechanisms such as competition for inputs, the less-competitive sectors will still be squeezed. For example, it is noteworthy that the balance (in current dollars) of U.S. trade in "high-technology" goods has grown almost exponentially since 1960, while the trade balance in all other manufactures is roughly its mirror image. There is no apparent discontinuity in this pattern between the 1960s and 1970s, except for a higher variability in the 1970s that probably reflects underlying macroeconomic fluctuations and large jumps in real exchange rates. . . .

CAUSES AND CONSEQUENCES OF PROTECTION

Freer trade was one widely anticipated advantage of flexible exchange rates that failed to materialize. The conventional wisdom predicted that exchange-rate flexibility would facilitate trade liberalization. . . . Yet the post-1973 period has in fact been marked by the proliferation of new and subtle trade-distorting measures. Furthermore, Bergsten and Williamson (1982) offer evidence that exchange-rate volatility has actually intensified the ever-present clamor for more and better protection from foreign competition.

According to the usual pre-1973 argument, exchange-rate flexibility would eliminate the perceived need for protection and in any case neutralize its benefits. This argument rested on errors concerning both the motives for protection and its consequences in a flexible-rate system. A floating rate obviates the perceived need for direct controls on foreign transactions only to the extent that protection is motivated by overall balance-of-payments considerations; it does not eliminate incentives for protection as a tool of macroeconomic stabilization or to achieve sector-specific goals. The implicit assumption that balance-of-payments considerations dominated trade-policy choices before 1973 may have stemmed from a confusion of the underlying motives for protection with the public rhetoric used to justify it. Since overall balance-of-payments considerations were in most instances merely a secondary motive for protection, the elimination of this motive has had only minor consequences for its use.

Sectoral Consequences of Protection

Gains achieved by protected domestic industries would be completely offset by resulting exchange-rate movements only under highly implausible circumstances. The notion that it is somehow irrational for industries to seek protection because it will be offset by currency appreciation . . . is another example of the misleading conclusions that are drawn from macroeconomic models with in-sufficient "structure." In both industrialized and developing countries, real-world protection is a microeconomic, industry-specific phenomenon. Although broad coalitions may form to support or oppose major changes in national trade legisla-tion, the level and type of actual protection are almost always determined on an industry-by-industry basis. Even the "across-the-board" tariff cuts achieved in the Kennedy Round of multilateral trade negotiations singled out numerous specific industries for exemptions from cuts. . . .

As soon as its industry-specific nature is recognized, the analysis of protection becomes identical to that of the industry-specific shocks discussed in the previous section. Protection of some tradables is likely to worsen the economic prospects of other, less-favored tradables. As before, whether the protection of some industries transforms others into lagging sectors depends in part on whether the exchange rate actually appreciates. In the case of protection, however, the outcome has an additional element of ambiguity, since some protective devices, such as "voluntary" export restraints, can cause a deterioration rather than an improvement in the trade balance and hence a depreciation rather than an apprecia-tion (to the extent that the trade balance does influence the exchange rate). . . .

Identification of sectoral consequences also helps to clarify the underly-ing rational motives for apparently irrational policies. One particularly interest-ing example is the prevalence of overvalued exchange rates among developing countries, along with extensive trade and credit controls. Taken together as a coherent policy package, this adds up to a hefty subsidy to a preferred sector, typically import-competing industrial production. While trade barriers protect domestic markets, an overvalued exchange rate allows required capital equipment and intermediate inputs to be purchased at bargain prices, and capital-export prohibitions facilitate access to low-cost credit. The resulting disadvantage to producers of other tradables is one important reason for the much-remarked failure of third-world agriculture to achieve the production levels suggested by its obvious comparative advantage. Like all generalizations regarding developing countries, this one clearly disregards many important national differences. However, the pattern seems to fit a large number of countries.

Volatility and Protectionism

The volatility of the dollar since 1973 has resulted in prolonged de-partures from purchasing power parity and large exogenous swings in the in-ternational competitiveness of U.S. producers of tradable goods. The unexpected increase in protectionism over the same period raises the question whether the current system has actually been an important *cause* of increased protectionism.

Bergsten and Williamson (1982) have recently suggested that there is a "ratchet" effect of exchange-rate fluctuations on the average level of protection. While prolonged overvaluation of the dollar gives rise to new arguments for all manner of sectoral protection, as in 1981 and 1982, any new protection is likely to persist long after the overvaluation has disappeared. Moreover, they argue, even undervaluation might add to protectionist pressures by attracting resources into industries with secularly declining international competitiveness, or at least slowing their exit. When the inappropriately low currency value finally moves upward again, protection will be demanded.

While this hypothesis is intuitively appealing and seems consistent with the recent protectionist fever in the U.S. Congress, there is again a problem of distinguishing appropriately between the underlying motives for protection and its public justification. The quest for favorable government intervention (in all forms, including, but certainly not limited to, trade policies) is a fact of economic life. As long as governments are responsive to demands for sectoral intervention, efforts to obtain, retain, and increase such benefits represent a capital investment comparable to research and development, advertising, and other intangibles that have a favorable impact on profits. (The analogy is imperfect, however, because investment in obtaining favorable government intervention is usually undertaken by a trade association or labor union and therefore has a "free rider" aspect that does not occur with most advertising or R & D.) However, managers, union officials, and the public do tend to view asymmetrically profits vs. losses and overtime vs. layoffs. Therefore, both the industry "demand" for government intervention and its politically determined "supply" may be expected to increase when national unemployment is high, as in 1981–82. Furthermore, while protection is only one possible type of favorable legislative or administrative action among many (including government procurement, regulatory or tax relief, technical assistance, and subsidized credit), the political cost of intervention in this particular form is probably less when the exchange rate is widely acknowledged to be overvalued, as in 1981–82. For these political-economic reasons, it is plausible to expect industry-specific intervention to increase when national unemployment is high and to take the specific form of new trade barriers when the dollar is overvalued.

Yet the actual cases cited to support this link between protection and overvaluation (e.g., textiles, steel, sugar, shoes) are ones with chronic competitiveness problems, not fundamentally healthy industries put temporarily into the red by an overvalued dollar. For some, protection from imports is a national vice extending back into the 1950s. This suggests that exchange-rate overvaluation can provide the politically expedient occasion for new protection of declining industries, interacting with other determinants of increased protectionism, without being the fundamental cause. . . .

CONCLUDING REMARKS

Much of the pre-1973 debate on international monetary reform proved to be irrelevant, for two reasons. First, international political realities precluded the "choice" or "design" of a new system. Perhaps Bretton Woods was a unique phenomenon, at least for modern times. But, more important, the post-1973 system of flexible exchange rates has functioned in ways that are markedly different from the predictions of most analysts on either side of the debate.

In many regards, the academic arguments in favor of increased flexibility never improved on Friedman's pioneering (1953) case. Yet Friedman, as well as most others, erred in their most fundamental prediction, that flexible rates would be stable if national monetary policies were stable. We live in times of too much daily economic "news" from other sources to avoid large fluctuations in market-determined exchange rates. As Mussa aptly remarked, "The smoothly adjusting exchange rate is, like the unicorn, a mythical beast" (1979, p. 9). Moreover, while these fluctuations probably do imply significant real costs to those engaged in international commerce, their effects on trade and investment flows are very different than anticipated. In particular, day-to-day movements in currency values offer an independent motive for international transactions, as a means of diversifying exchange risk. . . .

References

Bergsten, C. Fred, and John Williamson, "Exchange Rates and Trade Policy," paper prepared for the Institute for International Economics Conference on Trade Policy in the Eighties, Washington, D.C., June 23–25, 1982.

Corden, W. M., "Exchange Rate Protection," in R. N. Cooper *et al.*, eds., *The International Monetary System under Flexible Exchange Rates: Global, Regional, and National*, Cambridge, Mass., Ballinger, 1981.

Hooper, Peter, and Steven W. Kohlhagen, "The Effect of Exchange Rate Uncertainty on the Prices and Volume of International Trade," *Journal of International Economics, 8* (November 1978), 483–511.

Isard, Peter, "How Far Can We Push the 'Law of One Price'?" *American Economic Review, 67* (December 1977), 942–948.

Mussa, Michael, "Empirical Regularities in the Behavior of Exchange Rates and Theories of the Foreign Exchange Market," *Carnegie-Rochester Conference Series on Public Policy, 11* (1979), 9–55.

Neary, J. Peter, "Real and Monetary Aspects of the 'Dutch Disease,' " paper prepared for the International Economic Association Conference on Structural Adjustment in Trade-Dependent Advanced Economies, Yxtaholm, Sweden, Aug. 2–6, 1982.

22

The Overvalued Dollar

Rudiger Dornbusch

The strong dollar, large budget deficits, and high real interest rates are a major concern for U.S. domestic macroeconomic policy. The recovery has been strong, but it has not been shared by the traded goods sectors, which are suffering from the collapse in world trade and the continuing recession in Europe and the developing countries (LDCs), but, even more importantly, from a dramatic loss in external competitiveness. U.S. business has naturally reacted by calling for exchange rate protection, with particular attention given to the yen. Unfortunately, the discussion is focussing excessively on what Japan may be doing wrong rather than on our own policies. I will argue that it is our own unbalanced fiscal policies, above all, that make for a high dollar and a slow recovery of the world market for our goods. . . .

REASONS FOR DOLLAR APPRECIATION

Several reasons for the appreciation of the U.S. dollar have emerged from public discussion. The first is that the strengthening of the dollar reflects an improved competitive condition of the USA in the world economy. The improvement is claimed to have made the USA more competitive in international trade other than in manufacturing, specifically in the area of services. In the same spirit it is recognized that political and economic instability, in Europe and in Latin America, has led to international portfolio shifts towards the USA and dollar assets, away from foreign capital markets. The resulting incipient improvement in both the current and capital account, in this view, has led to and justifies the real appreciation of the dollar.

There can be little doubt that international capital has moved towards the USA and that gains in competitiveness in the service sector are manifest. But it is equally hard to believe that the full extent of the sustained dollar appreciation can be explained this way. The major part of the explanation therefore must lie elsewhere, and in particular either in market irrationality or in the systematic effects of international differences in the monetary-fiscal policy mix.

Much of the exchange rate literature of the last ten years has focussed on the short run implications of monetary policy changes for exchange rate movements. The standard argument is that exchange rates are determined in asset markets, and share the flexibility and volatility of interest rates and security prices.

From *Lloyds Bank Review*, no. 152 (April 1984) pp. 1–12. Reprinted by permission. Some text omitted or altered by the editors and some tables updated by the author.

Exchange rates share the volatility of asset prices and, therefore, often move very significantly relative to the much more sticky prices of goods. International investors, in choosing their portfolios, balance the gains from seeking high interest currencies against the potential loss from adverse movements in exchange rates. In such a setting, markets are in equilibrium when interest differentials between countries are matched by expected rates of currency depreciation. Therefore, monetary policy changes that affect interest rates also immediately move exchange rates.

A tightening of monetary policy, for example, leads in the short run to an increase in interest rates relative to those prevailing abroad and therefore attracts capital flows. The resulting payments surplus brings about appreciation of the exchange rate. The interesting point is that the exchange rate appreciation will typically be extreme — there will be overshooting. The reason is that the exchange rate must appreciate enough so that assets markets expect that future losses from a reversal of the appreciation just match the increased earnings on domestic securities. Over time, as goods prices adjust to the changed monetary conditions, the exchange rate then returns to its long run equilibrium value.

In the U.S. context this theory of exchange rate overshooting is an obvious candidate to explain the strong dollar appreciation. Clearly the sharply contractionary monetary policy of the post-1979 period is exactly the setting where we would expect exchange rate overshooting in the direction of appreciation, with the dollar becoming expensive in world markets even though our inflation rate had not become lower than that abroad. But the tight money story is not enough to explain the persistently high dollar. It explains why the dollar appreciated, but it cannot explain why the dollar remains high, unless one is willing to believe that the market continues to be surprised, month after month, by the persistence of tight money.

To have a complete explanation of the high dollar we must take into account not only monetary policy but also international differences in the stance of fiscal policy. Changes in full employment deficits change the full employment demand for goods and therefore affect both the real rate of interest *and* the real exchange rate. Crowding out in a closed economy perspective has always singled out the impact of fiscal policy on real interest rates. But, in an open economy, crowding out (at full employment) also takes place via the exchange rate. An increase in aggregate demand, because of increased government spending or tax cuts, creates an excess demand for goods and therefore brings about a real appreciation. The real appreciation discourages demand for domestic goods. It shifts consumers to goods produced abroad, and reduces exports, making room for investment just as the higher interest rate induces firms not to invest or households to increase saving, thus making room for an increased budget deficit.

The fiscal explanation is highly relevant to the U.S. situation because there has been an enormous shift in the relative fiscal position of the USA on one side and Europe and Japan on the other side. This shift in fiscal policies is shown in [Table 1]. The table reports the changes in the high employment or cyclically adjusted budget surplus as a percentage of GNP. Clearly the USA has moved to a

TABLE 1

Cumulative Changes in High Employment Budgets

	(Percent of GNP)	
	1976–79	[1980–85]*
U.S.A.	+ 2.1	[– 4.5]
Japan	– 1.3	[+ 3.2]
Germany	+1.3	[+ 4.2]

*Forecast

Source: OECD *Occasional Studies,* June 1983 and *Economic Outlook,* July 1983, and Rudiger Dornbusch, "Dollars, Debts, and Deficits," Statement before the Senate Budget Committee, U.S. Congress, February 21, 1985, p. 4.

strongly expansionary stance while Germany and Japan have moved in exactly the opposite direction. There is no surprise therefore that the dollar responded to the asynchronized fiscal policy by a sharp appreciation.

The fiscal interpretation of exchange rate movements does not suggest that U.S. fiscal expansion leads to higher U.S. real interest rates and lower real interest rates abroad. The world capital market is integrated and securities are highly substitutable. Therefore, except for transitory anticipated real exchange rate movements, the real rate of interest is internationally approximately equal. Fiscal expansion in the world, given tight money, will raise the *world* real rate of interest in response to the current and anticipated stimulus to demand. In addition, the currency of the country that is relatively more expansionary will appreciate.

A second point to note is that not only present changes in high employment budget deficits, but also anticipated future changes have an impact on the world rate of interest and on the exchange rate. This is a relevant consideration because also the medium-term fiscal stance in the USA is the opposite of that abroad. The anticipation of future increases in the full employment deficit, and therefore in the full employment demand for U.S. goods, creates the expectation of future crowding out and currency appreciation. In forward-looking asset and exchange markets, this crowding out is anticipated by an immediate appreciation.

It must be noted that the link between fiscal policy and exchange rates has three aspects: first international differences in the direction or extent of fiscal expansion, second the measurement of fiscal policy by changes in *full employment* budgets and finally the need to pay attention to anticipated future changes in fiscal policy. The failure to pay attention to these points explains why a recent U.S. Treasury study arrived at the opposite, though inappropriate, conclusion:

> There is no reliable empirical evidence to support the contention that large government budget deficits cause appreciation of the country's currency, at least as far as the dollar is concerned. As a matter of record the opposite hypothesis, if anything, appears to be better supported by historical data.[1]

The discussion has made no room, so far, for current account imbalances in the explanation of exchange rate movements. There are firm theoretical reasons for current account deficits to lead to depreciation and surpluses to bring about appreciation. However, the channels through which these effects operate and their quantitative magnitude make it empirically implausible that the current account should play a major role. But we must reserve the possibility that the market's belief that the current account does matter could lead to a collapse of the dollar. The uncomfortable part in this view is that the deficits have been so clearly predictable and predicted that the collapse should already have occurred.

EFFECTS OF THE APPRECIATION

The appreciation of the dollar has played a major role in helping reduce inflation in the USA, but also in deepening the recession and perhaps slowing the recovery. By reducing the level or the rate of inflation of import prices, and in particular the prices of materials, the appreciation has slowed down inflation. In this process it is worth separating out three distinct channels. First, dollar appreciation lowers the dollar prices of primary commodities in world trade and therefore reduces U.S. costs in producing manufactures, lowers producer prices and thus ultimately prices to consumers. Second, prices of manufactures produced abroad decline, or grow less, in dollar terms . . . which again lowers inflation.

The third channel emphasizes competitive effects. Dollar appreciation lowers import prices of manufactured goods relative to the prices of the same goods produced by domestic firms. This brings about pressure to cut domestic costs and prices in the affected industries. This effect is particularly significant because it was responsible for the break in wage patterns in the settlements in key industries exposed to severe competition by the persistently strong dollar. As a consequence, hourly earnings in manufacturing [in 1983 grew] at a rate significantly smaller than in the economy at large, thus reflecting the wage discipline features of appreciation.

The price effects of appreciation are brought out by the large differences in the cumulative price increases in the traded goods sector compared with the entire economy. In the period 1980–1983 (second quarter) the GNP deflator increased by 20.6 percent, the export deflator by only 12.6 percent and the import deflator actually fell by 6.9 percent. These price effects, of course, also reflect the behaviour of oil prices and of the world recession, but in good part must be attributed to the dollar. The overall effect of dollar appreciation on inflation in the USA has been estimated to be a reduction of about 1 to 1.5 percentage points per year over the past three years.

The counterpart of the disinflationary benefits is a sharp loss in international cost competitiveness and hence in output and employment. [Table 2] reports estimates of the cumulative losses in output and employment in the U.S. economy. It is worth emphasizing that the output and employment costs of dollar

TABLE 2

The Impact of Dollar Appreciation on the U.S. Economy (Cumulative Effect in 1980–1983, first quarter)

Real GNP	Employment	Unemployment rate
– 2.3%	– 1.1 million	+ 0.9%

Source: Data Resources Inc., *Review of the US Economy,* July 1983.

appreciation are concentrated on firms competing in world markets[, as suggested in Table 3,] or competing in the U.S. market with foreign producers. Moreover, the full adjustment to the overvaluation has, as yet, not been completed, and the growing losses in the international sector are exerting a drag on recovery elsewhere in the economy.

The gains from more rapid disinflation in the USA are offset abroad by increased inflationary pressure. The losses in output and employment here have as a counterpart export-led recovery in Europe and in Japan. Thus, for the rest of the world, dollar appreciation is a mixed blessing. Indeed, the inflationary impact has led many countries initially to tighten their policies to try and offset "imported inflation," thus steeply reinforcing the collapse in world activity. Dollar appreciation and the world recession have severely reinforced in LDCs the consequences of their own policy mistakes. Low real prices of commodities, increases in the real value of dollar debts and high real interest rates due to our poor monetary-fiscal mix have precipitated payments crises and are forcing unprecedented economic and social distress, especially in Latin America. Advocating belt-tightening *abroad* by the U.S. Treasury is an almost cynical misperception of the sources of the problem and the appropriate adjustments.

TABLE 3

U.S. Loss of Export Competitiveness in Manufacturing (Cumulative Percentage Change of Dollar Prices: 1980–84:I)

	U.S.	Japan	Germany
Machinery and transport equipment	20.0	–3.9	–19.5
Electrical machinery, apparatus and appliances	22.7	–1.0	–22.4
Nonelectrical machinery	13.1	–8.0	–19.6

Source: UN Monthly Bulletin of Statistics.

OVERVALUATION AND EXCHANGE RATE POLICY

The losses in output and employment which the U.S. economy is suffering in industries that are competing with the rest of the world and the vast deterioration in the trade balance suggest an overvalued dollar. Indeed, the affected industries have left no doubt that they consider the dollar overvalued and have recommended that their competitiveness be restored, especially by Japanese policies to appreciate the yen.

I define as the equilibrium real exchange rate the rate which, in conjunction with real interest rates and fiscal policy, yields full employment. This definition takes as a benchmark employment, not the current account or any other component of the external balance. It also emphasizes that exchange rates are only one of the key macroeconomic variables impinging on policy objectives.

With this definition in mind two points emerge. First, clearly the dollar is too high *and* real interest rates are too high because we do observe high unemployment. . . .

Second, high unemployment prevails not only in the USA but also abroad. In that sense all currencies are overvalued and, predictably, all countries seek competitive depreciation and might pursue such a policy aggressively were it not for the inflation costs following from currency depreciation.

The dollar appreciation and the increase in world real interest rates are part of the same anticipated adjustment to large high employment deficits and continuing tight money. If our fiscal policies persist, then *ultimately* the current real exchange rates and real interest rates are warranted. The joint problem of dollar overvaluation and excess long-term real interest rates thus reflects primarily a premature adjustment of asset prices to future equilibrium values: asset markets are too much forward-looking and monetary policy (perhaps wisely) is too un-accommodating.

The dollar overvaluation has led to [several] kinds of proposals. . . . Which is most appropriate depends on the relative importance of the various reasons for dollar appreciation discussed, whether competitiveness of U.S. services and assets, differential trends in U.S. and world monetary or fiscal policy, or current-account imbalances.

The case for *sterilized* foreign exchange market intervention is well established: in the face of international shifts in portfolios, in a circumstance where no real adjustments in the economy are called for, the optimal policy is to intervene in financial markets to absorb the securities investors wish to sell off and to sell the securities investors wish to buy. Intervention in these conditions prevents any and all undesirable spillover effects to exchange rates, money supplies and interest rates, and therefore seals off the real economy from the purely financial disturbance. Suppose, for example, investors lose confidence in the political stability of Germany and therefore attempt to shift out of Deutsche marks into dollar assets, in the process leading to a dollar appreciation. The correct response is to stabilize the exchange rate, buying German securities and selling dollar bonds. Note that the appropriate response is *sterilized* intervention. Printing money in response to an appreciation induced by portfolio shifts is an entirely and totally unsound policy response. Exchange-rate-oriented monetary policy is appropriate only when, implausibly, international currency substitution is the dominant source of monetary disturbances.[2]

Of course, there are macroeconomic disturbances that call for adjustments not only in the relative supplies of securities, but also in other macroeconomic variables. It is hard to think of an empirically important disturbance where the only appropriate response is to sustain exchange rates by expanding money in one country and contracting it abroad. As a rule we would expect adjustments in interest rates, in exchange rates and in fiscal policy in both countries. Dealing with disturbances exclusively by unsterilized intervention as the cure-all may in fact aggravate the consequences of asynchronized policies.

The large, cumulative movements of real exchange rates of the past three years have once again brought up proposals for some international arrangement that limits cumulative exchange rate movements within a given time period, that is, some form of exchange rate target zone. The specifics of the proposals — crawling pegs with soft bumpers — are often reminiscent of OSHA (Office of Safety and Health Administration) regulations.

Limiting real exchange rate fluctuations by international understandings on target zones would be a good idea under some circumstances. But such agreements without explicit and specific targets for real interest rates and the monetary-fiscal policy mix are a serious mistake.

Surely we have understood by now that implementing exchange rate targets requires changes in monetary and fiscal policy — the fundamentals. Even recognizing the potential for monetary policy to influence exchange rates, I believe it would be a mistake to leave fiscal policy out of an agreement on limits to the admissible range of key macroeconomic variables. . . .

Exchange-rate-oriented monetary policy, in the current U.S. conditions, would take a high dollar as a signal to expand money and would lead us to monetize fiscal deficits, rather than to correct the fiscal imbalance. Surely this must be considered extremely unwise policy advice even on the part of those who believe money is tight. On the contrary, the appropriate adjustment for the USA is to cut future deficits and for Europe to engage in transitory fiscal expansion. Given the difficulties, however, of reconciling fiscal targets, I believe there is no practical room for exchange rate targets. On the contrary, the extreme exchange rate overvaluation is an almost desirable check against persistence of the fiscal imbalance.

Aside from exchange-rate-oriented monetary policy there have been specific proposals to reduce the competitive pressure on U.S. business by causing a yen appreciation. The proposals involve various ways in which the world demand for yen securities would be increased, [thereby reducing Japan's capital-account deficit and reducing its current-account surplus] — Japanese financial liberalization, the yen as a world currency, invoicing world trade in yen, etc. The effectiveness of these proposals, unlike that of proposals in the area of trade and procurement liberalization, is vastly overrated and their merit is questionable. The experience with removal of exchange control in the UK or restrictions on U.S. private gold holdings does not suggest that changes in controls in fact lead to major changes in asset prices.

More basically the proposals involve the proposition that Japan should have higher unemployment and the USA less, unless Japan chooses to expand aggregate demand through fiscal policy. It is unreasonable that, faced with our own unbalanced fiscal policies, we should now recommend that Japan adjust. The more appropriate view is in the first place not to single out Japan, but to focus on the USA relative to other industrialized countries. This is appropriate because, as we saw above, the USA has got out of line. Any sensible cure of the dollar overvaluation requires restructuring world-wide fiscal policies to remove the extreme fiscal asynchronization already discussed above in [Table 2].

It may be useful to add that fiscal coordination could take the form of a long run cut in U.S. deficits, matched in Europe by a transitory, cyclical increase in high employment deficits. The lower long run U.S. deficits would reduce long run real interest rates and thus add to expansion, as would the European fiscal expansion. The world economy, and in particular the LDCs, would more certainly enjoy a sustained expansion. . . . A dollar depreciation that would be expected in such a policy package would prove inflationary for the USA, but it is certainly true that today we are in a much better position to accept some inflationary shock than another year into the recovery when commodities and labour markets will be much tighter.

REFORM OF THE INTERNATIONAL MONETARY SYSTEM

The world macroeconomy is in the process of dramatic experiments with inflation stabilization and fiscal imbalance, superimposed on sharp changes in sectoral international competitiveness. This is a very poor time to think of moving towards an exchange rate regime that limits exchange rate fluctuations without, at the same time, achieving a believable coordination of monetary and fiscal policy. The initial conditions vary widely between countries — Europe and Japan are tightening while the USA is expanding — inflation rates diverge significantly and the starting point is an overvalued dollar.

It is clear that the flexible exchange rate system is poorly suited to deal with asynchronized monetary and fiscal policy mixes: under these conditions flexible rates work poorly in the sense that they show large, cumulative movements away from levels justified by current levels of demand. But other exchange rate arrangements would cope as poorly. The problem is not the exchange rate system but the policy mix. Few would argue that bond markets need intervention just because real interest rates are unusually high. It is well understood, at least by those who understand, that this is a reflection of the policies that influence demand and supply conditions in the bond market. The same is true of the exchange market and [the] answer is more sensible policy mixes (monetary, fiscal and incomes policy), not schemes to fix interest rates or exchange rates.

Notes

1. See *Government Deficit Spending and Its Effects on Prices of Financial Assets,* Office of the Assistant Secretary for Economic Policy, Department of the Treasury, May 1983, p. 15. The study not only fails to make the distinction between actual and full employment budgets but also fails to understand the forward-looking nature of asset markets as evidenced on p. 7.
2. This point is well understood in the conduct of domestic monetary policy, but remains surprisingly controversial in a foreign exchange market context even today. See R. McKinnon, *Why Floating Exchange Rates Fail,* Stanford University, June 1983.

23

What Can Central Banks Do About the Value of the Dollar?

Dallas S. Batten and Mack Ott

. . . The purpose of this paper is to explain the fundamentals of central bank intervention in foreign exchange markets and the conditions required for it to be effective. First, the motives, mechanics and consequences of intervention are discussed. Next, the relationship between intervention and domestic monetary policy is investigated. Finally, some qualitative and quantitative evidence on the efficacy of intervention is reviewed.

WHY CENTRAL BANKS INTERVENE

The exchange rate is the price of one country's currency in terms of another. As the relative price of two assets (currencies), it is determined by the forces of demand and supply, as are the prices of other assets, such as stocks, bonds or real estate. Moreover, the relative valuations of and yields on noncurrency assets also have, as we shall see, large impacts on the exchange rate.

Unlike the prices of services or nondurable goods, asset prices reflect primarily the market's expectations about future economic conditions. Consequently, in the short run, exchange rates should be influenced predominantly by

From Federal Reserve Bank of St. Louis *Review* 66 (May 1984), pp. 16–25. Some text, footnotes, and references omitted or altered.

new information — that is, surprises — which alters expectations of future events; these surprises lead to highly unpredictable and often sizable movements in exchange rates. Because news can be incorrect and because markets can overreact to news even when it is correct, monetary authorities typically believe that much of the short-run volatility exhibited by foreign exchange markets is excessive. Consequently, intervention is frequently rationalized by central banks as a means to reduce the presumed excessive variability of exchange rate movements resulting from the variability of market expectations.

In the long run, movements of exchange rates tend toward a relationship among currencies known as purchasing power parity (PPP). That is, a dollar or yen or deutsche mark (DM) would each purchase the same amount of goods whether expended at home or abroad. Thus, a country with a relatively rapid inflation rate will have its currency decline in value relative to the currencies of countries with slower inflation rates.

Ignoring long-run considerations, frequent and offsetting exchange rate movements in the short or intermediate term can be more than just a nuisance to monetary authorities — they also can have real effects. For example, an appreciation of the exchange rate beyond that necessary to offset the inflation differential between two countries . . . raises the price of traded goods in the home country relative to the prices of traded goods[1] in the rest of the world. Thus, home country exports become less competitive in world markets and home country import substitutes less competitive in domestic markets. Consequently, sales of traded goods decline, generating unemployment in the traded goods sector and, subsequently, inducing a shift of resources from the traded to the nontraded goods sector.

This reallocation of resources is efficient for the economy if that portion of the exchange rate appreciation in excess of the inflation differential is permanent. If this excess portion of the exchange rate appreciation is short-lived (i.e., reversed in the near future), the corresponding movement of resources will be reversed, and the economy will have experienced unnecessary unemployment due to the costs of shifting resources, reallocating capital, laying off and hiring. Monetary authorities who wish to avoid such situations may intervene to oppose exchange rate movements that they believe will *not* persist. This is a feasible policy, however, only if they can distinguish temporary exchange rate fluctuations from permanent ones.

Exchange rate changes also affect the general price level and may generate some measured short-run inflation or disinflation as markets adjust to the changing relative price of traded to nontraded goods. In particular, an exchange rate depreciation raises the domestic currency price of imports and, thus, raises the domestic price level. Because the total impact of this change is not felt all at once, the price level continues to rise for some time. Thus, since exchange rate depreciation usually precedes changes in domestic prices, it may appear to cause inflation.

Finally, many domestic residents, firms and, especially, multinational corporations have financial assets and liabilities denominated in foreign currencies. Exchange rate changes, then, produce wealth effects since they generate capital losses and gains. For example, if the U.S. exchange rate unexpectedly appreciates, the dollar values of foreign-currency-denominated assets and liabilities fall. Hence, U.S. net monetary debtors in foreign currencies experience gains, and net creditors experience losses.

In sum, changes in exchange rates have consequences that monetary authorities may deem undesirable. Thus, having chosen not to allow exchange rates to be completely market-determined, many central banks intervene periodically in foreign exchange markets to mitigate what they believe to be transient but deleterious effects of exchange rate movements on the domestic economy.

HOW CENTRAL BANKS INTERVENE

The mechanics of central bank intervention in foreign exchange markets can take a variety of forms. The general purpose of each variant, however, is basically the same: augment the market demand for one currency by augmenting the market supply of another. An exhaustive explanation of the ways in which intervention can be conducted is beyond the scope of this paper.[2] Instead, we will describe the most frequently employed method — intervention by the monetary authority.

A Typical Example

Suppose that the dollar is believed to be overvalued. The Federal Reserve Bank of New York, which acts as the agent for U.S. foreign exchange market interventions, will purchase foreign currency, typically DM, with U.S. dollars.[3] It can do this simply by creating dollar reserves and using them to purchase DM. In particular, the Fed can purchase DM-denominated deposits of U.S. banks at German banks and pay for them by crediting the reserve accounts of these U.S. banks. The Fed then presents to the Bundesbank drafts drawn against accounts of these U.S. banks at German banks, which are subsequently cleared by the Bundesbank. The impact of this transaction on the financial institutions involved is outlined in [Table 1]. In general, the reserves of the U.S. banking system increase, while those of the German banking system fall. The changes in the reserve positions of the United States and Germany that result from this foreign exchange operation will cause the U.S. money stock to rise and Germany's money stock to fall.

Conversely, if the Bundesbank believes the DM to be undervalued (i.e., the dollar is overvalued), it could reduce the quantity of DM relative to dollars. This transaction is slightly more complicated than when the Fed intervenes in support of the DM. First, the Bundesbank must acquire dollars. It typically does this either by selling some of its non-negotiable U.S. Treasury securities to the Fed or by borrowing from the Fed in exchange for a dollar-denominated account through a swap arrangement already established between the two. These acquired dollars are then used to buy DM in the foreign exchange market.

In [Table 2] step 1 depicts the acquisition by the Bundesbank of a

TABLE 1
U.S. Intervention to Support the Deutsche Mark

Federal Reserve Banks (FRB)		U.S. commercial banks (cb)		Bundesbank (B)		German commercial banks (Gcb)	
+DM deposits at B	+Reserves of cb	+Reserves	−DM deposits at GcB		+DM deposits of FRB	−Reserves	−DM deposits of cb
					−Reserves of Gcb		

TABLE 2
German Intervention to Support the Deutsche Mark

Federal Reserve Banks (FRB)		U.S. commercial banks (cb)		Bundesbank (B)		German commercial banks (Gcb)	
(1) +Treasury securities	+$ deposit of B			−Treasury securities			
				+$ deposit at FRB			
(2) +Reserves of cb	−$ deposit of B	+Reserves	−DM deposits at Gcb	−$ deposit at FRB	−Reserves of Gcb	−Reserves	−DM deposits of cb

dollar-denominated deposit at the Fed. Since this transaction is between central banks, it does not affect the reserves of the banking system in either country and, hence, does not affect either country's domestic money supply. In step 2, the Bundesbank purchases DM-denominated deposits of U.S. commercial banks held at German commercial banks with dollars. This transaction is cleared by U.S. banks presenting to the Fed dollar-denominated claims against the Bundesbank and receiving reserves in return. (At the same time, the Fed reduces its deposit liabilities to the Bundesbank.) Likewise, the Bundesbank clears the draft it purchased from U.S. banks by lowering its reserve liabilities to German banks. And finally, German banks, presented with a draft against deposits of U.S. banks, reduce their deposit liabilities to these banks by the amount of the reduction in their reserve deposits at the Bundesbank. The final result is the same as in the preceding case — the reserves of the U.S. banking system rise, while those in the German banking system fall.

Sterilized vs. Unsterilized Intervention

The two examples discussed above are instances of unsterilized intervention; that is, the domestic money supplies have not been insulated from the foreign exchange market transaction. If unsterilized intervention is undertaken in large amounts, it will affect not only the money supplies of both countries, but domestic prices and interest rates as well. If monetary authorities do not want their foreign exchange market intervention to affect their domestic economies, they may sterilize its impact with an offsetting sale or purchase of domestic assets.

Sterilized intervention would be the preferred procedure if the Fed did not want the U.S. banking system's reserves to change. Thus, if the unsterilized intervention interfered with the goals of domestic monetary policy, the Fed could sell U.S. Treasury securities in U.S. financial markets equal to the amount of reserves created by the intervention. With this transaction, the level of reserves in the U.S. banking system would return to its preintervention level, and, as a result, there would be no subsequent change in the U.S. money supply.

Similarly, the Bundesbank could sterilize the impact of intervention on the German money supply by injecting new reserves into its banking system. If sterilized completely, the foreign exchange operation would not affect either country's money supply. Thus, in the case of a completely sterilized intervention, private portfolios would contain fewer DM-denominated securities and more dollar-denominated securities, while the Fed's portfolio would contain more DM-denominated securities and fewer dollar-denominated ones. . . .

Because sterilized intervention entails a substitution of dollar-denominated securities for DM-denominated ones, however, the exchange rate will be permanently affected only if the investors view domestic and foreign securities as being *imperfect* substitutes. If this is the case, investors will be unwilling to hold the new portfolio at unchanged exchange and interest rates. In fact, at the original exchange and interest rates, an excess demand for DM-denominated securities will arise. Consequently, investors will attempt to acquire additional DM-denominated securities in order to return their portfolios to the desired proportion of dollar-denominated securities, thereby placing downward pressure on the DM value of the dollar.

If investors consider these securities to be *perfect* substitutes, on the other hand, no change in either the exchange rate or in interest rates will be necessary to motivate investors to hold this portfolio. In summary, when two domestic money supplies have been unaffected by an intervention activity, the intervention can have a permanent impact on the exchange rate only if foreign and domestic securities are imperfect substitutes.

INTERVENTION AND DOMESTIC MONETARY POLICY

The foregoing discussion has emphasized that the relationship between domestic monetary policy and intervention depends on whether the intervention is sterilized. Domestic monetary policy cannot be conducted independently of unsterilized intervention since, as discussed above, it is tantamount to conducting monetary policy through foreign exchange market operations. Thus, the exchange rate is a third alternative monetary target variable to those more frequently considered — namely, monetary aggregates or interest rates.

Because there can be only one monetary policy stance, the role of unsterilized intervention depends crucially on the importance that policymakers place on the exchange rate as an objective for monetary policy. In particular, the use of unsterilized intervention necessarily implies that the monetary authority places relatively more importance on reducing the risks and real economic disturbances associated with exchange rate movements than achieving domestic targets for inflation and unemployment. The manipulation of monetary policy to achieve exchange rate objectives inevitably will conflict — occasionally or frequently — with the policy stance required to achieve these domestic objectives.

Furthermore, exchange rate movements may be motivated not only by changes in the desire to hold domestic currency (which probably should be offset by changes in the domestic money supply), but also by a host of other factors, especially the policies followed by foreign policymakers. Directing domestic monetary policy at an exchange rate target, then, subjects the domestic economy to disturbances from both domestic and foreign sources. Consequently, the monetary authority loses its ability to control its own money supply independently of foreign events.

The desire to influence exchange rate movements without losing control of the domestic money supply is the primary motivation for using sterilized intervention. Whether a monetary authority can separate exchange rate management from money stock control, however, depends on whether certain conditions are met. First, international assets (including currencies) must be imperfect substitutes. Second, the magnitude of sterilized intervention undertaken must be large enough — given the degree of imperfect substitutability — that market participants cannot undo this effect by engaging in offsetting transactions.

SOME EVIDENCE ON THE EFFECTIVENESS OF INTERVENTION

Assessing the efficacy of intervention is difficult because data on central bank intervention are not made available; in contrast to domestic central bank transactions, which are reported in great detail, international transactions are reported only in a nonsystematic, summary form. Three pieces of qualitative evidence, however, can be used to gauge the likely effectiveness of intervention. The first is an indirect assessment obtained by considering a domestic policy experiment, somewhat analogous to sterilized intervention, which occurred in the early 1960s. The second is an assessment of the potential for the U.S. monetary authorities to influence the foreign exchange market by comparing the volume of assets and the rate of transactions in these markets by private investors with the monetary authority's holdings and activities. The third is a direct assessment of U.S. and other central bank intervention activity revealed in a working group study prepared for the 1983 Williamsburg Economic Summit Meeting.

An Analogous Policy: Operation Twist

A historical example of a domestic policy experiment by the Federal Reserve that is similar to sterilized intervention is "Operation Twist." During 1961 62, the Federal Reserve sold short-term U.S. securities and used the proceeds to buy long-term U.S. securities; as with sterilized intervention, the transactions were offsetting so that the money supply was unchanged. The resulting increase in short-term government securities and the concomitant decline in long-term government securities in private portfolios were intended to raise the yield on short-term securities and lower the yield on long-term securities, thus, "twisting" the term structure.

In this effort, the first condition discussed above was met — namely, long-term securities bear higher interest rates than short-term securities, and, thus, the two assets are imperfect substitutes. Yet, the effort is generally judged to have failed primarily because the policy was not executed vigorously enough. The point . . . is that a central bank policy of affecting the term structure for interest rates depends, for its effectiveness, on two points: the bank's ability to affect significantly the relative supplies of short- and long-term financial assets and its willingness to do so. In this case of intervention in domestic asset markets, the extent of the activity was inadequate to have any significant impact.

Similarly, when sterilized intervention in foreign exchange markets is undertaken, the immediate distribution of currencies and securities denominated in those currencies is altered; two market activities, however, are thereby set in motion that tend to undo any impact on relative interest rates and the exchange rate. First, private entities — banks, primarily, but also individual traders — sell or buy securities denominated in the currencies that have been affected. Second, actual currency flows and options to buy or sell currencies or forward contracts are changed. Thus, unless the central bank is prepared to take sufficient actions to alter market expectations, it will be unlikely to affect the exchange rates by sterilized intervention.

The Potential: Foreign Asset Holdings and the Size of the U.S. Foreign Exchange Market

The likelihood that intervention can affect exchange rates may be assessed by comparing either private and central bank foreign asset holdings or central bank activity and the size of markets for foreign exchange. . . .

Chart 1 shows the stocks of foreign assets held by U.S. individuals and institutions, U.S. assets held by private foreigners, and the foreign reserves (minus gold) of the U.S. Federal Reserve System and the Treasury. It is clear that private

---

CHART 1

Relative Stocks of Holdings of Foreign Assets

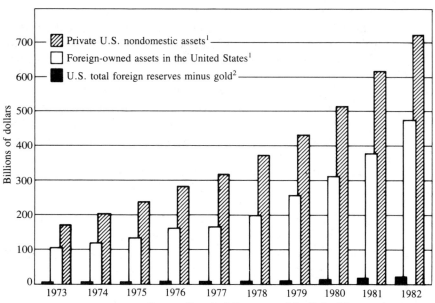

Sources: Board of Governors of the Federal Reserve System and U.S. Department of Commerce.

[1]Year-end outstanding.
[2]Annual averages of quarterly data.
Note: Direct investment data prior to 1977 do not reflect 1977 benchmark revision.

investors hold a much larger share of assets traded in international markets than do the Fed and the U.S. Treasury. Consequently, to change the price at which these assets are valued would require very aggressive intervention.

Many have argued that the primary impact of intervention is on the flow demands for the currencies involved. If so, one should compare the flows of transactions in these markets rather than asset holdings.[4] . . . From this perspective, consider the data in [Table 3], which reports the turnover statistics for U.S. banks engaging in significant volumes of foreign currency transactions.[5] As the table shows, both the volume (in the observed month) per bank and the number of banks with significant involvement in foreign currency markets have risen dramatically since 1977. The total volume has risen sevenfold, comprising a quadrupling in the per-bank volume (indicated by the changes in the activity of the banks originally surveyed in 1977) and a tripling (from 44 to 119) of the number of banks actively participating in foreign currency markets. If the volume in contracts during April 1983 is expressed in a daily average form, the market in U.S. banks alone is about $33.5 billion. Almost two-thirds of these contracts are spot currency exchanges.

In comparison, the table also reports the combined Federal Reserve–U.S. Treasury intervention for the full six-month period containing each of the three survey dates along with representative episodes of significant U.S. intervention. As even a cursory review of the data reveals, U.S. intervention activity has been trivial relative to the volume of bank trading in currencies; only rarely has intervention been more than a tiny fraction of the private market volume. Consequently, the notion that the central bank has influenced the market price of currencies — their exchange rate — purely by affecting the flow volume of exchange is inconsistent with the recent record.

Some Direct Evidence: Report of the Working Group on Exchange Market Intervention

Central bank intervention — whether in domestic asset markets or international currency markets — can be effective only if the market is convinced that the monetary authority is both able and willing to affect the flows of transactions. In view of the growing size of private currency markets and the conflict with domestic inflation policies that effective intervention would require, such an effect on market expectations also seems to be beyond the grasp of the U.S. authorities.

Support for this conclusion is provided by the study of exchange market intervention conducted by the working group established at the Versailles Summit in 1982.[6] This report is especially significant since it represents the most comprehensive analysis of the motives, methods and impacts of central bank intervention in foreign exchange markets that has been conducted using actual intervention data — data unavailable to most researchers.

TABLE 3

Market Volume in Foreign Currency Transactions and Federal Reserve-
Treasury Combined Intervention (millions of dollars)

FOREIGN CURRENCY TRANSACTIONS BY U.S. COMMERCIAL BANKS

	April 1977 (44 banks)	March 1980 (90 banks)	April 1983 (119 banks)
All banks surveyed			
Monthly average	$106,400	$491,300	$702,500
Daily average	5,300	23,400	33,500
Banks in 1977 survey	$103,100	$325,800	$432,600
	(41 banks)	(41 banks)	(40 banks)
Banks in 1980 survey	N/A	$484,000	$648,200
		(87 banks)	(87 banks)

COMBINED INTERVENTION BY THE FEDERAL RESERVE AND U.S. TREASURY

	February–July 1977	February–July 1980	February–July 1983
Total sales of currency	$212.4	$3,982.7	0
Monthly average	35.4	663.8	—
Daily average[1]	1.8	33.2	—
Total purchases of currency	$150.7	$6,266.9	$254.1[2]
Monthly average	25.1	1,044.5	—
Daily average[1]	1.3	52.2	42.4
Major episodes during period	April 15–May 4 Sold $34.8 DM	Mid-March–April 8 Purchased $1,396.2	July 29–August 5

N/A Not available

Note: Equivalent dollar values converted using exchange rates prevailing at date of transaction.

[1]Assumes 20 business days in the average month.

[2]Because the only transactions during the period were between July 29 and August 5, the period considered includes August 1–5. Consequently, the monthly average calculation is not applicable and the daily average is calculated only for these six days on which intervention took place.

Sources: Federal Reserve Bulletin, September 1977, September 1980, September 1983; Press Release, Federal Reserve Bank of New York, July 12, 1977, and June 23, 1980, and "Summary of Results of U.S. Foreign Exchange Market Turnover Survey Conducted in April 1983," Federal Reserve Bank of New York, September 8, 1983.

While the working group found that sterilized intervention is not totally ineffective, its effect was much smaller than that of unsterilized intervention. Furthermore, the group found that intervention could be effective in the face of persistent market pressures only if it was supported by complementary changes in domestic policy, especially monetary policy. When inconsistencies have arisen between domestic policy and exchange rate objectives, the group found that intervention (counter to the goals of domestic policy) was frequently useless and even counterproductive in the absence of supportive domestic policy. Consequently, the ministers, in their statement released with the working group's report, downplayed the importance of sterilized intervention as a separate policy tool:

> We have reached agreement [that], under the present circumstances, the role of [sterilized] intervention can only be limited. . . . Intervention will normally be useful only when complementing and supporting other policies.[7]

CONCLUSION

Most discussions of the effectiveness of central bank intervention focus on expectations of market participants and how intervention alters them. Yet, even if the central bank is capable of altering market expectations about its future policies, such a change can be brought about only if the market is convinced that other policy goals — the domestic inflation rate, level of interest rates, stability of domestic credit markets, etc. — are subordinate to exchange rate manipulation. For the United States, at least, such a policy stance would not be credible. Thus, the efficacy of exchange rate intervention would seem to be diminished greatly by the public's knowledge of the primacy of other monetary policy objectives.

Notes

1. Traded goods are those good that are *potentially* exportable or importable — whether or not they are actually consumed domestically or abroad. For instance, agricultural commodities, airplanes and steel are traded goods, while haircuts, legal services and housing are primarily nontraded goods. The importance of the distinction between traded and nontraded goods is that changes in foreign competition will directly affect production and sales both in the home and foreign markets in the traded goods sector, while only indirectly affecting production and sales in the nontraded goods sector.
2. See Balbach (1978) for a detailed analysis of various forms of intervention.
3. In the United States, the Federal Reserve Bank of New York intervenes for the Federal Reserve System and the U.S. Treasury. The decision to intervene, however, is made by the U.S. Treasury.
4. This leaves aside, for the moment, the indirect effect of intervention through changes in *expectations* of future central bank policy, which will be considered later.
5. The data in the first half of [Table 3] are from periodic surveys of U.S. banks that engage in significant foreign exchange market transactions. These surveys are conducted by the Federal Reserve Bank of New York. For more details about these surveys, see Revey (1981).
6. Report of the Working Group on Exchange Market Intervention (1983). What follows is a synopsis of the major conclusions drawn in this report.
7. Statement on the Report of the Working Group on Exchange Market Intervention (1983), p. 2.

References

Balbach, Anatol B. "The Mechanics of Intervention in Exchange Markets," this *Review* (February 1978), 2–7.
Report of the Working Group on Exchange Market Intervention established at the Versailles Summit of the Heads of State and Government, June 4, 5, and 6, 1982 (March 1983).
Revey, Patricia A. "Evolution and Growth of the United States Foreign Exchange Market," Federal Reserve Bank of New York *Quarterly Review* (Autumn 1981), 32–44.

24

The EMS and UK Membership

Geoffrey Dennis and Joseph Nellis

On the 13 March 1984, the European Monetary System (EMS) celebrated its fifth birthday. Contrary to the gloomy predictions made by many of its early critics, who feared that it would quickly collapse under both internal and external pressures, the system has survived intact. Given the turbulence in the international monetary system since 1979, this in itself is a considerable achievement.

Once the debate over the ability of the EMS to survive for any length of time had been silenced by events, much attention was focused on the possibility that Britain might, at some point in time, become a full member of the system. . . . Since the EMS's inception, successive governments in the UK have staunchly rejected the possibility of any greater involvement than membership in the European Monetary Cooperation Fund and the inclusion of sterling in the European Currency Unit (ECU). No decision has yet been taken for sterling to become a member of the exchange-rate mechanism of the system, which is, clearly, the most public element of the EMS.

THE SUCCESSES OF THE EMS

That the EMS has been able to overcome certain "crisis" periods in the past five years is testament to the flexibility inherent in the system's design and arrangements. This flexibility has had two main elements. First, the value of each member currency has been allowed to fluctuate within a 2.25 percent range on either side of its bilateral central rate against all other currencies (with Italy availing itself, as a nonmember of the previous snake arrangements, of fluctuation bands of 6 percent). These fluctuation bands have reduced the amount of intervention needed in

From *Lloyds Bank Review*, no. 154 (October 1984), pp. 13–31. Reprinted by permission. Some text and footnotes omitted or altered.

comparison to a system of immutably fixed parities. Secondly, as an arrangement of "adjustable" parities, necessary realignments of central rates were always envisaged if the divergence pressure between two or more currencies became too persistent to be accommodated at the existing central rates.

One notable success of the EMS has been the way in which the realignments of central rates have been carried out. Seven realignments have occurred to date and their details are set out in Table 1. . . . One trend has been the increasing complexity of these realignments as time has passed, culminating in the general reorganisation of parities in March 1983. With the exception, perhaps, of the Belgian franc devaluation in February 1982, the realignments have, however, been fairly modest in scale. The result has been a considerably lower volatility of member currencies than that generally experienced by other major currencies outside the EMS.

Table 2 . . . illustrates this argument[1], by demonstrating that the monthly changes in the effective exchange rates of EMS currencies have been significantly lower than those of the three major outside currencies in all years since 1979. . . . In 1979, 1980 and again in 1983-mid 1984, the limited volatility of EMS currencies was remarkable, with the average absolute monthly change being under one percent except for the Danish krone and Irish punt. Such a comparison of the volatility of exchange rates inside the EMS with outside currencies is a much more reliable guide to the success of the EMS in stabilising currency values than is any comparison with a period, such as prior to 1979, when the EMS was not in existence.

The timing of EMS realignments has frequently been linked to the performance of the U.S. dollar. Dollar weakness generally causes strains in the system as flows of money move out of the American currency and into the two major "hard" currency alternatives, namely the yen and, with implications for the EMS, the deutschemark. Given that these flows do not go into the other EMS currencies in similar quantities, upward pressure on the deutschemark in the system is inevitable. This experience illustrates that the desire of the founders of the EMS to achieve a situation where all EMS currencies would be considered as equal alternatives to the dollar has not yet materialized. Moreover, it is unlikely to do so given the existing institutional framework of the EMS. In contrast, it is widely agreed that the relative calm within the system since March 1983 has been due above all to the *strength* of the U.S. dollar relative to the deutschemark and also at times to a *weak* deutschemark within the EMS. This stresses the point that the EMS is crucially linked to the fortunes of an external currency.

A common criticism made of the EMS is that it has failed to bring about greater convergence of economic policies and performances. This is a complicated issue in many respects, not least concerning the definition of convergence and the debate over the standard against which EMS performance in this respect should be compared. Although, since 1980–81, virtually all European Community governments (apart from France and Italy who followed this trend somewhat later) have pursued restrictive monetary policies, at times supported by similar tightness

TABLE 1

Realignments of Exchange Rates Within the EMS, 1979–1984

	DATES OF REALIGNMENTS*						
	24 September 1979	30 November 1979	23 March 1981	5 October 1981	22 February 1982	14 June 1982	21 March 1983
Belgian franc/ Luxembourg franc	0	0	0	0	-8.5	0	+1.5
Danish krone	-2.9	-4.8	0	0	-3.0	0	+2.5
Deutschemark	+2.0	0	0	+5.5	0	+4.25	+5.5
French franc	0	0	0	-3.0	0	-5.75	-2.5
Irish pound (punt)	0	0	0	0	0	0	-3.5
Italian lira	0	0	-6.0	-3.0	0	-2.75	-2.5
Netherlands guilder	0	0	0	+5.5	0	+4.25	+3.5

*Calculated as the percentage change against the group of currencies whose bilateral parities remained unchanged in the realignment, except for the most recent realignment (21 March 1983) in which the bilateral central rates of all currencies were adjusted as shown — for details see *Bulletin of the European Communities* No. 3, Vol. 16, 1983.

Source: Commission of the European Communities.

TABLE 2

Variability* of EMS and other major currencies

	April–Dec 1979	1980	1981	1982	Jan 1983–June 1984	Apr 1979–June 1984
EMS CURRENCIES						
Deutschemark	0.823	0.906	1.471	0.665	0.923	0.962
Netherlands guilder	0.656	0.644	1.375	0.540	0.733	0.793
French franc	0.704	0.770	1.373	1.290	0.999	1.041
Italian lira	0.526	0.851	1.326	0.649	0.684	0.813
Belgian franc	0.538	0.683	0.712	1.783	0.701	0.934
Danish krone	1.183	1.031	1.493	1.220	0.966	1.164
Irish pound	0.836	1.137	1.365	1.513	1.270	1.246
OTHER MAJOR CURRENCIES						
British pound	1.962	1.161	1.698	1.110	1.478	1.458
U.S. dollar	1.063	1.619	1.875	1.993	1.306	1.595
Japanese yen	2.120	2.331	1.621	2.253	1.259	1.864

*Calculated as the average of monthly absolute percentage changes in the effective index for each currency. [The effective index is an index number measuring the average rate of change of a currency's exchange rates against all other currencies. The average is often "weighted," often by bilateral trade shares.]

Source: Bank of England.

in [fiscal policy], with the overriding objective of reducing inflation, there has been limited convergence of macroeconomic policy *design* arising from the EMS itself. Certainly the recent moves to achieve the de-indexation of wage increases in Belgium, France and Italy and the reversal of the policies of the Mitterrand administration may be in part attributable to the constraints of the EMS. However, the overall similarity of policy in this period was much more a reaction to the fear of high inflation — in the aftermath of the second round of oil-price increases and latterly to cope with the increasing strength of the U.S. dollar — than to any planned harmonization of policy to further the objectives of the EMS.

Convergence . . . is typically taken to mean a narrowing of monetary policy differentials in terms of either the intermediate objectives (monetary growth and rates of interest) or the goals of economic policy, notably inflation rates. As shown in the following section, the EMS was relatively unsuccessful on these terms . . . early in its life; however, since early 1982 a notable convergence of performances has been achieved.

A crucial point is that any judgment on convergence must be made in the light of the prevailing economic environment. The true comparison is between the EMS period and that same period had the EMS *not been* in existence. This requires a genuine counterfactual exercise which in the field of political economy is difficult if not impossible to undertake. In particular, any comparison of economic performance between the EMS era and the more tranquil 1975–78 period, as was the case when looking at exchange rate volatility, is biased against the EMS. What is clear, however, is that the EMS, by its very existence and the constraints built into it, has helped to prevent a *greater* divergence of economic developments in the member countries.

BRITISH GOVERNMENT ATTITUDES TO THE EMS

Although a member of the other institutional elements of the EMS, sterling has remained outside the exchange-rate mechanism [ERM] throughout its existence. Despite this consistency of action (or inaction), official justification for the refusal to link sterling to the EMS has changed . . . more than once since the system was first mooted. These, at times very subtle, changes of position may be easily identified from the study of official documents, speeches, etc. in the last five years.

At the time of the main EMS discussions in the autumn of 1978, a Green Paper was issued, setting out a number of characteristics that the EMS should possess, presumably before full membership by the UK would be contemplated by the then Labour government. Without listing all of these, the major requirements were that the EMS:

    i. should be durable;
    ii. should involve symmetrical adjustment obligations on both strong and weak members;

iii. should be truly European by aiding economic convergence in the Community; and

iv. should reinforce efforts to improve worldwide currency stability.

The British government hoped that the new arrangement would be sufficiently different from the old snake scheme in the sense that it would be flexible enough to cope with any initial differences of economic situation. Linked to this, and perhaps of even more immediate relevance, the authorities were clearly afraid that sterling would be unable to hold its position in the EMS once a decision to join had been taken. It was hoped that the flexibility of the EMS would help the system's overall cohesion and durability, in comparison with the snake, and increase the likelihood that sterling would not be faced with an early and embarrassing exit. In practice, the British government considered that the EMS was insufficiently innovative to provide this durability.

It is widely accepted that, like the Bretton Woods system of fixed exchange rates prior to December 1971, the snake arrangement had imposed greater adjustment responsibilities on countries with balance of payments deficits than on surplus nations. The British government wished to see a system established that would involve equal obligations on all divergent member states to intervene and make domestic policy adjustments. Such symmetrical adjustment would be best facilitated by what became known as the "basket" system of intervention rules, whereby intervention obligations would be determined by an exchange rate's position vis-a-vis the weighted average of other Community currencies (i.e. the ECU). In this situation, one currency *alone* could be considered "divergent." In contrast, many other Community governments proposed the introduction of a "parity grid" arrangement in which the crucial trigger would be a currency's position against any one or more other currencies, on an individual cross-rate basis. Under this alternative system, if one currency is too strong, the mirror image is that at least one other is too weak. In this situation, the burden of adjustment is unclear, but likely to fall primarily on the deficit country. The final compromise of parity grid with a "divergence indicator" based on the ECU basket was seen as sufficiently unsatisfactory for sterling not to join the exchange-rate mechanism. The aniticipated deflationary bias of such a system, with Germany widely expected to be the dominant country, was considered unacceptable to the government.

The third official concern was the ability of the EMS to achieve genuine convergence, which

> cannot be imposed by a particular exchange rate mechanism; it must develop from adequate coordination of economic policies. (Cmnd 7405, p. 7)

This argument was a throwback to the debate in . . . the 1960s between those economists who favoured convergence before exchange rates were fixed and those who held the view that this chain of events should be reversed. Although, like Ireland and Italy, the UK was offered special credit arrangements to facilitate sterling's transition to the EMS, these, along with certain regional policy initiatives were considered inadequate. Accordingly, they were used as a widely publicised reason for the failure of sterling to join the exchange-rate mechanism.

Finally, the absence of any attempt to design a co-ordinated strategy for outside currencies was seen as a considerable drawback. In particular, the weakness of the dollar was one of the factors behind the initial moves towards the EMS and yet no formal decision on a common dollar policy was reached.

A further argument that forcibly entered the discussion was advanced by the [labor unions], in particular, and fully supported by the government. It was that full membership of the EMS would restrict the scope of policy-making in the UK and specifically would remove the freedom to devalue the currency to create jobs in the face of declining industrial competitiveness.

These arguments, then, constituted the official British case for sterling remaining outside the ERM at the outset. There was little or no discussion of the now familiar arguments of the correct exchange rate for sterling's entry to the EMS or of its emerging petrocurrency status. Perhaps most surprisingly, given the introduction of money supply targets in 1976, there was little discussion of the issue of the independence of monetary policy. On the contrary, the authorities argued against the ability of a floating exchange rate to insulate an economy from overseas disturbances and stated that some stability of sterling's external value was important. Almost as an afterthought towards the end of the Green Paper, it was stated that

> there is the possibility of a conflict between a fixed exchange rate policy and a policy for control of the money supply. (Cmnd 7405, p. 19)

However, the perceived limits to this conflict were clear from the statement that

> the claim that joining the EMS would involve a loss of economic independence is only partially true. (Cmnd 7405, p. 19)

The proponents of the EMS hoped in May 1979 that the new Conservative government, with its more pro-European-Community views than the outgoing administration, would allow sterling, albeit a little belatedly, to join the EMS in full. That this did not happen was the result of a completely different set of arguments than those officially advanced only a few months previously.

One of the leading aims of the new government was the reduction of inflation through firm control of the money supply. . . . Despite a variety of other economic objectives, including the strengthening of economic incentives and other moves to improve the "supply-side" of the economy, there was to be no wavering from the path of monetary discipline, even in the event of unanticipated exogenous shocks (of which one, a substantial rise in the price of oil, had already occurred during 1979.) . . .

These early policy strictures amounted to the new world of rigid monetarism. The implications for all prices — including interest rates and exchange rates — of such extreme monetarism is that they are market-determined. Such crucial variables must be allowed to adjust fully in the unrelenting pursuit of money supply control. Given these views, membership of any fixed exchange rate scheme, even the EMS, with its inbuilt flexibility of fluctuation bands and the possibility of realignments, became unthinkable. . . .

[Another] argument against membership of the EMS was the effect of higher oil prices on the performance of sterling. Accompanying the most recent oil crisis in 1979 and its aftermath, sterling rose sharply in value, aided by the tough anti-inflationary stance of the new government. Many argued that sterling had become a petro-currency and, as such, would be buffetted by the vagaries of the oil market. This would make close links with the EMS currencies, none of which had this petro-status to any significant degree, very difficult. Furthermore, if sterling were to join the EMS at its inflated value of 1980–81, the loss of competitiveness in British industry would be severe. These arguments focused, therefore, on the possibility that sterling's petro-currency status [might] encourage deindustralisation. They were similar to those faced somewhat earlier by the Netherlands (the so-called "Dutch disease") as a result of that country's natural gas resources. The logical conclusion was to continue to allow sterling to float outside the EMS.

The first signs that some modification of this rigid approach to economic policy might be under way came early. . . . A radical adjustment . . . followed in the March 1982 Budget. . . . The overall approach set out in the 1982 Budget constituted a movement away from the uncompromising type of monetarism of the first months of the Tory government. As such, it became feasible once more to consider the possibility of the UK joining the EMS in full. . . .

. . . It is now widely agreed that the relative amount of autonomy over monetary policy given up in a fixed exchange rate arrangement is limited. Even under completely floating exchange rates, total insulation from real economic disturbances is unlikely to be achieved, particularly for a small, open economy in the EMS. On the other side of the argument, some monetary autonomy is likely to be retained under fixed rates due to the ability of monetary authorities to undertake short-term sterilization operations and the fact that capital is unlikely to be infinitely mobile internationally. The thrust of this argument is that this discussion is not therefore a comparison of two extremes. The adoption of an exchange rate target will only involve moving along a spectrum of policy choices.

This point is given further weight by the institutional details of the EMS. Despite the limitation on cross-rate variations of ± 2.25 percent around central rates and the constraints of the divergence indicator, the system has twice the flexibility of the defunct snake, while Italy makes use of even wider bands. Further, the operation of the EMS has been very flexible given the number of realignments and the tendency for the system to operate as a sophisticated form of "crawling peg." Combining these arguments it is notable that Germany, in particular, has successfully reconciled monetary targets with EMS membership as they have both been pursued with a degree of flexibility.

Despite the perceptible shift in the discussion of money supply targets

since the beginning of 1982, official pronouncements are little different in sub-
stance from those made at that time and UK entry into the EMS is clearly not
imminent. . . .

. . . Of great importance [in addition to the economic factors discussed
above], the British government's willingness to take up full membership in the
EMS may well depend on certain psychological and political factors. In essence,
these can be reduced to two key issues, namely that Britain seems to possess an
in-built aversion to being bracketed in the same monetary category as the rest of
Europe, and, secondly, the British authorities seem to have an innate reluctance to
consider formal devaluations of sterling. Some commentators go so far as to argue
that the EMS survives only as a "deutschemark bloc," such that the addition of
sterling would add to any disruptive pressures already present in the system.
British membership would result in the system embracing three of the world's
major currencies — the deutschemark, the French franc and sterling. The sheer
mechanics of keeping these currencies aligned *could* prove to be much more
difficult than maintaining stability between just two.

BRITISH MEMBERSHIP AND INSTITUTIONAL
DEVELOPMENT OF THE EMS

While the history of the EMS has seen considerable success in the operation of its
exchange-rate mechanism, the institutional development in the system has been
disappointing, with the notable exception of the increasing private role of the
ECU.

Full membership by sterling, and ultimately the Greek drachma, of the
EMS will significantly aid the process of financial integration in the EEC. In
particular, it is likely to facilitate the move to Stage 2 of the institutional development of the EMS. At the outset of the system, it was planned that [by early 1981],
the second stage involving the translation of the [European Monetary Cooperation
Fund] into the European Monetary Fund (EMF) and the full use of the ECU as a
reserve asset and means of settlement, would be achieved. In practice . . . there
were two main difficulties. First, the worsening economic situation exposed the
hollowness of such institutional moves and the German authorities, in particular,
were reluctant to consider such steps when economic performances were actually
diverging. Secondly, disagreement surfaced over how the powers and
responsibilities of the newly created EMF would be discharged and over the actual
route by which greater institutional integration would be achieved. The result was
an *impasse* which full British membership might . . . have helped to avoid.

In a wider sense, too, the cohesion of the [European Community] would
be aided by all member countries being full partners in the EMS. The design of the
Common Agricultural Policy . . . was always such that its optimum performance
would occur in a system of fixed exchange rates. . . .

A further point is that if the UK does not intend to become a member of
the EMS, whatever the circumstances, sterling should logically cease to be a

TABLE 3

International Bond Issues (by currency)

$ mn	1981	1982	1983	First half 1984
Dollars	25,761.2	42,228.2	39,230.4	27,272.5
Deutschemark	1,396.3	3,252.7	4,042.1	2,120.5
Sterling	535.0	845.6	2,152.5	1,801.4
ECUs	152.9	823.4	2,191.4	1,482.1
SDRs	429.6	—	—	—
Total issues	31,294.1	50,328.6	50,123.2	34,513.3
Shares (%) in total of				
ECUs	0.5	1.6	4.4	4.3
SDRs	1.4	—	—	—

Source: Organization for Economic Cooperation and Development

constituent of the ECU. It is claimed that one of the reasons for the, at times, unsatisfactory performance of the divergence indicator is the anomalous position of sterling being in the ECU but outside the exchange-rate mechanism of the EMS.

The rapidly increasing use of the ECU in private-sector transactions stands in marked contrast to this official slowness. Table 3 . . . shows the rapid expansion of international bond issues denominated in ECUs since 1981. In 1983 the ECU was the third most important currency, after the dominant dollar and the deutschemark, in the international bond markets. In particular, it is clearly the most important of the available currency baskets, with Special Drawing Rights (SDRs) having played no role at all in these markets since 1981.

The reason for the ECU's increasing private use is that, as with other currency baskets, it provides greater exchange-rate stability than the strongest and weakest currencies in the basket. It has, also, generally provided a relatively cheap form of finance in terms of both interest costs and exchange-rate risk.

CONCLUSION

Over five years after its formal establishment, the EMS is still very much in operation. The system has demonstrated an ability to overcome certain difficulties, not least through the agreement on major exchange rate realignments. However the EMS can, in no sense, be considered complete while Britain is not a full member. As we have set out in this paper, the ability of successive British governments to advance arguments against EMS membership has been remarkable. Notwithstanding this, the present configuration of relevant factors including the current design of macroeconomic policy, the level of sterling against EMS currencies and the gradual, but inevitable, decline of the petro-status of the pound makes full membership of the EMS particularly appropriate. . . .

Note

1. For more detailed results of this sort, including evidence that the volatility of the real (i.e., inflation-adjusted) exchange rates has also been lower in the EMS than outside, see also Ungerer, H. with Evans, O. and Nyberg, P., "The European Monetary System: The Experience, 1979–82," *International Monetary Fund,* Occasional Paper No. 19, May 1983.

VIII

Background and Issues in International Monetary Reform

Q. How's life in the lifeboats?
A. Not very comfortable, not very fast, and not very safe. But it's a lot better than the alternative.
Q. I'll bet you're all really looking forward to getting back on board a big ship again, aren't you?
A. Not if it's another *Titanic*.

This exchange illustrates the tension to be felt in the readings below. The reader's verdict from Part VII may have been that generalized floating works poorly. It may nevertheless be the best exchange-rate system possible in what Goldstein called the "harsh global operating environment" of the 1970s and 1980s. Corden especially defends this position in his contribution below, and Cooper respects it, too. But Cooper has hopes for a better ship, a reformed international monetary system. Corden, in turn, respects the possible value of Cooper's ideal, but wonders whether it would simply sink again, as did the ship built in Bretton Woods.

Cooper's vision for the year 2010 is for a currency area among the world's industrial democracies — a zone of credibly and inalterably fixed exchange rates, coming about essentially from the joint adoption of one common currency. His vision parallels fully the financial federalism enjoyed by the United States, as Corden observes. Industrial democracies would function like states of the (currency) union. Each would have independent fiscal policy, just as Pennsylvania and Texas do. None would have independent monetary policy. Instead, an international council of finance ministers would function like the Board of Governors of the Federal Reserve System. Currency issued by the "Federal Reserve Banks" of Italy and England would be perfectly substitutable, albeit distinguishable, just as is currency issued by the Federal Reserve Banks of Philadelphia and Dallas. Balance-of-payments adjustment on both current and capital accounts would take place among nations just as easily (or as painfully) as it does among states in the United States.

Cooper is sanguine but not naive about what it would take to achieve his vision. He mentions explicitly: time (at least 25 years);

convergence of political values; and gradual willingness of developed countries such as Sweden and the United States to submit to surveillance by a supranational agency like the International Monetary Fund.

Cooper suggests two practical steps to move toward his ideal. One is to make stabilization of real exchange rates have greater weight as a goal of monetary policy. This is a familiar recommendation from Part VII readings, and certain problems with it are discussed there (in the introduction and by Dunn). Cooper himself doubts at one point that governments know enough to do this predictably. Solomon points out yet another problem in commenting on Cooper's paper, also discussed by Dornbusch in Part VII. Cooper's suggestion, Solomon says, amounts practically to unsterilized intervention to iron out variation in nominal exchange rates, which is the principal cause of variation in real exchange rates (Corden). As such, Cooper's mechanism is a gold-standard style of adjustment to external shocks, with all its familiar disadvantages.

Cooper finds the alternative scenario to his ideal very unattractive. He labels it "piecemeal retroregression," since its key characteristic is increasing barriers to international trade and capital movements. These barriers would disintegrate the open world economy of the 1970s and 1980s and return it to its segmentation of earlier decades.

Cooper would have been more sanguine about his alternative scenario if he believed that barriers to capital movements due to "noisy news" could be imposed without inviting barriers to movements of goods and real capital. He even reminds the reader that this was the premise of the founders of the Bretton Woods system, who never envisioned convertibility of currency for *all* capital-account transactions. This is also the premise of those today who favor exchange-market transaction taxes and other capital controls (see Goldstein's and Dunn's contributions to Part VII). Cooper has grave doubts, however, about the ability to regulate some transactions but not others in today's trading environment. In rejecting the premise, he points to innovations in financial transfer (many offshore), to the sheer size of intracorporate international transactions, and to the inextricable link between financial-credit terms and current prices in durables trade.

Corden sees potential in Cooper's alternative scenario anyway, in spite of the inevitable problems that the current "nonsystem" has to overcome. He finds more logic in the "nonsystem" than at first appears. He also sees potential for Cooper's vision of credibly fixed exchange rates, but is less hopeful than Cooper for this ever coming to pass, even in 2010. Corden has a healthy respect for government's ability to fail worse than markets (Grubel calls this "nonmarket failure"), especially when attempting a joint effort as grandiose as Cooper's ideal. For example, Corden slyly identifies how familiar pleas for more policy coordination are like supporting motherhood, calling them "simpleminded prescriptions." If forced to make a choice, Corden would choose market failure over government failure.

Corden illustrates this preference most clearly in his skepticism about the second of Cooper's practical steps for getting from "here to 2010," namely "to breathe some life into the SDR by providing for a new allocation . . . plus making efforts to give the SDR an existence in the world of private finance." Try as he may, Corden cannot find any compelling reason to do so — *except* as a step toward Cooper's ideal. And since he doubts that Cooper's ideal is attainable, or even necessarily desirable, he is not quick to advocate stepping out toward it.

Corden painstakingly reveals an economist's insistence that government planners identify what the difficulty is with the market's solution to their problem, and that they explain why they would succeed better at solving it. Grubel's comment on Corden's paper is very much in this spirit. Grubel first enumerates several market inefficiencies in money creation. He uses these, arguing by analogy, to establish an economic case for a world central bank presiding over a single world money. Grubel then suggests rules and structures that would prevent the world central bank from "failing" due to bureaucratic abuse. His suggestions come very close to Cooper's ideal.

25

Is There a Need for Reform?

Richard N. Cooper

I. INTRODUCTION

The very notion of "reform of the international monetary system" is a very modern one in two respects. "Reform" is a conscious act, an act of volition and coordinated will, as distinguished from a series of piecemeal changes that occur as individual actors — banks, business firms, governments — respond to new circumstances, leading over time to change, but not to conscious reform. Second, the notion of an "international monetary system" reflects a distinctive perspective, an overview of

From *The International Monetary System: Forty Years After Bretton Woods,* Conference Series No. 28 (Boston: Federal Reserve Bank, 1984), pp. 19–39, 53–55. Some text omitted from A. Solomon's discussion.

how all of the pieces work together and a focus on the ultimate results from the behavior of individual agents, taken collectively, to be distinguished from how individual firms, banks or governments will or should behave in the international monetary domain, given its major features.

These two notions come naturally to us. But it was not always the case. It was perhaps the distinctive characteristic of the original Bretton Woods conference, and of the negotiations leading up to them, that this system-wide perspective, to be reformed, was adopted in full for the first time. The architects were addressing the structure of the international monetary system as a whole; and they were, as a collaborative act of volition, attempting to reform the entire system from the ground up. They had been shaken by the performance of the "nonsystem" of the 1930s and the short-lived gold exchange standard of the 1920s, and they wanted to build a stable, durable structure that would accommodate both the new commitment to activist macroeconomic policy at the national level, and a high degree of freedom for international trade at the international level.

To be sure, antecedents can be found here as in virtually all domains. There were several discussions during the nineteenth century of bimetalism, and how best to preserve it, but they were somewhat desultory. The 1922 Genoa conference was convened to figure out how to restore the prewar gold standard in view of the perceived global shortage of gold at postwar price levels. That conference clearly took a system-wide perspective, but the changes suggested were limited and piecemeal, designed to preserve as much as possible of the old structure. It was English-style evolutionary reform, rather than American-style constitutional reform, starting with the fundamentals rather than with what was inherited from the past.

In what follows I will comingle both types of reform. American-style or constitutional reform has the advantage of forcing thought with respect to what objectives are to be served. What do we really want out of the international monetary system? Evolutionary reform has the advantage of avoiding radical changes and building on what we are already accustomed to, yet adapting to new circumstances over time. It has the disadvantage that we can engage in it and at the same time avoid thinking about what are our basic objectives, running the risk that divergences in objectives become a hidden agenda in the efforts at piecemeal reform.

The plan of the paper is as follows. Part II offers a brief sketch of the main features of the Bretton Woods system and why it failed, drawing attention to two intrinsic flaws in the original conception. Part III briefly characterizes the present system and suggests that it is workable and even useful, but unstable in the long run — again, it suffers from two fundamental weaknesses. Part IV offers a technically workable scheme for the twenty-first century, which however calls for major political commitments to international collaboration by the key countries, commitments which are much too ambitious for the present time. Part V brings us back to the present and suggests what steps we might take in the near future with a view to reaching the longer term objective as it becomes politically possible. Part VI offers a few concluding remarks.

II. THE BRETTON WOODS SYSTEM

The system that emerged from Bretton Woods had five key structural features:

First, it provided a great deal of freedom consciously to pursue national economic objectives, with the objective of assuring full employment, price stability, economic growth, and so forth. The Bretton Woods agreement was produced in the same climate of opinion which resulted in the Beveridge Report in the United Kingdom, the Full Employment Act in the United States, and comparable legislation or statements of national policy in other countries, deriving directly from the experience of the 1930s and from the determination that that experience should never be repeated.

Second, the Bretton Woods system stipulated that exchange rates between currencies should be fixed. It was taken for granted that fixed exchange rates were desirable against the background of the turbulent periods of flexible exchange rates that prevailed in the early 1920s and again briefly in the early 1930s.

Third, currencies should be convertible one into another for current account transactions. Again, that stipulation was against the background of extensive use of exchange controls by Nazi Germany during the 1930s and the tight wartime restrictions on trade and payments levied by many countries and which the Bretton Woods architects considered it desirable to end as quickly as possible.

These three features taken together — autonomy of national policies, fixed exchange rates, and convertibility of currencies — were in conflict with one another. Countries could not frame their national economic policies independently and still maintain fixed exchange rates and currency convertibility except by luck and coincidence. The Bretton Woods architects recognized this conflict and therefore added two further features:

Fourth, provision was made for medium-term international lending to cover balance of payments deficits that might result temporarily from the combination of the first three features. A new institution, the International Monetary Fund, was created as a vehicle for this new lending.

Fifth, countries were allowed, and in time came to be encouraged, to alter their exchange rates if it became clear that imbalances in payments were not temporary in nature. In other words, if a "fundamental disequilibrium" emerged, the exchange rate was to be changed by a discrete amount, with international agreement, in recognition that it would be inappropriate to finance such imbalances indefinitely.

These then were the basic features of the Bretton Woods system. There were of course many additional details. Interestingly, however, there was no provision in the Bretton Woods system for secular growth in international liquidity beyond a somewhat ambiguous provision permitting what was called a "uniform change in par values," that is to say, a deliberate discrete rise in the price of gold. It was implicitly assumed that new gold production taken into monetary reserves would be sufficient to provide for a growth in international liquidity. In the event, the U.S. dollar came to provide for the needed liquidity, as well as emerging as the currency of intervention in a regime in which some operating mechanism was necessary to assure that exchange rates remained fixed.

During the quarter century between 1945 and 1970, world reserves outside the United States grew by $54 billion, averaging 4.5 percent per annum. Gold provided $13 billion of this increase, of which $9 billion was from the high gold reserves of the United States (70 percent of total world monetary gold reserves in the late 1940s) and $4 billion was from new gold production. Foreign exchange, which was overwhelmingly dollars, provided $30 billion of the growth in reserves. The IMF provided $11 billion, including $3 billion of the new SDRs in the last year, 1970. U.S. reserves of course declined during this period because a substantial part of its gold stock was lost to other countries.

As it emerged — though not as it was designed — the Bretton Woods system might be said to have involved a bargain between the United States, which in the late 1940s accounted for about half of world industrial production, and the rest of the world. The bargain was that the United States would maintain domestic economic stability, and other countries would fix their currencies to the dollar and would accumulate their reserves in gold-convertible dollars. After a relatively brief period of postwar redistribution of the world's monetary gold stock, they would not actually convert their dollars into gold. Under this bargain, other countries would import economic stability from the United States. If a country got out of line with the world norm, it would have to change the par value of its currency. The United States allegedly gained some seigniorage from this bargain, but that is far from clear. The dollar reserves were not held in currency or even for the most part in demand deposits; they were in dollar-denominated assets that carried market interest rates. But what is true is that the United States gained certain room for financial manoeuvre. That is to say, it did not have to be as concerned as other countries did about how to finance a balance of payments deficit. Indeed, the very notion of balance of payments deficit was an ambiguous one for the United States under these circumstances, although that did not keep the Commerce Department from publishing figures which it called the "deficit" for many years.

A second characteristic of this arrangement was that the dollar was over-valued relative to what it would have been without steady accretion of dollars in the reserves of other countries. That feature permitted some export-led growth by the rest of the world which would not have taken place under different monetary arrangements in which the United States itself would have been somewhat more competitive in world markets.

On this view of the world, the United States broke its part of the bargain in the late 1960s by inflating too much in connection with the Vietnam War and the Great Society programs. Some Europeans thought that the United States was inflating too much even in the early 1960s. On this point, they would have found much less agreement from Americans. Indeed, the disagreement over U.S. policy in the early 1960s indicated one of the weaknesses of the supposed bargain which I have just described, namely disagreement around the world over what represented economically stabilizing behavior by the United States.

The structure of the Bretton Woods system had two intrinsic flaws in it, so that it would have broken down sooner or later even without the burst of U.S. inflation in the late 1960s. First, the gold convertibility of the dollar was bound to become increasingly doubtful as dollar liabilities rose over time relative to the U.S. gold stock. To halt the accumulation of dollars in reserves would have stifled growth of the world economy. Yet to allow the accumulation to continue would have moved the system to an increasingly fragile foundation. Robert Triffin pointed out this dilemma as early as 1959. SDRs were finally created in the late 1960s as a long-run substitute for the dollar, thus offering a solution to the dilemma. But the solution came too late. This part of the system broke down in 1971 when gold convertibility of the dollar was suspended indefinitely. Two points are worth noting in passing. The first is that the U.S. dollar was the only currency that was convertible into gold, even though the Bretton Woods agreement was formally symmetrical with regard to all currencies. The second is that countries continued to accumulate dollars in their international reserves even after gold convertibility of the dollar was suspended.

The second flaw in the Bretton Woods system was its reliance on discrete changes in exchange rates to correct imbalances in payments. Once a disequilibrium persisted long enough to be "fundamental" rather than temporary in nature, it was clear to everyone and the system thus produced the celebrated one-way option for currency speculation. Since the remedy to a fundamental disequilibrium was a jump in the value of a currency, speculators could move into or out of the currency at relatively low cost when they thought the jump would occur and take their gains after it occurred. It is interesting to note that the architects had appreciated this problem, at least in principle, and they had stipulated that currencies should be convertible for current account transactions, but not for capital account transactions. The possibility was envisioned that countries might maintain controls on capital flows under the Bretton Woods system, and indeed countries were even enjoined to help other countries maintain and enforce their systems of capital controls. So capital controls were in principle allowed under the Bretton Woods system, and indeed in a certain sense they were required by the internal logic of the system.

This feature of the system did not anticipate the changes both in the nature of trade and in international capital movements that took place over time. With improved and cheaper communications, it became easy to move capital through telegraphic transfers around the world at relatively low cost. In addition, many firms, especially American firms, began to invest heavily abroad in the postwar period, so that many intracorporate transactions became international in nature. Finally, international trade gradually evolved away from traditional commodity trade toward trade involving special orders and long-lead-time items in which payments for trade and credit terms become inextricably mixed. For all of these reasons, it became increasingly difficult to separate capital from current account transactions and to maintain control on capital transactions.

The movement of funds that was associated with anticipated discrete changes in exchange rates became quite enormous and greatly complicated the management of domestic monetary policies. In many countries, they threatened the autonomy of domestic national policy which was to have been preserved by the Bretton Woods system. For example, Germany in 1969 experienced a 25 percent increase in its money supply in a single week due to the inflow of speculative funds across the foreign exchanges and the requirement that Germany maintain the fixed value of the mark in terms of other currencies. That was more than could be effectively sterilized given the instruments available to the German authorities at that time.

In truth, the free movement of capital is incompatible with a system of exchange rates that are occasionally changed by consequential amounts and in a predictable direction. This part of the Bretton Woods system broke down definitively in 1973, although the breakdown started earlier with the move to floating exchange rates by Canada in 1970 and by Britain in 1972.

The U.S. inflation of the late 1960s resulted in large dollar outflows in the early 1970s that strained the Bretton Woods system to the breaking point. But it should be clear by now that this was only the proximate cause of the breakdown of the Bretton Woods system. It was not the fundamental cause. The intrinsic flaws in the system would have come to the surface sooner or later, in response to one strain or another. It happened to come to the fore in 1971–73.

It is worth remarking that the breakdown of the Bretton Woods system was only partial. The International Monetary Fund is an important survivor, both as a lender and as a forum for managing the international monetary system. The convertibility of currencies and the continuing autonomy of national economic policies — both features of the Bretton Woods architecture — are still taken as desiderata in a well-functioning international monetary system. It is a measure of the success of that system that we take them for granted. It was the exchange rate features of the system that broke down, and the psychologically important but technically tenuous link to the historic gold standard via the gold convertibility of the leading currency.

III. PRESENT MONETARY ARRANGEMENTS

For the past decade, the world has had monetary arrangements that have permitted a variety of exchange rate arrangements, but in practice with a much higher degree of flexibility than prevailed under the Bretton Woods system. This "nonsystem" has served the world economy rather well during a turbulent decade. It is true that the overall economic performance during the past decade, whether measured in terms of inflation rates, growth rates, or unemployment rates, has been far inferior to what it was during the 1950s and 1960s. But it probably would have been even worse if governments had tried to maintain the Bretton Woods system through the period. In view of the large disturbances which the world economy has undergone, an attempt to maintain fixed but adjustable exchange rates would almost certainly have required a much higher degree of controls over not only capital but also current transactions than in fact prevailed. Thus exchange rate flexibility helped to preserve a relatively open trading and financial system.

During the decade, moveable exchange rates have generally corrected for differentials in national inflation rates, as economists predicted they would, but the movements in exchange rates have gone beyond that and affected "real" exchange rates as well — that is, the relative prices at which the goods of one country on average trade against the goods of another. An evaluation of the period as a whole is complicated and difficult. Many of the movements in real exchange rates followed textbook patterns, responding to imbalances in current accounts, or to dramatic changes in resource endowments (such as the discovery of North Sea oil), or they followed divergent movements in aggregate demand. But some of the movements in real exchange rates have not followed textbook patterns, and even when they have, they have often been viewed as unwelcome disturbances by some countries, especially following the sharp depreciation of the U.S. dollar in 1978, and again following the sharp appreciation of the U.S. dollar in 1981 and 1982. Perhaps for this reason, most countries of the world in fact have not allowed their exchange rates to float. Rather, they have fixed their exchange rates against something — against another currency, or a basket of currencies, or, in the case of the European Monetary System, against one another. Thus it is not entirely accurate to characterize current arrangements as involving floating exchange rates. In practice, the exchange rates of several major currencies — the U.S. dollar, the Japanese yen, the British pound, the Canadian dollar — do float more or less freely, but other currencies do not float, although they have shown greater flexibility than they would have under a Bretton Woods regime.

Movements in some key bilateral exchange rates have shown sharp short-run variations on occasion during the past decade, not keyed to fundamental economic developments in any obvious way. There have been occasional weeks of average daily variations in excess of 3 percent. Why such great variability? The asset approach to exchange rate determination emphasizes that stocks of foreign exchange are like other financial assets, whose current price reflects all the information available that may have a bearing on its future value. New information may then affect market prices (in this instance exchange rates) sharply as the "market" reappraises the future in the light of new information.

This focus on financial assets represents a valuable insight, and no doubt helps to explain the abruptness of some movements in exchange rates. But it hardly helps to explain month after month of sharp variability, up and down. Much "news" in a longer perspective in fact is noise, whose bearing on the price in question can reasonably be expected to be reversed in the near, if not immediate, future.

Abrupt up and down movements in exchange rates are not, by themselves, likely to affect trade and production very much, since they should reasonably be expected to be reversed soon if they are not clearly linked to more
fundamental economic developments. The difficulty with flexible exchange rates
is that another influence is also at work, which can transmute the influence of noisy
news into larger changes in exchange rates than otherwise would take place. It is
the presence of crowd or bandwagon effects in the trading community. Few know
how to interpret the news. Many use a movement in the exchange rate itself as a
source of information about market sentiment. So as to avoid being left behind,
they jump on the bandwagon, thus pushing the exchange rate further in the
direction it tended to go initially. Expectations feed on expectations. Economic
theorists have lately discovered this phenomenon and have called it a bubble, in
which prices can be rationally pushed beyond their long-run equilibrium values so
long as the participants expect the risk of relapse to fall short of the prospect of
further gain.

When this process is operating, even those who suspect the exchange rate
has gone too far will have an interest in holding their investments so long as the
prospect for further gain outweighs the probability of reversal. Thus a secondary
judgment, oriented toward market dynamics, is superimposed on the reassessment
based on the new information, and may come to dominate the movement in
exchange rates for a time. This would not be troublesome if there were no
consequential effect on the real economy. But in some periods expectations about
the "fundamentals" may be so weakly held that the rate can be dominated by purely
market dynamics for longish periods, measured in weeks or months. When that is
so, the exchange rate may in turn affect new information, such as the recorded
change in price indices that include a heavy imported content. Or it may set in
motion urgent risk-avoiding behavior, as when multi-national firms move to
protect their quarterly balance sheet (at the expense of the operating earnings of the
firm). So a vicious circle may temporarily be set in motion. And this vicious circle
may aggravate inflation rates and hence inflationary expectations or may divert
management attention away from real long-term investment to short-term balance-
sheet considerations. In either case an unnecessary and avoidable element of
instability is introduced into national economies.

Two features of present exchange rate arrangements will not be satisfactory over the long run. First, movements in real exchange rates have major
effects on national economies, effects which are not always welcome. Yet movements in real exchange rates, while they can be influenced by national economic
policy, cannot be easily controlled by use of the usual instruments of national
economic policy because the determinants of exchange rates are diverse and
complex. The result is that at any moment the influence of policy actions on
exchange rates is uncertain. Portfolio decisions with respect to financial assets play
a key role in the short-run determination of exchange rates; but the influence of
today's policy on portfolio decisions, via expectations, is uncertain. This marks a
substantial contrast with the influence of policy actions on the aggregate demand

for goods and services, where the linkages with policy are clearer. Despite this, we have not to date been able to eliminate the so-called business cycle. Unpredictable movements in real exchange rates and unpredictable responses of real exchange rates to government action greatly aggravate the problem of macroeconomic management.

At the same time, under a regime of flexible exchange rates there is a temptation, hence some tendency, to manipulate the exchange rate for macroeconomic purposes. This can be done either to fight inflation, since monetary tightening produces an immediate reward — at the expense of other countries, so long as others do not respond in kind — in terms of a decline in the inflation rate brought about via an appreciated currency. Or it can be used to combat unemployment, when expansionary monetary policy depreciates the currency — again, in general, at the expense of other countries. Of course, the same configuration of exchange rates may be satisfactory to all or most countries. But that would be a coincidence. In general, these represent self-centered national actions which simply pass the problem, either of inflation or of unemployment, to other countries. Members of the IMF have a general responsibility to avoid such manipulation of exchange rates, and the IMF has a general responsibility for surveillance over exchange rate practices, presumably with the aim of preventing such practices. But surveillance has not really gotten off the ground, and it is not clear under today's arrangements what the IMF can do, for example, when a Sweden deliberately depreciates its currency in order to increase output and employment, or when a United States achieves a substantial reduction in its inflation rate through a policy of tight money which has inter alia greatly appreciated the dollar against other currencies.

Just as present exchange rate arrangements are not really sustainable over the long run, neither are present arrangements for reserve management and in particular for reserve creation. The principal reserve medium is a national currency, the U.S. dollar, dependent in large part for its supply on the policies of the United States. This has been accepted, more or less grudgingly, because it has worked reasonably well and there is no clear feasible alternative. But it leaves a deep sense of uneasiness around the world, even when the United States in the judgment of others is relatively well-behaved; and the uneasiness grows dramatically when in such periods as 1970–71 and 1978 the rest of the world, or some parts of it, believe the United States is not well-behaved. Moreover, as the United States shrinks in relation to the rest of the world, as it is bound to do, the intrinsic weaknesses of reliance on the U.S. dollar will become more apparent, especially in the United States, where the possible reaction of foreign dollar holders will become an ever greater constraint in the framing of U.S. monetary policy. The United States is bound to shrink relative to the rest of the world, not because it is doing badly, but because the rest of the world may be expected to do well. The natural growth in the labor force and the rate of capital accumulation are both higher in many parts of the world than they are in the United States. Moreover, the possibility exists for closing the technological gap between the United States, which operates on the frontiers of modern technology, and the location far behind those frontiers at which many countries find themselves. Thus the simple arithmetic of economic growth will insure a gradual relative decline of the United States, for instance from about one-fourth of world GNP at present to around one-sixth 25 years from now if the United States grows on average at 3 percent a year and the rest of the world grows on average at 5 percent a year, both plausible numbers.

In short, the present set of monetary arrangements, while not in any immediate danger of collapse from their intrinsic features, as distinguished from some external unforeseen event, is not stable in the long run. It is not a durable system. It must evolve into something else. It must be "reformed."

But what will or should it evolve into? One possibility is that the frustrations arising from the sense of loss of control by national governments will lead to significant attempts to reassert national control by sharply reducing the openness and permeability of national economies to external influences. In a sense, the move to flexible exchange rates can be interpreted as such a response, since countries enjoyed even less control, especially as regards monetary policy, under a system of fixed exchange rates with high capital mobility. But we have now learned that flexible exchange rates, while they offer some greater national autonomy, do not do an effective job of insulating national economies from external influences, and may indeed in some instances, especially as regards worldwide shifts in preferences of asset holders, exacerbate the impact of external influences on national economic developments. So the frustrations at loss of national control continue, and alleviating them would require much stronger insulating material than flexible exchange rates alone provide. It would probably involve a reversion to extensive use of controls over capital movements. And since capital transactions cannot be effectively separated from current transactions, there would be a strong tendency to extend controls to current transactions as well. Indeed, there would be considerable independent pressure to do that as improved world telecommunications, transportation, and information flows increase international competition further.

But this paper is supposed to address the question of reform, not piecemeal retrogression. There is a normative component to reform, not merely a projection of likely trends. So I turn now to a different possible evolution of international monetary arrangements, which attempts to deal with what I have identified as the intrinsic problems with present arrangements which render them not stable in the long run. To fix the time frame, let us go forward 25 years, to the year 2010. That is far enough ahead so that many changes from now are plausible. Developments that are completely unrealistic in the next five or ten years can be contemplated. But it is not so far ahead that we cannot really contemplate it at all. Many of us will still be around and functioning at that time, and it is only as far ahead as the year 1960 is behind us, and no doubt that is still a fresh memory to most of us. I propose first to sketch a set of arrangements which I believe will deal with the problems in the present setup. If this proposed scheme is agreeable, we can then ask what interim steps will be useful to get from here to there.

IV. A MONETARY SCHEME FOR THE YEAR 2010

Before sketching the main features of the scheme, it is perhaps worth saying a word about the state of modern industrial economies in the year 2010. Populations and labor forces will of course be larger than they are today, but the labor force engaged in manufacturing production in today's OECD countries will probably not have changed much, and may actually have declined. Manufacturing is likely to go the way that agriculture has already gone, with a declining share of the labor force able to produce all of the goods that the rest of society needs. Real incomes per capita will be over 50 percent higher than they are today. The world will be very electronic. Thus not only will large-scale financial transactions be able to be made virtually instantaneously to any part of the world — we are close to that situation today — but even retail transactions in financial services and in goods will take place electronically. That is, householders will be able to purchase information about taxation, investments, retirement possibilities, or education by consulting electronic catalogues and information sources in their own home. Even goods will be able to be purchased by inspecting them on a television screen, placing the order electronically and having them delivered in a relatively short period of time. With higher real incomes and lower relative prices for long-distance transportation, much more travel will take place than occurs today. Reliable, high-speed, and low-cost communications over the globe will permit management control of production locations in many places. Lower transportation costs (relative to the price of other goods and services) will encourage trade. Less reliance on labor forces combined with these other factors will result in higher substitution rates in manufacturing production among locations, so real movements in exchange rates can be highly disruptive of production in any particular location. Yet financial factors, not international trade, will dominate exchange rate determination in the short run. In view of the greater sensitivity of production to changes in real exchange rates, governments must reduce arbitrary movements in the real exchange rates in order to maintain an open trading system. With widespread information and low transactions costs, an adjustable peg system of exchange rates that results in discretionary movements in market exchange rates is not likely to be tenable — indeed, did not prove to be tenable even under the technological conditions prevailing in the 1960s.

Taken together, these considerations lead me to conclude that we will need a system of credibly fixed exchange rates by that time if we are to preserve an open trading and financial system. Exchange rates can be most credibly fixed if they are eliminated altogether, that is, if international transactions take place with a single currency. But a single currency is possible only if there is in effect a single monetary policy, and a single authority issuing the currency and directing the monetary policy. How can independent states accomplish that? They need to turn over the determination of monetary policy to a supernational body, but one which is responsible to the governments of the independent states collectively. There is some precedent for this in the origins of the U.S. Federal Reserve System, which blended quite separate regions of the country and banks subject to diverse state banking jurisdictions into a single system, paralleling the increasingly national financial market. Similarly, we will need a world monetary system that parallels the increasingly global financial market. It will probably not be possible, even within the time scale envisaged here, to have a truly global Bank of Issue. But that will not be necessary either, and it may be possible to have a Bank of Issue which serves a more limited group of democratic countries, and which can serve as the core of an international system. More will be said about the membership in this core below.

The Monetary Authority

The tasks, the instruments, and the decision-making structure of the Bank of Issue could look something like the following:

The governing board would be made up of representatives of national governments, presumably finance ministers, who would vote according to the share of the national GNP in the total gross product of the community of nations participating in the monetary authority. These weights could be altered at five-year intervals to make allowance for different growth rates. If national membership in the monetary authority became so large that representatives from every country would make a committee unmanageable, the managing committee could be constituted on a representative basis, much as the International Monetary Fund is today.

The task of the monetary authority would be to stabilize the macroeconomic situation and to avoid or mitigate liquidity crises through a lender of last resort function, just as national central banks do today. The debate on the relative weights to be attached to output as opposed to price stabilization could continue just as they do at present, without prejudice.

The Bank of Issue would accomplish its tasks by engaging in open market operations in which it issued the new currency for the securities of member countries. It could also engage in rediscount operations, whereby it extended claims against itself in exchange for acceptable paper at the initiative of banks within the system, subject to its own acquiescence in those initiatives.

The Bank of Issue need not engage in detailed regulation of the banks throughout the system covered by the new currency. That could be left in the hands of national regulators. However, it would probably want to issue guidelines — minimum standards — to be followed by national regulators, and to maintain enough surveillance over banks to be sure of itself when it was called upon to act as a lender of last resort.

In the first instance, open market operations by the Bank of Issue could be distributed among the securities of national governments in proportion to their voting weight (i.e., their GNP share), but over time this limitation would probably cease to be necessary as financial markets evolved and securities issued by many national governments became virtually perfect substitutes one for another. In any case, the Bank of Issue's holdings of national government securities could be altered from GNP shares via the rediscounting facility, as needed.

Seigniorage in this system would automatically be distributed to national governments as their securities were purchased by the Bank of Issue, thereby giving them the purchasing power to buy goods and services. In addition, the Bank of Issue would run profits from its interest earnings, and those could be distributed from time to time to national governments on the basis of their voting shares.

The currency of the Bank of Issue could be practically anything, an evolution from the Canadian dollar, the Swedish krona, the ECU, or the SDR. Most natural would be an evolution from the present U.S. dollar, making use of the extensive dollar-based worldwide markets. But if that were not politically acceptable, it could be a synthetic unit which the public would have to get used to, as it had to get used to the metric system when that replaced numerous national systems. The key point is that monetary control — the issuance of currency and of reserve credit — would be in the hands of the new Bank of Issue, not in the hands of any national government, no matter what the historical origin of the new currency happened to be.

National Economic Policy

The peoples of the industrial democracies have placed high expectations on their national governments for economic management. Here governments are being asked to pass monetary policy to a supernational agency, the actions of which they can influence but not determine, taken one by one. Would national governments be giving up all of their macroeconomic control? The answer to this question is no, since they could still pursue fiscal policy at the national level. What they would be giving up is monetary financing of budget deficits beyond their prorated allocation from jointly agreed open market operations. In particular, they could not engage in inflationary finance to reduce the real value of outstanding debt at the national level, although the requisite majority could do so at the international level. To finance budget deficits, therefore, it would be necessary to go to the capital market. But the regime we have in mind would no doubt involve a very high degree of capital mobility among participants, especially since all securities would be denominated in a single, widely used currency. Of course, the influence of fiscal actions on national aggregate demand would be limited by leakages abroad through demand for imports, and at the outer limits by the extent to which individual governments could borrow in the capital market. Governments could also use their fiscal powers to attract internationally mobile firms via tax holidays or through covering the expenses of a portion of new investments. These practices have already emerged as a new form of fiscal action both within countries (e.g., industrial development bonds issued by the individual states within the United States) and between countries. With internationally mobile capital, these practices may indeed succeed in generating local employment in "depressed" areas without necessarily resulting in a misallocation of resources (see Cooper, 1974). Nonetheless, if these practices became too competitive among nations, they might want to put some collectively agreed limits on them, and even allow special differentiation under some circumstances, e.g., when unemployment rates were higher than some agreed norm.

One old-fashioned policy instrument for encouraging investment and employment is the use of tariffs to discriminate against goods from abroad. It would be logical if free trade accompanied this single currency regime. That would also be consistent with the collaborative political spirit that would be required to establish the single currency regime. Free trade would insure one market in goods as well as in financial instruments. But the scheme would be quite workable also with modest tariffs, at or below the levels that now generally prevail among OECD countries. Higher tariffs in the presence of a free flow of capital run the risk of leading to a gross misallocation of capital, even from the viewpoint of the tariff-imposing country, as tariffs draw capital and labor into what are by definition relatively inefficient industries. But the exact nature of the commercial regime is beyond the scope of this paper.

How the Regime Would Work

Governments could determine the balance between their expenditures and taxes as they do now, but beyond their prorated share of the Bank of Issue's open market purchases and profits they would have to borrow on the capital market to cover any budget deficits. Market access would be determined by a market assessment of the probability of repayment, which would assuredly be high within a plausible range of budgetary behavior. Both receipts and expenditures would be made in the common currency, as would the borrowing. Each country could set its own course independently, with no need for formal coordination of fiscal policy. Financial markets would "coordinate" to some extent, via interest rates, since if all governments decided to borrow heavily at once, in a period in which private demands for credit were also high, interest rates would rise and that would induce greater caution in borrowing. But the larger countries would certainly find it useful to exchange information on intentions with respect to future actions, so that each of them could take the actions of others into account. This exchange would over time no doubt evolve into an iterative process which was hardly distinguishable from coordination, although in the end each country would be free to act as it saw fit.

Monetary policy would be set for the community as a whole by a board of governors, who in practice would probably be finance ministers. No single country would be in control. A weighted majority of the governors would decide both the principles to govern monetary policy (e.g., how much weight to give to monetary magnitudes as opposed to other variables in framing monetary policy) and with respect to actual operations. The governors in turn would be accountable to legislatures. The Bank of Issue would have a certain autonomy by virtue of not being beholden to any single legislative or executive authority. Thus it could not be manipulated for particular electoral reasons. On the other hand, its actions would be determined by a majority of officials who would be individually accountable to legislatures or executives, so that if a (weighted) majority of them desired a shift in policy, it would occur.

Balance of payments adjustment within this regime would be as easy, or as difficult, as it is between regions of the United States or any other large country today. The adjustment would be automatic, except insofar as it was cushioned by capital inflows induced by fiscal actions. Automatic balance of payments adjustment sometimes leads to unemployment, as following a shift in demand away from the products of a particular region or country. Fiscal policy could be used to cushion such unemployment. In addition, my guess is that the present industrial democracies will have considerable net immigration by early in the next century, and the distribution of that flow of migrants would provide considerable flexibility to the labor force in the region as a whole.

This one-currency regime is much too radical to envisage in the near future. But it is not too radical to envisage 25 years from now, and indeed some such scheme, or its functional equivalent, will be necessary to avoid retrogression into greater reliance on barriers to international trade and financial transactions. Moreover, it is useful to have a "vision," MITI-style, to provide guidance for the steps that may be feasible in the near future. Thus some idea of where we would like to get to provides a sense of direction for the next steps.

V. NEXT STEPS FOR GETTING FROM HERE TO THERE

If the objective of a single currency is thought to be desirable, compared with the likely alternatives, are there steps we should be taking now to work toward that objective? The idea is so far from being politically feasible at present — in its call for a real pooling of monetary sovereignty — that it will require many years of consideration before people become accustomed to the idea. But the economic effect can be gradually approximated by giving greater weight to exchange rates in framing national monetary policy. Many countries — all those with fixed or semi-fixed rates — of course already do this. This injunction therefore applies mainly to the United States, Canada, Japan, the United Kingdom, and the EMS countries taken as a group. If monetary policy were governed in such a way as to limit wide swings in key exchange rates, this would tend also to reduce fluctuations in real exchange rates. This result could be accomplished by adopting one or another of the formal schemes that have been proposed from time to time, such as the target zone (Williamson, 1983), whereby countries undertake to confine market movements of the exchange rate within a specified band centered on a target rate, which target can if necessary be altered from time to time. The European monetary system is a variant of such a scheme, with central rates being subject to periodic renegotiation as they become questionable. Seven changes in central rates have been made in the period since 1979, and generally the changes have been sufficiently small so that market exchange rates were not immediately affected, or were affected only modestly.

It may not be possible to reach international agreement on a formal scheme for exchange rate management. But the process of official discussion of such schemes, each particular one of which is subject to defects under some circumstances, will appraise officials of the possibilities for accomplishing the principal objective, viz., to reduce undue fluctuations in real exchange rates. Thus launching a move toward "reform" of exchange rate arrangements may fail in the sense that no formal scheme is agreed on, but still succeed in its underlying purpose of establishing a more or less shared view of what exchange rates should be at a given time and a consensus to work toward keeping market rates within the neighborhood of the consensus rates.

This approach runs from monetary policy to exchange rates. But it does not rule out elements of an alternative approach, espoused especially by McKinnon (1984), running from exchange rates to monetary policy. If a country's real exchange rate is rising for reasons that are not associated with a clear change in economic fundamentals, that can be taken as prima facie evidence that the country's monetary policy is too tight relative to that of its trading partners. The opposite interpretation can be made for the countries whose real exchange rates are falling. The former country should ease and the latter countries should tighten their monetary policies, on this line of argument. While McKinnon's proposal is excessively monetaristic in its details — he would consolidate the money supplies of the United States, Japan, and West Germany, and have the consolidated money supply grow at a specified rate — the spirit is compatible with the target zone proposals and with the line of thought developed here, that monetary policy should be so managed to limit movements in real exchange rates.

N countries targeting N – 1 exchange rates leaves a degree of freedom, which can be used to determine the overall degree of monetary ease or tightness for the community of countries in question. Under the gold standard, this degree of freedom was used to tie currencies to a particular commodity, gold. Many academic proposals over the years would have retained that principle, but enlarged the list of commodities to some bundle or even to an index number of commodity prices (for a summary, see Cooper, 1982). McKinnon uses the degree of freedom by introducing a collective monetary rule, governing the growth of the joint money supply. A dollar-centered system has all countries other than the United States target an exchange rate, leaving it to the United States to determine monetary policy for the world. It was resistance to this last arrangement that contributed to the breakdown of the early 1970s and led to the introduction of floating exchange rates. What is necessary is some consultation among major countries on the overall "tone" of monetary policy. This is a politically difficult step and cannot be taken overtly any time soon, since each nation has its formal system of decision-making and channels of responsibilities for determining monetary policy. However, the same result can be accomplished informally, centered around discussion of exchange rate management, for which there seems to be a widespread desire, especially in business circles.

The previous section suggested that the choice of a currency for a one-currency regime is open and in a sense is arbitrary. It could be anything that is agreed upon, since money is above all a social convention. In fact the choice would be a politically charged issue, with strong if irrational objections to the choice of any national currency. If national currencies are ruled out, that leaves the ECU and SDR in today's world. The ECU might meet the same objections in the United States and Japan as the U.S. dollar would meet in Europe. That in turn leaves only the SDR, which is now a weighted average of five leading national currencies in value. We must distinguish between the SDR as a liability of the IMF, and the SDR as a unit of account. The new Bank of Issue could not issue IMF SDRs unless the Bank were the IMF itself (more will be said about this below). But the Bank could use the SDR as its unit of account, and issue its own liabilities in that unit, whether they be currency notes or reserve bank credit.

The future of the SDR as a currency would be immeasurably enhanced if private parties could transact in SDRs; indeed, that would be a necessary condition. It would also greatly facilitate the use of the SDR as a central bank currency, since the modus operandi of central banks in most cases is through private markets, and they need a medium which can be used in private markets. Thus the IMF-SDR would be enhanced if some mechanism could be found to make this possible. The IMF Articles would have to be amended to make the IMF-SDR directly holdable by private parties, including commercial banks. But Kenen (1983) has made an ingenious proposal, an extension and elaboration of one made earlier by Coats (1982), which would accomplish much the same result without formally amending the Articles. This is not an urgent step, but it should be done if the role of SDR is to be strengthened. Also, it would be desirable to issue more IMF-SDRs to keep that asset alive and in use. We will want it sometime in the future.

A key question concerning the new Bank of Issue is what countries should participate in its management, use its currency, and forswear monetary policy. We have come to think of the international monetary system, centered on the IMF with its 146 members, as a global system, albeit excluding most communist countries and Switzerland. That was certainly the conception at Bretton Woods, even though most of the negotiation had been between the Americans and the British. That was also the spirit of the times at Bretton Woods, when the wartime allies placed their hopes for a better world in the United Nations Organization and its functional satellites.

But there is serious question about whether one world money is either necessary or desirable. And it is certainly not feasible, even within our generous 25 year time frame. It is not feasible for two reasons. First, it is highly doubtful if the American public, to take just one example, could ever accept countries with oppressive autocratic regimes voting on the monetary policy that would affect monetary conditions in the United States. I believe that the same reservations would obtain in other democratic societies. For such a bold step to work at all, it presupposes a certain convergence of political values as reflected in the nature of political decision-making, and the basic confidence to which that gives rise.

Second, countries with different values, circumstances, and systems of governance are bound to introduce into negotiations leading toward a Bank of

Issue elements which are of greater interest to them, thus broadening the agenda for negotiation and rendering impossible an already difficult negotiation. For both reasons the proposal should be undertaken in the first instance by the United States, Japan, and the members of the European Community. This group represents the core of the monetary system at present and for some time to come. Other democracies would be free to join if they wished, and if they were willing to undertake the commitments involved, but no one should be obliged to join. Very likely many countries would find it attractive in the early stages not to join, but nonetheless to peg their currencies to the SDR or whatever was the unit of account of the Bank of Issue. They would retain the monetary freedom, however, which members had given up. Some countries would be reluctant to give up the seigniorage from monetary issue, which can be consequential where currency still bears a high ratio to GNP. . . .

In short, there would be an inner club accepting higher responsibilities, but open to additional members who met the requirements, and of value even to nonmembers by providing a stable monetary environment against which to frame their economic policies. But this arrangement would mark a formal break with the universalism that governs the de jure if not the de facto structure of the Bretton Woods system today.

VI. CONCLUSIONS

This paper addresses the question of the need for reform of existing international monetary arrangements by asking whether they are stable — that is, whether they are likely to survive over a considerable period of time, such as a couple of decades. My answer is negative. Dissatisfaction with both the very short-run and year-to-year movements in real exchange rates, combined with technological developments which will lead to further integration of the world economy, will force an alteration of existing arrangements. Unless that alteration is carefully managed, it will take the form of defensive, insulating measures involving controls over international transactions, both trade and finance. That would be politically divisive and economically costly.

I have put forward a radical alternative scheme for the next century: the creation of a common currency for all of the industrial democracies with a common monetary policy and a joint Bank of Issue to determine that monetary policy. Individual countries would be free to determine their fiscal policy actions, but those would be constrained by the need to borrow in the international capital market. Free trade is a natural but not entirely necessary complement to these macroeconomic arrangements.

This proposal is far too radical for the near future, but it could provide a "vision" or goal which can guide interim steps in improving international monetary arrangements, and by which we can judge the evolution of national economic policy.

In the meantime, we should design exchange rate arrangements and national economic management so as to reduce the variability of real exchange rates and to move toward some consensus on equilibrium values for exchange rates, necessarily to be altered from time to time. In addition, we will want eventually to move away from a dollar-based system, so we should breathe some life into the SDR by providing for a new allocation of SDRs plus making efforts to give the SDR an existence in the world of private finance. The SDR is perhaps the most suitable of several possible choices for the new, common currency.

By focusing on longer-run monetary arrangements, this paper has not addressed some issues that are usually thought of in connection with reforming the monetary system. In particular, it has not addressed foreign aid, external debt, or the substitution account, and the related question of multiple reserve currencies. We may some day want something that might be called a substitution account, but that should derive from the details of other, more basic arrangements that are being put in place. That issue can therefore be deferred until the right moment.

External debt is a serious, immediate issue. Growth in the world economy and maintenance of open markets are preconditions for managing the problem successfully. Given the highly diverse circumstances of the debtor countries — including the largest debtor, which is not Brazil, but the United States, which will borrow almost as much in 1984 from the rest of the world as Brazil's total external debt — and the politically charged atmosphere surrounding external debt, there is no practical alternative to a case-by-case approach for dealing with it. We need net new lending to cover at least a part of the interest that is due on outstanding debts, and that is entirely appropriate insofar as nominal interest rates carry an inflation premium. In addition, debts will have to be rescheduled from time to time, in conjunction with national stabilization programs. These arrangements against the background of a suitably buoyant world economy will probably be enough to get the monetary system through to the longer run which has been dealt with here.

References

Coats, Warren L., Jr. "The SDR as a Means of Payment," IMF *Staff Papers, 29* (September 1982), 422–36.

Cooper, Richard N. *Economic Mobility and National Economic Policy.* Stockholm: Almquist and Wiksell, 1974.

Cooper, Richard N. "The Gold Standard: Historical Facts and Future Prospects," *Brookings Papers on Economic Activity,* 1982, No. 1.

Kenen, Peter B. "Use of the SDR to Supplement or Substitute for Other Means of Finance" in George M. von Furstenberg, ed., *International Money and Credit: The Policy Roles.* Washington: IMF, 1983.

McKinnon, Ronald I. *An International Standard for Monetary Stabilization.* Washington: Institute for International Economics, 1984.

Williamson, John. *The Exchange Rate System.* Washington: Institute for International Economics, 1983.

DISCUSSION

Anthony M. Solomon

. . . The consequences of living with floating rates have created an understandable desire to see a reestablishment of stability. Exchange rate swings are often perceived to be inconsistent with changes in economic fundamentals, leading to unnecessary adjustment costs, including higher rates of unemployment and bankruptcies, and creating a general environment of uncertainty that lowers investment and trade.

Dick Cooper offers a radical answer to this dilemma, namely, the abandonment of national currencies and the establishment of a world money and world central bank. This proposal represents his vision of the ideal future arrangements for the monetary system. He also discusses some more pragmatic reforms of the present exchange rate system, which he paints as stepping stones on the way to his ideal system. I want to make some comments on both his ideal system of a world central bank and on his proposals for the transition.

Cooper sees the establishment of one global currency as a solution to anticipated future problems that will arise from basic forces now at work. These basic forces are, first, the continuing decline of the relative share of the United States in the world economy. This, presumably, undermines the dominant role of the dollar in the international system. The second basic force is the continuing adoption of telecommunications and other technologies that will aggravate the problems of volatile capital flows, and even goods flows, across national borders. The resulting swings in exchange rates will be greater in the future and will create a higher order of disruption. In his assessment, by the next generation these forces will make the present system of floating rates and dollar-based international finance incompatible with independent national monetary policies and free trade. No one can know the future, so it is possible to object that the basic forces will not carry disruption so far. But I am inclined to agree that those forces are at work and point in that direction.

Where I take issue with Cooper's ideal is in the nature of the adjustment process. If I understand him correctly, adjustment in a one-money world will be essentially similar to that under a gold standard. The rate of growth of world money will be fixed from the point of view of individual countries. We have to ask what will happen when fiscal policies are not coordinated — for experience teaches us that will certainly be the case at times. A nation following relatively expansive fiscal policies can postpone the day of reckoning by borrowing, but eventually it will reach a limit. Yet if domestic wages and prices are not sufficiently flexible — and nothing in Cooper's argument says they will be necessarily more flexible in the future than they are today — adjustment will be forced by reductions in output and employment, as in the gold standard. Clearly, the world central bank cannot run monetary policy to accommodate the most expansionary of national fiscal policies without creating global inflation.

This does not compare favorably with adjustment under a floating rate system. Changes in exchange rates can introduce a degree of price flexibility that is missing in domestic product and factor markets and can dampen the swings in output and employment that result during adjustment. For example, a country that must adjust back from too rapid an expansion can receive the trade balance benefits of a depreciating currency, which will moderate the effects of domestic recession. This is the strong point of the floating rate system, when it works well, that must be balanced against the problems caused by overshooting. Adjustment is likely to be an even more difficult business in Cooper's ideal system.

On the question of what steps can be taken to promote the transition to an ideal system, Cooper argues for two broad reforms: enhancing the role of the SDR, his candidate for world money, and giving greater weight to exchange rates in framing national monetary policies. I am basically sympathetic to both of these proposals, although with some important qualifications.

For promoting the SDR, Cooper stresses taking steps to privatize its use. I think there is a role for this and I have said so in the past. I also viewed the U.S. proposal for establishment of a substitution account as not just a practical measure to address the problem of reserve diversification in the late 1970s but also as a step promoting an expanded role for the SDR.

I also think there is a case for giving greater weight to exchange rates in monetary policy, but only if the mix of monetary and fiscal policies is appropriately balanced. Otherwise the flexibility of monetary policies to react to exchange rate developments can be seriously limited.

In fact, I think that a lot of what is perceived as exchange rate problems under floating reflects a lack of policy coordination that would have undesirable symptoms under any exchange rate system. Take the behavior of the dollar over the past two years, for example. Many view this as a striking example of the kind of currency misalignment that reform of the exchange rate system would avoid. But how much responsibility for the current dollar problem can we lay on the workings of the floating rate regime?

To the extent that the strength of the dollar reflects the U.S. fiscal-monetary policy mix, in particular unprecedentedly high federal deficits, it represents more a policy failure than a weakness of the exchange rate system. . . . If our policy mix and high real interest rates are largely responsible for the over-valued dollar, what could be a more effective way to restore a sustainable structure of exchange rates than a credible and specific plan to change the policy mix? Since a monetary accommodation of our huge federal deficits is ultimately going to be inflationary and would only add to uncertainty that already appears excessive, the action must come from the fiscal side. A credible plan to reduce our federal deficit substantially can do more at this time to lower real interest rates and eliminate the overvaluation of the dollar than a reform of the exchange rate system that imposes greater coordination on national monetary policies only. . . .

26

Is There an Important Role for an International Reserve Asset Such as the SDR?

W. M. Corden

The question set for this paper raises issues that are central to [international monetary reform]. The aims will be to highlight basic principles and underlying assumptions of various arguments and to focus on realities. But it must never be forgotten that today's dreams may become tomorrow's realities, so I shall also examine carefully the implications of various "dreams." I propose to avoid technicalities. . . .

Right from the beginning, one distinction must be stressed. This is between the concept of the special drawing right (SDR) as an internationally created reserve asset and its denomination as a currency basket. It was originally denominated in terms of a fixed quantity of gold valued at the official U.S. dollar price of gold. An internationally created asset could be denominated in various ways, for example, in terms of dollars or even commodities other than gold. Although much attention has been given recently to the matter of denomination, this is not the central issue. The use of a particular denomination — currently, a weighted-value average of a basket of five currencies — in the private market does not mean that there has been any international creation of a reserve asset. In general, I shall be concerned here with the reserve asset question, not the denomination question. . . . It is unfortunate that the same term is used both for the new kind of asset and for its denomination.

It seems best not to start with the "dreams" but with the current situation. The current situation is that the SDR does not have a very significant role in the international monetary system, making up only a small part of world reserves. This is so in spite of the intention expressed in the Articles of Agreement of the International Monetary Fund (IMF), since 1978, to make "the special drawing right the principal reserve asset in the international monetary system." At the time of writing, it does not appear that governments propose to move in the direction of fulfilling this intention. Thus, there is certainly a dramatic gap between realities and proclaimed intentions.

This "realities-intentions gap" could be interpreted in two ways. The first is that the supposed intention is simply a relic of circumstances that gave rise to the

From George M. von Furstenberg (ed.), *International Money and Credit: The Policy Rules* (Washington, D.C.: International Monetary Fund, 1983), pp. 213–237, 252–259. Reprinted by permission. Some text, footnotes, and references omitted or altered.

SDR and of theories that have gone out of fashion. Perhaps, in due course, the relic will be buried. The second is that the proclaimed intention lays the groundwork for a possible change in realities; it reflects a desire for change, though the kinds of change that would be appropriate in the new economic environment that has existed since the early seventies have not yet been envisaged. . . .

In either event, it would be necessary to examine aspects of the current system, including its inadequacies, if any, and to ask to what extent the large-scale creation of an international reserve asset could overcome these inadequacies either within, broadly, the current system (discussed in Section I) or possibly as part of a complete change in the system (discussed in Section II). . . . [The last] section summarizes the practical implications.

I. SDRs WITHIN THE CURRENT SYSTEM

The Current System — Chaotic "Nonsystem" with a Logic

Broadly, we have a decentralized international market system — one characterized by a kind of laissez-faire and under which governments and their central banks are major players, with their actions subject to few, if any, effective rules. The system has generated liquidity and reserves endogenously. Reserves can be earned in the international market, either by the net sale of goods and services — that is, through a current account surplus — or by the sale of bonds. When reserves are built up through a sale of bonds, there is an exchange of medium-term or long-term assets for short-term assets.

It would be wrong to say that reserves are determined by demand; rather, the level of reserves is the outcome of a demand-and-supply equilibrium. If increased reserves are to be earned through current account surpluses, there must be a corresponding willingness on the part of others to incur current account deficits (i.e., a willingness to sell financial assets for goods and services). Equilibrium is attained essentially through interest rate variations. If there is an excess demand for financial assets relative to goods, so that the algebraic sum of desired current account surpluses is positive, the interest rate will fall; this will increase real investment and perhaps reduce savings, thereby reducing desired surpluses and raising deficits until equilibrium is attained. If increased reserves are to be earned through medium-term and long-term borrowing, long-term rates will rise and short-term rates will fall until the private capital market chooses to supply what the central banks are demanding. At the same time, the changing structure of interest rates may lead the central banks to adjust their demands. Furthermore, the existence of the market provides liquidity — the potential availability of funds when needed — and thus reduces the need for owned reserves, whether private or public.

To the surprise of some, this market brought about the recycling of the oil surpluses. In fact, its emergence was completely unplanned and occurred at the very same time that lengthy official discussions were proceeding about the problems of reserve adequacy and the reconstruction of the whole system. Only a few economists noted the significance of the private capital market in generating reserves and in achieving an equilibrium between short-term and long-term assets for different countries and different financial institutions.

The prevailing exchange rate arrangement can also be described as a laissez-faire system under which governments, through their central banks, are important actors, intervening in the market as little or as much as they choose; perhaps fixing their exchange rates in a particular way — whether to another currency, to a trade-weighted basket, or even to the particular basket called the SDR; and fixing them for any period they choose. It is well known that the interventions in the markets of major countries that practice managed floating seem to have the general characteristic of "leaning against the wind," but the degree of "leaning" is optional and is different at different times. Also to be noted is the establishment of a regional par value system — a kind of "mini-Bretton Woods" — in the form of the European Monetary System.

The world system that has emerged is unplanned and apparently chaotic. It has been described as a nonsystem. In the view of some, it is desperately in need of "control" (especially control of the Eurocurrency market). But the point I wish to stress is that it nevertheless has some internal logic, essentially the logic of the market.[1] There are the same tendencies to equilibrium in the system as in any market, and it may well be efficient for the same reasons that — subject to qualifications — markets are generally or widely regarded as efficient ways of organizing economic relationships. The fact that a market is unplanned and uncontrolled does not mean that it is inadequate. Nor does the fact that public bodies, such as central banks, operate in it make it less of a market.

The standard market paradigm thus seems the best starting point for analysis. Given certain assumptions, markets lead to efficient solutions. Even though efficient, they are not necessarily "optimal" solutions, because they may lead to income and wealth distribution outcomes that are, by some criteria, inequitable or undesirable. Thus, ideally, an efficient market may need to be supplemented by redistributive arrangements; or, alternatively, intervention in the market may be justified if it has desirable redistributive consequences. In addition, the assumptions required for market efficiency may not be fulfilled. The various qualifications — externalities, public goods, information deficiencies, market power of major actors making them price makers rather than price takers, and introduction of oligopolistic effects — are well known.

It is also well known and important to note that the existence of market failure in itself does not justify just any kind of intervention. Intervention should be directed specifically at dealing with the relevant market failure. Furthermore, the operators of the intervention themselves become actors in the system, and their efficiency and motivations must be considered, so that the possibility of political or bureaucratic failure must be set against market failure.

I do not propose to pursue this approach to studying the international monetary system in a formal way, although it would be well worth doing, but I shall use it as a general framework. If one could assume that the system was efficient, there would be no need for an international reserve asset or any other kind of internationally coordinated action. The next step is to consider possible inadequacies of the system — that is, qualifications to the assumption — and in each case to ask whether the inadequacy might justify the establishment, or expansion in the supply, of an international reserve asset such as the SDR. I shall consider three possible inadequacies — namely (1) the instability of exchange rates, (2) the tendency for the system to give rise to inflation or recession, and (3) the inadequacies of the international capital market.

Instability of Exchange Rates — Multicurrency System and Substitution Account

A principal source of dissatisfaction with the current international monetary system is the instability of exchange rates, especially the large medium-term swings in nominal and real rates. A particular problem has arisen with the swings in the yen/dollar rate; whenever the yen depreciates in real terms, pressures for protectionism increase in the United States.

In general, the objection to severely fluctuating exchange rates is not so much that they may have adverse effects on trade and capital movements — for which there is, in fact, no clear evidence — but that they have unwelcome and politically awkward effects on the distribution of domestic incomes, as between different sectors. Real appreciations adversely affect profits and possibly employment in countries' export and import-competing industries. Real depreciations tend to lower real wages. If there is real wage resistance, nominal depreciations can give rise to "vicious circles." The rise in domestic prices resulting from depreciation generates nominal wage increases designed to restore real wages. To prevent these wage increases from causing unemployment, monetary expansion then follows, eliminating the initial benefits of the depreciation and thus leading to further depreciation and further price and wage rises.

The main causes of major exchange rate fluctuations appear to be divergences in monetary and fiscal policies, either in their impact on overall demand or in the policy mix leading to real interest rate divergences. When Japan follows a tight overall aggregate demand policy and the United States an expansionary one, the yen tends to appreciate. On the other hand, when policy mixes diverge (for any given overall demand outcome) — for example, tight money and easy fiscal policy in the United States and the opposite in Japan — the exchange rate is again influenced; in this example, the yen depreciates. These episodes are well known.

Countries follow policies designed primarily to suit domestic considerations, and their governments respond to political pressures and ideologies that differ between countries. Policies are also liable to change drastically as governments change. Exchange rate outcomes are essentially by-products of these domestically motivated policies, and the problem is that governments are unlikely to subordinate their domestic motives to the objective of exchange rate stability.

Furthermore, expectational effects may intensify or moderate the exchange rate outcomes. If expectations are correct, they anticipate changes that would otherwise take place, and they may smooth out fluctuations. It is widely believed, at least by advocates of exchange market intervention, that markets have a tendency to overreact to "news" and, in general, to expect more changes than underlying conditions justify. Nominal exchange rate fluctuations seem to lead to fluctuations in real rates, although the latter may be somewhat smaller in amplitude. The main sources of difficulty — especially because of their effects on the distribution of income between different domestic sectors — are the changes in real rates.

How does this problem relate to the question posed for this paper? The obvious solution is to deal with the underlying causes — unstable domestic macroeconomic policies and little coordination when changes are made in these policies. It is beyond the scope of this paper to discuss the practical implications of this simpleminded prescription. Here, I shall discuss only the implications for the reserve asset question.

First, the problem would disappear — almost by definition — if countries committed themselves (and adhered to their commitments) to a fixed exchange rate system. The implications of such a system for the reserve asset question will be discussed in Section II. Of course, while the exchange rate problem would disappear, if the underlying causes were not dealt with, the problem would manifest itself in other ways, essentially as balance of payments problems of individual countries. For the moment, I continue to assume that the world stays with its laissez-faire exchange rate system.

The second implication for the reserve asset question has to do with the development of a multicurrency [reserve] system. The familiar argument is that a multicurrency system increases exchange rate instability. If central banks held only one asset — ideally the SDR — instability would be reduced. This is the argument for the substitution account (ideally with compulsory substitution), with regard to existing foreign exchange assets, and for imposing rules on the acquisition of new assets, essentially designed to limit the scope for substitution between assets in response to fluctuations in expectations. The implication is that speculation by official holders is destabilizing.

There seem to be two reasons why one should be skeptical about the usefulness of a substitution account as a solution to the exchange stability problem.

First, not only would *official* holders have to be confined to one asset but something would also have to be done about private holders. Presumably their speculation would also be destabilizing. A severe restriction on market forces would have to be imposed. Japanese residents will always hold yen, and American residents dollars; far-reaching exchange controls would be needed to discourage the holding of each other's currencies, or bonds denominated in each other's currencies, when it appeared profitable. And, as one well remembers from the days when the postwar international capital market was in its infancy and exchange controls were very tight in Europe, there is always scope for leads and lags in payments.

Second, there is very little evidence that the gradual move from a dollar system to a multicurrency system has been a significant cause of exchange rate instability. Rather the instability of the dollar, caused by macroeconomic policy changes in the United States, and possibly other countries, has stimulated that move. The concern about the development of the multicurrency system was at its peak around 1978, when there was a dollar depreciation, the causes of which were macroeconomic policy divergences. It is also worth noting that the move has been mainly from dollars to deutsche marks, and not to yen; nevertheless, as mentioned earlier, there have been severe fluctuations in the yen/dollar rate — a major cause of international economic tensions. . . .

Inflation and Recession — Is the System to Blame?

The current international monetary nonsystem has developed more or less concurrently with the new era of inflation and recession that began in 1973. Therefore one must hesitate to suggest that such a system can possibly be efficient or optimal when its evolution has coincided with such a marked deterioration in the world economy. Is there an inadequacy in the system that is responsible for our current macroeconomic troubles? Are these troubles caused by exchange rate variability, by excessive or inadequate reserves, or perhaps by the growth of the international capital market? And, if so, could they be remedied by creation of more SDRs? In general, it seems to me that the answers must all be negative.

The world inflation originated during the operation of the Bretton Woods system and was exported from the United States and voluntarily imported by other countries through the mechanism of fixed rates. Countries could have insulated themselves by appreciating their currencies sufficiently relative to the dollar, but they chose not to do so. The variations in inflation rates that inevitably resulted made exchange rate flexibility inevitable. This is an oversimplified story, but it would be difficult to tell a story in which flexible exchange rates were the prime movers. Current unemployment can be attributed to the combination of real wage resistance and low productivity growth (resulting, perhaps, from low investment) and, in the last few years, relative monetary tightness in the major industrial countries.

Flexible exchange rates allow countries freedom in choosing their money supply policies. Insofar as nominal demand policies can affect real macroeconomic outcomes — as they usually can in the short run — flexible rates introduce a significant element of national independence. . . . For some countries, this freedom may make their problems worse, for others better. With regard to making it worse, it can certainly be argued convincingly that the inflationary explosions in 1973 and 1974 in some countries, such as the United Kingdom and Italy, were made possible by the removal of the balance of payments constraint of fixed rates. On the other hand, a degree of insulation became possible for the Federal Republic of Germany.

It could be argued that instabilities imported from abroad through terms of trade variations and through real exchange rate instability — the latter, in turn, caused or intensified by the international capital market — increase both inflation and unemployment. The mechanism is through asymmetric wage effects: increases in demand for the outputs of one industry increase wages and prices there, while decreases in demand for the outputs of other industries fail to lower wages but do raise unemployment. Yet it seems evident to me that this is not where the principal causes of inflation and unemployment since 1973 are to be found.

Is it possible that within the current laissez-faire exchange rate system, there are either excessive reserves — hence generating inflation — or too few reserves — hence causing unemployment? As stressed earlier, the reserve supply is essentially endogenous — the outcome of a demand-and-supply equilibrium — so the question is whether the process by which the system generates or destroys reserves is deflationary or inflationary. My answer is that *in the flexible-rate system,* the process is *not* necessarily deflationary or inflationary. I shall consider here the case where there is initially a perceived shortage of reserves, although the analysis could be applied symmetrically to the case where countries feel they have excessive reserves. . . .

What would happen if all countries wished to increase their reserves? . . . One can distinguish between the generation of reserves through financial asset transformation and the purchase of reserves through current account surpluses. The capital market can generate extra reserves by the private sector (principally the large international banks) exchanging assets with the world public sector (the central banks). This happens when central banks borrow to replenish their reserves. Insofar as this process raises medium-term and long-term interest rates, and hence reduces investment, it would be deflationary and would need to be offset within each country by appropriate monetary or fiscal expansion.

But let us now consider the example where all countries wish to run current account surpluses in order to increase reserves. Of course, they cannot achieve their objectives. The question is whether the effort of trying to achieve the inconsistent objectives need be deflationary. In a fixed-exchange-rate regime, it would be. But with flexible rates in a two-country world, we can imagine that both Country A and Country B buy each other's currency, aiming to depreciate their own currencies. This is a situation of competitive depreciation. Neither will achieve its exchange rate objective or its current account objective, but each will accumulate the currency of the other and thus will, incidentally, have succeeded in increasing its gross reserves.

There is no reason in this example why either country should actually reduce its absorption of goods and services. . . . The conclusion thus is that under the flexible-exchange-rate system, there is not an inevitable relationship between reserve adequacy and world deflation [or inflation, when there is a world excess of reserves]. The story is different, of course, in a fixed-rate system, and this I shall discuss later.

Here one might note a feature of the current system that may have led to money supply instability in major industrial countries other than the United States. The essential cause is the failure to allow exchange rates to float freely because of governments' desires to avoid severe real exchange rate changes that would have effects on the domestic distribution of income between sectors. Thus, policies of leaning-against-the-wind intervention are being followed. When the motive of intervention to moderate appreciation is to protect profits and employment in export and import-competing industries, the policy can be called "exchange rate protection."

The implications for the world money supply of such intervention policies have recently been noted by McKinnon (1982). When the dollar is expected to depreciate, for whatever reason, capital seeks to move out of the United States, and part of the effect is absorbed by depreciation of the dollar and part by monetary expansion in countries such as Japan and the Federal Republic of Germany. These countries do not succeed in sterilizing the domestic monetary effects, so their money supplies go up and inflation accelerates. At the same time, there is automatic sterilization in the United States. Thus, the world money supply rises unduly when the dollar depreciates (but *because* it does not depreciate enough) and similarly falls unduly when the dollar appreciates.

If one regards this outcome as undesirable and accepts both leaning-against-the-wind policies and nonsterilization (or inadequate sterilization) as inevitable, it is necessary to look at the causes of the expectational shifts that have fueled the actual and incipient capital movements. Are the changes in expectations rational or not? Furthermore, are the resultant capital movements encouraged or made possible by the multicurrency system? In fact, one comes back to the same issues that were discussed earlier. In general, it seems to me that instabilities in policies of major countries — caused by understandable and perhaps inevitable political factors — must be blamed for instabilities in expectations about exchange rates. And, with regard to the multicurrency system, the scope for speculation, whether rational or otherwise, would hardly alter if all official reserves were held in one currency, since the opportunities and motivations for private-sector speculation would still exist.

Is the International Capital Market Adequate?

The international capital market is the generator of official reserves and of liquidity, and the question is whether SDRs should supplement or replace it in some way. Presumably, there would be no need for SDRs if the capital market were entirely adequate. I shall explore three possible inadequacies and then go on to consider whether SDRs could do better.

To begin with, it must be noted that the international capital market is certainly perfect in the usually accepted sense of that term, or, at least, it must be one of the more perfect markets existing anywhere in the world. It absorbs and makes use of a vast amount of information and has given rise to a great information industry of its own. There is free entry. Its pricing is extremely flexible, as is reflected in the numerous and continuously changing margins for different borrowers and the term structure of interest rates. It has been remarkably neutral politically. Although there are some very large borrowers, lenders, and — above all — intermediaries, the market is in no sense monopolized. Let us now consider three possible inadequacies — namely, (1) unwise lending and borrowing, (2) inadequate insurance, and (3) failure to redistribute world income.

Unwise lending and borrowing. In the discussion of unwise lending and borrowing [underlying recent international debt problems], I shall first look backward and then forward.

With hindsight, we can see that some of the market participants have not shown foresight. We, and they, can now see that they may have been foolish or ignorant. Or perhaps they were only running some calculated risks. With respect to banks, good profits were made for many years by running risks. With respect to sovereign borrowers, political rewards were reaped by spending generously out of borrowed funds, or by postponing needed adjustments. Similarly, some private companies may have run undue risks or made misjudgments. But now there is trouble. Could these problems have been prevented or reduced by official controls of some kind, possibly by supervision from the Fund? . . . Here it has to be noted that governments of major lending countries strongly supported bank lending to some of the countries that subsequently turned out to have big debt problems.

In spite of this last factor, I suspect that if funds had been channeled through the Fund or through the central banks of major lending countries, they would have been more cautiously applied; and, in total, the flow of funds to developing countries would have been far less, with more going to governments and corporations in developed countries. In spite of current difficulties, it is not clear that this would have been a better outcome. From the point of view of world efficiency, quite apart from international income distribution considerations, the public bodies might have erred in the opposite direction from the private banks by being overcautious.

So much for looking backward. Now, what about the future? In view of current problems, the question must arise whether the role of the capital market in providing funds to many sovereign borrowers may be coming to an end. Although some lending may have been excessive in the past, we could be moving into a period of unwise or undesirably limited international lending, at least to developing countries. Because of a tendency to overreact, lending may be too limited . . . from a world efficiency point of view. . . . This implies, of course, that the private market may not be efficient and raises the related issue of whether supplementary public lending would compensate to the right extent or would overreact by providing funds too readily, at least to those sovereign borrowers viewed with favor by the political masters of the public agencies. . . . The issue . . . of arrangements for rescue, whether of sovereign borrowers or of international banks . . . is essentially an insurance issue, to which I come next.

Inadequate insurance. Although there is a private insurance market, one cannot insure against major liquidity crises or bankruptcy in this market. Domestic depositors in banks are usually protected, and the banks themselves have some degree of insurance through the lender-of-last resort commitments (insofar as these exist) of central banks. Because of the "moral hazard" problem, the insurer must exercise some degree of supervision, and this provides the logic for central bank supervision of private banks. . . .

Here, I want to focus specifically on the insurance problems of sovereign borrowers. It is not really possible for a nation to insure in the normal way against unexpected exogenous developments, such as deterioration in the terms of trade, or against the consequences of mistakes in policies. The problem is that the country may not be able to borrow in the international capital market because of unexpected circumstances that preclude such borrowing or because of prohibitive interest rates. A country may then be faced with major problems of reducing real expenditures. It is at this point that the Fund and international reserve assets come in.

The insurance is not just against unexpected developments affecting the particular country concerned but also against an unexpected tightening of conditions in the international capital market for whatever reason, or even against a breakdown in the market owing to a loss of confidence, possibly caused by defaults. This is the eventuality that, at least in its more moderate form, appears to be in prospect now. Governments insure against such situations by accumulating owned reserves. To that extent, the international capital market does provide the required service. But, in addition, governments provide mutual insurance for each other at no immediate cost by setting up swap arrangements and by creating international reserve assets.

Fund quotas can be regarded as part of a sovereign insurance system. Governments provide a line of credit, in effect, to the World Insurance Company (the IMF); and it, in turn, is prepared to come to the rescue of its customers. An insurance company, of course, must exercise some supervision to ensure that the customer tries to avoid getting into trouble, and if and when he does, that he puts his house in order and avoids mistakes in the future. There is a sovereign moral hazard problem that provides the logic for conditionality and for one of the principal activities of the Fund, surveillance.

Failure to redistribute world income. The private market discriminates against bad risks, in the worst cases by refusing to lend to them at all and more generally by charging higher interest rates. The bad risks tend to include the poorest nations, yet there is no inevitable relationship between a particular sovereign risk and the per capita gross national product of that country. Although this tendency of the market is not explicit discrimination against poor countries, . . . [it] does not help those whose poverty has pushed them out of the world market. . . .

. . . Efficiency considerations ignore income-distribution effects. It is legitimate to concentrate on efficiency if independent income distribution policies to implement a "world social welfare function" (something that can only be implicit) are being pursued. In practice, we know they are not, so there is at least a logical basis for taking world-income-distribution considerations into account when making various international arrangements, such as those under discussion here. This is the argument for a link [proposal — a proposal to link SDR creation to foreign aid]. On the other hand, some prefer to maintain a clear separation between the efficiency objective and the income-distribution objective and thus prefer international monetary arrangements to be directed at achieving (or moving closer to) world efficiency, while leaving redistribution objectives to other parts of the system, such as bilateral aid and the activities of the World Bank Group.

Capital Market Inadequacies and the SDR

I now consider the implications of these three possible capital market inadequacies for proposals to expand the role of the SDR.

First, something must be said about the fundamental characteristic of the SDR, as it exists now. A country that uses its SDRs is making use of a line of credit at a concessional rate of interest. The SDR interest rate is based on the short-term market rates of the five countries whose currencies make up the basket. For some borrowers, these interest rates are close to the rates at which they can actually borrow, so that there is little element of concession and hence little motive for using SDRs. On the other hand, for others, these five rates are well below the rates at which they can actually borrow, or at which they can always be certain they could borrow.

The certainty that this line of credit is always available is, in itself, a quality that the . . . private capital market does not provide. The certainty depends on the extent to which holders can be sure that the Fund will always designate some country to accept SDRs and that this country will always adhere to the obligations it incurred when it became a participant in the SDR scheme.

It has to be remembered that while the user of the SDR — that is, the borrower — is getting an implicit subsidy, the assigned recipient, the lender, may be paying an implicit tax. The extent to which there is such a tax is indicated by the extent to which countries are reluctant to hold SDRs, so that assignment (by designation of participants) is necessary. If the SDR interest rate were truly an appropriately weighted market rate for riskless bonds (and if there were no limitations on the use of SDRs by net acquirers), there should be no reluctance to accept SDRs, and hence no implicit tax on lenders. . . .

Would SDRs reduce unwise lending? If large issues of SDRs had been made in 1974 and every year thereafter, many sovereign borrowers would not have needed to go to the world capital market. . . .

The question is whether possibilities of unwise lending or borrowing would have been less. On the SDRs themselves, interest rates would have been less than in the capital market; to that extent, the strain would have been reduced. But the possibility would have remained that a country that was using its SDRs and thus committing itself to regular interest payments would not have been able to make them; the possibility of default would have remained. But this time the intermediary would not have been a private bank but rather the Fund. The Fund would have borne the risks, and its members would have covered any losses in proportion to their quotas. This might have been regarded as desirable, since there is a virtue in risk spreading. Furthermore, it could be argued that because of the greater potential power of the Fund, especially in a regime where it disposes of SDRs on a large scale, the risk that countries might default to the Fund is much less than the risk that they might default on debts to private lenders or individual governments. Thus, SDRs would reduce world risks — presumably leading to a world efficiency gain. . . .

On the other hand, the uniform interest rate on SDRs has to be contrasted with the varying margins that the private market charges. This seems to me an important consideration that weighs against SDRs. It is clearly efficient for interest rates to include margins for risk; in this important respect, then, the SDR is inefficient. The private market imposes margins and, in the limiting case, can actually refuse to lend to a really risky potential borrower. Thus, a strong incentive is provided for countries to maintain their creditworthiness by managing their economies sensibly and, above all, by not defaulting. By contrast, irrespective of the recipient's creditworthiness, SDRs are automatically issued to all participants. The probability of a participant defaulting on the interest payments cannot be taken into account when issuing SDRs. If the participant does default, he is no longer entitled to his share of SDRs.

Looking back, then, greater issues of SDRs would have led to a partial replacement of private lending by SDRs, with the consequences just discussed. Looking forward, the same analysis applies. If SDRs were issued on a large scale, to a considerable extent they would replace private lending, changing its pattern, presumably in the direction of those countries — primarily developing countries — that would be able to borrow little or nothing in the private market. In addition, there might be some net rise in total international lending. . . . As discussed earlier, whether this effect would be desirable depends on the extent to which the private market may be inefficiently *over*reacting to recent events by *under*lending to developing countries.

Quotas compared with SDRs as insurance mechanism — conditionality issue. Issues of SDRs are a form of insurance, as is any arrangement for mutual increases in owned reserves. The logic is the same as that for Fund quotas, which has already been discussed. Swap facilities under the General Arrangements to Borrow fall into the same category. If it is desired to increase the level of sovereign insurance, is this done better by an increase in quotas or an increase in SDRs?

This raises the question of how SDRs compare with quotas. . . . The key distinction between quotas and SDRs is that beyond the first credit tranche, the former involve conditionality and the latter do not. This refers to SDRs as at present issued. If they were issued not directly to participants but rather to the Fund itself, which could then use them for lender-of-last-resort lending subject to conditionality, the distinction would disappear. As discussed earlier, insurance always involves the problem of moral hazard, and this requires the insurance company to exercise some supervision. Hence a scheme with conditionality seems more appropriate than one without. . . .

If one accepts the case for associating conditionality with the international creation of official liquidity to supplement the private market on the grounds of the "insurance argument," it seems to follow that one must have reservations about a large-scale issue of unconditional SDRs. The case is stronger for increasing quotas or issuing SDRs directly to the Fund to strengthen its resources for conditional lending. . . .

SDRs as aid. A general issue of SDRs subsidizes borrowers and possibly taxes lenders. The subsidy benefit goes not only to those who would have been borrowers in the private market in any event but also to those who are able to borrow for the first time. Because the latter consist mainly or wholly of the poorest developing countries and the former also consist more of developing than developed countries (although this varies year by year, and a generalization is difficult), this particular international redistribution of income would probably tend to favor the poor over the rich — the latter including, notably, the OPEC low absorbers, the Federal Republic of Germany, and Japan. . . .

The SDR system provides the opportunity to introduce much more explicit discrimination into the system, thus raising the "link" issue. But a possibility of discrimination also exists in determining the size of Fund quotas (or the size of drawing rights relative to quotas), so that there is not necessarily a distinction between these two devices in this respect. It is understandable that developing countries prefer to receive unconditional liquidity — even though the interest rate on SDRs is much closer to market rates than it was once — rather than conditional liquidity. If aid is to be given in this form rather than through the usual channels, my own preference would be for conditionality, but this raises issues that go well beyond the scope of this paper.

Conclusion — SDRs Within the Present System

Suppose we stay within the present laissez-faire system. There will be a need for some officially owned reserves and certainly for liquidity. In this system, the international capital market has, until now, generated both as required. The problem of reserve adequacy or excess has not arisen. Because exchange rates can move, a country can choose its own monetary policies, and its reserve situation — which in any case is endogenous — need not determine domestic inflation or recession. . . .

There is an argument in favor of a substitution account designed to reduce exchange rate fluctuations, but I find this argument tenuous. The only connection between SDRs and the domestic macroeconomic disequilibria that have dominated countries since 1973 is through exchange rate variability; only if a substitution of SDRs for a multicurrency system actually succeeded in reducing exchange rate variability — itself a doubtful assumption — might SDRs also have some favorable effect — although hardly an overwhelming one — on domestic macro-economic situations.

It is doubtful that there is a really significant role for the SDR to play within the framework of the current system. This does not, of course, exclude a modest role. Possibly some weight should be given to the risk-spreading role of a large financial intermediary owned by all the world's governments that would have the ability to reduce, rather than merely shifting, world risks, and consequently to narrow interest rate margins. . . . But it may be justified to create some SDRs to compensate for a possible tendency of the international capital market to overreact to recent events and *under*lend to developing countries. If this is the motive, it would be logical to limit the SDR issue purely to developing countries.

The issue of SDRs or any kind of international reserve asset can be regarded as a desirable mutual insurance system, but here an association with conditionality seems to be appropriate, so that an increase in quotas, or of Fund resources possibly denominated in SDRs and available for conditional lending, is preferable to an increase in unconditional SDRs. This would also be a way of preparing for the possibility of reduced lending to sovereign borrowers by the international capital market. Finally, the issue of SDRs can have some effect, even if small, on international income distribution and the question is whether this could be better done through SDR allocations than through two alternatives — namely, differential quota arrangements associated with conditionality or explicit aid, bilateral or multilateral.

II. A FIXED-EXCHANGE-RATE WORLD

It seems unlikely that the major industrial nations will return to a system of fixed exchange rates, with or without occasional exchange rate adjustments. Now that they have tasted monetary policy freedom, it is improbable that they would give it up. This is so, even though much lip service is paid to the virtues of fixed rates and though it is clear that no one really likes fluctuating exchange rates. What national decision makers like is the monetary policy freedom that inevitably leads to fluctuating rates. Similarly, it seems unlikely that they will accept constraints on their use of the international capital market, including constraints on their choice of reserve assets. Nevertheless, one can, perhaps, envisage two different scenarios.

According to the first scenario, the world economy gradually calms down and stabilizes, essentially because of greater stability in macroeconomic policies and more successful ad hoc policy coordination between different countries aimed at avoiding the large medium-term exchange rate variations that the world has seen since 1973. But this would be the outcome not of formal international constraints or rules but of improved domestic policies. An agreement to fix nominal exchange rate relationships for as long as possible, without firm commitment — rather like an extended European Monetary System — might then be the result of such an essentially evolutionary process. The question is what implications this would have for the SDR.

It would mean that the choice of one currency basket over another would matter little to central banks. When there is reasonable certainty about future exchange rate relationships — a special case of which is certainty that rates will stay fixed to each other — there is less need to choose portfolios carefully, provided interest rates are flexible and capital markets (including forward markets) free. This means that countries would be more willing to subscribe voluntarily to a substitution account if there were some international pressure to do so. On the other hand, it also means that they might just as well hold dollars, or whatever was the favored reserve currency in that far-ahead halcyon era. In other words, the SDR might become more acceptable because it would matter less. These developments might lead to increased use of Fund-issued SDRs, or of private baskets denominated in SDRs, because world stability had been restored and not because such stability resulted from, or depended on, the SDR. We have no argument in favor of the SDR here; only an expectation of its innocuousness.

The second scenario — which seems rather less probable — is that exchange rate conditions get more and more unstable; elements of the international financial system "collapse"; and inflation and/or unemployment get worse. In other words, there is a crisis, whether slow or sudden. This may then lead to so much dissatisfaction — with blame being attached to the international monetary system — that policymakers will be psychologically ready to try a drastic change. One can imagine a great international conference designed to sort out all these problems. Possibly it would be preceded by major changes of governments, with the new governments all promising to come up with solutions. One can then conceive of a decision to establish a fixed-exchange-rate system with centralized determination of reserves and with the Fund turning into some kind of international central bank. The Fund might be instructed, or constitutionally committed, to follow a conservative monetary policy. The Keynes Plan or the various plans inspired by Triffin might then come into their own.

In current conditions, one finds this latter scenario hard to imagine. After all, if the major economies become more and more unstable, and especially if inflation and unemployment worsen, this is likely to occur mainly because governments have found it difficult to constrain their own citizens — that is, to impose constraints on sectional interests and to make compatible their excessive competing demands. Would it then be possible for the international community — in effect, a collective of major governments — to impose constraints on its constituent parts? But it is in such a situation that the SDR might come into its own, not because of its particular denomination but because of its status as the sole official international reserve asset, the regulation of which would ensure that world reserves were neither inadequate nor excessive. It is, of course, with fixed exchange rates that reserve levels determine, or at least influence, world inflation.

This is the Keynes–Triffin vision. As it has been spelled out so often, I hardly need go into it in detail here. Countries would still have some flexibility, since they would be able to borrow and lend in the world capital market. Presumably, the official sector would be prohibited from operating in the market directly, but budget deficits could be financed by sales of bonds at home; and, through the linking of capital markets, such deficits would, in effect, be financed on the world market. There would have to be compulsory substitution of existing reserve assets and a prohibition on central banks' dealing in gold. Although the dollar might still be the intervention currency, there would have to be a firm limit on the amount of dollars that could be held by central banks. Finally, and perhaps most importantly, the United States would have to be treated like any other country. It would have to settle its deficits in SDRs. To use the once-popular jargon, there would have to be "symmetry" through "asset settlement." . . .

The outside possibility of such a system being established suggests that there is a case for keeping SDRs going currently (quite apart from their use within the present system). They may not have a very significant current role, and possibly little future role, but it seems useful to have a device in operation that can be utilized and expanded should a real or perceived need for SDRs arise.

Finally, one cannot leave this discussion of a world-wide fixed-exchange-rate system and a world central bank without noting the underlying issue. This concerns the desirable degree of centralization of monetary decision making. At the one extreme is the present decentralized system, with the market, combined with ad hoc arrangements, coordinating the consequences of national governmental and private decisions. At the other extreme is internationally centralized decision making. The issue is not whether governments should intervene — they inevitably do so through their monetary and fiscal policies — but whether there should be a substantial element of "world government," with international voting or political bargaining within a centralized framework replacing the market and ad hoc bargaining.

This issue does not arise when various modest proposals for the SDR within the present system are discussed — for example, whether SDRs should be increased to a small extent, supplementing existing reserve assets, or whether there should be a voluntary substitution account. In that event, the Fund would become just another actor in the market. It arises only in connection with the ambitious Keynes–Triffin world central bank proposals that are only meaningful if exchange rates are fixed.

Let us put aside for the moment the question of which system of organization would be preferable from a world point of view. The prior question is whether there is the slightest chance that decentralized market forces can be prevented from operating. We know that even in socialist countries, it is difficult — in spite of all the authority of the state — to hold market forces down. It seems obvious that this must be so in the international community, where there is no effective state authority. The proposal really is to make the world — or perhaps the major industrial countries, combined with any other countries that choose to join — an area of monetary integration.

There are cases where sovereign nations have effectively been part of monetary unions; but in those cases the leadership — that is, the monetary decisions — has come from a major nation, to which others have voluntarily attached themselves and from which they have been free to detach themselves. Usually the minor partner has been an ex-colony or economic dependency of some kind. It is a different matter for genuinely sovereign nations, several of large economic size, to engage in monetary integration without prior or simultaneous political integration. These difficulties have been discussed in connection with proposals for European monetary integration. It has not been possible to bring about monetary integration in the European Community; it is unlikely to be possible for a much larger grouping.

Logically, one must distinguish the possible or probable from the desirable. Perhaps attainment of the Keynes–Triffin vision may not be very probable, but would it be desirable? The present system certainly leads to considerable disharmony and friction. Policies of particular governments with respect to their monetary, exchange rate, and fiscal policies may have adverse effects on other countries or, at least, on sectors of other countries. . . . The policies may also be unwise from the point of view of the interests of their own citizens. But would a world central bank do better? Would it produce steadier monetary growth? Presumably, it would have to estimate changes in the world demand for international money (SDRs) assuming zero or steady inflation, but this might present some difficulty if national moneys were still used domestically and, perhaps, if the private sector were still using national moneys in international trade and the capital market.

Governments are frequently faced with dilemmas. They have to balance increased unemployment in the short run against increased inflation later. Political judgments must be made to strike the balance, bearing in mind the need to maintain public support for policies, to avoid social tensions, and to maximize the present value of the expected real-income effects, perhaps weighted by income-distribution considerations. It seems to me that decisions like these are best made within the nation-state. Of course, the theory of optimum currency areas teaches us that a state can be too small, or its size at least nonoptimal, to conduct an independent monetary policy. At the moment, one can conceive of Western Europe making up an optimal currency area, but it seems to me highly unlikely that this could be said about a larger grouping that would include, in addition, North America and Japan, let alone the whole nonsocialist world. . . .

III. CONCLUSION

At the beginning of this paper, I noted the "realities-intentions gap" about the SDR and speculated whether the SDR was just a relic or whether the proclaimed intention to make the SDR "the principal reserve asset in the international monetary system" laid the groundwork for possible changes.

The greater part of the paper has been devoted to an analysis of the current international monetary nonsystem and to a detailed discussion of possible problems or limitations of this system and of the extent to which SDRs could deal with these problems. I then speculated whether a new fixed-rate system with centrally controlled reserves might be established and considered the implications of such a system. . . .

Let me conclude by summarizing the practical implications that seem to come out of this discussion.

First, there is always the outside possibility that at some stage the international community will decide to construct a new fixed-exchange-rate system with centralized determination of reserves. This might be the response to a major international crisis, though it is an outcome that seems unlikely. In that case, an international reserve asset such as the SDR would come into its own. It would then be useful if the SDR, and the various arrangements associated with it, already existed. Thus, even though the SDR might have little significant role or prospects within the present system, it might be a good idea to keep it going at a modest level should the situation change.

Second, it seems improbable that a voluntary substitution account would make much difference to the instability of exchange rates. The basic causes for instability can be found in the macroeconomic policies of the major countries. . . .

Third, the SDR can be an instrument of international income redistribution, especially for those countries that at present are not able to use the international capital market at all, or only to a very small extent. The number of these countries has increased lately. A case can, of course, be made for such redistribution. But if really large sums are to be involved, the donors — in fact, the potential acquirers of SDRs — would surely look for some degree of conditionality.

Fourth, it is possible that the effect of recent difficulties in the international capital market will be an undue reluctance by the private capital market to lend to developing countries. By "undue," I mean that lending would be too low from a world efficiency point of view, bearing in mind prospective risks. This can provide a qualified argument for an increase in SDRs within the present system. The issue might be limited to developing countries; possibly it ought to be associated with conditionality (through the issue being made to the Fund, which could then supplement or replace the lending of private banks, as appropriate); and it would certainly not represent a move toward "making the special drawing right the principal reserve asset of the international monetary system."

Fifth, and most important, the principal justification for the international creation of reserve assets is as a mutual insurance arrangement among nations. But this raises the issue of moral hazard, which calls for supervision by the World Insurance Company. It is here that one can see the key role of the Fund. The annual consultations can be regarded as a form of supervision before claims on the company are made, while conditionality is supervision associated with the controlled payment of claims. Perhaps the analogy can be pushed too far, but it does draw attention to the crucial role of conditionality.

SDRs are at present *unconditional* drawing rights, and I have suggested that — insofar as a significant expansion of international liquidity is justified on insurance grounds (and I believe that it is) — this would then be better done through increases in quotas or the expansion of the direct resources of the Fund.

This could, alternatively, be achieved by issuing SDRs initially to the Fund rather than directly to members. Hence, to that extent, there appears to be a clear potential role for an expansion of SDRs within the present system. But it has to be added that much the same objective could be achieved through the normal expansion of quotas or by the Fund borrowing on the capital market, in the latter case with members of the Fund collectively guaranteeing the loans.

The SDR does seem to be a relic of the visions of the recent past. If it did not exist already, we might now create it, but certainly with far less ambitious intentions than have prevailed at various times. In any event, given that the SDR exists, there is good reason for keeping it, at the minimum, in hibernation. . . .

DISCUSSION

Herbert G. Grubel

I am in general agreement with most of the points made in Professor Corden's paper, except for the most central one made in the conclusion of Section I. There, he describes how, in the present system of flexible exchange rates and a globally integrated capital market, private international liquidity has been provided in adequate amounts. From this he concludes that "The problem of reserve adequacy or excess has not arisen" and that "it is doubtful that there is really a significant role for the SDR to play within the framework of the current system.". . .

Corden's conclusions are based on the correct analysis that, in terms of what I would like to call static efficiency, a globally collective approach to liquidity creation through the International Monetary Fund has no distinct advantages and is beset by a number of technical and political problems which give the private solution an edge. My criticism of this analysis and conclusion is essentially that it is incomplete. It has neglected dynamic criteria of efficiency, which swing the balance to the advantage of the collective approach, if its operation is properly protected from the influence of political interest groups.

In the following, I develop my analysis by first drawing a parallel between the nature of domestic and international liquidity. Then I review the case for and against the use of central banks for the creation of domestic liquidity. In the next section, I make the case for SDRs on the same dynamic arguments used as a rationale for central banks. . . .

It will be obvious from the following analysis that it is designed to provide general and broad ideas about the future of special drawing rights and the Fund. It provides a compass setting for policies, rather than a road map. As such, it concentrates on the basic issue of whether the SDR system improves world welfare through increased efficiency in the operation of national economies in an economically interdependent world.

Similarity of domestic and international liquidity. Modern theory emphasizes the usefulness of money in carrying out purchases that have a stochastic time profile that is different from that of income. An analogous lack of synchronization in foreign exchange receipts and payments characterizes the international financial relations of all countries and gives international liquidity its utility.

This simple analogy is flawed, of course, because exchange rate changes and speculators can always equalize the demand for, and supply of, foreign exchange, so that in principle there is no need for a central authority to hold international money and arbitrage differences in the timing of income and expenditures. On this fact rests the case for freely floating exchange rates. In the following, I will disregard this case and simply assume that the efficiency of international exchange is enhanced by appropriate exchange rate stabilization efforts of national governments. Otherwise there is no need at all for analyzing questions of international liquidity. The assumption also allows me to concentrate on the question of whether the money for intervention should be provided by free market processes or by an institution created collectively by international agreement among nation-states.

The merit of central banks. It may be useful to set the stage for the following analysis by posing a question that is rarely found in the literature: What is so peculiar about money that its supply cannot be left to the private market? I find this not only a legitimate question but also an important one in our time, when economists have been rediscovering the merit of market solutions generally, even in the presence of externalities, because government programs seem inevitably to produce so-called nonmarket failures of their own. In my answer to this question, I distinguish static, dynamic, knowledge, and political criteria of efficiency.

STATIC EFFICIENCY. The great resource cost of commodity money makes it inevitable that even under complete laissez-faire, fiduciary money will take its place. However, there are significant externalities costs in the use of private coins and bank notes. The use of private currency forces transactors into generating expensive information about the creditworthiness of issuers. The information problem is complicated by the ease with which currency can be counterfeited.[2]

A central bank, as the monopoly issuer of legal-tender currency, internalizes these externalities in the service of society. In addition, it reaps the benefits of economies of scale in the production and surveillance of the currency. The excess profits earned by the central bank monopoly accrue to society as a whole, since the central bank is required to transfer them to general government use.

The case for the collective approach to the issue of currency on static efficiency grounds is almost unassailable in principle. The magnitude of the gains, however, is likely to be quite small in today's world, where the services of currency represent a tiny fraction of total income and where modern technology might well produce very efficient methods for dealing with the information externalities. A strong case for or against central banks must rest on the potentially much larger dynamic efficiency criteria.

DYNAMIC EFFICIENCY. Business cycles and random shocks to stability are an unalterable fact of economic life. While cycles have a certain beneficial cathartic effect, most economists believe that public welfare is greater, the smaller are the frequency and magnitude of business cycle fluctuations and the more readily economies adjust to other disturbances. There is strong historic evidence that free banking tends to contribute to cyclical instability. The reason is that bankers' behavior produces procyclical variations in the money supply, since their expectations are formed by much the same forces that make the rest of the economy alternate between unsustainable overspending and underspending. Historic evidence also suggests that sometimes, private banking systems have been unable to deal effectively with exogenous shocks, such as massive increases in gold supplies or harvest failures. To strengthen this conclusion, it is worth quoting Milton Friedman (1960, p. 8) on this subject: "Something like a moderately stable monetary framework seems an essential prerequisite for the effective operation of a private market economy. It is dubious that the market can by itself provide such a framework. Hence, the function of providing one is an essential governmental function on a par with the provision of a stable legal framework."

This dynamic case for the collective-money-supply solution is widely accepted in principle. Until recently, few economists other than F. v. Hayek (1976) appear to have doubted its quantitative importance. At any rate, the modern literature on money and banking is dominated by concern with the technique by which central banks can carry out their stabilization function. The basic rationale for these policies is rarely questioned.

KNOWLEDGE. Economists who believe in the social usefulness of central banks as dynamic stabilizing agents are divided into two groups. The first envisages the central bank making countercyclical policy, raising interest rates during booms and lowering them during recessions. The second is skeptical of the ability of central banks to make successful countercyclical policy because of the lags between changes in interest rates and because their effect on real variables is variable and unpredictable. Moreover, nominal interest rates often are a misleading guide for stabilization policies.

The disagreement over the efficacy of monetary policy in economic stabilization is at the heart of the continuing controversy between Keynesians and monetarists. The monetarist case has been articulated and documented by Friedman and his disciples. Their interpretation of history has led them to advocate that central banks be required to adhere to constant-money-supply-growth rules.

POLITICAL CRITERIA. The modern theory of regulation argues that it leads naturally to nonmarket failures, the social cost of which exceeds that of unregulated markets. This outcome stems from the power of interest groups which politicize the regulatory process and turn it to their advantage rather than that of society as a whole. In addition, there tends to be overregulation because its cost is diffuse and unlikely to injure the interests of the administrators using their considerable discretionary power.

The dangers of a politicized central bank have, of course, been recognized for a long time. They provide the other justification for the Friedman recommendation that the Federal Reserve System be required by law to follow a monetary growth rule. Most recently, it has been argued that the money supply should be governed by rules enshrined in the constitution to prevent them from becoming politicized by simple-majority voting. . . .

The case for collective international liquidity. The merit of institutions and agreements for the collective creation of international money, such as SDRs, can now be examined in the light of the preceding analysis of domestic issues. In doing so, I consider the pure case where countries hold only SDRs as reserves but use small inventories of key currencies for actual market intervention. Shortages or surpluses of such currencies are settled through SDR exchanges with the Fund.

Let us first consider *static efficiency*. It seems that, as is the case with most collective approaches, the exploitation of scale economies and the benefits of standardization give a slight edge to the collective solution and SDRs, while the dynamic innovation characteristics favor private suppliers. In the end, there is not enough difference to influence the choice decisively.

The problem of distributing the seigniorage which accrues to a monopoly issuer of money has been solved ingeniously by the method used to create SDRs and to charge and credit interest on them. Under the present method, seigniorage accrues to holders of reserves in proportion to their contribution to its existence. It is, therefore, distributionally neutral and approaches the market solution.

In terms of *dynamic efficiency,* the SDR system promises to offer the same kinds of external benefits as does the system of collectively managed domestic money supplies. Thus, SDRs could be created countercyclically and to deal with random disturbances. Above-normal increases in international reserves during global demand deficiencies would permit deficit countries to maintain demand and exchange rates at higher levels than they could in the absence of these reserve increases. As a result, global aggregate demand would either be maintained or would shrink less. Analogously, below-normal increases in reserves during global booms would limit excess demand. The principles of Keynesian countercyclical money-supply management and policies to deal with a wide variety of exogenous shocks are applicable directly to international reserve management. The welfare benefits from such policies are obvious.

However, the importance of the *knowledge* and *political problems* associated with collective solutions suggests that the actively countercyclical and shock-absorbing creation of reserves may give rise to serious nonmarket failures. For instance, the recent inability to reach agreement on a substitution account and on significant increases in SDR supplies may be interpreted as the result of the politicization of the process. Powerful interest groups, perceiving a threat to the rents they have obtained from existing arrangements, have effectively prevented policies that many neutral observers would view as enhancing global welfare.

By the same reasoning, of course, there exists also the threat that interest-group coalitions will develop which, at other times, will force the excess or procyclical creation of SDRs. The link proposal would encourage the formation of such coalitions. For this main reason it appears that the link would be detrimental to global welfare in the longer run.

To deal with the problems of politicization of the international money supply system, it seems important, therefore, to have SDRs created by rules similar to those recommended by monetarists for central banks. Countercyclical variations in interest rates under such a regime would serve to dampen the magnitude of cyclical fluctuations. Growth-rate rules for SDRs would produce additional benefits if, in fact, there were unknown lags from their creation to their effectiveness. On the other hand, such rules would reduce the ability of the system to respond to random disturbances. . . .

Summary and conclusions. Politicians and policymakers have been said to turn to economists for the same reason that drunks turn to lampposts, for support rather than illumination. The preceding analysis was designed to provide illumination. Unfortunately, it showed that determining the merit of collective solutions to liquidity creation involves very difficult conceptual and measurement problems, which economists have only begun to address. As a scholar, I cannot honestly interpret existing knowledge as lending strong support for either case.

However, in conclusion, I would like to give free reign to all of the psychological and historic influences that shape judgment, in contrast with scientifically rigorous knowledge. In doing so, I will provide a lamppost for some politicians and policymakers at this conference. In a nutshell, my judgment is that money and international liquidity are different from potatoes and air travel in essential ways that are relevant to the present problem. For this reason, I believe there is an important role for an international reserve asset, such as the SDR, to play in providing greater global stability.

The main specific policy conclusion based on the preceding analysis, mixed with personal judgment, is that SDR growth rates should be depoliticized as much as possible by the employment of growth rules. Any loss of benefits owing to countercyclical variation in SDR growth rates caused by the adoption of growth rules would be minor relative to the gains from reducing political influence on the SDR creation process, especially if unknown lags resulted in countercyclical policies achieving limited success. While the original setting and periodic review of rules are political in themselves, the use of qualified-majority voting can reduce the likelihood that the system will be abused by narrow interest groups and their coalitions.

In fact, of course, the Fund has already enacted the rule that increases in SDRs must be approved by members having a qualified majority of 85 percent of total votes. In addition, the distribution of approved increases in SDRs normally occurs in equal amounts over a period of years, a provision which is almost equivalent to a growth rule. My analysis suggests that these provisions are efficient and serve to protect the system from political abuse and the destabilization of the global economy. National politicians concerned about these potential costs of SDR creation can take comfort from the existence of these safeguards and support an increased role for SDRs in the international monetary system with much less concern than would be warranted otherwise.

Notes

1. The line of argument to follow, which runs through this paper, is developed more fully in Corden (1983).
2. Friedman (1960, page 8) notes that "the features of money that justify government intervention [are] the resource cost of a pure commodity currency and hence its tendency to become partly fiduciary; the peculiar difficulty of enforcing contracts involving promises to pay that serve as a medium of exchange and of preventing fraud in respect to them."

References

Corden, W. M., "The Logic of the International Monetary Non-System," in *Reflections on a Troubled World Economy,* ed. by F. Machlup and others (London: Macmillan (for the Trade Policy Research Center), 1983).

Friedman, Milton, *A Program for Monetary Stability* (New York: Fordham University Press, 1960).

McKinnon, Ronald I., "Currency Substitution and Instability in the World Dollar Market," *American Economic Review, 72* (June 1982), 320–33.

Hayek, Friedrich von, *Denationalization of Money,* Hobart Paper Special No. 70 (London: Institute of Economic Affairs, 1976).

IX

International Debt Problems

International debt problems hang like a sword over the international financial and trading systems. The debt crisis of 1982 was not so much overcome as tenuously suspended. Any new crisis of the same magnitude would generate chaotic shrinkage of trade and payments with major debtor countries. Some or all of them might be expected to default — that is, to cease paying interest on their debt, or perhaps even to repudiate it. Barriers to trade and financial payments would mushroom, reversing the trend of forty years. And some of the world's largest banks might fail.

Yet many commentators do not find a new debt crisis very likely. The sword will not fall, they believe, because it has been balanced by a mix of sensible actions taken by debtor and creditor governments, by international banks, and by the International Monetary Fund (IMF). This optimistic view is reflected by Cline and Mohammed in the readings below, although with considerable caution. Dornbusch is less optimistic, arguing that sooner or later the distributional sacrifices currently being made by debtors in favor of creditors, and by lower classes in favor of upper classes, will destabilize the balance. He alone speaks of the "equity problem" of current arrangements.

All agree that the "liquidity problem" of debtor countries — the problem of just paying interest on debt — has been ameliorated by a stretching out of interest payments (rescheduling), and by an astounding increase in exports and decrease in imports. Not all agree on whether debtor countries have a "solvency problem" — insufficient national wealth to ever pay back the stock of accumulated debt as well as interest on it. Cline (and implicitly Mohammed) dismiss any notion that there is a solvency problem. Dornbusch is more pessimistic, recognizing the political dimension of the sovereign solvency problem. *Any* debtor whose assets technically allow liabilities to be repaid may not want to become impoverished by doing so. When such a debtor is a sovereign government, no law, no bankruptcy court, no police force can force it legally to do what it or its political constituents refuse to do.

Differences like these among the authors make Cline and Mohammed content with the "case-by-case approach" to debt problems, which Dornbusch dismisses disdainfully as "muddling through." Cline and Mohammed see the IMF as a coordinating savior — monitoring debtor governments; prodding creditor banks into involuntary lending; making credit markets work in the midst of "free riding" and other classic reasons for market failure; communicating, cajoling, mediating. Dornbusch by contrast sees the IMF as administering a "classical mugging" to the debtor countries, and as presiding over the cartelization of the world banking system. Yet what would he recommend as a better set of solutions? He does not really say. Nor does he respond to any of Mohammed's four serious criticisms of "general solutions" to international debt problems.

The authors are in more agreement on diagnosis than prescription. All agree that external shocks and ill-advised policies in debtor countries were two fundamental causes of debt problems. Chief illustrations are the unexpected disinflation of the early 1980s and debtor-country currencies that were severely overvalued. The first is well known to penalize debtors and reward creditors — as long as debtors continue to pay (see Lamfalussy's reading in Part X). The second creates irresistible temptations for capital flight, or for excessive spending through trade deficits, or for both, as Dornbusch shows. He is also (not surprisingly) the only author to mention a third fundamental cause of debt problems — that "banks were falling all over themselves to persuade debtors to go yet deeper into debt."

What is the prognosis? External trends are more favorable at this time than Cline hoped and not as worrisome as Dornbusch feared. Interest rates and the foreign-exchange value of the dollar have begun to decline. Growth in developed countries has maintained Cline's threshold, and protection has not yet erupted. Yet the prospect for continued growth and suppression of protectionist surges is at best very fragile. Trends in debtor countries themselves are, by contrast, less favorable then Cline, Mohammed, or the IMF had hoped. They are very much what Dornbusch feared, and may yet be the undoing of the suspension of the debt crisis.

27

International Debt: From Crisis to Recovery?

William R. Cline

Since Mexico temporarily suspended payment in August 1982, the debt crisis has threatened the international financial system and crippled growth in developing countries. Emerging evidence and projection analysis suggest that the problem can be managed, however, if satisfactory growth in the industrial countries can be maintained.

I. ORIGINS, SYSTEMIC RISK, AND EMERGENCY RESPONSE

From 1973 to 1982, external debt of non-oil developing countries rose by $500 billion. Of this amount approximately $260 billion may be attributed to the exceptional rise in oil prices. Global recession in 1981–82 added another $100 billion through declines in the terms of trade and reduced export volume; and the excess of real interest rates in this period over historic averages cost them another $40 billion. External shocks thus accounted for a major portion of the debt crisis. Domestic factors also contributed, especially overvalued exchange rates and inadequate domestic interest rates that caused capital flight (Mexico, Venezuela, and Argentina).

Because debt tends to grow at the interest rate (by "inheritance" from past debt, unless the country runs a trade surplus to pay interest), exports need to grow at least this fast or else the burden of debt relative to exports increases. From 1973 to 1980, international interest rates (including a typical spread above LIBOR [London Interbank Offered Rate — an important reference interest rate]) averaged 10 percent, while nominal export growth from non-oil *LDCs* [Less-Developed Countries] averaged 21 percent. But in 1981–82, the interest rate rose to 16 percent while export growth averaged one percent. The debt problem may usefully be viewed as the consequence of the shift from low or negative real interest rates in the inflationary 1970's to the high real interest rates of the early 1980's, aggravated by declining real exports during the global recession.

In mid-1982, the nine largest U.S. banks had loans outstanding to developing countries and Eastern Europe amounting to 280 percent of their capital, and most had over 100 percent of capital in loans to just Brazil and Mexico. Large losses on *LDC* debt could cause technical insolvency in these banks. Attempts to bail out the banks could prove inflationary, while sharp cutbacks in bank capital

From *American Economic Review Papers and Proceedings* 75 (May 1985), pp. 185–190. Copyright © 1985 by the American Economic Association. Reprinted by permission of the publisher and author. Some text, footnotes, and references omitted.

would mean contractionary pressure as they cut back lending to maintain capital-asset ratios. Although some monetarists have argued that even the large banks could fail without adversely affecting the system if the Fed would maintain steady growth in the money supply, this approach would amount to a global roll of the dice.

Not being gamblers, policymakers responded to the debt crisis with emergency financial packages composed of: (1) a country adjustment program under IMF [International Monetary Fund] auspices; (2) continued new lending by banks; and (3) financial support from the IMF, central banks, and multilateral lending institutions.

II. MODELING DEBT VIABILITY

The premise underlying this policy response was that the debt crisis was one of illiquidity, requiring temporary financing, rather than one of insolvency, involving outright loss of a considerable portion of principal. To examine this question, in the spring of 1983, I developed a projection model for balance of payments and debt of the 19 largest debtor countries (see my 1983 study). . . .

Using this model, my estimates in mid-1983 indicated that the debt problem was indeed one of illiquidity rather than insolvency. Under central expectations for international economic variables (and politically acceptable growth rates in debtor countries), the projections showed that most major countries would show substantial improvement in balances of payments and relative debt burden, and that by the late 1980's, debt-export ratios would be back to levels previously associated with creditworthiness. A return to higher OECD [Organization for Economic Cooperation and Development] growth would increase export volume and prices, an eventual easing of interest rates would moderate interest payments, and a decline in the dollar from its seriously overvalued level would raise the dollar value of the export base. However, the analysis also indicated that a critical threshold of 2½ to 3 percent was required for OECD growth to avoid stagnation or severe deterioration in external deficits and debt-export ratios for debtor countries.

Even with gradual recovery from the debt crisis, however, there remains a difficult interim period during which major debtors will not yet have restored creditworthiness to levels necessary for normal capital market access. Where will financial flows come from in this period? Here I have suggested a model of "involuntary lending." In this model, although a country's creditworthiness is too weak for new creditors to risk lending, existing lenders with current exposure will be prepared to make modest new loans to shore up the quality of existing loans. Existing lenders will extend new credit as long as the expected benefit, the reduction in probability of default multiplied by the amount of outstanding exposure, exceeds the expected cost of new lending, the terminal default probability multiplied by the amount of the new loan.

This model predicts a relatively robust process of continued lending at modest rates. However, it is subject to breakdown because of the free-rider problem. Smaller banks are likely to judge their own actions to have little effect on default probability — even though in the aggregate their actions will affect the outcome.

In a historic departure, the IMF set as a precondition for its own lending that the banks as a group provide significant new lending. Central banks also apparently twisted some arms to ensure participation by smaller banks. These actions helped ensure burden sharing of the public good of increased lending. However, considering that up to two-thirds of bank exposure is held by perhaps 50 to 100 banks internationally, it is likely that a critical mass of banks would have found it in their own interest to provide additional lending even with less official intervention.

So far the mechanism of involuntary lending has held up relatively well. From June 1982 to June 1984, the exposure of U.S. banks in 6 major Latin American debtor countries rose by 9 percent, despite significant reductions in exposure in Argentina and Venezuela by banks other than the largest 24. . . .

For their part, debtor countries have cooperated and carefully avoided an aggressive debtors' cartel. Even though their interest payments exceed new borrowing, they have little incentive to default, because of immediate adverse consequences (drying up of trade credit, possible seizure of export shipments) and long-term damage to their credit reputation.

III. RECENT EVIDENCE

The emerging evidence in 1983–84 has tended to confirm the analysis that the debt problem is one of illiquidity and subject to improvement as international recovery takes place. In 1983, the 19 largest debtor countries (accounting for three-fourths of bank debt) cut their external current account deficits from $56 billion to $23 billion (an even sharper improvement than in my original projections). Mexico achieved a surplus of $5.5 billion instead of the deficit of $3 billion planned under its IMF program. On the strength of a large trade surplus, Brazil will have reduced its current account deficit from $14 billion in 1982 to less than $2 billion in 1984. And although cutbacks of imports have played an important role in these turn-arounds, rising exports have also been important. For 8 major Latin American debtors, after declining by 8 percent from 1981 to 1983, export earnings rose by 12 percent in 1984. (Brazil's exports rose by 21 percent, and Mexico's non-oil exports by 35 percent.) . . .

The centerpiece of debt recovery has materialized: recovery in the international economy. OECD growth has risen from –0.3 in 1982 to 2.3 percent in 1983, and nearly 5 percent in 1984. There have been adverse developments as well: interest rates rose by 2 percentage points in early 1984 (before moderating), and the dollar has continued to climb instead of depreciating. Nonetheless, the benefits from higher OECD growth have swamped these negative factors. Because one percent extra OECD growth offsets 3 percent additional interest charges for non-oil developing countries (in the first year, and more if sustained over several years — although the relationship is less favorable for more highly indebted countries), higher growth in 1984 would have more than compensated for even a sustained 2 percent rise in LIBOR for the year. The most serious setback has been in debtor country growth: Latin American income declined 3 percent in 1983 and per-capita income is 10 percent below the 1980 level. However, growth has once again begun in the region in 1984, with rates of 2 to 3 percent in the major debtor countries, and the prospects are for higher domestic growth in the future.

Projections using updated information through mid-1984 reconfirm the broad analysis that the debt problem is manageable (see my 1984 book, ch. 8). Even assuming some slowdown in OECD growth (2.7 percent in 1985, 2.3 percent in 1986, and 3 percent in 1987), relatively high interest rates (LIBOR at 12.5 percent in 1984, declining to 9.5 percent only by 1987); and assuming a 20 percent decline of the dollar phased over 1985–86 and oil at $29 per barrel, the ratio of net debt to exports of goods and services declines from 200 percent in 1983 to 140 percent by 1987 for the 19 largest debtor countries. For Mexico the decline is from 310 percent to 210 percent; for Brazil, from 370 percent to 230 percent; and for Argentina, from a high 490 percent to 320 percent. Moreover, these projections provide for debtor-country growth at politically acceptable rates of 4½ percent or more per year. And the projections indicate expansion of nominal export earnings at a faster average rate (14.2 percent, 1984–87) than the level of the interest rate (about 12.5 percent including spread), meeting this important test (even though, with trade surpluses, export growth could be lower without increasing the debt-export ratio).

At the end of 1984, it appears that the debtor countries whose debt has systemic consequences are on track for recovery from the debt crisis.[1] External performance has been extremely strong for Brazil and Mexico. Argentina, a source of great concern earlier in the year, has reached agreement with the IMF. Mexico and Venezuela have obtained multiyear rescheduling from the banks; Brazil is likely to do so soon; and Argentina has reached tentative agreement with the banks for a shorter period. Nonetheless, for a secondary tier of some smaller countries, external sector pressures are more serious, in part because their exports are concentrated in commodities with weak prices. Chile and Peru face severe difficulties, although these should moderate once dollar depreciation and/or interest rate reductions permit more normal recovery of metals prices. Bolivia, Nicaragua, Poland, Sudan, and Zaire — all on the bank regulators' list of "value impaired" — appear to have more protracted problems. Their aggregate debt is too small to threaten the system, however, and in some cases the best option may simply be to allow their arrears to accumulate. . . .

Some critics have challenged such projections on grounds that the chances are small that the international economic variables will turn out exactly as assumed. However, this criticism loses force if one considers that if departures from projected values of exogenous variables are randomly distributed, favorable departures in some (such as OECD growth in 1984) will offset adverse departures for others (such as interest rates and dollar strength in 1984).

Some important conceptual underpinnings of this outlook require clarification. First, it assumes interest payments will exceed new borrowing (there will be an "outward transfer of resources"). While some question the political viability of this assumption, this outcome is prudent and necessary to reduce debt-export ratios from levels associated with overborrowing in the past. Moreover, with domestic growth led by the export sector, an interim period of outward resource transfer need not mean slow domestic growth.

Second, the projections involve lower real import-*GDP* [Gross Domestic Product] ratios than in the early 1980's for some major countries. Argentina, Mexico, and Venezuela had bloated import levels now corrected by real depreciation, and even allowing for significant rebounds, imports should not return to earlier levels. Brazil's sharp increase in production of oil and other import substitutes has accomplished the same objective. Adjustment is shifting to the expenditure-switching phase (shift in resource allocation from nontradables to exports and import substitutes), so that domestic growth can be higher than in the earlier expenditure-reducing (recessionary) phase.

Third, a caveat is that domestic inflation may have already become a more binding constraint on growth than external debt. Brazil's inflation exceeds 200 percent and Argentina's 700, and monetary-fiscal restraint to reduce inflation may hold back near-term growth, while politically debt may be blamed.

IV. POLICY IMPLICATIONS

Despite favorable emerging economic reality, the debt problem remains politically vulnerable. The lagged effects of severe recession in 1983, and the runup in interest rates early in 1984, have caused political pressure, as shown by the emergence of the Cartagena group of Latin American debtor countries. The best strategy for the international financial system would be to pursue additional measures, to consolidate the gains made to date and insure against political disruption from possible future setbacks.

Macroeconomic policy in the North must ensure continued recovery. The U.S. fiscal deficits should be cut to permit more relaxed monetary policy, lower interest rates, and a lower dollar; and Europe and Japan should avoid further fiscal tightening until recovery is consolidated. A critical threshold of approximately 2½ percent for OECD growth is still the key to managing international debt (although the strong performance of 1984 leaves room for modest deceleration).

Sweeping measures on debt should be avoided. Write-downs and consolidation of debt in a new international agency would not only require scarce public capital and injure the debtors' credit ratings, but would also choke off the incentive for involuntary bank lending, as banks no longer would hold claims on the country. Interest forgiveness (such as a cut of all interest rates in half) would do great damage to the (highly leveraged) banks without providing much growth benefit for debtor countries (especially after deducting the loss of new lending).

For their part, banks need to continue aggregate new lending to developing countries at perhaps $20 billion annually. They should extend "Mexico-type" (September, 1984) packages of reduced spreads above LIBOR and multiyear reschedulings, especially to countries that demonstrate effective adjustment. In addition, the banks would do well to provide some insurance against interest rate surges by offering a "Reimbursable Interest-Averaging Cap," whereby interest above a given ceiling (set near the initial market rate) would be deferred if international interest rates rose, and repaid once rates declined again. Banks could charge some spread premium for this benefit, and even obtain private insurance of amounts deferred.

The International Monetary Fund could usefully introduce a Compensatory Finance Facility for interest rate surges, to complement its facility for export fluctuation. Expanded resources are necessary for lending by the World Bank, regional development banks, and export credit agencies, so that the official sector can help redress the excessive shift from official to private financial sources in the past several years. Finally, industrial countries must avoid increased protection against imports from developing countries.

In sum, the major debtor countries have made much progress in recovering from the debt crisis. International management of the crisis on a case-by-case basis has amounted to a coherent strategy that has in fact shown favorable results so far. Nonetheless, considerable risk remains. The most serious, but not necessarily most likely, risk is from a collapse in OECD growth, the motor force in debt recovery. The sharp slowdown in the U.S. economy in late 1984 is troubling. Nonetheless, the likely absence of further oil shocks in the 1980's, and the fact that growth now begins from a base of much-reduced inflation, suggest that international growth rates closer to those achieved in the 1950's and 1960's than those of 1974–82 should be attainable. Overall, a series of moderate measures along the lines suggested here should be sufficient to consolidate the political and economic basis for continued recovery from the debt crisis, making it possible for international lending to return to a much more normal basis by the late 1980's.

Note

1. Brazil ($92 billion total debt); Mexico ($88 billion); Argentina ($44 billion); and Venezuela ($34 billion) account for three-fourths of bank debt owed by countries with debt-servicing disruptions in 1982–84 (see my 1984 study, pp. 25; 165).

References

Cline, William R. "International Debt and the Stability of the World Economy," in *Policy Analyses in International Economics,* No. 4, Institute for International Economics, September 1983.

Cline, William R. *International Debt: Systemic Risk and Policy Response,* Washington: Institute for International Economics, 1984.

28

The Case by Case Approach to Debt Problems

Azizali F. Mohammed

THE FUND'S RECENT ROLE IN DEBT MANAGEMENT

The role of the Fund in assisting its member countries with their debt problems has changed since mid-1982, in response to a shift in the characteristics of the problems. In the preceding decade, countries with debt difficulties fell into one of two broad categories: (1) those more largely dependent upon officially financed or insured credits, and (2) others that borrowed mainly from private sources. For countries in both categories, debt problems were perceived as individual occurrences, without wider implications.

For the first category, a well-established set of procedures to redress the problems existed through the Paris Club framework for restructuring official debt. These were not formally codified rules, because creditor governments never did treat debt relief operations as anything but exceptional, undertaken at the express request of an individual debtor government, in the face of accumulating payments arrears and an evident inability to maintain debt-service payments. Before agreeing to modify the terms under a Paris Club renegotiation of debt, by stretching out maturities of principal and interest, creditor governments expected the debtor country to have negotiated a stabilization program supported by the Fund through a stand-by arrangement in the upper credit tranches (this has occurred without exception since 1977). Fund staff at Paris Club meetings were relied upon to furnish an objective assessment of recent economic performance, the main elements of a current adjustment program with the Fund, and the debtor's balance of payments prospects and external debt outlook.

The second category of cases consisted mainly of middle-income countries that ran into difficulties because of weak domestic policy or unanticipated exogenous developments, or a combination of both. Here solutions appeared to be achieved in two stages. First, private creditors, mostly commercial banks, were approached by the debtor government, especially when arrears on bank debt-service payments appeared earlier than on official obligations. However, the banks quickly came to realize that in negotiating with a sovereign borrower in this situation, it was not easy to work out conditions that would give them sufficient assurance that policy changes adequate to prevent a recurrence would be im-

From *Finance and Development*, 22 (March 1985), pp. 27–30.

plemented. It was therefore natural that in most of the bank debt renegotiations that were conducted between 1975 and 1978, the banks, as a second step, urged the debtor countries to undertake stabilization programs supported by the Fund. As a result, for five of the six countries negotiating with the banks during that period, a stand-by or extended arrangement was in effect when the banks signed the final agreement.

The banks also found that in the highly competitive environment in which they operated, it was difficult to reach common ground on the financial terms and conditions of debt relief. Often with 200 or 300 banks from a number of countries involved, the need for fair treatment required "lead" banks to make massive and often time-consuming efforts to obtain cooperation from all the creditor banks; this was particularly important given the "cross default" clauses in most agreements, which would have created a chain reaction if some banks declared a debtor country in default. Moreover, the anxiety of banks to ensure that their claims would be treated no less favorably than those of others often led to an insistence that the debtor government approach its official creditors through the Paris Club, if it had not already done so. Thus, four of the six countries that renegotiated their bank debt over 1975–78 concluded official debt restructurings, and three of these came into effect before agreement was reached with the banks. When an official restructuring took place, the Fund's role reverted to that described for the first category of countries. However, the Fund staff also participated in some of the negotiations with the banks, including (with the knowledge of the debtor) meetings in which the debtor was not present. On occasion, the Fund assumed a more active role, at the request of the debtor authorities, in facilitating discussions with the banks. The Fund also provided technical assistance to some of the countries in preparing their discussions with the banks and helped with the compilation of statistics.

The Polish debt crisis of 1981 moved the problem into a new phase, in which "contagion effects" became a factor. The commercial banks suddenly developed an intensified perception of risk in lending to the East European countries as a group; this affected Romania and Yugoslavia, both Fund members, and Hungary, which became a member in 1982. The countries concerned were able to provide assurance to the banks, by entering into stand-by arrangements with the Fund, that appropriate policies were being adopted to reduce the risk of default. Once an arrangement with the Fund was in place, the banks were found willing to proceed with new credits as well as with refinancing maturing debt.

Until this stage, the Fund's attitude was generally to try to help the debtor country devise a program that gave assurance that it could resolve its balance of payments difficulties in a medium-term framework. In some instances, the Fund staff did seek "indications of the likely magnitudes involved in a bank debt restructuring and also indicated to the banks the level of bank financing that it considered crucial to the success of a reasonable adjustment effort" (see IMF Occasional Paper No. 3, *External Indebtedness of Developing Countries*).

CHANGE IN CONDITIONS

As the debt problems of Mexico, and then those of Argentina and Brazil, became apparent, a perception developed that their reliance on commercial flows was so great that it entailed a distinct risk of program failure, unless the Fund could ensure that the financial assumptions on which the program was based were secured by explicit prior commitments from the banks to cover their share of the financing requirements of the program supported by the Fund.

It was the need to obtain agreement on the provision of additional bank and official finance *before* the approval of a Fund-supported arrangement that altered the role of the Fund in relation to commercial banks in the management of the debt problem. For, in addition to its certification function, the Fund developed a coordinating role as a mobilizer of funds from other lenders. This departure arose from several considerations. As noted earlier, the Mexican reliance upon bank financing was so large, and the assistance that could be furnished by the Fund so small relative to the need, that it was essential for the commercial banks not only to maintain their exposure but also to be prepared to enlarge it through the provision of additional financing. It was recognized that without such support, the compression of the economy, made unavoidable by lack of adequate external finance, might well make the situation unmanageable and render the Fund's own financial contribution ineffective.

Further, it was important to keep all elements of the banking industry involved. The major commercial banks understood that their stakes were so high that they could not afford to pull out without greatly reducing the quality of their own assets. The problem was to ensure that hundreds of other banks, especially the regional and smaller banks in the United States, would stay in the picture. If they did not, the major banks would be placed in the impossible position of having to explain (to shareholders, if not to depositors) why they were getting deeper into a country from which other banks were hastily extricating themselves. This was the issue of maintaining market discipline, i.e., preventing an uneven reduction in exposure by a large number of different lenders through, for example, withdrawal of short-term trade finance or the rundown of interbank deposits. There were also complex issues of intercreditor equity among banks with very different exposures, operating in different regulatory environments, and with varying accounting conventions, disclosure requirements, and funding constraints. These differences required formulas to be devised, in cooperation with the various national supervisory authorities, for allocating the net increase in exposure among the many banks from a number of national banking systems.

Finally, speed in decision making was imperative, requiring tight but credible deadlines. A series of highly complicated and closely articulated relationships had to be managed among a very large number of players — involving, in the case of Mexico, over 500 banks, their supervisory authorities in more than a dozen countries, governments of creditor countries, the Bank for International

Settlements, the World Bank, and, of course, Mexico. The Fund found itself at the center of this web of relationships, as it was later when similar arrangements were established for Brazil, the Philippines, and Argentina, among others.

In each case, an agreement with the Fund became the basis for mobilizing much larger sums by way of restructuring and new financing, than those it provided directly. This was natural since the adjustment effort mounted by the debtor country was the prime factor in assuring its creditors that corrective action was being taken, that it had the support of the international community through the Fund, and that its progress would be carefully monitored. The task had to be tackled country by country, and not only because of the obvious fact that the Fund could operate best through a stand-by or extended arrangement with each of its debtor member states. The fundamental judgment on the balance between adjustment and financing had to be made in each case, based on the initial conditions prevailing at the time of the debtor country's approach to the Fund; the level of its foreign exchange reserves and its accumulation of payments arrears; the types of claims involved; the proportions of debt owed to different creditors; the number, size, and national affiliation of the banks involved; and so forth.

Special problems arose with the interbank market in the case of the two largest debtors. Branches or affiliates of debtor country banks located in the main financial centers, especially New York and London, had borrowed substantial sums at very short maturities and re-lent them at longer maturities to their principals or to other borrowers in the (debtor) home country. These interbank deposits presented the most difficult problem of preventing the withdrawal of funds, let alone assuring a net increase in exposure. These differences in country situations often emerged in the course of managing the crisis and had to be resolved quickly and in a manner that protected the cohesion of the various interests engaged in the rescue effort.

GENERAL SOLUTIONS?

Various generalized solutions were proposed during this period, born of a conviction that the burden of debt servicing confronting a number of countries simply could not be managed in a world marked by deep recession, historically high interest rates, and a sharp curtailment of commercial lending. These schemes did not make much headway, however, for several reasons.

First, they proceeded from a perception about the global aggregates that was never true for the components. The existence or absolute magnitude of countries' borrowings was not in itself a reason for payments difficulties nor was the type of economy concerned. Recent data on debt and debt ratios for all developing countries, and equivalent figures for the different categories among developing countries, show that within each group were countries unaffected by a debt problem.

Among oil exporters that were OPEC members, two (Algeria and Indonesia) owed about 45 percent of the debt of their category, yet had no particular problem of market access. Of the net oil exporters among developing countries that were not OPEC members, Egypt and Malaysia accounted for about one fourth of the group's debt but, again, had no access difficulty. Among the net oil importers, about one half the debt was owed by the major exporters of manufactures, and four countries in this group (namely, Israel, Korea, Portugal, and South Africa), accounting for roughly one third of the total debt of the group, continued to borrow at very competitive terms throughout the period. In the low-income category, the two largest countries — China and India, which accounted for almost 40 percent of the debt — had no need for relief. Finally, in the residual group, at least three major borrowers had confronted their problems earlier and were already on the mend (Hungary, Romania, and Turkey), and two others (Colombia and Thailand) continued to have access on competitive terms. Any attempt to apply a general solution would have meant that countries whose creditworthiness was unimpaired would face interruptions of market access; a generalized approach could well create a new problem rather than provide a solution for an existing one.

A second factor militating against generalized solutions was that many of them implied large losses for commercial banks, inflicted in a manner that would prevent a gradual process of building up reserves and allowing write-offs over a period of time. Schemes to transfer bank claims on developing countries to international or national public entities would have involved either substantial public sector commitments or immediate and open losses for the banks. This would have risked breaking the nexus between commercial banks and their customers in the developing countries and destroying relationships built up over many years, if not decades. The debtor countries not only relied upon the international banks for normal trade financing but also expected to reactivate their access to markets for project and sectoral finance. Indeed, the promise of being able to attract new flows as existing credits were repaid was at the heart of the unflagging commitment that most debtors displayed in their approach to the debt problem. Generalized solutions tended to categorize problems mechanically according to quantitative criteria, such as levels of net capital flows or net resource transfers, whereas solutions to individual cases needed to be more sensitive to the organic interrelationships that underlay the financial magnitudes.

A third flaw of most generalized solutions lay in their assumption that support would be forthcoming from the governments of the major creditor countries. The political environment was not conducive to such use of public funds. In many countries, there was a drive to cut back on budget deficits, and any solutions that impeded the attainment of this objective were unlikely to find favor with financial officials and legislators. An even greater problem lay in a widespread public perception that the commercial banks had lent in an imprudent way, and that public funds should not be employed to rescue large private institutions from the consequences of their own errors of judgment. Similarly, while developing countries experienced serious adverse external conditions, their payments difficulties resulted in part from inadequate domestic economic policies. There was also a feeling that many of the countries that were in difficulty were among the most developed among the developing countries and that assisting them with public funds would skew the distribution of aid flows away from countries that were poorer, had little or no recourse to market borrowing from abroad, and stood perhaps in even greater need of external assistance for dealing with their problems.

A final difficulty with some generalized solutions concerned the time that their implementation would require. Many schemes would have required changes in national legislation or in the charters of international institutions whose amendment necessitated high voting majorities and large participation ratios to become effective. Yet in dealing with debt problems as they arose, time was of the essence and the constraints set by the need for urgent action meant that solutions had to be found within the bounds of existing legal and institutional arrangements.

THE INDIVIDUAL SOLUTION

With the passage of time, some evidence of the viability of the cooperative approach to debt management has begun to accumulate. In the 18 months ending in mid-1984, the external adjustment that has taken place in the nonoil developing countries has been characterized as "dramatic," and while it is recognized that sharp cuts in imports were involved, growth has resumed in a number of them.

On the financing side, the Fund (as of the end of 1984) had disbursed some $22 billion since the middle of 1982 to support adjustment in nearly 70 member countries, with another $8 billion of commitments outstanding under 31 current programs. In addition, new financing has been mobilized along with debt rescheduling. In 1983, some 30 developing countries (including 11 of the 25 largest borrowers) completed or were in the process of completing debt rescheduling agreements with official and commercial creditors. These agreements reduced the debt-service payments of nonoil developing countries by $23–24 billion in 1983, and by about the same amount in 1984. As a result, their debt-service ratios declined from a peak of 25 percent in 1982 to 22.3 percent in 1983. This compares with 27.6 percent, which would have applied in the absence of rescheduling. The maturity structure of debt has also been improving, with the ratio of short-term debt declining to 25 percent in 1983 from about 30 percent of exports of goods and services in 1982 and to an even lower ratio in 1984. In 1983, $13 billion of bank lending was also arranged in conjunction with Fund-supported adjustment programs.

Despite these encouraging developments in the debt situation and the recovery in the industrial world, considerable pessimism has persisted over the manageability of the debt problem. One explanation for this paradox is that lags exist between actions taken by debtor countries and the recognition of their positive results. A second reason is the concern over the prospect of a "hump" in countries' debt amortization in the next few years, resulting from the reschedulings of 1982–83. A third factor is the rise of about 2 percentage points in interest rates in the first half of 1984. This disturbing development has generated another spate of generalized solutions for "capping" interest rates and for reducing the burden of higher interest rates in other ways. There is no question that higher rates pose a risk to the viability of the solutions that have been found. However, before giving credence to the solutions proposed, two sets of factors must be kept in view, the first general and the second more specific.

At the more general level, there are several elements to be considered. First, the trough in imports of nonoil developing countries was reached in the fourth quarter of 1982, with imports from industrial countries falling by about 20 percent in U.S. dollar terms from early 1981 to late 1982. Thereafter, the financing packages put together in association with Fund programs were sufficient to stabilize the level of imports. Second, the exports of nonoil developing countries to the industrial countries began to recover from the fourth quarter of 1982 with the recovery in output in the industrial countries. As a result, the exports of these countries rose from some $190 billion (at an annual rate) in that quarter to some $240 billion in the first quarter of 1984. This expansion of exports helped bring about an improvement of around $70 billion (at an annual rate) in the trade balances of this group of countries. This is expected to result in a resumption in the growth of imports, projected to rise in volume terms by about 6 percent in both 1984 and 1985, despite any increase in the burden of interest charges on nonoil developing countries (net of interest earned).

At a more specific level, the effects of interest rate movements on dollar-denominated debt are sufficiently country-specific to require careful and individual analysis. There is, first of all, a wide variation in the reliance of countries on floating rate credit. Most of the poorer countries in Africa and Asia have not been significant users of such credit, some because they chose not to. Second, the proportion of variable rate debt in total debt has varied. Third, the interest rate factor has been offset to a varying extent by improvements in export receipts, following the strong upswing in North America that has accompanied the hardening of interest rates. The offsetting benefits have been greatest for countries such as Mexico, because of their proximity to the U.S. market, but the upswing has also helped countries farther away which have a highly diversified productive base, such as Korea, and possess the flexibility to adapt rapidly to the requirements of a booming North American market. There is a recognition that imaginative solutions may still become necessary were interest rates to rise or commodity prices to weaken further. However, there is an inclination to confine the search for such solutions to the banks negotiating with each debtor country, with support from the supervisory authorities of the banks and also from the Fund and the World Bank.

An application of this approach was the acceptance by the banks of the proposal advanced by the Fund's Managing Director in 1984 to consider a longer time frame for bank rescheduling arrangements for countries that have made or are making substantial progress toward adjustment, as a way of recognizing good performance, avoiding the necessity for repeated annual reschedulings, and restoring the conditions needed for the return to market access, as well as for rebuilding confidence in the system. The Managing Director proposed such an approach for

Mexico and expressed the hope that other countries whose performance is improving could also qualify, if their progress is sustained. The periods of consolidation, as well as of grace, would have to be longer for these advantages to be obtained and the terms and conditions would have to improve. The successful completion of multiyear restructuring agreements with Mexico and Venezuela illustrate the banks' readiness to adopt a forward-looking approach to debt restructuring, and represent an important step in preparing the way for countries' return to more normal market access. In the case of both countries there is a provision for the Fund to continue a monitoring role through its regular surveillance procedures, but on an enhanced basis.

The need for a longer-term perspective on debt management is important, and not only on the financial side. In spite of the progress already made, the debt problems are not going to vanish overnight. Their effective resolution will depend, first and foremost, upon continued action on the part of the indebted countries themselves aimed at strengthening their economies over a period of years. These efforts both need and deserve the support of the international community. The industrial countries need to make further progress toward a better and more stable world economic environment and the conditions in which international trade can flourish. Continued cooperation among financiers will also be required to ensure that determined adjustment efforts receive the necessary financial backing. The Fund, for its part, will have a role to play in all these areas in the years ahead.

29

Dealing with Debt in the 1980s

Rudiger Dornbusch

External debt problems, like wars, are common occurrences in a broader historical perspective. They occur every thirty or fifty years, much in the same circumstances. And when they do occur they put at odds the bond holder and the debtor and leave fundamental imprints on history. Hitler's Germany or Latin America's import substitution policy were the outgrowth of the last world debt crisis. Today Latin America is once again in a debt crisis and the debate confronts those who call for dramatic action, including even repudiation, and others who suggest the problem is minor and can be solved by time, adjustment and some tying-over finance — the "muddling-through" strategy.

From *Third World Quarterly* 7 (July 1985), pp. 532–551. Reprinted by permission. Some text and notes omitted.

In fact not much has changed from the debt crisis of the 1930s: today, the International Monetary Fund [IMF] plays the role of the League of Nations Financial Committee, the Bank Steering Committee replaces the Foreign Bank Holders Protective Council, and Bill Rhodes plays the role of Sir Otto Niemeyer.

Surprisingly, there was very little memory of debt history when the lending splurge of the 1970s got under way. Few remembered the terrible reputation of the U.S. in European credit markets following the defaults of the early 1840s which history relates as follows: "The vitriolic London *Times* indiscriminately denounced all Americans; and prophesied that the American name would not recover for half-a-century from the slur which had been cast upon it by the temporary or complete failure of some of the states to pay their debts."[1]

But closer to our topic virtually all Latin American states defaulted on their external debt in the 1920s and 1930s. Looking back over Latin [American] credit history, Winkler wrote in 1933:

> The fiscal history in Latin America, that stretch of territory lying south of the Rio Grande and housing about 110,000,000 inhabitants of various races and origins, is replete with instances of government defaults. Borrowing and default follow each other with almost perfect regularity. When payment is resumed, the past is easily forgotten and a new borrowing orgy ensues. This process started at the beginning of the past century and has continued down to the present day. It has taught us nothing.[2]

How little it has in fact taught us is apparent from a most peculiar story. In January 1983, banks joined to found The Institute of International Finance, Inc. which was intended to "improve the timeliness and quality of information available on sovereign borrowers. . . ." Apparently it was not even known to these good people that in 1928 they had done exactly the same thing: founding at New York University an Institute for International Finance for that very same purpose.

But there is one critical difference between the debt experience today and that of the 1930s. Today debts are continuing to be serviced and the burden of making that possible has been placed by the international financial system, with the assistance of the IMF, squarely on the debtors. In the 1930s bond holders lost and there was financial chaos. Today, real wage cuts in debtor countries assure the trade surpluses and dollar earnings that keep bank stockholders in the black. One might argue (or even believe) that this is essential to maintain order in the international financial system, but that of course raises the question of in whose interest the system works. For many who are paying the bill now there have been few benefits before and there are no obvious ones down the road.

The solution of the debt problem today is labelled economic, as if it did not have an overriding foreign policy dimension. Surely no one doubts that those who have fallen under the budget axe in the debtor countries distinguish between the IMF, the New York banks or the U.S. government. We would be wrong to believe that there is simply no politics to the immensely costly debt service that is being extracted today. This dimension is central to the call for some change in the muddling-through strategy that is being pursued at present.

Lord Lever has argued:[3]

> . . . we must not attempt to maintain the pretence that purely commercial lending is adequate for our purposes. It is defective in that it requires premature attempts at balance-of-payments surplus by the debtor countries not compatible with our political interests or theirs. Recent net transfers of resources from the debtors have been bought at the cost of economic slack and grave risk to political stability. They are too small to restore confidence but large enough to do serious damage to the debtors' economies and societies. They are neither desirable nor sustainable.

This paper places the debt problem first in terms of the facts: who are the debtors and creditors, what is the size of the debts, where do the debts come from? We then proceed to identify the debt "problem," the difficulties encountered in servicing the debts. Finally, we deal with the surprise of 1984 and the medium-term prospects for relief of the debt crisis.

THE FACTS

We start the discussion of facts with a look at some data to establish two points: first, that the debt problem is primarily a Latin American problem and not a problem of African or Asian less developed countries (LDCs). Second, on the other side, that it is a bank problem and primarily a "big bank" problem.

Table 1 shows data for LDC debts both in current and constant dollars as well as the ratio of debt to exports. The table brings out that debt grew for each of the regions, but that Latin America stands out by the large increase and the large ratio of debt to exports. It certainly compares strikingly with Asia where debts are large in absolute terms, but small relative to exports or GDP.

In Table 2 we go further to look at the debt problem in terms of debt service (interest plus amortisation) and interest payments in relation to exports and

TABLE 1

An Overview of LDC Debt (billion $U.S.)

	1973	1977	1980	1984
Nonoil developing countries	130.1	280.3	475.2	710.9
Debt in 1980 dollars	290.1	413.4	475.2	768.5
Long-term and short-term debt by area				
Africa (excluding South Africa)	NA	30.8	50.9	70.7
Asia	30.0	68.7	114.6	179.3
Europe	14.5	37.6	67.2	76.6
Middle East	8.7	21.9	36.3	56.2
Western Hemisphere	44.4	109.1	192.6	310.5

Source: IMF.

TABLE 2

The Debt Burden

	LOW-INCOME COUNTRIES		MAJOR BORROWERS		W. HEMISPHERE	
	1977	1983	1977	1983	1977	1983
Debt service						
% of Exports	12.1	13.3	19.1	29.9	29.2	44.0
% of GDP	1.0	0.7	3.4	6.5	3.9	8.4
Interest payments						
% of Exports	4.7	5.4	7.2	18.6	10.0	32.2
% of GDP	0.4	0.5	1.3	4.1	1.4	6.1

Source: IMF and OECD.

GDP. These are indicators of the debt burden. It is quite apparent that Latin America has a strikingly larger increase in debt burdens and a significantly larger absolute burden. The reason is two-fold. On the one hand, the debt represents a larger share of exports or GDP. On the other hand, Latin America pays significantly higher effective interest rates than Asian or African borrowers. This is the case since only a small part of [its] debt is official, at low or concessional fixed interest rates. The major part of Latin American debt is bank debt with the service linked to Libor plus spreads. In 1983, for example, the effective interest rate paid by Latin American borrowers was 10.8 percent while it was only 3.7 percent for low-income countries whose debt is primarily to official lenders rather than banks.

The difference between the debt burdens of Latin America and the poor countries is essential to recognise. It is this difference that leads us to argue that the debt problem today is specifically one of major borrowers and particularly Latin American — the upper middle-income countries. It is not a problem of most LDCs, and especially not of the "poor" LDCs.

The second point to be made is that on the lending side the debt problem is one of large banks. Table 3 shows the Latin American debts and the part that is due to banks, and to U.S. banks in particular. For the U.S. banking system at large the Latin American debts do not present a special problem since they amount to less than 5 percent of total assets. But the problem is acute for large banks where these debts represent, for the top groups, more than 200 percent of capital. Indeed, the top nine banks hold more than half of these debts and less than twenty-five banks account for almost 80 percent of the lending. The debt problem is thus very much a big bank problem.

We now turn to the sources of the debt accumulation. Here it is important to emphasise that there are two chief sources: one is the extraordinarily poor performance of domestic macroeconomic policy in 1979–82 in virtually every Latin American country: Pinochet's move to a fixed exchange rate despite continu-

TABLE 3

The Latin American Debt (billion $U.S., June 1983)

	TOTAL DEBT	DEBT TO BANKS	
		All banks	U.S. banks
Argentina	37.5	25.5	11.2
Brazil	89.5	62.8	23.3
Chile	18.0	10.9	5.2
Mexico	85.6	65.5	32.3
Venezuela	31.9	26.8	10.8
Total	263.3	191.5	82.8

Source: Bank for International Settlements, Morgan Guaranty and Board of Governors of the Federal Reserve System.

ing inflation and indexation, Martinez de Hoz's *tablita* that led to a gigantic overvaluation and capital flight, Portillo Lopez's squandering of oil revenues and Delfim Neto's mismanagement of growth, inflation and the external balance. The stories are not exactly the same, but they have common elements: excessive budget deficits, exchange rate overvaluation, capital flight, flight into importables, or failure to adjust to changing world prices.

Table 4 gives Mexico as an example. The budget deficit in 1981–82, as the Portillo Lopez administration comes to an end, moves to a vast deficit and the exchange rate is allowed to appreciate in real terms. As a result, capital flight takes place on a large scale and the current account deteriorates under the impact of record high imports. The spending binge and capital export is financed by borrowing from banks abroad to sustain the exchange rate. Accordingly gross external debt more than doubles between 1979 and 1982.

There are differences between countries in the relative role of capital flight and trade deficits: in Argentina, capital flight was the predominant counterpart of increased (gross) external debt. This has the curious implication that Argentina's external debt position is difficult only when one looks at the government's debt, forgetting about the sizeable private holdings of deposits, securities and real estate abroad of Argentinian residents. The same applies to Venezuela or to Mexico, where private dollar deposits with U.S. banks increased by as much as $4 billion between 1980 and 1982, not counting any other forms of capital flight. In Chile and Brazil, by contrast, capital outflows were of minor importance, trade deficits playing the chief role. In Chile, for example, the trade deficit of 1981 was almost three times larger than any other deficit of the last thirty years, reflecting a near-doubling of previous levels of consumer durable imports.

The other source of debt accumulation is the external shock of 1980–82 in the form of dollar appreciation, sharply increased real interest rates, reduced real

TABLE 4

Mexican Macroeconomic Indicators

	1978	1979	1980	1981	1982
Budget deficit (% of GDP)	5.5	6.0	6.9	13.6	16.3
Real exchange rate (index 1980 = 100)	117	113.5	100.0	90.6	137.9
External debt ($U.S. billions)	34.0	40.4	52.5	78.9	84.6

Source: *Informe Hacendario Mensual*, November 1983, IFS and Morgan Guaranty.

commodity prices and reduced demand for manufactured exports. This deterioration in the world trade and macroeconomic environment is, of course, due to the U.S. inflation stabilisation and the subsequent and continuing poor policy mix of tight money and over-easy fiscal policy. This shock has been particularly bad for Latin America because the debts are large, thus leading to large increases in interest bills. The effect is further reinforced because interest rates are floating rather than fixed.

Table 5 gives an indication of the macroeconomic problems in the world economy of the late 1970s. It compares those years to the episode of the early 1970s which was a period of debt liquidation as a consequence of a world boom. In the late 1970s, real interest rates were high, growth was stagnant at the centre, and an appreciating dollar increased the real burden of debt service.

How much of a contribution to the debt problem is due to the macroeconomic shock as opposed to domestic policies? One way to answer that question is to look at the debtors' deterioration in the ratio of debt to exports and measure the relative role in that deterioration of three factors:

TABLE 5

Two Episodes of the World Economy (annual average percentage rates)

	U.S. prime rate	Inflation in world trade	Growth of industrial countries	Dollar depreciation
1970–73	6.7	12.4	4.7	5.7
1979–82	15.5	4.4	1.1	−8.7

and
- noninterest current account deficits
- interest rates (including fees and spreads) in the world capital market,

- growth in export earnings.

The theory of debt dynamics shows that the ratio of debt to exports rises over time if a country runs noninterest current account deficits or if the effective interest rate exceeds the growth rate of export earnings.[4] If the interest rate exceeds the growth rate of export earnings, borrowing to finance interest payments makes the debt grow more rapidly than export revenue. Hence, the ratio of debt to exports grows over time. Periods of high interest rates and a collapse of world trade would therefore be cases where external shocks precipitate a debt crisis.

There is a simple way of constructing a counterfactual exercise to assess the significance of the external shock.[5] Suppose that throughout the 1970s the typical debtor country had every year balanced the current account except for interest payments, the latter being borrowed at prime rate. Suppose also that export earnings had increased at the rate they actually did for nonoil LDCs in the 1970s. In this counterfactual scenario it can be shown that the debt-export ratio would actually have declined substantially below the level of the early 1970s. The debt liquidation of the early 1970s, due to negative real interest rates, would have more than compensated for the shocks of the late 1970s. In fact, of course, the Latin American debt-export ratio increased sharply. This means that the noninterest current account and capital flight are an essential aspect of the debt crisis. That recognition is important because it has a bearing on acceptable policies of relief as viewed by tax payers in the centre countries.

THE DEBT PROBLEM[S]: [LIQUIDITY, SOLVENCY, EQUITY]

In evaluating debt problems it is important to ask whether we are addressing liquidity problems, solvency or equity issues. Liquidity problems involve an inability to service and amortise debts *now* on the time schedule and in the full amounts initially contracted. There is no question that that is a liquidity problem. Equity problems involve the question of how the burden of large, unanticipated increases in the costs of debt service should be borne between lenders and borrowers. Finally, solvency involves the question of whether the value of a country's liabilities exceeds the ability to pay *any* time. The ability to pay, however, is in large measure a political question involving the extent to which economic activity and living standards can be depressed in order to generate the foreign exchange revenues with which to service the external debt.

The present "muddling through" strategy is becoming increasingly doubtful as massive resource transfers from debtors to creditors are made at the cost of deep recession in the adjusting countries. There is much discussion of whether the debt crisis is a liquidity crisis or a solvency problem. But the definition of solvency for a nation is not as clear-cut as that for a corporation: given the exist-

ing size of debts, living standards in debtor countries could be depressed to levels
so low as to make it possible to service and even amortise the debts. The real issue
is whether the political systems can and should be made to stand the strain.

The chief difficulty of adjustment in Latin America today, and the source
of the debt problem, is that the region has been a *structural* importer of capital.
Deficits in the noninterest current account were the counterpart, at least until the
late 1970s, of a development strategy that used external resources to supplement
domestic saving in order to finance investment and growth. It was because these
countries had been structural importers of capital that the effort to rapidly generate
external surpluses turned out to be so costly. In a country where deficits in the
external accounts are due to a transitory overspending, correction is easy. All that
is required is to stop overspending and, without much effect on employment, the
external accounts return to balance. But, when development has been centred on a
growing home market, a rapid return to external balance meets with short-run
structural impediments that inevitably make unemployment the chief way of
generating surpluses.

A second difficulty in respect to debt service is that much of the adjustment effort falls on labour, whose real wage is reduced to achieve external
competitiveness. But the debt accumulation in many instances primarily reflects
benefits that accrued not to labour but rather to the upper middle class that engaged
in capital flight or the middle class that enjoyed an import spree. Thus in Argentina, Chile and Mexico the adjustment to service the debt involves a dramatic
inequity. In Brazil this is much less obvious, since the deficits that created the debt
reflected oil price policies and public sector investment, which also benefit the
working class.

The third issue is the long-run solvency question. Can Latin American
countries in the medium and long run service their debts as contracted *and* at the
same time enjoy growth in per capita incomes, having made up most of the losses
of 1981–84? This is the central question today and it is wide open. In part it
depends on domestic policies and the scope for effective mobilisation of resources
in the areas of import substitution and export promotion. But it clearly also
depends on the long-run external environment. If world real interest rates rapidly
return to low levels, growth of world trade is strong and sustained, and protectionism is not an issue, then debt problems can be solved by some sharing of the
short-run burdens.

There is no full assurance that long-run trends are favourable, but there is
also no particular reason to believe that in a five to fifteen year perspective
conditions are strongly adverse. The long-run solvency question therefore is
largely indeterminate and uninteresting. It is superseded by two other issues. One
is the increasing urgency to see the short-run problems caused by high interest rates
and a strong dollar as an equity problem. The second is the recognition that Latin
America for the next decade, and beyond, will be amortising debts: instead of
borrowing on average over and above the interest bill, Latin America will have to
be earning net exports to service and pay off debt. This is an implication of the fact

that commercial banks are seeking to reduce their exposure in real terms and that no other major source of development finance is available. This is an extraordinary change for the international financial system, running against common sense and good economics. This long-run implication of the debt problem has been over-shadowed by the short-run cyclical and financial aspects, but it deserves much more attention.

THE SURPRISE OF 1984

Even early in 1984 many observers felt that the debt crisis could not but get out of hand. Crisis management had carried the system already for more than a year, but developments in the world economy and the sharp economic setback in the debtor countries seemed to make some form of collapse of the "muddling through" strategy inevitable. It is true that there were optimists, in particular William Cline, whose cheerful forecasts would even turn out to be understatements, but by-and-large scepticism was the rule. For the moment, and perhaps for good, the sceptics proved to be way off the mark. Latin American countries turned their external imbalances so sharply into surpluses that they paid a large part of the 1984 interest bill and, what is perhaps even more surprising, did so under conditions of recovery and political stability. The year ended with a resumption of confidence and a long-term rescheduling of the major debtors at spreads significantly below those experienced in the past years. It is worth reviewing these developments in more detail.

In 1982 unanticipated credit rationing brought about the debt crisis. Debtors had come to expect that they could roll their debt, borrowing amortisation payments, interest payments and more almost automatically. The sharp increase in interest rates and the decline in export earnings led the debtor countries to call for financing out of line with what banks were willing to advance. The moment the financing gap became obvious, general credit rationing was immediately applied and the debtors and the banks were at a stand-off situation: banks were unwilling to lend and debtors were unable to pay. The international financial system was actively threatened by the possibility that borrowers would simply repudiate their debts in the way of the 1930s, thus throwing into chaos a banking system that had completely irresponsible supervision and inadequate capital.

The IMF set itself up to save the system, organising banks into a lender's cartel and holding the debtor countries up for a classical mugging. The IMF was immensely successful and immediately came to be thought of as central and essential to a well-functioning international financial system. There is little doubt that the strategy protected bank stockholders at the expense of the LDCs. It is wide open to discussion whether the debtors were net beneficiaries compared to a situation of international chaos. Similarly, it is open to discussion whether the IMF should not have shifted at least some of the burdens onto the banks, forcing them to accept loan losses.

There is a lot of discussion about involuntary lending. Banks wish they could sell off part of their loan portfolio because the existing spreads do not reward them sufficiently for the perceived risk that the stock market places on their exposure. Indeed, banks may be paying higher borrowing costs and thus experience reduced profitability on all their lending as a spill-over from the pollution of their portfolio via LDC debts. In that sense banks are paying too and sharing in the adjustment. It is indeed the case that Brazil today, were she to float $80 billion in bonds, using the proceeds to pay off the bank debts, would not be able to raise all the money at Libor plus one eight. But it is also true that the loans remain profitable in that they pay more than one per cent above Libor.

In any event, the process that evolved was a system of strict IMF conditionality with a counterpart of bank financing of part of the foreign exchange gap. The results were spectacular on the external balance side and dramatically negative on the domestic front. Trade surpluses of the debtor countries far exceeded expectation, and even targets, while growth turned dramatically negative.

Figure 1 shows the trade surplus and the service deficits of Latin America, the latter reflecting primarily interest payments; it highlights the large shift from the trade deficits of the 1970s to a large trade surplus. From 1982 to 1984, Latin America's trade balance improved by more than $30 billion, thus already covering in 1984 a large part of the service deficit. Table 6 shows the implications for per capita growth. Whereas on average in the past decade growth was above 3 percent, adjusting for the increase in population, it averaged –3 percent in 1981–84. Given poverty and the unequal distribution of income in Latin America, this recession implied a major reversal of social progress.

FIGURE 1

The Latin American External Balance

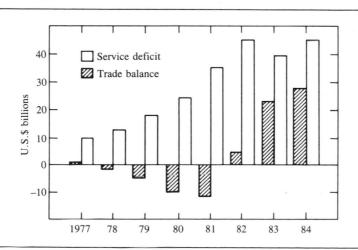

TABLE 6

Real per Capita Growth in Latin America (Average Annual Rate)

1967–76	1977–80	1981–84	1984
3.9	3.0	–3.0	0.2

Source: CEPAL.

Much of the scepticism of 1983–84 concerned the external balance: how could habitual dollar spenders turn rapidly into dollar earners? The surprise may be explained in terms of four factors:

- The debtor countries went into a severe recession, induced by tight money and fiscal policies. The recession automatically reduced import spending and freed domestic output for export.
- In the adjustment process the debtor countries had undergone a very significant real depreciation that increased external competitiveness. The gain in competitiveness promoted export earnings and made imports less competitive.
- The extraordinary growth of spending in the U.S. economy spilled over into imports from LDCs thus adding pull to the push of the debtors' recession and increased competitiveness.
- Finally, import substitution in the debtor countries, due to controls, earlier investment strategy, increased competitiveness and administrative decisions made possible an enormous contraction of imports.

It is not easy to assign a precise weight to each of these factors but it is certainly important to recognise the extent of the pull provided by U.S. growth. For example, in the year to June 1984, U.S. total import spending increased by 33 percent. Much of that increase in imports was supplied by Latin America. These cyclical effects are well understood and, in that sense, surprising only in magnitude.

The unanticipated event is the dramatic fall in imports. . . . [Take] Brazil as an example. Since 1980 import volume fell by more than half. The decline reflects in part a fall in investment associated with the recession and budget cuts in public sector enterprises. The major share however is apparently a reflection of successful import substitution. It is interesting to note that the Brazilian experience is not at all atypical. In fact, all of Latin America has experienced a dramatic reduction in import volume. Perhaps, just as in the 1930s, import substitution is once again providing a way for Latin America to shelter itself from external shocks.

The surprise of 1984 is not complete without a discussion of the costs of generating the external surpluses. The optimists had argued that the debt problem would not get out of hand because reduced interest rates and a collapse of the dollar would help pay the bills. Just as collapsing commodity prices, high interest rates and an appreciating dollar had helped make the crisis, the reversal would help solve it. But in fact none of this has happened: the dollar has grown stronger since 1983, interest rates have risen above their 1983 levels and commodity prices failed to show the typical cyclical rebound. All this is very important because it tells us that the turn around in the debtor countries' current accounts was achieved not with the aid of negative real interest rates and capital gains but entirely with hard work and forgone consumption or investment.

One cannot conclude comments on 1984 without noting that the good performance on debt and signs of recovery apply primarily to the major debtors. Indeed, there has been a division of performance. Smaller debtors, particularly Chile, Peru and Bolivia, did not share in the prospect of getting out of trouble. Their economies are far from a course of stability.

THE MEDIUM-TERM OUTLOOK

Is there any chance that the surprising ability of the debtor countries witnessed in 1984 will carry over to 1985 and beyond? If the debtor countries can both enjoy growth and meet their debt service commitments then there simply is no debt crisis. If, on the contrary, there is an almost clear-cut trade-off between growth and debt service, then the potential for a crisis remains.

Any prediction that the debt crisis is alive must somehow show that 1984 was particularly unusual in a manner that is unlikely to recur. A sensible framework for that question is to focus on the link between import availability and growth. It is widely accepted that without growth the debtor countries will, sooner or later, explode politically. The labour force in Mexico or Brazil grows at rates in excess of 3 percent. Adding productivity growth to that number suggests that without average growth rates of 5 to 6 percent, at the least, there will be still further deterioration of social performance. Growth is thus essential.

Consider first, import availability:

$$\text{Imports} = \text{exports} + \text{"new money"} - \text{debt service} \tag{1}$$

In Equation 1 import availability is interpreted as the constraining factor on growth and the problem is that "new money" from commercial banks falls short of debt service payments. Export revenues therefore are no longer available to finance imports, limiting import volume and therefore growth.

From Equation 1 it is apparent that strong export performance and low debt service due to lower interest rates and lower spreads are the recipe for the external constraint on growth to disappear. Strong export performance has three ingredients: first and paramount, there needs to be sustained growth in the centre countries. The number bandied around, without much justification, is an average growth rate in OECD countries of 3 percent. Such growth would open markets for manufactures from the debtor countries and, at the same time, improve the real prices of commodities which remain the chief exports in one form or another.

But, second, it is also important how that growth comes about. The favoured combination is [that it is] growth that causes the dollar to collapse in world markets. A fall of the dollar would raise dollar prices in world trade and thus, by the stroke of the pen, write down debts in real terms.

The third ingredient in loosening the external constraint is also linked to the policy mix. Since debt service is determined both by the outstanding stock of debt and the current interest rate it is essential that the policy mix be one of easy money. Debtors, not surprisingly, favour an environment of prosperity, world inflation and cheap credit, the more the better.

Macroeconomic predictions for the near term suggest about 3 percent OECD growth, although with a significant margin of uncertainty. Interest rates are predicted to rise somewhat from their present level, though not dramatically. Dollar decline continues to be expected, but no longer predicted. The world macro outlook decidedly does not offer the prospect of easy riding; inflation, low interest rates and a boom of the kind of the early 1970s. The LDCs may get out of their debt problems, but only by having conditions to pay, not by riding the waves of capital gains and inflationary write-offs.

The last consideration is how import availability translates into growth. . . . It suggests that we have no clear idea of import requirements for growth. There may have occurred in 1980–84 a once and for all decline in import requirements, both average and marginal. But the decline may also be only transitory, with no trend change in the high import content of growth that Latin America has experienced so far.

The 1984 recovery might lead us to believe that we can have both growth and debt service, suggesting that there is no painful trade-off. But that must be qualified in an important respect. In 1983–84, Brazil and Mexico transferred abroad an amount equal to 5 or 6 percent of their incomes. Chile's transfer came more nearly to 9 percent. The transfer represents the difference between the amount of output produced and income available for spending. It reflects the fact that the recovery in output in 1984 corresponds to increased employment, but not to increased domestic absorption of goods and services — people were able to find more employment by working for less. The ability to find employment is essential on the domestic side and must not be belittled. In itself it improves the distribution of adjustment and income. It also increases the chances that in the near-term the situation will not blow up. But that is primarily a comfort to the creditors, not relief for the debtors.

In the near term the debt question is whether the debtor countries' domestic ability can sustain the 1984 external performance under less favourable, but at the same time not outright impossible, external conditions. That leaves on the import side the question of whether controls and import substitution can be kept up. On the export side it raises the difficult issue of whether the export growth largely reflected the domestic depression of demand in debtor countries which, of course, would disappear in a recovery. Among the key questions is also the role of competitiveness. In 1982–84, the real wage was cut significantly, yielding reduced spending and increased competitiveness. Can these real wage cuts be sustained into a recovery? In Argentina that has proved impossible, in Brazil there is great doubt at present, and even in Mexico there are serious questions.

The debt problem has shifted to the debtor countries' domestic economies in at least three respects: first, the cuts in real wages associated with budget and external balance correction are huge and socially unacceptable. Workers now see themselves as paying for debt service on an external debt that reflects mismanagement and privilege from which they have had little benefit. For example, in Chile the real minimum wage is 30 percent below the 1981 level, and workers are clearly aware that they are paying a bill that is not their own.

The second serious issue is inflation. The adjustment to the external crisis involves, in all cases, a vast increase in inflation and with that an IMF intrusion in macro management. It is particularly clear in Argentina or Brazil that some measure for control of inflation is essential. It is much less apparent that IMF-style tight money and budget cutting is of much use in a highly indexed economy.

The third question is whether the deterioration in growth performance, compared to the last thirty years (see [Figure 2]), will have strongly adverse

---

[FIGURE 2]

Latin American Growth
(GDP growth, 3 year-centred moving average)

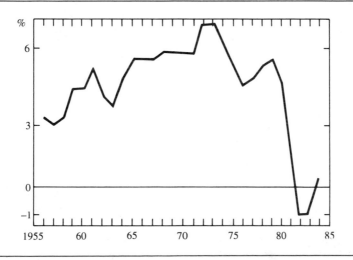

Source: IMF.

political consequences. Few would seriously disagree with the proposition that per capita growth in the decade of the 1980s will be approximately zero. By 1990 the working-class standard of living is unlikely to be much above where it was in 1980 and perhaps not even that. This outcome is all the more likely because the growth pattern has shifted quite a bit. In the past, LDCs offset a decline in the world economy by external borrowing, thus maintaining their growth rates at the cost of increased external debt. Now that possibility is limited and hence an external adversity will have to be borne much more by reduced growth rather than trade deficits. That fact cannot but force a reduced trend growth rate.

The optimistic outlook is that people quickly get accustomed to adversity and soon forget their previous peak real incomes or the growth rates they used to have. But that optimism may not be warranted in economies where it is increasingly perceived that poor performance is also due to a "system" that enforces, with IMF assistance, the interests of foreign banks over domestic prosperity and stability. There are also limits, as Mario Simonsen[6] has pointed out very forcefully:

> To keep developing debtor countries cooperating with the international financial community, a basic question should be addressed: under what conditions rational policy makers in debtor nations would prefer cooperation to retaliation? While precise rupture points are difficult to locate, a general principle remains valid: a growing economy with expanding exports hardly would seek confrontation with its creditors. In the same line, solvency at the expense of prolonged recession may be politically unsustainable.

CONCLUDING REMARKS

Solving debt problems is mostly politics, not economics. Yet today, unlike in the 1920s or 1930s, the problem is made to look as if it were solely an issue of economics: forecasts of interest rates, growth rates etc., are at the centre of the discussion to determine what are the domestic policies of debtor countries consistent with a dramatic reduction in their external indebtedness. Only four years ago banks were falling all over themselves to persuade debtors to go yet deeper into debt. Today we are told that there is an obvious over-indebtedness. The single premise of the "adjustment process" is the proposition that debts must stay intact and profitable in order to maintain the "system." Yet equity, good foreign policy, or simple long-run sense would indicate that some write-offs are in most people's interests.

The issue can be addressed simply by asking what the prospects are, thinking in terms of a decade, for Latin America. The standard view is that debtor countries will over several years work down their debts (relative to exports) by a combination of trade surpluses and export growth. One day, some day, banks will spontaneously decide that enough is enough, turn around and resume "voluntary lending." There is no assurance that this will happen and certainly no indication as to what is enough. Indeed, domestic regulators wince at the very thought that banks should think of renewed foreign lending. The priority is clearly that LDC debts should become a negligible item in both debtor countries' and commercial bank balance sheets. Until then, austerity.

But the prospect that commercial banks will seek to reduce their LDC exposure means that most of the interest will have to be earned rather than borrowed. The prospect combines with the unquestioned scarcity of official lending and the lack of significant direct investment. It adds up to the proposition that for the next decade Latin America will be a net exporter of resources. The notion that economic growth will be the same whether Latin America is borrowing resources or repaying, which is implicit in this thinking, runs against common sense and historical experience. Growth clearly will suffer simply because saving is inadequate to sustain investment levels at their historical trends. This scheme of things is somehow accepted as the inevitable short-run solution and, by extrapolation, as the medium-term outcome. The inevitability is not questioned, least of all by the IMF when it arranged for the cartelisation of banks and thus provided the essential mechanism to extract resources from Latin America.

But perhaps more disappointing is that policymakers in debtor countries themselves have come to accept the inevitability of this course of affairs. They have submitted to the IMF-sponsored case-by-case approach. Cartagena is remembered as an entirely embarrassing flop. They have agreed to make external debt a narrow technical problem (with vast domestic costs) rather than a burning international issue. Perhaps it is not surprising that Chile's Pinochet or Brazil's generals should avoid rocking the boat. But why did Mexico or Argentina go the same way? The answer is surely that any move on the external debt would potentially radicalise domestic politics of income distribution and property rights, perhaps beyond the precarious control of the present system?

Is the conclusion of all this that economics and politics combine to make the debt problem a dead issue? I do think that is the case, barring two possibilities. First, a major macroeconomic shock of the 1980–82 style could open up the issue of illiquidity and hence involve "impossible" adjustments. That might have happened in 1984–85 as a consequence of U.S. budget deficits colliding with tight money, but it simply has not happened. The rescuing factor presumably was skilful monetary policy in the U.S.

The other possibility, this one more plausible, is that creditor countries over the next decade find that they simply cannot live with the invasion of their home markets by exports from debtor LDCs that are required to pay the interest bill. Protection may well be the result. The protection issue, of course, was the main ingredient of the spreading in the 1930s of depression throughout the world economy:

> When the great creditor countries reduce their exports of capital . . . all their debtors must meet their obligations either in goods or in gold, instead of by fresh borrowing. Before this extraordinary situation had fully developed, however, a further check was imposed upon the capacity of the debtor countries to pay their external obligations. The increased export surpluses which they placed upon world markets caused concern in the importing creditor countries, which there-

upon imposed higher tariffs and supplemented them by additional restrictions on imports. There ensued in consequence an enormous shrinkage in world trade, and the logical consequence of this shrinkage has been a series of moratoria, suspensions of payment, and standstill agreements, as a result of which the credit of many debtor countries has been gravely impaired. (League of Nations, *World Economic Survey,* 1932.)

Notes

1. R. McCrane, *Foreign Bond Holders and American State Bonds,* London: Macmillan, 1933, p. 266.
2. M. Winkler, *Foreign Bonds. An Autopsy,* R. Swain & Co., 1933. Reprinted by Arno Press, 1976, p. 41.
3. Lord Lever "Begin to write down world debt," *Wall Street Journal* (New York) 7 June 1984.
4. See M. H. Simonsen, "The developing country debt problem," in G. Smith and J. Cuddington (eds.) *International Debt and the Developing Countries,* World Bank, Washington DC, 1985 for a development of this idea.
5. For details of the calculation, see R. Dornbusch and S. Fischer, "The world debt problem," *Journal of Development Planning* (forthcoming).
6. *Op cit.,* p. 41.

X

Structural and Institutional Change in International Finance

The readings in this part of the book might well have appeared first rather than last. The changes described here are at the root of problems with exchange-rate systems and international debt. Some would argue that they have even encouraged the surge of protectionist pressure described at the beginning of the book.

To summarize the readings briefly in the spirit of Lamfalussy's overview: financial capital has become internationally mobile at a far greater pace than real capital (direct investment) or goods; daily trade in financial assets dwarfs daily trade in commodities and services; financial markets are more integrated internationally today than any other markets; interest rates, bond and stock prices, and even capital gains move in increasingly parallel fashion from country to country. Lamfalussy says, "This is Bretton Woods turned upside down — a kind of topsy-turviness which . . . I view with some suspicion." So did the architects of the Bretton Woods system.

Some of the increasing mobility of financial capital is due to innovation. This is illustrated best in the readings from *Euromoney*, Fieleke, and Gendreau. Some of the innovation described there seems clearly beneficial. For example, the options market in foreign exchange opens the possibility for hedging contingencies, a valuable form of insurance against risk for international traders whose transactions must be submitted to a bidding process (military procurement) or to protracted negotiation (aircraft). Other innovations seem less clearly beneficial. Some are aimed quite consciously to avoid government regulation. Yet is such regulation necessarily bad? Both Lamfalussy and Dufey and Giddy worry about the ways that internationally mobile financial capital can undermine socially beneficial regulation.

Dufey and Giddy show clearly how the global integration of world banking is due to regulation of national money markets. Indeed that same integration can become a compelling force for deregulation, as they imply in their "law of maximum distortion." Their paper, written in 1978, is prescient in its discussion of this "law": for example, U.S. International Banking Facilities (IBFs) were created by statute in 1981 to compete more effectively with offshore banks by being freed from most U.S. banking regulations in dealing with nonresidents of the United States. Dufey and Giddy's paper was one of the earliest to describe modern Euro-banking simply as a competitive financial sector in which regulatory boundaries matter, but exchange rates and balances of payments need not. Older views of early Euro-banking, by contrast, focused more on its link to the balance of payments.

As one might expect when markets are becoming more global and competition more perfect, the identity of any one seller or buyer loses significance. Both Lamfalussy and the *Euromoney* writers comment on recent blurring of institutional distinctions. Investment banks look more and more like commercial banks, and conversely; bank loans look more and more like bonds, and so on. Even individuals are able to compete with large institutions as a specialized market such as the currency futures market springs up to serve them in parallel with the forward market.

One corollary of this trend deserves special attention. Financial transactions by central banks and regulatory authorities may lose any special significance, too, being swamped by the ocean of anonymous private transactions. Is this necessarily desirable? If not, then what should policy do? Lamfalussy raises the question, as did Corden and Grubel in their Part VIII readings. Lamfalussy only begins to answer, but alternative answers are scattered through many of the preceding readings, especially those of Goldstein, Dunn, Dornbusch, and Cooper.

30

The Changing Environment of Central Bank Policy

Alexandre Lamfalussy

. . . I propose to . . . you a few reflections on some of the more fundamental problems that monetary policymakers are facing today, both domestically and internationally, and for the handling of which they would be delighted to receive from the academic community some operationally usable advice — the stress being on "operationally usable."

I should like to focus my comments on two points. The first is that the financial systems of the main Western industrial countries are in the midst of not

From *American Economic Review Papers and Proceedings* 75 (May 1985), pp. 409–413. Copyright © 1985 by the American Economic Association. Reprinted by permission of the publisher and author. Some text omitted.

one but, in some cases, as many as four interconnected evolutionary processes: disinflation; internationalization; innovation; and deregulation. The second point is that . . . economic theory provides us with only limited guidance for managing our monetary affairs in such a complex process of structural adjustment and institutional change; nor can the observation of history give us much help towards understanding a situation which seems to be without precedent.

Let me begin with a few remarks on the management of the disinflation process. Under the impact of concerted anti-inflationary monetary policies initiated in 1979–80, inflation rates have over the last few years been declining more or less rapidly in all industrial countries. With the exception of a few countries they are, however, still at levels which would have been considered alarmingly high during the early 1960's. Moreover, what we know both from survey data and by inference from the level of interest rates suggests that inflationary expectations have been even slower to move downwards. The crux of the matter is that a slow process of disinflation of this kind carries with it, almost by definition, a good deal of uncertainty regarding future inflation rates — otherwise inflation could not be so sticky. This, in turn, implies that a considerable number of market participants are entering into contracts on terms that will inevitably prove costly for them; in other words, we are far from having seen the last of the casualties, either in the field of international lending or domestically, that are the normal corollary of disinflation. At the same time, the very slowness of the process also implies a continued high cost in terms of unused resources and unemployment. For both these reasons, there is the risk of a political reaction against the process of disinflation itself. On the other hand, an anti-inflationary shock treatment might well have been even more painful, with heavy costs being implied in both the short and long run.

These developments raise at least two sets of questions for policymakers. First, is there any practical alternative to slow disinflation? Is "shock treatment" a genuine alternative? Note that history provides us with good examples of quickly successful disinflation only after phases of hyperinflation, not after the sort of long-lasting, creeping inflationary process which has permeated and distorted most of our Western industrial countries over the last fifteen years or more. In the absence of historical precedents, can theory provide any guidance? There have been a few interesting pieces of analysis of the question of shock treatment vs. gradualism, but the academic debate has remained remarkably scant.

Second, on the assumption that the current policy course is the only practicable one, what are its implications for the prudential side of central banking policies? Can manifestations of financial fragility be taken care of by the normal market mechanism, or does their containment require specific lender-of-last-resort intervention by central banks in order to prevent domino effects? Here, too, I would much welcome a wide-ranging theoretical debate on the mechanics of financial adjustment during a slow process of disinflation, as distinct from crisis manifestations at cyclical turning points.

While I could imagine convincing answers to these questions when viewing the process of disinflation within one closed economy, my imagination begins to falter when I look at this process within the framework of the growing internationalization of domestic banking systems. Whatever ratios you care to consider — the share of external claims or liabilities in the total balance sheet, the relative importance of balance-sheet items in foreign currency, the size of income flows derived from international operations — they all point to a large and increasing international exposure of the domestic banking systems. The story of financial integration is also reflected in the cross-border transmission of interest rate developments. Interest rate parity holds almost instantaneously in the Euro-currency market; but, what is more important, there is growing statistical evidence of strong interconnections, even under floating exchange rates, between interest rate developments in the major domestic markets. Moreover, the fact that a number of countries, and within these countries private firms, are indebted in foreign currencies means that interest rate developments in these currencies can have a totally unexpected impact on the financial ratios of such debtors. In general, financial impulses emanating from the United States are transmitted remarkably quickly to other financial centers, despite fairly generalized floating. Interest rate "de-coupling" has been possible only within certain limits and by certain countries. Similarly, floating has not prevented strong international transmission links via the "real" side of the business cycle either.

. . . Much recent research has gone into analyzing the implications of this state of affairs for exchange rate determination and for the international transmission effects of shifts in the policy mix of a large country, in particular of the United States. This research confirms the day-to-day experience of policymakers, namely that in a financially integrated world no country can isolate itself from the others, no matter what its exchange rate regime. To mention just one example, even determined domestic anti-inflationary policies can be thrown off balance by a real effective exchange rate depreciation induced by capital flows. This clearly raises major policy issues to which there are no unequivocal answers. . . .

I do, however, have the uneasy impression that insufficient . . . work has been devoted to analyzing some other implications of international financial integration. One specific problem area concerns the question of whether the growing across-the-border interdependence increases, or, on the contrary, diminishes the fragility of the Western countries' banking systems. More perfect competition would seem to point to greater resilience, that is, to the ability of the system to take care of itself without any lender-of-last-resort intervention. On the other hand, it does not seem evident to me that more active competition in some fields (i.e., internationally), coupled with continued market imperfections in others (i.e., domestically), add up globally to more perfect competition. I shall return to this question shortly, when reflecting on the subject of deregulation. Another much broader area concerns the normative evaluation of the effects of greater financial integration (i.e., of speedier and much larger financial flows) on a world economy in which international direct investment flows remain limited and which at the same time is exposed to increasing trade barriers or to new types of trade distortions (for example, countertrade). This is Bretton Woods turned upside down — a kind of topsy-turviness which, in my physiocratic simplicity, I view with some suspicion.

The third evolutionary process has to do with the accelerating speed of financial innovations, particularly in North America and the United Kingdom, but also in quite a few other countries, though there, perhaps, attended by less publicity. This process is fueled by market participants' desire to hedge against the uncertainty generated by interest and exchange rate volatility (and is thus partly a reflection of inflationary developments), to circumvent regulations or to avoid taxes, to take up opportunities offered by deregulation or new technology, or simply to respond to market pressure. The result is a flow of new instruments and new techniques, and the blurring of dividing lines between institutions as well as between markets.

Central banks operating in such a fluid environment encounter a variety of problems. There is the problem of identifying suitable targets among the monetary aggregates, broad and narrow, and of recognizing circumstances when it seems appropriate to deviate from these targets. At a time when almost all bank liabilities are beginning to carry interest, I fear that the concept of transactions balances itself may be becoming elusive. Then, second, there are problems related to the narrowly defined monetary control techniques, that is, to the operational methods by which central banks try to hit their targets. Third, central banks would like to know whether and, if so, how the transmission mechanism from these targets to nominal income is affected, for example, by the proliferation of new instruments, the spreading use of floating interest rates or of financial futures.

Fourth, there are the prudential implications of innovation. What should be done, for instance, on a purely technical level, with a number of balance-sheet items listed as contingent liabilities, or with the host of intermediary balance-sheet items classed somewhere between equity and "traditional" liabilities? How should minimum capital ratios be established? Should such ratios be established at all? Are they not going to produce "evasive" innovations? What are the macroeconomic implications of assigning greater control responsibilities to the supervisory authorities? More fundamentally, we should try to assess the systemic effects of the redistribution of risk realized by means of some of these new techniques and instruments. You may argue that when risk-averse market participants shift risks associated with unexpected interest and exchange rate developments onto willing risk takers, everybody is going to be better off. This may well be the case, but increased collective happiness does not necessarily mean greater systemic stability. Or does it?

The difficulties in analyzing these problems and, therefore, in establishing policy-oriented value judgements are aggravated by two aspects of the current trend in innovations. One is that many of them also have an international dimension. Take the example of swapping a fixed interest claim in one currency on a foreign debtor against a variable interest claim in a different currency on a domestic borrower. Note, at the same time, that the legal obligations attached to a swap are so difficult to define, even within one legal system, let alone when several systems are involved, that the word itself cannot be translated unequivocally into the legally very precise French language. The point is that I am far from sure that all participants in these swaps fully appreciate the commitments they take on. Second, and more importantly, we are confronted here with a continuous *process,* rather than occasional discrete steps followed by a lengthy pause. There is no time for market participants to adjust themselves fully; the process is truly a dynamic one. Take, for instance, the gradual merging of the Euro-bond market with international bank lending, which is progressively eroding the usefulness of traditionally defined international banking statistics and removing the little transparency which we have managed to create in this particular field. What could be the consequences of this vanishing transparency for the decision-making process of market participants or for policymakers?

Let me now say a few words about deregulation — a topic of great interest in this country as well as in others. This, too, is an ongoing process, rather than a quantum jump from a fully regulated to an entirely free financial system. And if we consider the worldwide financial system, it becomes evident that we are condemned to live with a hybrid system even if the legislature of any single country were to accept such a quantum jump — a remote possibility anyway.

What guidance can theory offer to central banks managing their monetary policy or discharging their prudential duties in this environment? Note that the question is not only whether an entirely free financial system is more efficient (whatever that may mean), or more stable, or more easily "controlled" (in the sense of monetary control) than a regulated one. That is an interesting question but one of little immediate practical relevance. What I should like to know is, first, how the *process* of deregulation, with its inevitable lopsidedness and uncertainties as to the next steps, is working out in practice; and, second, how it could be improved. A deregulated world might be better than a fully regulated one, but a lot can happen on our way from the latter to the former.

I apologize for having presented such an indigestible menu of what might look like institutional trivialities, but I think that quite a lot is at stake. I have in mind in particular the need to preserve the useability of monetary policy as the main macroeconomic policy instrument. The practical or fundamental limitations of fiscal policy have become obvious: with government expenditure absorbing a very high proportion of resources, few Western European countries have any margins of maneuver for stimulatory fiscal policies, while, for reasons that you know only too well, the United States seems to have got stuck in the opposite direction. In such circumstances, impaired useability of monetary policy would surely have to be counted as a social cost to be set against the benefits of innovation and of deregulation in any global cost-benefit analysis.

Those of you who are familiar with ancient writings will by now have discovered my nostalgia for one of Schumpeter's main themes, namely that economic analysis should concern itself with the process of change, with its succession of cumulative or compensating imbalances, rather than with movements around some identifiable state of equilibrium. When I read his writings, more years ago than I care to remember, I hardly understood what he had in mind and dismissed it anyhow because I could not convert it into equations. As a professional participant[1] in the current process of change affecting financial markets, and having to advise central banks on how to operate in such an environment, I am beginning to have an inkling of what he was driving at — although I am less able than ever to put these thoughts into a rigorous theoretical framework. . . .

In the meantime — "en attendant" as we would say more appropriately in French — practitioners will have to continue to practice. They cannot simply resign and take up gardening, much though some of you might wish them to. For my part, in my advisory capacity, I try to prevent them from succumbing to two opposite temptations.

One temptation is to return to complete "*ad hoc*-ry," that is, to what the French would call "naviguer à vue." This would be a grave mistake. Full discretion cannot counteract uncertainty; in all likelihood it increases it. Rules, be they monetary aggregates or an exchange rate target, are needed to provide some anchor for the wildly fluctuating expectations of market participants; to make monetary policymakers accountable for their action, including their decisions to deviate from predetermined targets; and to give them leverage in their dealings with governments and parliaments.

The other temptation is to retreat into a world of rigid rules. I hope that I have made it abundantly clear why in the present world environment I do not believe in a monetary policy based on mechanical rules. It is difficult to define such rules; it is sometimes impossible to apply them; and it would often be irresponsible to stick to them.

The road to follow is somewhere in between: rules applied with a pragmatic sense of discretion. Admittedly, this is more easily said than done, but then monetary policy, like all other policies, remains an art, not a science.

Note

1. Dr. Lamfalussy is General Manager of the Bank for International Settlements.

31

The International Money Market: Perspective and Prognosis

Gunter Dufey and Ian H. Giddy

I. WHAT'S SO SPECIAL ABOUT THE EUROCURRENCY MARKETS?

There are few important aspects about the international money market that cannot be explained with reference to the following ideas:

1. The external (Eurocurrency) and internal (domestic) money markets are merely competing segments of the larger markets for the assets and liabilities of financial intermediaries.
2. Financial institutions in the external market are largely free of both informal constraints (such as pressures to allocate credit to certain borrowers) and formal regulations (such as reserve requirements). Eurobanks can therefore operate on narrower margins than can domestic banks.
3. On the other hand, from the point of view of the depositor or borrower, deposits in and loans from Eurobanks are generally riskier, because transactions with Eurobanks are subject to restrictions on funds transfers and for credit extension by *two* political jurisdictions, whereas domestic transactions are subject to the political risk of only one government. Hence Eurobanks — as a rule — offer more attractive deposit and loan rates than do domestic banks.
4. While entry to virtually all national banking systems is restricted, in effect if not *de jure*, there is no limit to participation by any financial institution in external financial intermediation.
5. The close links between the domestic and external credit markets in a particular currency may be partially broken when capital controls restrict transfers of funds into and out of the country of that currency.
6. The links between segments of the Eurocurrency markets denominated in different currencies are governed by exchange-rate expectations. Arbitrage within the Eurocurrency market occurs through the foreign exchange markets, whereby the interest differentials equal the respective forward exchange premium or discount.

From Gunter Dufey and Ian H. Giddy, *The International Money Market,* © 1978, pp. 259–268. Reprinted by permission of Prentice-Hall, Inc., Englewood Cliffs, New Jersey. Adapted by permission.

The Eurocurrency markets do differ from domestic markets in ways other than those summarized above. In most cases, however, these differences can be explained as the result of one or another of the basic features noted or can be dismissed as not being fundamental features of the external markets per se. *In all other respects, therefore, there is nothing special about the Eurocurrency markets.*

Indeed, most aspects of the external market can be explained by means of an analogy with a particular segment of the domestic banking market. There are many aspects of the international money market that we have, by intent or omission, neglected to discuss. But we have attempted to provide the reader with the tools with which to dissect virtually any problem relating to the market. The basic rule is this: if the problem cannot be interpreted by analogy with a segment of the domestic market, it must be the result of one of the six distinguishing characteristics we have listed. We have found this to be a remarkably powerful principle.

II. DOMESTIC AND EXTERNAL CREDIT MARKETS AND THE INTERNATIONAL FINANCIAL SYSTEM

The fact that the international money markets involve few concepts that are not already familiar to students of money or banking does not reduce their central role in the modern international financial system. The Euromarkets serve as the bridge between the financial markets of countries and currencies. They enable, for the first time, the *currency of denomination* of an asset to be separated from the *country of jurisdiction*. Stated differently, they enable borrowers and lenders to systematically separate the *currency risk* from the *political risk* of an asset or liability.

It is therefore instructive to examine precisely how the domestic and external markets for credit and the foreign exchange markets fit into the international financial system in general. Table 1 provides a schematic summary of the issues arising from the existence of international payments, capital flows, and financial markets. Let us explore some of these questions.

In a fundamental sense the financial system performs two functions: (1) the collection of savings and the allocation of resources into real investments, and (2) the facilitation of payment for transactions. Efficient performance of both functions requires financial assets and money balances, serving as convenient stores of value and means of payments, respectively. Internationally, there exists a need for the same services. Differences in the intertemporal preferences of economic transactors in different countries can be efficiently evened out through the international exchange of financial assets (international capital flows). And the working balances that financial institutions hold in other countries make possible an efficient transfer of funds to settle various kinds of international transactions. However, virtually all money balances are of a strictly national character, reinforced by national monopolies on issuance of currency and buttressed by legal

TABLE 1

Role of the External Markets in the International Financial System

Phenomenon	Function
Existence of financial assets	Satisfies intertemporal preferences
Existence of money balances	Minimizes uncertainty and cost associated with future payments
Use of a vehicle currency	Reduces the costs and uncertainties involved in international payments
Currency denomination of financial assets and liabilities	Guards the international purchasing power and stability of portfolios
Extent of financial intermediation	Reconciles different risk and maturity preferences of borrowers and lenders
Determination of external versus internal intermediation	Reflects relative cost and risk perceptions
Market for spot and forward foreign exchange	Reconciles currency preferences and expectations
Arbitrage between domestic and external markets and among Eurocurrency markets	Assures equality of effective interest rates in the absence of controls

tender laws. If trade and payments were effected only on a bilateral basis, using only the currency of the transactors, every international company or bank would be forced to hold money balances in all countries where payments might have to be made. Hence the use of a common vehicle currency considerably improves the efficiency of the system for international payments because it permits transactors to economize on the number and amount of foreign money balances held. The choice of a national currency as a vehicle currency depends largely on three factors: (1) the relative number of "natural transactions" favoring large countries; (2) the availability of an efficient money market that permits transactors to adjust their liquidity positions at a low incremental cost; and (3) a strong expectation that the authorities will not restrict nonresidents in their use of working balances (technically this is known as the *maintenance of nonresident convertibility*).

Although the existence of money balances in a certain foreign currency will also promote the denomination of financial assets in that currency, because transactions cost (conversion costs) will be minimized, in a world of uncertainty of exchange rates and international consumption, it is considerations of portfolio diversification that determine the currency denomination of financial assets and liabilities.

Such assets and liabilities are issued either directly by (ultimate) investors as a means of obtaining funds for productive assets, or by financial intermediaries who interject themselves between savers and investors, performing a risk and maturity transformation. The extent of financial intermediation relative to the total savings-investment process depends largely on the ability of such institutions to better reconcile different risk and maturity preferences of borrowers and lenders than would be possible through organized securities markets. Given the institutional barriers involved in international capital flows, it is not surprising that financial intermediaries play a dominant role in the international flow of credit.

International capital flows, however, do not explain the existence and growth of extensive external ("Euro-") financial intermediation sectors; these phenomena are explained by different cost structures and risk perceptions relative to domestic financial intermediation. However, because of the special operating conditions, external financial intermediaries play an important role in the collection of savings and the allocation of credit, both internationally and in respect to the national financial market, of which they represent the external sector.

It is the special operating characteristics of the Eurocurrency markets that make them the integrating mechanism of what are basically different, and to a certain extent independent, functions: the international transmission of credit and payments. To the extent that payments are made in the future, markets for foreign means of payments and international credit markets are linked through arbitrage: the foreign exchange market, where currency preferences and expectations are reconciled, determines the relationship among various segments of the external markets, which, in turn, tie together national financial systems. How close these links are depends largely on the extent of governmental controls on international payments and credit transactions.

III. HOW DO THE EUROMARKETS AFFECT ECONOMIC GROWTH AND THE DISTRIBUTION OF INCOME?

. . . The development of large, competitive financial markets facilitates the transfer of resources from ultimate savers to ultimate investors at low cost, and so promotes economic growth. As broad, competitive, and liquid financial markets, the Eurocurrency markets contribute to the efficient transfer and allocation of resources to their most productive use. The Eurobanks enlarge the financial sector of those countries whose currencies are used to denominate the assets and liabilities of external financial intermediaries. As a result of their diversity of geographical location and national origin, these Eurobanks may have a less domestically oriented bias in seeking out borrowers and depositors. Thus there is a strong presumption that they may contribute more to the efficient *international* allocation of credit than would the growth of an equal volume of intermediation in purely domestic markets.

But is there anything about the fundamental nature of the Eurocurrency system which suggests that its effect on economic growth and its distribution might differ from that of domestic markets? The answer is "yes," and the basis for that answer is grounded in two facts: (1) Eurobanks are not subject to pressures and legal constraints on investment behavior, and (2) they allow both international investors and borrowers to separate their choice of political risk from the choice of currency in which the asset or liability is to be denominated.

How do these features affect the growth and distribution of output? Consider first the effect on the distribution of credit, and therefore of income, in a purely domestic context. Domestic banks are almost universally expected to allocate a portion of their loan and bond portfolios to "socially preferred" borrowers who are less able to compete for funds in the open credit market. In addition, domestic banks are required to hold non-interest-bearing reserves, which are obligations of the government (in effect, a free loan to the public). Each of these constraints means that banks earn less on their portfolios, given the level of risk, than they would otherwise choose to do. Each constraint, therefore, implies (1) a transfer of income to preferred borrowers (including the government itself) from the bank's shareholders and depositors, and (2) a suboptimal allocation of credit, in the sense that the bank is prevented from allocating funds to their most profitable and productive uses.[1] By conducting their business in the external rather than the domestic market, banks escape such constraints, with the result that there is a redistribution of credit away from privileged borrowers and in favor of more productive borrowers and therefore in favor of economic growth.

Similar reasoning applies to the international as opposed to domestic allocation of credit through the external markets. Since the class of privileged borrowers (whose credit needs are perforce favored by domestic banks) seldom extends to foreign borrowers, the latter are, when credit-worthy and productive, favored by the effective removal of political constraints on bank portfolios. The redistribution and growth-promoting effect of the Euromarkets occurs on an international as well as on a domestic scale.

It would be a mistake to infer from this argument that the growth of Eurocurrency banking is necessarily accompanied by a capital flow from countries with an external market to those without one. Although this may occur — developing countries, for example, now have freer access to dollar credit than might otherwise have been the case — the flow of loans to such countries may well be offset by a flow of deposits from the same countries to the Euromarkets. And such flows are even more likely now that savers are able to invest in dollar assets, for example, without necessarily placing their funds in the United States.

This brings us to our second point. International capital flows tend to increase total (world) welfare by equalizing the marginal efficiency of capital, differences in preferences for present as opposed to future consumption, and differences in preferences for liquidity. It may be argued . . . that the Eurocurrency markets increase the international mobility of capital and hence enhance economic welfare and growth. The reason lies partly in the institutional mechanism (it is easier to switch currencies in a single institution, place and time zone), but also in the separation of currency risk from political risk. An individual may respond to an attractive yield differential by switching his deposit or loan from one currency to another without altering the nature of the jurisdiction in which his deposit or loan is booked; the same would not be true in the absence of the Euromarket.

IV. BANK REGULATION AND THE EUROCURRENCY MARKET

If it is true that the external market enables banks to circumvent the government's efforts to allocate credit by way of the private financial system, what can we conclude about the need for, and nature of, a response on the part of the regulatory authorities? For although the Euromarkets may redistribute credit in such a way as to promote economic growth, one cannot be sure that such a redistribution actually is in the social interest of any particular country. A redistribution that increases total output does not necessarily increase total welfare. All one can say is that if a government is to tax some citizens to improve the income of others, the tax should not be levied in such a way as to discourage efficient use of resources.

The simple answer, then, to the dilemma posed by unregulated external markets is for the government to impose a *direct* tax and provide a *direct* subsidy to favored sectors or institutions. In this way the transfer of income would be effected without additional distortions in financial markets occurring. Instead, however, the usual method is to increase the burden of credit allocation on those institutions that remain subject to domestic regulatory influences, thus distorting domestic financial markets even further. But there is a limit to the extent to which authorities, such as the U.S. government, can increase the burden of indirect credit allocation on domestic institutions without forcing *them* into the external market. This limit may be stated in terms of the *law of maximum distortion: for a given level of restrictions on international capital flows, there is a limit on the extent to which a government can distort domestic financial markets.*

The reasoning behind this statement is quite simple. A government can force financial markets and institutions to allocate credit in a suboptimal fashion to a certain degree, even if an external market exists and capital inflows and outflows are relatively unrestricted. If the manipulation of banks' portfolios or market decisions is carried too far, however, depositors and other investors will find themselves receiving returns insufficiently high for the level of risk involved. Therefore, either the financial markets and institutions themselves will shift to the external market (taking borrowers and depositors with them), or they will lose intermediation business to the external markets. Taking the United States as an example, let us assume that there is a given volume of credit intermediated in dollars. Part of the dollar credit system is external: the Eurodollar market. The more the U.S. authorities impose restraints and regulations on the rates that domestic banks can pay for deposits or obtain on assets, the greater the proportion of credit that will be intermediated externally. And the more dollar credit intermediation occurs outside the U.S. authorities' jurisdiction, the more difficult it will be to allocate credit domestically. The only recourse for the U.S. government is to accept the limits to market distortion, or to impose restrictions on investing or borrowing abroad — that is, to raise the level of capital controls. And a policy of financial isolationism has its own costs, which we need not discuss here.

What can we conclude? Since . . . there is little that the U.S. government or even the major industrial countries' governments in concert can do about controlling the Eurodollar market directly, domestic financial institutions will continue to bear a disproportionate burden of regulation. Reserve requirements and other nonmarket constraints on banks' asset or liability decisions can be regarded as an indirect tax.[2] The existence of external markets means that this tax falls more heavily on domestic banks, their owners and depositors, than would be the case in the absence of external markets. This is not necessarily "unfair," because many domestic banks benefit from protected markets that result solely from regulation-related barriers to entry. But it does suggest that such a tax might be more equitably and efficiently collected by some means other than the distortion of credit markets.

Indeed, some observers have suggested that the only way for the U.S. authorities to regain controls over financial markets is to allow domestic institutions to be sufficiently competitive to attract credit intermediation business back to the United States. This could be done, for example, by (1) removing reserve requirements on bank time deposits, (2) by paying a competitive interest rate on the required reserves, and (3) by eliminating most of the explicit and informal constraints on portfolio choices that banks face. Under this scheme, both domestic banks and Eurobanks could, for a fee, buy deposit insurance such as that offered by a deposit insurance institution such as the FDIC in the United States, and be subject to examination. But these higher costs would mean that depositors who favored such banks would have to accept a slightly lower interest rate.

V. THE CONDITIONS FOR EXISTENCE OF EXTERNAL CREDIT MARKETS

The Eurocurrency market is a creature of regulation and as such depends largely for its existence on the nature and degree of banking regulations and capital controls. Of course, it is not regulation per se that matters, only regulation that imposes a greater cost than it provides benefits. The banking authorities of many countries provide supervision and examination of domestic banks that is regarded as a useful service by the consumers of banking services. And the test of such effects of regulation is when both borrowers and depositors are willing to accept less favorable interest rates in return for the assurance that the bank's books are subject to regular review by competent and objective authorities. The most successful of the Eurobanks, then, tend to be those that are subject to such review.

But domestic banking regulation that imposes a cost without any associated benefits provides an incentive for the banking public to avoid this cost, and it does so by means of the external money market. We conclude that, other things being equal,

Size of external credit market relative to total credit market in that currency
= a function of Costs of domestic banking regulation
– Benefits from domestic banking regulation

It follows that if domestic banking regulation were to disappear, there would be little incentive for the Eurocurrency markets to exist. Yet we need not go so far. Even in the presence of banking regulation, most of the external market would shift back to the domestic market if banking regulation were such that it did not distort financial decisions.[3]

This raises a related question: If the size and existence of external markets are largely a function of the burden of domestic regulation, why is it that external credit markets have not developed in the many currencies whose countries distort banks' decisions to a much greater degree than does the United States? Why is there not a large Eurocurrency market in Brazilian cruzeiros, Indian rupees, or even Japanese yen? The answer lies in the mechanism of the market. Every transfer of funds into, out of, or between Eurobanks is made by means of a transfer in domestic banks; hence the ability to undertake such transfers is an absolute prerequisite for the existence of a Euromarket in a particular currency. To the extent that financial transactions between domestic residents and nonresidents are restricted, it becomes more difficult to establish and maintain an active external credit market. Thus it is a mistake to suppose that the Eurodollar market grew during the 1960s because of the U.S. capital controls; more accurately, it grew in spite of them. At no time, however, did the United States restrict *nonresident convertibility* — that is, foreigners were always free to increase or decrease their balances in U.S. domestic banks. . . .

There is another reason for the absence of external credit markets in most of the world's currencies. This reason is that paradoxically, one can obtain Euroloans or Eurodeposits in any particular currency without there actually being a Euromarket in that currency. How can this be? The answer lies in the fact that an asset or liability in, say, dollars, can be effectively converted into any other currency by buying or selling that currency in the forward market. . . . Assume, for example, that a Mexican resident wishes to hold a Europeso deposit in London but discovers that no Europeso market exists and that even if it did, it would be narrow, illiquid, and inefficient. What he can do, instead, is sell his pesos for dollars in the spot foreign exchange market, deposit the dollars in a Eurobank, and simultaneously buy Mexican pesos forward. He will now effectively own a peso-denominated asset earning an interest rate that equals the Eurodollar rate plus the forward discount on the Mexican peso.[4]

Taken to its logical extreme, this argument implies that when an external market in one currency (such as the U.S. dollar) exists, there is no need for parallel deposit markets in any other currency, since Eurodollars can be "swapped" into any given currency as long as a forward market exists for that currency. Alternatively, since transactions in external deposit markets are perfect substitutes for forward foreign exchange transactions, the depth and liquidity of the market for forward foreign exchange is greatly enhanced by the existence of the Euromarkets.

VI. SOME UNRESOLVED ISSUES

As long as the Euromarkets continue to exist in their present form, we will be able to employ the framework laid out in Section I to reinterpret any issues that arise. But the answers to specific questions in particular instances frequently depend on purely empirical issues. Indeed, it is our belief that differences in various research-ers' interpretations of the market would be largely resolved if they could reach agreement on certain empirical characteristics of the external markets and their linkages with domestic credit markets. And such knowledge would certainly improve policymakers' understanding of how to respond to the Eurocurrency phenomenon.

What are these questions? The first concerns simply the size of various segments of the Eurocurrency market and related aggregates. What, for example, is the effective size of the external market in each currency, after taking into account the conversion from one currency into another through forward hedging? What fraction of the total *comparable* credit market in each currency does the external market form? And how does the inclusion of the external market alter various domestic monetary aggregates?

The next set of questions concerns the size of interest elasticities, or the responsiveness of capital flows between the domestic and external markets, and between various external markets, to a given change in interest rates in one market. And what is the impact on interest rates of a given shift in deposits? Related questions are: How much credit business shifts from the domestic to the external market (or vice versa) in response to a given change in domestic regulations, such as reserve requirements? How sensitive are Eurocurrency depositors to a given change in the political risk associated with a particular offshore market location? In what way, if at all, are lending practices of banks affected by the geographical location of deposits?

Next, how much exactly is the distribution of credit and economic growth affected by a given shift of deposits out of or into the external credit market? What is the additional cost to domestic banks of being obliged to bear the burden of "taxes" in one form or another imposed by the regulatory authorities?

Finally, there remain several empirical issues relating to the quantitative effect of various attempts to control the Eurocurrency markets and their im-plications for the cost and efficacy of conducting domestic banking and monetary policies. To what extent, for example, would the imposition of small reserve requirements on one particular segment of Eurobanks cause business to shift to other segments or geographical locations? And what is the impact of a given proportion of credit being intermediated externally on the domestic credit multi-plier — its size and variability, the lags involved, and the difficulty of gauging the final impact on total credit of a given reserve change?

These are the kinds of issues that we do not propose to resolve here but which will provide grist for the mill of anyone who believes that no interesting questions remain concerning the international money market.

Notes

1. Of course, domestic banking regulations often protect banks from competition, too; so the final effect of being subject to domestic regulations on a particular bank's profitability cannot be stated unequivocally.
2. This tax is akin to a sales tax rather than a tax on income or profits.
3. Even in the absence of costly regulations, however, some credit business would continue to be intermediated externally as a result of *fear* of the later imposition of restrictions on domestic banks.
4. Note, however, that this example or any similar transaction presupposes some degree of freedom for capital transfers into and out of the country in question.

32

The One-World Capital Market

From *Euromoney Magazine*

The world's capital markets are experiencing a revolution. . . . [The early 1980s has witnessed] the progressive demise of barriers and regulations which hinder the movement of capital around the world. This process, combined with some powerful new financing techniques, is creating an almost global capital market.

The lines of demarcation between domestic and international capital markets are increasingly blurred, as are those between the different instruments for raising capital: equity, bonds and loans. The structure of the financial institutions serving the markets is also changing. And the pace of change, in the structure of the markets, the instruments and the institutions, is accelerating.

The advent of currency and interest rate swaps[1] has brought domestic and international capital markets closer together, almost to the point where they are indistinguishable; a borrower can tap a domestic capital market and swap that debt with a foreign counterparty. Some new equity issues, particularly large issues for well-known multinationals, are being sold simultaneously in different markets by different underwriting syndicates to give a more global shareholder base, and in much the same way that bonds and loans are syndicated. More companies seek foreign stock exchange listings and make share issues directly into major foreign markets. Increasingly, participations in syndicated credits are being traded around the world much like bonds or shares. A steadily increasing volume of corporate Eurobond issues is convertible into shares in the corporation. This unique financing survey shows how deregulation and the invention of new instruments are making an enormous impact on the international markets. . . .

From *Euromoney,* the London-based journal of the international capital markets, October 1984, pp. 106–110. Reprinted by permission. Some text and charts omitted.

The abolition of U.S. withholding tax on foreign holders of U.S. bonds has ushered in what should be the final phase in the elimination of barriers. That decision drew an immediate response from the West Germans who announced plans to examine the possibility of abolishing their 25 percent withholding tax.

The universal abolition of withholding tax would rapidly internationalize the leading domestic capital markets as international investor interest created a wider base of demand. Even though the abolition of withholding tax in the U.S. is an obvious move by the Treasury to attract some of the funds that are now invested in Eurobonds,[2] it will have the side-effect of making the U.S. domestic bond market more international.

Traditionally, Eurobonds have yielded slightly less than equivalent instruments in the U.S. domestic market, because they are not subject to withholding tax and because they are bearer instruments.[3] But that edge will disappear with the abolition of withholding tax and the new regulations which will allow U.S. corporations to issue bearer bonds.

The better known issuers of bonds already switch between their domestic market, foreign markets and the Euromarket, depending on where they can get the best deal. U.S. corporations are probably the most mobile, moving in and out of their domestic market with considerable ease. [In 1983], domestic U.S. corporate bond issues amounted to $52.4 billion, compared with $44 billion in 1982. In the first six months of [1984] U.S. domestic bond volume amounted to $26.7 billion. Over the same period the volume of Eurobonds from U.S. issuers amounted to $13.3 billion in 1982, declining to $6.2 billion in 1983, offset by the increase in domestic financings, but in the first half of [1984], their volume shot up to $6.8 billion.

Swaps in theory allow any borrower, and any investor for that matter, access to any capital market in the world. They can do this without breaking down barriers between markets; in fact they rely on the arbitrage from market to market, instrument to instrument and borrower to borrower. The swap market has developed so fast — some estimates say $75 billion worth will have been written by the end of [1984] — that their full impact on, say, the Eurobond market, or the Swiss capital market, is probably still being underestimated.

During some months of 1984 around 80 percent of the Eurobonds issued were swap-related — with sharp repercussions on pricing and secondary market performance. But the classic interest-rate swap, with a bank Eurobond issue on one side and a U.S. corporate or thrift institution on the other, now probably accounts for less than a quarter of the market.

In the U.S., a thriving domestic market has grown up with regional banks and thrifts taking new swaps and reversing old ones. Matching counterparties is no longer regarded as necessary or businesslike by many of the major arranging banks. Banks and investment banks in New York and London act as principals, taking swaps on their own books and laying them off later. . . . U.S. investment banks are pressing for interest rate swaps to become a tradeable commodity; the commercial banks see each swap as linked to a credit decision and therefore not tradeable, but perhaps assignable by negotiation.

Despite this obstacle, an active secondary market in interest-rate swaps has grown up, driven by U.S. thrifts and corporates taking cash gains by selling swaps written [during 1983] at lower interest rates. However, many thrifts originally made the swaps to fund fixed-rate assets with fixed-rate liabilities. Having now sold them to return to floating-rate assets, some of them could be in trouble if U.S. interest rates don't fall, but rise. U.S. regulators are growing concerned about the speculative use of swaps by thrifts and nonbanks and may write new rules soon. Swaps for many institutions are becoming an interest rate hedging tool more than a means of credit arbitrage. With their own view on interest rates they can write swaps, even without any underlying debt. About a tenth of the market now includes an asset swap element, whereby an investor can change his income stream from floating to fixed, Swiss francs to dollars, and so on.

Currency swaps are by tradition more complex but they are moving closer to, and even assisting, banks' medium-term foreign exchange transactions. Citicorp and Paribas are quoting currency swaps both ways in the major currencies.

Like the greatest inventions, the swap principle has caused a revolution, even though the concept is simple and could have been applied years earlier. Even after two or three years' concentration by the most creative minds in investment banking, new applications are being tested every day, like the zero coupon swap, swap options, swaps off Spanish commercial paper, perhaps a swap with the U.S. Treasury itself?

For the houses like Salomon Brothers, who like to trade everything, the swap throws all interest-bearing instruments everywhere in the world into one melting pot. Everyone's debt and everyone's asset becomes fungible. For the global universal banks, like Citicorp, swaps are both a way to service their clients and a way to fund and improve their own balance sheet around the world. The investment banks and commercial banks are therefore fighting a battle to establish their very different uses of the swap market as the norm.

Swaps enable banks, as well as everyone else, to manage their liabilities to best advantage; bank assets, too, are increasingly managed on the basis of their tradeability. Some loans are now structured to resemble publicly traded securities rather than traditional loans. The main instruments of the capital markets now bear little relation to what they looked like as recently as five years ago. The basic instruments have spawned numerous offspring in response to the changes that have had to be made to accommodate all sides of the market — borrowers, lenders and investors.

The Eurobond has probably undergone the greatest change, which is why the market didn't contract to anything like the same extent as the Euroloan market [in 1983]. In 1982, Eurobond volume was $47.3 billion and [in 1983], although marginally down on 1982 volume at $47.2 billion, total volume was higher than

Euroloan volume for the first time, as syndicated lending contracted sharply [due to international debt problems]. . . .

That the Eurobond market was able to maintain volume was entirely the result of the performance of the floating rate note [FRN][4] sector. The FRN market took off [in 1983]. Issue volume amounted to $14.7 billion and accounted for nearly a third of total Eurobond volume. Issue size was increased to syndicated loan proportions. Sweden launched a $1.2 billion floater in January. This was followed by a $1.8 billion issue for the European Economic Community in July, which still ranks as the largest-ever Eurobond issue. The success of these issues showed that sovereign borrowers could raise as much money through FRNs as through loans. And being liquid instruments, FRNs provided cheaper money than loans.

The market was able to digest such large amounts because a new class of investor came in to buy the notes, to supplement the bank purchasers who have traditionally bought most FRNs. Institutional investors became heavy buyers of triple-A sovereign FRNs, attracted by the increased liquidity which came with the jumbo-sized issues. Pension funds, insurance companies and corporations bought the notes and held them for brief periods, treating them like short-term money market instruments.

The FRN market has continued to grow this year and new records continue to be set . . . Although there have been no FRN jumbos [in 1984] to match those from the EEC and Sweden . . . total volume in the first six months of the year amounted to $13.3 billion, which is not far short of the total for the whole of last year. . . .

Despite all its attractions, the FRN doesn't provide the same flexibility as some other instruments, which can be priced lower. As swaps become more refined, borrowers are able to raise funds at a cost below Libor [the London Interbank Offered Rate, an important reference interest rate]. Also, a number of other instruments such as revolving underwriting facilities (RUFs), and Euronotes can be cheaper than FRNs, and may have added flexibility. And loans can be arranged on a standby or backup basis, which is not possible with an FRN because it is a debt offering. So the FRN is not likely to completely replace other floating-rate borrowing instruments, even for prime sovereign borrowers, who are now able to borrow in the FRN market at around 20 basis points over Libor. . . .

Not all the innovation in the bond market has been on the floating rate side. In March, Texaco launched a $1 billion convertible issue with four separate underwriting syndicates to handle the issue in Switzerland, Germany, Asia and the rest of the world outside the U.S. That successful issue is regarded as the first truly global syndication of a Eurobond issue. . . . It was both the largest fixed-rate issue and the largest convertible the market had ever seen.

The Euroloan market is also changing and drawing closer to the bond market. Bank loans are becoming more liquid, and are growing to resemble securities. Whereas, at one time, a bank would participate in a loan syndicate and keep the amount of its participation on its books for the life of that loan, there is now a flourishing market in unwanted loan participations. Many banks, hurt by the rash of reschedulings in the last two years, are not prepared to lend for longer than three years, but borrowers still want to borrow for up to 10 years. The market in trading loan participations bridges that gap. Most of the larger banks are prepared to provide medium-term funds, but they have active marketing departments selling a growing proportion of those assets on to other, smaller banks.

The gain for the larger banks is considerable: they restrict their own asset growth, while keeping the front-end fees on loans, and taking a margin on the sale. And the small, purchasing bank gains assets with the reassuringly short maturity of one or two years.

Loan syndication is no longer the driving force of the Euromarket banks. They are keen to provide a number of other instruments for the increasingly knowledgeable borrower. RUFs are one of the instruments that they are keen to promote. A RUF provides the borrower with medium-term funds at a lower cost than a loan, financed through the sale of short-term notes, which are underwritten by banks. Spain, for example, recently raised $500 million through a RUF, showing that RUFs, like FRNs, are displacing syndicated loans.

The RUF has been a useful instrument in the international capital markets because it has brought into the market, as underwriters, a wide range of banks that would not otherwise have been involved. Bank of China heads the list of underwriters who have participated in RUFs since their launch in 1981. . . .

The keenness of banks to provide new instruments in the Euroloan market doesn't mean that the traditional syndicated loan has outlived its usefulness, even if some of the bigger loans are now hybrid financings, combining note insurance with traditional lending. In volume terms, the Euroloan is still the major contributor of funds to the international capital markets. After a setback . . . [in 1983] because less-developed-country borrowers were mostly excluded from the market, the syndicated loan market came roaring back this year, led by the merger and acquisition fever that struck the U.S. in the early part of [1984]. The number of loans signed in the first half of the year was 590, compared with 526 in the same period of 1983. But the U.S. oil companies were largely responsible for pushing volume up from $43.9 billion to $90.7 billion. . . .

The top tier of lead managers in syndicated lending is now the preserve of U.S. banks. But for all their expertise in putting together attractive financing packages for mergers and acquisitions, the lead managers of syndicated loans don't get a look-in when it comes to advising the respective parties in a merger or an acquisition, particularly if it is a cross-border transaction. International mergers and acquisitions are on the increase and a small, select group of U.S. investment banks and British merchant banks have cornered the market in providing advice. That they have been able to achieve this preeminence is a result of their presence in most of the leading international markets and their enviable, worldwide client base.

While swaps have drawn together international and domestic bond markets and mergers and acquisitions have drawn together the international corporate sector, the upsurge in trading in international equities is doing the same for leading stock markets. Equity finance is the last capital-raising instrument to embrace internationalism. The leading companies in many countries have long had listings on foreign exchanges, but with the possible exception of South African gold mining companies listed on the London Stock Exchange, there has not, until recently, been an active market.

That changed [in 1983] as share prices in the leading markets started rising and portfolio managers saw good foreign investment opportunities. In some cases, the flow of funds to a particular market was large enough to determine the direction of stock market price movements. In most leading equity markets, share prices were pushed to record levels. Corporate issuers of equity took the opportunity to place equity in overseas markets, with London and New York as the main destinations. [In 1983], equity issues by foreign corporations — excluding Canadians — in the U.S. amounted to $1 billion, compared with $239 million in 1982, although activity has slumped to $162.8 million, from five issues, in the first half of [1984].

The first truly international equity issues were launched by two Canadian companies, Alcan Aluminum and Bell Canada Enterprises, last year. Each issue was launched simultaneously in three separate markets — Canada, the U.S. and Europe — with three separate underwriting syndicates. The issues were generally well received in each of the markets and active trading followed. The gain for such issuers is that an active market in shares listed on foreign exchanges opens their options in raising new capital.

Notes

1. A *swap* is a simultaneous sale of one asset (or liability) and purchase of another of the same value. When the currencies in which the two assets are denominated differ, a *currency swap* has taken place. When interest-rate provisions differ (e.g., when one asset bears a fixed rate and one a floating rate), an *interest-rate swap* has taken place.
2. A Eurobond is a bond denominated in the currency of one country but issued in some other country, thereby avoiding regulation in each over own-currency bond markets.
3. Bearer bonds are physically portable and transferable among holders.
4. A floating rate note is a Eurobond whose maturity is divided into subperiods, during which the interest rate is constant, but between which it can be adjusted.

33

The Rise of the Foreign Currency Futures Market

Norman S. Fieleke

Among the many remarkable developments in financial markets in recent years, one of the most intriguing is the rise of trading in futures contracts for foreign currencies and financial instruments. Although active markets in futures contracts for physical commodities such as grain had existed for many years, the market for foreign currency futures was not launched until 1972. Markets for financial instruments such as U.S. Treasury bills soon followed. . . . Both the foreign currency market and the markets for financial instruments have exhibited rapid growth since their inauguration.

What are foreign currency futures? Why has the market for them expanded so rapidly? What are the social benefits, if any, from this financial innovation?

Broadly defined, a futures contract is simply an agreement to buy or sell a specified quantity of a particular asset for delivery at a future date at a designated price. Many agreements fall into this category, including such everyday undertakings as a homeowner's order for furniture to be delivered c.o.d. the following week. The futures contracts treated in this article, however, are those entered into through a centralized market exchange, the International Monetary Market (IMM) in Chicago, and are for foreign currencies. . . .

Foreign currency futures trading can be undertaken not only for the purposes of hedging or speculation, but also for the purpose of arbitrage. In particular, some traders are quick to take advantage of any profitable differential that arises between rates quoted in the futures market and in the so-called "forward market" for the same currency.

THE FUTURES MARKET AND THE FORWARD MARKET

Long before the IMM was even a gleam in the eyes of its founders, a vast, efficient, and well-established forward market for foreign exchange served essentially the same purposes as futures trading. Why the seeming duplication?

In fact, the forward market and the futures market differ in some notable ways. To be sure, in both markets, foreign exchange is bought and sold for future delivery. In the forward market, however, a party wishing to buy or sell typically enters into an agreement to do so with any one of a large number of banks (which in

From Federal Reserve Bank of Boston, *New England Economic Review,* March/April 1985, pp. 38–47. Some notes, tables, charts, and text omitted.

turn may deal with other banks), while in the futures market the agreement, or contract, is arranged through a broker and the market-clearing mechanism of the IMM. A futures broker who takes an order for a particular contract undertakes to acquire it at the IMM at the lowest available price from some other broker who has received an order to sell the same contract. Once the deal is negotiated, the IMM guarantees to deliver the currency on schedule if the seller defaults or to acquire it if the buyer defaults, thus obviating any doubts that the buyer or seller might otherwise entertain about the creditworthiness of the other. A bank dealing in the forward market also must satisfy itself that the party with whom it is contracting is creditworthy (willing and able to deliver the currency promised on the due date), but banks generally discourage speculation by individuals. The futures broker is prepared to accommodate speculative transactions; but he requires a margin deposit (a percentage of the contract value) from a customer seeking to enter a futures contract, and may require a deposit above the going minimum if the customer's creditworthiness is questionable.

In the forward market a large bank will quote to its customer the exchange rate at which it will buy or sell, while in the futures market the customer must first place an order to buy or sell a certain number of contracts and then accept the price that subsequently prevails in the auction bidding process employed at the IMM (although the customer can specify the minimum or maximum contract price at which he is willing to deal). Moreover, a single forward contract can be arranged for the precise amount and maturity that the bank's customer desires, while a single futures contract is available only in a predetermined amount and for one of several specified maturity dates.

As these differences indicate, the forward market and the futures market are far from identical; they are not perfect substitutes, even though there is competition between them. Rather, the forward market contract is to the futures market contract as a custom-built machine is to one produced on an assembly line, or as a tailor-made suit is to a ready-made. The product, or typical contract, of the forward market is much less standardized, and its final assembly much less centralized, than is true of the contract produced in the futures market. Because the amount and the maturity date of a forward contract is tailored precisely to the customer's specifications at a price quoted in advance, and because the customer's creditworthiness must be established with the bank involved, the relationship between the contracting parties is more intimate in the forward market than in the futures market. Also, the typical transaction in the forward market probably is notably larger than that in the futures market.

History teaches that a standardized, mass-produced item is preceded by a custom-made counterpart, and the foreign currency futures contract is no exception. Just as custom-built automobiles preceded the standardized variety, the forward contract preceded the futures contract. This is true not just for foreign currency but for other items traded in futures markets; forward contracts were in use at least as early as the seventeenth century, while futures markets did not emerge until the nineteenth century. The explanation of this sequence is that as the demand for a forward contract expands, economies of scale can be realized by standardizing the contract and centralizing its trading, that is, by launching a new futures contract; thus, profit-seeking entrepreneurs organize a centralized exchange such as the IMM.

If it is true that futures markets achieve economies of scale, that is, achieve lower unit operating costs from centrally trading a large volume of standardized contracts, it should be less expensive to enter into a futures contract than to enter into a similar forward contract, other things equal. However, as we have noted, futures and forward contracts are not equivalent. In particular, while the forward market offers a greater variety of contract terms than the futures market — a feature that tends to make forward contracting more expensive — the futures market much more readily accommodates the small-scale speculator — a feature that tends to make futures contracting more expensive by promoting relatively small transactions. . . .

DOES SOCIETY BENEFIT?

There is widespread sentiment that futures markets are essentially casinos whose social utility is little, if any, greater than the utility yielded by gambling. Although it may be true that some participants enter the market at least partly to satisfy their gambling instincts, a well-functioning futures market provides social services not to be found in any of the gaming houses.

To begin with, the foreign currency futures market, like the forward market, provides a mechanism whereby offsetting exchange rate risks can be matched and thus neutralized or whereby a risk that cannot be neutralized can be shifted from someone who finds it relatively unsettling to another who is more inclined to bear it. . . .

To be sure, the basic functions performed by the futures market are little different from those provided by the forward market. However, the forward market may well be rendered more efficient by competition from the futures market. Moreover, the futures market nicely complements the forward market in several important respects. In particular, the futures market provides a more standardized, easily liquidated contract geared to accommodate the small scale business or speculator as well as larger scale operators who are willing to tolerate the degree of exchange rate risk that could be eliminated by the tailor-made contracts of the forward market.

CONCLUSION

Foreign currency futures contracts, like forward contracts, are acquired for the purposes of hedging, speculation, or arbitrage. Speculation commonly meets with disdain; but if no one were willing to speculate in foreign currency, the exports and imports of every country would have to be in balance continuously, precluding net capital flows from countries with relatively low rates of return on investment to those offering higher rates.

While foreign currencies are bought and sold for future delivery in both the futures and the forward markets, the futures market is much more highly centralized and standardized and caters more to the smaller customer, including the personal speculator. Standardization within the futures market is facilitated by the fact that the futures price and the spot price for a currency converge as the futures contract nears maturity, providing a link between the two prices that allows hedging to take place with relatively few maturity dates for futures contracts.

Bid-asked spreads, one measure of market efficiency, do not seem to differ radically between the futures and the forward markets. However, if broker-age commissions are added to the bid-asked spreads, the "cost" of using the futures market seems significantly higher than the cost of using the forward market. Cost comparisons are difficult because the two markets provide somewhat different services.

The rapid growth in the number of futures contracts outstanding is attributable partly to the increase in the volume of contracts traded and partly to the increase in the value of U.S. imports, among other things. Although there would be no reason for the foreign currency futures market if the dollar prices of foreign currencies did not vary, it is doubtful that the size of the market is related in any simple way to the size of variation in foreign exchange rates.

The foreign currency futures market provides another mechanism whereby business firms can hedge against the risk of exchange rate change. If a firm is freed from the need to make short-term exchange rate forecasts, it can specialize more completely in its chosen principal line of business, attaining greater expertise and efficiency. Similarly, if the futures market elicits skilled speculative activity, futures prices will provide useful signals to firms on how to allocate resources for future production.

34

New Markets in Foreign Currency Options

Brian Gendreau

INTRODUCTION

In recent years, exchanges and banks have developed a variety of new financial instruments designed to give customers the option to buy or sell foreign currencies. Exchanges in Amsterdam, Montreal, and Philadelphia opened trading in standardized options on foreign currencies in late 1982. Banks responded by resurrecting an old practice of writing tailor-made foreign currency options for their customers. And in January, 1984 the Chicago Mercantile Exchange opened trading in the newest instrument, an option on its Deutsche mark *futures* contract.

How do these new currency options work? What do options allow traders to do that they cannot do already in foreign currency markets? Under what circumstances will they do well in the marketplace? As a first step toward examining these issues, it is important to understand exactly what options are.

WHAT ARE OPTIONS?

An option is a contract that gives its holder the right, but not the obligation, to buy or sell an asset on or before a future date at a specified price. In this regard options differ crucially from forward and futures contracts, which are firm commitments to buy or sell an asset at a fixed price on a future date. Once forward and futures contracts are made, they must be fulfilled whether prices have moved favorably or not.[1]

An option that can be exercised only on its expiration date is called a European option; one that can be exercised anytime up to expiration is called an American option. Theoretically, options can be written on any asset or commodity, be it a crop, real estate, a security, or a futures contract. With foreign currency options, the underlying asset is a specified quantity of a foreign currency, say, 12,500 British pounds or 62,500 Swiss francs.

Foreign currency options, like all other options, involve two transactions. The first transaction is the purchase or sale of the *option* itself: one party buys from the other the right to exchange dollars for foreign currency in the future at a set price, known as the exercise or striking price. The person obtaining the right to make the future exchange is known as the option buyer or holder, and the person

From Federal Reserve Bank of Philadelphia, *Business Review*, July/August 1984, pp. 3–12. Reprinted by permission. Some notes and text omitted.

granting the right is known as the option seller or writer. To have the privilege of exchanging the currency at the price specified in the option contract, the buyer must pay the seller a fee, called a premium.

The second transaction in an option is the future exchange of the underlying *asset:* the foreign currency. This exchange may be one of two kinds. In a *call* option, dollars may be exchanged for a specified quantity of the foreign currency; a call is thus a contract for the right to buy the foreign currency. In a *put* option, a specified quantity of the foreign currency may be exchanged for dollars; it is a contract for the right to sell the foreign currency. Because options may be bought or sold for the right to buy or sell foreign currency, four basic trading positions are possible. A market participant can:

1. buy a call, obtaining the right to purchase the foreign currency;
2. sell a call, standing ready to sell the foreign currency at the option buyer's discretion;
3. buy a put, obtaining the right to sell the foreign currency; or
4. sell a put, standing ready to buy the foreign currency at the option buyer's discretion.

Each of these four positions exposes the trader to different risks and returns. Why a trader would choose to take on any of these positions may be best explained with examples, beginning with foreign currency calls.

RISKS AND REWARDS IN TRADING CURRENCY OPTIONS

Call Options

Suppose a trader has good reason to think that the Swiss franc will rise relative to the dollar by more than the market expects. One way to profit from that information is to buy a call option on francs. The trader could, for example, buy a call in March giving him the right to purchase 62,500 francs at a price of $.46 apiece in June, paying (for example) a $560 premium for the option. If the trader is correct and by March the franc rises — say to $.48 — the trader can exercise the option, buy the francs from the option writer at the exercise price, $.46, then sell them in the spot market at $.48 for a profit of $1,250 — more than enough to cover the premium. If, instead, the franc does not rise above the option's exercise price, the trader will let the option lapse and lose the premium. In no event, however, will the buyer lose more than the $560 paid for the premium.

Put Options

In contrast to calls, in which buyers gain from unexpected rises in the spot price, puts enable buyers to gain from unexpected *declines* in the spot price. Specifically, the buyer of a put held to expiration will profit if the price of the underlying currency falls below the exercise price by more than enough to cover the cost of the premium. If the currency price does not fall below the option's exercise price, the buyer will lose the premium.

To see how puts can be used to profit from exchange rate declines, imagine a trader who believes that the Japanese yen will drop relative to the dollar by more than the rest of the market expects. The trader could bet on the extra decline by paying, say, a $225 premium for a June put on 6,250,000 yen with an exercise price of $.0042. If by June the yen falls unexpectedly, say to $.0040, the trader will find it profitable to exercise the put and sell the yen purchased in the spot market at $.0040 to the option seller at the exercise price of $.0042 for a gain of $1,250, an amount that more than offsets the cost of the premium.

These examples illustrate two important features of option trading. First, the amount the option buyer stands to gain depends on the movement of the spot price of the underlying currency relative to the option's exercise price. Second, the risks in option trading are asymmetric. The most the option buyer stands to lose is the premium, while his potential gains are limited only by the subsequent movement of the underlying currency's exchange rates. By the same token, the most the option seller can gain is the premium, though his potential losses are bounded only by the range of future exchange rate movements.[2] In effect, the option buyer is paying the seller to take on his risk, and the premium will rise to a value that compensates the seller for assuming that risk.

In contrast to options, the upside and downside risks in trading forward and futures contracts are symmetric. The buyer of a forward contract held to maturity will lose, dollar for dollar, as much when the spot price falls below the contract price as he will gain when the spot price rises above the contract price. Options are thus likely to attract traders who wish to profit from movements of prices in one direction while limiting their losses from adverse price movements. In addition, options are likely to attract traders who wish to profit from misalignments between prices on forward or futures contracts and prices on options. Option and forward foreign exchange prices, therefore, are not independent. (See the APPENDIX: PUT-CALL PARITY).

USING OPTIONS TO HEDGE CONTINGENCIES

The asymmetries between potential gains and losses in options allow them to be used — in ways that forwards and futures cannot — to hedge *contingencies:* transactions that are not certain to materialize. Consider, for example, a U.S. firm that has submitted a competitive bid in pounds to supply communications equipment in Britain. If it wins the bid, it will receive pounds, which it will then want to convert into dollars. Until the bids are awarded, the firm is exposed to the risk of a decline in the value of the pound, which would reduce the value of the contract award if it wins the bid. The firm would like to hedge against this risk. Forward or futures contracts are not the right hedging instruments in this case because it is not certain that the firm will actually be awarded the bid. If the firm tries to hedge the bid by selling pounds under a forward contract, and then fails to win the bid, it will be left with a forward contract but no matching business transaction in the foreign currency. The firm will have started out trying to reduce its foreign exchange risk, only to wind up with a foreign currency exposure after all.

To hedge a contingent transaction like a competitive bid a firm should use an option; in this case it should buy a put. If the anticipated transaction does occur, the firm can exercise the option and sell the foreign currency it receives at a set price. If, instead, the transaction falls through, the firm can simply let the option expire. From the firm's perspective, buying an option is like buying insurance against foreign exchange risk by paying the option seller a premium to cover its risk.

Contingent transactions are not uncommon in international finance. The terms of an investment in a foreign firm, for example, may include the acquisition of warrants to buy the firm's shares at a fixed price in the future, with payment in the foreign currency. In another case, a firm's future foreign currency requirements may hinge upon whether it decides to take advantage of an option it has obtained to purchase a foreign asset — say, the right to purchase a hotel in Bavaria. Or a firm may anticipate receiving a future award in a foreign currency depending upon the outcome of a lawsuit in a foreign court. Each of these possible, but not certain, future claims or liabilities in a foreign currency can be hedged with options. The warrants and hotel option can be covered by buying calls, and the potential receipt of a lawsuit award covered by buying a put.

THE DEMAND FOR CURRENCY OPTIONS

Despite the advantages currency options have over forward and futures contracts in some situations, no markets existed for these options until recently. An unsuccessful effort had been made to start a market for puts and calls on foreign currencies in New York in the 1920s, and U.S. banks have occasionally arranged currency options privately for customers since the 1940s. But by and large, the market for currency options was dormant until the European Options Exchange (Amsterdam), the Montreal Exchange, and the Philadelphia Stock Exchange opened trading in currency options in late 1982. Once currency option trading was established on these exchanges, banks began writing substantial quantities of currency options for customers, creating an over-the-counter market parallel to the exchange markets.

The recent demand for currency options can be attributed to two factors: increased exchange rate volatility and the growth of international trade. Prior to 1971, exchange rates were not as variable as they are now. At the Bretton Woods conference in 1944, the industrial nations agreed to have their central banks buy and sell dollars to keep exchange rate movements within fairly narrow bounds. As a result, traders expected little variability in exchange rates. Under these circumstances, few market participants were willing to pay for option contracts to provide protection against adverse exchange rate movements: the costs to maintaining uncovered foreign currency positions were small, as were the fees writers could have earned by producing option coverage.

After this system of nearly-fixed exchange rates collapsed in 1971, most major currencies began to float with market forces and exchange rates became more volatile. The average monthly range of fluctuations of the Deutsche mark to the dollar, for example, widened from .44 cents over the 1959 to 1971 period to 5.66 cents between 1971 and 1982 — a more than twelvefold increase. At the same time that exchange rates were becoming more variable, the volume of trade in goods and services and financial flows between nations continued to grow. The sum of exports and imports in the U.S. alone grew from $135.9 billion in 1971 to $265.7 billion in 1982 in constant (inflation adjusted) dollars. Forward and futures contracts could have been used to hedge the lion's share of these international transactions. Some portion of foreign trade, however, is carried out under contingent contracts, for which options are the desired hedging tool. Assuming that the proportion of contingencies in international trade is constant, the combination of volatile exchange rates and growing trade meant inevitably that a market for foreign currency options to hedge those contingencies would also grow. It was to meet this expanding market that exchanges and banks began to offer options.

CREATORS OF CURRENCY OPTION MARKETS

Exchange Options

The Amsterdam, Montreal, and Philadelphia exchanges have devoted resources to providing centralized trading floors, and have adopted the open outcry system for matching option buyers to sellers. . . . To open trading in currency options to a wide range of participants, the exchanges have adopted contract designs and trading safeguards that have proven successful on futures exchanges and common stock option exchanges. To begin with, currency options on all three exchanges were designed as American options with standardized trading units and expiration dates. (See [Table 1]). Contract standardization helps to reduce the number of dimensions over which buyers and sellers must agree. Some flexibility is lost as a result, but standardization is probably necessary for contract trading in a central marketplace: matching customers with a wide range of quantity and maturity preferences would be an administrative nightmare. By standardizing the contract terms the exchanges have made it possible to trade options in a secondary market — a market in which options can be bought and sold many times before expiration. Indeed, exchange options are so readily accepted by traders that no distinction exists between new and resold options: all are traded interchangeably on the exchange floor.

The greatest obstacle to achieving widespread participation in option trading is credit risk: option buyers are at risk that sellers will default when the options are exercised. To assure buyers that sellers will fulfill their contracts, the exchanges restrict trading privileges to members and provide clearing corporation

---

TABLE 1

Contract Specifications on the Amsterdam, Montreal, and Philadelphia Exchanges[a]

The European Options Exchange (Amsterdam), the Montreal Exchange, and the Philadelphia Stock Exchange all offer trading in standardized puts and calls on foreign currencies. The following table gives the number of foreign currency units underlying each option contract offered on the three exchanges:

TRADING UNITS

CURRENCY	European Options Exchange (Amsterdam)	Montreal Exchange	Philadelphia Stock Exchange
British pounds	£5,000	£5,000	£12,500
Canadian dollars	b	CD50,000	CD50,000
Deutsche marks	$10,000	DM25,000	DM62,500
Japanese yen	b	¥2,500,000	¥6,250,000
Swiss francs	b	SF25,000	SF62,500
Dutch guilders	$10,000	b	b

[a]Payment for all options on the Montreal and Philadelphia exchanges is in U.S. dollars. Payment for each of the options offered on the Amsterdam exchange, however, is in a different currency. The Amsterdam exchange offers an option on British pounds with payment in U.S. dollars, an option on U.S. dollars with payment in Dutch guilders, and an option on U.S. dollars with payment in Deutsche marks. Contracts on all three exchanges are issued with maturities of 3, 6, and 9 months, with expiration dates set in March, June, September, and December to coincide with the maturity dates of the CME's International Monetary Market's foreign currency futures contracts. Option contract sizes are also compatible with the IMM's futures contracts; the Philadelphia exchange's options, for example, are exactly one half the size of the corresponding IMM futures contracts. Making currency option contracts compatible with futures contracts facilitates cross-trading between the two kinds of instruments, encouraging trading volume growth in both markets.
[b]Indicates that the contract is not offered on that exchange.

guarantees for their options. Exchange rules require the public to trade currency options through exchange member firms, who are liable to other members for their customers' trades. In the event that an option seller defaults, then, the seller's member firm is responsible for completing the contract with the buyer's member firm. As a result, members have an incentive to execute trades only for customers they believe are willing and able to honor their contracts. The clearing corporation guarantees, however, provide an even stronger safeguard for traders. All organized options exchanges are affiliated with a clearing corporation, a nonprofit organization of member firms that clears trades on the exchange. Though customers trade options with each other through member firms on the exchange, options are legally contracts with the clearing corporation, not other customers. In effect, the clearing corporation inserts itself between the buyer and seller of every option, giving each party a contract with the clearing corporation. The clearing corporation guarantees all trades, and stands ready to assess its member firms to cover losses resulting from a default by a member firm. To protect itself from losses, the clearing corporation requires that a security deposit known as a margin be posted by exchange members that have sold options; the members in turn generally require their customers to make margin deposits with them. By providing for clearing corporation guarantees, the exchanges have created an option instrument that people can trade without worrying about each other's creditworthiness.

Options on Currency Futures

Recently, the Chicago Mercantile Exchange (CME) introduced a new option instrument to compete with the currency options offered by exchanges and banks: an option on a foreign currency futures contract. This option contract gives the holder the right to buy or sell a futures contract for Deutsche marks, rather than the marks themselves. When a buyer exercises this option, he or she receives a futures contract to buy or sell 125,000 Deutsche marks on the CME's International Monetary Market at a set price. The futures contract can either be offset immediately to take the gain, or can be held to maturity. Like the currency options offered on other exchanges, the CME's option has standardized delivery dates and is guaranteed by a clearing corporation.

At first glance, an option on a futures contract rather than on the underlying currency appears to be an unnecessarily cumbersome instrument. . . . Futures prices and spot currency prices are closely correlated, [however,] so that an option on a futures contract is for most purposes as effective a hedging instrument as an option on the currency itself. Moreover, . . . an option on a futures contract makes it easy for traders to shift between options and futures to take advantage of temporary price misalignments between the two markets. The CME hopes that its option on a futures contract will be attractive to the kinds of traders who currently trade currency options and will appeal to new groups of traders as well.

Bank Options

The bank market for foreign currency options is composed of large U.S. banks which write options for their corporate customers. When banks write puts and calls, they are creating a market individually by buying and selling for their own account. Banks provide no trading floors for the exchange of orders; instead, they quote prices directly to customers, often by telephone. Usually, banks only sell options, and write the contracts as European options. Because the option seller is commonly a bank with whom the customer has had a long-standing relationship, the customer generally has little concern that the bank will default on the option.

Banks write currency options on an individual basis, tailoring the contracts to the specific currency, quantity, and maturity needs of each customer. Not surprisingly, no secondary market yet exists for bank options: creating a secondary market would require banks to agree to some minimal contract standardization conventions, and reaching such an agreement is likely to take some time. Banks sometimes reduce the risks they have taken in selling options, however, by buying currency options on an exchange. When banks completely offset their option sales in this way, they are acting as middlemen between their customer and the ultimate sellers of the contract. When banks choose instead not to offset options written for customers, they are acting as insurers, bearing their customers' exchange risk in return for fee income. . . .

CONCLUSION

Since late 1982, traders have been able to use options on foreign currencies in addition to forward and futures contracts to manage their exchange rate risk. These options allow traders to profit from favorable exchange rate changes while avoiding the risks of adverse movements. Because they convey the right, but not the obligation, to buy or sell a foreign currency, options can be used to hedge transactions that are not certain to occur, a task for which forward and futures contracts are not well suited.

Continued volatility in exchange rates and growth in international trade will ensure a demand for currency options. Exchange options and over-the-counter bank options are likely to coexist for some time because they are different instruments and appeal to different customers. Many exchange options, however, are close substitutes for each other. The experience with futures markets suggests that not all exchanges' options will prosper, and that traders will increasingly give their business to the market able to offer the greatest volume and lowest cost trades.

APPENDIX: PUT-CALL PARITY

Though options and forward contracts are distinct instruments, their prices are linked together by the actions of traders who buy and sell both instruments in search of profits. The basic trading strategy for profiting from a price difference between option and forward markets is called a *reversal*. With this strategy, a trader simultaneously buys a call and sells a put, both for the same expiration date and exercise price E. This strategy will give the trader a pattern of gains and losses that duplicates that on a forward contract to purchase the currency on that expiration date at the exercise price E. The trader will, by maturity, gain dollar-for-dollar on the call by the amount the spot price rises above E, or lose dollar-for-dollar on the put by the amount the spot price falls below E, just as he would on a forward contract. The price at which the trader has effectively purchased currency forward, however, should take into account the interest cost of borrowing the difference between the premium C paid for the call and the premium P received for the put (if C is greater than P) over the life of the contracts. Assuming the trader can borrow at an interest rate i, the price at which the trader is buying the currency forward under the reversal will be:

$$E + (C - P)(1 + i) \tag{1}$$

where C and P are measured per quantity of currency traded.

If the cost of obtaining the currency using this strategy is cheaper than buying it under a forward contract at the going forward rate F, the trader will, by coupling the reversal with a forward sale, earn a profit of π_r:

$$\pi_r = F - E - (C - P)(1 + i) \tag{2}$$

Alternatively, if the cost of buying currency under a forward contract is cheaper than obtaining it by combining puts and calls, the trader could profit by executing the mirror image trade of the reversal called a *conversion*. Here the trader would create an artificial contract to sell the currency forward by buying a put, selling a call, and investing the difference (if it is positive) between the two premiums in a money market instrument paying a rate of interest i. This strategy will, coupled with a forward purchase, produce a profit of π_c:

$$\pi_c = E + (C - P)(1 + i) - F \tag{3}$$

As many traders try to take advantage of price differentials between the forward and options markets, they will drive the call prices up and put prices down when executing reversals (and drive call prices down and put prices up in executing conversions) until no more profits can be made with these strategies ($\pi_r = \pi_c = 0$). This implies that in equilibrium the difference between the call and put premiums for an option at an exercise price E will be equal to the difference between the forward exchange rate F and E, discounted to the market interest rate or:

$$C - P = (F - E)/(1 + i) \tag{4}$$

This relationship is called *put-call parity*. How close does it come to describing the relationship we see in reported option and forward prices? A complete answer requires a careful statistical study, but a rough idea can be obtained by seeing how close the put-call parity theory comes to predicting the actual price differences between puts and calls on one of the Philadelphia Stock Exchange's most active contracts on a recent date. On July 17, 1984, at 10:11 a.m., calls on the Deutsche mark contract with a \$.36 striking price and September expiration were trading for \$318.75, while puts on that contract were trading for \$631.25. These prices are the average bid-offer prices on recent trades, kindly provided by the Financial Options Group, Inc. A 2-month forward contract made on July 17th would be settled on the same date the options expired, and the average bid-offer rate on this contract posted by Citibank's New York office was \$.3555. The 2-month CD rate, taken here to be a representative interest rate, was 11.63 percent, or 1.85 percent for 2 months.

Inserting the figures for the forward rate, the exercise price, and the interest rate into the put-call parity formula gives a predicted difference between the call and put premiums of −\$276.14:

$$\text{Predicted } (C - P) = [(F - E) \times 62{,}500]/(1 + i)$$

$$= [(.3555 - .36) \times 62{,}500]/(1.0185)$$

$$= -\$276.14$$

The difference between the forward price and the exercise price $(F - E)$ was multiplied by the number of Deutsche marks in the Philadelphia Stock Exchange's contract to put these prices in the same units as the premium.

The actual difference between the call and put options on July 17th was –\$312.50. So the parity formula used with market data gives a close prediction of what the relationship among call, put, and forward prices was on the date. Could traders have executed reversals and conversions at the time the market data were taken to profit from the price difference? The answer is no: inserting the appropriate bid and offer prices into the reversal condition formulas (equations (2) and (3)) revealed no profit opportunities. In addition, the formulas do not take brokerage costs — which are on the order of \$13 to \$16 per option — into account. At the time the market data were collected, the September Deutsche mark option with a \$.36 striking price was not mispriced relative to the forward market.

Notes

1. Forward and futures contracts can be fulfilled either by delivering the currency specified in the contract or by making a second, offsetting contract. Forward contracts for foreign exchange are generally made with commercial banks and can be tailored to specific customer needs. Futures contracts are similar to forward contracts, but are traded in standardized quantities with regular maturities on organized exchanges, are guaranteed by the exchanges, and generally require a security deposit (called a "margin"). See K. Alec Chrystal, "A Guide to Foreign Exchange Markets," Federal Reserve Bank of St. Louis *Review,* Vol. 66, No. 3 (March 1984) pp. 5–18.
2. Puts and calls can also be combined in a number of complex strategies to bet on price volatility, rather than on the direction of a price movement. For a discussion of these strategies in currency option markets, see Ian H. Giddy, "Foreign Exchange Options," *The Journal of Futures Markets,* Vol. 3, No. 2 (1983) pp. 143–166.

Index

Adjustable par values. *See* Bretton Woods system; European Monetary System
Adjustment assistance. *See also* Trade adjustment assistance
  GATT recommendations on, 207–208
  model, 40, 43
  and private adjustment costs, 78
  protectionism and, 54–56
  and world trade, 200
Adjustment costs, 4, 15, 18n, 59
  and attrition, 81
  and debt crisis, 406–409
  empirical tests of trade policy and, 47
  measurement, 75–78
  private, 77–78
  between surplus and deficit countries, 263–264
  trade policies and, 32–34, 43, 44, 75–78
Aerospace industry, world share of, 238
AFL-CIO, protectionism and, 150–151
Agricultural trade
  GATT recommendations on, 202–203
  protectionism and LDCs and, 229–230
  and subsidies to U.S. exports, 130
  trade liberalization and, 146
American Selling Price (ASP) system of customs valuation, 155
Andean Common Market (ANCOM), 191
Anti-Dumping Act, 115, 155
Anti-Monopoly Act, 123–124
Antitrust policies, strategic trade policy and, 105
Apparel. *See* Textiles and apparel
Arbitration, international, of investment disputes, 196
Automation, unemployment and, 89

Automobile trade, 49, 62–74, 186–190
  protectionism and, 55
  and VERs, 55, 66–74
  world share of, 239

Balance of payments
  and Bretton Woods system, 339
  and crawling exchange rates, 287
  and flexible exchange rates, 279, 300
  and protectionism, 301
Bank of Issue proposal, 348–349, 350–351, 353
Bank Steering committee, 399
Banking, global integration of, 415–416
Beggar-your-neighbor policies, 27, 160
Beveridge Report, 339
Bretton Woods system, 266, 268–269, 290–294, 303–304, 329, 335, 338–343, 418–419
Budget deficits, impact of, 2, 19, 24–25

Cabotage, 170
Cambridge Economic Policy Group, 295
Canadian Industrial Renewal Board, 82
Capital controls, 265–267, 285, 286, 295–296
Capital flight, 385, 402
Capital flows, 274. *See also* International capital market
  adjustment costs and, 76
  Bretton Woods system and, 341–342
  and exchange market tax, 286
  and exchange rates, 274, 284–285, 287, 294–295
  trade deficits and, 24–26
  world welfare and, 426
Capital-labor ratios, 15–17

Capital losses and gains, exchange rate changes and, 314–315
Cargo preference, 171
Cartels, in Japan, 124, 126–127. *See also* OPEC
Chemical industry, 240, 246
Clothing. *See* Textiles and apparel
Coal and oil industries, 150
Code of Liberalization of Capital Movements, 178, 182
Code of Liberalization of Current Invisible Operations, 172, 178
Code on Liner Conferences, 177
Code on Subsidies and Countervailing Duties, 134–135
Committee on International Investment and Multinational Enterprises, 195
Committee on Invisible Exports, 164
Committee on Liberalization of Trade in Services, 175
Commodity Credit Corporation (CCC), 130
Common Agricultural Policy (CAP), 115, 119, 121
Common Market. *See* European Economic Community
Comparative advantage, 2, 4–5, 16–18, 30–31, 40, 65
    adjusting to changes in, *see* Adjustment costs
    determinants of, 132–133
    free trade and, 85
    increased competition and, 226–227
    of MNCs, 250–252
    performance of U.S. manufacturing and, 8–14
    public policy and, 122
    U.S.-Japan trade and, 22–23, 28–29
Compensatory Finance Facility, 390
Compensatory financing, 33
Competition, imperfect. *See* Monopoly; Oligopolistic industries; Strategic trade policy
Competitiveness, 19–38
    efficiency and employment and, 26–28, 227
    and exchange rates, 25–26, 260, 297–301, 308–309, 311–312
    gains from improvement of, 31
    in labor-intensive industries, 54–55
    between LDCs, 227–228
    minimum wage laws and, 132
    and MNCs, 233–234

in oligopolistic industries, 55
    trade adjustment assistance and, 79–80
    trade policy and, 32–34, 95
Computers, 163, 168–170
Content requirements, 183, 186, 195
Contingent transactions, 443–444
Convertibility, nonresident, 424
Costs. *See also* Adjustment costs
    economies of scale and, 102–103
    of import substitution activities, 221
    of protectionism, 60–61, 86–88
    of trade liberalization, 148
Countervailing duties, 135–136, 196
Crawling exchange rates, 286–287
Credit allocation
    Eurocurrency markets and, 427–428
    in Japan, 29
Credit risk, and option trading, 444–445
Currency-substitution argument, 283
Currency swaps, 431–436
Current account. *See* Balance of payments; Capital flows
Customs unions, GATT rules on, 206

Debt crisis. *See* International debt problems
Deindustrialization of U.S., myth of, 5–8
Demand elasticities, 272, 280, 297–298
Democratic party, and U.S. trade policy, 143–151
Depletion allowances, 131
Deregulation, 431. *See also* Regulation
    and central bank policy, 420
    impact on international money market, 417–420, 431–436
Developing countries. *See* Less-developed countries
Dillon Round, 144, 159
Direct investment. *See* Foreign direct investment
DISC (Domestic International Sales Corporation), 129–130, 154
Discriminatory trade restrictions, 50–52, 203
Disinflation. *See* also Inflation
    and central bank policy, 417–420
    exchange rates and, 308–309, 314, 418–419
Displaced workers. *See* Unemployment
Disputes, 161
    common interests and, 199–200
    and decline in U.S. hegemony, 159–160
    GATT recommendations on settlement of, 210–211

and performance requirements, 195–196
and unfair trade, 116–117
Distribution. *See* Income distribution
Documentation requirements, 50
Dollar appreciation. *See* Overvaluation
Dual exchange rates, 285–286
Dumping, 115, 147, 155–157, 203
Duopoly firms, and VERs, 104

Economies of scale, 102–103, 112, 227
Effective rates, and empirical tests of trade
    policy, 46, 222n
Elasticities. *See* Demand elasticities
Electronics and appliances industry, 243, 247
Employment. *See also* Unemployment
    blue, white collar, 53–54
    composition of, 21
    deindustrialization and, 10
    dollar appreciation and, 308–309
    exports and, 26–28
    manufacturing's share of, 1–2, 3–4, 7, 11,
        12
    productivity increases and, 53
    protectionism and, 52–54, 60, 83–89
    structural change in U.S. manufacturing
        and, 14–18
    and trade adjustment assistance, 83–84
    and U.S. investment overseas, 190
    VERs on Japanese automobiles and, 72–74
Entry promotion and deterrence, trade policy
    and, 106
Escape clause, 147, 149, 152, 203
Eurobanks. *See* Euro-currency market
Eurobond market, 431–434
Euro-currency market, 360, 431–436
    bank regulation and, 427–430
    compared with domestic money markets,
        422–423
    and economic growth and income distribu-
        tion, 425–6
European Currency Unit (ECU), 324
    European Monetary System and, 332–333
    and international monetary reform, 353
European Economic Community (EEC), 206,
    236
    agricultural policy, 115, 119, 121
    and decline in U.S. hegemony, 158–159,
        160
    GATT and, 117
    and growth of business and financial com-
        munities, 236–247

impact of Multifiber Arrangement on, 50–51
    manufacturing employment in, 52
European Free Trade Association, 206
European Monetary Fund (EMF), 324, 332
European Monetary System (EMS), 256, 325–
    334, 360
    flexible exchange rates and, 259
    UK membership in, 324, 328–332
Exchange rate instability, 260, 361–371
    and demand for foreign currency options,
        444–445, 448
    effects of, 314–315, 361
    inflation and recession and, 363–365
    multicurrency system and, 362–363
    and restrictions on international capital
        flows, 266–267
Exchange rates. *See also* Crawling exchange
    rate; Dual exchange rates; Exchange rate
    instability; Flexible exchange rates; In-
    ternational monetary reform; Over-
    valuation; Real exchange rates
    Bretton Woods system and, 293–294,
        339
    central bank intervention and, 313–323
    debt crisis and, 385
    devaluation, 297–299
    disinflation and, 418–419
    fiscal interpretation of, 306–308
    fixed, 154, 288–289, 347–348, 371–374
    and Japanese automobile industry, 66
    and Latin American debt problem, 402
    misalignment of, 256–257
    presumptive indicators for, 265–266, 287–
        288
    prices and, 85, 297–301
    and protectionism, 90–91
    purchasing power parity and, 269 270, 272–
        275, 314
    and target zones, 268
    trade balance and, 25–26, 28–30
    volatility of, 283–285
Export and Import Trading Act, 124
Export-Import Bank of Japan, 124, 130, 154
Export orientation
    criticisms of, 225–230
    and fallacy of composition, 227–228
    promotion by LDCs, 115, 215, 217–231
Export subsidies, 106, 135–136, 147
    in agriculture, 202–203
    and GATT Code, 134–135
    harmonization of, 136–137
Export tax, 101

Exports. *See also* Export orientation
 debt crisis and, 409–412
 earnings instability, 5
 employment and, 26–28
 high-technology, 17–18
 U.S. government policy and, 129–132
External currency. *See* Euro-currency market
External shocks, debt crisis and, 385, 402–403

Fair trade legislation, 156, 159. *See* Unfair
  trade practices
Fiscal Investment and Loan Program (FILP),
  124, 126, 127
Fiscal policies
 dollar appreciation and, 306–307, 312
 exchange rate fluctuations and, 361–362
 forward-looking, 255–256
 world trade and, 212–213
Flexible exchange rates, 259–260, 274, 279,
  290–297. *See also* Exchange rates
 and adjustments to real shocks, 300–301
 and business cycles, 270–271, 278
 and current and capital account adjustment,
  274
 evaluation of, 262–264
 expected performance of, 268–274, 280–
  285, 303–304
 and goals of Bretton Woods, 291–294
 inflation and recession and, 363–365
 international debt problems and, 397
 and monetarism, 269–270, 281–283
 and oligopoly, 281
 and overshooting, 282–283
 and protectionism, 301–303
 and purchasing power parity, 268–269, 272–
  274, 342–346
 real consequences of, 290–304
 sectoral consequences of changes in, 298–
  299
 volatility of, 283–285
Floating exchange rates. *See* Flexible exchange
  rates
Floating rate notes (FRN), 434
Foreign aid, 129. *See also* World Bank
Foreign Bank Holders Protective Council, 399
Foreign Corrupt Practices Act of 1979, 172
Foreign direct investment. *See also* Multinational corporations
 barriers to, 190–192
 and exchange rates, 295–297
 liberalization of, 181–183, 192–194

Mexican automobile industry and, 186–188,
  190
 and nontariff barriers, 180
 performance requirements, 183–189
 in protected markets, 55–56, 192–194
 U.S. policy toward, 180–198
Foreign policy, trade liberalization and, 145
Forward market, 437–439. *See also* Futures
  market; Options
Free-rider problem, 158
Free trade. *See also* Trade liberalization
 adjustment and, 75–78, 81
 arguments for, 85–91, 226–227
 and unfair trade practices, 118
Friendship, Commerce, and Navigation (FCN)
  treaties, 196
Futures market in foreign currency, 437–450.
  See also Forward market; Options

GATT (General Agreement on Tariffs and
  Trade), 82, 94, 133–135, 144, 148–149,
  158, 160, 167
 and EEC policies, 119
 and Japanese industrial policy, 119–121,
  125
 and liberalization of direct foreign investment, 182–183
 and liberalization of trade, 181
 and NTBs, 155
 and performance requirements, 195–198
 and service sector trade, 161–162, 172–179
 and unfair trade practices, 114–115, 116–
  117
General Adjustment Assistance Program
  (GAAP), 78
Generalized System of Preferences, 49
Gold standard, and return to fixed parities,
  288–289

Harmonization, 138
Havana Charter for the International Trade
  Organization (ITO), 181, 190
Hecksher-Ohlin goods, 15–17
Hedging contingencies, options and, 443–444
Hedonic model, 70–71
Hegemonic model of regime change, 148,
  157–158, 160
High-technology goods, 15–17
 bilateral imbalance in U.S.-Japan trade, 22
 comparative advantage in, 2
 government support for, 127

and Japanese industrial policy, 126
U.S. share of world trade, 19n
Houdaille relief petition, 120

IMF. *See* International Monetary Fund
Imperfectly competitive environments
  and concept of "equilibrium," 111
  economies of scale with, 102–103
  and strategic trade policy, 96–106
Import quotas. *See* Protectionism; Quotas;
  Voluntary export restraints
Import substitution
  economic growth of LDCs and, 215–231
  transition to export orientation, 223–224
Income distribution
  and Euromarkets, 425–426
  and exchange-rate instability, 361
  protectionism and, 52
  strategic trade policies and, 106
Indexation, 14, 273
Industrial policy, 122–140
Industrialization strategy for LDCs, 216–222
Infant-industry argument, 32
Inflation. *See also* Disinflation
  Bretton Woods system and, 340–341, 342
  EMS policies and, 328, 330–331
  and exchange rates, 263, 269–270, 272–
    274, 279, 280, 287, 297–299, 308,
    314, 345, 363–365
  Latin American debt crisis and, 411
Injury clause, 141, 152
Innovation, and international finance, 417–420
Interest group pressures
  and NTBs, 156–157
  model of, 41–42, 46–47
  protectionism and, 58, 59, 143, 149–51
Interest rate swaps, 419–420, 431–436
Interest rates
  capital formation and, 25
  "capping," 396–397
  debt crisis and, 385
  and EMS, 330–331
  exchange rates and, 90–91, 274, 281–283,
    306
  and oil shock, 57
  productivity growth and, 26
  on SDRs, 369
International Air Transport Association
  (IATA), 171
International capital market. *See also* Capital
  Flows
  adequacy of insurance in, 366–367

evaluation of, 365–370
lending and borrowing in, 366
restricting, 266–267
SDRs and inadequacies of, 368–370
and world income distribution, 367–368
International debt problems, 57, 383–414
  case-by-case vs. generalized approach to,
    391–398
  historical comparisons, 398–400
  Latin American focus of, 400–403
  liquidity, solvency, equity and, 404–406
  medium-term outlook, 385–390, 409–412
  Mexico and, 393–394
  origins of, 385–386
  Paris Club, 391
  policy implications, 389–390
International liquidity
  collective, 379–380
  exchange rates and, 259
  and international debt problems, 404–406
International Monetary Fund (IMF), 5, 342,
  383, 399
  Articles of Agreement, 291–293
  and exchange rates, 290–291, 298, 345
  and GATT, 213
  and international debt problems, 386, 390,
    391–398, 406–409
  quotas, 367–360
International monetary reform, 335–381. *See*
  also SDRs
  and criticism of Bretton Woods system,
    339–342
  debt crisis and, 389–390
  and fixed exchange rates, 371–374
  and present monetary arrangements, 342–
    346
  presumptive indicators and, 265–266, 287–
    288
  target zones, 268
  types of, 338
International money market. *See* Euro-currency
  market
International reserve asset, 358–381. *See also*
  SDRs; International monetary reform
International Trade Commission (ITC), 82,
  118, 147, 150, 152–156
International Trade Organization (ITO), 115,
  116, 147, 181, 190
Intervention, in foreign exchange market, 317–
  321
Investment. *See* Foreign direct investment;
  Capital Flows; International capital market

Investment income, receipts from services and, 164
Investment tax credit, 105, 130
ITC. *See* International Trade Commission

Japan
  and automobile industry, 64–74
  and decline in U.S. hegemony, 159–160
  and exchange rates, 305, 311–312
  and growth of business and financial communities, 236–247
  industrial performance, 8–14
  management practices, 22
  Ministry of International Trade and Industry (MITI), 120, 124
  and Orderly Market Agreement, 51
  pollution control, 126
  service sector trade, 175–176
  Social security system, 126
  unfair trade and industrial policy, 119–127
  U.S. competition with, 19–35
Japan Development Bank (JDB), 124, 125
Joint ownership, MNCs and, 249–250
Jones Act of 1920, 170

Kennedy Round, 115, 144, 155, 158, 159, 211

Labor. *See* Employment; Labor unions; Unemployment
Labor Industry Coalition for International Trade, 138
Labor unions, 15
  imports and, 26
  trade policy and, 150–151
  and U.S. investment overseas, 190
Latin America, debt crisis and, 399–403, 405–409. *See also* International debt problems
Law of one price, 297–298. *See also* Purchasing power parity
LDCs. *See* Less-developed countries
League of Nations Financial committee, 399
Less-developed countries (LDCs). *See also* International debt problems
  agricultural protection and, 229–230
  export promotion, 215–231, 222–223
  and foreign direct investment, 182, 185–189, 191–196, 248–254
  GATT recommendations on, 207
  import substitution, 215–231
  and performance requirements, 185–89, 191–192, 195–196

protectionism and, 56–59, 85–86, 87
special treatment in GATT rules, 199–200, 208–209
trade, 177–178
Less-than-fair-value cases, 155
Licensing, 167
Liquidity. *See* International liquidity
Local content requirements, 183, 186, 195

Macroeconomic policies. *See also* Fiscal policies; Monetary policies
  and Bretton Woods system, 292–293
  exchange rates and, 255, 260–263, 267, 271, 289, 362
  international coordination of, 142
  and international debt problems, 389–390
Manufactures, and trade balance, 4–18, 158
Maritime trade, regulation of, 130, 170–171
Marketing agreements, and conformity with GATT rules, 203
Metal products industry, 242, 244, 247
MFN (Most-Favored-Nation) tariffs, 49, 208–209
Minimum wage laws, 132
Ministry of International Trade and Industry (MITI), 120, 124
Misalignment. *See* Exchange rates
Mobility of resources, adjustment costs and, 75–78
Monetarism, and flexible exchange rates, 269–270, 281–283
Monetary policies
  and exchange rates, 278, 306, 311
  real exchange rates and, 277–278
  service sector trade and, 166
Money, one world, 353–354
Money markets, 318, 422–425
Monopoly, protectionism and, 83–84
Motion pictures, protection for, 172
Multicurrency system, exchange rate instability and, 362–363
Multifiber Arrangement (MFA), 50–52, 53, 142, 204
Multilateral trade negotiations (MTN). *See* Trade negotiations
Multinational corporations (MNCs), 51, 112, 233–254. *See also* Foreign direct investment
  comparative advantage of, 250–252
  cross-penetration, 224–225
  and development of LDCs, 248–254

multinationalization of, 233, 236–237, 248–249

National Advisory Council, 181
National Aeronautics and Space Development Agency (NASA), 126
National Foreign Trade Council, 193–194
National Industrial Development Plan, 186
National security and U.S. trade policy, 85, 90, 143, 150
Newly industrializing countries (NICs), 50–52, 127
Nontariff trade barriers (NTBs), 49, 121
and foreign direct investment, 180
GATT recommendations on, 205–206
increased use of, 143, 154–157
and service sector trade, 172–173, 174
and unfair trade practices, 114–115, 116–117

OECD (Organization for Economic Cooperation and Development), 125, 171, 172, 182, 236
and negotiations on service sector trade, 177–178
and performance requirements, 194, 195
and recovery from debt crisis, 387–389
screening mechanisms for foreign direct investment, 191–192
trade policies, 49–59
Official reserves. *See* International monetary reform; SDR
Oil prices, 126, 131, 331. *See also* OPEC
Oil surpluses, recycling of, 359–360
Oligopolistic industries, 55, 58. *See also* Strategic trade policy
and antitrust policies, 105
economies of scale and, 102–103
and policy precommitments, 98–101
and supernormal profits, 97–98
theory, 158–159
OPEC, debt problems of, 394–395. *See also* Oil prices
Operation Twist, 319–321
Options, 441, 445–447. *See also* Forward market; Futures market
Orderly Marketing Agreements (OMAs), 51, 57, 203
Organization for Economic Cooperation and Development. *See* OECD
Overshooting, 282–283, 306

Overvaluation
central bank intervention and, 315, 317
of dollar, 305–313
exchange rate policy and, 310–312
fiscal policies and, 312
protectionism and, 302–303
and reform of international monetary system, 312–313

Paris Club, 391
Parity, put-call, in options market, 448–450
Performance requirements, for direct foreign investment, 185–189, 190, 194. *See also* Trade-related performance requirements
Peril point provision, 149
Pharmaceuticals industry, 245, 247
Political economy of protection, 39–47, 58–59
Preferential tariffs for LDCs, 208–209. *See also* Generalized System of Preferences
Presumptive indicators and exchange rates, 265–266, 287–288
Prices. *See also* Inflation
impact of discriminatory restrictions on, 50–52
models for, 69–71
protectionism and, 83, 84, 87
of U.S. automobiles, VERs and, 68–72
of U.S. exports, 5
Primary products, export subsidies on, 205
Product-cycle goods, 15
Productivity growth, 4, 28
employment and, 53
exchange rates and, 263
interest rates and, 26
international comparisons, 13
in motor vehicle industry, 68
in manufacturing, 7
Profits, and the case for trade policy, 97–101
Protection. *See also* Nontariff barriers; Trade liberalization; VERs
adjustment costs and, 32–34, 43, 44, 75–78
and AFL-CIO, 150–151
arguments for and against, 59–61, 85–91
and capital-labor substitution, 53
cheap foreign labor and, 89
effective rate of, 46, 222n
employment and, 52–54, 60, 83–89
and exchange rates, 90–91, 301–303
impact on structural adjustment, 54–56
and import substitution, 216–217
and LDCs, 56–59
models of, tested, 46–47

and national security, 85, 90, 143, 150
political and economic determinants of, 39–
47, 58–59
and service sector trade, 161–179
trade adjustment assistance versus, 79–84,
143
and trade flows and prices, 50–52
wages and, 54, 58
Public goods, trade liberalization and, 148
Purchasing power parity (PPP), 269–270, 272–
275, 297–298, 314

Quotas. See also Protectionism
and empirical tests of trade policy, 46
and service sector trade, 172
and U.S. automobile industry, 62–74

Real exchange rates, 311, 361
and flexible exchange rates, 269–270, 275–
278
gains and losses from changing, 276–277
and monetary policy independence, 277–278
stabilization of, 256–258
Real interest rates, and overvaluation, 310
Real shocks, and floating exchange rates, 300–
301
Real wages, Latin American debt crisis and,
411
Reallocation of resources, exchange rate movements and, 314
Recession, 3–4
debt crisis and, 385
exchange rates and, 308, 363–365
Reciprocity, export subsidies and, 136–137
Recycling of oil surpluses, 359–360
Regulation. See also Deregulation
banks, 168, 427–430
government, 64–65, 131–132, 168–171, 177
Reinsurance, 168
Republican party, and trade policy, 143, 146,
147, 149–151
Research and development, 7, 11, 13
government expenditures on, 129, 131
and high-technology goods, 17–18
Japanese industrial policy and, 22, 126
joint ventures, 105
as performance requirement, 193
subsidies, 105
and supernormal profits, 97
and trade balance, 17–18
trade policy and, 111

Reserves. See International monetary reform;
SDRs
Resource-intensive goods, comparative advan-
tage in, 2
Retaliation, 107–110, 115. See also Tit for Tat
strategy
Ricardo goods, 15–17

SDRs (Special Drawing Rights) 333, 341. See
also International monetary reform
denomination, 358–359
in fixed-exchange-rate world, 371–374
and flexible exchange rates, 361–371
possible benefits of, 374–381
role within current monetary system, 359,
370–371
Service sector trade, 161–179. See also Transport and travel
current restrictions on, 164, 166–172
GATT recommendations on, 209–210
insurance companies, 167–168
international comparisons of, 163–166
meaning of, 162–164
negotiations on, 141, 172–179
Smoot-Hawley Tariff of 1930, 145
Snake arrangement, 329
Special drawing rights. See SDRs
Special interests. See Interest group pressures
Speculation, 288
Stainless steel flatware industry, 80
State-owned industrial enterprises, 127
Steel industry, 55, 58, 89, 157
Sterilized intervention by central bank, 317–
321
Stolper-Samuelson theorem, 42
Strategic trade policy, 95–112
antitrust policies and, 105
and consumption effects, 101–102
and economies of scale, 102–103
and imperfectly competitive market environ-
ment, 96–106
income redistribution and, 105–106
Tit for Tat, 114–118, 121
and voluntary export restraints, 104
Structural adjustment. See Adjustment costs;
Adjustment assistance
Subsidies, 87, 170, 203
for American exports, 129–132
and empirical tests of trade policy, 46
GATT and, 133–135
and service sector trade, 172

and unfair trade practices, 118
and world trade, 204–205
Swaps, interest rate, 419–420, 431–436
Syndicated loans, RUFs and, 434–435

Target zones. *See* International monetary reform
Tariffs, 116, 137, 144, 224. *See also* OECD trade policies; Protection; Trade liberalization
Tax Act (1984), 130
Technology
    and labor adjustment costs, 74
    transfer requirements, 183
Telecommunications, 163, 168–170
Temporary trade protection, 79–83
Textiles and apparel, 53–55, 117–118, 149–150
Tit for Tat strategy, 114–118, 121
Tokyo Round, 49, 82, 116–117, 134, 136, 141, 144, 155, 158, 161, 163, 173–174, 180, 196, 204, 211
Trade Act of 1974, 151, 154, 155, 156–157, 174
Trade Act of 1979, 156
Trade adjustment assistance (TAA), 32–34, 79–83, 153
Trade Agreements Act of 1979, 154, 196
Trade Agreements Extension Act of 1955, 153
Trade balance. *See* Balance of payments; Capital flows
Trade liberalization. *See also* Dillon Round; Kennedy Round; Protection; Tokyo Round
    adjustment costs, 32–34
    AFL-CIO leadership and, 150–151
    benefits of, 29–31
    and congressional restraints on President, 151–154
    Democratic party support for, 145–147
    and foreign direct investment, 181–198
    history, 141–147
    and nontariff trade-distorting measures, 154–157
    political parties and, 149–151
    and public goods, 148
    and service sector, 161–179
    U.S. hegemonic leadership, 144–149, 152–160
Trade negotiations, 116. *See also* Dillon Round; GATT; Kennedy Round; Tokyo Round

and direct foreign investment, 181–183
    need for new round of, 211
    service sector trade and, 172–174
Trade-related performance requirements (TRPRs). *See also* Performance requirements
    extent of use of, 186
    in Canada, 188–189
    U.S. policy response to, 194–198
Training programs, 79. *See also* Adjustment costs
Transport and travel services, 170–171, 177
Treaty of Rome, 175
Trigger pricing, 109, 118, 157

UNCTAD (United Nations Conference on Trade & Development), 171, 177
Unemployment. *See also* Employment
    adjustment costs and, 76–77
    exchange rates and, 263, 310, 314
    free trade and, 32
    protection and, 52–54, 80–81
Unfair trade practices, 114–121, 156. *See also* Trade-related performance requirements
    dispute settlement mechanisms, 116–117
    and EEC policies, 119
    and export subsidies, 133–140
    GATT and ITO and, 147
    Japanese industrial policy and, 119–121, 123–127
    and Tit for Tat strategy, 117–118
Unions. *See* Labor unions
United States economy
    and Bretton Woods system, 340–341
    and costs of trade liberalization, 148
    decline in hegemony of, 157–160, 247
    and dollar appreciation, 305–313
    and investment abroad, 25
    post–World War II hegemony, 145–146
United States trade
    determinants of, 3–18
    high-technology, 17–18
    in manufactured goods with Japan, 22–23, 28–29
United States Trade Representative (USTR), 186
United States Treasury Department, and enforcement of trade laws, 153–154
Unsterilized intervention by central bank, 317–319

VERs (Voluntary Export Restraints), 51, 52,
    53, 86, 104, 142, 203
  automobile industry and, 53, 66–74
  and conformity with GATT rules, 203
Versailles Economic Summit meeting, 175
Vietnam War, 340
VLSI (very large-scale integrated circuit) project, 126
Volatility. *See* Flexible exchange rates
Voluntary export restraints. *See* VERs

Wages
  adjustment costs and, 75–76, 77

and exchange rates, 272–273, 299
in manufacturing and automobile industries,
    65–66, 72
protection and, 54, 58, 89
Williamsburg Economic Summit Meeting,
    319
Withholding tax abolition, 432
Working Group on Investment Policies, 195
World Bank, 129
  and GATT, 213
  and trade-related performance requirements,
    194, 197